Fourth Conference on Machine Translation (WMT 2019)

Volume 3: Shared Task Papers, Day 2

Florence, Italy
1-2 August 2019

ISBN: 978-1-5108-9291-0

WMT 2019

**Fourth Conference on
Machine Translation**

Proceedings of the Conference

Volume 3: Shared Task Papers, Day 2

Introduction

The Fourth Conference on Machine Translation (WMT 2019) took place on Thursday, August 1 and Friday, August 2, 2019 in Florence, Italy, immediately following the 57th Annual Meeting of the Association for Computational Linguistics (ACL 2019).

This is the fourth time WMT has been held as a conference. The first time WMT was held as a conference was at ACL 2016 in Berlin, Germany, the second time at EMNLP 2017 in Copenhagen, Denmark, and the third time at EMNLP 2028 in Brussels, Belgium. Prior to being a conference, WMT was held 10 times as a workshop. WMT was held for the first time at HLT-NAACL 2006 in New York City, USA. In the following years the Workshop on Statistical Machine Translation was held at ACL 2007 in Prague, Czech Republic, ACL 2008, Columbus, Ohio, USA, EACL 2009 in Athens, Greece, ACL 2010 in Uppsala, Sweden, EMNLP 2011 in Edinburgh, Scotland, NAACL 2012 in Montreal, Canada, ACL 2013 in Sofia, Bulgaria, ACL 2014 in Baltimore, USA, and EMNLP 2015 in Lisbon, Portugal.

The focus of our conference is to bring together researchers from the area of machine translation and invite selected research papers to be presented at the conference.

Prior to the conference, in addition to soliciting relevant papers for review and possible presentation, we conducted 8 shared tasks. This consisted of four translation tasks: Machine Translation of News, Biomedical Translation, Robust Machine Translation, and Similar Language Translation, two evaluation tasks: Metrics and Quality Estimation, as well as the Automatic Post-Editing and Parallel Corpus Filtering tasks.

The results of all shared tasks were announced at the conference, and these proceedings also include overview papers for the shared tasks, summarizing the results, as well as providing information about the data used and any procedures that were followed in conducting or scoring the tasks. In addition, there are short papers from each participating team that describe their underlying system in greater detail.

Like in previous years, we have received a far larger number of submissions than we could accept for presentation. WMT 2019 has received 48 full research paper submissions (not counting withdrawn submissions). In total, WMT 2019 featured 12 full research paper oral presentations and 102 shared task poster presentations.

The invited talk was given by Marine Carpuat from the University of Maryland, College Park, USA. It was titled "Semantic, Style & Other Data Divergences in Neural Machine Translation".

We would like to thank the members of the Program Committee for their timely reviews. We also would like to thank the participants of the shared task and all the other volunteers who helped with the evaluations.

Ondřej Bojar, Rajen Chatterjee, Christian Federmann, Mark Fishel, Yvette Graham, Barry Haddow, Matthias Huck, Antonio Jimeno Yepes, Philipp Koehn, André Martins, Christof Monz, Matteo Negri, Aurélie Névéol, Mariana Neves, Matt Post, Marco Turchi, and Karin Verspoor

Co-Organizers

Marine Carpuat (University of Maryland)
Francisco Casacuberta (Universitat Politècnica de València)
Sheila Castilho (Dublin City University)
Rajen Chatterjee (Apple Inc)
Boxing Chen (Alibaba)
Colin Cherry (Google)
Mara Chinea-Rios (Universitat Politècnica de València)
Chenhui Chu (Osaka University)
Ann Clifton (Spotify)
Marta R. Costa-jussà (Universitat Politècnica de Catalunya)
Josep Crego (SYSTRAN)
Raj Dabre (NICT)
Steve DeNeefe (SDL Research)
Michael Denkowski (Amazon)
Mattia A. Di Gangi (Fondazione Bruno Kessler)
Miguel Domingo (Universitat Politècnica de València)
Kevin Duh (Johns Hopkins University)
Marc Dymetman (Naver Labs Europe)
Hiroshi Echizen'ya (Hokkai-Gakuen University)
Sergey Edunov (Faceook AI Research)
Marcello Federico (Amazon AI)
Yang Feng (Institute of Computing Technology, Chinese Academy of Sciences)
Andrew Finch (Apple Inc.)
Orhan Firat (Google AI)
George Foster (Google)
Alexander Fraser (Ludwig-Maximilians-Universität München)
Atsushi Fujita (National Institute of Information and Communications Technology)
Juri Ganitkevitch (Google)
Mercedes García-Martínez (Pangeanic)
Ekaterina Garmash (KLM Royal Dutch Airlines)
Jesús González-Rubio (WebInterpret)
Isao Goto (NHK)
Miguel Graça (RWTH Aachen University)
Roman Grundkiewicz (School of Informatics, University of Edinburgh)
Mandy Guo (Google)
Jeremy Gwinnup (Air Force Research Laboratory)
Thanh-Le Ha (Karlsruhe Institute of Technology)
Nizar Habash (New York University Abu Dhabi)
Gholamreza Haffari (Monash University)
Greg Hanneman (Amazon)
Christian Hardmeier (Uppsala universitet)
Eva Hasler (SDL Research)
Yifan He (Alibaba Group)
John Henderson (MITRE)
Christian Herold (RWTH Aachen University)
Felix Hieber (Amazon Research)
Hieu Hoang (University of Edinburgh)

Vu Cong Duy Hoang (The University of Melbourne)
Bojie Hu (Tencent Research, Beijing, China)
Junjie Hu (Carnegie Mellon University)
Mika Hämäläinen (University of Helsinki)
Gonzalo Iglesias (SDL)
Kenji Imamura (National Institute of Information and Communications Technology)
Aizhan Imankulova (Tokyo Metropolitan University)
Julia Ive (University of Sheffield)
Marcin Junczys-Dowmunt (Microsoft)
Shahram Khadivi (eBay)
Huda Khayrallah (Johns Hopkins University)
Douwe Kiela (Facebook)
Yunsu Kim (RWTH Aachen University)
Rebecca Knowles (Johns Hopkins University)
Julia Kreutzer (Department of Computational Linguistics, Heidelberg University)
Shankar Kumar (Google)
Anoop Kunchukuttan (Microsoft AI and Research)
Surafel Melaku Lakew (University of Trento and Fondazione Bruno Kessler)
Ekaterina Lapshinova-Koltunski (Universität des Saarlandes)
Alon Lavie (Amazon/Carnegie Mellon University)
Gregor Leusch (eBay)
William Lewis (Microsoft Research)
Jindřich Libovický (Charles University)
Patrick Littell (National Research Council of Canada)
Qun Liu (Huawei Noah's Ark Lab)
Samuel Läubli (University of Zurich)
Pranava Madhyastha (Imperial College London)
Andreas Maletti (Universität Leipzig)
Saab Mansour (Apple)
Sameen Maruf (Monash University)
Arne Mauser (Google, Inc)
Arya D. McCarthy (Johns Hopkins University)
Antonio Valerio Miceli Barone (The University of Edinburgh)
Paul Michel (Carnegie Mellon University)
Aaron Mueller (The Johns Hopkins University)
Kenton Murray (University of Notre Dame)
Tomáš Musil (Charles University)
Mathias Müller (University of Zurich)
Masaaki Nagata (NTT Corporation)
Toshiaki Nakazawa (The University of Tokyo)
Preslav Nakov (Qatar Computing Research Institute, HBKU)
Graham Neubig (Carnegie Mellon University)
Jan Niehues (Maastricht University)
Nikola Nikolov (University of Zurich and ETH Zurich)
Xing Niu (University of Maryland)
Tsuyoshi Okita (Kyushuu institute of technology)
Daniel Ortiz-Martínez (Technical University of Valencia)

Myle Ott (Facebook AI Research)
Santanu Pal (Saarland University)
Carla Parra Escartín (Unbabel)
Pavel Pecina (Charles University)
Stephan Peitz (Apple)
Sergio Penkale (Lingo24)
Mārcis Pinnis (Tilde)
Martin Popel (Charles University, Faculty of Mathematics and Physics, UFAL)
Maja Popović (ADAPT Centre @ DCU)
Matīss Rikters (Tilde)
Annette Rios (Institute of Computational Linguistics, University of Zurich)
Jan Rosendahl (RWTH Aachen University)
Raphael Rubino (DFKI)
Devendra Sachan (CMU / Petuum Inc.)
Elizabeth Salesky (Carnegie Mellon University)
Hassan Sawaf (Amazon Web Services)
Jean Senellart (SYSTRAN)
Rico Sennrich (University of Edinburgh)
Patrick Simianer (Lilt)
Linfeng Song (University of Rochester)
Felix Stahlberg (University of Cambridge, Department of Engineering)
Dario Stojanovski (LMU Munich)
Katsuhito Sudoh (Nara Institute of Science and Technology (NAIST))
Felipe Sánchez-Martínez (Universitat d'Alacant)
Aleš Tamchyna (Charles University in Prague, UFAL MFF)
Gongbo Tang (Uppsala University)
Jörg Tiedemann (University of Helsinki)
Antonio Toral (University of Groningen)
Ke Tran (Amazon)
Marco Turchi (Fondazione Bruno Kessler)
Ferhan Ture (Comcast Applied AI Research)
Nicola Ueffing (eBay)
Masao Utiyama (NICT)
Dušan Variš (Charles University, Institute of Formal and Applied Linguistics)
David Vilar (Amazon)
Ivan Vulić (University of Cambridge)
Ekaterina Vylomova (University of Melbourne)
Wei Wang (Google Research)
Weiyue Wang (RWTH Aachen University)
Taro Watanabe (Google)
Philip Williams (University of Edinburgh)
Hua Wu (Baidu)
Joern Wuebker (Lilt, Inc.)
Hainan Xu (Johns Hopkins University)
Yinfei Yang (Google)
François Yvon (LIMSI/CNRS)
Dakun Zhang (SYSTRAN)
Xuan Zhang (Johns Hopkins University)

Table of Contents

Conference Program

Thursday, August 1, 2019

8:45–9:00   *Opening Remarks*

9:00–10:30   **Session 1: Shared Tasks Overview Presentations I (chair: Barry Haddow)**

9:00–9:35   *Findings of the 2019 Conference on Machine Translation (WMT19)*
Loïc Barrault, Ondřej Bojar, Marta R. Costa-jussà, Christian Federmann, Mark Fishel, Yvette Graham, Barry Haddow, Matthias Huck, Philipp Koehn, Shervin Malmasi, Christof Monz, Mathias Müller, Santanu Pal, Matt Post and Marcos Zampieri

9:35–9:50   *Test Suites*

9:50–10:10   *Results of the WMT19 Metrics Shared Task: Segment-Level and Strong MT Systems Pose Big Challenges*
Qingsong Ma, Johnny Wei, Ondřej Bojar and Yvette Graham

10:10–10:30   *Findings of the First Shared Task on Machine Translation Robustness*
Xian Li, Paul Michel, Antonios Anastasopoulos, Yonatan Belinkov, Nadir Durrani, Orhan Firat, Philipp Koehn, Graham Neubig, Juan Pino and Hassan Sajjad

10:30-11:00   *Coffee Break*

11:00–12:30   **Session 2: Shared Task Poster Session I**

11:00–12:30   *Shared Task: News Translation*

The University of Edinburgh's Submissions to the WMT19 News Translation Task
Rachel Bawden, Nikolay Bogoychev, Ulrich Germann, Roman Grundkiewicz, Faheem Kirefu, Antonio Valerio Miceli Barone and Alexandra Birch

GTCOM Neural Machine Translation Systems for WMT19
Chao Bei, Hao Zong, Conghu Yuan, Qingming Liu and Baoyong Fan

Machine Translation with parfda, Moses, kenlm, nplm, and PRO
Ergun Biçici

Neural Machine Translation for English–Kazakh with Morphological Segmentation and Synthetic Data
Antonio Toral, Lukas Edman, Galiya Yeshmagambetova and Jennifer Spenader

The LMU Munich Unsupervised Machine Translation System for WMT19
Dario Stojanovski, Viktor Hangya, Matthias Huck and Alexander Fraser

Combining Local and Document-Level Context: The LMU Munich Neural Machine Translation System at WMT19
Dario Stojanovski and Alexander Fraser

IITP-MT System for Gujarati-English News Translation Task at WMT 2019
Sukanta Sen, Kamal Kumar Gupta, Asif Ekbal and Pushpak Bhattacharyya

The University of Helsinki Submissions to the WMT19 News Translation Task
Aarne Talman, Umut Sulubacak, Raúl Vázquez, Yves Scherrer, Sami Virpioja, Alessandro Raganato, Arvi Hurskainen and Jörg Tiedemann

Microsoft Research Asia's Systems for WMT19
Yingce Xia, Xu Tan, Fei Tian, Fei Gao, Di He, Weicong Chen, Yang Fan, Linyuan Gong, Yichong Leng, Renqian Luo, Yiren Wang, Lijun Wu, Jinhua Zhu, Tao Qin and Tie-Yan Liu

The En-Ru Two-way Integrated Machine Translation System Based on Transformer
Doron Yu

DFKI-NMT Submission to the WMT19 News Translation Task
Jingyi Zhang and Josef van Genabith

11:00–12:30   *Shared Task: Test Suites*

Linguistic Evaluation of German-English Machine Translation Using a Test Suite
Eleftherios Avramidis, Vivien Macketanz, Ursula Strohriegel and Hans Uszkoreit

A Test Suite and Manual Evaluation of Document-Level NMT at WMT19
Kateřina Rysová, Magdaléna Rysová, Tomáš Musil, Lucie Poláková and Ondřej Bojar

Evaluating Conjunction Disambiguation on English-to-German and French-to-German WMT 2019 Translation Hypotheses
Maja Popović

The MuCoW Test Suite at WMT 2019: Automatically Harvested Multilingual Contrastive Word Sense Disambiguation Test Sets for Machine Translation
Alessandro Raganato, Yves Scherrer and Jörg Tiedemann

SAO WMT19 Test Suite: Machine Translation of Audit Reports
Tereza Vojtěchová, Michal Novák, Miloš Klouček and Ondřej Bojar

11:00–12:30   *Shared Task: Metrics*

WMDO: Fluency-based Word Mover's Distance for Machine Translation Evaluation
Julian Chow, Lucia Specia and Pranava Madhyastha

Meteor++ 2.0: Adopt Syntactic Level Paraphrase Knowledge into Machine Translation Evaluation
Yinuo Guo and Junfeng Hu

YiSi - a Unified Semantic MT Quality Evaluation and Estimation Metric for Languages with Different Levels of Available Resources
Chi-kiu Lo

EED: Extended Edit Distance Measure for Machine Translation
Peter Stanchev, Weiyue Wang and Hermann Ney

Filtering Pseudo-References by Paraphrasing for Automatic Evaluation of Machine Translation
Ryoma Yoshimura, Hiroki Shimanaka, Yukio Matsumura, Hayahide Yamagishi and Mamoru Komachi

11:00–12:30   *Shared Task: Robustness*

Naver Labs Europe's Systems for the WMT19 Machine Translation Robustness Task
Alexandre Berard, Ioan Calapodescu and Claude Roux

NICT's Supervised Neural Machine Translation Systems for the WMT19 Translation Robustness Task
Raj Dabre and Eiichiro Sumita

System Description: The Submission of FOKUS to the WMT 19 Robustness Task
Cristian Grozea

CUNI System for the WMT19 Robustness Task
Jindřich Helcl, Jindřich Libovický and Martin Popel

NTT's Machine Translation Systems for WMT19 Robustness Task
Soichiro Murakami, Makoto Morishita, Tsutomu Hirao and Masaaki Nagata

JHU 2019 Robustness Task System Description
Matt Post and Kevin Duh

Robust Machine Translation with Domain Sensitive Pseudo-Sources: Baidu-OSU WMT19 MT Robustness Shared Task System Report
Renjie Zheng, Hairong Liu, Mingbo Ma, Baigong Zheng and Liang Huang

Improving Robustness of Neural Machine Translation with Multi-task Learning
Shuyan Zhou, Xiangkai Zeng, Yingqi Zhou, Antonios Anastasopoulos and Graham Neubig

12:30–14:00   *Lunch*

14:00–15:30   **Panel on "Open Problems in Machine Translation" (chair Ondrej Bojar): Alex Fraser (Ludwig-Maximilians-Universität München), Alon Lavie (Unbabel), Marcin Junczys-Dowmunt (Microsoft), Yvette Graham (Dublin City University)**

15:30–16:00   *Coffee Break*

16:00–17:30   **Session 4: Research Papers on Modeling and Analysis (chair: Matthias Huck)**

16:00–16:15   *Saliency-driven Word Alignment Interpretation for Neural Machine Translation*
Shuoyang Ding, Hainan Xu and Philipp Koehn

16:15–16:30   *Improving Zero-shot Translation with Language-Independent Constraints*
Ngoc-Quan Pham, Jan Niehues, Thanh-Le Ha and Alexander Waibel

16:30–16:45   *Incorporating Source Syntax into Transformer-Based Neural Machine Translation*
Anna Currey and Kenneth Heafield

11:00–12:30   Session 2: Shared Task Poster Session I

11:00–12:30   *Shared Task: Quality Estimation*

RTM Stacking Results for Machine Translation Performance Prediction
Ergun Biçici

Unbabel's Participation in the WMT19 Translation Quality Estimation Shared Task
Fabio Kepler, Jonay Trénous, Marcos Treviso, Miguel Vera, António Góis, M. Amin
Farajian, António V. Lopes and André F. T. Martins

QE BERT: Bilingual BERT Using Multi-task Learning for Neural Quality Estimation
Hyun Kim, Joon-Ho Lim, Hyun-Ki Kim and Seung-Hoon Na

MIPT System for World-Level Quality Estimation
Mikhail Mosyagin and Varvara Logacheva

NJU Submissions for the WMT19 Quality Estimation Shared Task
Hou Qi

Quality Estimation and Translation Metrics via Pre-trained Word and Sentence Embeddings
Elizaveta Yankovskaya, Andre Tättar and Mark Fishel

SOURCE: SOURce-Conditional Elmo-style Model for Machine Translation Quality Estimation
Junpei Zhou, Zhisong Zhang and Zecong Hu

11:00–12:30   *Shared Task: Automatic Post-Editing*

Transformer-based Automatic Post-Editing Model with Joint Encoder and Multi-source Attention of Decoder
WonKee Lee, Jaehun Shin and Jong-Hyeok Lee

Unbabel's Submission to the WMT2019 APE Shared Task: BERT-Based Encoder-Decoder for Automatic Post-Editing
António V. Lopes, M. Amin Farajian, Gonçalo M. Correia, Jonay Trénous and André F. T. Martins

Friday, August 2, 2019 (continued)

USAAR-DFKI – The Transference Architecture for English–German Automatic Post-Editing
Santanu Pal, Hongfei Xu, Nico Herbig, Antonio Krüger and Josef van Genabith

APE through Neural and Statistical MT with Augmented Data. ADAPT/DCU Submission to the WMT 2019 APE Shared Task
Dimitar Shterionov, Joachim Wagner and Félix do Carmo

Effort-Aware Neural Automatic Post-Editing
Amirhossein Tebbifakhr, Matteo Negri and Marco Turchi

UdS Submission for the WMT 19 Automatic Post-Editing Task
Hongfei Xu, Qiuhui Liu and Josef van Genabith

11:00–12:30   *Shared Task: Biomedical Translation*

Terminology-Aware Segmentation and Domain Feature for the WMT19 Biomedical Translation Task
Casimiro Pio Carrino, Bardia Rafieian, Marta R. Costa-jussà and José A. R. Fonollosa

Exploring Transfer Learning and Domain Data Selection for the Biomedical Translation
Noor-e- Hira, Sadaf Abdul Rauf, Kiran Kiani, Ammara Zafar and Raheel Nawaz

Huawei's NMT Systems for the WMT 2019 Biomedical Translation Task
Wei Peng, Jianfeng Liu, Liangyou Li and Qun Liu

UCAM Biomedical Translation at WMT19: Transfer Learning Multi-domain Ensembles
Danielle Saunders, Felix Stahlberg and Bill Byrne

BSC Participation in the WMT Translation of Biomedical Abstracts
Felipe Soares and Martin Krallinger

11:00–12:30   *Shared Task: Similar Languages*

The MLLP-UPV Spanish-Portuguese and Portuguese-Spanish Machine Translation Systems for WMT19 Similar Language Translation Task
Pau Baquero-Arnal, Javier Iranzo-Sánchez, Jorge Civera and Alfons Juan

Low-Resource Corpus Filtering Using Multilingual Sentence Embeddings
Vishrav Chaudhary, Yuqing Tang, Francisco Guzmán, Holger Schwenk and Philipp Koehn

Quality and Coverage: The AFRL Submission to the WMT19 Parallel Corpus Filtering for Low-Resource Conditions Task
Grant Erdmann and Jeremy Gwinnup

Webinterpret Submission to the WMT2019 Shared Task on Parallel Corpus Filtering
Jesús González-Rubio

Noisy Parallel Corpus Filtering through Projected Word Embeddings
Murathan Kurfalı and Robert Östling

Filtering of Noisy Parallel Corpora Based on Hypothesis Generation
Zuzanna Parcheta, Germán Sanchis-Trilles and Francisco Casacuberta

Parallel Corpus Filtering Based on Fuzzy String Matching
Sukanta Sen, Asif Ekbal and Pushpak Bhattacharyya

The University of Helsinki Submission to the WMT19 Parallel Corpus Filtering Task
Raúl Vázquez, Umut Sulubacak and Jörg Tiedemann

12:30–14:00   *Lunch*

Findings of the WMT 2019 Shared Task on Quality Estimation

Erick Fonseca
Instituto de Telecomunicações, Portugal
erick.fonseca@lx.it.pt

Lisa Yankovskaya
University of Tartu, Estonia
lisa.yankovskaya@ut.ee

André F. T. Martins
Instituto de Telecomunicações
& Unbabel, Portugal
andre.martins@unbabel.com

Mark Fishel
University of Tartu, Estonia
fishel@ut.ee

Christian Federmann
Microsoft, USA
chrife@microsoft.com

Abstract

We report the results of the WMT19 shared task on Quality Estimation, i.e. the task of predicting the quality of the output of machine translation systems given just the source text and the hypothesis translations. The task includes estimation at three granularity levels: word, sentence and document. A novel addition is evaluating sentence-level QE against human judgments: in other words, designing MT metrics that do not need a reference translation. This year we include three language pairs, produced solely by neural machine translation systems. Participating teams from eight institutions submitted a variety of systems to different task variants and language pairs.

1 Introduction

This shared task builds on its previous seven editions to further examine automatic methods for estimating the quality of machine translation (MT) output at run-time, without the use of reference translations. It includes the (sub)tasks of word-level, sentence-level and document-level estimation. In addition to advancing the state of the art at all prediction levels, our more specific goals include to investigate the following:

- The predictability of missing words in the MT output. As in last year, our data include this annotation.

- The predictability of source words that lead to errors in the MT output, also as in last year.

- Quality prediction for documents based on errors annotated at word-level with added severity judgments. This is also like in last year.

- The predictability of individual errors within documents, which may depend on a larger

context. This is a novel task, building upon the existing document-level quality estimation.

- The reliability of quality estimation models as a proxy for metrics that depend on a reference translation.

- The generalization ability of quality estimation models to different MT systems instead of a single ones

We present a simpler setup in comparison to last edition, which featured more language pairs, statistical MT outputs alongside neural ones, and an additional task for phrase-based QE. This simplification reflects a more realistic scenario, in which NMT systems have mostly replaced SMT ones, making phrase-level predictions less interesting.

We used both existing data from the previous edition as well as new data. For word and sentence level, we reused the English-German dataset from last year, but also added a new English-Russian one. For document level, we reused last year's English-French data for training and validation, but introduce a new test set from the same corpus. For QE as a metric we ran the evaluation jointly with the WMT19 metrics task, which meant applying the QE systems to news translation submissions and evaluating them against the human judgments collected this year.

2 Tasks

This year we present three tasks: Task 1 for word-level and sentence-level quality estimation, Task 2 for document-level, and Task 3 for quality estimation as a metric. In contrast to previous editions, in which there were data from statistical translation systems, all datasets come from neural machine translation systems.

1

Proceedings of the Fourth Conference on Machine Translation (WMT), Volume 3: Shared Task Papers (Day 2) pages 1–10
Florence, Italy, August 1-2, 2019. ©2019 Association for Computational Linguistics

2.1 Task 1

The aim of Task 1 is to estimate the amount of human post-editing work required in a given sentence. It is comprised of word-level and sentence-level subtasks, both of which annotated as in last year.

2.1.1 Word Level

At the word level, participants are required to produce a sequence of tags for both the source and the translated sentences. For the source, tokens correctly translated should be tagged as OK, and the ones mistranslated or ignored as BAD. For the translated sentence, there should be tags both for words and *gaps* – we consider gaps between each two words, plus one in the beginning and another in the end of the sentence. Words correctly aligned with the source are tagged as OK, and BAD otherwise. If one or more words are missing in the translation, the gap where they should have been is tagged as BAD, and OK otherwise.

As in previous years, in order to obtain word level labels, first both the machine translated sentence and the source sentence are aligned with the post-edited version. Machine translation and post-edited pairs are aligned using the TERCOM tool (`https://github.com/jhclark/tercom`);[1] source and post-edited use the IBM Model 2 alignments from `fast_align` (Dyer et al., 2013).

Target word and gap labels Target tokens originating from insertion or substitution errors were labeled as BAD (i.e., tokens absent in the post-edit sentence), and all other tokens were labeled as OK. Similarly to last year, we interleave these target word labels with *gap* labels: gaps were labeled as BAD in the presence of one or more deletion errors (i.e., a word from the source missing in the translation) and OK otherwise.

Source word labels For each token in the post-edited sentence deleted or substituted in the machine translated text, the corresponding aligned source tokens were labeled as BAD. In this way, deletion errors also result in BAD tokens in the source, related to the missing words. All other words were labeled as OK.

Evaluation As in last year, systems are evaluated primarily by F_1-Mult, the product of the F_1 scores for OK and BAD tags. There are separate scores for source sentences and translated sentences, with the latter having word and gap tags interleaved. Systems are ranked according to their performance on the source side.

Additionally, we compute the Matthews correlation coefficient (MCC, Matthews 1975), a metric for binary classification problems particularly useful when classes are unbalanced. This is the case in QE, in which OK tags are much more common than BAD tags (see Table 2 for the statistics on this year's data). It is computed as follows:

$$
\begin{aligned}
S &= \frac{TP + FN}{N} \\
P &= \frac{TP + FP}{N} \\
MCC &= \frac{\frac{TP}{N} - SP}{\sqrt{SP(1-S)(1-P)}},
\end{aligned}
\tag{1}
$$

where TP, TN, FP and FN stand for, respectively, true positives, true negatives, false positives and false negatives; and N is the total number of instances to be classified.

2.1.2 Sentence Level

At the sentence level, systems are expected to produce the Human Translation Error Rate (HTER), which is the minimum ratio of edit operations (word insertions, deletions and replacements) needed to fix the translation to the number of its tokens, capped at maximum 1.

In order to obtain the number of necessary operations, we run TERCOM on the machine translated and post-edit sentences, with a slightly different parametrization (see footnote 1).

Evaluation Also as in last year, systems are primarily evaluated by the Pearson correlation score with the gold annotations. Mean absolute error (MAE), rooted mean squared error (RMSE) and Spearman correlation are also computed.

2.2 Task 2

The goal of Task 2 is to predict document-level quality scores as well as fine-grained annotations, identifying which words and passages are incorrect in the translation.

Each document contains zero or more errors,

---

[1] For back-compatibility with last year's datasets, when computing word-level labels, we disabled shifts in TERCOM; but for sentence-level, shifts were allowed.

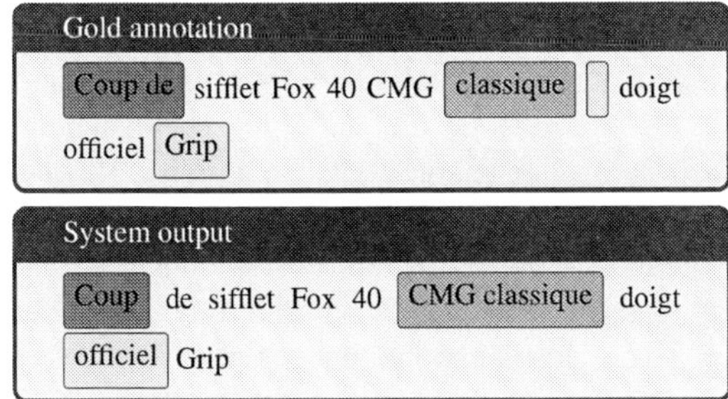

Figure 1: Example of fine-grained document annotation. Spans in the same color belong to the same annotation. Error severity and type are not shown for brevity.

Gold	R	System	P
Coup de	0.57	Coup	1
classique	1	CMG classique	0.69
Grip	0	officiel	0
Mean Recall			0.52
Mean Precision			0.56
F$_1$			0.54

Table 1: Scores for the example system output shown in Figure 1. **R** stands for recall and **P** for precision, and are computed based on character overlap.

annotated according to the MQM taxonomy[2], and may span one or more tokens, not necessarily contiguous. Errors have a label specifying their type, such as wrong word order, missing words, agreement, etc. They provide additional information, but do not need to be predicted by the systems. Additionally, there are three severity levels for errors: *minor* (if it is not misleading nor changes meaning), *major* (if it changes meaning), and *critical* (if it changes meaning and carries any kind of implication, possibly offensive).

Figure 1 shows an example of fine-grained error annotations for a sentence, with the ground truth and a possible system prediction. Note that there is an annotation composed by two discontinuous spans: a whitespace and the token *Grip* — in this case, the annotation indicates wrong word order, and *Grip* should have been at the whitespace position.

The document-level scores, called MQM scores, are determined from the error annotations and their severity:

$$\text{MQM} = 1 - \frac{n_{minor} + 5n_{major} + 10n_{crit}}{n}. \quad (2)$$

Notice that the MQM score can be negative depending on the number and severity of errors; we truncate it to 0 in that case. Also notice that, while the MQM score can be obtained deterministically from the fine-grained annotations, participants are allowed to produce answers for both subtasks inconsistent with each other, if they believe their systems to work better estimating a single score for the whole document.

MQM Evaluation MQM scores are evaluated in the same way as the document-level HTER scores: primarily with Pearson correlation with the gold values, and also with MAE, RMSE and Spearman's ρ.

Fine-grained Evaluation Fine-grained annotations are evaluated as follows. For each error annotation a_i^s in the system output, we look for the gold annotation a_j^g with the highest overlap in number of characters. The precision of a_i^s is defined by the ratio of the overlap size to the annotation length; or 0 if there was no overlapping gold annotation. Conversely, we compute the recall of each gold annotation a_j^g considering the best matching annotation a_k^s in the system output[3], or 0 if there was no overlapping annotation. The document precision and recall are computed as the average of all annotation precisions in the corresponding system output and recalls in the gold output; and therewith we compute the document F$_1$. The final score is the unweighted average of the F$_1$ for all documents. Table 1 shows the precision and recall for each annotation in the example from Figure 1.

2.3 Task 3

Task 3 on applying QE as a metric had several purposes:

- To find out how well QE results correlate with general human judgments of MT quality. This mainly means shifting the application focus of quality estimation from professional translators (whose primary interest is the expected number of post-edits to perform,

---

[2]Multidimensional Quality Metrics; see http://www.qt21.eu/mqm-definition/ definition-2015-12-30.html for details.

[3]Notice that if a gold annotation a_j^g has the highest overlap with a system annotation a_i^s, it does not necessarily mean that a_i^s has the highest overlap with a_j^g.

as estimated by the HTER score) to MT developers and general users.

- To test the generalization ability of QE approaches in a massive multi-system scenario, instead of learning to estimate the quality of just a single MT system

- To directly compare QE models to MT metrics and see how far one can get without a reference translation, or in other words, how much does one gain from having a reference translation in terms of scoring MT outputs

As part of this task sentence-level QE systems were applied to pairs of source segments and translation hypotheses submitted to the WMT19 news translation shared task. System-level results were also computed via averaging the sentence score over the whole test set.

Submission was handled jointly with the WMT19 metrics task. Two language pairs were highlighted as the focus of this task: English-Russian and English-German; however, the task was not restricted to these, and other news translation task languages were also allowed.

Results of this task were evaluated in the same way as MT metrics, using Kendall rank correlation for sentence-level and Spearman rank correlation for system-level evaluations. The overall motivation was to measure how often QE results agree or disagree with human judgments of MT quality.

3 Datasets

3.1 Task 1

Two datasets were used in this task: an English-German, the same as in last year with texts from the IT domain; and a novel English-Russian dataset with interface messages present in Microsoft applications. The same data are used for both word-level and sentence-level evaluations.

Table 2 shows statistics for the data. Both language pairs have nearly the same number of sentences, but EN-DE has substantially longer ones. The ratio of BAD tokens in the word-level annotation is also similar in both datasets, as well as the mean HTER, with a increased standard deviation for EN-RU.

3.2 Task 2

There is only one dataset for this task. It is the same one used in last year's evaluation, but with a new unseen test set and some minor changes in the annotations; last year's test set was made available as an additional development set. The documents are derived from the Amazon Product Reviews English-French dataset, a selection of Sports and Outdoors product titles and descriptions. The most popular products (those with more reviews) were chosen. This data poses interesting challenges for machine translation: titles and descriptions are often short and not always a complete sentence. The data was annotated for translation errors by the Unbabel community of crowd-sourced annotators.

Table 3 shows some statistics of the dataset. We see that the new test set has a mean MQM value higher than last year, but actually closer to the training data. On the other hand, the average number of annotations per document is smaller.

3.3 Task 3

Task 3 did not use a specially prepared dataset, as evaluations were done via the human judgments collected in the manual evaluation phase of the news translation shared task.

Suggested training data included last years' WMT translation system submissions and their collected human judgments, as well as any other additional resources including HTER-annotated QE data, monolingual and parallel corpora.

4 Baselines

These are the baseline systems we used for each subtask.

4.1 Word Level

For word-level quality estimation, we used the NuQE (Martins et al., 2017) implementation provided in OpenKiwi (Kepler et al., 2019), which achieved competitive results on the datasets of previous QE shared tasks. It reads sentence pairs with lexical alignments, and takes as input the embeddings of words in the target sentence concatenated with both their aligned counterparts in the source and neighboring words. It then applies linear layers and an RNN to the embedded vectors, outputting a softmax over OK and BAD tags.

4.2 Sentence Level

The sentence-level baseline is a linear regressor trained on four features computed from word-level tags. At training time, it computes the features from the gold training data; at test time, it uses the

Split	Pair	Sentences	Words	BAD source	BAD target	HTER
Train	EN-DE	13,442	234,725	28,549 (12.16%)	37,040 (7.06%)	0.15 ($\pm$0.19)
	EN-RU	15,089	148,551	15,599 (10.50%)	18,380 (6.15%)	0.13 ($\pm$0.24)
Dev	EN-DE	1,000	17,669	2,113 (11.96%)	2,654 (6.73%)	0.15 ($\pm$0.19)
	EN-RU	1,000	9,710	1,055 (10.87%)	1,209 (6.17%)	0.13 ($\pm$0.23)
Test	EN-DE	1,023	17,649	2,415 (13.68%)	3,136 (8.04%)	0.17 ($\pm$0.19)
	EN-RU	1,023	7,778	1,049 (13.49%)	1,165 (7.46%)	0.17 ($\pm$0.28)

Table 2: Statistics of the datasets used in Task 1. Number of sentences is always the same in source and target; number of words refer to the source. Values shown for HTER are mean and standard deviation in parentheses.

Split	Documents	Sentences	Words	MQM	Annotations
Train	1,000	6,003	158,393	29.47 ($\pm$ 24.42)	23.17 ($\pm$ 29.46)
Dev	200	1,301	33,959	19.29 ($\pm$ 23.28)	28.11 ($\pm$ 42.94)
Test 2018	268	1,640	46,564	18.11 ($\pm$ 23.52)	27.74 ($\pm$ 35.04)
Test 2019	180	949	26,279	26.60 ($\pm$ 26.80)	19.24 ($\pm$ 23.94)

Table 3: Statistics of the datasets used in Task 2. The column Annotations shows the average number of annotations per document in the dataset. The values for MQM and Annotations are the mean with standard deviation in parentheses

output produced by the word-level baseline. We found this setup to work better than training the regressor with the automatically generated output. The features used are:

1. Number of BAD tags in the source;

2. number of BAD tags corresponding to words in the translation;

3. number of BAD tags corresponding to gaps in the translation;

4. number of tokens in the translation.

During training, we discarded all sentences with an HTER of 0, and during testing, we always answer 0 when there are no BAD tags in the input. This avoids a bias towards lower scores in the case of a high number of sentences with HTER 0, which is the case in the EN-RU data.[4]

4.3 Document Level

For the document-level task, we first cast the problem as word-level QE: tokens and gaps inside an error annotation are given BAD tags, and all others are given OK. Then, we train the same word-level estimator as in the baseline for Task 1. At test time, for the fine-grained subtask, we group consecutive BAD tags produced by the word-level baseline in a single error annotation and always give it severity *major* (the most common in the training data). As such, the baseline only produces error annotations with a single error span.

For the MQM score, we consider the ratio of bad tags to the document size:

$$\text{MQM} = 1 - \frac{n_{bad}}{n} \quad (3)$$

This simple baseline contrasts with last year, which used QuEst++ (Specia et al., 2015), a QE tool based on training an SVR on features extracted from the data. We found that the new baseline performed better than QuEst++ on the development data, and thus adopted it as the official baseline.

4.4 QE as a Metric

The QE as a metric task included two baselines, both unsupervised. One relied on pre-trained vector representations; the metric consisted of computing LASER (Artetxe and Schwenk, 2018) sentence embeddings for the source segment and the

---

[4]While in principle sentences with no BAD tags should have an HTER of 0, this is not always the case. When pre-processing the shared task data, word-level tags were determined in a case-sensitive fashion, while sentence-level scores were not. The same issue also happened last year, but unfortunately we only noticed it after releasing the training data for this edition.

hypothesis translation and using their cosine similarity.

The second baseline consisted of using bilingually trained neural machine translation systems to calculate the score of the hypothesis translation, when presented with the source segment as input. Thus, instead of decoding and looking for the best translation with the MT models, we computed the probability of each subword in the hypothesis translation and based on these computed the overall log-probability of the hypothesis under the respective MT model.

5 Participants

In total, there were eight participants for Tasks 1 and 2, but not all participated in all of them. Here we briefly describe their strategies and which subtasks they participated in.

There were four participants for Task 3, each team provided two different systems. The description of their methods are presented together with the metrics task[5].

5.1 MIPT

MIPT only participated in the word-level EN-DE task. They used a BiLSTM, BERT and a baseline hand designed-feature extractor to generate word representations, followed by Conditional Random Fields (CRF) to output token labels. Their BiLISTM did not have any pretraining, unlike BERT, and combined the source and target vectors using a global attention mechanism. Their submitted runs combining the baseline features with the BiLSTM and with BERT.

5.2 ETRI

ETRI participated in Task 1 only. They pretrained bilingual BERT (Devlin et al., 2019) models (one for EN-RU and another for EN-DE), and then finetuned them to predict all the outputs for each language pair, using different output weight matrices for each subtask (predicting source tags, target word tags, target gap tags, and the HTER score). Training the same model for both subtasks effectively enhanced the amount of training data.

5.3 CMU

CMU participated only in the sentence-level task. Their setup is similar to ETRI's, but they pretrain

a BiLSTM encoder to predict words in the target conditioned on the source. Then, a regressor is fed the concatenation of each encoded word vector in the target with the embeddings of its neighbours and a mismatch feature indicating the difference between the prediction score of the target word and the highest one in the vocabulary.

5.4 Unbabel

Unbabel participated in Tasks 1 and 2 for all language pairs. Their submissions were built upon the `OpenKiwi` framework: they combined linear, neural, and predictor-estimator systems (Chollampatt and Ng, 2018) with new transfer learning approaches using BERT (Devlin et al., 2019) and XLM (Lample and Conneau, 2019) pre-trained models. They proposed new ensemble techniques for word and sentence-level predictions. For Task 2, they combined a predictor-estimator for word-level predictions with a simple technique for converting word labels into document-level predictions.

5.5 UTartu

UTartu participated only in the sentence-level task. They combined BERT (Devlin et al., 2019) and LASER (Artetxe and Schwenk, 2018) embeddings to train a regression neural network model. In the second proposed method, they used not only pretrained embeddings as input features, but also a log-probability score obtained from a neural MT system.

5.6 NJUNLP

NJUNLP participated only in the sentence-level EN-DE task. In order to generate word representation vectors in the QE context, they trained transformer models to predict source words conditioned on the target and target words conditioned on the source. Then, they run a recurrent neural network over these representations and a regressor on their averaged output vectors.

5.7 BOUN

BOUN turned in a late submission. For word-level predictions, they used referential machine translation models (RTM), which search the training set for instances close to test set examples, and try to determine labels according to them. For sentence level, they used different regressors trained on features generated by their word-level model.

---

[5]http://statmt.org/wmt19/metrics-task.html

For document level, they treat the whole document as a single sentence and apply the same setup.

5.8 USAAR-DFKI

USAAR-DFKI participated only in the sentence-level EN-DE task, and used a CNN implementation of the predictor-estimator based quality estimation model (Chollampatt and Ng, 2018). To train the predictor, they used WMT 2016 IT domain translation task data, and to train the estimator, the WMT 2019 sentence level QE task data.

6 Results

The results for Task 1 are shown in Tables 4, 5, 6 and 7. Systems are ranked according to their F_1 on the target side. The evaluation scripts are available at `https://github.com/deep-spin/qe-evaluation`.

We computed the statistical significance of the results, and considered as winning systems the ones which had significantly better scores than all the rest with $p < 0.05$. For the word-level task, we used randomization tests (Yeh, 2000) with Bonferroni correction[6] (Abdi, 2007); for Pearson correlation scores used in the sentence-level and MQM scoring tasks, we used William's test[7].

In the word-level task, there is a big gap between Unbabel's winning submission and ETRI's, which in turn also had significantly better results than MIPT and BOUN. Unfortunately, we cannot do a direct comparison with last year's results, since i) we now evaluate a single score for target words and gaps, which were evaluated separately before, and ii) only two systems submitted results for source words last year.

The newly proposed metric, MCC, is very well correlated with the F_1-Mult. If we ranked systems based on their (target) MCC, the only difference would be in the EN-RU task, in which BOUN would be above the baseline. Since this metric was conceived especially for unbalanced binary classification problems, it seems reasonable to use it as the primary metric for the next editions of this shared task.

In the sentence-level task, Unbabel achieved again the best scores, but with a tighter gap to the other participants. For EN-RU, their second submission is statistically tied to ETRI's first. Comparing to last year's results in EN-DE, in which the best system had a Pearson correlation of 0.51 and the median was 0.38, we see a great improvement overall. This is likely due to the more powerful pre-trained models, such as BERT and ELMo, that are common now.

In the document-level task, Unbabel achieved the best scores again. Unbabel was also the only participant in the fine-grained annotation subtask, but surpassed the baseline by a large margin. As for the MQM scoring, last year used a different test set, making results not directly comparable, but the best system achieved a Pearson correlation of 0.53. The test set this year is arguably easier because its mean MQM is closer to the training set (see Table 3).

Results for Task 3 are presented together with the metrics task[8].

7 Conclusions

We presented our findings in this year's shared task on translation quality estimation. This year, the main novelties were a new task that assesses quality estimation as a metric (Task 3), a new subtask related to document-level quality estimation (Task 2) where the goal is to predict error annotations and their severities, and a new dataset for English-Russian used in Task 1.

Following similar trends in other NLP tasks, a common choice from the participants this year was the usage of contextual and pre-trained embedding models such as BERT and XLM along with transfer learning, which includes the systems that obtained the best results. In the future, we plan to implement some strategies to reduce the gap for participants to enter Task 2, as this year we only had two participants. One possibility is to make available pre-processed data or word-level predictions, so that participants can focus more easily on document-level details.

Acknowledgments

We would like to thank Ramon Astudillo, Frédéric Blain, Carolina Scarton, and Lucia Specia for answering several questions regarding the organization of previous year's shared task, as well as the Linguistic Services and Platform teams at Unbabel

---

[6]We adapted the implementation from `https://gist.github.com/varvara-l/d66450db8da44b8584c02f4b6c79745c`

[7]We used the implementation from `https://github.com/ygraham/nlp-williams`

[8]`http://statmt.org/wmt19/metrics-task.html`

| | Target | | Source | |
Model	F_1	MCC	F_1	MCC
† UNBABEL Ensemble	0.4752	0.4585	0.4455	0.4094
UNBABEL Stacked	0.4621	0.4387	0.4284	0.3846
ETRI BERT Multitask A	0.4061	0.3778	0.3946	0.3426
ETRI BERT Multitask B	0.4047	0.3774	0.396	0.3446
MIPT Neural CRF Transformer	0.3285	0.2896	0.2662	0.1811
MIPT Neural CRF RNN	0.3025	0.2601	0.26	0.1748
Baseline	0.2974	0.2541	0.2908	0.2126
BOUN RTM GLMd*	0.1846	0.1793	0.0957	0.0372

Table 4: Word-level results for EN-DE. † indicates the winning system.* indicates late submissions that were not considered in the official ranking.

| | Target | | Source | |
Model	F_1	MCC	F_1	MCC
† UNBABEL Ensemble 2	0.478	0.4577	0.4541	0.4212
† UNBABEL Ensemble	0.4629	0.4412	0.4174	0.3729
† ETRI BERT Multitask A	0.4515	0.4294	0.4202	0.3732
ETRI BERT Multitask B	0.43	0.4082	0.4114	0.3644
Baseline	0.2412	0.2145	0.2647	0.1887
BOUN RTM GLMd*	0.1952	0.2271	0.0871	0.0698

Table 5: Word-level results for EN-RU. † indicates the winning systems. * indicates late submissions that were not considered in the official ranking.

Model	Pearson	Spearman
† UNBABEL Ensemble	0.5718	0.6221
CMULTIMLT	0.5474	0.5947
NJUNLP BiQE BERT Ensemble	0.5433	0.5694
NJUNLP BiQE	0.5412	0.5665
ETRI	0.526	0.5745
Baseline	0.4001	0.4607
UTARTU LABE	-0.319	-0.3768
UTARTU LABEL	0.2487	0.2531
USAAR-DFKI CNNQE	0.2013	0.2806
BOUN RTM1*	0.4734	0.5307
BOUN RTM2*	0.1799	0.2779

Table 6: Sentence-level results for EN-DE. † indicates the winning system. * indicates late submissions that were not considered in the official ranking.

Model	Pearson	Spearman
† UNBABEL Ensemble 2	0.5923	0.5388
† UNBABEL Ensemble	0.5889	0.5411
ETRI	0.5327	0.5222
CMULTIMLT	0.4575	0.4039
CMULTIMLT 2	0.4292	0.3628
UTARTU LABEL	0.4014	0.3364
Baseline	0.2601	0.2339
UTARTU LACLAS	0.0424	0.1735
BOUN RTM 1*	0.2817	0.2067
BOUN RTM 2*	0.2314	0.1082

Table 7: Sentence-level results for EN-RU. † indicates the winning system. * indicates late submissions that were not considered in the official ranking.

Model	F_1
UNBABEL BERT	0.48
Baseline	0.38

Table 8: Document-level fine grained annotation results for EN-FR

Model	Pearson
UNBABEL LINBERT	0.37
UNBABEL BERT	0.37
Baseline	0.35
BOUN RTM 1*	0.22
BOUN RTM 2*	0.05

Table 9: Document-level MQM results for EN-FR. † indicates the winning system. * indicates late submissions.

for helping creating and annotating the new test set used for Task 2. We also thank Microsoft for the preparation of the new post-edited dataset for Task 1. This work was partly funded by the European Research Council (ERC StG DeepSPIN 758969), the European Union's Horizon 2020 research and innovation programme under grant agreement No. 825303, the Estonian Research Council grant no. 1226 and by the Fundação para a Ciência e Tecnologia through contract UID/EEA/50008/2019.

References

H. Abdi. 2007. Bonferroni and Šidák corrections for multiple comparisons. In N. J. Salkind, editor, *Encyclopedia of Measurement and Statistics*, pages 103–107. Sage, Thousand Oaks, CA.

Mikel Artetxe and Holger Schwenk. 2018. Massively multilingual sentence embeddings for zero-shot cross-lingual transfer and beyond. *CoRR*, abs/1812.10464.

Shamil Chollampatt and Hwee Tou Ng. 2018. Neural quality estimation of grammatical error correction. In *Proceedings of the 2018 Conference on Empirical Methods in Natural Language Processing*, Brussels, Belgium.

Jacob Devlin, Ming-Wei Chang, Kenton Lee, and Kristina Toutanova. 2019. Bert: Pre-training of Deep Bidirectional Transformers for Language Understanding. In *Proceedings of NAACL*.

Chris Dyer, Victor Chahuneau, and Noah A. Smith. 2013. A simple, fast, and effective reparameterization of IBM model 2. In *Proceedings of NAACL*.

Fábio Kepler, Jonay Trénous, Marcos Treviso, Miguel Vera, and André F. T. Martins. 2019. OpenKiwi: An open source framework for quality estimation. In *Proceedings of ACL 2019 System Demonstrations*.

Guillaume Lample and Alexis Conneau. 2019. Cross-lingual Language Model Pretraining. *arXiv preprint arXiv:1901.07291*.

André F. T. Martins, Marcin Junczys-Dowmunt, Fabio N. Kepler, Ramón Astudillo, Chris Hokamp, and Roman Grundkiewicz. 2017. Pushing the Limits of Translation Quality Estimation. *Transactions of the Association for Computational Linguistics*, 5:205–218.

B.W. Matthews. 1975. Comparison of the predicted and observed secondary structure of t4 phage lysozyme. *Biochimica et Biophysica Acta (BBA) - Protein Structure*, 405(2):442 – 451.

Lucia Specia, Gustavo Paetzold, and Carolina Scarton. 2015. Multi-level translation quality prediction with quest++. In *Proceedings of ACL-IJCNLP*

2015 System Demonstrations, pages 115–120, Beijing, China. Association for Computational Linguistics and The Asian Federation of Natural Language Processing.

Alexander Yeh. 2000. More accurate tests for the statistical significance of result differences. In *Coling-2000: the 18th Conference on Computational Linguistics*, pages 947–953.

Findings of the WMT 2019 Shared Task on Automatic Post-Editing

Rajen Chatterjee[1], **Christian Federmann**[2] **Matteo Negri**[3], **Marco Turchi**[3]

[1] Apple Inc., Cupertino, CA, USA
[2] Microsoft Cloud+AI, Redmond, WA, USA
[3] Fondazione Bruno Kessler, Trento, Italy

Abstract

We present the results from the 5th round of the WMT task on MT Automatic Post-Editing. The task consists in automatically correcting the output of a "black-box" machine translation system by learning from human corrections. Keeping the same general evaluation setting of the previous four rounds, this year we focused on two language pairs (English-German and English-Russian) and on domain-specific data (Information Technology). For both the language directions, MT outputs were produced by neural systems unknown to participants. Seven teams participated in the **English-German** task, with a total of 18 submitted runs. The evaluation, which was performed on the same test set used for the 2018 round, shows further progress in APE technology: 4 teams achieved better results than last year's winning system, with improvements up to -0.78 TER and +1.23 BLEU points over the baseline. Two teams participated in the **English-Russian** task submitting 2 runs each. On this new language direction, characterized by a higher quality of the original translations, the task proved to be particularly challenging. Indeed, none of the submitted runs improved the very high results of the strong system used to produce the initial translations (16.16 TER, 76.20 BLEU).

1 Introduction

MT Automatic Post-Editing (APE) is the task of automatically correcting errors in a machine-translated text. As pointed out by (Chatterjee et al., 2015), from the application point of view the

task is motivated by its possible uses to:

- Improve MT output by exploiting information unavailable to the decoder, or by performing deeper text analysis that is too expensive at the decoding stage;

- Cope with systematic errors of an MT system whose decoding process is not accessible;

- Provide professional translators with improved MT output quality to reduce (human) post-editing effort;

- Adapt the output of a general-purpose MT system to the lexicon/style requested in a specific application domain.

In its 5th round, the APE shared task organized within the WMT Conference on Machine Translation kept the same overall evaluation setting of the previous four rounds. Specifically, the participating systems had to automatically correct the output of an unknown "black box" MT system by learning from human revisions of translations produced by the same system.

This year, the task focused on two language pairs (English-German and English-Russian) and, in continuity with the last three rounds, on data coming from the Information Technology domain. While in 2018 one of the proposed subtasks was still focusing on the correction of phrase-based MT output, this year only neural MT (NMT) output has been considered. However, this year's campaign allows both for a fair assessment of the progress in APE technology and for tests in more challenging conditions. On one side, reusing the same test English-German set used last year, the evaluation framework allows us for a direct comparison with the last year's outcomes at least on one language. On the other side, dealing with a

Proceedings of the Fourth Conference on Machine Translation (WMT), Volume 3: Shared Task Papers (Day 2) pages 11–28
Florence, Italy, August 1-2, 2019. ©2019 Association for Computational Linguistics

difficult language like Russian and only with high-quality NMT output, also this round presented participants with an increased level of difficulty with respect to the past.

Seven teams participated in the English-German task, submitting 18 runs in total. Two teams participated in the English-Russian task, submitting 2 runs each. Similar to last year, all the teams developed their systems based on neural technology, which confirms to be the state-of-the-art approach to APE. Only in one case, indeed, a participating team achieved its highest results (but with no improvement over the baseline) with a phrase-based APE system. In most of the cases, participants experimented with the Transformer architecture (Vaswani et al., 2017), either directly or by adapting it to the task (see Section 3). Another common trait of the submitted systems is the reliance on the consolidated multi-source approach (Zoph and Knight, 2016; Libovický et al., 2016), which is able to exploit information from both the MT output to be corrected and the corresponding source sentence. The third aspect common to all submissions is the exploitation of synthetic data, either those provided together with the task data (Negri et al., 2018; Junczys-Dowmunt and Grundkiewicz, 2016) or similar, domain-specific resources created *ad-hoc* by participants.

In the English-German task, the evaluation was performed on the same test set used in 2018, whose "gold" human post-edits were kept undisclosed to participants for the sake of future comparisons. Evaluating on the same benchmark allowed to observe further technology improvements over the past. Last year, the largest gain over the baseline (16.84 TER, 74.73 BLEU) was -0.38 TER (16.46) and +0.8 BLEU (75.53). This year, four teams achieved better results than last year's best submission. The top-ranked system achieved 16.06 TER (-0.78 with respect to the baseline) and 75.96 BLEU (+1.23). Most noticeably, the fact that the TER/BLEU differences between the top four primary submissions are not statistically significant indicates that the observed progress is not isolated.

The newly proposed English-Russian task represents a more challenging evaluation scenario, mainly due to the higher quality of the NMT output to be corrected. In this case, even the best submission (16.59 TER, 75.27 TER) was unable to beat the baseline (16.16 TER, 76.20 BLEU). These results confirm one of the main findings of previous rounds (Bojar et al., 2017; Chatterjee et al., 2018a): improving high-quality MT output remains the biggest challenge for APE. This motivates further research on precise and conservative solutions able to mimic human behaviour by performing only the minimum amount of edit operations needed.

2 Task description

In continuity with all the previous rounds of the APE task, participants were provided with training and development data consisting of (*source*, *target*, *human post-edit*) triplets, and were asked to return automatic post-edits for a test set of unseen (*source*, *target*) pairs.

2.1 Data

This year, the evaluation was performed on two language pairs, English-German and English-Russian. For both the subtasks, data were selected from the Information Technology (IT) domain. As emerged from the previous evaluations, the selected target domain is specific and repetitive enough to allow supervised systems to learn from the training set useful correction patterns that are also re-applicable to the test set.

The released training and development sets consist of (*source*, *target*, *human post-edit*) triplets in which:

- The source (SRC) is a tokenized English sentence;

- The target (TGT) is a tokenized German/Russian translation of the source, which was produced by a black-box system unknown to participants. For both the languages, translations were obtained from neural MT systems:[1] this implies that their overall quality is generally high, making the task harder compared to previous rounds, which

---

[1] For **English-German**, the NMT system was trained with generic and in-domain parallel training data using the attentional encoder-decoder architecture (Bahdanau et al., 2014) implemented in the Nematus toolkit (Sennrich et al., 2017). We used byte-pair encoding (Sennrich et al., 2016) for vocabulary reduction, mini-batches of 100, word embeddings of 500 dimensions, and gated recurrent unit layers of 1,024 units. Optimization was done using Adam and by re-shuffling the training set at each epoch. For **English-Russian**, the NMT system used was the Microsoft Translator production system, which was trained with both generic and in-domain parallel training data.

<table>
<tr><td></td><td colspan="4">Number of instances</td></tr>
<tr><td></td><td>Training</td><td>Development</td><td>Test</td><td>Additional Resources</td></tr>
<tr><td>English-German</td><td>13,442</td><td>1,000</td><td>1,023</td><td>eSCAPE-PBSMT: 7,258,533
eSCAPE-NMT: 7,258,533
Artificial: 4.5M</td></tr>
<tr><td>English-Russian</td><td>15,089</td><td>1,000</td><td>1,023</td><td>eSCAPE-NMT: 7.7 M</td></tr>
</table>

Table 1: Data statistics.

focused only (until 2017) or also (as in 2018) on the correction of the output of phrase-based systems.

- The human post-edit (PE) is a manually-revised version of the target, which was produced by professional translators.

Test data consists of (*source, target*) pairs having similar characteristics of those in the training set. Human post-edits of the test target instances are left apart to measure system performance.

For the **English-German** subtask, the same in-domain data[2] collected for last year's round of the task have been used. The *training* and *development* set respectively contain 13,442 and 1,000 triplets, while the *test* set consists of 1,023 instances. Participants were also provided with two additional training resources, which were widely used in last year's round. One (called "Artificial" in Table 1) is the corpus of 4.5 million artificially-generated post-editing triplets described in (Junczys-Dowmunt and Grundkiewicz, 2016). The other resource is the English-German section of the eSCAPE corpus (Negri et al., 2018). It comprises 14.5 million instances, which were artificially generated both via phrase-based and neural translation (7.25 millions each) of the same source sentences.

For the **English-Russian** subtask, Microsoft Office localization data have been used. This material, which mainly consists of short segments (menu commands, short messages, etc.), is shared with the English-Russian Quality Estimation shared task.[3] The *training* and *development* set respectively contain 15,089 and 1,000 triplets, while the *test* set comprises 1,023 instances. For this language pair, the eSCAPE corpus has been extended to provide participants with additional

training material.[4]

Table 1 provides basic statistics about the data of the two subtasks.

2.1.1 Complexity indicators: repetition rate

Table 2 provides a view of the data from a task difficulty standpoint. For each dataset released in the five rounds of the APE task, it shows the repetition rate of SRC, TGT and PE elements, as well as the TER (Snover et al., 2006) and the BLEU score (Papineni et al., 2002) of the TGT elements (i.e. the original target translations).

The repetition rate measures the repetitiveness inside a text by looking at the rate of non-singleton n-gram types (n=1...4) and combining them using the geometric mean. Larger values indicate a higher text repetitiveness and, as discussed in (Bojar et al., 2016; Bojar et al., 2017; Chatterjee et al., 2018a), suggest a higher chance of learning from the training set correction patterns that are applicable also to the test set. In the previous rounds of the task, we considered the large differences in repetitiveness across the datasets as a possible explanation for the variable gains over the baseline obtained by participants. In this perspective, the low system performance observed in the APE15 task and in the APE17 German-English subtask was in part ascribed to the low repetition rate in the data. In contrast, much higher repetition rates in the data likely contributed to facilitate the problem in the APE16 task and in the APE17 English-German subtask, in which most of the participants achieved significant gains over the baseline. Although in both the APE18 subtasks the repetition rate values were relatively high, evaluation results shown that the influence of data repetitiveness on final APE performance is marginal. Indeed, while in the last year's PBSMT subtask the improvements over the baseline were impressive (-

---

	2015	2016	2017	2017	2018	2018	2019	2019
Language	En-Es	En-De	En-De	De-En	En-De	En-De	En-De	En-Ru
Domain	News	IT	IT	Medical	IT	IT	IT	IT
MT type	PBSMT	PBSMT	PBSMT	PBSMT	PBSMT	NMT	NMT	NMT
Repet. Rate SRC	2.905	6.616	7.216	5.225	7.139	7.111	7.111	18.25
Repet. Rate TGT	3.312	8.845	9.531	6.841	9.471	9.441	9.441	14.78
Repet. Rate PE	3.085	8.245	8.946	6.293	8.934	8.941	8.941	13.24
Baseline TER	23.84	24.76	24.48	15.55	24.24	16.84	16.84	16.16
Baseline BLEU	n/a	62.11	62.49	79.54	62.99	74.73	74.73	76.20

Table 2: Basic information about the APE shared task data released since 2015: languages, domain, type of MT technology, repetition rate and initial translation quality (TER/BLEU of TGT). Grey columns refer to data covering different language pairs and domains with respect to this year's evaluation round.

6.24 TER, +9.53 BLEU points), in the NMT sub-task (whose data were reused this year) the quality gains were considerably smaller (-0.38 TER and +0.8 BLEU points). As discussed in Section 4.1, also this year we observe a similar situation: especially for English-Russian, the high repetition rate values reported in Table 2, which are the highest ones across all the APE data released so far, are not enough to determine quality improvements comparable to previous rounds. This suggests that, although it used to play an important role when dealing with lower quality MT output in the first rounds of the APE task, text repetitiveness has less influence on final performance compared to other complexity indicators.

2.1.2 Complexity indicators: MT quality

Indeed, another important aspect that determines the difficulty of APE is the initial quality of the MT output to be corrected. This can be measured by computing the TER ($\downarrow$) and BLEU ($\uparrow$) scores (last two rows in Table 2) using the human post-edits as reference.

As discussed in (Bojar et al., 2017; Chatterjee et al., 2018a), numeric evidence of a higher quality of the original translations can indicate a smaller room for improvement for APE systems (having, at the same time, less to learn during training and less to correct at test stage). On one side, indeed, training on good (or near-perfect) automatic translations can drastically reduce the number of learned correction patterns. On the other side, testing on similarly good translations can drastically reduce the number of corrections required and the applicability of the learned patterns, thus making the task more difficult. As observed in the previous APE evaluation rounds, there is a noticeable correlation between translation quality

and systems' performance. In 2016 and 2017, on English-German data featuring a similar level of quality (24.76/24.48 TER, 62.11/62.49 BLEU), the top systems achieved significant improvements over the baseline (-3.24 TER and +5.54 BLEU in 2016, -4.88 TER and +7.58 BLEU in 2017). In 2017, on higher quality German-English data (15.55 TER, 79.54 BLEU), the observed gains were much smaller (-0.26 TER, +0.28 BLEU). In 2018, the correction of English-German translations produced by a phrase-based system (24.24 TER, 62.99 BLEU) yielded much larger gains (up to -6.24 TER and +9.53 BLEU) compared to the correction of higher-quality neural translations (16.84 TER, 74.73 BLEU), which resulted in TER/BLEU variations of less than 1.00 point. As discussed in Section 4, also this year's results confirm the strict correlation between the quality of the initial translations and the actual potential of APE.

2.1.3 Complexity indicators: TER distribution

Further indications about the difficulty of the two subtasks are provided by Figures 1 and 2, which plot the TER distribution for the items in the two test sets. As shown in Figure 1, the distribution for English-German is quite skewed towards low TER values, with almost 50% of the test test items having a TER between 0 and 10 that indicates their very high quality (in other terms, they require few edits). In particular, the proportion of "perfect" test instances having TER=0 (i.e. items that should not be modified by the APE systems) is quite high (25.2% of the total).[5] For these test

---

[5] This value is considerably lower than the proportion observed in the challenging APE17 German-English test set (45.0%) but still a considerably higher value compared to "easier" test sets released for other rounds of the task.

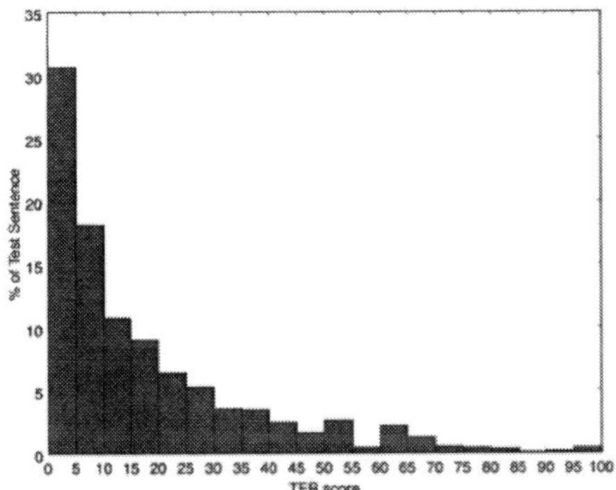

Figure 1: TER distribution in the **English-German** test set

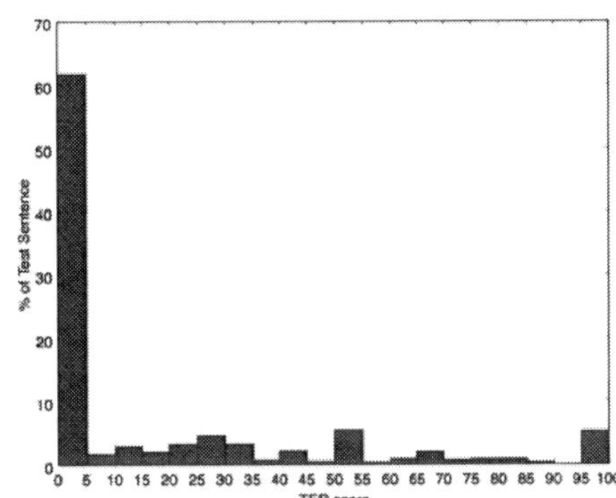

Figure 2: TER distribution in the **English-Russian** test set

items, any correction made by the APE systems will be treated as unnecessary and penalized by automatic evaluation metrics. This problem calls for conservative and precise systems able to properly fix errors only in the remaining test items, leaving the "perfect" ones unmodified.

Data skewedness is exacerbated in the English-Russian test set, in which 63.5% of the instances have a TER between 0 and 10 (in particular, 61.4% of them are perfect translations). Together with the high BLEU score, this contributes to make the English-Russian task considerably more difficult compared to the English-German one (as well as compared to most of the APE test sets released so far).

As discussed in Section 4, also this year's evaluation results confirm the strict correlation between the quality of the initial translations and the actual potential of APE.

2.2 Evaluation metrics

System performance was evaluated both by means of automatic metrics and manually. Automatic metrics were used to compute the distance between *automatic* and *human* post-edits of the machine-translated sentences present in the test sets. To this aim, TER and BLEU (case-sensitive) were respectively used as primary and secondary evaluation metrics. Systems were ranked based on the average TER calculated on the test set by using the TERcom[6] software: lower average TER scores correspond to higher ranks. BLEU was computed using the multi-bleu.perl package[7] available

---

[6]`http://www.cs.umd.edu/~snover/tercom/`
[7]`https://github.com/moses-smt/`
`mosesdecoder/blob/master/scripts/`

in MOSES.

Manual evaluation was conducted via source-based direct human assessment (Graham et al., 2013; Cettolo et al., 2017; Bojar et al., 2018) as implemented by Appraise (Federmann, 2012). Details are discussed in Section 6.

2.3 Baseline

In continuity with the previous rounds, the official baseline results were the TER and BLEU scores calculated by comparing the raw MT output with the human post-edits. In practice, the baseline APE system is a *"do-nothing"* system that leaves all the test targets unmodified. Baseline results, the same shown in Table 2, are also reported in Tables 4 and 5 for comparison with participants' submissions.[8]

For each submitted run, the statistical significance of performance differences with respect to the baseline was calculated with the bootstrap test (Koehn, 2004).

3 Participants

Seven teams submitted a total of 18 runs for the English-German subtask. Two of them participated also in the English-Russian subtask by sub-

---

`generic/multi-bleu.perl`

[8]In addition to the *do-nothing* baseline, in the first three rounds of the task we also compared systems' performance with a re-implementation of the phrase-based approach firstly proposed by Simard et al. (2007), which represented the common backbone of APE systems before the spread of neural solutions. As shown in (Bojar et al., 2016; Bojar et al., 2017), the steady progress of neural APE technology has made the phrase-based solution not competitive with current methods reducing the importance of having it as an additional term of comparison. In 2018, we hence opted for considering only one baseline.

ID	Participating team
ADAPT_DCU	ADAPT Centre & Dublin City University, Ireland (Shterionov et al., 2019)
FBK	Fondazione Bruno Kessler, Italy (Tebbifakhr et al., 2019)
POSTECH	Pohang University of Science and Technology, South Korea (Lee et al., 2019)
UDS	Saarland University, Germany (Xu et al., 2019)
UNBABEL	Unbabel, Portugal (Lopes et al., 2019)
USAAR_DFKI	Saarland University & German Research Center for Artificial Intelligence, Germany (Pal et al., 2019)
IC_USFD	Imperial College London & University of Sheffield, United Kingdom

Table 3: Participants in the WMT19 Automatic Post-Editing task.

mitting 2 runs each. Participants are listed in Table 3, and a short description of their systems is provided in the following.

ADAPT Centre & Dublin City University. The ADAPT_DCU team participated in both the subtasks proposed this year. Their submissions pursue two main objectives, namely: *i)* investigating the effect of adding extra information in the form of prefix tokens in a neural APE system; and *ii)* assessing whether an SMT-based approach can be effective for post-editing NMT output. The neural APE system exploits a multi-source approach based on Marian-NMT.[9] Training data were augmented with two types of extra context tokens that identify partitions of the training set that may be relevant to guide system's behaviour (i.e. to identify features in the dataset with a very close relation to the editing patterns the system is supposed to learn). Such partitions are based on sentence length and topic information. Hence, the prepended tokens respectively state the data partition based on the number of source tokens and the topic induced via LDA clustering (Blei et al., 2003). The statistical APE models, which are based on Moses (Koehn et al., 2007), were trained to explore the idea of interleaving different MT technologies to improve NMT output quality. All the models are built by taking advantage of both the released training material and the provided artificial data (Negri et al., 2018; Junczys-Dowmunt and Grundkiewicz, 2016).

Fondazione Bruno Kessler. Also FBK participated in both the subtasks. Their submissions focus on mitigating the "over-correction" problem in APE, that is the systems' tendency to rephrase and correct MT output that is already acceptable, thus producing translations that will be penalized by evaluation against human post-edits. Following (Chatterjee et al., 2018b), the underlying idea is that over-correction can be prevented by inform-

ing the system about the predicted quality of the MT output or, in other terms, the expected amount of corrections needed. The proposed solution is based on prepending a special token to the source text and the MT output, so to indicate the required amount of post-editing. Three different tokens are used, namely "no post-edit" (no edits are required), "light post-edit" (minimal edits are required), and "heavy post-edit" (a large number of edits are required). At training time, the instances are labelled based on the TER computed between the MT output and its post-edited version, with the boundary between light and heavy post-edit set to TER=0.4 based on the findings reported in (Turchi et al., 2013; Turchi et al., 2014). At test time, tokens are predicted with two approaches. One is based on a classifier obtained by fine-tuning BERT (Devlin et al., 2018) on the in-domain data. The other approach exploits a retrieval-based method similar to (Farajian et al., 2017): given a query containing the source and the MT output to be post-edited, it: *i)* retrieves similar triplets from the training data, *ii)* ranks them based on the sentence level BLEU score between the MT output and the post-edit, and *iii)* creates the token based on the TER computed between the MT output and the post-edit of the most similar triplet. The backbone architecture is the multi-source extension of Transformer (Vaswani et al., 2017) described in (Tebbifakhr et al., 2018), which is trained both on the task data and on the available artificial corpora.

Pohang University of Science and Technology. POSTECH's system (English-German subtask) is a multi-source model that extends the Transformer implementation of the OpenNMT-py (Klein et al., 2017) library. It includes: *i)* a joint encoder that is able to generate joint representations reflecting the relationship between two input sources (SRC, TGT) with optional future masking to mimic the general decoding process of machine translation systems, and *ii)* two types of multi-source attention layers in the decoder that computes the atten-

---

[9]`https://marian-nmt.github.io/`

tion between the decoder state and the two outputs of the encoder. Therefore, four different model variants were suggested in terms of the existence of the encoder future mask and the type of the multi-source attention layer in the decoder. The eSCAPE corpus (Negri et al., 2018) was filtered to contain similar statistics as the official training dataset. During training, various teacher-forcing ratios were adjusted to alleviate the exposure bias problem. After training four variants with various teacher-forcing ratios, the final submissions were obtained from an ensemble of models. These are: 1) the primary submission that ensembles the variants with the two best TER scores in each architecture, 2) the contrastive submission that ensembles the variants with the best TER scores in each architecture, 3) the contrastive submission that ensembles two variants from each architecture, achieving the best TER and BLEU, respectively.

Saarland University. UdS's participation (English-German subtask) is based on a multi-source Transformer model for context-level machine translation (Zhang et al., 2018) implemented with the Neutron implementation (Xu and Liu, 2019) for the Transformer translation model (Vaswani et al., 2017). To improve the robustness of the training, and inspired by (Cheng et al., 2018), the APE task is jointly trained with the de-noising encoder task, which adds noises distribution directly to the post-editing results' embedding as machine translation outputs and tries to recover the original post-editing results. Both Gaussian noise and uniform noise were tried for the de-noising encoder task. The synthetic eSCAPE corpus (Negri et al., 2018) was also used for the training. Contrastive submissions were generated with the best averaged models of 5 adjacent checkpoints of 2 kinds of noise, and the primary submission is obtained with the ensemble of 5 models (4 averaged models + 1 model saved for every training epoch).

Unbabel. Following (Correia and Martins, 2019), Unbabel's submission (English-German subtask) adapts BERT (Devlin et al., 2018) to the APE task with an encoder-decoder framework. The system consists in a BERT encoder initialised with the pretrained model's weights and a BERT decoder initialised analogously, where the multi-head context attention is initialised with the self-attention weights. Additionally, source embeddings, target embeddings and projection layer (Press and Wolf, 2017) are shared, as well as the self-attention weights of the encoder and decoder. The system exploits BERT training schedule with streams A and B: the encoder receives as input both the source and the MT output separated by the special symbol "[SEP]", assigning to the first "A" segment embeddings and to the latter "B" segment embeddings. Regarding the BERT decoder, they use just the post-edit with "B" segment embeddings. In addition, as the NMT system has a strong in-domain performance, a conservativeness factor to avoid over-correction is explored. Similarly to (Junczys-Dowmunt and Grundkiewicz, 2016), a penalty is added during beam decoding (logits or log probabilities) to constrain the decoding to be as close as possible to the input – both the source and the MT output are considered, which allows to copy from the source – in order to avoid over edition of the MT segment. This penalty is tuned over the development set. In addition to the shared task in-domain data, system training exploits a variant of the eSCAPE corpus built on a closer in-domain parallel corpus (IT domain) provided by the Quality Estimation shared task.

Saarland University & German Research Center for Artificial Intelligence. USAAR_DFKI's participation (English-German subtask) is based on a multi-encoder adaptation of the Transformer architecture. The system consists in: *i)* a Transformer encoder block for the source sentence, followed by *ii)* a Transformer decoder block, but without masking, for self-attention on the MT segment, which effectively acts as second encoder combining source and MT output, and *iii)* feeds this representation into a final decoder block generating the post-edit. The intuition behind the proposed architecture is to generate better representations via both self- and cross- attention and to further facilitate the learning capacity of the feed-forward layer in the decoder block. Also in this case, model training takes advantage of the eSCAPE synthetic data (Negri et al., 2018).

University of Sheffield & Imperial College London. IC_USFD's submission (English-German subtask) is based on the dual-source Transformer model (Junczys-Dowmunt and Grundkiewicz, 2018), which was re-implemented in the

Tensor2Tensor (Vaswani et al., 2017) toolkit. The model was enriched with a copying mechanism that prevents unnecessary corrections. In addition to the main training data, the primary submission uses the EN-DE eSCAPE data (Negri et al., 2018). The contrastive submission uses data triplets where source and target are genuine data, and MT is a modified target (200K). This modified target mimics MT by simulating errors in the task training data. Sentences where error simulation is possible are selected from in-domain corpora (eSCAPE, as well as the in-domain data released with the WMT18 Quality Estimation task).

4   Results

Participants' results are shown in Tables 4 (English-German) and 5 (English-Russian). The submitted runs are ranked based on the average TER (case-sensitive) computed using human post-edits of the MT segments as reference, which is the APE task primary evaluation metric ("*TER (pe)*"). The two tables also report the BLEU score computed using human post-edits ("*BLEU (pe)*" column), which represents our secondary evaluation metric. These results are discussed in Section 4.1.

Table 4 includes four additional columns, which show the TER/BLEU scores computed using external references ("*TER (ref)*" and "*BLEU (ref)*") as well as the multi-reference TER/BLEU scores computed using human post-edits and external references ("*TER (pe+ref)*" and "*BLEU (pe+ref)*"). In Section 4.2, these figures are respectively used to discuss systems' capability to reflect the post-editing style of the training data and their tendency to produce unnecessary corrections of acceptable MT output. Since external references are available only for German, this analysis was not feasible for the English-Russian task.

4.1   Automatic metrics computed using human post-edits

Different from the past, this year the primary ("*TER (pe)*") and secondary evaluation metric ("*BLEU (pe)*") produce slightly different rankings.[10] For English-German, system results are quite close to each other, up to the point that *i)* TER differences between the top eight submissions are not statistically significant and *ii)* all the

submissions with a TER score equal or lower than the baseline are concentrated in a performance interval of less than 0.8 TER points and less than 1.2 BLEU points. This compression can contribute to explain the ranking differences, especially at higher ranks where discriminating between strong systems with almost identical performance is particularly difficult. However, for the sake of future analysis or alternative views of this year's outcomes, it's worth remarking that the 2nd, 3rd and 5th runs in terms of TER (all by the same team –POSTECH) respectively represent the top three submissions in terms of BLEU.

For English-Russian, the distance between the top and the worst submissions is larger, but also in this case the BLEU-based ranking is not identical to the TER-based one. Though with a negligible margin, the worst run in terms of TER would rank 2nd in terms of BLEU.

English-German subtask.   In order to measure the progress with respect to last year's round of the APE task, for this language pair the evaluation has been performed with the same data used for the NMT subtask in 2018. Last year, the majority of the participants' scores fell in a range of less than one TER/BLEU point improvement over the *do-nothing* baseline (16.84 TER, 74.73 BLEU), being 16.46 TER (-0.38) and 75.53 BLEU (+0.8) the scores and the corresponding quality gains achieved by the top submission. This year, eight submissions achieved a TER reduction larger than 0.4 points and a BLEU increase of more than 0.9 points. The top submission, in particular, obtained improvements up to -0.78 TER and +1.23 BLEU points over the baseline. Although correcting the output of a neural MT system still proves to be quite hard, we take the fact that 4 teams achieved better results than last year's winning system as an indicator of technology advancements.

English-Russian subtask.   This subtask proved to be more challenging compared to the English-German subtask. Final results are indeed much worse: none of the four runs submitted by the two participating teams was able to beat the *do-nothing* baseline (16.16 TER, 76.2 BLEU). Even for the top submission (16.59 TER, 75.27 BLEU), results' difference with respect to the baseline is statistically significant. One possible cause of the higher difficulty of the English-Russian subtask is the fact that dealing with a morphology-rich lan-

---

[10]The correlation between the ranks obtained by the two metrics is 0.97 for the English-German subtask and 0.7 for the English-Russian subtask.

ID	TER (pe)	BLEU (pe)	TER (ref)	BLEU (ref)	TER (pe+ref)	BLEU (pe+ref)
UNBABEL Primary	16.06*	75.96	41.66	44.95	15.58	78.1
POSTECH Primary	16.11*	76.22	42.04	44.57	15.68	78.08
POSTECH Contrastive (var2Ens8)	16.13*	76.21	42.09	44.53	15.73	78.05
USAAR_DFKI Primary	16.15*	75.75	41.84	44.65	15.69	77.84
POSTECH Contrastive (top1Ens4)	16.17*	76.15	42.09	44.52	15.74	78.01
UNBABEL Contrastive (2)	16.21*	75.7	41.59	45.08	15.72	77.98
UNBABEL Contrastive (1)	16.24*	75.7	41.62	45.01	15.76	77.97
FBK Primary	16.37*	75.71	42.18	44.39	15.90	77.54
FBK Contrastive	16.61†	75.28	42.12	44.49	16.1	77.43
UDS Primary	16.77†	75.03	42.64	43.78	16.34	76.83
IC_USFD Contrastive	16.78†	74.88	42.45	44.01	16.31	76.82
UDS Contrastive (Gaus)	16.79†	75.03	42.55	44.0	16.33	76.87
UDS Contrastive (Uni)	16.80†	75.03	42.66	43.79	16.37	76.85
IC_USFD Primary	16.84†	74.8†	42.58	43.86	16.41	76.68
Baseline	16.84	74.73	42.24	44.2	16.27	76.83
ADAPT_DCU Contrastive (SMT)	17.07	74.3	42.40	44.14	16.54	76.36
ADAPT_DCU Primary	17.29	74.29	42.41	44.09	16.81	76.51
USAAR_DFKI Contrastive	17.31	73.97	42.45	43.71	16.87	76.06
ADAPT_DCU Contrastive (LEN)	17.41	74.01	42.44	44.01	16.91	76.2

Table 4: Results for the WMT19 APE **English-German subtask** – average TER (↓), BLEU score (↑). The symbol "*" indicates results differences between runs that are not statistically significant. The symbol "†" indicates a difference from the MT baseline that is not statistically significant.

ID	TER (pe)	BLEU (pe)
Baseline	16.16	76.2
ADAPT_DCU Contrastive	16.59	75.27
ADAPT_DCU Primary	18.31	72.9
FBK Primary	19.34	72.42
FBK Contrastive	19.48	72.91

Table 5: Results for the WMT19 APE **English-Russian subtask** – average TER (↓), BLEU score (↑).

guage like Russian is problematic not only for MT but also from the APE standpoint. Under similar data conditions (the training sets of the two subtasks differ by ∼1,650 instances), the training set of a morphology-rich language is likely to be more sparse compared to other languages. The other possible explanation lies in the higher quality of the original translations (our second complexity indicator discussed in Section 2.1.2), which reduces the room for improvement with APE and, at the same time, increases the possibility to damage MT output that is already correct. From the MT quality point of view, according to the baseline results shown in Table 2, the English-Russian dataset used for this year's campaign is the second most difficult benchmark released in five rounds of the APE task. Also the TER distribution of the test set instances (our third complexity indica-

tor discussed in Section 2.1.3) indicates the higher difficulty of the task, which is characterized by the highest number of perfect translations across the five rounds of the APE shared task (61.4%). In terms of repetition rate, as observed in Section 2.1.1, English-Russian data considerably differ from those released for the previous rounds of the task. The much larger values shown in Table 2 are not surprising considering that this material is drawn from Microsoft Office localization data that mainly consist of short segments (e.g. menu commands), which are likely produced based on standardized guidelines. However, also this year text repetitiveness seems to have a smaller influence on final performance compared to quality of the initial translations. Besides all these elements, the higher difficulty of the English-Russian subtask is also indirectly suggested by the low number of participants. Likely, poor results observed on the development set during system development (i.e. the difficulty to beat the *do-nothing* baseline) discouraged other potential participants.

4.2 Automatic metrics computed using external references

By learning from (SRC, TGT, PE) triplets, APE systems' goal is to perform a "monolingual translation" from raw MT output into its correct version. In this translation process, the same sentence can be corrected in many possible ways that make the space of possible valid outputs potentially very large. Ideally, from this space, APE systems should select solutions that reflect as much as possible the post-editing style of the training data (in real-use settings, this can be the style/lexicon of specific users, companies, etc.). However, nothing prevents to end up with outputs that partially satisfy this constraint. In light of these considerations, TER and BLEU scores computed using human post-edits as reference represent a reliable measure of quality but:

1. They provide us with partial information on how systems' output reflects the post-editing style of the training data;

2. They are not informative at all about the amount of valid corrections that are not present in the human post-edits.

In order to shed light on these aspects, in previous rounds of the task, further analysis was performed by taking advantage of reference translations. In continuity with the past, in Sections 4.2.1 and 4.2.2 we re-propose this analysis for the English-German subtask, the only one for which external references are available.

4.2.1 Output style

To gain further insights on point 1. (i.e. system's capability to learn the post-editing style of the training data), the *"TER (ref)"* and *"BLEU (ref)"* columns in Table 4 show the TER and BLEU scores computed against independent reference translations. The rational behind their computation is that differences in TER/BLEU(pe) and TER/BLEU(ref) can be used as indicators of the "direction" taken by the trained models (i.e. either towards humans' post-editing style or towards a generic improvement of the MT output).

Since independent references are usually very different from conservative human post-edits of the same TGT sentences, all the TER/BLEU scores measured using independent references are expected to be worse. However, if our hypothesis holds true, visible differences in the baseline improvements measured with TER/BLEU(pe) and TER/BLEU(ref) should indicate system's ability to model the post-editing style of the training data. In particular, larger gains measured with TER/BLEU(pe) will be associated to this desired ability.

As can be seen in Table 4, systems' results on English-German show this tendency. Looking at the improvements over the baseline, those measured by computing TER and BLEU scores against human post-edits (i.e. TER/BLEU(pe)) are often larger than those computed against independent references (i.e. TER/BLEU(ref)). In terms of TER, this holds true for most of the submitted runs, with the best system that shows a difference of 0.2 TER points in the gains over the baseline computed with TER(pe) (-0.78) and those computed with TER(ref) (-0.58). On average, for the runs achieving improvements over the baseline, the difference in the gains over the baseline computed with TER(pe) and TER(ref) is respectively -0.41 and -0.08. In terms of BLEU, the differences are more visible. The best system improves over the baseline by 1.23 points with BLEU(pe) and 0.75 points with BLEU(ref), while the average difference in the gains over the baseline is 0.8 with BLEU(pe) and 0.2 with BLEU (ref). The larger (0.32/0.6) average improvements over the baseline observed with TER/BLEU computations against human post-edits can be explained by systems' tendency to reflect the post-editing style of the training data.

4.2.2 Over-corrections

To shed light on point 2. (i.e. system's tendency to produce unnecessary corrections of acceptable MT output), the *"TER (pe+ref)"* and *"BLEU (pe+ref)"* columns in Table 4 show the multi-reference TER and BLEU scores computed against post-edits and independent references. The rational behind their computation is that differences in TER/BLEU(pe) and TER/BLEU(pe+ref) can be used to analyze the quality of the unnecessary corrections performed by the systems (or, in other words, to study the impact of systems' tendency towards "over-correction"). APE corrections of a given MT output can indeed be of different types, namely: *i)* correct edits of a wrong passage, *ii)* wrong edits of a wrong passage, *iii)* correct edits of a correct passage and *iv)* wrong edits of a correct passage. TER/BLEU scores computed against human post-edits work reasonably well in capturing cases *i)-ii)* by matching APE systems' output with human post-edits: for wrong MT output passages (i.e. those changed by the post-editor), they inform us about the general quality of automatic corrections (i.e. how close they are to the post-editor's actions). Cases *iii)-iv)*, in contrast, are more problematic since any change performed by the system to a correct passage (i.e. those that were not changed by the post-editor) will always be penalized by automatic comparisons with human post-edits. Although discriminating between the two types of unnecessary corrections is hard, we hypothesize that a comparison between TER/BLEU(pe) and TER/BLEU(pe+ref) can be used as a proxy to quantify those belonging to type *iii)*. In general, due to the possibility to match more and longer n-grams in a multi-reference setting, TER/BLEU(pe+ref) scores are expected to be higher than TER/BLEU(pe) scores. However, if our hypothesis holds true, visible differences in the increase observed for the baseline and for the systems should indicate systems' tendency to produce acceptable over-corrections (type *iii)*). In particular, larger gains observed for the APE systems will be associated to their over-correction tendency towards potentially acceptable edits that should not be penalized by automatic evaluation metrics.

As expected, Table 4 shows that, on English-German data, multi-reference evaluation against post edits and external references (TER/BLEU(pe+ref)) yields better results compared to single reference evaluation with post-edits only (TER/BLEU(pe)). The variations of the *do-nothing* baseline are -0.57 TER (from 16.84 to 16.27) and 2.1 BLEU (from 74.73 to 76.83) points. In contrast, systems' scores vary by -0.46 TER and +2.01 BLEU points on average. In comparison with the larger variation observed for the baseline, this indicates that, for most of the submissions, the multi-reference evaluation does not indicate a tendency to produce unnecessary but acceptable corrections. On a positive note, while last year this was true for all the systems, this year four runs perform slightly better than

the baseline in terms of BLEU(pe+ref). Though minimal, these differences suggest that a certain amount of corrections made by the top systems still represent acceptable modifications of the original translations.

5 System/performance analysis

As a complement to global TER/BLEU scores, also this year we performed a more fine-grained analysis of the changes made by each system to the test instances.

5.1 Macro indicators: modified, improved and deteriorated sentences

Tables 6 and 7 show the number of modified, improved and deteriorated sentences, respectively for the English-German and the English-Russian subtasks. It's worth noting that, as in the previous rounds and in both the settings, the number of sentences modified by each system is higher than the sum of the improved and the deteriorated ones. This difference is represented by modified sentences for which the corrections do not yield TER variations. This grey area, for which quality improvement/degradation can not be automatically assessed, contributes to motivate the human evaluation discussed in Section 6.

English-German subtask. As shown in table 6, the amount of sentences modified by the participating systems varies considerably. With values ranging from 4.01% to 39.1%, the average proportion of modifications (23.53%) is lower compared to last year (32.7%). Considering that about 25.2% (i.e. 257) of the test instances are to be considered as "perfect" (see Figure1), also this year the reported numbers are, for most of the submissions, far below the target percentage of modifications (74.8%). Overall, system's aggressiveness does not correlate with the final ranking: among both the top ranked systems and those with lower performance, large differences in the proportion of modified sentences can be observed. Indeed, as expected, what makes the difference is system's precision (i.e. the proportion of improved sentences out of the total amount of modified test items). Overall, the average precision is 45.92%, which represents a significant increase from last year's value (34.3%). While in 2018 none of the systems showed a precision higher than 50.0%, this year seven runs are above this value. As a

Systems	Modified	Improved	Deteriorated
UNBABEL Primary	366 (35.78%)	187 (51.09%)	110 (30.05%)
POSTECH Primary	207 (20.23%)	127 (61.35%)	41 (19.81%)
POSTECH Contrastive (var2Ens8)	210 (20.53%)	125 (59.52%)	45 (21.43%)
USAAR_DFKI Primary	301 (29.42%)	157 (52.16%)	83 (27.57%)
POSTECH Contrastive (top1Ens4)	213 (20.82%)	125 (58.69%)	47 (22.07%)
UNBABEL Contrastive (2)	400 (39.1%)	202 (50.50%)	121 (30.25%)
UNBABEL Contrastive (1)	393 (38.42%)	195 (49.62%)	117 (29.77%)
FBK Primary	200 (19.55%)	115 (57.50%)	50 (25.00%)
FBK Contrastive	363 (35.48%)	164 (45.18%)	131 (36.09%)
UDS Primary	96 (9.38%)	42 (43.75%)	36 (37.50%)
IC_USFD Contrastive	41 (4.01%)	21 (51.22%)	16 (39.02%)
UDS Contrastive (Gaus)	125 (12.22%)	54 (43.20%)	51 (40.80%)
UDS Contrastive (Uni)	112 (10.95%)	49 (43.75%)	41 (36.61%)
IC_USFD Primary	72 (7.04%)	29 (40.28%)	35 (48.61%)
ADAPT_DCU Contrastive (SMT)	120 (11.73%)	29 (24.17%)	61 (50.83%)
ADAPT_DCU Primary	368 (35.97%)	116 (31.52%)	169 (45.92%)
USAAR_DFKI Contrastive	391 (38.22%)	135 (34.53%)	168 (42.97%)
ADAPT_DCU Contrastive (LEN)	354 (34.60%)	101 (28.53%)	169 (47.74%)

Table 6: Number of test sentences modified, improved and deteriorated by each run submitted to the **English-German subtask**.

Systems	Modified	Improved	Deteriorated
ADAPT_DCU Contrastive	92 (8.99%)	17 (18.48%)	49 (53.26%)
ADAPT_DCU Primary	245 (23.95%)	57 (23.27%)	130 (53.06%)
FBK Primary	147 (14.37%)	49 (33.33%)	67 (45.58%)
FBK Contrastive	26 (2.54%)	5 (19.23%)	18 (69.23%)

Table 7: Number of test sentences modified, improved and deteriorated by each run submitted to the **English-Russian subtask**.

consequence, the percentage of deteriorated sentences out of the total amount of modified test items shows a significant drop. On average, a quality decrease is observed for 35.11% of the test items, while last year the average was 47.85%.

English-Russian subtask. As shown in table 7, also in this subtask the amount of sentences modified by the submitted systems varies considerably and does not correlate with systems' ranking. On average, the proportion of modifications is 12.46% (much less compared to the English-German subtask). With values ranging from 2.54% to 23.95%, all the four runs are far from the expected value of 38.6% modifications (recall that 61.4% of the test items are perfect translations). Systems' precision is also lower compared to the English-German task. The average proportion of improved sentences is 23.58%, while the deteriorated ones are on average 55.28%, thus confirming the higher difficulty of the English-Russian evaluation setting.

Overall, the analysis confirms that correcting high-quality translations still remains a hard task, especially when dealing with higher-quality English-Russian outputs. On one side, systems' low precision is an evident limitation. On the other side, one possible explanation is that the margins of improvement to the input sentences are reduced to types of errors (e.g. lexical choice) on which APE systems are less reliable. The analysis proposed in Section 5.2 aims to explore also this aspect.

5.2 Micro indicators: edit operations

In previous rounds of the APE task, the possible differences in the way systems corrected the test set instances were analyzed by looking at the distribution of the edit operations done by each system (insertions, deletions, substitutions and shifts). Such distribution was obtained by computing the TER between the original MT output and the output of each system taken as reference (only for the primary submissions). This analysis has been performed also this year but it turned out to be scarcely informative, as shown in Figure 3.

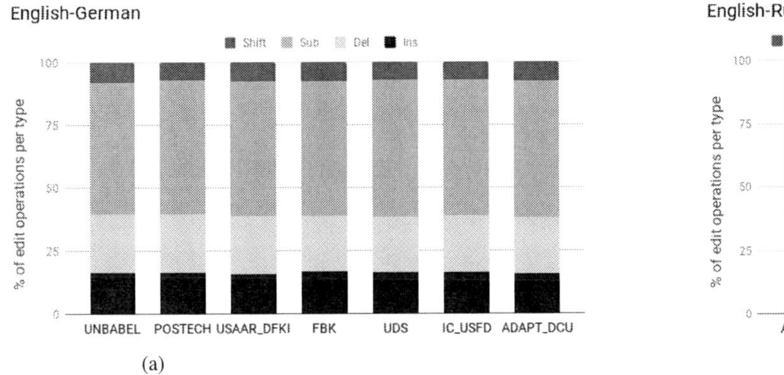

Figure 3: System behaviour (primary submissions) for **English-German** (a) and **English-Russian** (b) – TER(MT, APE)

For both the subtasks, the differences in system's behaviour are indeed barely visible, mainly due to the fact that, in most of the cases, the submitted neural APE models implement similar solutions (multi-source, Transformer-based models trained with the same in-domain and artificial corpora). All the submitted runs are characterized by a large number of substitutions (on average, 53.6% for English-German and 59.7% for English-Russian), followed by the deletions (22.6% for English-German and 26.4% for English-Russian), the insertions (respectively 16.3% and 9.4%) and finally the shifts (7.4% and 4.5%). These results are in line with previous findings. Also in 2018, for instance, the high fluency of neural translations induced the trained models to perform few reordering operations leaving lexical choice as a main direction of improvement, as suggested by the larger amount of substitutions performed by all the systems.

6 Human evaluation

In order to complement the automatic evaluation of APE submissions, a manual evaluation of the primary systems submitted (seven for English-German, five for English-Russian) was conducted. Similarly to the manual evaluation carried out for last year APE shared task, it was based on the direct assessment (DA) approach (Graham et al., 2013; Graham et al., 2017). In this Section, we present the evaluation procedure as well as the results obtained.

6.1 Evaluation procedure

The manual evaluation carried out this year involved 32 native German speakers with full professional proficiency in English. All annotators were paid consultants, sourced by a linguistic service provider company. Each evaluator had experience with the evaluation task through previous work using the same evaluation platform in order to be familiar with the user interface and its functionalities. A screenshot of the evaluation interface is presented in Figure 4.

We measure post-editing quality using *source-based direct assessment* (src-DA), as implemented in Appraise (Federmann, 2012). Scores are collected as $x \in [0, 100]$, focusing on adequacy (and not fluency, which previous WMT evaluation campaigns have found to be highly correlated with adequacy direct assessment results).

The original DA approach (Graham et al., 2013; Graham et al., 2014) is reference-based and, thus, needs to be adapted for use in our paraphrase assessment and translation scoring scenarios. Of course, this makes translation evaluation more difficult, as we require bilingual annotators. Src-DA has previously been used, e.g., in (Cettolo et al., 2017; Bojar et al., 2018).

Direct assessment initializes mental context for annotators by asking a priming question. The user interface shows two sentences:

- the source (src-DA, reference otherwise); and

- the candidate output.

Annotators read the priming question and both sentences and then assign a score $x \in [0, 100]$ to the candidate shown. The interpretation of this score considers the context defined by the priming question, effectively allowing us to use the same annotation method to collect assessments wrt. the different dimensions of quality as defined above. Our priming questions are shown in Table 8.

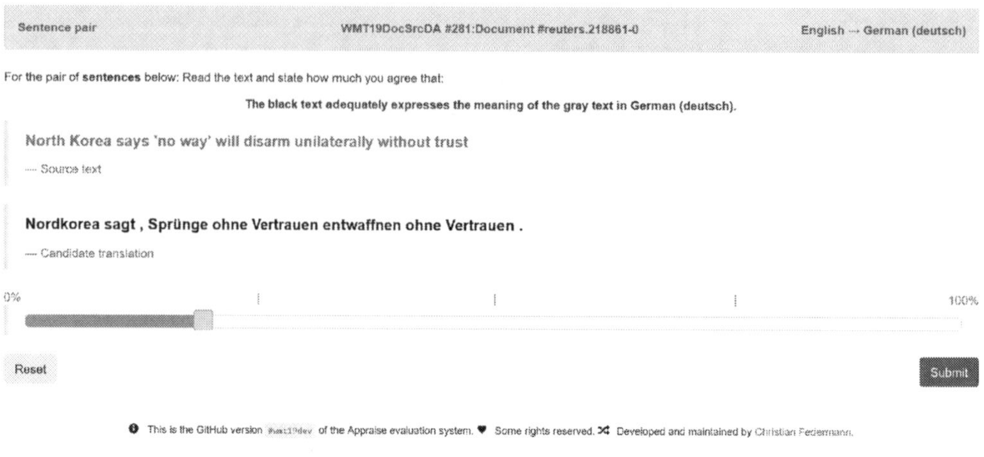

Figure 4: Screenshot of the direct assessment user interface.

Eval mode	Priming question used
Post-editing adequacy	How accurately does the above candidate text convey the original semantics of the source text? Slider ranges from *Not at all* (left) to *Perfectly* (right).

Table 8: Priming question used for human evaluation of post-editing adequacy.

For adequacy, we ask annotators to assess semantic similarity between source and candidate text, labeled as "source text" and "candidate translation", respectively. The annotation interface implements a slider widget to encode perceived similarity as a value $x \in [0, 100]$. Note that the exact value is hidden from the human, and can only be guessed based on the positioning of the slider. Candidates are displayed in random order, preventing bias.

For our human evaluation campaign, we also include human post-editing output (`test.tok.pe`) and unedited, neural machine translation output (`test.tok.nmt`). We expect human post-editing to be of higher quality than output from automatic post-editing submissions, which in turn should outperform unedited, neural machine translation output.

6.2 Human Evaluation results

English-German subtask. Score convergence over time for English-German assessments is presented in Figure 5. This figure tracks average system adequacy (as measured by Src-DA) over time, as assessments come in from human annotators. Note that we use the so-called *alternate HIT layout* as named in the WMT18 findings paper, using an 88:12 split between actual assessments and those reserved for quality control. All annotators have proven reliable, passing qualification tests.

The results of Src-DA for the English-German subtask are presented in Table 9. Our main findings are as follows:

- Human post-editing outperforms all auotmatic post-editing systems, the quality difference is significant;

- UNBABEL achieves best APE performance;

- USAAR_DFKI comes in second;

- POSTECH comes in third;

- All but one APE systems outperform unedited NMT output;

- Difference to the remaining APE system is not statistically significant.

Human evaluation does only result in very coarse result cluster. Thus, in order to order submissions by their respective post-editing quality, as perceived by human annotators, we also present *win-based results* in Table 10.

English-Russian subtask. For 2019, we did not run any human evaluation for the English-Russian subtask, due to lack of participation. Instead, we focused annotation efforts on English-German.

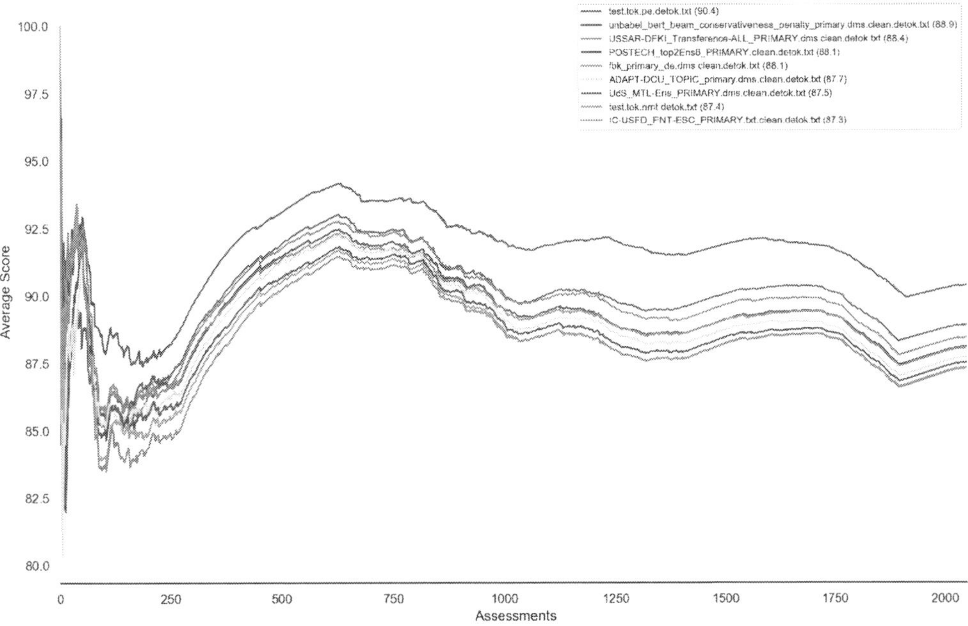

Figure 5: Score convergence over time for English-German assessments.

#	Systems	Ave %	Ave z
1	Human post-edit	90.39	0.154
2	UNBABEL	88.87	0.056
	USAAR_DFKI	88.45	0.027
	POSTECH	88.11	-0.006
	FBK	88.05	-0.014
	ADAPT_DCU	87.70	-0.037
	UDS	87.54	-0.043
	NMT output	87.35	-0.054
	IC_USFD	87.31	-0.059

Table 9: DA Human evaluation results for the **English-German subtask** in terms of average raw DA (Ave %) and average standardized scores (Ave z). Dashed lines between systems indicate clusters according to Wilcoxon signed-rank test at p-level $p \leq 0.05$.

#	Systems	Wins	Ave %	Ave z
1	Human post-edit	8	90.39	0.154
2	UNBABEL	4	88.87	0.056
3	USAAR_DFKI	3	88.45	0.027
4	POSTECH	1	88.11	-0.006
5	FBK	0	88.05	-0.014
	ADAPT_DCU	0	87.70	-0.037
	UDS	0	87.54	-0.043
	NMT output	0	87.35	-0.054
	IC_USFD	0	87.31	-0.059

Table 10: DA Human evaluation results for the **English-German subtask** in terms of average raw DA (Ave %) and average standardized scores (Ave z). Dashed lines between systems indicate clusters according to number of wins.

7 Conclusion

We presented the results from the fifth shared task on Automatic Post-Editing. This year, we proposed two subtasks in which the neural MT output to be corrected was respectively generated by an English-German system and by an English-Russian system. Both the subtasks dealt with data drawn from the information technology domain. Seven teams participated in the English-German task, with a total of 18 submitted runs, while two teams participated in the English-Russian task submitting two runs each. Except in one case (a contrastive run produced with a phrase-based system), the submissions are based on neural approaches, which confirm to be the state-of-the-art in APE. Most of them rely on multi-source models built upon the Transformer and trained by taking advantage of the synthetic corpora released as additional training material.

For the English-German subtask the evaluation was carried out on the same test set used last year, whose human post-edits were not released for the sake of future comparisons. The results on these data, indicate further technology improvements with respect to the 2018 round. This is shown by: *i)* the top result (-0.78 TER and +1.23 BLEU points over the baseline), which is significantly better than last year (-0.38 TER and +0.8 BLEU), and *ii)* the fact that four teams achieved higher results than last year's winning system.

The newly proposed English-Russian subtask proved to be more challenging. None of the submitted runs was able to beat the baseline, whose high TER (16.16) and BLEU (76.2) indicate a very high quality of the initial translations. This is also confirmed by the very skewed TER distribution of the test set items. With more than 60.0% of the translations with TER=0 (the highest value across all the APE datasets released so far), the chance of damaging a perfect MT output is extremely high. Despite the high repetition rate of the English-Russian data (also in this case, the highest across all datasets), the difficulty of handling such a high level of quality contributes to explain the lower results achieved by the two participating teams.

Overall, also this year the main open problem remains to mitigate systems' tendency towards over-correction. In light of the steady progress of NMT technology, handling increasingly better translations calls for conservative and precise solutions able to avoid the unnecessary modification of correct MT output.

Acknowledgments

We would like to thank Apple and Microsoft for their support and sponsorship in organizing the 2019 APE shared task. We are also particularly grateful to the anonymous Appraise annotators that contributed their human intelligence to this activity.

References

Dzmitry Bahdanau, Kyunghyun Cho, and Yoshua Bengio. 2014. Neural Machine Translation by Jointly Learning to Align and Translate. *arXiv preprint arXiv:1409.0473*.

David M. Blei, Andrew Y. Ng, Michael I. Jordan, and John Lafferty. 2003. Latent dirichlet allocation. *Journal of Machine Learning Research*, 3:2003.

Ondřej Bojar, Rajen Chatterjee, Christian Federmann, Yvette Graham, Barry Haddow, Matthias Huck, Antonio Jimeno Yepes, Philipp Koehn, Varvara Logacheva, Christof Monz, Matteo Negri, Aurelie Neveol, Mariana Neves, Martin Popel, Matt Post, Raphael Rubino, Carolina Scarton, Lucia Specia, Marco Turchi, Karin Verspoor, and Marcos Zampieri. 2016. Findings of the 2016 conference on machine translation. In *Proceedings of the First Conference on Machine Translation*, pages 131–198, Berlin, Germany, August. Association for Computational Linguistics.

Ondřej Bojar, Rajen Chatterjee, Christian Federmann, Yvette Graham, Barry Haddow, Shujian Huang, Matthias Huck, Philipp Koehn, Qun Liu, Varvara Logacheva, Christof Monz, Matteo Negri, Matt Post, Raphael Rubino, Lucia Specia, and Marco Turchi. 2017. Findings of the 2017 Conference on Machine Translation (WMT17). In *Proceedings of the Second Conference on Machine Translation, Volume 2: Shared Task Papers*, pages 169–214, Copenhagen, Denmark, September. Association for Computational Linguistics.

Ondej Bojar, Christian Federmann, Mark Fishel, Yvette Graham, Barry Haddow, Matthias Huck, Philipp Koehn, and Christof Monz. 2018. Findings of the 2018 conference on machine translation (wmt18). In *Proceedings of the Third Conference on Machine Translation, Volume 2: Shared Task Papers*, pages 272–307, Belgium, Brussels, October. Association for Computational Linguistics.

Mauro Cettolo, Marcello Federico, Luisa Bentivogli, Jan Niehues, Sebastian Stüker, Katsuhito Sudoh, Koichiro Yoshino, and Christian Federmann. 2017. Overview of the iwslt 2017 evaluation campaign. In *Proc. of IWSLT*, Tokyo, Japan.

Rajen Chatterjee, Marion Weller, Matteo Negri, and Marco Turchi. 2015. Exploring the Planet of the APEs: a Comparative Study of State-of-the-art Methods for MT Automatic Post-Editing. In *Proceedings of the 53rd Annual Meeting of the Association for Computational Linguistics)*, Beijing, China.

Rajen Chatterjee, Matteo Negri, Raphael Rubino, and Marco Turchi. 2018a. Findings of the WMT 2018 shared task on automatic post-editing. In *Proceedings of the Third Conference on Machine Translation: Shared Task Papers*, pages 710–725, Belgium, Brussels, October. Association for Computational Linguistics.

Rajen Chatterjee, Matteo Negri, Marco Turchi, Frédéric Blain, and Lucia Specia. 2018b. Combining quality estimation and automatic post-editing to enhance machine translation output. In *Proceedings of the 13th Conference of the Association for Machine Translation in the Americas (Volume 1: Research Papers)*, pages 26–38, Boston, MA, March. Association for Machine Translation in the Americas.

Yong Cheng, Zhaopeng Tu, Fandong Meng, Junjie Zhai, and Yang Liu. 2018. Towards robust neural machine translation. In *Proceedings of the 56th Annual Meeting of the Association for Computational Linguistics (Volume 1: Long Papers)*, pages 1756–1766, Melbourne, Australia, July. Association for Computational Linguistics.

Gonçalo Correia and André Martins. 2019. A simple and effective approach to automatic post-editing with transfer learning. In *To appear at Proceedings of the 57th annual meeting on association for computational linguistics*. Association for Computational Linguistics.

Jacob Devlin, Ming-Wei Chang, Kenton Lee, and Kristina Toutanova. 2018. BERT: pre-training of deep bidirectional transformers for language understanding. *CoRR*, abs/1810.04805.

M Amin Farajian, Marco Turchi, Matteo Negri, and Marcello Federico. 2017. Multi-domain neural machine translation through unsupervised adaptation. In *Proceedings of the Second Conference on Machine Translation*, pages 127–137.

Christian Federmann. 2012. Appraise: An open-source toolkit for manual evaluation of machine translation output. *The Prague Bulletin of Mathematical Linguistics*, 98:25–35, September.

Yvette Graham, Timothy Baldwin, Alistair Moffat, and Justin Zobel. 2013. Continuous Measurement Scales in Human Evaluation of Machine Translation. In *Proceedings of the 7th Linguistic Annotation Workshop and Interoperability with Discourse*, pages 33–41, Sofia, Bulgaria, August. Association for Computational Linguistics.

Yvette Graham, Timothy Baldwin, Alistair Moffat, and Justin Zobel. 2014. Is machine translation getting better over time? In *Proceedings of the 14th Conference of the European Chapter of the Association for Computational Linguistics*, pages 443–451.

Yvette Graham, Timothy Baldwin, Alistair Moffat, and Justin Zobel. 2017. Can machine translation systems be evaluated by the crowd alone. *Natural Language Engineering*, 23(1):3–30.

Marcin Junczys-Dowmunt and Roman Grundkiewicz. 2016. Log-linear Combinations of Monolingual and Bilingual Neural Machine Translation Models for Automatic Post-Editing. In *Proceedings of the First Conference on Machine Translation*, pages 751–758, Berlin, Germany, August.

Marcin Junczys-Dowmunt and Roman Grundkiewicz. 2018. Microsoft and University of Edinburgh at WMT2018: Dual-Source Transformer for Automatic Post-Editing. In *Proceedings of the Third Conference on Machine Translation*, Brussels, Belgium, October.

Guillaume Klein, Yoon Kim, Yuntian Deng, Jean Senellart, and Alexander Rush. 2017. OpenNMT: Open-Source Toolkit for Neural Machine Translation. In *Proceedings of ACL 2017, System Demonstrations*, pages 67–72. Association for Computational Linguistics.

Philipp Koehn, Hieu Hoang, Alexandra Birch, Chris Callison-Burch, Marcello Federico, Nicola Bertoldi, Brooke Cowan, Wade Shen, Christine Moran,

Richard Zens, Chris Dyer, Ondrej Bojar, Alexandra Constantin, and Evan Herbst. 2007. Moses: Open Source Toolkit for Statistical Machine Translation. In *Proceedings of the 45th Annual Meeting of the Association for Computational Linguistics Companion Volume Proceedings of the Demo and Poster Sessions*, pages 177–180, Prague, Czech Republic.

Philipp Koehn. 2004. Statistical Significance Tests for Machine Translation Evaluation. In *Proceedings of EMNLP 2004*, pages 388–395, Barcelona, Spain.

WonKee Lee, Jaehun Shin, and Jong-Hyeok Lee. 2019. Transformer-based Automatic Post-Editing Model with Joint Encoder and Multi-source Attention of Decoder. In *Proceedings of the Fourth Conference on Machine Translation (WMT19)*, Florence, Italy, August.

Jindřich Libovický, Jindřich Helcl, Marek Tlustý, Ondřej Bojar, and Pavel Pecina. 2016. CUNI at Post-editing and Multimodal Translation Tasks. In *Proceedings of the 11th Workshop on Statistical Machine Translation (WMT)*.

António V. Lopes, M. Amin Farajian, Gonçalo M. Correia, Jonay Trénous, and André F. T. Martins. 2019. Unbabel's Submission to the WMT2019 APE Shared Task: BERT-based Encoder-Decoder for Automatic Post-Editing. In *Proceedings of the Fourth Conference on Machine Translation (WMT19)*, Florence, Italy, August.

Matteo Negri, Marco Turchi, Rajen Chatterjee, and Nicola Bertoldi. 2018. eSCAPE: a Large-scale Synthetic Corpus for Automatic Post-Editing. In *Proceedings of the Eleventh International Conference on Language Resources and Evaluation (LREC 2018)*, Miyazaki, Japan, May 7-12, 2018.

Santanu Pal, Nico Herbig, Antonio Krüger, and Josef van Genabith. 2019. USAAR-DFKI – The Transference Architecture for English–German Automatic Post-Editing. In *Proceedings of the Fourth Conference on Machine Translation (WMT19)*, Florence, Italy, August.

Kishore Papineni, Salim Roukos, Todd Ward, and Wei-Jing Zhu. 2002. BLEU: A Method for Automatic Evaluation of Machine Translation. In *Proceedings of the 40th Annual Meeting on Association for Computational Linguistics*, ACL '02, pages 311–318.

Ofir Press and Lior Wolf. 2017. Using the Output Embedding to Improve Language Models. In *Proceedings of the 15th Conference of the European Chapter of the Association for Computational Linguistics: Volume 2, Short Papers*, pages 157–163, Valencia, Spain, April. Association for Computational Linguistics.

Rico Sennrich, Barry Haddow, and Alexandra Birch. 2016. Neural Machine Translation of Rare Words with Subword Units. In *Proceedings of the 54th Annual Meeting of the Association for Computational*

Linguistics (Volume 1: Long Papers), pages 1715–1725, Berlin, Germany, August.

Rico Sennrich, Orhan Firat, Kyunghyun Cho, Alexandra Birch, Barry Haddow, Julian Hitschler, Marcin Junczys-Dowmunt, Samuel Läubli, Antonio Valerio Miceli Barone, Jozef Mokry, and Maria Nadejde. 2017. Nematus: a Toolkit for Neural Machine Translation. In *Proceedings of the Software Demonstrations of the 15th Conference of the European Chapter of the Association for Computational Linguistics*, pages 65–68, Valencia, Spain, April.

Dimitar Shterionov, Joachim Wagner, and do Carmo Félix. 2019. APE through neural and statistical MT with augmented data. ADAPT/DCU submission to the WMT 2019 APE Shared task. In *Proceedings of the Fourth Conference on Machine Translation (WMT19)*, Florence, Italy, August.

Michel Simard, Cyril Goutte, and Pierre Isabelle. 2007. Statistical Phrase-Based Post-Editing. In *Proceedings of the Annual Conference of the North American Chapter of the Association for Computational Linguistics (NAACL HLT)*, pages 508–515, Rochester, New York.

Matthew Snover, Bonnie Dorr, Richard Schwartz, Linnea Micciulla, and John Makhoul. 2006. A Study of Translation Edit Rate with Targeted Human Annotation. In *Proceedings of Association for Machine Translation in the Americas*, pages 223–231, Cambridge, Massachusetts, USA.

Lucia Specia, Kim Harris, Aljoscha Burchardt, Marco Turchi, Matteo Negri, and Inguna Skadina. 2017. Translation Quality and Productivity: A Study on Rich Morphology Languages. In *Proceedings of the 16th Machine Translation Summit*, Nagoya, Japan, September.

Amirhossein Tebbifakhr, Ruchit Agrawal, Rajen Chatterjee, Matteo Negri, and Marco Turchi. 2018. Multi-source Transformer with Combined Losses for Automatic Post-Editing. In *Proceedings of the Third Conference on Machine Translation*, Brussels, Belgium, October.

Amirhossein Tebbifakhr, Matteo Negri, and Marco Turchi. 2019. Effort-Aware Neural Automatic Post-Editing. In *Proceedings of the Fourth Conference on Machine Translation (WMT19)*, Florence, Italy, August.

Marco Turchi, Matteo Negri, and Marcello Federico. 2013. Coping with the subjectivity of human judgements in MT quality estimation. In *Proceedings of the Eighth Workshop on Statistical Machine Translation*, pages 240–251, Sofia, Bulgaria, August. Association for Computational Linguistics.

Marco Turchi, Matteo Negri, and Marcello Federico. 2014. Data-driven annotation of binary MT quality estimation corpora based on human post-editions. *Machine Translation*, 28(3):281–308.

Ashish Vaswani, Noam Shazeer, Niki Parmar, Jakob Uszkoreit, Llion Jones, Aidan N Gomez, Lukasz Kaiser, and Illia Polosukhin. 2017. Attention is All you Need. In I. Guyon, U. V. Luxburg, S. Bengio, H. Wallach, R. Fergus, S. Vishwanathan, and R. Garnett, editors, *Advances in Neural Information Processing Systems 30*, pages 5998–6008. Curran Associates, Inc.

Hongfei Xu and Qiuhui Liu. 2019. Neutron: An Implementation of the Transformer Translation Model and its Variants. *arXiv preprint arXiv:1903.07402*, March.

Hongfei Xu, Qiuhui Liu, and Josef van Genabith. 2019. UdS Submission for the WMT 19 Automatic Post-Editing Task. In *Proceedings of the Fourth Conference on Machine Translation (WMT19)*, Florence, Italy, August.

Jiacheng Zhang, Huanbo Luan, Maosong Sun, Feifei Zhai, Jingfang Xu, Min Zhang, and Yang Liu. 2018. Improving the transformer translation model with document-level context. In *Proceedings of the 2018 Conference on Empirical Methods in Natural Language Processing*, pages 533–542, Brussels, Belgium, October-November. Association for Computational Linguistics.

Barret Zoph and Kevin Knight. 2016. Multi-source neural translation. *arXiv preprint arXiv:1601.00710*.

Findings of the WMT 2019 Biomedical Translation Shared Task: Evaluation for MEDLINE Abstracts and Biomedical Terminologies

Rachel Bawden[*]
School of Informatics,
University of Edinburgh,
Scotland

K. Bretonnel Cohen[*]
Biomedical Text Mining Group
University of Colorado
School of Medicine
Aurora, CO, USA

Cristian Grozea[*]
Fraunhofer Institute
FOKUS,
Berlin, Germany

Antonio Jimeno Yepes[*]
IBM Research Australia
Melbourne, Australia

Madeleine Kittner[*]
Knowledge Management
in Bioinformatics
Humboldt-Universität
zu Berlin, Germany

Martin Krallinger[*]
Barcelona Supercomputing
Center, Spain

Nancy Mah[*]
Charité-Universitätsmedizin,
Berlin-Brandenburger Centrum
für Regenerative Therapien (BCRT)
Berlin, Germany

Aurélie Névéol[*]
LIMSI, CNRS,
Université Paris-Saclay
Orsay, France

Mariana Neves[*]
German Centre for the Protection
of Laboratory Animals (Bf3R),
German Federal Institute for
Risk Assessment (BfR),
Berlin, Germany

Felipe Soares[*]
Barcelona Supercomputing
Center, Spain

Amy Siu[*]
Beuth University of
Applied Sciences,
Berlin, Germany

Karin Verspoor[*]
University of Melbourne,
Australia

Maika Vicente Navarro[*]
Maika Spanish Translator
Melbourne, Australia

Abstract

In the fourth edition of the WMT Biomedical Translation task, we considered a total of six languages, namely Chinese (zh), English (en), French (fr), German (de), Portuguese (pt), and Spanish (es). We performed an evaluation of automatic translations for a total of 10 language directions, namely, zh/en, en/zh, fr/en, en/fr, de/en, en/de, pt/en, en/pt, es/en, and en/es. We provided training data based on MEDLINE abstracts for eight of the 10 language pairs and test sets for all of them. In addition to that, we offered a new sub-task for the translation of terms in biomedical terminologies for the en/es language direction. Higher BLEU scores (close to 0.5) were obtained for the es/en, en/es and en/pt test sets, as well as for the terminology sub-task. After manual validation of the primary runs, some submissions were judged to be better than the reference translations, for instance, for de/en, en/es and es/en.

1 Introduction

Machine translation (MT) holds the promise to unlock access to textual content in a wide range of languages. In the biomedical domain, the bulk of the literature is available in English, which provides two interesting applications for machine translation: first, providing patients, scientists and health professionals with access to the literature in their native language and second, assisting scientist and health professionals in writing reports in English, when it is not their primary language. Furthermore, important health information can be found in the free text of electronic health records and social media. As these sources are increasingly available to patients and health professionals, MT can be leveraged to widen access beyond

---

[*] The author list is alphabetical and does not reflect the respective author contributions. The task was coordinated by Mariana Neves.

Proceedings of the Fourth Conference on Machine Translation (WMT), Volume 3: Shared Task Papers (Day 2) pages 29–53
Florence, Italy, August 1-2, 2019. ©2019 Association for Computational Linguistics

language barriers. Other situations in the health care domain, such as emergency response communications, have expressed the need for translation technologies to improve patient-provider communication (Turner et al., 2019). However, the recurring conclusion of practical studies is that progress is still needed. The goal of this shared task is to bring machine translation of biomedical text to a level of performance that can help with these medical challenges.

In recent years, many parallel corpora in the biomedical domain have been made available, which are valuable resources for training and evaluating MT systems. Examples of such corpora include Khresmoi (Dušek et al., 2017), Scielo (Neves et al., 2016), Full-Text Scientific Articles from Scielo (Soares et al., 2018a), MeSpEn (Villegas et al., 2018), thesis and dissertations (Soares et al., 2018b), and clinical trials (Neves, 2017). These corpora cover a variety of language pairs and document types, such as scientific articles, clinical trials, and academic dissertations.

Many previous efforts have addressed MT for the biomedical domain. Interesting previous work includes a comparison of performance in biomedical MT to Google Translate for English, French, German, and Spanish (Wu et al., 2011). Pecina et al. applied MT for the task of multilingual information retrieval in the medical domain (Pecina et al., 2014). They compared various MT systems, including Moses, Google Translate, and Bing Translate. Later, Pecina et al. utilized domain adaptation of statistical MT for English, French and Greek (Pecina et al., 2015). The field of MT has experienced considerable improvements in the performance of systems, and this is also the case for biomedical MT. Our more recent shared tasks show an increasing number of teams that relied on neural machine translation (NMT) to tackle the problem (Jimeno Yepes et al., 2017; Neves et al., 2018).

We found some commonalities in the work above. On the one hand, clinical vocabularies are under development, as well as data sets based on scientific publications. On the other hand, there is little or no work on languages that do not have typical Indo-European morphology, e.g. in the isolating direction (no Chinese), and in the agglutinating direction (no Hungarian, Turkish, Finnish, Estonian). There is also little previous research in MT for electronic health records (EHR).

The translation of technical texts requires considerable specific knowledge, not only about linguistic rules, but also about the subject of the text that is being translated. The advantage of terminology management can be seen in its important role in the process of acquiring, storing and applying linguistic and subject-specific knowledge related to the production of the target text.

Terminologies can also be extremely useful in data mining pipelines, where one might be interested in identifying specific terms or diseases, for example. In addition, terminologies can be used to improve the quality of machine translation and help in the normalization of vocabulary use. Terminological resources in the field of biomedicine and clinic are of crucial importance for the development of natural language processing systems and language technologies in the field of health, among them the semantic network called Unified Medical Language System (UMLS). This resource contains terminological subsets of a wide variety of subject areas and specialties such as health sciences, life sciences and pharmacology.

For instance, at present only 13% of the concepts included in UMLS have entries for Spanish, while the vast majority of concepts have an equivalent in English. Therefore, one of the coverage expansion strategies is based on the translation of terms related to UMLS entries from English into Spanish.

Over the past three years, the aim of the biomedical task at WMT has been to focus the attention of the community on health as a specialized domain for the application of MT (Bojar et al., 2016; Jimeno Yepes et al., 2017; Neves et al., 2018). This forum has provided a unique opportunity to review existing parallel corpora in the biomedical domain and to further develop resources in language pairs such as English and Chinese, French, Spanish, Portuguese (Névéol et al., 2018).

In this edition of the shared task, we continued this effort and we addressed five language pairs in two translation directions, as follows: Chinese/English (zh/en and en/zh), French/English (fr/en and en/fr), German/English (de/en and en/de), Portuguese/English (pt/en and en/pt), and Spanish/English (es/en and en/es). Herein we describe the details of the fourth edition of the WMT Biomedical Task which includes the following:

- construction of training data and the official test sets, including statistics and an evaluation of the quality of the test sets (Section 2);

- a description of the three baselines that we developed for comparison (Section 3);

- an overview of the participating teams and their systems (Section 4);

- the results obtained by the submitted runs based on our automatic evaluation (Section 5);

- the results of the manual evaluation of selected translations from each team (Section 6);

- and a discussion of various topics, especially the quality of the test sets and of the automatic translations submitted by the teams (Section 7).

2 Training and Test Sets

We made training and test sets available to support participants in the development and evaluation of their systems. We provided two types of test set, scientific abstracts from Medline and terms from biomedical terminologies. Both data and test sets are available for download.[1] Table 1 provides some basic characteristics of the training and test sets, and we provide details of their construction in this section.

2.1 Medline training and test sets

We provided training data based on Medline data for eight of the language pairs that we addressed, namely, fr/en, en/fr, de/en, en/de, pt/en, en/pt, es/en, and en/es. We released test sets for all 10 language pairs, which are the official test sets used for the shared task. The creation of the Medline training and test sets was as follows.

Document retrieval. For the training data, we downloaded the Medline database[2] that included the citations available until the end of 2018. For the test sets, we downloaded the Medline update files available for 2019 until the end of February.

XML parsing. We parsed the Medline files using a Python XML library.[3] Based on the metadata available, we selected the citations that contained abstracts both in English and in at least one of the foreign languages addressed in the shared task, namely, Chinese (zh), French (fr), German (de), Portuguese (pt), and Spanish (es).

Language detection. Even though the citations in Medline include the language of the abstracts, we found some mistakes in the data from last year in which some abstracts were tagged with the wrong language, e.g. Italian instead of German. Therefore, we automatically detected the language of the article using the Python langdetect library.[4] For instance, when building the training data, we detected a total of 156 abstracts that were identified with the wrong language. For the training data, this was the data that was released to the participants after removal of the abstracts in the wrong language. When building the test sets, we kept only 100 articles for each language pair, i.e. 50 articles for each direction es/en and en/es.

Sentence splitting. For the test sets, we considered only the abstracts in the Medline citations and segmented them into sentences, which is a necessary step for automatic sentence alignment. For all language pairs except for zh/en, we used the syntok Python library[5]. For zh/en, we used LingPipe's Medline-specific API[6] to segment the English abstracts. Splitting the Chinese ones by the language-specific period punctuation "。" (using our own script) was sufficient.

Sentence alignment. For the test sets in all language pairs except for zh/en, we automatically aligned the sentences using the GMA tool.[7] We relied on the same configuration and stopword lists used for the test sets in 2018 (Neves et al., 2018). For zh/en, we used the Champollion tool[8], also relying on the same configurations and stopword lists used in 2018.

Manual validation. We performed a manual validation of the totality of the aligned sentences in the test sets using the Quality Checking task in

---

[1]https://drive.google.
com/drive/u/0/folders/
1x4689LkvdJTyAxsB6tYu12MJzxgiyDZ_

[2]https://www.nlm.nih.gov/databases/
download/pubmed_medline.html

[3]https://github.com/titipata/pubmed_
parser

[4]https://pypi.org/project/langdetect/

[5]https://github.com/fnl/syntok

[6]http://alias-i.com/lingpipe/demos/
tutorial/sentences/read-me.html

[7]https://nlp.cs.nyu.edu/GMA/

[8]http://champollion.sourceforge.net/

Language pairs	Medline training		Medline test		Terminology test
	Documents	Sentences	Documents	Sentences	Terms
de/en	3,669	40,398	50	589	-
en/de			50	719	-
es/en	8,626	100,257	50	526	-
en/es			50	599	6,624
fr/en	6,540	75,049	50	486	-
en/fr			50	593	-
pt/en	4,185	49,918	50	491	-
en/pt			50	589	-
zh/en	-	-	50	283	-
en/zh			50	351	-

Table 1: Number of documents, sentences, and terms in the training and test sets.

the Appraise tool. We present statistics concerning the quality of the test set alignments in Table 2.

For each test sets of each language pair, we released the abstracts in the source language and kept the ones in the target language for the both the automatic and manual evaluations, the so-called "reference translations". For instance, for the test set for de/en, we released the abstracts in German to the participants during the evaluation period and kept the ones in English for the evaluation.

2.2 Terminology

For the terminology dataset, a total of 6624 terms in English were manually translated to Spanish by domain experts. The terms were extracted from the scientific literature using the DNorm (Leaman et al., 2013) Named Entity Recognition and medical glossaries.

3 Baselines

Baseline 1: Marian NMT

This represents a low-experience, minimal effort submission based on current methods. We develop "baseline1" using the tutorial written for the MT Marathon 2018 Labs[9] and the Marian NMT framework (Junczys-Dowmunt et al., 2018).

As training data we used the UFAL medical corpus (UFA), and as validation data we used Khresmoi (Dušek et al., 2017). The Khresmoi data did not overlap with the UFAL corpus, despite being mentioned as one of the sources. The UFAL corpus was filtered to remove lower quality data. Specifically, we removed the "Subtitles" subset, as it is of lower quality than the rest, less medically oriented (if at all), and contains dialogue rather

than narrative. Two of the targeted languages, Portuguese and Chinese, are not present in UFAL. For Portuguese we therefore trained our model on the Scielo corpus (Neves et al., 2016) and tested on the Brazilian thesis corpus (Soares et al., 2018b). For Chinese we used the United Nations Parallel Corpus (Ziemski et al., 2016).

The data was preprocessed using standard tools from the Moses toolkit (Koehn et al., 2007): tokenisation, cleaning of training data and truecasing. Subword segmentation (Sennrich et al., 2015) was then trained jointly over both source and target languages and applied using FastBPE.[10] The number of merge operations for BPE was set to 85000.

The models trained were shallow RNN encoder-decoders.[11] They were trained on a GTX 1080 Ti with 8 GPUs. Validation using cross-entropy and BLEU was performed every 10,000 updates, and models were trained until there was no improvement on either metric for 5 consecutive updates. Training of a single model took approximately 2 days.

Discussion. Compared to the traditional domain of news translation, biomedical MT poses additional challenges; biomedical texts contain a large amount of specialised, in-domain vocabulary, and in-domain training data is less readily available.

Baselines 2 and 3: OpenNMT

We also provide two additional baselines trained using OpenNMT-py (Klein et al., 2017)[12], one with a small network size, and a second one with a higher number of hidden units. The data used

---

[9] `https://marian-nmt.github.io/examples/mtm2018-labs`

[10] `https://github.com/glample/fastBPE`

[11] 1 encoder layer, 1 decoder layer, both with with GRU cells, embedding dimension of 512, hidden state of dimension 1024, using layer normalization, implemented using Marian NMT and trained using the Adam optimizer.

[12] `http://opennmt.net/OpenNMT-py/`

Language	OK	Source>Target	Target>Source	Overlap	No Align.	Total
de/en	808 (67.8%)	69 (5.8%)	126 (10.6%)	42 (3.5%)	147 (12.3%)	1192
es/en	825 (78.6%)	33 (3.1%)	67 (6.4%)	28 (2.7%)	96 (9.1%)	1049
fr/en	857 (82.6%)	21 (2.0%)	64 (6.2%)	9 (0.9%)	87 (8.4%)	1038
pt/en	833 (78.9%)	31 (2.9%)	77 (7.3%)	7 (0.7%)	107 (10.1%)	1055
zh/en	469 (84.4%)	53 (9.5%)	12 (2.2%)	5 (0.9%)	17 (3.1%)	556

Table 2: Statistics (number of sentences and percentages) of the quality of the automatic alignment for the Medline test sets. For each language pair, the total of sentences corresponds to the 100 documents that constitute the two test sets (one for each language direction).

for training was the Medline abstracts corpora. We trained these two baselines using the following parameters:

- 2-layer LSTM for both the encoder and decoder (300 and 500 hidden units)
- Vocabulary size: 32,000
- Training steps: 100,000
- Batch size: 64
- Optimization: SGD
- Dropout: 0.3
- Embedding size: 500

The models were trained on a PC with Intel Xeon E-2124 processor and NVIDIA GeForce GTX 1060 GPU and are available for download.[13]

4 Teams and Systems

This year, the task attracted the participation of 11 teams from six countries (China, Germany, Japan, Pakistan, Spain and United Kingdom) from two continents. As opposed to previous years, no team from the Americas participated in the task. We list the teams and their affiliation (where available) in Table 3. We received a total of 59 run submissions as presented in Table 4.

System descriptions were solicited by email from the participating teams in the form of a system paper and a summary paragraph. Below we provide a short description of the systems for which a corresponding paper is available or for which we received a description from the participants. Two teams ('peace' and 'Radiant') did not provide system descriptions.

Table 5 provides an overview of the methods, implementations and training corpora used by the participants. While two teams used the statistical machine translation toolkit Moses (MT-UOC-UPF and UHH-DS), the most popular translation

method relied on neural networks and the transformer architecture.

ARC (Wei et al., 2019). The ARC team's systems were based on the Transformer-big architecture (Vaswani et al., 2017). The relied on both general (news translation task, OPUS, UM, Wikipedia) and in-domain (EMEA, UFAL, Medline) corpora. For en/zh, they also used in-house training data. In order to improve the overall training data quality, they filtered noisy and misaligned data, and to improve vocabulary coverage they trained their subword segmentation model on the BERT multilingual vocabulary. They experimented with over 20 different models with various combinations of training data and settings and chose the best ones when submitting their runs.

BCS (Soares and Krallinger, 2019). The team's systems were also based on the Transformer-big architecture, which were trained using the OpenNMT-py toolkit. They relied on resources from both the general domain (books corpus), as well as from the biomedical domain, such as parallel terminologies from UMLS and various corpora (Scielo, UFAL medical, EMEA, theses and dissertations abstracts, and the Virtual Health Library).

KU. The KU team's systems were based on the Transformer-big architecture, trained using the Tensor2Tensor toolkit (Vaswani et al., 2018). Training data was carefully cleaned to remove encoding errors, bad translations, etc. They did not perform standard ensemble translation, but obtained a small BLEU improvement by taking a "majority vote" on the final translations for different checkpoints.

MT-UOC-UPF. The MT-UOC-UPF team's systems were deep RNN-based encoder-decoder models with attention, trained using Marian (and with layer normalisation, tied embeddings and

---

[13]10.6084/m9.figshare.8094119

Team ID	Institution
ARC	Huawei Technologies (China),
BSC	Barcelona Supercomputing Center (Spain)
KU	Kyoto University (Japan)
MT-UOC-UPF	Universitat Oberta de Catalunya (Spain)
NRPU	Fatima Jinnah Women University (Pakistan), Manchester Metropolitan University (UK)
OOM	Beijing Atman Technology Co. Ltd. (China)
peace	(unknown)
Radiant	Harbin Institute of Technology (China)
Talp_upc	Universitat Politècnica de Catalunya (Spain)
UCAM	University of Cambridge (UK)
UHH-DS	University of Hamburg (Germany)

Table 3: List of the participating teams.

Teams	de/en	en/de	en/es	en/fr	en/pt	en/zh	es/en	fr/en	pt/en	zh/en	Total
ARC	M3	M3		M3		M3		M3		M3	18
BSC			M1		M1		M1		M1		4
KU				M1						M1	2
MT-UOC-UPF			M1T1				M1				3
NRPU				M1				M1			2
OOM						M2				M2	4
peace						M1				M1	2
Radiant						M3					3
Talpc_upc			M3				M3				6
UCAM	M3	M3	M3				M3				12
UHH-DS							M3				3
Total	6	6	9	5	1	9	11	4	1	7	59

Table 4: Overview of the submissions from all teams and test sets. We identify submissions to the MEDLINE test sets with an "M" and to the terminology test set with a "T". The value next to the letter indicates the number of runs for the corresponding test set, language pair, and team.

Teams	MT method	Package, library or system	Training corpus
ARC	NMT	Transformer-big architecture	**general:** news translation task, OPUS, UM, Wikipedia; **in-domain:** EMEA, MEDLINE, UFAL
BSC	NMT	Transformer-big, OpenNMT-py	**general:** books corpus; **in-domain:** EMEA, Scielo, UFAL, UMLS, theses and dissertations abstracts, and the Virtual Health Library
KU	NMT	Transformer-big architecture, Tensor2Tensor toolkit	**in-domain**
MT-UOC-UPF	SMT, NMT	Moses, RNN-based Marian NMT	**in-domain**
NRPU	NMT	OpenNMT-py, transfer learning	**general:** News-Commentary; **in-domain:** EMEA, MEDLINE, Scielo, UFAL
OOM	NMT	Transformer architecture	**general** and **in-domain:** MedRA
peace	NA	NA	NA
Radiant	NA	NA	NA
Talpc_upc	NMT	Transformer architecture, BabelNet dictionary	**in-domain:** MEDLINE
UCAM	NMT	Transformer-big architecture, Tensor2Tensor toolkit, transfer learning	**general:** news translation task; **in-domain:** MEDLINE, Scielo, UFAL
UHH-DS	SMT	Moses	**in-domain:** biomedical task 2018 corpus

Table 5: Overview of the methods implemented by each team. We report the general translation method, specific package, library or implementation used and training corpus used. The letters "NA" are used when this information was not available at the time of writing.

residual connectors). The systems were trained with several medical corpora and glossaries. For the terminology translation task, they trained a Moses system using the same corpus as for the Marian NMT system. The translation table was queried for the English terms and when they were not found, they were translated using the NMT system if all subwords in the term were known and with the SMT Moses system if not.

NRPU (Noor-e-Hira et al., 2019). The NRPU team applied transfer learning and selective data training to build NMT systems. The goal of their approach is to mine biomedical data from general domain corpus and show its efficacy for the biomedical domain. The books corpus was used as the main out-of-domain corpus. News-Commentary (NC) (Tiedemann, 2012) was used as general domain corpus to perform information retrieval for selective data selection. The data selection procedure was performed as reported in Abdul-Rauf et al. (2016). In-domain MEDLINE titles were used as queries to retrieve biomedical related sentences from the general domain NC corpus. They had a total of 627,576 queries for data selection. Top n ($1<n<10$) relevant sentences were ranked against each query. The data selection process was done on both French and English.

OOM. Their system was based on the Transformer architecture trained on various parallel and monolingual corpora from in-domain and out-of-domain corpora. In the fine-tuning phase, the models were first tuned with the in-domain data and then fine-tuned with a curriculum learning mechanism for several rounds. Several model instances were ensembled to generate the translation candidates followed by a re-ranking model to select the best one. In addition to the standard sentences used in the training, terminological resources such as MedDRA were used as a constraint in the decoding phase to keep translation accuracy and consistency of key words.

Talp_upc (Pio Carrino et al., 2019). The Talp_upc team's submission was based on a Transformer and on the BabelNet multilingual semantic dictionary (Navigli and Ponzetto, 2012). From the Medline training data, they extracted a list of biomedical terms. They proposed *bpe-terms segmentation*, which consists of segmenting sentences as a mixture of subwords and term tokens in order to take into account domain-specific terms. They experimented with three systems: (i) terminology-aware segmentation (run2 for es/en and run2 for en/es), (ii) terminology-aware segmentation with a word-level domain feature (run3 for es/en and run1 for en/es), and (iii) terminology-aware segmentation, shared source and target vocabularies and shared encoder-decoder embedding weights (run1 for es/en and run3 for en/es).

UCAM (Saunders et al., 2019). The UCAM team relied on transfer learning and used the Tensor2Tensor implementation of the Transformer model. For each language pair, they used the same training data in both directions. Regarding training data, for en/de and de/en, they reused general domain models trained on the WMT19 news data and biomedical data (UFAl and Medline). For es/en and en/es, they trained on Scielo, UFAL, and Medline. Their three runs use the following: (i) the best single system trained on biomedical data, (ii) a uniform ensemble of models on two en/de and three es/en domains, and (iii) an ensemble with Bayesian Interpolation.

UHH-DS. The team submitted three runs for the Spanish-English language pair. Their SMT systems were developed using the Moses toolkit (Koehn et al., 2007) and trained on the same data as their submission from last year. Data selection was used to sub-sample two general domain corpora using a ratio of 50% sentences. Detailed descriptions of the methods are presented in (Duma and Menzel, 2016a) (run 1), (Duma and Menzel, 2016b) (run2) and (Duma and Menzel) (run 3). The first two methods rely on Paragraph Vector (Le and Mikolov, 2014) for sentence representation and scoring formulas based on the cosine similarity, and the third method focuses on the relative differences between term frequencies. All methods are unsupervised and produce fast results.

5 Automatic Evaluation

For each language pair, we compared the submitted translations to the reference translations. BLEU scores were calculated using the MULTI-EVAL tool and tokenization as provided in Moses. For Chinese, character-level tokenization was used via a minor modification to the tool. Although an ideal tokenization would take into account that Chinese words consist of a varying number of characters, achieving such an ideal tokenization requires a sophisticated dictionary (Chang et al., 2008) – including biomedical terms – and is beyond the scope of this shared task. Further, using character-level tokenization for BLEU purposes is in accordance with current practice (Wang et al., 2018; Xu and Carpuat, 2018).

Table 6 shows BLEU scores for all language pairs when considering all sentences in our test sets. Table 7 only considers the sentences that have been manually classified as being correctly aligned (cf. Section 2). As expected, certain results improve considerably (by more than 10 BLEU points) when only considering the sentences that are correctly aligned.

Most teams outperformed the three baselines, except the NRPU team's submissions for en/fr and fr/en. Baseline1, trained using Marian NMT, obtained results not far behind the best performing team, while the two other baselines were not very competitive. We rank the various runs according to the results that they obtained followed by a short discussion of the results with regard to the methods that they used.

- de/en: baseline2,3 < baseline1 < UCAM, ARC

- en/de: baseline2,3 < baseline1 < UCAM, ARC

- es/en: baseline2,3 < baseline1 < UHH-DS < MT-UOC-UPF < BSC, Talp_upc runs2,3 < Talp_upc run1 < UCAM

- en/es: baseline2,3 < baseline1 < MT-UOC-UPF < Talp_upc, BSC < UCAM

- en/fr: baseline2,3 < NRPU < baseline1, KU < ARC runs2,3 < ARC run1

- fr/en: baseline2,3 < NRPU < baseline1 < ARC

- pt/en: baseline2,3 < baseline1 < BSC

- en/pt: baseline2,3 < baseline1 < BSC

- zh/en: baseline1 < peace < KU < ARC < OOM

- en/zh: Radiant < peace < ARC < OOM

de/en. All submitted runs from both ARC and UCAM teams outperformed our three baselines. The runs from ARC were slightly superior to those from UCAM. Both teams used Transformer models but the ARC also used BERT multilingual embeddings. We observed no significant difference between the submissions from team ARC but runs based on the ensemble of models from team UCAM (i.e. runs 2 and 3) obtained a higher score than their single best systems.

en/de. Results were similar to those for en/de: the runs from team ARC outperformed the runs from team UCAM. Similarly, we observed no difference between the runs from team ARC and slightly higher scores for the runs based on ensemble systems from team UCAM.

es/en. All submitted runs outperformed our baselines. The best performing systems from the Talp_upc, UCAM, and BSC teams were Transformer models, the one based on Marian NMT from the MT-UOC-UPF team, an finally the SMT Moses systems from UHH-DS. We did not observe significant differences between the various runs from single teams, except for run1 from Talp_upc team (terminology-aware segmentation, shared source and target vocabularies and shared encoder-decoder embedding weights), which outperformed their other two runs.

en/es. All submitted runs outperformed our baselines. As opposed to results for en/es, the Transformer system from the UCAM team slightly outperformed the one developed by the Talp_upc team, which obtained a similar performance to the OpenNMT system from the BSC team.

fr/en. Baselines 2 and 3 were outperformed by all submitted runs, whereas baseline 1, which is trained using Marian, was only outperformed by team ARC, whose system uses the Transformer model. We observed no significant difference between the three runs from the ARC team.

en/fr. Similar to fr/en, baselines 2 and 3 were outperformed by all submitted runs, while baseline 1 was similar to the run from the KU team, which uses the Transformer model. All runs from the ARC team outperformed our baseline 1. Run1 from the ARC performed significantly better than the other two runs, although details about the difference between the runs do not seem to be available.

pt/en. The run from the BSC team based on OpenNMT performed slightly better than baseline 1. However, their performance was far superior to baselines 2 and 3, which were also trained using OpenNMT but only trained on the Medline training data.

en/pt. Results for en/pt from the BSC were almost 10 points higher than the ones for pt/en. The run from the BSC team based on OpenNMT outperfomed with some difference the baseline based on Marian NMT, maybe because of the many resources that the team trained its system on. Further, they were much superior to the baselines 2 and 3 also based on OpenNMT but only trained on the Medline training data.

zh/en. All submitted runs outperformed the only baseline that we prepared. The three best-performing teams's submissions were Transformer models. The system developed by the OOM team slightly outperformed ARC's submission. Little difference in the results for the runs for the two teams was observed. A significant difference, however, was observed between results from the ARC and OOM teams and the Transformer system of the KU team.

en/zh. The Transformer-based system from team OOM significantly outperformed the transformer systems of team ARC. The latter had a similar performance to the runs for the other two teams (Radiant and peace) for which we do not know the details.

Table 8 presents the results of the automatic evaluation of the terminology test set. The evaluation considered the accuracy of translation (on lower-cased terms), rather than BLEU. The choice of accuracy was due to the fact that the terms are usually very short and having at least one different word from the reference translation can lead to a complete different meaning.

6 Manual Evaluation

For the Medline test sets, we performed manual evaluation of the primary runs, as identified by the participants, for all teams and language pairs. We carried out pairwise comparisons of translations taken either from a sample of the translations from the selected primary runs or the reference translations. Specifically, sets of translation pairs, consisting of either two automatic translations for a given sentence (derived from submitted results), or one automatic translation and the reference translation for a sentence, were prepared for evaluation. Table 9 presents the primary runs that we considered from each team. We performed a total of 62 validations of pairwise datasets.

We relied on human validators who were native speakers of the target languages and who were either members of the participating teams or colleagues from the research community. We also preferred to use validators who were familiar enough with the source language so that the original text could be consulted in case of questions about the translations, and for most language pairs this was the case.

We carried out the so-called 3-way ranking task in our installation of the Appraise tool (Federmann, 2010).[14]. For each pairwise dataset, we checked a total of 100 randomly-chosen sentence pairs. The validation consisted of reading the two translation sentences (A and B) and choosing one of the options listed below:

- A<B: the quality of translation B is higher than translation A;

- A=B: both translations have similar quality;

- A>B: the quality of translation A was higher than translation B;

- Flag error: the translations do not seem to come from the same source sentence, probably due to errors in the corpus alignment.

Table 10 summarizes the manual evaluation for the Medline test sets. We did not perform manual evaluation for any of our baselines. We ranked the runs and reference translations among themselves based on the number of times that one validation was carried out by the evaluators. When the superiority of a team (or reference translation) over another team was not very clear, we decided to put both of them together in a block without the "lower than" sign (<) between them. However, in these situations, the items are listed in ascending order of possible superiority in relation to the others. The various runs were ranked as listed below:

- de/en: reference, ARC, UCAM

- en/de: UCAM < ARC < reference

[14]https://github.com/cfedermann/Appraise

Teams and Runs	de/en	en/de	es/en	en/es	en/fr	fr/en	pt/en	en/pt	zh/en	en/zh
ARC-run1	0.2871	0.2789	-	-	0.3995	0.3551	-	-	0.3007	0.3547
ARC-run2	0.2879	0.2786	-	-	0.3667	0.3551	-	-	0.3005	0.3547
ARC-run3	0.2882*	0.2785*	-	-	0.3619*	0.3556*	-	-	0.3005*	0.3547*
BSC-run1	-	-	0.3769*	0.4421*	-	-	0.3990*	0.4811*	-	-
KU-run1	-	-	-	-	0.3114*	-	-	-	0.2489*	-
MT-UOC-UPF-run1	-	-	0.3659*	0.3974*	-	-	-	-	-	-
NRPU-run1	-	-	-	-	0.1587*	0.1972*	-	-	-	-
OOM-run1	-	-	-	-	-	-	-	-	0.3413	0.4234
OOM-run2	-	-	-	-	-	-	-	-	0.3413*	0.4234*
peace-run1	-	-	-	-	-	-	-	-	0.2266*	0.3379*
Radiant-run1	-	-	-	-	-	-	-	-	-	0.3266
Radiant-run2	-	-	-	-	-	-	-	-	-	0.3265
Radiant-run3	-	-	-	-	-	-	-	-	-	0.3294*
Talp_upc-run1	-	-	0.3941	0.4301*	-	-	-	-	-	-
Talp_upc-run2	-	-	0.3792*	0.4340	-	-	-	-	-	-
Talp_upc-run3	-	-	0.3721	0.4392	-	-	-	-	-	-
UCAM-run1	0.2741	0.2651	0.4241	0.4492	-	-	-	-	-	-
UCAM-run2	0.2863	0.2716	0.4303	0.4539	-	-	-	-	-	-
UCAM-run3	0.2850*	0.2641*	0.4290*	0.4558*	-	-	-	-	-	-
UHH-DS-run1	-	-	0.3561*	-	-	-	-	-	-	-
UHH-DS-run2	-	-	0.3585	-	-	-	-	-	-	-
UHH-DS-run3	-	-	0.3586	-	-	-	-	-	-	-
baseline1	0.2473	0.2202	0.3306	0.3722	0.3056	0.2927	0.3812	0.4115	0.1519	-
baseline2	0.0954	0.0347	0.2373	0.0614	0.0211	0.1406	0.2280	0.2264	-	-
baseline3	0.0962	0.0367	0.2373	0.0614	0.0221	0.1572	0.2394	0.2328	-	-

Table 6: BLEU scores when considering all sentences in the test sets. Runs are presented in alphabetical order of the team's name, while the baseline results are shown at the bottom of the table. * indicates the primary run, as indicated by the participants, in the case of multiple runs.

Teams and Runs	de/en	en/de	es/en	en/es	en/fr	fr/en	pt/en	en/pt	zh/en	en/zh
ARC-run1	0.3866	0.3539	-	-	0.4241	0.3818	-	-	0.3215	0.3709
ARC-run2	0.3880	0.3528	-	-	0.3889	0.3818	-	-	0.3216	0.3709
ARC-run3	0.3884*	0.3526*	-	-	0.3829*	0.3824*	-	-	0.3216*	0.3709*
BSC-run1	-	-	0.4356*	0.4701*	-	-	0.4617*	0.4951*	-	-
KU-run1	-	-	-	-	0.3292*	-	-	-	0.2716*	-
MT-UOC-UPF-run1	-	-	0.4159*	0.4219*	-	-	-	-	-	-
NRPU-run1	-	-	-	-	0.1745*	0.2105*	-	-	-	-
OOM-run1	-	-	-	-	-	-	-	-	0.3561	0.4392
OOM-run2	-	-	-	-	-	-	-	-	0.3561*	0.4392*
peace-run1	-	-	-	-	-	-	-	-	0.2518*	0.3508*
Radiant-run1	-	-	-	-	-	-	-	-	-	0.3405
Radiant-run2	-	-	-	-	-	-	-	-	-	0.3416
Radiant-run3	-	-	-	-	-	-	-	-	-	0.3424*
Talp_upc-run1	-	-	0.4509	0.4568*	-	-	-	-	-	-
Talp_upc-run2	-	-	0.4355*	0.4609	-	-	-	-	-	-
Talp_upc-run3	-	-	0.4270	0.4683	-	-	-	-	-	-
UCAM-run1	0.3669	0.3328	0.4770	0.4834	-	-	-	-	-	-
UCAM-run2	0.3807	0.3469	0.4833	0.4891	-	-	-	-	-	-
UCAM-run3	0.3799*	0.3379*	0.4811*	0.4896*	-	-	-	-	-	-
UHH-DS-run1	-	-	0.3969*	-	-	-	-	-	-	-
UHH-DS-run2	-	-	0.3999	-	-	-	-	-	-	-
UHH-DS-run3	-	-	0.3997	-	-	-	-	-	-	-
baseline1	0.3277	0.2806	0.3765	0.4037	0.3253	0.2989	0.4298	0.4275	0.1667	-
baseline2	0.1250	0.0410	0.2724	0.0633	0.0228	0.1553	0.2666	0.2284	-	-
baseline3	0.1287	0.0436	0.2724	0.0633	0.0236	0.1730	0.2727	0.2345	-	-

Table 7: BLEU scores when considering only the correctly aligned sentences in the test sets. Runs are presented in alphabetical order of the team's name, while the baseline results are shown at the bottom of the table. * indicates the primary run, as indicated by the participants, in the case of multiple runs.

Teams	Runs	en/es
MT-UOC-UPF	1	47.55

Table 8: Accuracy results for the terminology test set.

- en/es: reference, MT-UOC-UPF < BSC, Talp_upc, UCAM

- en/fr: NRPU < KU < ARC, reference

- en/pt: reference, BSC

- en/zh: no possible ranking

- es/en: UHH-DS < MT-UOC-UPF < BSC, UCAM < reference, Talp_upc

- fr/en: NRPU < reference < ARC

- pt/en: BSC, reference

- zh/en: KU < ARC, peace < reference, OOM

The ranks for the manual validation were usually consistent with the ones that we obtained for the automatic validation. We discuss differences that we found in the discussion of the results for each language pair below.

de/en. The reference translations and the runs from teams ARC and UCAM were of similar quality and we did not observe huge differences between them. For this reason, we have grouped them into a single block, ordering them according to increasing performance. The UCAM team's submission was seen to be marginally better than the reference translations (33 vs. 23). We did not observe any differences in the respective order of teams compared to that of the automatic evaluation.

en/de. The reference translation was clearly superior to the runs from the ARC and UCAM teams (41 vs. 19, and 44 vs. 16, respectively). The translations from the ARC submission were more frequently judged better than the ones from the UCAM team (37 vs. 16). While we found no significant difference in the BLEU scores for teams ARC and UCAM, the manual evaluation showed that translations from team ARC were of superior quality to those of team UCAM.

en/es. The runs from the MT-UOC-UPF and BSC teams were judged as of similar quality to the reference translations, while the ones from Talp_upc and UCAM were deemed superior to the reference translations. The manual validation did not indicate much difference between runs from teams BSC, Talp_upc and UCAM. The ranking of the teams did not change significantly between that of the automatic evaluation.

en/fr. The reference translations were clearly superior to the runs from the KU and the NRPU teams, however, they were found only marginally superior to the ARC run. We therefore decided to put the ARC runs and reference translations in a single block. As for the comparison of the ARC runs to the KU and NRPU runs, superiority of ARC was higher when compared to the NRPU team (82 vs. 2) than for team KU (42 vs. 21). Indeed, the translations from the KU team were validated as far superior (73 vs. 9) to team NRPU. We did not observe any differences in the ranking of teams with respect to the automatic evaluation.

en/zh. We could not rank the runs from the various teams because of inconsistencies when comparing results from the various pairwise validations. For instance, the translations from the OOM team were judged better than the the reference translations, and the latter better that the ones from the ARC team. However, the translation from the ARC team were considered better than the ones from the OOM team. We also found differences in the rankings found in the automatic validation. For instance, the team that obtained the lowest BLEU scores (peace), had their translation judged to be as good as the ones from the Radiant and OOM teams, two of the teams that obtained high BLEU scores.

en/pt. The translations from the BSC team were validated as slightly superior (29 vs. 25) to the reference translations. We therefore grouped both of them in a single block.

es/en. The reference translations were judged as of similar quality to the ones from the Talp_upc teams, followed by the translations from the BSC and UCAM teams. The only difference to the ranking from the automatic evaluation was that the runs from the Talp_upc were considered better than those from the UCAM team while the latter obtained a higher BLEU score.

Teams	de/en	en/de	en/es	en/fr	en/pt	en/zh	es/en	fr/en	pt/en	zh/en	Total
ARC	run3	run3		run3		run3		run3		run3	6
BSC			run1		run1		run1		run1		4
KU				run1						run1	2
MT-UOC-UPF			run1				run1				2
NRPU				run1				run1			2
OOM						run2				run2	2
peace						run1				run1	2
Radiant						run3					1
Talpc_upc			run1				run2				2
UCAM	run3	run3	run3				run3				4
UHH-DS							run1				1
Total	2	2	4	3	1	4	5	2	1	4	28
Pairwise	3	3	10	6	1	10	15	3	1	10	62

Table 9: Overview of the primary runs that were considered for manual validation. The last columns shows the number of runs that we validated for each team. The last rows in the tables show the total number of runs and of pairwise combinations between runs and the reference translations.

fr/en. The reference translations were consistently validated as superior to the one from team NRPU's submissions, whereas the ones from team ARC were judged to be better than the reference translations.

pt/en. The reference translations were validated as slightly superior (29 vs. 24) to the ones from team BSC. Therefore, we grouped both of them in a single block.

zh/en. Only the translation from the OOM team, the runs that obtained the highest BLEU scores, were judged as of similar quality to the reference translations. The only main difference compared to the ranking from the automatic translation was with regard to team peace's submission, which obtained the lowest BLEU score, but for which the translations were ranked higher than the ones from the KU team and of similar quality to the ARC team according to the manual evaluation.

7   Discussion

In this section we discuss important topics related to the shared task, such as a short analysis of best performing methods, lack of sufficient resources for some language pairs and the quality of the test sets and the submitted translations.

7.1   Analysis of results and methods

Across all language pairs, the best performing runs were those based on the Transformer architecture trained on as much data as possible from the general and biomedical domain (cf. the submissions by the ARC, Talp_upc, and UCAM teams). En-sembled runs tended to perform well and generally outperformed using the single best system (cf. OOM, Talp_upc, and UCAM).

Differences in the amount of training data available across languages appeared to have a direct impact on translation quality. The Scielo and Medline corpora are larger for es/en and en/es than for the other languages, which is reflected in the BLEU scores. For example, results for team UCAM were more than 10 points higher for es/en and en/es than for de/en and en/de, results which were mirrored for baseline 1.

Regarding zh/en and en/zh for which we do not yet provide any training data, results were inferior to the best-performing language pairs (es/en and en/es), but still surprisingly good. However the best-performing teams trained on additional in-house data (cf. ARC's submission), which was not available to the community.

We compared results for this year's shared task in comparison to the previous year's (Neves et al., 2018). The addition of the Medline training data this year resulted in an improvement for en/de (from 24.30 to almost 28.00), but not for de/en. Similarly, we observed no real improvement for es/en and en/es, the highest BLEU scores for both remained in the range of 43-45 points. However, a considerably improvement occurred for en/fr, whose scores increased from almost 25 to almost 40 points, and for fr/en from almost 27 to around 35 points. Finally, the scores for en/pt showed an improvement from 43 to 49 points, while the scores remained constant for pt/en on 46 points.

In the shared task that we organized last year (Neves et al., 2018), for the first time certain runs outperformed the reference translations in the

Languages	Runs (A vs. B)	Total	A>B	A=B	A<B
de/en	reference vs. ARC	94	31	30	33
	reference vs. UCAM	93	23	37	33
	ARC vs. UCAM	100	20	60	20
en/de	reference vs. ARC	92	41	32	19
	reference vs. UCAM	92	44	32	16
	ARC vs. UCAM	100	37	47	16
en/es	reference vs. BSC	100	10	78	12
	reference vs. MT-UOC-UPF	100	25	49	26
	reference vs. Talp_upc	100	7	74	19
	reference vs. UCAM	100	18	62	28
	BSC vs. MT-UOC-UPF	100	26	59	15
	BSC vs. Talp_upc	100	9	80	11
	BSC vs. UCAM	100	9	86	5
	MT-UOC-UPF vs. Talp_upc	98	6	77	15
	MT-UOC-UPF vs. UCAM	100	6	75	19
	Talp_upc vs. UCAM	100	11	82	7
en/fr	reference vs. ARC	98	36	34	28
	reference vs. KU	98	61	21	16
	reference vs. NRPU	99	79	18	2
	ARC vs. KU	100	42	37	21
	ARC vs. NRPU	100	86	12	2
	KU vs. NRPU	99	73	17	9
en/zh	reference vs. ARC	95	55	12	28
	reference vs. OOM	100	28	28	44
	reference vs. peace	93	50	18	25
	reference vs. Radiant	99	24	14	61
	ARC vs. OOM	96	52	7	37
	ARC vs. peace	96	52	7	37
	ARC vs. Radiant	93	45	6	42
	OOM vs. peace	100	33	38	29
	OOM vs. Radiant	100	68	16	16
	peace vs. Radiant	98	43	7	48
en/pt	reference vs. BSC	99	25	45	29
es/en	reference vs. BSC	98	40	30	28
	reference vs. MT-UOC-UPF	90	36	36	10
	reference vs. Talp_upc	95	27	42	26
	reference vs. UCAM	99	30	45	24
	reference vs. UHH-DS	96	55	33	8
	BSC vs. MT-UOC-UPF	97	32	39	26
	BSC vs. Talp_upc	100	19	43	38
	BSC vs. UCAM	99	29	48	22
	BSC vs. UHH-DS	100	55	29	16
	MT-UOC-UPF vs. Talp_upc	95	15	46	34
	MT-UOC-UPF vs. UCAM	100	24	35	41
	MT-UOC-UPF vs. UHH-DS	100	51	36	13
	Talp_upc vs. UCAM	100	33	42	25
	Talp_upc vs. UHH-DS	100	55	35	10
	UCAM vs. UHH-DS	98	54	34	10
fr/en	reference vs. ARC	96	23	32	41
	reference vs. NRPU	95	72	20	3
	ARC vs. NRPU	99	80	19	0
pt/en	reference vs. BSC	96	29	43	24
zh/en	reference vs. ARC	100	47	29	24
	reference vs. KU	100	36	37	27
	reference vs. OOM	100	12	43	12
	reference vs. peace	100	33	32	25
	ARC vs. KU	100	36	44	20
	ARC vs. OOM	100	13	41	46
	ARC vs. peace	100	31	38	31
	KU vs. OOM	100	9	40	51
	KU vs. peace	100	25	42	33
	OOM vs. peace	100	49	45	6

Table 10: Results for the manual validation for the Medline test sets. Values are absolute numbers (not percentages). They might not sum up to 100 due to the skipped sentences.

Pair	=	>
de/en	ARC, UCAM	-
en/de	-	-
en/es	MT-UOC-UPF	BSC, Talp_upc, UCAM
en/fr	ARC	-
en/pt	BSC	-
en/zh	-	-
es/en	Talp_upc	-
fr/en	-	ARC
pt/en	BSC	-
zh/en	OOM	-

Table 11: List of teams with runs of a similar quality to the reference translations or that outperformed them.

manual validation (e.g. for en/es) or were of similar quality (e.g. de/en). This year there were more such cases (cf. Table 11), which confirms the improvements of the participating systems.

7.2 Quality of the test sets

To evaluate the quality of the MEDLINE test sets, we performed an evaluation of the sentence alignment using Appraise to classify sentence pairs between "OK", "Target > Source", "Source > Target" and "No Alignment". During this process, we also noted any observation on the quality of the reference translation. Of note for this dataset, the reference translation is produced by the original authors of the papers who are scientists with likely no training in translation and whose writing competence in the languages involved is unknown. We can make the hypothesis that the authors have acquired English as a second language while they have native or near-native competence in the non English language.

The quality of the alignment in the Medline test sets varied from as low as around 68% (for de/en and en/de) to as high as 84.4% (for zh/en and en/zh). Therefore, the rate of misaligned sentences did not vary much across the language pairs. Part of this problem was due to incorrectly considering the titles of the citations, when usually there is no translation for these available in Medline.

Some of the segments assessed as correctly aligned ("OK") sometimes exhibited sentence segmentation error that were similar in the two languages. For example, there were segments where pairs of sentences were aligned, instead of being split into two aligned segments.

Interestingly, except for zn/en and en/zh, we observed an average of twice more sentences classified as "Target > Source" than as "Source > Target". This might suggest that authors of the ar-

ticles might have added more information in the English version of the article than in the version in the foreign language.

During our manual validation of the test sets (cf. Section 2), we identified the non-aligned sentences with the specific label 'No Alignment'. However, almost 1/3 of these not aligned sentences correspond to other issues: (a) misalignment between titles to nothing or something else; (b) misalignment of complete, different sentences (even though these were rather rare); and (c) misalignment of section+sentences wrongly aligned to only the section name in the other language. The latter was also sometimes classified as either "Target > Source" or "Source > Target". Regarding these two labels, i.e., "Target > Source" and "Source > Target", these were often utilized for the following situations: (a) section+sentence automatically aligned only to sentence (the opposite of the above); (b) reference to an entity (e.g. a disease), while referred only to the pronoun (e.g. it) in the other language; (c) mention of a particular information (e.g. a method or a time range) in one language, while not in the other language; and (d) the English version included notes in squared brackets which were not part of the foreign sentence.

We also identified problems in the reference translation when performing the manual validation. Some issues were related to the sentence splitting, for instance, p-values were often split, so that "(p=0.5)" would be split on the ".". In those cases, the preceding sentence ended in "... (p=0." and the next sentence started with "5) ...". Others were related to the content of the reference translations themselves, including non-literal translations that alter the meaning of the original sentence when out of context (Example 1), wrong translations (as in Example 2) and even poor formatting and punctuation.

(1) *Source:* Toutes **ces personnes**, et en particulier dans le monde du sport amateur...
   Ref: **These athletes**, especially, the amateurs...
   Correct: All of **these people**, especially in the amateur sports world...[15]

(2) *Source:* Les crises épileptiques sont imprévisibles et peuvent se produire

---

[15] Relevant parts of the translation are indicated in bold. The same holds for Example 2.

43

n'importe où.

Ref: Epileptic seizures occur with unpredictable frequency **in unexpected place**.

Correct: Epileptic seizures are unpredictable and can occur **anywhere**.

A further problem identified was the presence of very short sentences often formed of a single word (e.g. titles or listed items such as "Conclusions", "Objective", or "Clinical Case"), which are in general correctly translated. Including such items for evaluation could influence quality assessments, inflating the scores, since their translation is more similar to terminology translation rather than sentential translation.

7.3 Quality of the system translations

English (from Chinese). As the first year receiving submissions addressing the Chinese language, the overall quality of the translations was delightfully high. For an English sentence to offer the same level of fluency, the order of phrases is often different from those in the source Chinese sentence. Many of the submitted translations successfully captured this behavior, as in the example below.

在健康风险和生理及心理自我调节能力评估讨论的背景下解读 HRV 节律。
(Order of terms: health risk, physiological and psychological self-regulation, interpretation, HRV rhythms.)
– Source

Interpretation of heart rate variability rhythms in the context of health risk and physiological and psychological self-regulatory capacity assessment is discussed.
– Reference translation

HRV rhythms are interpreted in the context of health risks and assessment of physiological and psychological self-regulation.
– Translation

Errors that disrupt the meaning of the translations most are incorrectly translated biomedical terms, presumably due to an inadequate Chinese biomedical dictionary. For instance, 人智医学 or *anthroposophic healthcare* was, based on the literal meanings of the individual Chinese characters making up the term, variably translated

as *human intellectual healthcare*, *psychiatric care* and even *humane healthcare*. Other literal but incorrect translations include *horse's syndrome* for 马方综合征 (Mafran's syndrome) due to the 马 character (a horse), and *parasitic therapy* for 槲寄生疗法 (mistletoe therapy) due to 寄生 (parasitic). In some cases, such terms, which were presumably absent from the dictionary, were entirely omitted in the translations.

Improvements to the translations could be made in two areas. Firstly, singular and plural markings could be made consistent within one translated abstract. In Chinese, with very few exceptions, nouns are not inflected to indicate plurality. Hence where an earlier sentence in an abstract mentions, for instance, 两名患者 (*two patients*) and in a later sentence only 患者, a correct English translation should remain consistent with the plural *patients*, not the singular *patient*. Secondly, non-biomedical terms with connotations specific to scientific abstracts could be more precisely translated. For instance, beginning the final sentence in an abstract with 总之 would be better translated as *in conclusion* than *in general*.

English (from French). The overall translation quality was high for this language direction, and it was often difficult to distinguish between the MT output and the reference translation in terms of quality, in some cases indicative of the good quality of automatic translation, and in others of the presence of problems in the reference translations themselves.

An aspect that could have contributed to a translation being considered better or worse was the handling of complex noun phrases (e.g. *case monitoring* versus a prepositional phrase complement *monitoring of cases*). Whereas many prescriptivists would prescribe the noun compound variant, these were actually often perceived to be more natural and appropriate for academic or scientific writing.

Noun compound	PP complement
robust case monitoring	robust monitoring of cases
stool culture results	results of stool culture
treatment trajectories	trajectories of treatments

Table 12: Examples of equally grammatical noun compounds and prepositional phrase (PP) complements in the fr/en manually evaluated data.

English (from German). The quality of the translations from German to English was generally good. German sentences, which have a typically different structure and word order than English sentences, were usually re-arranged with conjunctions and subordinate clauses in proper written English. In a few cases, the greater context of the German corpus at hand appeared to influence the translation of the individual checked sentences, as additional information, which was not part of the original German sentence, was integrated into the English translation. For example:

Bei 3,6% war schon einmal eine psychosomatische Reha durchgeführt worden und dennoch vom Konsiliararzt eine Wiederholungsreha als sinnvoll erachtet. ***Patienten, die bereits einmal in Reha waren sind kränker und haben mehr Fähigkeits- und Teilhabeprobleme.***
Von 35 Patienten, bei denen der Konsiliararzt die Neubeantragung einer psychosomatischen Rehabilitation empfahl, wurde bei 13 im Verlauf der folgenden 6 Monate ein Antrag gestellt.
– Source

Patients who had already been in inpatient rehabilitation in the past 5 years were more severely ill and had more severe participation problems.
– Translation

As the appraiser was blinded to the source of the translations, it was not possible to determine if such sentences were machine-translated or human-translated.

Pro-forms were also successfully used in the German to English translations, such as *sie* to *OCT*, referring to *optical coherence tomography*, and *In den aufgearbeiteten Fällen* to *In our cases*. These two examples make sense and appear to be correctly translated. However, other pro-forms were not, such as German *er* to English *he* instead of the gender-neutral pronoun *it*. German pronouns present a challenge for automated translation, as all nouns in the German language are assigned a gender, whereas in English, only persons are given gendered pronouns.

While most German words were correctly translated to their English equivalents, there were some interesting cases, ranging from completely off-topic to understandable yet odd equivalents. For example, the German word *Möpsen* (English: *pugs*) was incorrectly translated many times to *seagulls* or *cups*. *Konsiliararzt* (English: *consultant*) was translated to different terms but never correctly: *siliconist* or *silicone doctor*. Interestingly, the adverb *konsiliarärztlich* was correctly interpreted to describe a recommendation from a doctor in the English translation, but unfortunately this doctor was translated to be a *silicone doctor*:

Bei 64% der Patienten mit chronischen psychischen Erkrankungen war bislang keine psychosomatische Reha erfolgt und auch keine Indikation gegeben. ***Bei 27% wurde bislang noch keine Rehamaßnahme durchgeführt, wurde jetzt aber konsiliarärztlich erstmals empfohlen.***
Bei 3,6% war schon einmal eine psychosomatische Reha durchgeführt worden und dennoch vom Konsiliararzt eine Wiederholungsreha als sinnvoll erachtet.
– Source

At 27%, no rehab has been performed yet, but has now been recommended for the first time by a silicone doctor.
– Translation

Improvements to automated translation could be made if translations of medical or technical words could be constrained to the context. When describing the torso of the human body, *Rumpf* was translated to the aviation term *fuselage* and *Säugezeit* was literally translated to *mammalian period* instead of *suckling period*. In peculiar yet comprehensible translations, the German *befragte Person* was translated to *repliers* instead of *respondents*. The English translation of *Lebensqualität* was mistaken as the phonetic *quality of live* instead of *quality of life*. On a positive note, the German false friend *evtl.* was indeed correctly translated to the English word *possible*. Some abbreviations were not even translated at all (*AÄ, OÄ, KP*), yet the procedure *Zementsakroplastie (ZSP)* was correctly constructed as *Cement Sacroplasty (CSP)* in English. *Vitien* (English: *cardiac defect*), which is actually Latin, was wrongly translated to *vials* or *vii*. Overall, German scientific and medical terms and abbreviations were occasionally difficult to translate correctly.

In a handful of examples, the English translations appeared to be too colloquial for a written scientific context. This includes phrases such as *so you always have to ask about it* and *but there are no studies on that* and using the verb *got* instead of *received*. From the appraiser's point of view, the origin of these phrases - automatic translation or manually curated gold standard - is not clear.

In a few cases, the English translations, despite being grammatically correct, altered the intended meaning of the original German sentence. The compound word *Teilhabebeeinträchtigungen* was wrongly translated to *partial impairment* instead of *participation impairment*. In another example, a long German sentence ending in *Antrag gestellt* was incorrectly interpreted to mean *received an application*. The same original text was further mistakenly interpreted in another translation to imply that the actual rehabilitation had been started, when in fact the German original indicated that only an application for rehabilitation had been initiated:

> *Patienten, die bereits einmal in Reha waren sind kränker und haben mehr Fähigkeits- und Teilhabeprobleme.*
> ***Von 35 Patienten, bei denen der Konsiliararzt die Neubeantragung einer psychosomatischen Rehabilitation empfahl, wurde bei 13 im Verlauf der folgenden 6 Monate ein Antrag gestellt.***
> *SCHLUSSFOLGERUNG*
> – Source

> *Of 35 patients in whom the consultant recommended the reapplication of psychosomatic rehabilitation, 13 received an application during the following 6 months.*
> – Translation A

> *In 13 out of 35 patients who got a recommendation for a new psychosomatic rehabilitation, this rehabilitation was initiated within 6 months after the consult.*
> – Translation B

> *Of the 35 patients in whom the silicone doctor recommended a new application for psychosomatic rehabilitation, 13 were applied for during the following 6 months.*
> – Translation C

In fact, Translation C was the most correct about the 13 patients, except the error that *Konsiliararzt* was translated as *silicone doctor*.

In a last example, the words *nachhaltigen Effekt* were translated to two different possibilities: *sustainable effect* (the fact that the effect is able to be sustained) and *sustained effect* (an effect that held continuously at a certain level). There is a subtle difference in meaning of these two English terms, whereas the German word (*nachhaltigen*) could used to describe both situations. This complicates a straight-forward translation because the correct interpretation heavily depends on the whole context of the matter:

> *Berufsgruppenbedingte Unterschiede im klinischen Alltag und individueller Karrierefortschritt üben einen Einfluss auf Art, Umsetzung und Wahrnehmung der Lehrtätigkeit aus.* ***Hinweise auf einen nachhaltigen Effekt ermutigen zur Fortsetzung und Weiterentwicklung des TTT-Konzepts.***
> *Er wurde in den letzten acht Jahren auf ähnliche Symptome untersucht.*
> – Source

> *Indications of a sustained effect encourage the continuation and further development of the TTT concept.*
> – Translation A

> *Indications of a sustainable effect encourage the continuation and further development of the TTT concept.*
> – Translation B

From the appraiser's point of view, it is not possible to ascertain the author's true meaning of *nachhaltigen* from these short excerpts.

English (from Spanish). The translations into English from Spanish were notably improved this year , and judgments were much more subtle in many cases. There were still a few occurrences of untranslated words appearing in the translations, but far fewer than in previous years.

Lexical choice was often a differentiating factor between translations, e.g. *accomplish several goals* was preferred to *achieving various goals*.

Grammar differences were also visible, in particular for complex noun phrases, e.g. *creative alternatives management* vs. *creative management alternatives*.

Some differences in the translations hinged on treatment of acronyms; without further context (i.e., the expansion of the acronym) or specific domain knowledge it was sometimes difficult to decide which acronym should be preferred.

Reference translations were sometimes clearly identifiable due to including information from other parts of the text outside of the focus sentence, leaving out some details in the original, or completely rephrasing an idea; in general translations more faithful to the original sentence were preferred, as long as the translation was basically fine.

Sometimes neither translation being compared was ideal, and assessment came down to a judgment call. For instance, comparing the two translations A: *In the **double cerclage**, surgery time was shorter (average 38 minutes), and the range of motion showed improvement **since** the first month.* and B: *In the **cerclage double**, the time of surgery was shorter (average 38 minutes), and the range of motion demonstrated improvement **from** the first month.*, A has the more accurate grammar for *double cerclage*, but *from the first month* is more correctly expressed. In this case, B was picked because the error in the noun phrase is easier to compensate for.

Another such example was the translation of *Existen desigualdades de género en la provisión de cuidados informales a mayores dependientes en Gipuzkoa, mostrando las mujeres un mayor impacto en su salud y CVRS que los hombres.* as A: *There are gender inequalities in the provision of informal care to dependent older adults in Gipuzkoa, showing that women have a greater impact on their health and HRQOL than men.* and B: *Gender inequalities exist in the provision of informal care to elderly dependent in Gipuzkoa, showing women a greater impact on their health and HRQL than men..* Both translations are imperfect, however A provides a better treatment of *mayores dependientes (the dependent elderly)* than B – although B is close, it requires a plural *dependents*. However, *showing that women* is not a natural way to express the relationship between the gender inequalities (*desigualdades de género*) in the first half of the sentence and the impact of women in the second half; a better translation would be *indicating that women* or *with women having*. On balance, though, translation A is overall more readable than B.

Some differences were only in relation to spacing, i.e. one translation included "patients,14%" while the other had "patients, 14%". This suggests the use of character-level modeling in the algorithms having occasional hiccups. One particularly problematic translation was *Univariate and **multivariateanalyses** were performed through a Multilayer **Perceptronnetwork** and a logistic regression model **EmpiricalBayesian** penalized type LASSO Elastic net.* On the flip side, these algorithms were sometimes able to correct spacing problems in the source text.

Chinese. The quality of translations from all four participating systems was very high, and the translations were generally fluent and accurate. When comparing the translations from the various systems, shorter sentences were typically highly similar, differing only in certain formulations. However, such differences could suffice to distinguish one translation as better than another, because a wording (e.g. 新努力 *new efforts*) more precisely captures the source (exactly *new efforts*) than alternative wordings (新进展 *new developments*). For longer sentences, more noticeable differences surfaced, particularly in different orderings of phrases. These orderings sometimes impacted the fluency of the translation, but in generally were merely different but valid arrangements of the same content.

In terms of serious errors, only in rare cases were phrases completely dropped in the translations. As for incorrect translation of biomedical terms, they occurred far less frequently in the en/zh direction than zh/en. One might hypothesize that the dictionary in the en/zh direction was more complete. However, the fact that translating into Chinese has the option of retaining the original term in English is also a contributing factor, which leads us to the next point.

Currently there is no consensus in how much of a technical term in English should be preserved in the Chinese translation. Take *Functional electronic stimulation (FES)* in a source as an example. Valid translations in Chinese include having only the Chinese term (功能性电刺激); with the acronym (功能性电刺激 *(FES)*); as well as with full term plus acronym (功能性电刺激 *(Functional electronic stimulation, FES)*). Gene names, on the other hand, are uncontentiously retained in English (e.g. *AMP* and *CK2 α* in source, reference, and submitted translations alike).

German. Compared to last year again in general translations were of very high quality. Only rarely we found untranslated bits from the source language, while automatic systems were mostly able to differentiate between sequences that should be translated or not (e.g. citations, links). The use of capitalization was correct in almost all cases. Therefore, the decision for a better translation was mostly based on the correct translation of technical terms, in general a more appropriate use of German words or word order.

Mostly usage of technical terms was decisive: grayscale ultrasound is *Schwarz-Weiß-Ultraschall* instead of *Graustufen-Ultraschall*, or similarly *mandibular advancement device* is a *Unterkieferprotrusionsschiene* instead of the rather word-by-word but wrong translation *mandibulären Fortschrittsgerät*. Other examples rather concern the appropiate use of German words. For instance, *disease attenuation* is rather a *Abschwächung* than a *Dämpfung* of a disease. It seems that automatic systems could not deal with more complex syntax such as coordination as in *tumor mass and symptom reduction*. Instead of *Tumormassenreduktion und Symptomlinderung*, the automatic translations did not identify the coordination structure and produces an incorrect (word-by-word) translation *Tumormasse und Symptomreduktion*.

Similar to last year, cases when automatic systems were judged better than the reference, the reference contained additional information or missed information while translation usually contained the complete content of the source sentence.

We were not able to define clear patterns for differences between the two automatic systems. However, ARC seems to be more capable of providing proper German syntax (e.g. *Steifigkeitsschwankungen* for *stiffness variation* or *Patienten mit Bauchspeicheldrüsenkrebs* for *pancreatic cancer patients* than UCAM. On the other hand, ARC seems to have difficulty identifying acronyms at the beginning of a sentence and did not keep them all capitalized. ARC even provided a false translation for *Sleep is ... unrefreshing* as *Schlaf ist ... erfrischend* instead of *nicht erfrischend*. UCAM did not show the last two issues.

French. Although the quality of the translations was generally uneven, some systems offered mostly fluent translations.

A number of errors were easily identified as untranslated segments, or repeated words. However, a category of serious errors occurred in otherwise fluent sentences where missense or erroneous information was introduced. This is the case for example when a significant piece of information is omitted in the translation: *We used inverse proportional weighting* translated by *Nous avons utilisé un facteur de pondération proportionnelle* (omission de *inverse*) or when numbers are substituted: *data from adolescents aged 15-18 years* translated by *données des adolescents âgés de 12 à 25 ans*. Arguably, in these cases, no translation would be preferable to a translation error that could easily go undetected.

One notable improvement over previous years was the processing of acronyms, which were often directly expanded or translated with suitable equivalents: for example, *long-lasting insecticidal nets (LLINs)* was translated by *moustiquaires imprégnées d'insecticide de longue durée (MILD)* or *moustiquaires imprégnées à longue durée d'action (MILDA)*. Further assessment should take context beyond a single sentence into account, so that the consistency of use of acronyms can be evaluated over a document. It can also be noted that in some cases, the context of a sentence is not enough to make an assessment. For example, the phrases *Elle survient le plus souvent...* ou *Il se développe le plus souvent...* could be acceptable translations for *It occurs most frequently...*, depending on the grammatical agreement between *Elle/Il* and the translation of the antecedent.

Portuguese. As shown in the results for manual validation (cf. table 6), the automatic translations for Portuguese were of very good quality and often with similar or higher quality as the reference translations. However, we still found some mistakes and issues. Similar to previous years, we still find some acronyms, words or phrases (e.g. Leo G. Reeder Award) that were not translated and remained in the English format. We also found some small mistakes when referring to particular values or parameters from the study, usually between parenthesis. For instance, the passage "88% para T2-0,535 cm)" instead of the complete statement "88% para RM ponderada em T2 (viés = 0,52 cm2; p = 0,735)".

We identified few terms that were translated literally into Portuguese. For intance the term "scrub nurses" was translated into "enfermeiros esfregadores" instead of "enfermeiros/instrumentadores". In many situations, both sentences were correct but we identified as better the sentences that utilized a more scientific language, more appropriate for a publication, e.g., "nivel de escolaridade" instead of just "escolaridade". In another of such cases, we chose the term "longevos" as more appropriate than "mais velhos" when referring to elderly people. We also found errors due to nominal concordance with the number, such "dividido" when related to plural nouns, when it should have been "divididos".

Some mistakes were very subtle, such as the translation shown below which includes the verb "apresentaram" twice in the same sentence. Further, in the translated sentence, it is not clear whether the first instance of the verb "apresentaram" (present) refers just to the second or both subjects, while this information is clear in the reference translation, i.e. that it should refer just to "casos". However, this ambiguity is also present in the original English sentence.

> ***Tumors larger than 2cm and cases that presented angiolymphatic invasion had...***
> – Source
>
> *Tumores maiores do que 2cm e casos com invasão angiolinfática apresentaram...*
> – Reference translation
>
> *Tumores maiores que 2cm e casos que apresentaram invasão angiolinfática apresentaram...*
>   Translation

Another subtle mistake that we found relates to the meaning of the sentence which changed in the translation. In the first sentence below, the subject of the sentence is unknown, while in the second one it is clear that the elderly people are the ones who provide the information.

> *Identificar e hierarquizar as dificuldades referidas no desempenho das atividades de vida diária de idosos.*
> – Sentence 1
>
> *Identificar e hierarquizar as dificuldades relatadas pelos idosos na realização das atividades de vida diária.*
> – Sentence 2

Spanish. The overall quality of the Spanish translations was uneven across all four systems submitted to the challenge. BSC and Talp_upc MT systems had a very good performance when compared to the reference translation, with being BSC the best of the four. UCAM MT's system had a reasonable performance but MT-UOC-UPF was the most irregular.

Sentence structure and word order have shown very good results in all systems for short sentences as shown in the following example.

> ***Isotretinoin is still the best treatment for severe nodulocystic acne.***
> – Source
>
> *la isotretinoína todavía es el mejor tratamiento para el acné noduloquístico severo.*
> – Reference translation
>
> *La isotretinoína sigue siendo el mejor tratamiento para el acné noduloquístico severo.*
> – Translation C

However this was not the case of all sentences, some of which followed English word order, resulting in grammatical correct but unnatural sentences in the target language. Other frequent problems include the handling of acronyms (e.g. *EDs*) and additional information included in the reference translation that was not present in the source, as shown in the example below. (cf. *N = 480*)

> ***Ten Eds will be randomly assigned to the intervention group and 10 to the***

control group.
– Source

*Se asignará de forma aleatoria 10
SU (N = 480) al grupo de intervención
y 10 SU (N = 480) al grupo de control.*
– Reference translation

*Diez EDs se asignarán aleatoria-
mente al grupo de intervención y 10 al
grupo de control.*
– Translation D

Erroneous word order translation for technical terms has been observed resulting in mistranslation of the English source (e.g. *FE-IV*) sentence as shown bellow.

Additionally, system A has translated *fixed-effects instrumental-variable* as *efectos fijos variable instrumental*, that not only is a mistranslation of this technical term, but also changes the overall meaning of the sentence.

Fixed-effects instrumental-variable (FE-IV) pseudo-panel estimation from three rounds of the Mexican National Health and Nutrition Survey (2000, 2006 and 2012).
– Source

*Estimación de pseudopanel de variables
instrumentales de efectos fijos (FE-IV)
en tres rondas de la Encuesta Nacional
de Salud y Nutrición de México (2000,
2006 y 2012).*
– Reference translation

*Los efectos fijos variable instru-
mental (FE-VI) se estimaron en tres
rondas de la Encuesta Nacional de
Salud y Nutrición de México (2000,
2006 y 2012).*
– Translation A

Subject-verb agreement mistakes have been observed in some MT translations, such as the one that follows.

**Each group will enroll 480 patients,
and the outcomes will be compared
between groups.**

– Source

*Cada grupo incluirán 480 pacientes y
los resultados serán comparados entre
grupos.*
– Translation B

Other issues found, more common in longer sentences, are missing information in the translation or wrongly parsed and separated terms, especially if the source sentence also suffers from the same problem.

**For the 5-year time horizon, the
incrementalcost per patient with
mirabegron 50 mg versustolterodine
was 195.52 and 157.42, from theN-
ational Health System (NHS) and
societal perspectivesrespectively, with a
gain of 0.0127 QALY withmirabegron.**
– Source

*Para el horizonte temporal de 5
años, el incremento por paciente con
mirabegron 50 mg versustolterodina fue
195,52 y 157,42 , del Sistema Nacional
de Salud (SNS) y de la perspectiva social respectivamente, con una ganancia
de 0,0127 AVAC con mirabegron.*
– Translation D

8   Conclusions

We presented the 2019 edition of the WMT shared task for biomedical machine translation. Participants were challenged to provide automatic translations for medical texts from the literature in ten language pairs as well as for terminology content from English to Spanish. We prepared three baseline systems based on neural toolkits and received 59 runs from 11 teams. Overall, submissions were received for all test sets that were offered. Some of the results obtained by the participants could outperform the scores from previous editions of the shared task and some submissions were judged better than the reference translations created by the authors of the papers in the test set. We also identified some limitations of this shared task, such as issues with the quality of the test sets that we plan to improve in the next edition of the task. Other planned improvements include manual evaluation of the submission based on direct assessment as opposed to the current pairwise comparison of two sentences.

Acknowledgments

We would like to thank all participants in the challenges, and especially those who supported us for the manual evaluation, including Melana Uceda (es/en). We also would like to thank the participants Aihu Zhang (team OOM), Antoni Oliver Gonzalez (team MT-UOC-UPF), Fabien Cromières (team KU), Sadaf Abdul-Rauf (team NRPU) and Stefania Duma (team UHH-DS) for providing summaries about their systems, which we included in the manuscript. MK and FS acknowledge support from the *encargo de gestión* SEAD-BSC-CNS of Plan for the Advancement of Language Technology (Plan TL) and the Interreg Sudoe ICTUSnet project.

References

UFAL medical corpus 1.0. `https://ufal.mff.cuni.cz/ufal_medical_corpus`. Accessed: 2018-07-24.

Sadaf Abdul-Rauf, Holger Schwenk, Patrik Lambert, and Mohammad Nawaz. 2016. Empirical use of information retrieval to build synthetic data for smt domain adaptation. *IEEE/ACM Transactions on Audio, Speech and Language Processing (TASLP)*, 24(4):745–754.

Ondřej Bojar, Rajen Chatterjee, Christian Federmann, Yvette Graham, Barry Haddow, Matthias Huck, Antonio Jimeno Yepes, Philipp Koehn, Varvara Logacheva, Christof Monz, Matteo Negri, Aurelie Neveol, Mariana Neves, Martin Popel, Matt Post, Raphael Rubino, Carolina Scarton, Lucia Specia, Marco Turchi, Karin Verspoor, and Marcos Zampieri. 2016. Findings of the 2016 Conference on Machine Translation. In *Proceedings of the First Conference on Machine Translation: Volume 2, Shared Task Papers*, pages 131–198.

Pi-Chuan Chang, Michel Galley, and Christopher D. Manning. 2008. Optimizing Chinese Word Segmentation for Machine Translation Performance. In *Proceedings of the Third Workshop on Statistical Machine Translation*, pages 224–232, Columbus, Ohio.

Mirela-Stefania Duma and Wolfgang Menzel. Translation of Biomedical Documents with Focus on Spanish-English. In *Proceedings of the Third Conference on Machine Translation: Shared Task Papers*.

Mirela-Stefania Duma and Wolfgang Menzel. 2016a. Data Selection for IT Texts using Paragraph Vector. In *Proceedings of the First Conference on Machine Translation*, pages 428–434, Berlin, Germany.

Mirela-Stefania Duma and Wolfgang Menzel. 2016b. Paragraph Vector for Data Selection in Statistical Machine Translation. In *Proceedings of the 13th Conference on Natural Language Processing KONVENS 2016*, pages 84–89, Bochum, Germany.

Ondřej Dušek, Jan Hajič, Jaroslava Hlaváčová, Jindřich Libovický, Pavel Pecina, Aleš Tamchyna, and Zdeňka Urešová. 2017. Khresmoi Summary Translation Test Data 2.0. LINDAT/CLARIN digital library at the Institute of Formal and Applied Linguistics (ÚFAL), Faculty of Mathematics and Physics, Charles University.

Christian Federmann. 2010. Appraise: An Open-Source Toolkit for Manual Phrase-Based Evaluation of Translations. In *Proceedings of the Seventh conference on International Language Resources and Evaluation*, pages 1731–1734, Valletta, Malta.

Antonio Jimeno Yepes, Aurelie Neveol, Mariana Neves, Karin Verspoor, Ondrej Bojar, Arthur Boyer, Cristian Grozea, Barry Haddow, Madeleine Kittner, Yvonne Lichtblau, Pavel Pecina, Roland Roller, Rudolf Rosa, Amy Siu, Philippe Thomas, and Saskia Trescher. 2017. Findings of the WMT 2017 Biomedical Translation Shared Task. In *Proceedings of the Second Conference on Machine Translation*, pages 234–247, Copenhagen, Denmark.

Marcin Junczys-Dowmunt, Roman Grundkiewicz, Tomasz Dwojak, Hieu Hoang, Kenneth Heafield, Tom Neckermann, Frank Seide, Ulrich Germann, Alham Fikri Aji, Nikolay Bogoychev, André F. T. Martins, and Alexandra Birch. 2018. Marian: Fast Neural Machine Translation in C++. In *Proceedings of the 56th Annual Meeting of the Association for Computational Linguistics: System Demonstrations*, pages 116–121, Melbourne, Australia.

Guillaume Klein, Yoon Kim, Yuntian Deng, Jean Senellart, and Alexander M. Rush. 2017. OpenNMT: Open-Source Toolkit for Neural Machine Translation. In *Proceedings of the 55th Annual Meeting of the Association for Computational Linguistics: System Demonstrations*, pages 67–72, Vancouver, Canada.

Philipp Koehn, Hieu Hoang, Alexandra Birch, Chris Callison-Burch, Marcello Federico, Nicola Bertoldi, Brooke Cowan, Wade Shen, Christine Moran, Richard Zens, Chris Dyer, Ondřej Bojar, Alexandra Constantin, and Evan Herbst. 2007. Moses: Open Source Toolkit for Statistical Machine Translation. In *Proceedings of the 45th Annual Meeting of the ACL on Interactive Poster and Demonstration Sessions*, pages 177–180, Prague, Czech Republic.

Quoc Le and Tomas Mikolov. 2014. Distributed Representations of Sentences and Documents. In

Proceedings of the 31st International Conference on International Conference on Machine Learning - Volume 32, ICML'14, pages II–1188–II–1196. JMLR.org.

Robert Leaman, Rezarta Islamaj Doğan, and Zhiyong Lu. 2013. DNorm: disease name normalization with pairwise learning to rank. *Bioinformatics*, 29(22):2909–2917.

Roberto Navigli and Simone Paolo Ponzetto. 2012. BabelNet: The automatic construction, evaluation and application of a wide-coverage multilingual semantic network. *Artificial Intelligence*, 193:217–250.

Aurélie Névéol, Antonio Jimeno Yepes, Mariana Neves, and Karin Verspoor. 2018. Parallel corpora for the biomedical domain. In *Proceedings of the Eleventh International Conference on Language Resources and Evaluation (LREC-2018)*. European Language Resource Association.

Mariana Neves. 2017. A parallel collection of clinical trials in portuguese and english. In *Proceedings of the 10th Workshop on Building and Using Comparable Corpora*, pages 36–40. Association for Computational Linguistics.

Mariana Neves, Antonio Jimeno Yepes, Aurélie Névéol, Cristian Grozea, Amy Siu, Madeleine Kittner, and Karin Verspoor. 2018. Findings of the wmt 2018 biomedical translation shared task: Evaluation on medline test sets. In *Proceedings of the Third Conference on Machine Translation: Shared Task Papers*, pages 324–339. Association for Computational Linguistics.

Mariana Neves, Antonio Jimeno Yepes, and Aurélie Névéol. 2016. The scielo corpus: a parallel corpus of scientific publications for biomedicine. In *Proceedings of the Tenth International Conference on Language Resources and Evaluation (LREC 2016)*, Paris, France. European Language Resources Association (ELRA).

Noor-e-Hira, Sadaf Abdul Rauf, Kiran Kiani, Ammara Zafar, and Raheel Nawaz. 2019. Translation of Medical texts using Transfer Learning and Selective Data Training: NRPU-FJ Participation in WMT19. In *Proceedings of the Fourth Conference on Machine Translation*. Association for Computational Linguistics.

Pavel Pecina, Ondřej Dušek, Lorraine Goeuriot, Jan Hajič, Jaroslava Hlaváčová, Gareth J.F. Jones, Liadh Kelly, Johannes Leveling, David Mareček, Michal Novák, Martin Popel, Rudolf Rosa, Aleš Tamchyna, and Zdeňka Urešová. 2014. Adaptation of machine translation for multilingual information retrieval in the medical domain. *Artificial Intelligence in Medicine*, 61(3):165 – 185. Text Mining and Information Analysis of Health Documents.

Pavel Pecina, Antonio Toral, Vassilis Papavassiliou, Prokopis Prokopidis, Ales Tamchyna, Andy Way, and Josef van Genabith. 2015. Domain adaptation of statistical machine translation with domain-focused web crawling. *Language resources and evaluation*, 49(1):147–193. 26120290[pmid].

Casimiro Pio Carrino, Bardia Rafieian, Marta R. Costa-jussà, and José A. R. Fonollosa. 2019. Terminology-aware segmentation and domain feature data enriching strategy for the WMT19 Biomedical Translation Task. In *Proceedings of the Fourth Conference on Machine Translation*. Association for Computational Linguistics.

Danielle Saunders, Felix Stahlberg, and Bill Byrne. 2019. UCAM Biomedical translation at WMT19: Transfer learning multi-domain ensembles. In *Proceedings of the Fourth Conference on Machine Translation*. Association for Computational Linguistics.

Rico Sennrich, Barry Haddow, and Alexandra Birch. 2015. Neural machine translation of rare words with subword units. *CoRR*, abs/1508.07909.

Felipe Soares and Martin Krallinger. 2019. BSC participation in the WMT biomedical task. In *Proceedings of the Fourth Conference on Machine Translation*. Association for Computational Linguistics.

Felipe Soares, Viviane Moreira, and Karin Becker. 2018a. A large parallel corpus of full-text scientific articles. In *Proceedings of the Eleventh International Conference on Language Resources and Evaluation (LREC-2018)*. European Language Resource Association.

Felipe Soares, Gabrielli Harumi Yamashita, and Michel Jose Anzanello. 2018b. A parallel corpus of theses and dissertations abstracts. In *International Conference on Computational Processing of the Portuguese Language*, pages 345–352. Springer.

Jörg Tiedemann. 2012. Parallel data, tools and interfaces in opus. In *Proceedings of the Eight International Conference on Language Resources and Evaluation (LREC'12)*, Istanbul, Turkey. European Language Resources Association (ELRA).

Anne M Turner, Yong K Choi, Kristin Dew, Ming-Tse Tsai, Alyssa L Bosold, Shuyang Wu, Donahue Smith, and Hendrika Meischke. 2019. Evaluating the usefulness of translation technologies for emergency response communication: A scenario-based study. *JMIR Public Health Surveill*, 5(1):e11171.

Ashish Vaswani, Samy Bengio, Eugene Brevdo, Francois Chollet, Aidan Gomez, Stephan Gouws, Llion Jones, Łukasz Kaiser, Nal Kalchbrenner, Niki Parmar, Ryan Sepassi, Noam Shazeer, and Jakob Uszkoreit. 2018. Tensor2Tensor for neural machine translation. In *Proceedings of the 13th Conference of the Association for Machine Translation in the*

Americas (Volume 1: Research Papers), pages 193–199, Boston, MA. Association for Machine Translation in the Americas.

Ashish Vaswani, Noam Shazeer, Niki Parmar, Jakob Uszkoreit, Llion Jones, Aidan N. Gomez, Łukasz Kaiser, and Illia Polosukhin. 2017. Attention is all you need. In *Advances in Neural Information Processing Systems 30*, pages 5998–6008. Curran Associates, Inc.

Marta Villegas, Ander Intxaurrondo, Aitor Gonzalez-Agirre, Montserrat Marimón, and Martin Krallinger. 2018. The mespen resource for english-spanish medical machine translation and terminologies: Census of parallel corpora, glossaries and term translations. In *Proceedings of the Eleventh International Conference on Language Resources and Evaluation (LREC 2018)*, Paris, France. European Language Resources Association (ELRA).

Mingxuan Wang, Li Gong, Wenhuan Zhu, Jun Xie, and Chao Bian. 2018. Tencent neural machine translation systems for WMT18. In *Proceedings of the Third Conference on Machine Translation: Shared Task Papers*, pages 522–527, Belgium, Brussels. Association for Computational Linguistics.

Peng Wei, Liu Jianfeng, Li Liangyou, and Liu Qun. 2019. Huawei's NMT systems for the WMT 2019 biomedical translation task. In *Proceedings of the Fourth Conference on Machine Translation*. Association for Computational Linguistics.

Cuijun Wu, Fei Xia, Louise Deleger, and Imre Solti. 2011. Statistical machine translation for biomedical text: are we there yet? *AMIA ... Annual Symposium proceedings. AMIA Symposium*, 2011:1290–1299. 22195190[pmid].

Weijia Xu and Marine Carpuat. 2018. The university of Maryland's Chinese-English neural machine translation systems at WMT18. In *Proceedings of the Third Conference on Machine Translation: Shared Task Papers*, pages 535–540, Belgium, Brussels. Association for Computational Linguistics.

Michał Ziemski, Marcin Junczys-Dowmunt, and Bruno Pouliquen. 2016. The united nations parallel corpus v1.0. In *Proceedings of the Tenth International Conference on Language Resources and Evaluation (LREC 2016)*, Paris, France. European Language Resources Association (ELRA).

Findings of the WMT 2019 Shared Task
on Parallel Corpus Filtering for Low-Resource Conditions

Philipp Koehn
Johns Hopkins University
phi@jhu.edu

Francisco Guzmán
Facebook AI
fguzman@fb.com

Vishrav Chaudhary
Facebook AI
vishrav@fb.com

Juan Pino
Facebook AI
juancarabina@fb.com

Abstract

Following the WMT 2018 Shared Task on Parallel Corpus Filtering (Koehn et al., 2018), we posed the challenge of assigning sentence-level quality scores for very noisy corpora of sentence pairs crawled from the web, with the goal of sub-selecting 2% and 10% of the highest-quality data to be used to train machine translation systems. This year, the task tackled the low resource condition of Nepali–English and Sinhala–English. Eleven participants from companies, national research labs, and universities participated in this task.

1 Introduction

Machine Translation (MT) has experienced significant advances in recent years thanks to improvements in modeling, and in particular neural models (Bahdanau et al., 2015; Gehring et al., 2016; Vaswani et al., 2017). Unfortunately, today's neural machine translation models, perform poorly on *low-resource* language pairs, for which clean, parallel training data is high-quality training data is lacking, by definition (Koehn and Knowles, 2017).

Improving performance on low resource language pairs is very impactful considering that these languages are spoken by a large fraction of the world population. This is a particular challenge for industrial machine translation systems that need to support hundreds of languages in order to provide adequate services to their multilingual user base.

In face of the scarcity of clean parallel data, learning to translate from any multilingual noisy data such as web-crawls (e.g. from Wikipedia, Paracrawl[1]) is an important option.

Recently, there is an increased interest in the filtering of noisy parallel corpora to increase the amount of data that can be used to train translation systems (Koehn et al., 2018). While the state-of-the-art methods that use NMT models have proven effective in mining parallel sentences (Junczys-Dowmunt, 2018) for high-resource languages, their effectiveness has not been tested in low-resource languages. The implications of low availability of training data for parallel-scoring methods is not known yet.

The Shared Task on Parallel Corpus Filtering at the Conference for Machine Translation (WMT 2019) was organized to promote research to learning from noisy data more viable for low-resource languages. Compared to last year's edition (Koehn et al., 2018), we only provide about 50-60 million word noisy parallel data, as opposed to 1 billion words. We also provide only a few million words of clean parallel data of varying quality, instead of over 100 million words of high-quality parallel data. Participants developed methods to filter web-crawled Nepali–English and Sinhala–English parallel corpora by assigning a quality score for each sentence pair. These scores are used to filter the web crawled corpora down to fixed sizes (1 million and 5 million English words), trained statistical and neural machine translation systems on these subsets, and measured their quality with the BLEU score on a test set of multi-domain Wikipedia content (Guzmán et al., 2019).

This paper gives an overview of the task, presents the results for the participating systems and provides analysis on additional subset sizes and the average sentence length of sub-selected data.

---

[1]http://www.paracrawl.eu/

Proceedings of the Fourth Conference on Machine Translation (WMT), Volume 3: Shared Task Papers (Day 2) pages 54–72
Florence, Italy, August 1-2, 2019. ©2019 Association for Computational Linguistics

2 Related Work

Although the idea of crawling the web indiscriminately for parallel data goes back to the 20th century (Resnik, 1999), work in the academic community on extraction of parallel corpora from the web has so far mostly focused on large stashes of multilingual content in homogeneous form, such as the Canadian Hansards, Europarl (Koehn, 2005), the United Nations (Rafalovitch and Dale, 2009; Ziemski et al., 2015), or European Patents (Täger, 2011). A nice collection of the products of these efforts is the OPUS web site[2] (Tiedemann, 2012).

2.1 Parallel Corpus Acquisition

The Paracrawl project is currently engaged in a large-scale effort to crawl text from the web. That work is funded by the European Union via the Connecting Europe Facility. The Paracrawl infrastructure was used to generate the noisy parallel data for this shared task. In previous years, as part of the Paracrawl effort, a shared task on document alignment (Buck and Koehn, 2016) and a shared task on parallel corpus filtering was organized (Koehn et al., 2018).

Acquiring parallel corpora from the web typically goes through the stages of identifying web sites with parallel text, downloading the pages of the web site, aligning document pairs, and aligning sentence pairs. A final stage of the processing pipeline filters out non parallel sentence pairs. These exist either because the original web site did not have any actual parallel data (garbage in, garbage out), only partial parallel data, or due to failures of earlier processing steps.

2.2 Filtering Noisy Parallel Corpora

In 2016, a shared task on sentence pair filtering[3] was organized, albeit in the context of cleaning translation memories which tend to be cleaner than the data at the end of a pipeline that starts with web crawls.

There is a robust body of work on filtering out noise in parallel data. For example: Taghipour et al. (2011) use an outlier detection algorithm to filter a parallel corpus; Xu and Koehn (2017) generate synthetic noisy data (inadequate and non-fluent translations) and use this data to train a classifier to identify good sentence pairs from a noisy corpus; and Cui et al. (2013) use a graph-based random walk algorithm and extract phrase pair scores to weight the phrase translation probabilities to bias towards more trustworthy ones.

Most of this work was done in the context of statistical machine translation, but more recent work targets neural models. Carpuat et al. (2017) focus on identifying semantic differences in translation pairs using cross-lingual textual entailment and additional length-based features, and demonstrate that removing such sentences improves neural machine translation performance.

As Rarrick et al. (2011) point out, one type of noise in parallel corpora extracted from the web are translations that have been created by machine translation. Venugopal et al. (2011) propose a method to watermark the output of machine translation systems to aid this distinction, with a negligible loss of quality. Antonova and Misyurev (2011) report that rule-based machine translation output can be detected due to certain word choices, and statistical machine translation output can be detected due to lack of reordering. It is notable that none of the participants in our shared task have tried to detect machine translation.

There is a rich literature on data selection which aims at sub-sampling parallel data relevant for a task-specific machine translation system (Axelrod et al., 2011). van der Wees et al. (2017) find that the existing data selection methods developed for statistical machine translation are less effective for neural machine translation. This is different from our goals of handling noise since those methods tend to discard perfectly fine sentence pairs that are just not relevant for the targeted domain. Our task is focused on data quality that is relevant for all domains.

2.3 Impact of Noise on Neural Machine Translation

Belinkov and Bisk (2017) investigate the impact of noise on neural machine translation. They focus on creating systems that can *translate* the kinds of orthographic errors (typos, misspellings, etc.) that humans can comprehend. In contrast, Khayrallah and Koehn (2018) examine noisy *training* data and focus on types of noise occurring in web-crawled corpora. They carried out a study about how noise that occurs in crawled parallel text impacts statistical and neural machine translation.

---

[2]http://opus.nlpl.eu
[3]NLP4TM 2016: Shared task
http://rgcl.wlv.ac.uk/nlp4tm2016/shared-task/

Neural machine translation model training may combine data selection and model training, taking advantage of the increasing quality of the model to better detect noisy data or to increasingly focus on cleaner parts of the data (Wang et al., 2018; Kumar et al., 2019).

2.4 Sentence Embeddings

Bouamor and Sajjad (2018) learned sentence embeddings for the source and target languages and selected the nearest translation from a list of candidate sentences for a given source sentence using a classifier. Guo et al. (2018) leveraged hard negatives to correctly identify translation pairs.

Artetxe and Schwenk (2018) use multilingual sentence embeddings to compute cosine similarity between the source and the target sentence. They further normalize the score by the average cosine similarity of the nearest neighbors for the given sentence pair. Their method has shown promising results in filtering WMT Paracrawl data and has achieved state-of-the-art performance on the BUCC corpus mining task.

2.5 Findings of the 2018 Shared Task

The WMT 2018 Shared Task on Parallel Corpus Filtering (Koehn et al., 2018) attracted 18 submissions in a high resource setup. Not surprisingly, due to the large number of submissions, many different approaches were explored for this task. However, most participants used a system using three components: (1) pre-filtering rules, (2) scoring functions for sentence pairs, and (3) a classifier that learned weights for feature functions.

Pre-filtering rules. Some of the training data can be discarded based on simple deterministic filtering rules. These may include rules may consider sentence length, number of real words vs. other tokens, matching names, numbers, dates, email addresses, or URLs, too similar sentences (copied content), and language identification (Pinnis, 2018; Lu et al., 2018; Ash et al., 2018).

Scoring functions. Sentence pairs that pass the pre-filtering stage are assessed with scoring functions which provide scores that hopefully correlate with quality of sentence pairs. Participants used a variety of such scoring functions, including language models, neural translation models and lexical translation probabilities, e.g., IBM Model 1 scores. (Junczys-Dowmunt, 2018; Rossenbach et al., 2018; Lo et al., 2018).

Learning weights for scoring functions. Given a large number of scoring functions, simply averaging their resulting scores may be inadequate. Learning weights to optimize machine translation system quality is computationally intractable due to the high cost of training these systems to evaluate different weight settings. A few participants used instead a classifier that learns how to distinguish between high-quality and low-quality sentence pairs. High-quality sentence pairs are selected from existing high-quality parallel corpora, while low-quality sentence pairs are either synthesized by scrambling high-quality sentence pairs or by using the raw crawled data (Sánchez-Cartagena et al., 2018).

Use of embeddings. While the participant's methods were dominated by non-neural components, sometimes using neural machine translation outputs and scores, some participants used word and sentence embeddings. Given cross-lingual word embeddings, sentence match scores based on the difference between the average of the word embeddings (Paetzold, 2018), or, for each word in the sentence, the closest match in the corresponding sentence (Hangya and Fraser, 2018). Matching of word embeddings may also be done monolingually, after machine translating the foreign sentence into English (Lo et al., 2018). Cross-lingual word embeddings were obtained using uses monolingual word embedding spaces which were aligned with an unsupervised method, or using pre-trained cross-lingual word embeddings. Littell et al. (2018) used monolingual sentence embedding spaces to discount outliers. Pham et al. (2018) use a neural model that takes a sentence pair and predicts a matching score.

Some participants made a distinction between unsupervised methods that did not use existing parallel corpora to train parts of the system, and supervise methods that did. Unsupervised methods have the advantage that they can be readily deployed for language pairs for which no seed parallel corpora exist.

3 Low-Resource Corpus Filtering Task

The shared task tackled the problem of filtering parallel corpora. Given a noisy parallel corpus (crawled from the web), participants developed methods to filter it to a smaller size of high quality sentence pairs.

Specifically, we provided a very noisy 50-60 million word (English token count) Nepali–English and Sinhala–English corpora crawled from the web using the Paracrawl processing pipeline (see Section 4.4 for details). We asked participants to generate sentence-level quality scores that allow selecting subsets of sentence pairs that amount to (a) 1 million words, and (b) 5 million words, counted on the English side. These values were chosen as an approximation to the conditions on the WMT 2018 task. The resulting subsets were scored by building a statistical phrase-based machine translation system (Koehn et al., 2007) and a neural machine translation system (Ott et al., 2019) trained on this data, and then measuring their BLEU score on the `flores` Wikipedia test sets (Guzmán et al., 2019).

Participants in the shared task submitted a file with quality scores, one per line, corresponding to the sentence pairs. Scores are only required to have the property that higher scores indicate better quality. The scores were uploaded to a Google Drive folder which remains publicly accessible.[4]

For development purposes, we released configuration files and scripts that mirror the official testing procedure with a development test set. The development pack consists of:

- A script to subsample corpora based on quality scores.
- A Moses configuration file to train and test a statistical machine translation system.
- `fairseq` scripts to train and test a neural machine translation system.
- The `flores-dev` set of Wikipedia translations as development set.
- The `flores-devtest` set of Wikipedia translations as development test set.

The web site for the shared task[5] provided detailed instructions on how to use these tools to replicate the official testing environment.

4 Data

We provided three types of data for this shared task: (1) clean parallel and monolingual data, including related language data in Hindi, to train models that aid with the filtering task, (2) the noisy

Corpus	Sentence Pairs	English Words
Bible (two translations)	61,645	1,507,905
Global Voices	2,892	75,197
Penn Tree Bank	4,199	88,758
GNOME/KDE/Ubuntu	494,994	2,018,631
Nepali Dictionary	9,916	25,058

Table 1: Provided clean parallel data for Nepali.

parallel data crawled from the web which participants have to score for filtering, and (3) development and test sets that are used to evaluate translation systems trained on filtered data.

4.1 Clean Parallel Data

The main distinction between this year's version of the parallel corpus filtering task and last year's version is the amount of provided clean parallel data. For both Nepali–English and Sinhala–English, only few parallel corpora are available and these are of questionable relevance due to their peculiar domains.

For Nepali (see Table 1 for detailed statistics), the largest data sets are the Bible which we provided with two English translations and the GNOME/KDE/Ubuntu localization data collected by OPUS[6] (Tiedemann, 2012). The type of text found in these corpora are quite different from language found on the Internet. The data sets with more conventional language, a partial translation of the Penn Tree Bank by the Language Resource Association (GSK) of Japan and International Development Research Center (IDRC) of Canada, through PAN Localization project[7] and the citizen journalist news sites Global Voices[8], are much smaller (less than 100,000 words each). We also provide a Nepali–English bilingual dictionary with 9,916 entries (Pavlick et al., 2014).

For Sinhala (see Table 2 for detailed statistics), we only provide two data sources: a fairly large corpus of volunteer translation of subtitles and the GNOME/KDE/Ubuntu localization data collected by OPUS. The Open Subtitles corpus is of mixed quality and most of the language is casual.

---

[4]`https://bit.ly/2IoOXOr`
[5]`http://www.statmt.org/wmt19/`
`parallel-corpus-filtering.html`

[6]`http://opus.nlpl.eu/`
[7]`http://www.PANL10n.net/`
[8]`https://globalvoices.org/`

Corpus	Sentence Pairs	English Words
Open Subtitles	601,164	3,594,769
GNOME/KDE/Ubuntu	45,617	150,513

Table 2: Provided clean parallel data for Sinhala.

Corpus	Sentences	Words
Wikipedia		
Sinhala	155,946	4,695,602
Nepali	92,296	2,804,439
English	67,796,935	1,985,175,324
CommonCrawl		
Sinhala	5,178,491	110,270,445
Nepali	3,562,373	102,988,609
English	380,409,891	8,894,266,960

Table 3: Provided clean monolingual data.

Corpus	Sentences	Words
Hindi–English	1,492,827	20,667,240
Hindi	67,796,935	1,985,175,324

Table 4: Hindi corpora released as related language data from the IIT Bombay English-Hindi Corpus.

	Sentence Pairs	English Words
Nepali	2,235,512	58,537,167
Sinhala	3,357,018	60,999,374

Table 5: Noisy parallel data to be filtered (de-duplicated raw output Paracrawl pipeline).

4.2 Clean Monolingual Data

Monolingual data is always available in much larger quantities, and we provided data from two sources: Wikipedia and CommonCrawl. Both contain language that is similar to what is expected in the noisy web data to be filtered.

We filtered the data to eliminate overlap with the development and test sets. See Table 3 for detailed statistics.

4.3 Related Language Data

Nepali uses the same Devanagari script as Hindi and the languages are closely related. Neural machine translation models for low-resource language pairs have particularly benefited from training data in other language pairs, so parallel Hindi–English data and monolingual Hindi data may be beneficial to train models for our shared task.

As shown in Table 4, we provide a relatively large 20 million word parallel corpus and almost 2 billion words of monolingual Hindi. This data was created from a variety of public domain sources and corpora developed at the Center for Indian Language Technology, IIT Bombay (Kunchukuttan et al., 2018).

4.4 Noisy Parallel Data

The noisy parallel corpora from Paracrawl are the outcome of a processing pipeline that aimed at high recall at the cost of precision, so they are very noisy. They exhibit noise of all kinds: wrong language in source and target, sentence pairs that are not translations of each other, bad language (incoherent mix of words and non-words), incomplete or bad translations, etc.

We used the processing pipeline of the Paracrawl project to create the data, using the clean parallel data to train underlying models such as the dictionary used by Hunalign (Varga et al., 2007) and a statistical translation model used by the document aligner. One modification was necessary to run the pipeline for Nepali due to the end-of-sentence symbol of the script that was previously not recognized by the sentence splitter.

The provided parallel corpus is the raw output of the crawling pipeline, with sentence pairs deduplicated but otherwise no further filtering performed. See Table 5 for statistics of the corpus and Table 6 for some example sentences.

4.5 Development and Test Sets

For test and development purposes, we use the `flores` Wikipedia data-sets for Nepali–English and Sinhala–English (Guzmán et al., 2019). These sets are multi-domain, that is they were sampled from Wikipedia documents with a diverse set of topics. In Table 7 we present the statistics of these sets.

The official scoring of machine translation systems generated from the subsampled data sources is done on the *test* set.

5 Evaluation Protocol

The testing setup mirrors the development environment that we provided to the participants.

Source	previous आधारभूत कुराहरू तपाईंले हाउस सुधार गर्न के गर्न सकेन
Target	previous Basic Things You Could Do To Improve Your House
Source	यो भिडियो Batesville मा एक चेला अब सम्मेलन हो, सुश्री. कृपया भिडियो र अडियो गुणस्तर क्षमा
Target	This video is from a Disciple Now conference in Batesville, MS. Please forgive the video and audio quality

Source	Paintballing, හා තවත් බොහෝ!
Target	Paintballing, and many more!
Source	සම්පත් මුල් පිටුව » සම්පත් » ගැසට් පත් ර අංක 2061/10 – 2018 මාර්තු 05 වැනි සඳුදා – 2018.03.05
Target	Home » Resources » Gazette NO. 2061/10 – MONDAY, MARCH 05, 2018

Table 6: Examples of good sentence pairs from the noisy corpus for Nepali–English and Sinhala–English.

	Nepali		**Sinhala**	
	Sentence Pairs	**English Words**	**Sentence Pairs**	**English Words**
dev	2,559	46,274	2,898	53,479
dev test	2,835	51,458	2,766	50,985
test	2,924	54,062	2,905	52,851

Table 7: Statistics for the `flores` test sets used to evaluate the machine translation systems trained on the subsampled data sets. Word counts are obtained with `wc` on tokenized text.

5.1 Participants

We received submissions from 11 different organizations. See Table 8 for the complete list of participants. The participant's organizations are quite diverse, with 4 participants from the United States, 2 participants from Spain, and 1 participant each from Canada, Sweden, India, and Finland. 5 of the participants are universities, 4 are companies, and 2 are national research organizations. There was little overlap between this year's shared task and last year's high-resource shared task. Only AFRL, NRC, and Webinterpret participated also last year.

Each participant submitted up to 4 different sets of scores, typically a primary and contrastive submission, resulting in a total of 21 different submissions for Nepali and 23 different submissions for Sinhala that we scored.

5.2 Methods used by Participants

Almost all submissions used basic filtering rules as a first filtering step. These rules typically involve language identification and length consid-

erations to remove too long or length-wise mismatched sentence pairs. Some also remove sentence pairs where a specific number occurred on one side but not the other. For some submissions this removed over 80% of the data (Kurfalı and Östling, 2019; Soares and Costa-jussà, 2019).

A novel method that was central to the best-performing submission was the use of cross-lingual **sentence embeddings** that were directly trained from parallel sentence pairs (Chaudhary et al., 2019). Other submissions used monolingual **word embeddings**. These were first trained monolingually for each language from monolingual data. The resulting embedding spaces were mapped either in an unsupervised fashion (Soares and Costa-jussà, 2019) or based on a dictionary learned from the parallel data (Kurfalı and Östling, 2019). Bernier-Colborne and Lo (2019) use both monolingually trained word embeddings aligned in an unsupervised fashion and bilingually trained word embeddings.

Another approach is to first train a translation

Acronym	Participant and System Description Citation
AFRL	Air Force Research Lab, USA (Erdmann and Gwinnup, 2019)
DiDi	DiDi, USA (Axelrod, 2019)
Facebook	Facebook, USA (Chaudhary et al., 2019)
Helsinki	University of Helsinki, Finland (Vázquez et al., 2019)
IITP	Indian Institute of Technology Patna, India (Sen et al., 2019)
Webinterpret	WebInterpret Inc., USA (González-Rubio, 2019)
NRC	National Research Council, Canada (Bernier-Colborne and Lo, 2019)
Stockholm	Stockholm University, Sweden (Kurfalı and Östling, 2019)
SUNY Buffalo	State University of New York, USA (System description not submitted)
Sciling	Sciling S.L., Spain (Parcheta et al., 2019)
TALP-UPC	TALP, Universitat Politècnica de Catalunya, Spain (Soares and Costa-jussà, 2019)

Table 8: Participants in the shared task.

system on the clean data, then use it to **translate the non-English side** into English and use monolingual matching methods to compare it against the English side of the parallel corpus. Different matching metrics were used: METEOR (Erdmann and Gwinnup, 2019), Levenshtein distance (Sen et al., 2019), or BLEU (Parcheta et al., 2019),

Several submissions considered vocabulary **coverage** in their methods, preferring to add sentence pairs to the limited set that increase the number of words and n-grams covered (Erdmann and Gwinnup, 2019; Bernier-Colborne and Lo, 2019; González-Rubio, 2019).

One of the best-performing methods under last year's high resource setting was **dual conditional cross-entropy**, i.e. building neural machine translation models on the clean data and considering the translation scores from forced translation of the parallel corpus. One submission used this method Chaudhary et al. (2019), while others applied the same idea to monolingual language model scores (Axelrod, 2019; Parcheta et al., 2019).

Several **other scoring functions** were used, to name a few: cross-lingual language models (Bernier-Colborne and Lo, 2019), monolingual language models (Vázquez et al., 2019), IBM Model 1 word translation scores (González-Rubio, 2019), and the existing off-the-shelf tools like Zipporah and Bicleaner (Chaudhary et al., 2019).

Some submissions combined multiple scoring functions with **ensemble** methods which may be optimize to distinguish between clean parallel data and synthetic noise data (Chaudhary et al., 2019; Bernier-Colborne and Lo, 2019; Vázquez et al., 2019).

AFRL Erdmann and Gwinnup (2019) use a coverage metric and quality metric. The coverage metric discourages the addition of sentence pairs that have vocabulary already included in the selected set. The quality metric is based on comparing the machine translation of the foreign sentence with the English sentence using the METEOR machine translation metric.

DiDi Axelrod (2019) uses dual cross-entropy based on monolingual language models to find sentence pairs where each side has similar probability. They also employ so-called cynical data selection that prefers to select a representative subset. Additional simple features are length ratio and using character set-based language identification.

Facebook Chaudhary et al. (2019) use an ensemble of methods: matching of cross-lingual sentence embeddings (their best feature), dual cross entropy based on neural translation model scores, and the open source tools Zipporah and Bicleaner.

IITP Sen et al. (2019) build a statistical machine translation systems on the clean parallel data, translate each non-English sentence of the parallel corpus and use scores based on the Levenshtein distance between the machine translation and the English sentence in the parallel corpus. They also use filtering rules based on language identification and sentence length that filter out more than 70% of the data.

NRC Bernier-Colborne and Lo (2019) first employ filtering rules based on language ID, length ratio, mismatched numbers, and near-duplicates. They use the cross-lingual semantic evaluation metric Yisi-2 that relies on cross-lingual word embeddings and a Transformer model based on cross-lingual language model pre-training (XLM) that is optimized to distinguish between clean parallel data and synthetic noisy parallel data. Final scores are re-ranked to increase coverage.

Sciling Parcheta et al. (2019) build machine translation models on the clean data , including the use of the Hindi–English corpus (removing some sentence pairs based on cross-entropy language model scores), translate the non-English side of the noisy data and measure the similarity of the machine translation and the given English sentence with the BLEU score. They also use filtering rules for sentence length, or much overlap between source and target sentence, and language identification.

Stockholm Kurfalı and Östling (2019) first use filtering rules based on excessive amount of numbers or too few actual words (vs. non-word tokens), sentence length, wrong script, and too long words. This removes over 80% of the data. They build monolingual word embeddings using FastText and learn a projection between the spaces based on word translations distilled from word alignments of the parallel data. Sentence similarity is computed based on the cosine between each English word's word vector and the best matching projected word vectors in the other language.

TALP-UPC Soares and Costa-jussà (2019) employ an unsupervised approach (ignoring the clean parallel data). They train monolingual word embeddings using FastText and align them in unsupervised fashion. Sentence pairs are scored based on Word Mover's Distance. They also use basic filtering rules based on sentence length, language identification, and number mismatches which altogether removes over 80% of the data.

Helsinki Vázquez et al. (2019) first clean the provided clean parallel data by employing a number of filtering rules based on sentence length, sentences with long words (over 40 characters), sentences with XML or HTML tags, and sentences in the wrong script (Latin, Devanagari, or Sinhala). This removes about 20% of the data which is then word aligned to obtain bilingual dictionaries. In addition to a word alignment score, the noisy training data is filtered with several scoring functions: language models, language identification, ratio of characters in the correct script, punctuation, number matching, and length mismatch.

Webinterpret González-Rubio (2019) first apply filtering rules based on language identification and sentence length. Coverage ranking incrementally adds sentence pairs to increase vocabulary and n-gram coverage. Adequacy ranking considers IBM Model 1 word translation scores.

5.3 Subset Selection

We provided to the participants a file containing one sentence pair per line (see Section 4.4) each for the two languages. A submission to the shared task consists of a file with the same number of lines, with one score per line corresponding to the quality of the corresponding sentence pair.

To evaluate a submitted score file, we selected subsets of a predefined size, defined by the number of English words (1M or 5M).

Selecting a subset of sentence pairs is done by finding a threshold score, so that the sentence pairs that will be included in the subset have a quality score at and above this threshold. In some cases, a submission assigned this threshold score to a large number of sentence pairs. Including all of them would yield too large a subset, excluding them yields too small a subset. Hence, we randomly included some of the sentence pairs with the exact threshold score to get the desired size in this case.

5.4 Evaluation System Training

Given a selected subset of a given size for a system submission, we built statistical (SMT) and neural machine translation (NMT) systems to evaluate the quality of the selected sentence pairs.

SMT For statistical machine translation, we used Moses (Koehn et al., 2007) with fairly basic settings, such as Good-Turing smoothing of phrase table probabilities, maximum phrase length

```
--arch transformer
--share-all-embeddings
--encoder-layers 5
--decoder-layers 5
--encoder-embed-dim 512
--decoder-embed-dim 512
--encoder-ffn-embed-dim 2048
--decoder-ffn-embed-dim 2048
--encoder-attention-heads 2
--decoder-attention-heads 2
--encoder-normalize-before
--decoder-normalize-before
--dropout 0.4
--attention-dropout 0.2
--relu-dropout 0.2
--weight-decay 0.0001
--label-smoothing 0.2
--criterion label_smoothed_cross_entropy
--optimizer adam
--adam-betas '(0.9, 0.98)'
--clip-norm 0
--lr-scheduler inverse_sqrt
--warmup-update 4000
--warmup-init-lr 1e-7
--lr 1e-3 --min-lr 1e-9
--max-tokens 4000
--update-freq 4
--max-epoch 100
--save-interval 10
```

Figure 1: The baseline `flores` model settings[9] for the NMT training with `fairseq`

of 5, maximum sentence length of 80, lexicalized reordering (*hier-mslr-bidirectional-fe*), fast-align for word alignment with *grow-diag-final-and* symmetrization, tuning with batch-MIRA, no operation sequence model, 5-gram language model trained on the English side of the subset with no additional data, and decoder beam size of 5,000 hypotheses.

NMT For neural machine translation, we used `fairseq` (Ott et al., 2019) transformer model with the parameter settings shown in Figure 1. Preprocessing was done with sentence piece for a 5000 subword vocabulary on tokenized text using the Moses tokenizer (but no truecasing was used). Decoding was done with beam size 5 and length normalization 1.2. Training a system for the 1 million, and 5 million subsets took about 3, and 13 hours, respectively, on a single GTX 1080ti GPU. Scores on the test sets were computed with Sacrebleu (Post, 2018). We report case-insensitive scores.

---

6   Results

In this section we present the final results of the shared task evaluation. We added an additional condition at 2 million English words, to better observe tendencies.

6.1   Core Results

The official results are reported in Table 9 (Nepali) and Table 10 (Sinhala). The tables contains the BLEU scores for

- development test set and final test set
- statistical and neural machine translation
- 1, 2, and 5 million word subsets.

The official scoring is for the 1 million and 5 million word data settings on the final test set. In the table, we highlight cells for the best scores for each of these settings, as well as scores that are close to it. Results for the unofficial 2 million word baseline are shown without highlighting.

For both language pairs, the best scores are achieved for the 1 million word data condition for the neural machine translation model (6.9 for Nepali and 6.4 for Sinhala). This is not the case for all submissions. The better performance for neural systems than for statistical systems with this little data is contrary to earlier findings (Koehn and Knowles, 2017), indicating that recent progress, such as the Transformer model (Vaswani et al., 2017), have addressed this challenge to some degree. However, for some submissions, such as AFRL 50k, SMT scores are higher than NMT scores (4.0 vs. 2.7 for Nepali, 3.8 vs. 3.0 for Sinhala for AFRL 50k).

Scores between the submissions differ more for neural machine translation systems than for statistical machine translation systems. For instance, for the Nepali 1 million word data condition, the difference between the best and the second best participant's submission is 0.2 for SMT but 1.4 for NMT. For the Nepali 5 million word data condition, almost all systems have BLEU scores around 4 for SMT, but NMT scores range from 0.2 to 3.4. This confirms earlier findings (cite noise) that statistical machine translation is more robust towards noise. So better quality for neural machine translation under low resource conditions requires good noise filtering methods.

For statistical machine translation, the bigger and noisier 5 million subsets yield better BLEU

Nepali	1 million				2 million				5 million			
	SMT		NMT		SMT		NMT		SMT		NMT	
Submission	test	devt	test	devt	test	devt	test	devt	test	devt	test	devt
AFRL 50k	4.0	3.8	2.7	2.5	4.2	3.8	3.6	3.6	4.5	4.4	3.4	3.2
AFRL 150k	1.5	3.6	2.3	2.4	4.1	4.0	2.0	2.0	4.7	4.4	2.7	2.5
Facebook main	4.2	4.0	6.8	6.9	4.6	4.3	5.9	6.3	4.6	4.1	2.8	2.9
Facebook contrastive	4.2	4.0	6.9	6.6	4.6	4.3	5.9	6.1	4.6	4.0	2.5	2.4
Helsinki	3.2	3.1	0.9	0.9	3.9	3.5	1.4	1.5	4.3	4.0	1.1	1.1
Helsinki contrastive	1.3	1.2	0.1	0.1	2.0	1.6	0.1	0.1	3.8	3.8	0.9	0.8
IITP	3.8	3.6	5.5	5.9	4.4	4.0	3.3	3.6	4.3	4.0	1.3	1.2
IITP geom	3.9	3.6	5.3	5.6	4.3	4.1	3.6	3.9	4.3	4.0	1.3	1.2
NRC ensemble	4.1	3.7	4.6	4.5	4.5	4.2	3.3	3.4	4.3	4.2	1.1	1.2
NRC xlm	3.9	3.5	4.0	3.8	4.3	3.9	3.2	3.1	4.5	4.2	1.4	1.4
NRC yisi-2-sup	3.5	3.3	3.1	3.1	3.9	3.9	1.5	1.4	4.1	4.0	1.3	1.4
NRC yisi-2-unsup	4.0	3.5	3.7	3.8	4.2	4.2	2.4	2.3	4.1	4.4	1.0	1.0
Stockholm	4.0	3.4	4.2	4.2	4.0	3.6	3.2	3.1	3.8	3.5	1.2	1.2
Stockholm ngram	2.8	2.7	0.3	0.3	3.1	2.7	0.6	0.6	3.6	3.5	0.6	0.6
SUNY Buffalo	1.8	1.4	0.1	0.1	3.0	2.7	0.1	0.1	4.1	4.0	0.8	0.8
Sciling	2.9	2.5	3.5	3.6	3.4	3.2	5.1	5.5	4.1	3.9	3.3	3.2
TALP-UPC primary	0.5	0.5	0.0	0.0	1.2	1.1	0.1	0.1	3.1	3.0	0.2	0.2
TALP-UPC secondary	0.1	0.1	0.1	0.1	0.2	0.1	0.2	0.1	0.4	0.5	0.2	0.1
Webinterpret primary	3.4	3.2	3.1	2.8	3.9	3.8	2.4	2.5	3.3	3.0	2.6	2.5
Webinterpret cov	2.9	2.9	0.5	0.3	3.7	3.5	1.6	1.7	4.2	4.1	2.4	2.3
Webinterpret prob	3.5	3.4	3.6	3.0	4.0	3.7	2.2	2.2	4.2	4.1	2.4	2.3

Table 9: Results for Nepali: BLEU scores are reported for systems trained on 1, 2, and 5 million word subsets of the data, subsampled based on the quality scores provided by the participants.

Sinhala	1 million				2 million				5 million			
	SMT		NMT		SMT		NMT		SMT		NMT	
System	test	devt	test	devt	test	devt	test	devt	test	devt	test	devt
AFRL 50k	3.8	4.4	3.0	3.5	3.9	4.6	4.2	5.0	4.5	5.2	4.4	4.9
AFRL 150k	4.1	4.7	3.6	4.1	4.2	4.9	4.5	5.2	4.6	5.4	4.4	4.7
DiDi	1.3	1.6	0.2	0.2	1.8	2.2	0.1	0.1	3.1	3.7	0.1	0.1
DiDi lmdiff	1.2	1.3	0.1	0.1	1.8	1.7	0.1	0.1	2.8	3.1	0.1	0.1
DiDi lratio	2.5	2.8	0.2	0.1	3.2	3.5	0.2	0.2	3.7	4.2	0.2	0.3
Facebook main	4.3	5.0	6.4	7.2	4.8	5.2	6.5	7.3	4.9	5.7	4.0	5.0
Facebook contrastive	4.3	4.8	6.2	6.8	4.5	5.2	6.1	6.7	4.7	5.5	3.8	4.1
Helsinki	3.3	3.4	1.1	1.4	3.5	4.1	1.1	1.2	4.2	4.7	0.7	0.8
Helsinki contrastive	2.3	2.4	0.3	0.2	3.2	3.8	0.5	0.4	4.0	4.6	0.6	0.7
IITP	3.1	3.6	3.2	3.7	4.0	4.6	5.3	6.5	4.4	5.1	3.9	4.5
IITP geom	3.0	3.5	3.0	3.4	4.0	4.6	5.4	6.2	4.4	5.2	4.3	5.1
NRC ensemble	4.2	4.7	4.1	4.6	4.3	4.8	2.8	3.2	4.5	5.1	1.4	1.5
NRC xlm	3.8	4.0	1.6	2.0	4.1	4.5	1.5	1.8	4.4	5.0	0.9	1.2
NRC yisi-2-sup	3.9	4.7	5.0	5.9	4.2	5.4	4.6	5.2	4.4	5.2	1.6	1.9
NRC yisi-2-unsup	3.1	3.9	2.4	2.9	3.8	4.4	1.8	2.3	4.3	4.9	0.7	0.9
Stockholm	3.8	4.3	2.9	3.2	4.1	4.6	2.2	2.4	4.0	4.8	0.5	0.5
Stockholm ngram	3.3	4.0	2.2	2.5	3.5	4.1	1.7	1.8	3.6	4.3	0.4	0.4
Sciling	2.4	2.5	2.5	2.6	3.0	3.0	3.5	3.7	3.8	4.1	3.4	3.8
TALP-UPC primary	0.9	0.9	0.0	0.0	1.4	1.5	0.1	0.1	2.7	3.0	0.1	0.1
TALP-UPC sec.	0.3	0.2	0.1	0.0	0.2	0.2	0.0	0.0	0.8	0.7	0.2	0.2
Webinterpret primary	3.7	4.2	2.1	2.3	3.8	4.6	2.0	2.6	4.1	4.8	1.7	1.9
Webinterpret cov	2.6	3.0	0.1	0.1	3.6	4.0	0.2	0.2	4.0	4.5	1.2	1.4
Webinterpret prob	3.9	4.6	2.9	3.5	4.2	5.0	4.1	4.7	4.1	4.7	1.4	1.6

Table 10: Results for Sinhala: BLEU scores are reported for systems trained on 1, 2, and 5 million word subsets of the data, subsampled based on the quality scores provided by the participants.

scores than the smaller and cleaner 1 million subsets, for almost all submissions. However, for neural machine translation the opposite is true.

This is a pretty striking piece of evidence that the adage of *more data is better data* of the statistical world of yesteryears is no longer true in todays neural age. The best submission's NMT score drops from 6.9 to 2.5 BLEU for Nepali and from 6.4 to 4.0 BLEU for Sinhala between the 1 million and the 5 million conditions. More data may be quite harmful, if it is of lesser quality. Alternatively, more research is needed into making neural machine translation models robust to noise in training.

6.2 Additional Subset Sizes

Since we were interested in the shape of the curve of how different corpus sizes impact machine translation performance, we selected additional subset sizes. Specifically, in addition to the 1, 2 and 5 million word corpora, we also selected subset 0.5, 0.7, 1.5, and 3 million words.

See Figure 2 for results for neural machine translation systems (also broken down by each individual test set) and Figure 3 for statistical machine translation systems. We only computed results for 7 systems due to the computational cost involved.

The additional data points refine the observation for the three original subset sizes. For neural machine translation, submissions have different optimal subset sizes, ranging from 0.7 million to 3 million words.

For Nepali, most of the submissions show peak translation quality with 1 million words, although Stockholm's submission peaks at 700,000, Sciling's and AFRL's submission at 3 million. For most submission translation quality deteriorates several BLEU points off their peak.

For Sinhala, the picture is similar. Most of the submission show peaks at 2 million words, indicating that there is more useful data for this data condition. Peaks range from 1 million for Stockholm's submission to 3 million for Sciling's submission. The curves are somewhat shallower than for Nepali.

The curves for statistical machine translation look very different. All submissions tend to improve with additional data, outperforming neural machine translation at 5 million, and showing no sign of stopping there. This demonstrates that sta-

Nepali Submission	1 million		5 million	
	Sent.	W/S	Sent.	W/S
AFRL 50k	51932	19.3	241513	20.7
AFRL 150k	50422	19.8	236966	21.1
Facebook main	36331	27.5	115673	43.2
Facebook contr.	36397	27.5	115771	43.2
Helsinki	48020	20.8	253834	19.7
Helsinki contr.	50801	19.7	251983	19.8
IITP	56868	17.6	200725	24.9
IITP geom	53821	18.6	185978	26.9
NRC ensemble	31675	31.6	154622	32.3
NRC xlm	28348	35.3	191203	26.2
NRC yisi-2-sup	42922	23.3	161022	31.1
NRC yisi-2-unsup	40951	24.4	148072	33.8
Sciling	85253	11.7	314196	15.9
Stockholm	46529	21.5	272605	18.3
Stockholm ngram	141732	7.1	419335	11.9
SUNY Buffalo	93063	10.7	300627	16.6
TALP-UPC	75423	13.3	246875	20.3
TALP-UPC sec.	84978	11.8	375387	13.3
Webinterpret	34873	28.7	400441	12.5
Webinterpret cov	29575	33.8	400441	12.5
Webinterpret prob	52271	19.1	400441	12.5

Table 11: Number of sentences and the corresponding average sentence length (counting English words) for Nepali.

tistical machine translation is more robust to noise.

Compared to last year's high resource version of the shared task, the peak data selection sizes are smaller. Best translation quality is achieved with about 2–6% of the full set, compared to 10% or more for German–English. This is likely due to the fact that the raw data is noisier, but may be also attributed to the difficulty of devising good quality metrics with little evidence of good translations.

6.3 Average Sentence Length

Given the quality scores, subsets are selected by including the highest ranked sentence pairs until the total number of English words in these sentences reaches the specified size. So, if a quality scores prefers shorter sentences, more sentences are selected. It is not clear in general, all things being otherwise equal, if shorter or longer sentences are better for training machine translation systems.

What choices did the participants make in their quality scores? Table 11 and Table 12 show the number of sentences and the corresponding average number of words per sentence for the official subsets for all submissions.

The numbers show that the submissions have quite different preferences with regard to sentence length. Even among the best submissions for Nepali, to give two examples, the Facebook main submission in the 5 million data condition includes

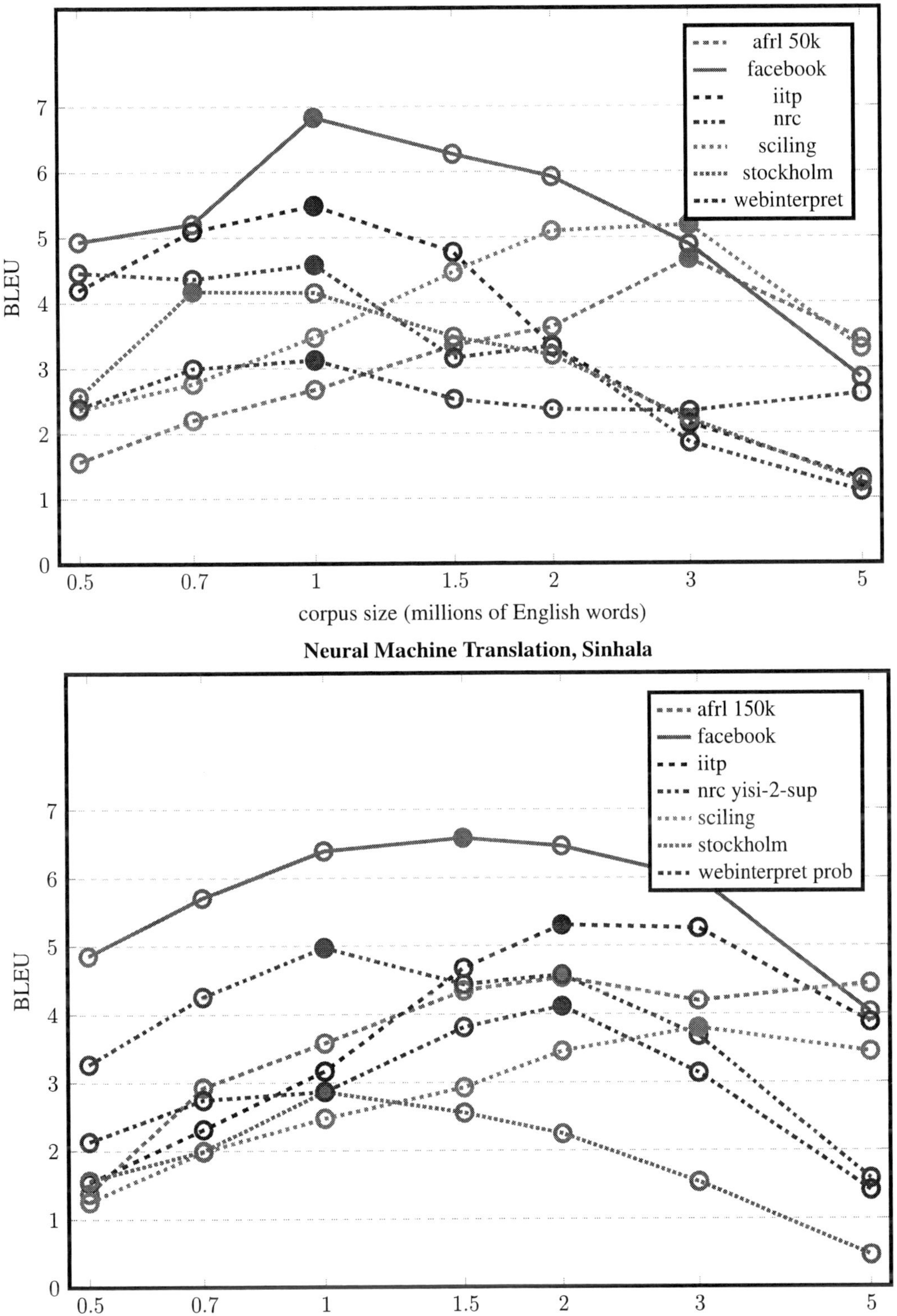

Figure 2: **Additional subsets, neural machine translation.** The charts plot BLEU scores against the size of the subselected corpus (in millions of English words). Different submissions have very different optima, ranging from 1 to 3 million words. The optimal subset size is lower for Nepali (mostly around 1 million) than for Sinhala (mostly around 2 million). Only the 7 best submissions are shown.

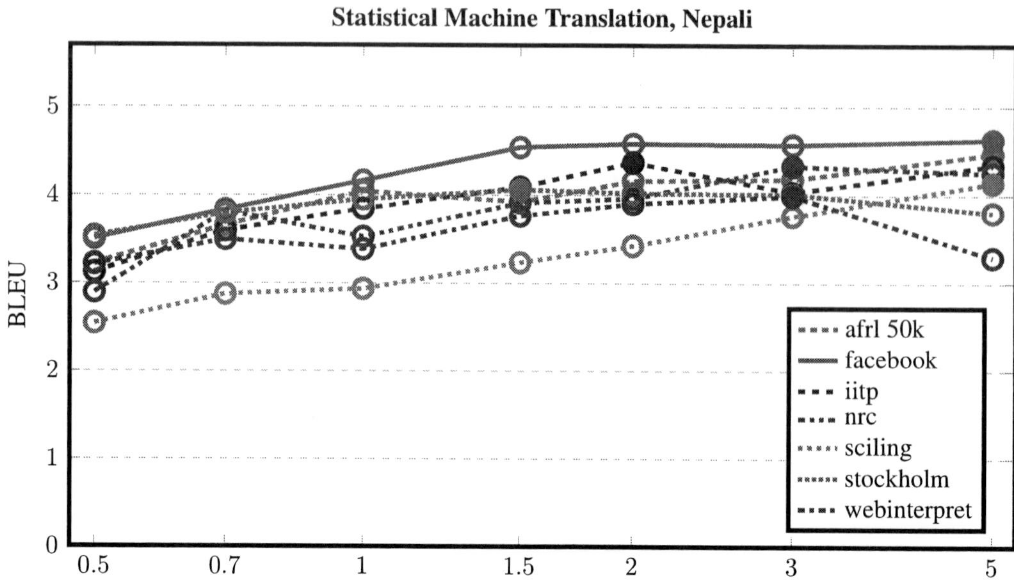

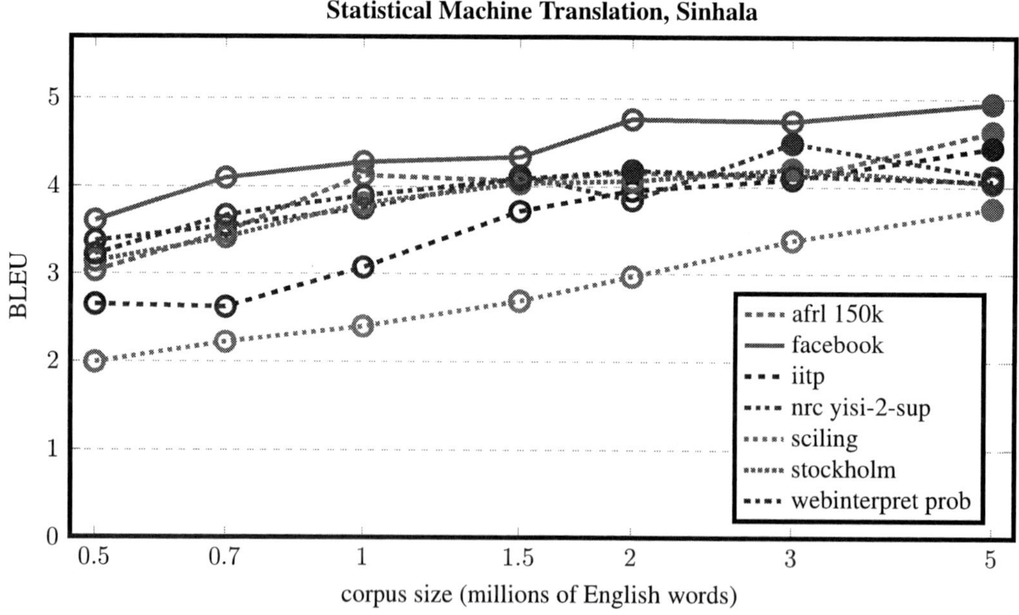

Figure 3: **Additional subsets, statistical machine translation.** The charts plot BLEU scores against the size of the subselected corpus (in millions of English words). All submissions tend to improve with additional data, outperforming neural machine translation at 5 million. This demonstrates that statistical machine translation is more robust to noise.

Sinhala Submission	1 million		5 million	
	Sent.	W/S	Sent.	W/S
AFRL 50k	61,605	16.2	292,912	17.1
AFRL 150k	59,593	16.8	276,633	18.1
DiDi	24,324	41.1	134,769	37.1
DiDi lratio	26,191	38.2	143,744	34.8
DiDi lmdiff	25,974	38.5	170,848	29.3
Facebook main	55,829	17.9	159,924	31.3
Facebook contr.	43,895	22.8	159,723	31.3
Helsinki	87,547	11.4	341,489	14.6
Helsinki contr.	78,579	12.7	345,108	14.5
IITP	70,114	14.3	264,271	18.9
IITP geom	67,888	14.7	249,275	20.1
NRC ensemble	30,533	32.8	172,643	29.0
NRC xlm	24,961	40.1	195,332	25.6
NRC yisi-2-sup	55,757	17.9	192,017	26.0
NRC yisi-2-unsup	60,594	16.5	215,421	23.2
Sciling	120,399	8.3	332,120	15.1
Stockholm	55,293	18.1	250,767	19.9
Stockholm ngram	46,529	21.5	444,106	11.3
TALP-UPC	89,785	11.1	2896,74	17.3
TALP-UPC sec.	114,990	8.7	437,636	11.4
Webinterpret	35,684	28.0	328,620	15.2
Webinterpret cov	29,678	33.7	318,360	15.7
Webinterpret prob	64,115	15.6	345,536	14.5

Table 12: Number of sentences and the corresponding average sentence length (counting English words) for Sinhala.

sentences with an average number of 43.2 words per sentence, while AFRL's 50k submission averages at just 20.7.

For other data conditions, differences are not that extreme but do spread out mainly in the range of under 20 to over 30 words per sentence. There is no clear pattern in the preference for shorter and longer sentence lengths for the 1 million and 5 million word subset — for most submissions these two numbers are quite similar. There are outliers, however, such as Facebook's Nepali submission (average length 27.5 vs. 43.2) and Webinterpret's Nepali submission (28.7 vs. 12.5).

6.4 Diversity of Submissions

The different submissions subselect different sentences, but how different are they?

Table 13–16 give detailed statistics about how many sentence pairs the subsets of any two submissions for the two languages and two data conditions have in common.

There is no clear trend. For Nepali, there is more overlap in the 1 million word data condition than the 5 million word data condition. For Sinhala, the opposite is the case. Among the best-performing submissions, roughly half of the subselected sentence pairs are the same. But what submissions are similar may change drastically

between the data conditions.

7 Conclusion

We report on the findings of the WMT 2019 Shared Task on Parallel Corpus Filtering. Eleven participants used a variety of methods that gave quite different results, as measured by translation quality, optimal subset sizes, suitability for SMT and NMT, sentence length, etc. We hope that this task provides a benchmark for future research and improvements on this task.

References

Alexandra Antonova and Alexey Misyurev. 2011. Building a web-based parallel corpus and filtering out machine-translated text. In *Proceedings of the 4th Workshop on Building and Using Comparable Corpora: Comparable Corpora and the Web*, pages 136–144, Portland, Oregon. Association for Computational Linguistics.

Mikel Artetxe and Holger Schwenk. 2018. Margin-based Parallel Corpus Mining with Multilingual Sentence Embeddings. *arXiv preprint arXiv:1912.10464*.

Tom Ash, Remi Francis, and Will Williams. 2018. The speechmatics parallel corpus filtering system for wmt18. In *Proceedings of the Third Conference on Machine Translation, Volume 2: Shared Task Papers*, pages 866–872, Belgium, Brussels. Association for Computational Linguistics.

Amittai Axelrod. 2019. Dual monolingual cross-entropy delta filtering of noisy parallel data. In *Proceedings of the Fourth Conference on Machine Translation (WMT)*.

Amittai Axelrod, Xiaodong He, and Jianfeng Gao. 2011. Domain adaptation via pseudo in-domain data selection. In *Proceedings of the 2011 Conference on Empirical Methods in Natural Language Processing*, pages 355–362, Edinburgh, Scotland, UK. Association for Computational Linguistics.

D. Bahdanau, K. Cho, and Y. Bengio. 2015. Neural machine translation by jointly learning to align and translate. In *International Conference on Learning Representations (ICLR)*.

Yonatan Belinkov and Yonatan Bisk. 2017. Synthetic and natural noise both break neural machine translation. *CoRR*, abs/1711.02173.

Gabriel Bernier-Colborne and Chi-kiu Lo. 2019. Nrc parallel corpus filtering system for wmt 2019. In *Proceedings of the Fourth Conference on Machine Translation (WMT)*.

Submission	Total	Unique	AFRL 50k	AFRL 150k	Facebook main	Facebook contr.	Helsinki	Helsinki contr.	IITP	IITP geom	NRC ensemble	NRC xlm	NRC yisi-2-sup	NRC yisi-2-unsup	Sciling	Stockholm	Stockholm ngram	SUNY Buffalo	TALP-UPC	TALP-UPC sec.	Webinterpret	Webinterpret cov	Webinterpret prob
AFRL 50k	51932	2.4%		92.0%	34.0%	34.0%	12.6%	2.5%	36.8%	36.5%	27.5%	23.0%	34.8%	34.4%	36.2%	26.5%	19.0%	4.7%	3.2%	0.5%	20.1%	6.1%	27.8%
AFRL 150k	50422	2.8%	94.8%		34.3%	34.3%	12.4%	2.3%	36.6%	36.3%	27.9%	23.6%	34.9%	34.6%	35.4%	26.2%	18.3%	4.6%	3.0%	0.5%	20.3%	6.3%	27.6%
Facebook main	36331	0.0%	48.6%	47.6%		99.9%	21.5%	3.9%	63.8%	63.6%	59.2%	52.3%	64.7%	62.5%	29.5%	56.0%	31.5%	3.6%	2.9%	0.3%	45.0%	14.8%	53.4%
Facebook contr.	36397	0.0%	48.5%	47.5%	99.7%		21.5%	3.9%	63.8%	63.5%	59.1%	52.2%	64.6%	62.4%	29.5%	55.9%	31.6%	3.6%	2.9%	0.3%	44.9%	14.8%	53.4%
Helsinki	48020	15.0%	13.7%	13.0%	16.3%	16.3%		27.2%	17.6%	17.0%	16.6%	14.5%	13.9%	12.5%	11.3%	23.8%	26.7%	26.5%	19.5%	0.7%	17.5%	13.4%	19.8%
Helsinki contr.	50801	40.4%	2.6%	2.3%	2.8%	2.8%	25.7%		3.2%	2.9%	1.6%	1.7%	1.5%	1.5%	2.3%	9.1%	10.0%	13.6%	30.8%	0.6%	2.7%	4.5%	3.2%
IITP	56868	2.5%	33.6%	32.5%	40.8%	40.8%	14.9%	2.9%		93.7%	35.8%	30.3%	45.6%	44.8%	27.2%	35.1%	22.7%	4.5%	3.5%	0.4%	32.4%	10.7%	53.2%
IITP geom	53821	0.2%	35.2%	34.0%	42.9%	43.0%	15.2%	2.7%	99.0%		37.5%	31.9%	47.9%	46.8%	27.8%	36.4%	23.1%	4.3%	3.2%	0.4%	33.9%	11.0%	54.7%
NRC ensemble	31675	3.7%	45.1%	44.5%	67.9%	67.9%	25.1%	2.6%	64.2%	63.8%		73.8%	74.8%	71.2%	21.2%	56.7%	29.8%	7.5%	1.3%	0.1%	54.4%	22.0%	58.9%
NRC xlm	28348	7.0%	42.1%	41.9%	67.0%	67.0%	24.5%	3.1%	60.9%	60.6%	82.4%		69.3%	67.8%	15.9%	55.7%	27.8%	8.0%	0.7%	0.0%	56.0%	25.5%	55.8%
NRC yisi-2-sup	42922	9.1%	42.1%	41.0%	54.8%	54.8%	15.5%	1.8%	60.5%	60.1%	55.2%	45.8%		73.6%	24.2%	42.9%	26.8%	3.2%	2.9%	0.1%	39.1%	13.0%	49.2%
NRC yisi-2-unsup	40951	7.2%	43.6%	42.7%	55.4%	55.5%	14.7%	1.8%	62.2%	61.5%	55.0%	47.0%	77.1%		24.2%	41.5%	22.9%	2.8%	2.7%	0.1%	39.6%	13.6%	49.5%
Sciling	85253	52.4%	22.1%	20.9%	12.6%	12.6%	6.4%	1.4%	18.1%	17.5%	7.9%	5.3%	12.2%	11.6%		11.0%	15.2%	4.3%	3.9%	1.1%	5.4%	1.1%	12.7%
Stockholm	46529	16.4%	29.6%	28.4%	43.7%	43.7%	24.6%	9.9%	42.9%	42.1%	38.6%	34.0%	39.6%	36.5%	20.1%		38.2%	10.0%	6.9%	0.2%	32.7%	13.1%	38.8%
Stockholm ngram	141732	55.5%	7.0%	6.5%	8.1%	8.1%	9.1%	3.6%	9.1%	8.8%	6.7%	5.6%	8.1%	6.6%	9.2%	12.6%		19.2%	6.7%	1.1%	5.2%	1.2%	8.7%
SUNY Buffalo	93063	44.9%	2.6%	2.5%	1.4%	1.4%	13.7%	7.4%	2.8%	2.5%	2.6%	2.4%	1.5%	1.2%	3.9%	5.0%	29.3%		9.0%	2.1%	4.9%	7.2%	5.0%
TALP-UPC	75423	52.9%	2.2%	2.0%	1.4%	1.4%	12.4%	20.8%	2.6%	2.3%	0.6%	0.2%	1.6%	1.5%	4.4%	4.2%	12.6%	11.1%		1.9%	0.4%	0.5%	2.0%
TALP-UPC sec.	84978	93.9%	0.3%	0.3%	0.1%	0.1%	0.4%	0.4%	0.3%	0.3%	0.0%	0.0%	0.1%	0.1%	1.1%	0.1%	1.8%	2.3%	1.7%		0.0%	0.0%	0.1%
Webinterpret	34873	0.0%	29.9%	29.3%	46.8%	46.8%	24.1%	4.0%	52.9%	52.3%	49.5%	45.5%	48.2%	46.4%	13.2%	43.6%	21.2%	13.2%	0.9%	0.0%		54.0%	82.0%
Webinterpret cov	29575	18.0%	10.8%	10.8%	18.2%	18.2%	21.7%	7.7%	20.5%	20.1%	23.6%	24.5%	18.8%	18.8%	3.2%	20.6%	5.5%	22.5%	1.3%	0.0%	63.7%		42.6%
Webinterpret prob	52271	11.1%	27.6%	26.6%	37.1%	37.2%	18.2%	3.1%	57.9%	56.3%	35.7%	30.2%	40.4%	38.8%	20.7%	34.5%	23.6%	9.0%	3.0%	0.2%	54.7%	24.1%	

Table 13: **Overlap for Nepali, 1 million word data condition.** For each submission, a row in the table lists the total number of sentence pairs, the ratio of unique sentence pairs that are in included in no other submission, and the ratio of sentence pairs shared with each of the other submissions.

Submissions from different participants share up to 67.9% of sentence pairs (NRC ensemble and Facebook main).

Submission	Total	Unique	AFRL 50k	AFRL 150k	Facebook main	Facebook contr.	Helsinki	Helsinki contr.	IITP	IITP geom	NRC ensemble	NRC xlm	NRC yisi-2-sup	NRC yisi-2-unsup	Sciling	Stockholm	Stockholm ngram	SUNY Buffalo	TALP-UPC	TALP-UPC sec.	Webinterpret	Webinterpret cov	Webinterpret prob
AFRL 50k	241513	1.7%	-	86.4%	32.6%	32.6%	34.5%	30.4%	39.4%	38.8%	30.6%	30.9%	31.0%	31.9%	61.5%	25.7%	26.0%	29.6%	26.7%	12.8%	38.9%	38.9%	38.9%
AFRL 150k	236966	1.9%	88.0%	-	31.1%	31.2%	36.1%	32.4%	38.8%	37.7%	30.8%	31.2%	31.4%	32.4%	60.8%	25.2%	25.9%	29.5%	25.7%	11.7%	38.5%	38.5%	38.5%
Facebook main	115673	0.0%	68.0%	63.8%	-	99.9%	42.5%	34.4%	44.6%	44.8%	43.9%	43.8%	40.0%	44.1%	54.3%	32.5%	28.9%	34.5%	30.0%	9.0%	40.5%	40.5%	40.5%
Facebook contr.	115771	0.0%	68.0%	63.8%	99.9%	-	42.5%	34.4%	44.6%	44.8%	43.9%	43.8%	40.0%	44.1%	54.3%	32.5%	28.9%	34.5%	30.0%	9.0%	40.5%	40.5%	40.5%
Helsinki	253834	0.1%	32.8%	33.7%	19.4%	19.4%	-	86.6%	34.5%	32.5%	32.4%	39.1%	28.5%	26.9%	36.7%	52.2%	64.4%	50.6%	50.0%	27.6%	36.5%	36.5%	36.5%
Helsinki contr.	251983	0.5%	29.2%	30.5%	15.8%	15.8%	87.3%	-	32.1%	30.1%	28.5%	35.1%	26.3%	24.4%	33.3%	50.6%	62.7%	45.8%	51.0%	27.8%	31.0%	31.0%	31.0%
IITP	200725	0.6%	47.4%	45.8%	25.7%	25.7%	43.6%	40.4%	-	89.5%	44.9%	45.7%	44.2%	42.6%	41.5%	45.9%	41.0%	46.6%	35.1%	10.6%	52.1%	52.1%	52.1%
IITP geom	185978	0.1%	50.4%	48.1%	27.9%	27.9%	44.4%	40.8%	96.6%	-	47.0%	47.4%	46.9%	45.5%	42.4%	45.1%	39.3%	45.0%	33.9%	9.5%	51.8%	51.8%	51.8%
NRC ensemble	154622	0.3%	47.8%	47.3%	32.9%	32.9%	53.2%	46.4%	58.3%	56.6%	-	85.1%	64.9%	62.8%	40.7%	47.6%	43.2%	55.6%	37.5%	8.5%	44.9%	44.9%	44.9%
NRC xlm	191203	1.6%	39.1%	38.7%	26.5%	26.5%	51.9%	46.2%	48.0%	46.1%	68.8%	-	48.5%	47.7%	36.4%	46.1%	53.0%	51.2%	36.4%	12.1%	42.2%	42.2%	42.2%
NRC yisi-2-sup	161022	4.6%	46.5%	46.1%	28.7%	28.8%	44.9%	41.1%	55.1%	54.2%	62.4%	57.6%	-	69.4%	37.4%	38.9%	36.0%	40.2%	30.0%	5.9%	36.8%	36.8%	36.8%
NRC yisi-2-unsup	148072	2.7%	52.0%	51.9%	34.5%	34.5%	46.0%	41.6%	57.7%	57.1%	65.5%	61.6%	75.5%	-	40.0%	36.3%	30.4%	43.1%	30.1%	5.6%	38.7%	38.7%	38.7%
Sciling	314196	21.1%	47.2%	45.9%	20.0%	20.0%	29.6%	26.7%	26.5%	25.1%	20.0%	22.1%	19.2%	18.9%	-	28.2%	30.8%	25.3%	25.5%	15.3%	34.2%	34.2%	34.2%
Stockholm	272605	1.0%	22.8%	21.9%	13.8%	13.8%	48.6%	46.7%	33.8%	30.8%	27.0%	32.4%	23.0%	19.7%	32.5%	-	87.1%	49.5%	43.3%	23.4%	35.4%	35.4%	35.4%
Stockholm ngram	419335	17.3%	15.0%	14.6%	8.0%	8.0%	39.0%	37.7%	19.6%	17.4%	15.9%	24.2%	13.8%	10.7%	23.0%	56.6%	-	41.0%	29.3%	19.4%	26.0%	26.0%	26.0%
SUNY Buffalo	300627	11.9%	23.8%	23.3%	13.3%	13.3%	42.7%	38.4%	31.1%	27.9%	28.6%	32.6%	21.5%	21.2%	26.5%	44.8%	57.2%	-	31.3%	19.9%	36.2%	36.2%	36.2%
TALP-UPC	246875	3.7%	26.1%	24.7%	14.1%	14.1%	51.4%	52.1%	28.5%	25.5%	23.5%	28.2%	19.5%	18.1%	32.5%	47.8%	49.8%	38.1%	-	39.8%	30.6%	30.6%	30.6%
TALP-UPC sec.	375387	53.2%	8.2%	7.4%	2.8%	2.8%	18.7%	18.6%	5.7%	4.7%	3.5%	6.2%	2.5%	2.2%	12.8%	17.0%	21.7%	15.9%	26.2%	-	14.8%	14.8%	14.8%
Webinterpret	400441	0.0%	23.4%	22.8%	11.7%	11.7%	23.1%	19.5%	26.1%	24.1%	17.3%	20.2%	14.8%	14.3%	26.8%	24.1%	27.2%	27.2%	18.9%	13.9%	-	100.0%	100.0%
Webinterpret cov	400441	0.0%	23.4%	22.8%	11.7%	11.7%	23.1%	19.5%	26.1%	24.1%	17.3%	20.2%	14.8%	14.3%	26.8%	24.1%	27.2%	27.2%	18.9%	13.9%	100.0%	-	100.0%
Webinterpret prob	400441	0.0%	23.4%	22.8%	11.7%	11.7%	23.1%	19.5%	26.1%	24.1%	17.3%	20.2%	14.8%	14.3%	26.8%	24.1%	27.2%	27.2%	18.9%	13.9%	100.0%	100.0%	-

Table 14: **Overlap for Nepali, 5 million word data condition.** For each submission, a row in the table lists the total number of sentence pairs, the ratio of unique sentence pairs that are in included in no other submission, and the ratio of sentence pairs shared with each of the other submissions.

There is much less overlap for this data condition, compared to the 1 million word subset. The NRC/Facebook overlap dropped to 32.9% (from 67.9%), NRC's submissions now have more in common with other submissions.

Submission	Total	Unique	AFRL 50k	AFRL 150k	DiDi	DiDi lratio	DiDi lmdiff	Facebook main	Facebook contr.	Helsinki	Helsinki contr.	IITP	IITP geom	NRC ensemble	NRC xlm	NRC yisi-2-sup	NRC yisi-2-unsup	Sciling	Stockholm	Stockholm ngram	TALP-UPC	TALP-UPC sec.	Webinterpret	Webinterpret cov	Webinterpret prob
AFRL 50k	61605	7.6%	-	81.3%	3.2%	6.0%	2.3%	36.2%	31.7%	16.0%	5.1%	51.0%	49.6%	15.6%	10.6%	30.8%	24.5%	45.2%	16.6%	15.5%	4.8%	1.4%	11.1%	4.2%	29.8%
AFRL 150k	59593	2.3%	84.0%	-	3.7%	7.1%	2.8%	40.7%	34.6%	18.0%	6.1%	50.4%	48.8%	18.1%	12.6%	34.2%	27.1%	44.5%	19.2%	18.1%	5.3%	1.4%	12.7%	4.9%	32.9%
DiDi	24324	35.4%	8.2%	9.1%	-	36.2%	26.5%	5.1%	4.1%	10.2%	9.5%	1.2%	1.1%	10.4%	10.8%	3.7%	1.4%	2.5%	7.0%	7.2%	3.5%	0.2%	7.9%	11.6%	4.3%
DiDi lratio	26191	15.9%	14.1%	16.1%	33.6%	-	18.3%	16.9%	14.2%	25.5%	12.6%	6.3%	6.0%	22.8%	21.6%	11.8%	5.5%	6.5%	19.4%	19.7%	4.5%	0.4%	21.5%	23.7%	14.6%
DiDi lmdiff	25974	43.5%	5.6%	6.5%	24.8%	18.4%	-	4.6%	3.3%	9.7%	8.9%	0.9%	0.8%	10.3%	9.3%	4.1%	2.1%	2.4%	6.9%	7.4%	3.2%	0.2%	8.5%	10.7%	5.2%
Facebook main	55829	2.1%	40.0%	43.5%	2.2%	7.9%	2.2%	-	59.5%	30.8%	11.9%	40.7%	39.3%	29.0%	18.7%	47.7%	34.3%	40.3%	37.0%	29.9%	7.3%	1.3%	22.1%	7.0%	48.4%
Facebook contr.	43895	4.4%	44.5%	47.0%	2.3%	8.5%	2.0%	75.7%	-	25.5%	9.0%	45.3%	44.0%	31.7%	22.1%	50.5%	37.9%	38.2%	32.4%	26.5%	6.3%	1.2%	24.2%	9.1%	42.4%
Helsinki	87547	22.5%	11.3%	12.3%	2.8%	7.6%	2.9%	19.7%	12.8%	-	37.7%	8.6%	8.0%	11.2%	7.0%	12.4%	8.2%	21.3%	21.9%	19.0%	20.7%	2.4%	8.9%	4.8%	16.7%
Helsinki contr.	78579	36.9%	4.0%	4.7%	3.0%	4.2%	3.0%	8.5%	5.0%	42.0%	-	2.9%	2.7%	5.5%	3.6%	5.3%	3.0%	10.0%	13.6%	12.3%	21.9%	2.2%	4.7%	2.3%	7.7%
IITP	70114	1.1%	44.8%	42.8%	0.4%	2.3%	0.3%	32.4%	28.4%	10.7%	3.3%	-	94.6%	11.1%	7.2%	29.6%	25.0%	45.6%	13.4%	10.9%	3.3%	0.9%	9.8%	3.1%	34.1%
IITP geom	67888	0.6%	45.0%	42.8%	0.4%	2.3%	0.3%	32.3%	28.5%	10.4%	3.2%	97.7%	-	11.1%	7.2%	29.1%	24.4%	45.4%	13.1%	10.6%	3.2%	0.9%	9.9%	3.1%	34.5%
NRC ensemble	30533	3.4%	31.5%	35.3%	8.3%	19.5%	8.8%	53.1%	45.5%	32.1%	14.0%	25.6%	24.7%	-	58.2%	52.5%	30.8%	17.0%	39.1%	35.7%	1.5%	0.1%	38.8%	19.6%	42.0%
NRC xlm	24961	10.0%	26.1%	30.2%	10.5%	22.6%	9.7%	41.9%	38.8%	24.4%	11.4%	20.1%	19.6%	71.2%	-	39.6%	22.9%	8.4%	32.2%	29.8%	0.5%	0.0%	38.2%	24.9%	32.7%
NRC yisi-2-sup	55757	8.1%	34.0%	36.6%	1.6%	5.5%	1.9%	47.7%	39.8%	19.5%	7.5%	37.3%	35.5%	28.7%	17.7%	-	61.7%	34.0%	24.3%	21.0%	6.2%	0.7%	19.0%	7.2%	34.2%
NRC yisi-2-unsup	60594	21.3%	24.9%	26.6%	0.6%	2.4%	0.9%	31.6%	27.5%	11.9%	3.9%	29.0%	27.4%	15.9%	9.4%	56.7%	-	32.1%	13.3%	11.5%	7.1%	1.0%	12.5%	5.4%	24.8%
Sciling	120399	37.0%	23.1%	22.0%	0.5%	1.4%	0.5%	18.7%	13.9%	15.5%	6.5%	26.5%	25.6%	4.3%	1.7%	15.7%	16.2%	-	12.4%	8.6%	8.1%	1.8%	2.9%	0.5%	16.4%
Stockholm	55293	15.6%	18.4%	20.7%	3.1%	9.2%	3.2%	37.4%	25.7%	34.7%	19.3%	16.9%	16.0%	21.6%	14.5%	24.6%	14.6%	26.9%	-	43.8%	12.3%	1.2%	17.1%	7.2%	29.8%
Stockholm ngram	46529	12.5%	20.5%	23.2%	3.8%	11.1%	4.2%	35.9%	25.0%	35.7%	20.8%	16.5%	15.5%	23.5%	16.0%	25.1%	14.9%	22.3%	52.0%	-	12.7%	1.8%	17.3%	8.6%	27.3%
TALP-UPC	89785	50.0%	3.3%	3.5%	0.9%	1.3%	0.9%	4.5%	3.1%	20.2%	19.2%	2.6%	2.4%	0.5%	0.1%	3.9%	4.8%	10.8%	7.6%	6.6%	-	9.1%	0.4%	0.6%	2.9%
TALP-UPC sec.	114990	90.6%	0.8%	0.7%	0.0%	0.1%	0.0%	0.6%	0.5%	1.8%	1.5%	0.5%	0.5%	0.0%	0.0%	0.3%	0.5%	1.9%	0.6%	0.7%	7.1%	-	0.0%	0.0%	0.3%
Webinterpret	35684	5.1%	19.1%	21.1%	5.4%	15.8%	6.2%	34.6%	29.7%	21.8%	10.4%	19.3%	18.7%	33.2%	26.7%	29.6%	21.3%	9.9%	26.5%	22.6%	1.1%	0.1%	-	44.1%	64.1%
Webinterpret cov	29678	24.7%	8.8%	9.9%	9.5%	21.0%	9.4%	13.1%	13.5%	14.1%	6.0%	7.4%	7.1%	20.1%	20.9%	13.4%	11.0%	2.1%	13.4%	13.5%	1.8%	0.1%	53.1%	-	22.8%
Webinterpret prob	64115	11.8%	28.7%	30.6%	1.6%	6.0%	2.1%	42.2%	29.1%	22.8%	9.4%	37.2%	36.6%	20.0%	12.7%	29.7%	23.4%	30.8%	25.7%	19.8%	4.0%	0.6%	35.7%	10.6%	-

Table 15: **Overlap for Sinhala, 1 million word data condition.** For each submission, a row in the table lists the total number of sentence pairs, the ratio of unique sentence pairs that are in included in no other submission, and the ratio of sentence pairs shared with each of the other submissions.

There is less overlap between submissions, compared to Nepali. The submissions share almost always below half of the sentence pairs.

Submission	Total	Unique	AFRL 50k	AFRL 150k	DiDi	DiDi lratio	DiDi lmdiff	Facebook main	Facebook contr.	Helsinki	Helsinki contr.	IITP	IITP geom	NRC ensemble	NRC xlm	NRC yisi-2-sup	NRC yisi-2-unsup	Sciling	Stockholm	Stockholm ngram	TALP-UPC	TALP-UPC sec.	Webinterpret	Webinterpret cov	Webinterpret prob
AFRL 50k	292912	0.8%	-	90.9%	8.4%	12.1%	10.8%	38.0%	41.1%	33.0%	33.0%	58.7%	55.6%	28.1%	26.5%	35.1%	35.1%	58.5%	24.0%	26.5%	20.7%	13.2%	44.3%	37.4%	44.9%
AFRL 150k	276633	0.2%	96.2%	-	10.6%	14.1%	11.7%	39.1%	42.0%	33.2%	33.2%	59.4%	56.5%	29.5%	27.6%	35.6%	34.6%	58.6%	24.0%	25.7%	20.0%	12.6%	43.8%	36.7%	44.5%
DiDi	134769	4.1%	18.3%	21.7%	-	77.5%	47.0%	21.4%	16.3%	38.2%	35.9%	24.1%	22.6%	39.7%	38.4%	30.2%	21.8%	21.5%	38.3%	32.9%	27.0%	8.9%	25.8%	26.6%	25.4%
DiDi lratio	143744	0.3%	24.7%	27.2%	72.7%	-	44.1%	27.7%	22.6%	45.7%	41.0%	32.3%	30.4%	47.1%	46.0%	34.6%	26.6%	31.2%	50.0%	42.0%	31.3%	11.4%	42.7%	44.1%	42.2%
DiDi lmdiff	170848	9.4%	18.6%	18.9%	37.1%	37.1%	-	18.6%	13.3%	34.4%	32.6%	23.6%	31.8%	32.1%	29.2%	25.0%	26.1%	34.7%	35.8%	28.3%	10.5%	31.2%	31.9%	31.2%
Facebook main	159924	4.8%	69.5%	67.7%	18.0%	24.9%	19.9%	-	69.5%	45.6%	41.2%	60.0%	57.8%	49.8%	47.0%	51.5%	44.7%	52.0%	35.5%	35.2%	24.0%	10.1%	49.5%	41.4%	50.2%
Facebook contrastive	159723	2.4%	75.4%	72.8%	13.8%	20.3%	16.4%	69.6%	-	39.9%	37.8%	60.7%	58.3%	40.8%	38.3%	46.5%	45.1%	56.0%	30.4%	29.5%	23.9%	11.5%	50.7%	44.5%	50.7%
Helsinki	341489	0.1%	28.3%	26.9%	15.1%	19.2%	17.2%	21.4%	18.7%	-	91.3%	28.3%	26.5%	26.6%	30.7%	23.6%	20.9%	31.7%	36.7%	63.0%	42.7%	26.2%	37.8%	36.2%	40.9%
Helsinki contr.	345108	1.1%	28.0%	26.6%	14.0%	17.1%	16.2%	19.1%	17.5%	90.3%	-	27.5%	25.8%	23.6%	27.5%	21.5%	19.1%	30.2%	33.9%	60.6%	41.8%	25.9%	34.2%	32.7%	37.2%
IITP	264271	0.2%	65.0%	62.2%	12.3%	17.6%	16.4%	36.3%	36.7%	36.6%	35.9%	-	92.6%	35.5%	34.9%	41.3%	40.4%	56.2%	31.5%	31.7%	21.3%	10.0%	57.0%	49.8%	57.9%
IITP geom	249275	0.1%	65.3%	62.7%	12.2%	17.5%	16.2%	37.1%	37.4%	36.3%	35.8%	98.2%	-	35.6%	35.1%	41.4%	40.1%	56.1%	31.1%	31.2%	20.5%	9.7%	57.3%	49.8%	58.2%
NRC ensemble	172643	0.2%	47.7%	47.3%	31.0%	39.2%	31.5%	46.2%	37.7%	52.7%	47.2%	54.4%	51.5%	-	82.5%	65.4%	51.9%	49.5%	47.6%	41.5%	32.3%	10.2%	57.7%	54.5%	58.3%
NRC xlm	195332	1.1%	39.8%	39.1%	26.5%	33.9%	28.0%	38.5%	31.3%	53.6%	48.7%	47.2%	44.8%	72.9%	-	50.0%	43.4%	44.2%	47.1%	47.8%	34.8%	13.1%	53.2%	50.5%	54.4%
NRC yisi-2-sup	192017	1.9%	53.6%	51.3%	21.2%	25.9%	26.0%	42.9%	38.7%	41.9%	38.6%	56.8%	53.7%	58.8%	50.8%	-	65.4%	47.7%	33.4%	32.0%	27.8%	9.8%	50.6%	47.5%	51.1%
NRC yisi-2-unsup	215421	5.6%	47.7%	44.5%	13.6%	17.7%	19.8%	33.2%	33.5%	33.2%	30.6%	49.6%	46.4%	41.6%	39.3%	58.3%	-	44.4%	26.1%	27.2%	30.2%	12.2%	50.0%	47.5%	50.2%
Sciling	332120	11.7%	51.6%	48.8%	8.7%	13.5%	13.4%	25.0%	26.9%	32.6%	31.4%	44.7%	42.1%	25.7%	26.0%	27.6%	28.8%	-	29.2%	29.9%	25.3%	15.0%	50.6%	46.9%	50.7%
Stockholm	250767	2.7%	28.1%	26.4%	20.6%	28.6%	23.6%	22.6%	19.3%	49.9%	46.6%	33.2%	30.9%	32.8%	36.7%	25.6%	22.4%	38.7%	-	73.4%	41.4%	21.0%	46.1%	45.6%	47.4%
Stockholm ngram	444106	17.5%	17.5%	16.0%	10.0%	13.6%	13.8%	12.7%	10.6%	48.4%	47.1%	18.9%	17.5%	16.1%	21.0%	13.8%	13.2%	22.4%	41.5%	-	29.8%	20.2%	28.9%	27.8%	31.7%
TALP-UPC	289674	3.5%	20.9%	19.1%	12.5%	15.5%	16.7%	13.2%	13.2%	50.4%	49.8%	19.5%	17.7%	19.2%	23.5%	18.4%	22.5%	29.0%	35.8%	45.7%	-	49.6%	39.4%	41.9%	40.8%
TALP-UPC sec.	437636	56.3%	8.8%	8.0%	2.8%	3.7%	4.1%	3.7%	4.2%	20.4%	20.4%	6.0%	5.5%	4.0%	5.8%	4.3%	6.0%	11.4%	12.0%	20.5%	32.8%	-	14.3%	16.2%	15.1%
Webinterpret	328620	0.0%	39.4%	36.9%	10.6%	18.7%	16.2%	24.1%	24.7%	39.3%	35.9%	45.9%	43.5%	30.3%	31.6%	29.5%	32.8%	51.1%	35.2%	39.1%	34.7%	19.0%	-	85.7%	96.0%
Webinterpret cov	318360	1.9%	34.4%	31.9%	11.3%	19.9%	17.1%	20.8%	22.3%	38.8%	35.5%	41.3%	39.0%	29.5%	31.0%	28.7%	32.1%	48.9%	35.9%	38.8%	38.1%	22.3%	88.4%	-	86.5%
Webinterpret prob	345536	1.3%	38.1%	35.6%	9.9%	17.6%	15.4%	23.2%	23.4%	40.4%	37.2%	44.3%	42.0%	29.1%	30.7%	28.4%	31.3%	48.7%	34.4%	40.7%	34.2%	19.1%	91.3%	79.7%	-

Table 16: **Overlap for Sinhala, 5 million word data condition.** For each submission, a row in the table lists the total number of sentence pairs, the ratio of unique sentence pairs that are in included in no other submission, and the ratio of sentence pairs shared with each of the other submissions.

For Nepali, there was less overlap in the 5 million word data condition, compared to the 1 million word data condition. Here, for Sinhala, the trend goes the other way.

Houda Bouamor and Hassan Sajjad. 2018. H2@bucc18: Parallel sentence extraction from comparable corpora using multilingual sentence embeddings. In *Proceedings of the Eleventh International Conference on Language Resources and Evaluation (LREC 2018)*, Paris, France. European Language Resources Association (ELRA).

Christian Buck and Philipp Koehn. 2016. Findings of the wmt 2016 bilingual document alignment shared task. In *Proceedings of the First Conference on Machine Translation*, pages 554–563, Berlin, Germany. Association for Computational Linguistics.

Marine Carpuat, Yogarshi Vyas, and Xing Niu. 2017. Detecting cross-lingual semantic divergence for neural machine translation. In *Proceedings of the First Workshop on Neural Machine Translation*, pages 69–79, Vancouver. Association for Computational Linguistics.

Vishrav Chaudhary, Yuqing Tang, Francisco Guzmán, Holger Schwenk, and Philipp Koehn. 2019. Low-resource corpus filtering using multilingual sentence embeddings. In *Proceedings of the Fourth Conference on Machine Translation (WMT)*.

Lei Cui, Dongdong Zhang, Shujie Liu, Mu Li, and Ming Zhou. 2013. Bilingual data cleaning for SMT using graph-based random walk. In *Proceedings of the 51st Annual Meeting of the Association for Computational Linguistics (Volume 2: Short Papers)*, pages 340–345, Sofia, Bulgaria. Association for Computational Linguistics.

Grant Erdmann and Jeremy Gwinnup. 2019. Quality and coverage: The afrl submission to the wmt19 parallel corpus filtering for low-resource conditions task. In *Proceedings of the Fourth Conference on Machine Translation (WMT)*.

Jonas Gehring, Michael Auli, David Grangier, and Yann N Dauphin. 2016. A convolutional encoder model for neural machine translation. *arXiv preprint arXiv:1611.02344*.

Jesús González-Rubio. 2019. Webinterpret submission to the wmt2019 shared task on parallel corpus filtering. In *Proceedings of the Fourth Conference on Machine Translation (WMT)*.

Mand y Guo, Qinlan Shen, Yinfei Yang, Heming Ge, Daniel Cer, Gustavo Hernand ez Abrego, Keith Stevens, Noah Constant, Yun-hsuan Sung, Brian Strope, and Ray Kurzweil. 2018. Effective parallel corpus mining using bilingual sentence embeddings. In *Proceedings of the Third Conference on Machine Translation: Research Papers*, pages 165–176, Belgium, Brussels. Association for Computational Linguistics.

Francisco Guzmán, Peng-Jen Chen, Myle Ott, Juan Pino, Guillaume Lample, Philipp Koehn, Vishrav Chaudhary, and Marc'Aurelio Ranzato. 2019. Two new evaluation datasets for low-resource machine translation: Nepali-english and sinhala-english. *arXiv preprint arXiv:1902.01382*.

Viktor Hangya and Alexander Fraser. 2018. An unsupervised system for parallel corpus filtering. In *Proceedings of the Third Conference on Machine Translation, Volume 2: Shared Task Papers*, pages 895–900, Belgium, Brussels. Association for Computational Linguistics.

Marcin Junczys-Dowmunt. 2018. Dual conditional cross-entropy filtering of noisy parallel corpora. In *Proceedings of the Third Conference on Machine Translation: Shared Task Papers*, pages 888–895, Belgium, Brussels. Association for Computational Linguistics.

Huda Khayrallah and Philipp Koehn. 2018. On the impact of various types of noise on neural machine translation. In *Proceedings of the 2nd Workshop on Neural Machine Translation and Generation*, pages 74–83. Association for Computational Linguistics.

Philipp Koehn. 2005. Europarl: A parallel corpus for statistical machine translation. In *Proceedings of the Tenth Machine Translation Summit (MT Summit X)*, Phuket, Thailand.

Philipp Koehn, Hieu Hoang, Alexandra Birch, Chris Callison-Burch, Marcello Federico, Nicola Bertoldi, Brooke Cowan, Wade Shen, Christine Moran, Richard Zens, Chris Dyer, Ondřej Bojar, Alexandra Constantin, and Evan Herbst. 2007. Moses: Open source toolkit for statistical machine translation. In *Proceedings of the 45th Annual Meeting of the Association for Computational Linguistics Companion Volume Proceedings of the Demo and Poster Sessions*, pages 177–180, Prague, Czech Republic. Association for Computational Linguistics.

Philipp Koehn, Huda Khayrallah, Kenneth Heafield, and Mikel L. Forcada. 2018. Findings of the wmt 2018 shared task on parallel corpus filtering. In *Proceedings of the Third Conference on Machine Translation: Shared Task Papers*, pages 726–739, Belgium, Brussels. Association for Computational Linguistics.

Philipp Koehn and Rebecca Knowles. 2017. Six challenges for neural machine translation. In *Proceedings of the First Workshop on Neural Machine Translation*, pages 28–39, Vancouver. Association for Computational Linguistics.

Gaurav Kumar, George Foster, Colin Cherry, and Maxim Krikun. 2019. Reinforcement learning based curriculum optimization for neural machine translation. In *Proceedings of the 2019 Conference of the North American Chapter of the Association for Computational Linguistics: Human Language Technologies, Volume 1 (Long and Short Papers)*, pages 2054–2061, Minneapolis, Minnesota. Association for Computational Linguistics.

Anoop Kunchukuttan, Pratik Mehta, and Pushpak Bhattacharyya. 2018. The IIT Bombay English-Hindi Parallel Corpus.

Murathan Kurfalı and Robert Östling. 2019. Noisy parallel corpus filtering through projected word embeddings. In *Proceedings of the Fourth Conference on Machine Translation (WMT)*.

Patrick Littell, Samuel Larkin, Darlene Stewart, Michel Simard, Cyril Goutte, and Chi-kiu Lo. 2018. Measuring sentence parallelism using mahalanobis distances: The nrc unsupervised submissions to the wmt18 parallel corpus filtering shared task. In *Proceedings of the Third Conference on Machine Translation, Volume 2: Shared Task Papers*, pages 913–920, Belgium, Brussels. Association for Computational Linguistics.

Chi-kiu Lo, Michel Simard, Darlene Stewart, Samuel Larkin, Cyril Goutte, and Patrick Littell. 2018. Accurate semantic textual similarity for cleaning noisy parallel corpora using semantic machine translation evaluation metric: The nrc supervised submissions to the parallel corpus filtering task. In *Proceedings of the Third Conference on Machine Translation, Volume 2: Shared Task Papers*, pages 921–929, Belgium, Brussels. Association for Computational Linguistics.

Jun Lu, Xiaoyu Lv, Yangbin Shi, and Boxing Chen. 2018. Alibaba submission to the wmt18 parallel corpus filtering task. In *Proceedings of the Third Conference on Machine Translation, Volume 2: Shared Task Papers*, pages 930–935, Belgium, Brussels. Association for Computational Linguistics.

Myle Ott, Sergey Edunov, Alexei Baevski, Angela Fan, Sam Gross, Nathan Ng, David Grangier, and Michael Auli. 2019. fairseq: A fast, extensible toolkit for sequence modeling. In *Proceedings of the 2019 Conference of the North American Chapter of the Association for Computational Linguistics (Demonstrations)*, pages 48–53, Minneapolis, Minnesota. Association for Computational Linguistics.

Gustavo Paetzold. 2018. Utfpr at wmt 2018: Minimalistic supervised corpora filtering for machine translation. In *Proceedings of the Third Conference on Machine Translation, Volume 2: Shared Task Papers*, pages 936–940, Belgium, Brussels. Association for Computational Linguistics.

Zuzanna Parcheta, Germán Sanchis-Trilles, and Francisco Casacuberta. 2019. Filtering of noisy parallel corpora based on hypothesis generation. In *Proceedings of the Fourth Conference on Machine Translation (WMT)*.

Ellie Pavlick, Matt Post, Ann Irvine, Dmitry Kachaev, and Chris Callison-Burch. 2014. The language demographics of Amazon Mechanical Turk. *Transactions of the Association for Computational Linguistics*, 2(Feb):79–92.

Minh Quang Pham, Josep Crego, and Jean Senellart. 2018. Systran participation to the wmt2018 shared task on parallel corpus filtering. In *Proceedings of the Third Conference on Machine Translation, Volume 2: Shared Task Papers*, pages 947–951, Belgium, Brussels. Association for Computational Linguistics.

Marcis Pinnis. 2018. Tilde's parallel corpus filtering methods for wmt 2018. In *Proceedings of the Third Conference on Machine Translation, Volume 2: Shared Task Papers*, pages 952–958, Belgium, Brussels. Association for Computational Linguistics.

Matt Post. 2018. A call for clarity in reporting bleu scores. In *Proceedings of the Third Conference on Machine Translation: Research Papers*, pages 186–191, Belgium, Brussels. Association for Computational Linguistics.

Alexandre Rafalovitch and Robert Dale. 2009. United Nations General Assembly resolutions: A six-language parallel corpus. In *Proceedings of the Twelfth Machine Translation Summit (MT Summit XII)*. International Association for Machine Translation.

Spencer Rarrick, Chris Quirk, and Will Lewis. 2011. MT detection in web-scraped parallel corpora. In *Proceedings of the 13th Machine Translation Summit (MT Summit XIII)*, pages 422–430. International Association for Machine Translation.

Philip Resnik. 1999. Mining the web for bilingual text. In *Proceedings of the 37th Annual Meeting of the Association of Computational Linguistics (ACL)*.

Nick Rossenbach, Jan Rosendahl, Yunsu Kim, Miguel GraÃ§a, Aman Gokrani, and Hermann Ney. 2018. The rwth aachen university filtering system for the wmt 2018 parallel corpus filtering task. In *Proceedings of the Third Conference on Machine Translation, Volume 2: Shared Task Papers*, pages 959–967, Belgium, Brussels. Association for Computational Linguistics.

Víctor M. Sánchez-Cartagena, Marta Bañón, Sergio Ortiz Rojas, and Gema Ramírez. 2018. Prompsit's submission to wmt 2018 parallel corpus filtering shared task. In *Proceedings of the Third Conference on Machine Translation: Shared Task Papers*, pages 955–962, Belgium, Brussels. Association for Computational Linguistics.

Sukanta Sen, Asif Ekbal, and Pushpak Bhattacharyya. 2019. Parallel corpus filtering based on fuzzy string matching. In *Proceedings of the Fourth Conference on Machine Translation (WMT)*.

Felipe Soares and Marta R. Costa-jussà. 2019. Unsupervised corpus filtering and mining. In *Proceedings of the Fourth Conference on Machine Translation (WMT)*.

Wolfgang Täger. 2011. The sentence-aligned european patent corpus. In *Proceedings of the 15th International Conference of the European Association for Machine Translation (EAMT)*, pages 177–184.

Kaveh Taghipour, Shahram Khadivi, and Jia Xu. 2011. Parallel corpus refinement as an outlier detection algorithm. In *Proceedings of the 13th Machine Translation Summit (MT Summit XIII)*, pages 414–421. International Association for Machine Translation.

Jörg Tiedemann. 2012. Parallel data, tools and interfaces in opus. In *Proceedings of the Eighth International Conference on Language Resources and Evaluation (LREC-2012)*, pages 2214–2218, Istanbul, Turkey. European Language Resources Association (ELRA). ACL Anthology Identifier: L12-1246.

Dániel Varga, Péter Halácsy, András Kornai, Viktor Nagy, László Németh, and Viktor Trón. 2007. Parallel corpora for medium density languages. *Amsterdam Studies In The Theory And History Of Linguistic Science Series 4*, 292:247.

Ashish Vaswani, Noam Shazeer, Niki Parmar, Jakob Uszkoreit, Llion Jones, Aidan N Gomez, Ł ukasz Kaiser, and Illia Polosukhin. 2017. Attention is all you need. In I. Guyon, U. V. Luxburg, S. Bengio, H. Wallach, R. Fergus, S. Vishwanathan, and R. Garnett, editors, *Advances in Neural Information Processing Systems 30*, pages 5998–6008. Curran Associates, Inc.

Raúl Vázquez, Umut Sulubacak, and Jörg Tiedemann. 2019. The university of helsinki submission to the wmt19 parallel corpus filtering task. In *Proceedings of the Fourth Conference on Machine Translation (WMT)*.

Ashish Venugopal, Jakob Uszkoreit, David Talbot, Franz Och, and Juri Ganitkevitch. 2011. Watermarking the outputs of structured prediction with an application in statistical machine translation. In *Proceedings of the 2011 Conference on Empirical Methods in Natural Language Processing*, pages 1363–1372, Edinburgh, Scotland, UK. Association for Computational Linguistics.

Wei Wang, Taro Watanabe, Macduff Hughes, Tetsuji Nakagawa, and Ciprian Chelba. 2018. Denoising neural machine translation training with trusted data and online data selection. In *Proceedings of the Third Conference on Machine Translation: Research Papers*, pages 133–143, Belgium, Brussels. Association for Computational Linguistics.

Marlies van der Wees, Arianna Bisazza, and Christof Monz. 2017. Dynamic data selection for neural machine translation. In *Proceedings of the 2017 Conference on Empirical Methods in Natural Language Processing*, pages 1411–1421. Association for Computational Linguistics.

Hainan Xu and Philipp Koehn. 2017. Zipporah: a fast and scalable data cleaning system for noisy webcrawled parallel corpora. In *Proceedings of the 2017 Conference on Empirical Methods in Natural Language Processing*, pages 2935–2940. Association for Computational Linguistics.

Michał Ziemski, Marcin Junczys-Dowmunt, and Bruno Pouliquen. 2015. The united nations parallel corpus v1.0. In *International Conference on Language Resources and Evaluation (LREC)*.

RTM Stacking Results for Machine Translation Performance Prediction

Ergun Biçici

ergun.bicici@boun.edu.tr

Electrical and Electronics Engineering Department, Boğaziçi University

orcid.org/0000-0002-2293-2031

Abstract

We obtain new results using referential translation machines with increased number of learning models in the set of results that are stacked to obtain a better mixture of experts prediction. We combine features extracted from the word-level predictions with the sentence- or document-level features, which significantly improve the results on the training sets but decrease the test set results.

1 Referential Translation Machines for Machine Translation Performance Predicion

Quality estimation task in WMT19 (Specia et al., 2019) (QET19) address machine translation performance prediction (MTPP), where translation quality is predicted without using reference translations, at the sentence- and word- (Task 1), and document-levels (Task 2). The tasks contain subtasks involving English-German, English-Russian, and English-French machine translation (MT). The target to predict in Task 1 is HTER (human-targeted translation edit rate) scores (Snover et al., 2006) and binary classification of word-level translation errors and the target in Task 2 is multi-dimensional quality metrics (MQM) (Lommel, 2015). Table 1 lists the number of sentences in the training and test sets for each task and the number of instances used as interpretants in the RTM models (M for million).

We use referential translation machine (RTM) (Biçici, 2018; Biçici and Way, 2015) models for building our prediction models. RTMs predict data translation between the instances in the training set and the test set using interpretants, data close to the task instances. Interpretants provide context for the prediction task and are used during the derivation of the features measuring the closeness of the test sentences to the

Task	Train	Test	RTM interpretants	
			Training	LM
Task 1 (en-de)	14442	1000		
Task 1 (en-ru)	16089	1000	0.250M	5M
Task 2 (en-fr)	1468	180		

Table 1: Number of instances and interpretants used.

training data, the difficulty of translating them, and to identify translation acts between any two data sets for building prediction models. With the enlarging parallel and monolingual corpora made available by WMT, the capability of the interpretant datasets selected by RTM models to provide context for the training and test sets improve as can be seen in the data statistics of `parfda` instance selection (Biçici, 2019). Figure 1 depicts RTMs and explains the model building process. RTMs use `parfda` for instance selection and machine translation performance prediction system (MTPPS) for obtaining the features, which includes additional features from word alignment and also from GLMd for word-level prediction.

We use ridge regression, kernel ridge regression, k-nearest neighors, support vector regression, AdaBoost (Freund and Schapire, 1997), gradient tree boosting, gaussian process regressor, extremely randomized trees (Geurts et al., 2006), and multi-layer perceptron (Bishop, 2006) as learning models in combination with feature selection (FS) (Guyon et al., 2002) and partial least squares (PLS) (Wold et al., 1984) where most of these models can be found in `scikit-learn`.[1] We experiment with:

- including the statistics of the binary tags obtained as features extracted from word-level tag predictions for sentence-level prediction,

- using KNN to estimate the noise level for

---

[1] http://scikit-learn.org/

Proceedings of the Fourth Conference on Machine Translation (WMT), Volume 3: Shared Task Papers (Day 2) pages 73–77
Florence, Italy, August 1-2, 2019. ©2019 Association for Computational Linguistics

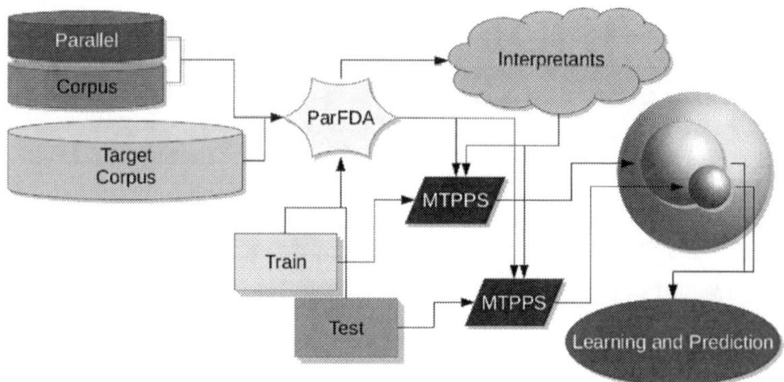

Figure 1: RTM depiction: parfda selects interpretants close to the training and test data using parallel corpus in bilingual settings and monolingual corpus in the target language or just the monolingual target corpus in monolingual settings; an MTPPS use interpretants and training data to generate training features and another use interpretants and test data to generate test features in the same feature space; learning and prediction takes place taking these features as input.

SVR, which obtains accuracy with 5% error compared with estimates obtained with known noise level (Cherkassky and Ma, 2004) and set $\epsilon = \sigma/2$.

Martins et al. (2017) used a hybrid stacking model to combine the word-level predictions from 15 predictors using neural networks with different initializations together with the previous features from a linear model. The neural network architecture they used is also hybrid with different types of layers: input word embedding use 64 dimensional vectors, the next three layers are two feedforward layers with 400 nodes and a bidirectional gated recurrent units layer with 200 units, followed by similar three layers with half nodes, followed by a feedforward layer with 50 nodes and a softmax layer.

We use Global Linear Models (GLM) (Collins, 2002) with dynamic learning (GLMd) (Biçici, 2018) for word- and phrase-level translation performance prediction. GLMd uses weights in a range $[a, b]$ to update the learning rate dynamically according to the error rate. Evaluation metrics listed are Pearson's correlation (r), mean absolute error (MAE), and root mean squared error (RMSE).

2   Mixture of Experts Models

We use prediction averaging (Biçici, 2018) to obtain a combined prediction from various prediction outputs better than the components, where the performance on the training set is used to obtain weighted average of the top k predictions, $\hat{y}$ with

evaluation metrics indexed by $j \in J$ and weights with w:

$$
\begin{aligned}
w_{j,i} &= \tfrac{w_{j,i}}{1 - w_{j,i}} \\
\hat{\boldsymbol{y}}_{\mu_k} &= \tfrac{1}{k} \sum_{i=1}^{k} \hat{\boldsymbol{y}}_i & \text{MEAN} \\
\hat{\boldsymbol{y}}_{j,w_k^j} &= \tfrac{1}{\sum_{i=1}^{k} w_{j,i}} \sum_{i=1}^{k} w_{j,i}\, \hat{\boldsymbol{y}}_i \\
\hat{\boldsymbol{y}}_k &= \tfrac{1}{|J|} \sum_{j \in J} \hat{\boldsymbol{y}}_{j,w_k^j} & \text{MIX}
\end{aligned}
\tag{1}
$$

We assume independent predictions and use $p_i/(1 - p_i)$ for weights where p_i represents the accuracy of the independent classifier i in a weighted majority ensemble (Kuncheva and Rodríguez, 2014). We only use the MIX prediction if we obtain better results on the training set. We select the best model using r and mix the results using r, RAE, MRAER, and MAER. We filter out those results with higher than 1 relative evaluation metric scores.

We also use stacking to build higher level models using predictions from base prediction models where they can also use the probability associated with the predictions (Ting and Witten, 1999). The stacking models use the predictions from predictors as features and build second level predictors.

For the document-level RTM model, instead of running separate MTPPS instances for each training or test document to obtain specific features for each document, we concatenate the sentences from each document to obtain a single sentence representing each and then run an RTM model. This conversion decreases the number of features and obtains close results (Biçici, 2018).

Before model combination, we further filter prediction results from different machine learn-

				r_P	MAE	RAE	MAER	MRAER
2019	sentence	en-de		0.4908	0.1102	0.8017	0.8721	0.7554
			+word tags	0.9608	0.0237	0.1725	0.1388	0.1823
		en-ru		0.2724	0.1548	0.8769	0.9064	0.7736
			+word tags	0.9481	0.028	0.1587	0.1541	0.1553
	document	en-fr		0.3959	17.982	0.8564	0.933	0.7908
			+word tags	0.478	17.1015	0.8144	0.8921	0.7564
2018	sentence	en-de SMT		0.4386	0.1368	0.8675	0.9103	0.8168
			+word tags	0.9424	0.0391	0.248	0.1716	0.2969
		en-de NMT		0.4613	0.1109	0.8066	0.8414	0.7347
			+word tags	0.9589	0.0244	0.1777	0.144	0.1901
		de-en SMT		0.5636	0.1355	0.7903	0.9173	0.7826
			+word tags	0.9276	0.0485	0.2828	0.2413	0.3378
		en-cs SMT		0.5397	0.1506	0.8084	0.8203	0.7886
			+word tags	0.9356	0.0477	0.256	0.1825	0.3021
		en-lv SMT		0.4006	0.1329	0.8832	0.9316	0.8059
			+word tags	0.9452	0.0342	0.2271	0.1768	0.2625
		en-lv NMT		0.5779	0.1441	0.7831	0.8679	0.7768
			+word tags	0.9571	0.0398	0.2163	0.1778	0.2573
	document	en-fr		0.2141	40.7359	0.9324	1.2074	0.7573
			+word tags	0.2254	41.6591	0.9535	1.0849	0.7783

Table 2: RTM train results in sentence- and document-level MTPP. r_P is Pearson's correlation.

ing models based on the results on the training set to decrease the number of models combined and improve the results. A criteria that we use is to include results that are better than the best RR model's results. In general, the combined model is better than the best model in the set and stacking achieves better results than MIX.

3 Results

We tokenize and truecase all of the corpora using Moses' (Koehn et al., 2007) processing tools.[2] LMs are built using `kenlm` (Heafield et al., 2013). The comparison of results on the training set are in Table 2 and the results on the test set we obtained after the competition are in Tables 3 and 5. Official competition results of RTMs are similar.

We convert MQM annotation to word-level tags to train GLMd models and obtain word-level predictions. Addition of the tagging features from the word-level prediction improves the training results significantly but does not improve the test results at the same rate, which indicates overfitting. The reason for the overfitting with the word-level features is due to their high correlation with the target. Table 4 lists some of the top individual feature

correlations for en-ru in Task1. Top 26 highly correlated features belong to word-level features.

We also obtained new results on QET18 datasets and experimented adding features from word-level predictions on the QET18 sentence-level results. QET18 results in Table 3 are improved overall.

4 Conclusion

Referential translation machines pioneer a language independent approach and remove the need to access any task or domain specific information or resource and can achieve top performance in automatic, accurate, and language independent prediction of translation scores. We present RTM results with stacking.

Acknowledgments

The research reported here received financial support from the Scientific and Technological Research Council of Turkey (TÜBİTAK).

References

Ergun Biçici. 2018. RTM results for predicting translation performance. In *Third Conf. on Statistical Machine Translation (WMT18)*, Brussels, Belgium.

			r_P	MAE	RAE	MAER	MRAER
2019	sentence	en-de		0.4617	0.1176	0.8066	0.7755	0.7338
			+word tags	0.1842	0.1612	1.1056	1.1472	1.1771
		en-ru		0.269	0.187	0.8468	0.7827	0.7232
			+word tags	0.2423	**0.1868**	**0.8461**	0.7919	0.7681
	document en-fr			0.3064	21.6283	0.9044	1.3233	0.8565
			+word tags	0.2162	22.2011	0.9283	**1.2688**	0.8861

				r_P	r_S	MAE	RMSE
2018	sentence	en-de SMT		0.4165 (11)	0.4236 (9)	0.1368 (10)	0.1734 (10)
			+word tags	0.2689 (16)	0.2780 (12)	0.1659 (15)	0.2192 (15)
			top	0.7397	0.7543	0.0937	0.1362
		en-de NMT		0.4752 (3)	0.5556 (4)	0.1173 (3)	0.1753 (5)
			+word tags	0.1645 (16)	0.3752 (10)	0.1501 (11)	0.2239 (14)
			top	0.5129	0.6052	0.1114	0.1719
		de-en SMT		0.5773 (9)	0.5144 (8)	0.1326 (10)	0.1687 (9)
			+word tags	0.3936 (12)	0.3530 (9)	0.1603 (13)	0.2155 (13)
			top	0.7667	0.7318	0.0945	0.1315
		en-cs SMT		0.5007 (6)	0.5037 (5)	0.1544 (6)	0.1988 (6)
			+word tags	0.4469 (8)	0.4384 (7)	0.1775 (11)	0.2331 (11)
			top	0.6918	0.7105	0.1223	0.1693
		en-lv SMT		0.3560 (7)	0.2884 (8)	0.1395 (5)	0.1867 (4)
			+word tags	0.3097 (10)	0.2578 (8)	0.1598 (6)	0.2155 (8)
			top	0.6188	0.5766	0.1202	0.1602
		en-lv NMT		0.5394 (4)	0.4963 (4)	0.1533 (2)	0.2009 (2)
			+word tags	0.4132 (7)	0.4007 (7)	0.1841 (7)	0.2466 (8)
			top	0.6819	0.6665	0.1308	0.1747
	document en-fr			0.0068 (4)		58.4664 (4)	88.1198 (4)
			+word tags	**0.0112** (4)		**58.0524** (4)	**86.3416** (4)
			top	0.5337		56.2264	85.2319

Table 3: RTM stacking results on the test set where **bold** indicate results that improve with the addition of features from word-level predictions. (#) indicates the rank. r_S is Spearman's correlation.

r_P train	r_P test	feature
0.937	0.2369	avg number of 1s in tags
0.5941	0.1838	std of the number of 1s in tags
0.0773	0.055	translation average BLEU

Table 4: Word-level prediction features are highly correlated with the target in the training set for en-ru in Task1.

Ergun Biçici. 2019. Machine translation with `parfda`, moses, `kenlm`, `nplm`, and pro. In *Fourth Conf. on Statistical Machine Translation (WMT19)*, Florence, Italy.

Ergun Biçici and Andy Way. 2015. Referential translation machines for predicting semantic similarity. *Language Resources and Evaluation*, pages 1–27.

Christopher M. Bishop. 2006. *Pattern Recognition and Machine Learning*.

Vladimir Cherkassky and Yunqian Ma. 2004. Practical selection of svm parameters and noise estimation for svm regression. *Neural Networks*, 17(1):113–126.

Michael Collins. 2002. Discriminative training methods for hidden markov models: theory and experiments with perceptron algorithms. In *ACL-02 Conf. on Empirical methods in natural language processing*, EMNLP '02, pages 1–8, Stroudsburg, PA, USA.

Yoav Freund and Robert E Schapire. 1997. A decision-theoretic generalization of on-line learning and an application to boosting. *Journal of Computer and System Sciences*, 55(1):119–139.

Pierre Geurts, Damien Ernst, and Louis Wehenkel. 2006. Extremely randomized trees. *Machine Learning*, 63(1):3–42.

Isabelle Guyon, Jason Weston, Stephen Barnhill, and Vladimir Vapnik. 2002. Gene selection for cancer classification using support vector machines. *Machine Learning*, 46(1-3):389–422.

	model	r_P	r_S	MAE	RMSE
sentence	en-de +word tags	0.4617	0.5279	0.1176	0.1757
		0.1842	0.3308	0.1612	0.2334
	top	0.5718	0.6221		
	en-ru +word tags	0.2690	0.2677	0.187	0.2827
		0.2423	0.1474	0.1868	0.3048
	top	0.5923	0.5388		
document	en-fr +word tags	0.3065	0.3642	21.6282	26.1010
		0.2162	0.2460	22.2011	27.0249
	top	0.3744			

Table 5: RTM test results and the top result.

Kenneth Heafield, Ivan Pouzyrevsky, Jonathan H. Clark, and Philipp Koehn. 2013. Scalable modified Kneser-Ney language model estimation. In *51st Annual Meeting of the Assoc. for Computational Linguistics*, pages 690–696, Sofia, Bulgaria.

Philipp Koehn, Hieu Hoang, Alexandra Birch, Chris Callison-Burch, Marcello Federico, Nicola Bertoldi, Brooke Cowan, Wade Shen, Christine Moran, Richard Zens, Chris Dyer, Ondrej Bojar, Alexandra Constantin, and Evan Herbst. 2007. Moses: Open source toolkit for statistical machine translation. In *45th Annual Meeting of the Assoc. for Computational Linguistics Companion Volume Demo and Poster Sessions*, pages 177–180.

Ludmila I. Kuncheva and Juan J. Rodríguez. 2014. A weighted voting framework for classifiers ensembles. *Knowledge and Information Systems*, 38(2):259–275.

Arle Lommel. 2015. Multidimensional quality metrics (mqm) definition. *URL http://www. qt21. eu/mqm-definition/definition-2015-12-30. html*.

André F.T. Martins, Marcin Junczys-Dowmunt, Fabio N. Kepler, Ramón Astudillo, Chris Hokamp, and Roman Grundkiewicz. 2017. Pushing the limits of translation quality estimation. *Transactions of the Association for Computational Linguistics*, 5:205–218.

Matthew Snover, Bonnie Dorr, Richard Schwartz, Linnea Micciulla, and John Makhoul. 2006. A Study of Translation Edit Rate with Targeted Human Annotation. In *Assoc. for Machine Translation in the Americas*.

Lucia Specia, Frédéric Blain, Varvara Logacheva, Ramón F. Astudillo, and André Martins. 2019. Findings of the wmt 2019 shared task on quality estimation. In *Fourth Conf. on Machine Translation*, Florence, Italy.

Kai Ming Ting and Ian H. Witten. 1999. Issues in stacked generalization. *Journal of Artificial Intelligence Research*, 10:271–289.

S. Wold, A. Ruhe, H. Wold, and III Dunn, W. J. 1984. The collinearity problem in linear regression. the partial least squares (pls) approach to generalized inverses. *SIAM Journal on Scientific and Statistical Computing*, 5:735–743.

Unbabel's Participation
in the WMT19 Translation Quality Estimation Shared Task

Fábio Kepler
Unbabel

Jonay Trénous
Unbabel

Marcos Treviso
Instituto de Telecomunicações

Miguel Vera
Unbabel

António Góis
Unbabel

M. Amin Farajian
Unbabel

António V. Lopes
Unbabel

André F. T. Martins
Unbabel

{kepler, sony, miguel.vera}@unbabel.com
{antonio.gois, amin, antonio.lopes, andre.martins}@unbabel.com
marcosvtreviso@gmail.com

Abstract

We present the contribution of the Unbabel team to the WMT 2019 Shared Task on Quality Estimation. We participated on the word, sentence, and document-level tracks, encompassing 3 language pairs: English-German, English-Russian, and English-French. Our submissions build upon the recent OpenKiwi framework: we combine linear, neural, and predictor-estimator systems with new transfer learning approaches using BERT and XLM pre-trained models. We compare systems individually and propose new ensemble techniques for word and sentence-level predictions. We also propose a simple technique for converting word labels into document-level predictions. Overall, our submitted systems achieve the best results on all tracks and language pairs by a considerable margin.

1 Introduction

Quality estimation (QE) is the task of evaluating a translation system's quality without access to reference translations (Blatz et al., 2004; Specia et al., 2018). This paper describes the contribution of the Unbabel team to the Shared Task on Word, Sentence, and Document-Level (QE Tasks 1 and 2) at WMT 2019.

Our system adapts OpenKiwi,[1] a recently released open-source framework for QE that implements the best QE systems from WMT 2015-18 shared tasks (Martins et al., 2016, 2017; Kim et al., 2017; Wang et al., 2018), which we extend to leverage recently proposed pre-trained models

via transfer learning techniques. Overall, our main contributions are as follows:

- We extend OpenKiwi with a Transformer predictor-estimator model (Wang et al., 2018).

- We apply transfer learning techniques, fine-tuning BERT (Devlin et al., 2018) and XLM (Lample and Conneau, 2019) models in a predictor-estimator architecture.

- We incorporate predictions coming from the APE-BERT system described in Correia and Martins (2019), also used in this year's Unbabel's APE submission (Lopes et al., 2019).

- We propose new ensembling techniques for combining word-level and sentence-level predictions, which outperform previously used stacking approaches (Martins et al., 2016).

- We build upon our BERT-based predictor-estimator model to obtain document-level annotation and MQM predictions via a simple word-to-annotation conversion scheme.

Our submitted systems achieve the best results on all tracks and all language pairs by a considerable margin: on English-Russian (En-Ru), our sentence-level system achieves a Pearson score of 59.23% (+5.96% than the second best system), and on English-German (En-De), we achieve 57.18% (+2.44%).

2 Word and Sentence-Level Task

The goal of the word-level QE task is to assign quality labels (OK or BAD) to each *machine-translated word*, as well as to *gaps* between words

---

[1] https://unbabel.github.io/OpenKiwi.

78

(to account for context that needs to be inserted), and *source words* (to denote words in the original sentence that have been mistranslated or omitted in the target). The goal of the Sentence-level QE task, on the other hand, is to predict the quality of the whole translated sentence, based on how many edit operations are required to fix it, in terms of HTER (Human Translation Error Rate) (Specia et al., 2018). We next describe the datasets, resources, and models that we used for these tasks.

2.1 Datasets and Resources

The data resources we use to train our systems are of three types: the QE shared task corpora, additional parallel corpora, and artificial triplets (`src`, `pe`, `mt`) in the style of the eSCAPE corpus (Negri et al., 2018).

- The En-De QE corpus provided by the shared task, consisting of 13,442 `train` triplets.

- The En-Ru QE corpus provided by the shared task, consisting of 15,089 `train` triplets.

- The En-De parallel dataset of 3,396,364 sentences from the IT domain provided by the shared task organizers. which we extend in the style of the eSCAPE corpus to contain artificial triplets. To do this, we use OpenNMT with 5-fold jackknifing (Klein et al., 2017) to obtain unbiased translations of the source sentences.

- The En-Ru eSCAPE corpus (Negri et al., 2018) consisting of 7,735,361 artificial triplets.

2.2 Linear Sequential Model

Our simplest baseline is the linear sequential model described by Martins et al. (2016, 2017). It is a discriminative feature-based sequential model (called LINEARQE). The system uses a first-order sequential model with unigram and bigram features, whose weights are learned by using the max-loss MIRA algorithm (Crammer et al., 2006). The features include information about the words, part-of-speech tags, and syntactic dependencies, obtained with TurboParser (Martins et al., 2013).

2.3 NuQE

We used NUQE (NeUral Quality Estimation) as implemented in `OpenKiwi` (Kepler et al., 2019) and adapted it to jointly learn MT tags, source tags and also sentence scores. We use the original architecture with the following additions. For learning sentence scores, we first take the average of the MT tags output layer and than pass the result through a feed-forward layer that projects the result to a single unit. For jointly learning source tags, we take the source text embeddings, project them with a feed-forward layer, and then sum the MT tags output vectors that are aligned. The result is then passed through a feed-forward layer, a bi-GRU, two other feed-forward layers, and finally an output layer. The layer dimensions are the same as in the normal model. It is worth noting that NUQE is trained from scratch using only the shared task data, with no pre-trained components, besides Polyglot embeddings (Al-Rfou et al., 2013).

2.4 RNN-Based Predictor-Estimator

Our implementation of the RNN-based prediction estimator (PREDEST-RNN) is described in Kepler et al. (2019). It follows closely the architecture proposed by Kim et al. (2017), which consists of two modules:

- a *predictor*, which is trained to predict each token of the target sentence given the source and the left and right context of the target sentence;

- an *estimator*, which takes features produced by the *predictor* and uses them to classify each word as OK or BAD.

Our predictor uses a biLSTM to encode the source, and two unidirectional LSTMs processing the target in left-to-right (LSTM-L2R) and right-to-left (LSTM-R2L) order. For each target token t_i, the representations of its left and right context are concatenated and used as query to an attention module before a final softmax layer. It is trained on the large parallel corpora mentioned above. The estimator takes as input a sequence of features: for each target token t_i, the final layer before the softmax (before processing t_i), and the concatenation of the i-th hidden state of LSTM-L2R and LSTM-R2L (after processing t_i). We train this system with a multi-task architecture that allows us to predict sentence-level HTER scores. Overall, this system is capable to predict sentence-level scores and all word-level labels (for MT words, gaps, and source words)—the source word labels are produced by training a predictor in the reverse direction.

2.5 Transformer-Based Predictor-Estimator

In addition, we implemented a Transformer-based predictor-estimator (PREDEST-TRANS), following Wang et al. (2018). This model has the following modifications in the *predictor*: (i) in order to encode the source sentence, the bidirectional LSTM is replaced by a Transformer encoder; (ii) the LSTM-L2R is replaced by a Transformer decoder with future-masked positions, and the LSTM-R2L is replaced by a Transformer decoder with past-masked positions. Additionally, the Transformer-based model produces the "mismatch features" proposed by Fan et al. (2018).

2.6 Transfer Learning and Fine-Tuning

Following the recent trend in the NLP community leveraging large-scale language model pre-training for a diverse set of downstream tasks, we used two pre-trained language models as feature extractors, the multilingual BERT (Devlin et al., 2018) and the Cross-lingual Language Model (XLM) (Lample and Conneau, 2019). The predictor-estimator model consists of a predictor that produces contextual token representations, and an estimator that turns these representations into predictions for both word level tags, and sentence level scores. As both of these models produce contextual representations for each token in a pair of sentences, we simply replace the predictor part by either BERT or XLM to create new QE models: PREDEST-BERT and PREDEST-XLM. The XLM model is particularly well suited to the task at hand, as its pre-training objective already contains a translation language modeling part.

For improved performance, we employ a pre-fine-tuning step by continuing their language model pre-training on data that is closer to the domain of the shared task. For the En-De pair we used the in-domain data provided by the shared task, and for the En-Ru pair we used the eSCAPE corpus (Negri et al., 2018).

Despite the shared multilingual vocabulary, BERT is originally a monolingual model, treating the input as either being from one language or another. We pass both sentences as input by concatenating them according to the template: `[CLS] target [SEP] source [SEP]`, where `[CLS]` and `[SEP]` are special symbols from BERT, denoting beginning of sentence and sentence separators, respectively. In contrast, XLM is a multilingual model which receives two sentences from different languages as input. Thus, its usage is straightforward.

The output from BERT and XLM is split into target features and source features, which in turn are passed to the regular *estimator*. They work with word pieces rather than tokens, so the model maps their output to tokens by selecting the first word piece of each token. For En-Ru the mapping is slightly different, it is done by taking the average of the word pieces of each token.

For PREDEST-BERT, we obtained the best results by ignoring features from the other language, that is, for predicting target and gap tags we ignored source features, and for predicting source tags we ignored target features. On the other hand, PREDEST-XLM predicts labels for target, gaps and source at the same time. As the predictor-estimator model, PREDEST-BERT and PREDEST-XLM are trained in a multi-task fashion, predicting sentence-level scores along with word-level labels.

2.7 APE-QE

In addition to traditional QE systems, we also use Automatic Post-Editing (APE) adapted for QE (APE-QE), following Martins et al. (2017). An APE system is trained on the human post-edits and its outputs are used as pseudo-post-editions to generate word-level quality labels and sentence-level scores in the same way that the original labels were created.

We use two variants of APE-QE:

- PSEUDO-APE, which trains a regular translation model and uses its output as a pseudo-reference.

- An adaptation of BERT to APE (APE-BERT) with an additional decoding constraint to reward or discourage words that do not exist in the source or MT.

PSEUDO-APE was trained using `OpenNMT-py` (Klein et al., 2017). For En-De, we used the IT domain corpus provided by the shared task, and for En-Ru we used the Russian eSCAPE corpus (Negri et al., 2018).

For APE-BERT, we follow the approach of Correia and Martins (2019), also used by Unbabel's APE shared task system (Lopes et al., 2019), and adapt BERT to the APE task using the QE in-domain corpus and the shared task data as input, where the source and MT sentences are the encoder's input and the post-edited sentence is the decoder's output. In addition, we also employ a conservativeness penalty (Lopes et al., 2019), a

Method	Target F_1
Stacked Linear	43.88
Powell	44.61

Table 1: Performance of the stacked linear ensemble and Powell's method on the WMT17 dev set (F_1-MULT on MT tags). The ensemble is over the same set of models[3] reported in the release of the OpenKiwi (Kepler et al., 2019) framework. To estimate the performance of Powell's method, the dev set was partitioned into 10 folds f_i. We ran Powell's method 10 times, leaving out one fold at a time, to learn weights w_i. Predicting on fold f_i using weights w_i and calculating F_1 performance over the concatenation of these predictions gives an approximately unbiased estimate of the performance of the method.

beam decoding penalty which either rewards or penalizes choosing tokens not in the `src` and `mt`, with a negative score to encourage more edits of the MT.

2.8 System Ensembling

We ensembled the systems above to produce a single prediction, as described next.

Word-level ensembling. We compare two approaches:

- A stacked architecture with a feature-based linear system, as described by Martins et al. (2017). This approach uses the predictions of various systems as additional features in the linear system described in §2.2. To avoid overfitting on the training data, this approach requires jackknifing.

- A novel strategy consisting of learning a convex combination of system predictions, with the weights learned on the development set. We use Powell's conjugate direction method (Powell, 1964)[2] as implemented in `SciPy` (Jones et al., 2001) to directly optimize for the task metric (F_1-MULT).

Using the development set for learning carries a risk of overfitting; by using k-fold cross-validation we avoided this, and indeed the performance is equal or superior to the linear stacking ensemble (Table 1), while being computationally cheaper as only the development set is needed to learn an ensemble, avoiding jackknifing.

---

[2]This is the method underlying the popular MERT method (Och, 2003), widely used in the MT literature.

Sentence-level ensembling. We have systems outputting sentence-level predictions directly, and others outputting word-level probabilities that can be turned into sentence-level predictions by averaging them over a sentence, as in (Martins et al., 2017). To use all available features (sentence score, gap tag, MT tag and source tag predictions from all systems used in the word-level ensembles), we learn a linear combination of these features using ℓ_2-regularized regression over the development set. We tune the regularization constant with k-fold cross-validation, and retrain on the full development set using the chosen value.

3 Document-Level Task

Estimating the quality of an entire document introduces additional challenges. The text may become too long to be processed at once by previously described methods, and longer-range dependencies may appear (e.g inconsistencies across sentences).

Both sub-tasks were addressed: estimating the MQM score of a document and identifying character-level annotations with corresponding severities. Note that, given the correct number of annotations in a document and their severities, the MQM score can be computed in closed form. However, preliminary experiments using the predicted annotations to compute MQM did not outperform the baseline, hence we opted for using independent systems for each of these sub-tasks.

3.1 Dataset

The data for this task consists of Amazon reviews translated from English to French using a neural MT system. Translations were manually annotated for errors, with each annotation associated to a severity tag (minor, major or critical).

Note that each annotation may include several words, which do not have to be contiguous. We refer to each contiguous block of characters in an annotation as a span, and refer to an annotation with at least two spans as a multi-span annotation. Figure 1 illustrates this, where a single annotation is comprised of the spans *bandes* and *parfaits*.

Across training set and last year's development and test set, there are 36,242 annotations. Out of these, 4,170 are multi-span, and 149 of the multi-span annotations contain spans in different sentences. The distribution of severities is 84.12% of major, 11.74% of minor and 4.14% of critical.

Source: *resistance bands are great for home use, gym use, offices, and are ideal for travel.*

Target: *les bandes de résistance sont parfaits pour l'usage domestique, l'utilisation de la salle de gym, bureaux et sont idéales pour les voyages.*

Figure 1: Example of a multi-span annotation containing two spans: *parfaits* does not agree with *bandes* due to gender—it should be *parfaites*. This mistake corresponds to a single annotation with severity "minor".

3.2 Implemented System

To predict annotations within a document the problem is first treated as a word-level task, with each sentence processed separately. To obtain gold labels, the training set is tokenized and an OK/BAD tag is attributed to each token, depending on whether the token contains characters belonging to an annotation. Note that besides token tags, we will also have gap tags in between tokens. A gap tag will only be labeled as BAD if a span begins and ends exactly in the borders of the gap. Our best-performing model for the word-level part is an ensemble of 5 BERT models. Each BERT model was trained as described in §2.6, but without pre-fine-tuning. Systems were ensembled by a simple average.

Later, annotations may be retrieved from the predicted word-level tags by concatenating contiguous BAD tokens into a single annotation. This is done for token-tags, while each gap-tag can be directly mapped to a single annotation without attempting any merge operation. Note that this immediately causes 4 types of information loss, which can be addressed in a second step:

- Severity information is lost, since all three severity labels are converted to BAD tags. As a baseline, all spans are assigned the most frequent severity, "major."

- Span borders are defined on character-level, whose positions may not match exactly the beginning or ending of a token. This will cause all characters of a partially correct token to be annotated with an error.

- Contiguous BAD tokens will always be mapped to a single annotation, even if they belong to different ones.

- Non-contiguous BAD tokens will always be mapped to separate annotations, even if they belong to the same one.

Pair	System	Target F_1	Source F_1	Pearson
En-De	Linear	0.3346	0.2975	-
	APE-QE	0.3740	0.3446	0.3558
	APE-BERT	0.4244	0.4109	0.3816
	PredEst-RNN	0.3786	-	0.5020
	PredEst-Trans	0.3980	-	0.5300
	PredEst-XLM	0.4144	0.3960	0.5810
	PredEst-BERT	0.3870	0.3310	0.5190
	Linear Ens.	0.4520	0.4116	-
	(*)Powell's Ens.	0.4872	0.4607	0.5968
En-Ru	Linear	0.2839	0.2466	-
	APE-QE	0.2592	0.2336	0.1921
	APE-BERT	0.2519	0.2283	0.1814
	NuQE	0.3130	0.2000	-
	PredEst-RNN	0.3201	-	-
	PredEst-Trans	0.3414	-	0.3655
	PredEst-XLM	0.3799	0.3280	0.4983
	PredEst-BERT	0.3782	0.3039	0.5000
	(*)Ensemble 1	0.3932	0.3640	0.5469
	(*)Ensemble 2	0.3972	0.3700	0.5423

Table 2: Word and sentence-level results for En-De and En-Ru on the validation set in terms of F_1-MULT and Pearson's r correlation. (*) Lines with an asterisk use Powell's method for word level ensembling and ℓ_2-regularized regression for sentence level. As the weights are tuned on the dev set, their numbers can not be directly compared to the other models

Although more sophisticated approaches were tested for predicting severities and merging spans into the same annotation, these approaches did not result in significant gains, hence we opted by using the previously described pipeline as our final system. To predict document-level MQM, each sentence's MQM is first predicted and used to get the average sentence MQM (weighting the average by sentence length degraded results in all experiments). This is used together with 3 percentages of BAD tags from the word-level model (considering token tags, gap tags and all gaps) as features for a linear regression which outputs the final document-level MQM prediction. The percentage of BAD tags is obtained from the previously described word-level predictions, whereas the sentence MQMs are obtained from an ensemble of 5 BERT models trained for sentence-level MQM prediction. Again, each BERT model was trained as described in §2.6 without pre-fine-tuning, and the ensembling consisted of a simple average.[4]

4 Experimental Results

4.1 Word and Sentence-Level Task

The results achieved by each of the systems described in §2 for En-De and En-Ru on the valida-

---

[4]Using the approach of Ive et al. (2018) proved less robust to this year's data due to differences in the annotations. Particularly some outliers containing zero annotations would strongly harm the final Pearson score when mis-predicted.

PAIR	SYSTEM	TARGET F_1	TARGET MCC	SOURCE F_1	SOURCE MCC	PEARSON
	Baseline	0.2412	0.2145	0.2647	0.1887	0.2601
En-Ru	ENSEMBLE 1	0.4629	0.4412	0.4174	0.3729	0.5889
	ENSEMBLE 2	0.4780	0.4577	0.4541	0.4212	0.5923
	Baseline	0.2974	0.2541	0.2908	0.2126	0.4001
En-De	LINEAR ENSEMBLE	0.4621	0.4387	0.4284	0.3846	-
	POWELL'S ENSEMBLE	0.4752	0.4585	0.4455	0.4094	0.5718

Table 3: Word and sentence-level results for En-De and En-Ru on the test set in terms of F_1-MULT and Pearson's r correlation.

tion set are shown in Table 2. We tried the following strategies for ensembling:

- For En-De, we created a word-level ensembled system with Powell's method, by combining one instance of the APE-BERT system, another instance of the PSEUDO-APE-QE system, 10 runs of the PREDEST-XLM model (trained jointly for all subtasks), 6 runs of the same model without pre-fine-tuning, 5 runs of the PREDEST-BERT model (trained jointly for all subtasks), and 5 runs of the PREDEST-TRANS model (trained jointly for MT and sentence subtasks, but not for predicting source tags). For comparison, we report also the performance of a stacked linear ensembled word-level system. For the sentence-level ensemble, we learned system weights by fitting a linear regressor to the sentence scores produced by all the above models.

- For En-Ru, we tried two versions of word-level ensembled systems, both using Powell's method: EMSEMBLE 1 combined one instance of the APE-BERT system, 5 runs of the PREDEST-XLM model (trained jointly for all subtasks), one instance of the PREDEST-BERT model (trained jointly for all subtasks), 5 runs of the NUQE models (trained jointly for all subtasks), and 5 runs of the PREDEST-TRANS model (trained jointly for MT and sentence subtasks, but not for predicting source tags). EMSEMBLE 2 adds to the above predictions from the PSEUDO-APE-QE system. In both cases, for sentence-level ensembles, we learned system weights by fitting a linear regressor to the sentence scores produced by all the above models.

The results in Table 2 show that the transfer learning approach with BERT and XLM benefits the QE task. The PREDEST-XLM model, which has been pre-trained with a translation ob-

	DEV	DEV0	TEST
F_1 ANN. (BERT)	0.4664	0.4457	0.4811
MQM (BERT)	0.3924	-	0.3727
MQM (LINBERT)	-	0.4714	0.3744

Table 4: Results of document-level submissions, and their performance of the dev and dev0 validation sets.

jective, has a small but consistent advantage over both PREDEST-BERT and PREDEST-TRANSF. A clear takeaway is that ensembling of different systems can give large gains, even if some of the sub-systems are weak individually.

Table 3 shows the results obtained with our ensemble systems on the official test set.

4.2 Document-Level Task

Finally, Table 4 contains results for document-level submissions, both on validation and test set submissions. On F_1 annotations, results across all data sets are reasonably consistent. On the other hand, MQM Pearson varies significantly between dev and dev0. Differences in the training of the two systems shouldn't explain this variation, since both have equivalent performance on the test set.

5 Conclusions

We presented Unbabel's contribution to the WMT 2019 Shared Task on Quality Estimation. Our submissions are based on the `OpenKiwi` framework, to which we added new transfer learning approaches via BERT and XLM pre-trained models. We also proposed a new ensemble technique using Powell's method that outperforms previous strategies, and we convert word labels into span annotations to obtain document-level predictions. Our submitted systems achieve the best results on all tracks and language pairs.

Acknowledgments

The authors would like to thank the support provided by the EU in the context of the PT2020 project (contracts 027767 and 038510), by the European Research Council (ERC StG DeepSPIN 758969), and by the Fundação para a Ciência e Tecnologia through contract UID/EEA/50008/2019.

References

Rami Al-Rfou, Bryan Perozzi, and Steven Skiena. 2013. Polyglot: Distributed Word Representations for Multilingual NLP. *arXiv preprint arXiv:1307.1662*.

John Blatz, Erin Fitzgerald, George Foster, Simona Gandrabur, Cyril Goutte, Alex Kulesza, Alberto Sanchis, and Nicola Ueffing. 2004. Confidence Estimation for Machine Translation. In *Proc. of the International Conference on Computational Linguistics*, page 315.

Gonçalo Correia and André Martins. 2019. A Simple and Effective Approach to Automatic Post-Editing with Transfer Learning. In *Proc. of the 57th annual meeting on association for computational linguistics*. Association for Computational Linguistics.

Koby Crammer, Ofer Dekel, Joseph Keshet, Shai Shalev-Shwartz, and Yoram Singer. 2006. Online Passive-Aggressive Algorithms. *Journal of Machine Learning Research*, 7:551–585.

Jacob Devlin, Ming-Wei Chang, Kenton Lee, and Kristina Toutanova. 2018. Bert: Pre-training of Deep Bidirectional Transformers for Language Understanding. *arXiv preprint arXiv:1810.04805*.

Kai Fan, Bo Li, Fengming Zhou, and Jiayi Wang. 2018. "Bilingual Expert" Can Find Translation Errors. *arXiv preprint arXiv:1807.09433*.

Julia Ive, Carolina Scarton, Frédéric Blain, and Lucia Specia. 2018. Sheffield Submissions for the WMT18 Quality Estimation Shared Task. In *Proc. of the Third Conference on Machine Translation: Shared Task Papers*, pages 794–800.

Eric Jones, Travis Oliphant, Pearu Peterson, et al. 2001. SciPy: Open source scientific tools for Python. [Online; accessed on May 17th, 2019].

Fábio Kepler, Jonay Trénous, Marcos Treviso, Miguel Vera, and André F. T. Martins. 2019. OpenKiwi: An Open Source Framework for Quality Estimation. In *Proc. of the Annual Meeting of the Association for Computational Linguistics, System Demonstration*. Association for Computational Linguistics.

Hyun Kim, Jong-Hyeok Lee, and Seung-Hoon Na. 2017. Predictor-Estimator using Multilevel Task Learning with Stack Propagation for Neural Quality Estimation. In *Conference on Machine Translation (WMT)*.

Guillaume Klein, Yoon Kim, Yuntian Deng, Jean Senellart, and Alexander M Rush. 2017. OpenNMT: Open-Source Toolkit for Neural Machine Translation. *arXiv preprint arXiv:1701.02810*.

Guillaume Lample and Alexis Conneau. 2019. Cross-lingual Language Model Pretraining. *arXiv preprint arXiv:1901.07291*.

António V. Lopes, M. Amin Farajian, Gonçalo Correia, Jonay Trenous, and André F. T. Martins. 2019. Unbabel's Submission to the WMT2019 APE Shared Task: Bert encoder-decoder for Automatic Post-Editing. In *Under review*.

André F. T Martins, Miguel B. Almeida, and Noah A. Smith. 2013. Turning on the Turbo: Fast Third-Order Non-Projective Turbo Parsers. In *Proc. of the Annual Meeting of the Association for Computational Linguistics*.

André F. T. Martins, Ramon Astudillo, Chris Hokamp, and Fábio Kepler. 2016. Unbabel's Participation in the WMT16 Word-Level Translation Quality Estimation Shared Task. In *Conference on Machine Translation (WMT)*.

André F. T. Martins, Marcin Junczys-Dowmunt, Fabio Kepler, Ramon Astudillo, Chris Hokamp, and Roman Grundkiewicz. 2017. Pushing the Limits of Translation Quality Estimation. *Transactions of the Association for Computational Linguistics (to appear)*.

Matteo Negri, Marco Turchi, Rajen Chatterjee, and Nicola Bertoldi. 2018. eSCAPE: a Large-scale Synthetic Corpus for Automatic Post-Editing. *arXiv preprint arXiv:1803.07274*.

Franz Josef Och. 2003. Minimum Error Rate Training in Statistical Machine Translation. In *Proceedings of the 41st Annual Meeting on Association for Computational Linguistics-Volume 1*, pages 160–167. Association for Computational Linguistics.

Michael J. D. Powell. 1964. An Efficient Method for Finding the Minimum of a Function of Several Variables without Calculating Derivatives. *The Computer Journal*, 7(2):155–162.

Lucia Specia, Carolina Scarton, and Gustavo Henrique Paetzold. 2018. Quality Estimation for Machine Translation. *Synthesis Lectures on Human Language Technologies*, 11(1):1–162.

Jiayi Wang, Kai Fan, Bo Li, Fengming Zhou, Boxing Chen, Yangbin Shi, and Luo Si. 2018. Alibaba Submission for WMT18 Quality Estimation Task. In *Conference on Machine Translation (WMT)*.

QE BERT: Bilingual BERT using Multi-task Learning
for Neural Quality Estimation

Hyun Kim and **Joon-Ho Lim** and **Hyun-Ki Kim**
SW & Contents Research Laboratory,
Electronics and Telecommunications Research Institute (ETRI), Republic of Korea
{h.kim, joonho.lim, hkk}@etri.re.kr

Seung-Hoon Na
Computer Science and Engineering,
Chonbuk National University, Republic of Korea
nash@jbnu.ac.kr

Abstract

For translation quality estimation at word and sentence levels, this paper presents a novel approach based on BERT that recently has achieved impressive results on various natural language processing tasks. Our proposed model is re-purposed BERT for the translation quality estimation and uses *multi-task learning* for the sentence-level task and word-level subtasks (i.e., source word, target word, and target gap). Experimental results on Quality Estimation shared task of WMT19 show that our systems show competitive results and provide significant improvements over the baseline.

1 Introduction

Translation quality estimation (QE) has become an important research topic in the field of machine translation (MT), which is used to estimate quality scores and categories for a machine-translated sentence without reference translations at various levels (Specia et al., 2013).

Recent Predictor-Estimator architecture-based approaches (Kim and Lee, 2016a,b; Kim et al., 2017a,b, 2019; LI et al., 2018; Wang et al., 2018) have significantly improved QE performance. The Predictor-Estimator (Kim and Lee, 2016a,b; Kim et al., 2017a,b, 2019) is based on a modified neural encoder architecture that consists of two subsequent neural models: 1) a word prediction model, which predicts each target word given the source sentence and the left and right context of the target word, and 2) a quality estimation model, which estimates sentence-level scores and word-level labels from features produced by the predictor. The word prediction model is trained from additional large-scale parallel data and the quality estimation model is trained from small-scale QE data.

Recently, BERT (Devlin et al., 2018) has led to impressive improvements on various natural language processing tasks. BERT is a bidirectionally trained language model from large-scale "monolingual" data to learn the "monolingual" context of a word based on all of its surroundings (left and right of the word).

Both BERT that is based on the Transformer architecture (Vaswani et al., 2017) and the word prediction model in the Predictor-Estimator that is based on the attention-based recurrent neural network (RNN) encoder-decoder architecture (Bahdanau et al., 2015; Cho et al., 2014) have some common ground utilizing generative pretraining of sentence encoder.

In this paper, we propose a "bilingual" BERT using multi-task learning for translation quality estimation (called the QE BERT). We describe how we have applied BERT (Devlin et al., 2018) to the QE task to make much improvements. In addition, for recent QE task, which consists of one sentence-level subtask to predict HTER scores and three word-level subtasks to detect errors for each source word, target (mt) word, and target (mt) gap, we also have applied multi-task learning (Kim et al., 2019, 2017b) to enhance the training data from other QE subtasks[1]. The results of experiments conducted on the WMT19 QE datasets show that our proposed QE BERT using multi-task learning provides significant improvements over the baseline system.

2 QE BERT

In this section, we describe two training steps for QE BERT: pre-training and fine-tuning. Figure 1 shows QE BERT architecture to predict HTER scores in sentence-level subtask and to detect errors in word-level source word, mt word, and mt gap subtasks. The sentences are tokenized using

---

[1] Kim et al. (2019, 2017b) use multi-task learning to take into account the training data of other QE subtasks as alternative route of handling the insufficiency of target training data.

Proceedings of the Fourth Conference on Machine Translation (WMT), Volume 3: Shared Task Papers (Day 2) pages 85–89
Florence, Italy, August 1-2, 2019. ©2019 Association for Computational Linguistics

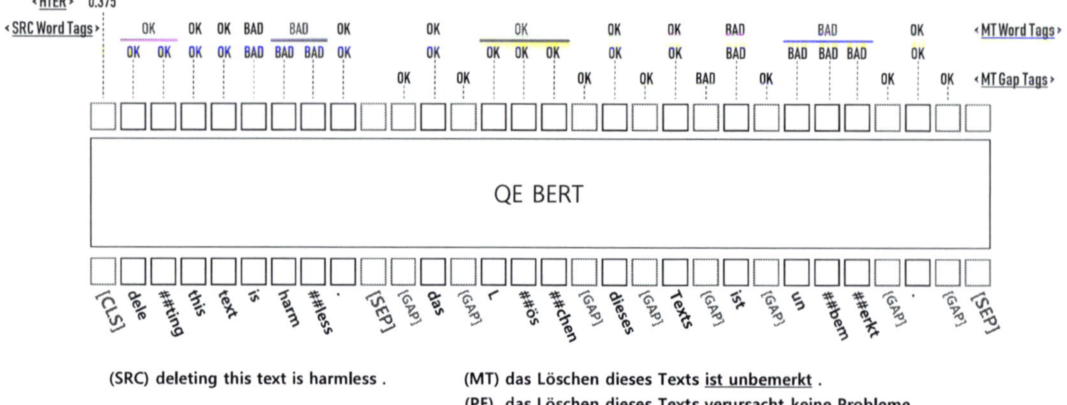

Figure 1: QE BERT architecture.

WordPiece tokenization.

2.1 Pre-training

The original BERT (Devlin et al., 2018) is focused on "monolingual" natural language understanding using generative pretraining of sentence encoder. QE BERT, which is focused on "bilingual" natural language understanding[2], is pre-trained from parallel data to learn the bilingual context of a word based on all of its left and right surroundings.

In pre-training, a default [SEP] token is used to separate source sentence and target sentence of parallel data. In addition, [GAP] tokens, which are newly introduced in this paper for word-level target gap, are inserted between target words.

As a pre-training task of QE BERT, only the masked LM task between parallel sentences is conducted where 15% of the words are replaced with a [MASK] token and then original values of the masked words are predicted[3]. The pre-training enables to make a large-scale parallel data helpful to QE task. As an initial checkpoint of pre-training, we used the released multilingual model[4].

2.2 Fine-tuning

QE BERT is fine-tuned from QE data with the above pre-trained model for a target-specific QE task.

Similar to the pre-training step, a [SEP] token is used to separate source sentence and machine translation sentence of QE data. [GAP] tokens are inserted between words of the machine translation sentence.

2.2.1 Word-level QE

To compute a word-level QE, the final hidden state (h_t) corresponds to each token embedding is used as follows:

$$P = \mathrm{softmax}(W_{\bullet} \, h_t) \tag{1}$$

where P is the label probabilities and W is the weight matrix used for word-level fine-tuning. Because word-level QE task consists of source word, mt word, and mt gap subtasks, three different types of weight matrix are used for each task: $W_{src.word}$, $W_{mt.word}$, and $W_{mt.gap}$.

Because each word of sentences could be tokenized to several tokens, we primarily compute the token-level labels as follows:

$$\mathrm{QE_{token}} = \begin{cases} \mathrm{OK} \;\; , & \text{if } \mathrm{argmax}(P) = 1 \\ \mathrm{BAD}, & \text{if } \mathrm{argmax}(P) = 0. \end{cases} \tag{2}$$

And then, we compute word-level labels from the token-level labels. In training, if a word is labeled as 'BAD', all of tokens in the word boundary have 'BAD' labels. In inference, if any token in the word boundary is labeled as 'BAD', the output of the word-level QE has a 'BAD' label.

2.2.2 Sentence-level QE

To compute a sentence-level QE, the final hidden state (h_s) corresponds to the [CLS] token embed-

---

[2]In Lample and Conneau (2019), translation language model (TLM) pretraining is used for cross-lingual understanding by concatenating parallel sentences.

[3]In Devlin et al. (2018), two pre-training tasks – masked LM and next sentence prediction – are conducted simultaneously.

[4]"BERT-Base Multilingual Cased" model, released in https://github.com/google-research/bert.

ding, which is a fixed-dimensional pooled representation of the input sequence, is used as follows:

$$QE_{sent} = \text{sigmoid}(W_s \, h_s) \qquad (3)$$

where W_s is the weight matrix used for sentence-level fine-tuning.

2.2.3 Multi-task learning

The QE subtasks at word and sentence levels are highly related because their quality annotations are commonly based on the HTER measure. Quality annotated data of other QE subtasks could be helpful in training a QE model specific to a target QE task (Kim et al., 2019). To take into account the training data of other QE subtasks as a route of supplementation of target training data, we apply multi-task learning (Kim et al., 2019, 2017b).

For multi-task learning of word-level QE, we use a linear summation of word-level objective losses as follows:

$$\mathcal{L}_{WORD} = \mathcal{L}_{src.word} + \mathcal{L}_{mt.word} + \mathcal{L}_{mt.gap}$$

where most QE BERT components are common across word-level source word, mt word, and mt gap subtasks except for the output matrices $W_{src.word}$, $W_{mt.word}$, and $W_{mt.gap}$.

Kim et al. (2019) showed that it is helpful to use word-level training examples for training a sentence-level QE model. For multi-task learning of sentence-level QE, we combine sentence-level objective loss and word-level objective losses by simply performing a linear summation of the losses for each task as follows:

$$\mathcal{L}_{SENT} = \mathcal{L}_{hter} + \mathcal{L}_{src.word} + \mathcal{L}_{mt.word} + \mathcal{L}_{mt.gap}$$

where most QE BERT components are common across sentence-level and word-level tasks except for the output matrices of each task.

3 Experimentation

3.1 Experimental settings

The proposed learning methods were evaluated on the WMT19 QE Shared Task[5] of word-level and sentence-level English-Russian and English-German.

We used parallel data provided for the WMT19 news machine translation task[6] to pre-train QE BERT. The English-Russian parallel data set consisted of the ParaCrawl corpus, Common Crawl corpus, News Commentary corpus, and Yandex Corpus. The English-German parallel data set consisted of the Europarl corpus, ParaCrawl corpus, Common Crawl corpus, News Commentary corpus, and Document-split Rapid corpus.

In pre-training, we used the default hyperparameter setting of the released multilingual model. In fine-turing, a sequence length of 512 was used to cover the length of QE data.

To make ensembles, we combined five instances having different hyperparameter weight for 'BAD' label (i.e., 1:10, 1:15, 1:20, 1:25, and 1:30). For word-level ensemble results, we voted the predicted labels from each instance. For sentence-level ensemble results, we averaged the predicted HTER scores from each instance.

3.2 Comparison of learning methods

Tables 1 and 2 show the experimental results obtained from the QE BERT using the different learning methods for the WMT19 word-level and sentence-level QE tasks. For both language pairs, using multi-task learning consistently improves the scores.

We made ensembles by combining five instances of QE BERT models. The word-level results of ensemble A are based on mixtures of the best performance systems on each subtasks (i.e., source word, mt word, and mt gap tasks). On the other hand, the word-level results of ensemble B are based on an all-in-one system using a unified criterion[7] with same model parameters for all word-level subtasks.

Finally, Tables 3 and 4 show the results obtained in the WMT19 test set for our submitted systems and official baseline systems.

4 Conclusion

In this paper, we explored an adaptation of BERT for translation quality estimation. Because the quality estimation task consists of one sentence-level subtask to predict HTER scores and three word-level subtasks to detect errors for each source word, target word, and target gap, we also applied multi-task learning to enhance the training data from other subtasks. The results of experiments conducted on WMT19 quality estimation datasets strongly confirmed that our proposed bilingual BERT using multi-task learning

---

[5] http://www.statmt.org/wmt19/qe-task.html

[6] http://www.statmt.org/wmt19/translation-task.html

[7] The averaged performance on source word, mt word, and mt gap tasks is used as the unified criterion to select model parameters of the all-in-one system.

Word level	Source Word			MT (All)		
	(F_1-**Mult** ↑	F_1-BAD ↑	F_1-OK ↑)	(F_1-**Mult** ↑	F_1-BAD ↑	F_1-OK ↑)
<**English-Russian**>						
QE-BERT Word	0.3344	0.3663	0.9128	0.3895	0.4051	0.9617
QE-BERT Multitask-Word	0.3513	0.3780	0.9294	0.3943	0.4076	0.9673
QE-BERT Multitask-Word Ensemble A*	<u>0.3600</u>	0.3861	0.9326	<u>0.4128</u>	0.4275	0.9657
QE-BERT Multitask-Word Ensemble B*	0.3452	0.3700	0.9331	0.3934	0.4071	0.9665
<**English-German**>						
QE-BERT Word	0.3755	0.4113	0.9130	0.4028	0.4198	0.9595
QE-BERT Multitask-Word	0.3918	0.4288	0.9138	0.4074	0.4258	0.9567
QE-BERT Multitask-Word Ensemble A*	<u>0.4044</u>	0.4391	0.9210	<u>0.4318</u>	0.4501	0.9593
QE-BERT Multitask-Word Ensemble B*	0.3916	0.4262	0.9189	0.4288	0.4466	0.9602

Word level	MT Word			MT Gap		
	(F_1-**Mult** ↑	F_1-BAD ↑	F_1-OK ↑)	(F_1-**Mult** ↑	F_1-BAD ↑	F_1-OK ↑)
<**English-Russian**>						
QE-BERT Word	0.4215	0.4561	0.9240	0.1609	0.1631	0.9863
QE-BERT Multitask-Word	0.4313	0.4616	0.9344	0.1734	0.1758	0.9866
QE-BERT Multitask-Word Ensemble A*	<u>0.4354</u>	0.4642	0.9381	<u>0.1791</u>	0.1812	0.9884
QE-BERT Multitask-Word Ensemble B*	0.4180	0.4446	0.9403	0.1710	0.1730	0.9882
<**English-German**>						
QE-BERT Word	0.4307	0.4640	0.9283	0.2729	0.2765	0.9871
QE-BERT Multitask-Word	0.4365	0.4724	0.9241	0.2936	0.2983	0.9840
QE-BERT Multitask-Word Ensemble A*	0.4429	0.4766	0.9293	<u>0.3060</u>	0.3107	0.9849
QE-BERT Multitask-Word Ensemble B*	<u>0.4443</u>	0.4767	0.9320	0.2884	0.2930	0.9845

* Our submissions at the WMT19 QE task

Table 1: Results of the QE BERT model on the *development* set of the WMT19 *word-level* QE task.

Sentence level	Pearson's r ↑	Spearman's ρ ↑	MAE ↓	RMSE ↓
<**English-Russian**>				
QE-BERT Sent	0.4683	0.4524	0.1151	0.2072
QE-BERT Multitask-Sent-Word	0.4948	0.4908	0.1106	0.2056
QE-BERT Multitask-Sent-Word Ensemble*	<u>0.5229</u>	0.5102	0.1080	0.2016
<**English-German**>				
QE-BERT Sent	0.4849	0.5401	0.1072	0.1698
QE-BERT Multitask-Sent-Word	0.5199	0.5859	0.1026	0.1670
QE-BERT Multitask-Sent-Word Ensemble*	<u>0.5450</u>	0.6229	0.0978	0.1665

* Our submissions at the WMT19 QE task

Table 2: Results of the QE BERT model on the *development* set of the WMT19 *sentence-level* QE task.

Word level	Source Word F_1-**Mult** ↑	MT (All) F_1-**Mult** ↑
<**English-Russian**>		
Baseline	0.2647	0.2412
QE-BERT Multitask-Word Ensemble A*	<u>0.4202</u>	<u>0.4515</u>
QE-BERT Multitask-Word Ensemble B*	0.4114	0.4300
<**English-German**>		
Baseline	0.2908	0.2974
QE-BERT Multitask-Word Ensemble A*	0.3946	<u>0.4061</u>
QE-BERT Multitask-Word Ensemble B*	<u>0.3960</u>	0.4047

* Our submissions at the WMT19 QE task

Table 3: Results of the QE BERT model on the *test* set of the WMT19 *word-level* QE task.

Sentence level	Pearson's r ↑	Spearman's ρ ↑
<**English-Russian**>		
Baseline	0.2601	0.2339
QE-BERT Multitask-Sent-Word Ensemble*	<u>0.5327</u>	0.5222
<**English-German**>		
Baseline	0.4001	0.4607
QE-BERT Multitask-Sent-Word Ensemble*	<u>0.5260</u>	0.5745

* Our submissions at the WMT19 QE task

Table 4: Results of the QE BERT model on the *test* set of the WMT19 *sentence-level* QE task.

achieved significant improvements. Given this promising approach, we believe that BERT-based quality estimation models can be further advanced with more investigation.

Acknowledgments

This work was supported by Institute for Information & Communications Technology Planning & Evaluation (IITP) grant funded by the Korea government (MSIT) (No.2013-2-00131, Development of Knowledge Evolutionary WiseQA Platform Technology for Human Knowledge Augmented Services).

References

Dzmitry Bahdanau, Kyunghyun Cho, and Yoshua Bengio. 2015. Neural machine translation by jointly learning to align and translate. In *ICLR 2015*.

Kyunghyun Cho, Bart van Merrienboer, Caglar Gulcehre, Dzmitry Bahdanau, Fethi Bougares, Holger Schwenk, and Yoshua Bengio. 2014. Learning phrase representations using rnn encoder–decoder for statistical machine translation. In *Proceedings of the 2014 Conference on Empirical Methods in Natural Language Processing (EMNLP)*, pages 1724–1734, Doha, Qatar. Association for Computational Linguistics.

Jacob Devlin, Ming-Wei Chang, Kenton Lee, and Kristina Toutanova. 2018. BERT: pre-training of deep bidirectional transformers for language understanding. *CoRR*, abs/1810.04805.

Hyun Kim, Hun-Young Jung, Hongseok Kwon, Jong-Hyeok Lee, and Seung-Hoon Na. 2017a. Predictor-estimator: Neural quality estimation based on target word prediction for machine translation. *ACM Trans. Asian Low-Resour. Lang. Inf. Process.*, 17(1):3:1–3:22.

Hyun Kim and Jong-Hyeok Lee. 2016a. Recurrent neural network based translation quality estimation. In *Proceedings of the First Conference on Machine Translation*, pages 787–792, Berlin, Germany. Association for Computational Linguistics.

Hyun Kim and Jong-Hyeok Lee. 2016b. A recurrent neural networks approach for estimating the quality of machine translation output. In *Proceedings of the 2016 Conference of the North American Chapter of the Association for Computational Linguistics: Human Language Technologies*, pages 494–498, San Diego, California. Association for Computational Linguistics.

Hyun Kim, Jong-Hyeok Lee, and Seung-Hoon Na. 2017b. Predictor-estimator using multilevel task learning with stack propagation for neural quality estimation. In *Proceedings of the Second Conference on Machine Translation, Volume 2: Shared Task Papers*, pages 562–568, Copenhagen, Denmark. Association for Computational Linguistics.

Hyun Kim, Jong-Hyeok Lee, and Seung-Hoon Na. 2019. Multi-task stack propagation for neural quality estimation. *ACM Trans. Asian Low-Resour. Lang. Inf. Process.*, 18(4):48:1–48:18.

Guillaume Lample and Alexis Conneau. 2019. Cross-lingual language model pretraining. *CoRR*, abs/1901.07291.

Maoxi LI, Qingyu XIANG, Zhiming CHEN, and Mingwen WANG. 2018. A unified neural network for quality estimation of machine translation. *IEICE Transactions on Information and Systems*, E101.D(9):2417–2421.

Lucia Specia, Kashif Shah, Jose G.C. de Souza, and Trevor Cohn. 2013. Quest - a translation quality estimation framework. In *Proceedings of the 51st Annual Meeting of the Association for Computational Linguistics: System Demonstrations*, pages 79–84, Sofia, Bulgaria. Association for Computational Linguistics.

Ashish Vaswani, Noam Shazeer, Niki Parmar, Jakob Uszkoreit, Llion Jones, Aidan N. Gomez, Lukasz Kaiser, and Illia Polosukhin. 2017. Attention is all you need. *CoRR*, abs/1706.03762.

Jiayi Wang, Kai Fan, Bo Li, Fengming Zhou, Boxing Chen, Yangbin Shi, and Luo Si. 2018. Alibaba submission for wmt18 quality estimation task. In *Proceedings of the Third Conference on Machine Translation, Volume 2: Shared Task Papers*, pages 822–828, Belgium, Brussels. Association for Computational Linguistics.

MIPT System for World-Level Quality Estimation

Mikhail Mosyagin
MIPT, Russia
`mosyagin.md@phystech.edu`

Varvara Logacheva
Neural Networks and Deep Learning Lab
MIPT, Russia
`logacheva.vk@mipt.ru`

Abstract

We explore different model architectures for the WMT 19 shared task on word-level quality estimation of automatic translation. We start with a model similar to Shef-bRNN (Ive et al., 2018), which we modify by using conditional random fields (CRFs) (Lafferty et al., 2001) for sequence labelling. Additionally, we use a different approach for labelling gaps and source words. We further develop this model by including features from different sources such as BERT (Devlin et al., 2018), baseline features for the task (Specia et al., 2018) and transformer encoders (Vaswani et al., 2017). We evaluate the performance of our models on the English-German dataset for the corresponding task.

1 Introduction

Current methods of assessing the quality of machine translation, like BLEU (Papineni et al., 2002), are based on comparing the output of a machine translation system with several gold reference translations. The tasks of quality estimation at the WMT 19 conference aims at detecting errors in automatic translation without a reference translation at various levels (word-level, sentence-level and document-level). In this work we predict word-level quality.

In the task the participants are given a source sentence and its automatic translation and are asked to label the words in the machine translation as *OK* or *BAD*. The machine translation system could have omitted some words in the translated sentence. To detect such errors participants are also asked to label the gaps in the automatic translation. A target sentence has a gap between every pair of neighboring words, one gap in the beginning of the sentence and one gap at the end of the sentence. We are also interested in detecting the words in the source sentence that led to

errors in the translation. For this purpose participants are also asked to label the words in source sentences. The source labels were obtained based on the alignments between the source and the post-edited target sentences. If a target token is labeled as *BAD* in the translation, then all source tokens aligned to it are labeled as *BAD* as well.

In section 2 we introduce our base model, which is a modified version of phrase-level Shef-bRNN (Ive et al., 2018), and further develop it by using different methods of extracting features from the input alongside the bi-RNN features. In section 3 we write about our experimental setup and in section 4 we present the scores achieved by our models. In section 5 we summarize our work and propose ways for further development.

2 Models

All of our models have two stages: feature extraction and tag prediction. The first stage uses different neural architectures like bi-LSTM encoder and BERT (Devlin et al., 2018) to extract features from the input sequences. Some models also use human-crafted features alongside the automatically generated ones. The second stage feeds the sequence of extracted features into a CRF (Lafferty et al., 2001) to obtain labels for words or gaps in the automatic translation.

2.1 RNN Features

Our base model is similar to phrase-level Shef-bRNN (Ive et al., 2018). We chose the phrase-level version of Shef-bRNN over the word-level version because we found it to be more understandable and intuitive.

The model is given a sequence of source tokens $s_1, \ldots, s_n$ and a sequence of target tokens $t_1, \ldots, t_m$. The source sequence is fed into the source encoder, which is a bidirectional LSTM.

Proceedings of the Fourth Conference on Machine Translation (WMT), Volume 3: Shared Task Papers (Day 2) pages 90–94
Florence, Italy, August 1-2, 2019. ©2019 Association for Computational Linguistics

Thus, for every word s_j in the source a source vector $h_j^{\text{src}} = \left[\vec{h}_j^{\text{src}}, \overleftarrow{h}_j^{\text{src}}\right]$ is produced, where $\vec{h}_j^{\text{src}}$ and $\overleftarrow{h}_j^{\text{src}}$ are the corresponding hidden states of the forward and backward LSTMs and $[x, y]$ is the concatenation of vectors x and y. Similarly, the target sequence is fed into the target encoder, which is also a bidirectional LSTM, to obtain a target vector h_j^{tgt} for every word t_j in the target sequence. Global attention (Luong et al., 2015) is used to obtain context vector c_j for every target vector h_j^{tgt}:

$$\alpha_{ij} = h_i^{\text{src}\top} h_j^{\text{tgt}},$$

$$a_{ij} = \frac{\exp(\alpha_{ij})}{\sum_{k=1}^{n} \exp(\alpha_{kj})},$$

$$c_j = \sum_{k=1}^{n} a_{kj} h_k^{\text{src}}.$$

The vector c_j gives a summary of the source sentence, focusing on parts which are most relevant to the target token. Using the same technique, we obtain self-context vector sc_j for every target vector h_j^{tgt} by computing global attention for h_j^{tgt} over $h_i^{\text{tgt}}, i \neq j$. The resulting feature vector is denoted as $f_j^{\text{RNN}} = \left[h_j^{\text{tgt}}, c_j, sc_j\right]$ for every word t_j in the target sequence.

2.2 Baseline Features

Specia et al. (2018) use a CRF (Lafferty et al., 2001) with a set of human-crafted features as the baseline model for the same task at WMT 18. The WMT 18 and WMT 19 tasks use the same English-German dataset, so we can use the baseline features provided with the WMT 18 dataset to further improve the performance our model.

For every word t_j in the target sequence baseline features represent a sequence of 34 values: $b_j^1, \ldots, b_j^{34}$, some of which are numerical – like the word count in source and target sentences – and the others are categorical – like the target token, aligned source token and their part-of-speech (POS) tags. We represent categorical features using one-hot encoding. In this case if a value of a categorical feature occurs less than min_occurs times in the train dataset, then this value is ignored (i.e. it is represented by a zero vector). After the conversion all features are concatenated into a single feature vector f_j^{Base}

2.3 BERT Features

BERT is a model for language representation presented by Delvin et al. (2018) which demonstrated state of the art performance on several NLP tasks. BERT is trained on a word prediction task and, as shown in (Kim et al., 2017), word prediction can be helpful for the quality estimation task. Pretrained versions of BERT are publicly available and we use one of them to generate features for our models.

To extract BERT features the target sequence is fed into a pretrained BERT model. It is important to note that we do not fine-tune BERT and just use its pretrained version as-is. BERT utilizes WordPiece tokenization (Wu et al., 2016), so for each target token t_j it produces k_j output vectors $\text{BERT}_j^1, \ldots, \text{BERT}_j^{k_j}$. However, we can only use a fixed size feature vector for each source token. We noticed that about 83% of target tokens produce less than three BERT tokens. This means that by using only two of the produced tokens we will preserve most of the information. To obtain the BERT feature vector, we decided to concatenate the first and the last BERT outputs $f_j^{\text{BERT}} = \left[\text{BERT}_j^1, \text{BERT}_j^{k_j}\right]$. We chose the first and the last outputs, because this approach was the easiest to implement.

2.4 Transformer Encoder

We tried replacing bi-RNN encoders with transformer encoders (Vaswani et al., 2017) to include more contextual information in the encoder outputs.

The source transformer encoder produces embeddings $h_1^{\text{src}}, \ldots, h_n^{\text{src}}$ for the source sequence and the target transformer encoder produces outputs $h_1^{\text{tgt}}, \ldots, h_m^{\text{tgt}}$ for the target sequence. After that, similarly to 2.1, a context vector c_j is obtained for every word in the target sequence. For transformer encoder we do not compute self-context vectors as the transformer architecture itself utilizes the self-attention mechanism.

The resulting feature vector is denoted as $f_j^{\text{Trf}} = \left[h_j^{\text{tgt}}, c_j\right]$.

2.5 Word Labelling

After the feature vectors for the target sequence have been obtained, they are fed into a CRF that labels the words in the translation. In this paper we explore architectures that use the following feature vectors:

- RNN: f_j^{RNN};

- RNN+Baseline:

$$f_j^{\text{RNN+Baseline}} = \left[f_j^{\text{RNN}}, f_j^{\text{Base}}\right];$$

- RNN+BERT:

$$f_j^{\text{RNN+BERT}} = \left[f_j^{\text{RNN}}, f_j^{\text{BERT}}\right];$$

- RNN+Baseline+BERT:

$$f_j^{\text{RNN+Baseline+BERT}} =$$
$$= \left[f_j^{\text{RNN}}, f_j^{\text{Base}}, f_j^{\text{BERT}}\right];$$

- Transformer: f_j^{Trf}.

- Transformer+Baseline+BERT:

$$f_j^{\text{Transformer+Baseline+BERT}} =$$
$$= \left[f_j^{\text{Trf}}, f_j^{\text{Base}}, f_j^{\text{BERT}}\right];$$

To label words in the source sequence we use the alignments between the source sentence and the machine translation provided with the dataset. Specifically, if a source word s_j is aligned with a target word t_j, which is labeled as *BAD* then we label s_j as *BAD* as well. In case when s_j is aligned with multiple target words, we label s_j as *BAD* if at least one of the aligned target words is labeled *BAD*.

2.6 Gap Labelling

Unlike word-level Shef-bRNN, we refrain from using a dummy word to predict gap tags, because increasing the input sequence length might make it difficult for encoders to carry information between distant words. Instead, we train different models for word labelling and gap labelling.

To modify a word labelling architecture *Arch*, where *Arch* is either *RNN+Baseline+BERT* or *Transformer+Baseline+BERT*, to label gaps, we construct a new sequence of features:

$$fg_j^{\text{Arch}} = \left[f_j^{\text{Arch}}, f_{j+1}^{\text{Arch}}\right]$$

for $j = 0, \ldots, m$. Here we assume f_0^{Arch} and f_{m+1}^{Arch} to be zero vectors.

After the new sequence has been constructed, we feed it into a CRF to label the gaps.

3 Experimental Setup

We train and evaluate our models on the WMT 19 Word-Level Quality Estimation Task English-German dataset. In our experiments we did not utilize pre-training or multi-task learning unlike some versions of Shef-bRNN. All our models were implemented in PyTorch, the code is available online. [1]

For RNN feature extraction we use OpenNMT (Klein et al., 2017) bi-LSTM encoder implementation with 300 hidden units in both backward and forward LSTMs for models that label words and 150 hidden units for models that label gaps. We used FastText models (Grave et al., 2018) for English and German languages to produce word embeddings.

Baseline features were provided with the dataset. In our experiments we used min_occurs $= 4$ when building baseline feature vocabularies.

Pretrained BERT model was provided by the *pytorch-pretrained-bert* package. [2] In our experiments we used the *bert-base-multilingual-cased* version of BERT.

We used the OpenNMT (Klein et al., 2017) transformer encoder implementation with the following parameters: num_layers $= 3$, d_model $= 300$, heads $= 4$, d_ff $= 600$ (or d_ff $= 300$ for gap labelling), dropout $= 0.1$.

We trained our models using PyTorch implementation of the ADADELTA algorithm (Zeiler, 2012) with all parameters, except the learning rate, set to their default values. For the train loss to converge we used the learning rate of 1 for the *RNN* and *Transformer* models, the learning rate of 0.3 for the *RNN+Baseline* model and the learning rate of 0.1 for *RNN+Bert*, *RNN+Baseline+Bert* and *Transformer+Baseline+Bert* models. The inputs were fed into the model in mini-batches of 10 samples.

4 Results

We used the English-German dataset provided in the WMT 19 Shared task on Word-Level Quality Estimation. The primary metric for each type of tokens – source words, target words and gaps – is

---

[1] https://github.com/Mogby/
QualityEstimation
[2] https://github.com/huggingface/
pytorch-pretrained-BERT

F_1 *Mult* which is the product of F_1 scores for *BAD* and *OK* labels.

The scores for each system are presented in Table 1 (participation results), Table 2 (target words), Table 3 (source words) and Table 4 (gaps). For the WMT 19 task we submitted the *RNN+Baseline+BERT* and *Transformer+Baseline+BERT* models which correspond to the *Neural CRF RNN* and *Neural CRF Transformer* entries in the public leaderboard.

We don't have the scores for the WMT 18 Baseline system and the Shef-bRNN system on the development dataset, so we can compare them directly with only two of our systems from table 1. Both of these systems perform on par with Shef-bRNN and the *Transformer+Baseline+BERT* model was able to achieve a slightly better score for target classification. Word-level Shef-bRNN seems to outperform all of our other systems, most likely, because it uses a more appropriate architecture for the task. All of our systems, seem to outperform the WMT 18 baseline system.

The BERT features turned out to improve the performance a little – an increase of 0.02 for target labelling and an increase of 0.01 for source labelling. The baseline features, on the other hand, have a greater impact on the model's performance, increasing the score by 0.05 for target labelling and by 0.04 for source labelling. Replacing the bi-RNN encoder with a transformer encoder also improved the score by 0.03 in case of the *RNN+Baseline+BERT* configuration.

5 Conclusion

We applied different neural systems to the task of word-level quality estimation. We measured their performance in comparison to each other and the baseline system for the task. All of our systems outperformed the WMT 18 baseline on the development dataset and can be trained in a couple of hours on a single Tesla K80 GPU.

Our models can be further improved by fine-tuning BERT and utilizing multi-task learning as proposed in (Kim et al., 2017).

References

Jacob Devlin, Ming-Wei Chang, Kenton Lee, and Kristina Toutanova. 2018. BERT: pre-training of deep bidirectional transformers for language understanding. *CoRR*, abs/1810.04805.

Edouard Grave, Piotr Bojanowski, Prakhar Gupta, Armand Joulin, and Tomas Mikolov. 2018. Learning word vectors for 157 languages. In *Proceedings of the International Conference on Language Resources and Evaluation (LREC 2018)*.

Julia Ive, Carolina Scarton, Frédéric Blain, and Lucia Specia. 2018. Sheffield submissions for the WMT18 quality estimation shared task. In *Proceedings of the Third Conference on Machine Translation: Shared Task Papers, WMT 2018, Belgium, Brussels, October 31 - November 1, 2018*, pages 794–800.

Hyun Kim, Jong-Hyeok Lee, and Seung-Hoon Na. 2017. Predictor-estimator using multilevel task learning with stack propagation for neural quality estimation. pages 562–568.

Guillaume Klein, Yoon Kim, Yuntian Deng, Jean Senellart, and Alexander M. Rush. 2017. Opennmt: Open-source toolkit for neural machine translation. In *Proc. ACL*.

John D. Lafferty, Andrew McCallum, and Fernando C. N. Pereira. 2001. Conditional random fields: Probabilistic models for segmenting and labeling sequence data. In *Proceedings of the Eighteenth International Conference on Machine Learning (ICML 2001), Williams College, Williamstown, MA, USA, June 28 - July 1, 2001*, pages 282–289.

Minh-Thang Luong, Hieu Pham, and Christopher D. Manning. 2015. Effective approaches to attention-based neural machine translation. *CoRR*, abs/1508.04025.

Kishore Papineni, Salim Roukos, Todd Ward, and Wei-Jing Zhu. 2002. Bleu: a method for automatic evaluation of machine translation. In *Proceedings of 40th Annual Meeting of the Association for Computational Linguistics*, pages 311–318, Philadelphia, Pennsylvania, USA. Association for Computational Linguistics.

Lucia Specia, Frédéric Blain, Varvara Logacheva, Ramón Astudillo, and André F. T. Martins. 2018. Findings of the wmt 2018 shared task on quality estimation. In *Proceedings of the Third Conference on Machine Translation: Shared Task Papers*, pages 689–709, Belgium, Brussels. Association for Computational Linguistics.

Ashish Vaswani, Noam Shazeer, Niki Parmar, Jakob Uszkoreit, Llion Jones, Aidan N. Gomez, Lukasz Kaiser, and Illia Polosukhin. 2017. Attention is all you need. *CoRR*, abs/1706.03762.

Yonghui Wu, Mike Schuster, Zhifeng Chen, Quoc V. Le, Mohammad Norouzi, Wolfgang Macherey, Maxim Krikun, Yuan Cao, Qin Gao, Klaus Macherey, Jeff Klingner, Apurva Shah, Melvin Johnson, Xiaobing Liu, Lukasz Kaiser, Stephan Gouws, Yoshikiyo Kato, Taku Kudo, Hideto Kazawa, Keith Stevens, George Kurian, Nishant Patil, Wei Wang, Cliff Young, Jason Smith, Jason

Model	Target F_1 Mult	Source F_1 Mult
RNN + Baseline + BERT	0.30	0.26
Transformer + Baseline + BERT	**0.33**	**0.27**

Table 1: Final results on the test dataset.

Model	Dataset	F_1 OK	F_1 BAD	F_1 Mult
WMT 18 Baseline	test	0.20	0.92	0.18
Shef-bRNN (Word-Level)	test	0.86	0.35	0.30
RNN	dev	0.88	0.26	0.23
RNN + Baseline	dev	0.91	0.31	0.28
RNN + BERT	dev	0.88	0.29	0.25
RNN + Baseline + BERT	dev	0.88	0.34	0.30
Transformer	dev	0.90	0.25	0.23
Transformer + Baseline + BERT	dev	0.89	0.37	**0.33**

Table 2: Models scores on WMT 19 English-German dataset, target prediction. The baseline scores are taken from (Specia et al., 2018) and the Shef-bRNN scores are taken from (Ive et al., 2018)

Model	Dataset	F_1 OK	F_1 BAD	F_1 Mult
Shef-bRNN (Word-Level)	test	0.87	0.33	0.29
RNN	dev	0.88	0.22	0.19
RNN + Baseline	dev	0.90	0.25	0.23
RNN + BERT	dev	0.87	0.23	0.20
RNN + Baseline + BERT	dev	0.88	0.29	**0.25**
Transformer	dev	0.88	0.23	0.20
Transformer + Baseline + BERT	dev	0.89	0.28	**0.25**

Table 3: Models scores on WMT 19 English-German dataset, source prediction. The Shef-bRNN scores are taken from (Ive et al., 2018)

Model	Dataset	F_1 OK	F_1 BAD	F_1 Mult
Shef-bRNN (Word-Level)	test	0.99	0.12	0.12
RNN + Baseline + BERT	dev	0.98	0.14	0.14
Transformer + Baseline + BERT	dev	0.99	0.14	**0.14**

Table 4: Models scores on WMT 19 English-German dataset, gap prediction. The Shef-bRNN scores are taken from (Ive et al., 2018)

Riesa, Alex Rudnick, Oriol Vinyals, Greg Corrado, Macduff Hughes, and Jeffrey Dean. 2016. Google's neural machine translation system: Bridging the gap between human and machine translation. *CoRR*, abs/1609.08144.

Matthew D. Zeiler. 2012. ADADELTA: an adaptive learning rate method. *CoRR*, abs/1212.5701.

NJU Submissions for the WMT19 Quality Estimation Shared Task

Qi Hou, Shujian Huang,* Tianhao Ning, Xinyu Dai and **Jiajun Chen**
National Key Laboratory for Novel Software Technology, Nanjing, China
Nanjing University, Nanjing, China
{houq, huangsj, ningth, daixy, chenjj}@nlp.nju.edu.cn

Abstract

In this paper, we describe the submissions of the team from Nanjing University for the WMT19 sentence-level Quality Estimation (QE) shared task on English-German language pair. We develop two approaches based on a two-stage neural QE model consisting of a feature extractor and a quality estimator. More specifically, one of the proposed approaches employs the translation knowledge between the two languages from two different translation directions; while the other one employs extra monolingual knowledge from both source and target sides, obtained by pre-training deep self-attention networks. To efficiently train these two-stage models, a joint learning training method is applied. Experiments show that the ensemble model of the above two models achieves the best results on the benchmark dataset of the WMT17 sentence-level QE shared task and obtains competitive results in WMT19, ranking 3rd out of 10 submissions.

1 Introduction

Sentence-level Quality Estimation (QE) of Machine Translation (MT) is a task to predict the quality scores for unseen machine translation outputs at run-time, without relying on reference translations. There are some interesting applications of sentence-level QE, such as deciding whether a given translation is good enough for publishing, informing readers of the target language only whether or not they can rely on a translation, filtering out sentences that are not good enough for post-editing by professional translators, selecting the best translation among multiple MT systems and so on.

The common methods formalize the sentence-level QE as a supervised regression task. Traditional QE models (Specia et al., 2013, 2015) have

two independent modules: feature extractor module and machine learning module. The feature extractor module is used to extract human-crafted features, which describe the translation quality, such as source fluency indicators, translation complexity indicators, and adequacy indicators. And the machine learning module serves for predicting how much effort is needed to post-edit translations to acceptable results as measured by the Human-targeted Translation Edit Rate (HTER) (Snover et al., 2006) based on extracted features above.

With the great success of deep neural networks in a number of tasks in natural language processing (NLP), some researches have begun to apply neural networks to QE task and these neural approaches have shown promising results. Shah et al. (2015, 2016) combine neural features, such as word embedding features and neural network language model (NNLM) features with other features produced by QuEst++ (Specia et al., 2015). Kim and Lee (2016); Kim et al. (2017a,b) apply modified recurrent neural network (RNN) based neural machine translation (NMT) model (Bahdanau et al., 2014) to the sentence-level QE task, which does not require manual effort for finding the best relevant features. Wang et al. (2018) replace the above NMT model with modified self-attention mechanism based transformer model (Vaswani et al., 2017). This approach achieves the best result we know so far in the WMT17 sentence-level QE task on English-German language pair.

In this paper, we present two different approaches for the sentence-level QE task, which employ bi-directional translation knowledge and large-scale monolingual knowledge to the QE task, respectively. Also, a simple ensemble of them can help to achieve better quality estimation performance in the sentence-level QE task. The remainder of this paper is organized as follows. In Section 2 and Section 3, we separately describe

---

* Corresponding author.

Proceedings of the Fourth Conference on Machine Translation (WMT), Volume 3: Shared Task Papers (Day 2) pages 95–100
Florence, Italy, August 1-2, 2019. ©2019 Association for Computational Linguistics

the two proposed QE models above. In Section 4, we report experimental results and conclude our paper in Section 5.

2 Employing Bi-directional Translation Knowledge

Sennrich et al. (2015) apply the idea of back-translation to improve the performance of NMT model by extending the parallel corpus with monolingual data. Kozlova et al. (2016) propose two types of features including pseudo-references features for source sentence and back-translations features for machine translation to enrich the baseline features in sentence-level QE task. Inspired by these successful practices, we present a Bi-directional QE model, as depicted in Figure 1.

2.1 Model Architecture

The Bi-directional QE model contains a neural feature extractor and a neural quality estimator. The feature extractor relies on two symmetric word predictors to extract quality estimation feature vectors (QEFVs) of the source sentence and target sentence (i.e., machine translation output). The quality estimator is based on two identical Bi-directional RNN (BiRNN) (Schuster and Paliwal, 1997) for predicting quality scores using QEFVs as inputs.

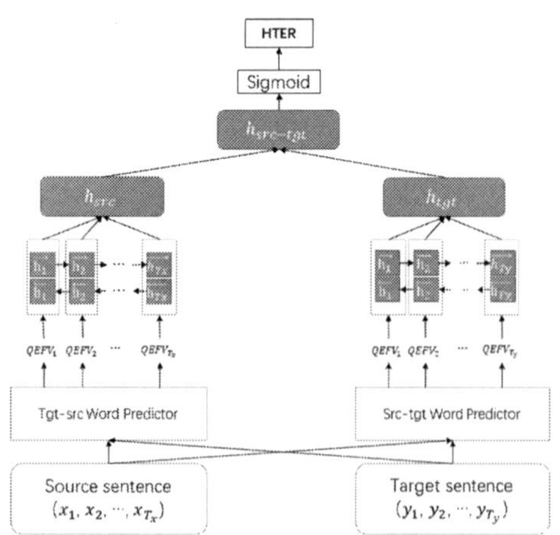

Figure 1: An illustration of the architecture of the proposed Bi-directional QE model.

The source-to-target word predictor modifies self-attention mechanism based transformer model (Vaswani et al., 2017) to i) apply additional backward decoder for the target sentence with the right to left masked self-attention and ii) generate QEFVs for target words as outputs, which is similar with QEBrain model as described in Wang et al. (2018). It is a conditional probabilistic model that generates a target word y at j-th position via the source context $\mathbf{x} = (x_1, ..., x_{T_x})$ and target context $y_{-j} = (y_1, ..., y_{j-1}, y_{j+1}, ..., y_{T_y})$ as follows:

$$P(y_j \mid y_{-j}, \mathbf{x}; \theta) = \text{softmax}([\overrightarrow{s_j}; \overleftarrow{s_j}])$$
$$= \frac{\exp(w_j^\text{T} W s_j)}{\sum_{k=1}^{K_y} \exp(w_k^\text{T} W s_j)} \quad (1)$$

where T_x and T_y are the length of the source and target sentences. $s_j = [\overrightarrow{s_j}; \overleftarrow{s_j}]$ is the concatenation of $\overrightarrow{s_j}$ and $\overleftarrow{s_j}$, $\overrightarrow{s_j}$ is the hidden state at the last layer of forward decoder and $\overleftarrow{s_j}$ is the hidden state of backward decoder. $w_j \in \mathbb{R}^{K_y}$ is the one-hot representation of the target word, and K_y is the vocabulary size of the target language. $W \in \mathbb{R}^{K_y \times 2d}$ is the weight matrix, and d is the size of a unidirectional hidden layer.

To describe how well a target word y_j in a target sentence is translated from a source sentence, the QEFV_j is defined as follows:

$$\text{QEFV}_j = [(w_j^\text{T} W) \odot s_j^\text{T}]^\text{T} \quad (2)$$

where $\odot$ is an element-wise multiplication.

Similarly, the target-to-source word predictor encodes a target sentence as input and decodes every word for source sentence step by step. We use the identical modified transformer model to generate QEFV_i for every source word x_i as output.

The quality estimator firstly uses the Bi-directional Long Short-term Memory (BiLSTM) (Hochreiter and Schmidhuber, 1997) model to encode given QEFVs of the source and target sentences such that

$$\overrightarrow{h_{1:T_x}}, \overleftarrow{h_{1:T_x}} = \text{BiLSTM}(\{\text{QEFV}_i\}_{i=1}^{i=T_x}) \quad (3)$$

$$\overrightarrow{h_{1:T_y}}, \overleftarrow{h_{1:T_y}} = \text{BiLSTM}(\{\text{QEFV}_j\}_{j=1}^{j=T_y}) \quad (4)$$

Secondly, the quality estimator compresses the concatenation of two sequential hidden states along the depth direction to a single one by averaging them respectively as follows:

$$h_{src} = \frac{1}{T_x} \sum_{i=1}^{i=T_x} ([\overrightarrow{h_i}; \overleftarrow{h_i}]) \quad (5)$$

$$h_{tgt} = \frac{1}{T_y} \sum_{j=1}^{j=T_y} ([\overrightarrow{h_j}; \overleftarrow{h_j}]) \quad (6)$$

Finally, sentence-level quality score of a translation sentence is calculated as follows:

$$QE_{\text{sentence}}(y, x) = \sigma(\mathbf{v}^{\text{T}}[h_{src}; h_{tgt}]) \qquad (7)$$

where $\mathbf{v}$ is a vector, σ denotes the logistic sigmoid function.

In general, the word predictors in both directions can supervise each other and jointly complete the goal of feature extractor, which enhances the representation ability of the whole QE model. At the same time, bi-directional translation knowledge is transferred from feature extractor to quality estimator, which can be deemed to data augmentation of the original parallel corpus. Therefore, this approach can increase the diversity of training samples and improve the robustness of QE model.

2.2 Model Training

The training objective of Bi-directional QE model is to minimize the Mean Average Error (MAE) between the gold standard labels and predicted quality scores over the QE training samples. Because the training set for QE task is not sufficient for training the entire QE model, we need to use large-scale parallel corpus in source-to-target direction and reverse (target-to-source) direction to pre-train two word predictors respectively. Then, the parameters of the whole Bi-directional QE model are trained jointly with the training samples of sentence-level QE task.

3 Employing Monolingual Knowledge

In fact, most language pairs do not have a large amount of parallel corpus to train the modified NMT model. But finding monolingual data for any language is relatively easy. Therefore, we propose a QE model to integrate monolingual knowledge, as depicted in Figure 2.

3.1 Model Architecture

The BERT-based QE model also consists of a neural feature extractor and a neural quality estimator. The feature extractor is implemented by a pre-training representation learning model for language understanding called Multilingual-BERT (Devlin et al., 2018), which extracts hidden states corresponding to the last attention block as QEFVs for the sentence pair of source sentence and target sentence. Further, we can use a self-attention based transformer model (Vaswani et al.,

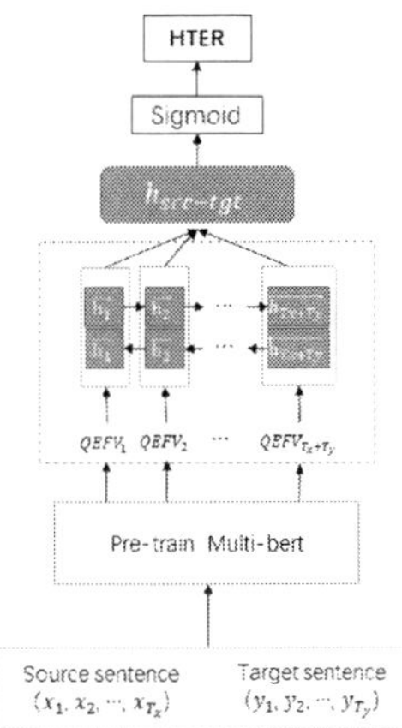

Figure 2: An illustration of the architecture of the proposed BERT-based QE model.

2017) to translate the source sentence to pseudo-reference, which is the same language as the target sentence. Then, the input of feature extractor is replaced with the sentence pair of pseudo-reference and target sentence.

The quality estimator applies BiLSTM based model to predict quality scores using QEFVs as inputs such that

$$\overrightarrow{h_{1:T_x+T_y}}, \overleftarrow{h_{1:T_x+T_y}} = \text{BiLSTM}(\{\text{QEFV}_i\}_{i=1}^{i=T_x+T_y})$$
$$(8)$$

$$h_{src-tgt} = \frac{1}{T_x + T_y} \sum_{i=1}^{i=T_x+T_y} ([\overrightarrow{h_i}; \overleftarrow{h_i}]) \qquad (9)$$

$$QE_{\text{sentence}}(x, y) = \sigma(\mathbf{v}_1^{\text{T}} h_{src-tgt}) \qquad (10)$$

where $\mathbf{v}_1$ is a vector.

3.2 Model Training

Consistently, the pre-trained feature extractor and initialized quality estimator of BERT-based QE model are trained jointly over the training samples of sentence-level QE task by minimizing the MAE loss function.

4 Experiments

4.1 Dataset and Metrics

The bilingual parallel corpus that we used for training word predictors is officially released by the WMT17 Shared Task: Machine Translation of News[1], including Europarl v7, Common Crawl corpus, News Commentary v12, and Rapid corpus of EU press releases. The newstest2016 was used

---

[1] http://www.statmt.org/wmt17/translation-task.html

	Train	Dev	Test 2017
Sentences	23,000	1,000	2,000

Table 1: Statistics of the en-de dataset of the WMT17 sentence-level QE task.

	Train	Dev	Test 2019
Sentences	13,442	1,000	1,023

Table 2: Statistics of the en-de dataset of the WMT19 sentence-level QE task.

as development dataset. Pre-processing script can be found at github[2].

To test the performance of the proposed QE models, we conducted experiments on the WMT17 and WMT19 sentence-level QE task for English-to-German (en-de) direction. Because the gold standard labels of testing data on the WMT18 sentence-level QE task are unobtainable. The statistics of the dataset are shown in Tables 1 and 2.

Pearson's correlation coefficient (Pearson) (as primary metric), Mean Average Error (MAE) and Root Mean Squared Error (RMSE) are used to evaluate the correlation between the predicted quality scores and the true HTER scores.

4.2 Experimental Setting

Both of the word predictors of Bi-directional QE Model hold the same parameters. The number of layers for the self-attention encoder and forward/backward self-attention decoder are all set as 6, where we use 8-head self-attention in practice. The dimensionality of word embedding and self-attention layers are all 512 except the feed-forward sub-layer is 2048. The dropout rate is set as 0.1. Worth mentioning, the normal transformer model introduced in BERT-based QE model is trained using the same parallel corpus and parameter settings as word predictors.

For quality estimator module, the number of hidden units for forward and backward LSTM is 512. And we uniformly use a minibatch stochastic gradient descent (SGD) algorithm together with Adam (Kingma and Ba, 2014) to train all models described.

These proposed models were compared with the traditional QE framework QuEst++ (Specia et al., 2015), the neural network features based

[2]https://github.com/zhaocq-nlp/MT-data-processing

QE model SHEF/QUEST-EMB (Shah et al., 2016) and the QE model combined with NMT model, including POSTECH (Kim et al., 2017b), QE-Brain (Wang et al., 2018), and UNQE (Li et al., 2018).

4.3 Experimental Results

In this section, we will report the experimental results of our approaches for WMT17 and WMT19 sentence-level QE task in English-German direction. For WMT17 QE task, we tried to verify our proposed models and chose the best two models to participate in WMT19 QE task. In Table 3 and Table 4, results of WMT17 and WMT19 QE tasks are listed respectively.

Method	test 2017 en-de		
	Pearson ↑	MAE ↓	RMSE ↓
Baseline	0.397	0.136	0.175
SHEF/QUEST-EMB	0.496	0.126	0.166
POSTECH Single	0.6599	0.1057	0.1450
QEBrain Single	0.6837	0.1001	0.1441
UNQE Single	0.700	-	-
Bi-directional QE	**0.7097**	0.1028	0.1352
BERT-based QE	0.6827	0.1081	0.1456
+NMT	**0.703**	0.1007	0.1377
POSTECH Ensemble	0.6954	0.1019	0.1371
QEBrain Ensemble	0.7159	0.0965	0.1384
UNQE Ensemble	0.710	-	-
Ours Ensemble	**0.7337**	0.0964	0.1294

Table 3: Results of the models on the WMT17 sentence-level QE. "BERT-based QE model" represents the original model with the sentence pair of source sentence and target sentence as inputs. "+NMT" represents that we use the sentence pair of pseudo-reference and target sentence as inputs of BERT-based QE model. And the rest of these two models remain the same.

Method	test 2019 en-de	
	Pearson ↑	Rank
Baseline	0.4001	
Bi-directional QE	0.5412	4
Ours Ensemble	0.5433	3

Table 4: Results of submitted models on the WMT19 sentence-level QE.

From the results listed in Table 3, our proposed single models, Bi-directional QE and BERT-based QE (+NMT) can outperform all the other compared single models for the primary metric. Then, we ensemble the two best single models above, where corresponding weights are tuned according to Pearson's correlation coefficient on the development dataset. The ensemble model can be comparable or better than the state-of-the-art (SOTA) ensemble models of WMT17 sentence-level QE task.

Considering the experimental results obtained from WMT17 QE task, we submitted the ensemble model and Bi-directional QE model to WMT19 sentence-level QE task, and ranked 3rd and 4th respectively according to WMT19 QE website.

5 Conclusion

This paper introduces two proposed QE models, Bi-directional QE model and BERT-based QE model, for the WMT19 sentence-level Quality Estimation shared task on English-German language pair. They can be used selectively in situations where parallel corpus and/or monolingual corpus are available. Experimental results showed that our ensemble model outperformed the SOTA results on WMT17 sentence-level QE task in English-German direction and ranked 3rd in WMT19 QE task. In future work, we would like to explore how to apply our approaches for finer-grained QE task, such as phrase-level and word-level.

References

Dzmitry Bahdanau, Kyunghyun Cho, and Yoshua Bengio. 2014. Neural machine translation by jointly learning to align and translate. *arXiv preprint arXiv:1409.0473*.

Jacob Devlin, Ming-Wei Chang, Kenton Lee, and Kristina Toutanova. 2018. Bert: Pre-training of deep bidirectional transformers for language understanding. *arXiv preprint arXiv:1810.04805*.

Sepp Hochreiter and Jürgen Schmidhuber. 1997. Long short-term memory. *Neural Computation*, 9(8):1735–1780.

Hyun Kim, Hun-Young Jung, Hongseok Kwon, Jong-Hyeok Lee, and Seung-Hoon Na. 2017a. Predictor-estimator: Neural quality estimation based on target word prediction for machine translation. *ACM Transactions on Asian and Low-resource Language Information Processing*, 17(1):3.

Hyun Kim and Jong-Hyeok Lee. 2016. Recurrent neural network based translation quality estimation. In *Proceedings of the 1st Conference on Machine Translation*, pages 787–792.

Hyun Kim, Jong-Hyeok Lee, and Seung-Hoon Na. 2017b. Predictor-estimator using multilevel task learning with stack propagation for neural quality estimation. In *Proceedings of the 2nd Conference on Machine Translation*, pages 562–568.

Diederik P Kingma and Jimmy Ba. 2014. Adam: A method for stochastic optimization. *arXiv preprint arXiv:1412.6980*.

Anna Kozlova, Mariya Shmatova, and Anton Frolov. 2016. Ysda participation in the wmt16 quality estimation shared task. In *Proceedings of the 1st Conference on Machine Translation*, pages 793–799.

Maoxi Li, Qingyu Xiang, Zhiming Chen, and Mingwen Wang. 2018. A unified neural network for quality estimation of machine translation. *IEICE Transactions on Information and Systems*, E101.D(9):2417–2421.

Mike Schuster and Kuldip K Paliwal. 1997. Bidirectional recurrent neural networks. *IEEE Transactions on Signal Processing*, 45(11):2673–2681.

Rico Sennrich, Barry Haddow, and Alexandra Birch. 2015. Improving neural machine translation models with monolingual data. *arXiv preprint arXiv:1511.06709*.

Kashif Shah, Fethi Bougares, Loïc Barrault, and Lucia Specia. 2016. Shef-lium-nn: Sentence level quality estimation with neural network features. In *Proceedings of the 1st Conference on Machine Translation*, volume 2, pages 838–842.

Kashif Shah, Raymond WM Ng, Fethi Bougares, and Lucia Specia. 2015. Investigating continuous space language models for machine translation quality estimation. In *Proceedings of the 2015 Conference on Empirical Methods in Natural Language Processing*, pages 1073–1078.

Matthew Snover, Bonnie Dorr, Richard Schwartz, Linnea Micciulla, and John Makhoul. 2006. A study of translation edit rate with targeted human annotation. In *Proceedings of Association for Machine Translation in the Americas*, pages 223–231.

Lucia Specia, Gustavo Paetzold, and Carolina Scarton. 2015. Multi-level translation quality prediction with quest++. *Proceedings of the 53rd Annual Meeting of the Association for Computational Linguistics: System Demonstrations*, pages 115–120.

Lucia Specia, Kashif Shah, José GC De Souza, and Trevor Cohn. 2013. Quest-a translation quality estimation framework. In *Proceedings of the 51st Annual Meeting of the Association for Computational Linguistics: System Demonstrations*, pages 79–84.

Ashish Vaswani, Noam Shazeer, Niki Parmar, Jakob Uszkoreit, Llion Jones, Aidan N Gomez, Łukasz Kaiser, and Illia Polosukhin. 2017. Attention is all you need. In *Advances in Neural Information Processing Systems*, pages 5998–6008.

Jiayi Wang, Kai Fan, Bo Li, Fengming Zhou, Boxing
Chen, Yangbin Shi, and Luo Si. 2018. Alibaba submission for wmt18 quality estimation task. In *Proceedings of the 3rd Conference on Machine Translation*, pages 809–815.

Quality Estimation and Translation Metrics via Pre-trained Word and Sentence Embeddings

Lisa Yankovskaya   **Andre Tättar**   **Mark Fishel**
Institute of Computer Science
University of Tartu, Estonia
{lisa.yankovskaya,andre.tattar,fishel}@ut.ee

Abstract

We propose the use of pre-trained embeddings as features of a regression model for sentence-level quality estimation of machine translation. In our work we combine freely available BERT and LASER multilingual embeddings to train a neural-based regression model. In the second proposed method we use as an input features not only pre-trained embeddings, but also log probability of any machine translation (MT) system. Both methods are applied to several language pairs and are evaluated both as a classical quality estimation system (predicting the HTER score) as well as an MT metric (predicting human judgements of translation quality).

1 Introduction

Quality estimation (Blatz et al., 2004; Specia et al., 2009) aims to predict the quality of machine translation (MT) outputs without human references, which is what sets it apart from translation metrics like BLEU (Papineni et al., 2002) or TER (Snover et al., 2006). Most approaches to quality estimation are trained to predict the post-editing effort, i.e. the number of corrections the translators have to make in order to get an adequate translation. The effort is measured by the HTER metric (Snover et al., 2006) applied to human post-edits.

In this paper, we introduce a light-weight neural method with pre-trained embeddings, that means it does not require any pre-training. The second proposed method is the extension of the first one: besides pre-trained embeddings, it takes log probability from any MT system as an input feature.

In addition to the official datasets provided for this year's WMT sentence level shared task, we analyze the performance of our methods against the extended datasets made from previous years data. Using the extended datasets allows to get a more reliable score and avoid skewed distributions of the predicted metrics.

Besides that we apply our method to predict direct human assessment (DA) (Graham et al., 2017). In direct human assessment humans compare the machine translation output with a reference translation not seeing a source translation. Usually MT metrics (Ma et al., 2018) are compared to DA, but we decided to compare our predictions as well, because there is a difference between a number of post-edits and a human assessment. For example, if everything in a translation is perfect except one thing: all indefinite articles are missed, the number of post-edits may be large enough and a score will be low whereas humans likely give it a high score. The main difference between MT metrics and quality estimation is that quality estimation is computing without reference sentences.

2 Architecture

Our method performs sentence-level quality estimation of machine translation. As other state-of-the-art methods (Kim et al., 2017; Fan et al., 2018), we use a neural-based architecture. However, compared to the other neural-based methods, we do not train embeddings from scratch, that usually takes a lot of data and computational resources. Instead of that, we use already well trained and freely available embeddings.

For our method we have picked BERT (Devlin et al., 2018) and LASER (Artetxe and Schwenk, 2018) multilingual embeddings toolkits. We extract both BERT and LASER embeddings and feed them into a feed-forward neural network. A sigmoid output layer produces the desirable score. In case of HTER prediction we can add log probability score obtained from a neural MT system as an additional feature to the described above feed-forward neural network. The whole architecture of our system is depicted in Fig.1.

Proceedings of the Fourth Conference on Machine Translation (WMT), Volume 3: Shared Task Papers (Day 2) pages 101–105
Florence, Italy, August 1-2, 2019. ©2019 Association for Computational Linguistics

BERT embeddings are extracted from a deep bidirectional transformer encoder, which is pre-trained on Wikipedia data, with the aim of generating a general-purpose "language understanding". LASER embeddings are extracted from bidirectional word-level recurrent encoder, where sentence embeddings are extracted from max-pooled word embeddings, trained on publicly available parallel corpora.

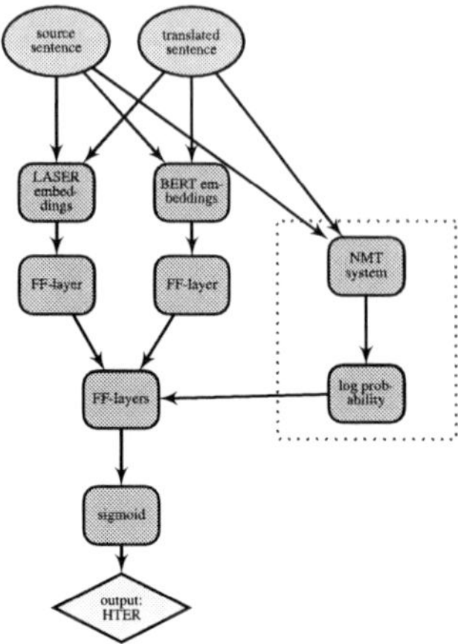

Figure 1: The proposed methods: LABEL: it requires LASER and BERT to get embeddings and NMT system to compute log probability and LABE: it requires only LASER and BERT to get embeddings.

3 Experimental Settings

In this section we analyze the performance of proposed methods on different prediction outputs (HTER and DA) and different datasets and compare them with another neural method DeepQuest (Ive et al., 2018) that does not require additional data.

To predict HTER we take a dataset that contains source sentences, their translated outputs and HTER scores. It is domain-specific: IT or pharmaceutical depending on the language pair. As there is no large enough corpus with DA labels, we use a dataset that consists only of source sentences and their machine translation output. The domain of this corpus is more general and source sentences have taken from the open resources.

3.1 Experiments

We have implemented our methods using the Keras toolkit. As a regression model we have used four-layered feed-forward neural network with sigmoid as a final activation function.

To obtain a log probability score, we trained neural MT systems using sockeye toolkit. We used Transformer (Vaswani et al., 2017) as a network architecture with six layers in encoder and decoder, word vectors of size 512, batch size 50, and Adam (Kingma and Ba, 2015) as optimizer with an initial learning rate of 0.0002.

We present two models with different set of features:

- **LABE**: embeddings extracted from LASER and BERT

- **LABEL**: embeddings extracted from LASER and BERT and log probability obtained from Transformer NMT model

BERT embeddings are extracted for multilingual cased BERT model. Only the last layer of embeddings is extracted. BERT gives 728-dimension embeddings for each word, source and target embeddings are separated by a special token and then average pooling is used to get sentence embeddings for source and target sentences.

3.2 Data and Results of HTER Prediction

Data

We gathered the data from WMT16 - WMT18 shared tasks on sentence-level quality estimation for English-German (En-De) (Bojar et al., 2016a, 2017a; Specia et al., 2018), from WMT17 - WMT18 German-English (De-En) and from WMT 18 English-Czech (En-Cs).

The En-De data contains translations from neural and statistical MT systems and De-En and En-Cs datasets contain outputs only from statistical MT. However, for our method there is no difference between neural and statistical MT output. En-De and En-Cs sentences on the IT domain and De-En — on the pharmaceutical domain.

We removed duplicated sentences and randomly split data into training, dev and test sets in the 70/20/10 ratio. As a result, we got the following number of sentences:

- **En-De**: ≈ 55K/16K/8K

- **De-En**: ≈ 37K/10K/5K

- **En-Cs**: ≈ 29K/8K/4K

We intentionally increased the size of the test sets to reduce the impact of skewed distributions towards high quality translations. These fluent translation have the HTER score equalled zero and make up 70% of all data. Such distribution where we have 70% of zeros and other 30% of data is uniform from 0 to 1 is hard to learn with a regression model.

Results

Below we describe the results of our systems for two test datasets: the extended dataset is described above and the second one is the small dataset (around 1K sentences) provided by organizers of WMT19.

Results for extended datasets The resulting Pearson and Spearman coefficients for the all given language pairs are presented in Table 1. As one can see the highest values were obtained by applying the models `LABEL`, but the difference of the computing values is small. The obtained numbers for En-De and En-Cs are close to each other whereas the resulting coefficients for De-En are noticeably higher. Both our models showed the better performance than `deepQuest`.

	LABE		LABEL		deepQuest	
	PCC	SCC	PCC	SCC	PCC	SCC
DEEN	0.599	0.586	0.64	0.615	0.368	0.347
ENDE	0.533	0.566	0.542	0.57	0.294	0.305
ENCS	0.542	0.532	0.557	0.549	0.446	0.433

Table 1: Pearson and Spearman correlation coefficients for the monolingual models LABE and LABEL, and `deepQuest` . For models LABE and LABEL we show PCC and SCC between ensemble of five runs and HTER.

Results for WMT 2019 The results for the small WMT dataset do not look so impressive (Table 2) compared to the results of extended datasets. Without knowledge of data, it is difficult to say what the reason for it. We can assume that it may be due to the skewed distribution of the given dataset. It is worth noting that the same En-De (nmt) dataset was given also in WMT18 shared task and looking at the results[1], we can see a drop in performance for this dataset as well.

3.3 Data and Results for human assessment prediction

Data

We took data from News Translation Tasks 2015-2018 years (Bojar et al., 2015, 2016a,

	LABE		LABEL	
	PCC	SCC	PCC	SCC
ENDE	0.319	0.377	0.249	0.253
ENRU	0.401	0.336	-	-

Table 2: Pearson and Spearman correlation coefficients for the monolingual models LABE and LABEL. Test set: official test set of WMT19. We show PCC and SCC between ensemble of five runs and HTER.

2017a, 2018) for En-De, English-Finnish (En-Fi), English-Russian (En-Ru) (both directions for all three language pairs) and En-Cs. The data consists of source sentences and their translation. The number of unique source sentences ($\approx$10-11K for each language pair) are significantly less than the number of translation, because every source sentence has several translations obtained from different systems. We randomly split the data into training and dev sets in the ratio 80/20:

- **En-De**: $\approx$ 141K/35K

- **De-En**: $\approx$ 111K/28K

- **En-Fi**: $\approx$ 100K/25K

- **Fi-En**: $\approx$ 73K/18K

- **En-Ru**: $\approx$ 95K/24K

- **Ru-En**: $\approx$ 94K/24K

- **En-Cs**: $\approx$ 113K/28K

As test sets we used DAseg-newstest2016 (Bojar et al., 2016b) that consists of 560 sentences for each language pair. As fine-tuning sets we took DAseg-newstest2015 (Stanojević et al., 2015) and DAseg-newstest2017 (Bojar et al., 2017b) that gave us around 1K sentences per each language pair.

Results

Below we describe the obtained results for newstest2016 (Bojar et al., 2016b) and compare them with results of metrics tasks. At the time of publication of the article, results of newstest2019 were not yet available.

Results for DAseg-newstest2016 The both proposed methods are supervised, so to train models we need labels. As DA data is scarce resource we trained models using chrF++ (Popović, 2017) (with default hyper-parameters) as labels.

To investigate how the number of language pairs affects the performance of models, we trained several models: with one language pair in the training

---

[1] `http://statmt.org/wmt18/`
`quality-estimation-task.html#results`

set, with four (De-En, En-De, En-Cs, En-Ru) and with seven language pairs. As can be seen in the Figure 2, the best results were achieved with the mono language pair models, although the difference between mono- and multimodels is not large.

We also fine-tuned our models by using human assessment data. Fine-tuned models showed a little bit better results compared to the non-tuned models (Figure: 2).

We compared the obtained results to the metrics results. For De-En the best resulting Pearson correlation coefficient for metrics is 0.601 and for En-Ru is 0.666 (Bojar et al., 2016b), whereas the best scores of our models are 0.520 and 0.668 for De-En and En-Ru respectively. Our results are comparable to the metrics results, despite the fact that we did not use reference sentences in contrast to the metrics task.

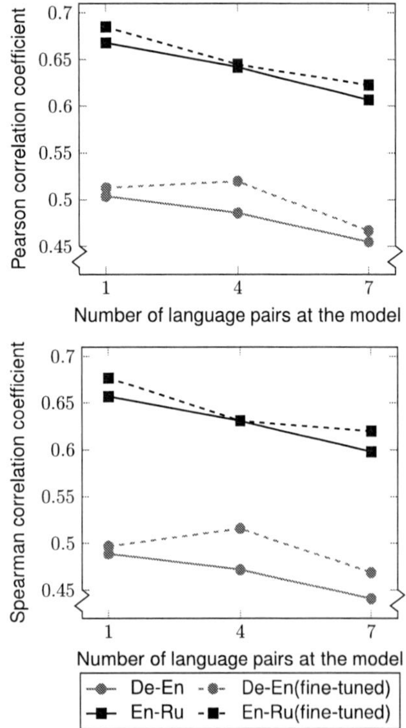

Figure 2: Pearson and Spearman correlation coefficients for LABE model and different number of language pairs in training dataset. We show average over three runs. Test dataset: newstest2016

Results for DAseg-newstest2019 We prepared scores for all language pairs described in 3.3 by using non-tuned models trained on seven language pairs and for De-En, En-Ru, Ru-En, Fi-En by using fine-tuned models. Results of this submission

will be available (Fonseca et al., 2019).

4 Conclusions

We proposed neural-based models for quality estimation of machine translation. One of our models requires only freely available embeddings (LASER and BERT) and the second needs also log probability from any MT system (in our experiments, we use Transformer MT system).

We analyzed performance of both models on different language pairs and different prediction outputs and compared them to another neural quality estimation system. Both our methods showed better results compared to another light-weight approach deepQuest and we got comparable results with the metrics tasks even without using references.

Acknowledgments

This work was supported in part by funding from the European Union's Horizon 2020 research and innovation programme under grant agreement No. 825303 as well as the Estonian Research Council grant no. 1226

References

Mikel Artetxe and Holger Schwenk. 2018. Massively multilingual sentence embeddings for zero-shot cross-lingual transfer and beyond. *arXiv preprint arXiv:1812.10464*.

John Blatz, Erin Fitzgerald, George Foster, Simona Gandrabur, Cyril Goutte, Alex Kulesza, Alberto Sanchis, and Nicola Ueffing. 2004. Confidence estimation for machine translation. In *Proceedings of the 20th international conference on Computational Linguistics*, page 315. Association for Computational Linguistics.

Ondřej Bojar, Rajen Chatterjee, Christian Federmann, Yvette Graham, Barry Haddow, Shujian Huang, Matthias Huck, Philipp Koehn, Qun Liu, Varvara Logacheva, et al. 2017a. Findings of the 2017 conference on machine translation (wmt17). In *Proceedings of the Second Conference on Machine Translation*, pages 169–214.

Ondřej Bojar, Rajen Chatterjee, Christian Federmann, Yvette Graham, Barry Haddow, Matthias Huck, Antonio Jimeno Yepes, Philipp Koehn, Varvara Logacheva, Christof Monz, et al. 2016a. Findings of the 2016 conference on machine translation. In *Proceedings of the First Conference on Machine Translation: Volume 2, Shared Task Papers*, volume 2, pages 131–198.

Ondrej Bojar, Rajen Chatterjee, Christian Federmann, Barry Haddow, Matthias Huck, Chris Hokamp, Philipp Koehn, Varvara Logacheva, Christof Monz, Matteo Negri, Matt Post, Carolina Scarton, Lucia Specia, and Marco Turchi. 2015. Findings of the 2015 workshop on statistical machine translation. In *WMT@EMNLP*.

Ondřej Bojar, Christian Federmann, Mark Fishel, Yvette Graham, Barry Haddow, Philipp Koehn, and Christof Monz. 2018. Findings of the 2018 conference on machine translation (WMT18). In *Proceedings of the Third Conference on Machine Translation: Shared Task Papers*, pages 272–303, Belgium, Brussels. Association for Computational Linguistics.

Ondřej Bojar, Yvette Graham, and Amir Kamran. 2017b. Results of the WMT17 metrics shared task. In *Proceedings of the Second Conference on Machine Translation*, pages 489–513, Copenhagen, Denmark. Association for Computational Linguistics.

Ondřej Bojar, Yvette Graham, Amir Kamran, and Miloš Stanojević. 2016b. Results of the wmt16 metrics shared task. In *Proceedings of the First Conference on Machine Translation: Volume 2, Shared Task Papers*, volume 2, pages 199–231.

Jacob Devlin, Ming-Wei Chang, Kenton Lee, and Kristina Toutanova. 2018. Bert: Pre-training of deep bidirectional transformers for language understanding. *arXiv preprint arXiv:1810.04805*.

Kai Fan, Bo Li, Fengming Zhou, and Jiayi Wang. 2018. "bilingual expert" can find translation errors. *CoRR*, abs/1807.09433.

Erick Fonseca, Lisa Yankovskaya, André F. T. Martins, Mark Fishel, and Christian Federmann. 2019. Findings of the wmt 2019 shared task on quality estimation. In *Proceedings of the Fourth Conference on Machine Translation*.

Yvette Graham, Timothy Baldwin, Alistair Moffat, and Justin Zobel. 2017. Can machine translation systems be evaluated by the crowd alone. *Natural Language Engineering*, 23(1):3–30.

Julia Ive, Frédéric Blain, and Lucia Specia. 2018. Deepquest: a framework for neural-based quality estimation. In *Proceedings of the 27th International Conference on Computational Linguistics*, pages 3146–3157.

Hyun Kim, Jong-Hyeok Lee, and Seung-Hoon Na. 2017. Predictor-estimator using multilevel task learning with stack propagation for neural quality estimation. In *Proceedings of the Second Conference on Machine Translation*, pages 562–568.

Diederik P Kingma and Lei Ba. 2015. J. adam: a method for stochastic optimization. In *International Conference on Learning Representations*.

Qingsong Ma, Ondřej Bojar, and Yvette Graham. 2018. Results of the wmt18 metrics shared task: Both characters and embeddings achieve good performance. In *Proceedings of the Third Conference on Machine Translation: Shared Task Papers*, pages 671–688.

Kishore Papineni, Salim Roukos, Todd Ward, and Wei-Jing Zhu. 2002. Bleu: a method for automatic evaluation of machine translation. In *Proceedings of the 40th annual meeting on association for computational linguistics*, pages 311–318. Association for Computational Linguistics.

Maja Popović. 2017. chrf++: words helping character n-grams. In *Proceedings of the second conference on machine translation*, pages 612–618.

Matthew Snover, Bonnie Dorr, Richard Schwartz, Linnea Micciulla, and John Makhoul. 2006. A study of translation edit rate with targeted human annotation. In *Proceedings of association for machine translation in the Americas*, volume 200.

Lucia Specia, Frédéric Blain, Varvara Logacheva, Ramón F. Astudillo, and André Martins. 2018. Findings of the wmt 2018 shared task on quality estimation. In *Proceedings of the Third Conference on Machine Translation, Volume 2: Shared Task Papers*, Brussels, Belgium. Association for Computational Linguistics.

Lucia Specia, Marco Turchi, Nicola Cancedda, Marc Dymetman, and Nello Cristianini. 2009. Estimating the sentence-level quality of machine translation systems. In *13th Conference of the European Association for Machine Translation*, pages 28–37.

Miloš Stanojević, Amir Kamran, Philipp Koehn, and Ondřej Bojar. 2015. Results of the wmt15 metrics shared task. In *Proceedings of the Tenth Workshop on Statistical Machine Translation*, pages 256–273.

Ashish Vaswani, Noam Shazeer, Niki Parmar, Jakob Uszkoreit, Llion Jones, Aidan N Gomez, Łukasz Kaiser, and Illia Polosukhin. 2017. Attention is all you need. In *Advances in Neural Information Processing Systems*, pages 5998–6008.

SOURCE: SOURce-Conditional Elmo-style Model
for Machine Translation Quality Estimation

Junpei Zhou[*]   **Zhisong Zhang**[*]   **Zecong Hu**[*]

Language Technologies Institute

Carnegie Mellon University

{junpeiz, zhisongz, zeconghu}@andrew.cmu.edu

Abstract

Quality estimation (QE) of machine translation (MT) systems is a task of growing importance. It reduces the cost of post-editing, allowing machine-translated text to be used in formal occasions. In this work, we describe our submission system in WMT 2019 sentence-level QE task. We mainly explore the utilization of pre-trained translation models in QE and adopt a bi-directional translation-like strategy. The strategy is similar to ELMo, but additionally conditions on source sentences. Experiments on WMT QE dataset show that our strategy, which makes the pre-training slightly harder, can bring improvements for QE. In WMT-2019 QE task, our system ranked in the second place on En-De NMT dataset and the third place on En-Ru NMT dataset.

1 Introduction

The quality of machine translation systems have been significantly improved over the past few years (Chatterjee et al., 2018), especially with the development of neural machine translation (NMT) models (Sutskever et al., 2014; Bahdanau et al., 2014). Despite such inspiring improvements, some machine translated texts are still error-prone and unreliable compared to those by professional humans. It is often desirable to have human experts perform post-editing on machine-translated text to achieve a balance between cost and correctness. Correspondingly, we may also want to develop automatic quality estimation systems to judge the quality of machine translation outputs, leading to the development of the Machine Translation Quality Estimation task. The task of QE aims to evaluate the output of a machine translation system without access to reference translations. It would allow human experts to concentrate

on translations that are estimated of low-quality, further reducing post-editing cost.

In this work, we focus on sentence-level QE and describe our submission to the WMT 2019 QE task. Sentence-level QE aims to predict a score for the entire source–translation pair that indicates the effort required for further post-editing. The goals of the task are two-fold: 1) to predict the required post-editing cost, measured in HTER (Snover et al., 2006); 2) to rank all sentence pairs in descending translation quality.

In previous works, including the participating systems in previous WMT shared tasks, there have been various methods to tackle this problem. Traditional linear models are based on hand-crafted features, while recent state-of-the-art systems adopt end-to-end neural models (Kim and Lee, 2016; Wang et al., 2018). The neural systems are usually composed of two modules: the bottom part is an MT-like source–target encoding model pre-trained with large parallel corpora, stacked with a top-level QE scorer based on the neural features extracted by the bottom model. Especially, Wang et al. (2018) adopted the "Bilingual Expert" model (Fan et al., 2018) for pre-training the bottom model and obtained several best results in WMT 2018. In this work, we improve the "Bilingual Expert" model with a SOURce-Conditional ELMo-style (SOURCE) strategy: instead of predicting target words based on contexts from both sides, we train two conditioned language (translation) models, each restricted to context from one side only. This harder setting may force the model to condition more on the source. Experiments show that this strategy can bring improvements for QE.

---

[*]equal contribution

Proceedings of the Fourth Conference on Machine Translation (WMT), Volume 3: Shared Task Papers (Day 2) pages 106–111
Florence, Italy, August 1-2, 2019. ©2019 Association for Computational Linguistics

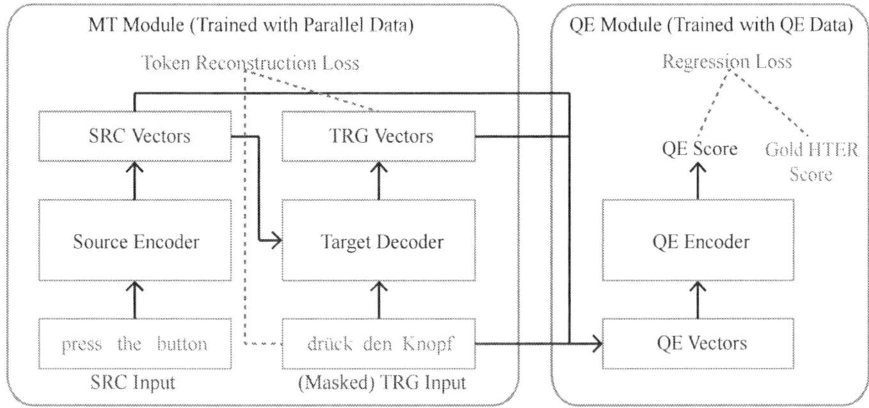

Figure 1: The architecture of our QE system, which consists of two modules: 1) the MT Module encodes the bilingual information and can be pre-trained with large parallel data, 2) the QE Module adopts the source and target representations from the MT Module and further encodes those information followed by a final linear layer for QE scoring.

2 System

2.1 Basic Framework

We follow previous works and adopt the end-to-end styled model for the QE scoring task. The overall system architecture is shown in Figure 1. The system consists of two components: 1) a pre-trained MT module which learns the representations of the source and target sentences, 2) a QE scorer which takes the representations from the MT module as inputs and predicts the translation quality score.

The MT module is pre-trained on large parallel corpus. It is trained to predict each token in the translated sentence by using the information in source sentence and tokens in the translated sentence. Details of the model will be described in Section 2.2.

In the QE scorer module, the problem can be cast as a regression task, where the QE score is predicted given the source and target sentences. The original inputs are encoded by the pre-trained MT module, whose outputs are taken as input features for this module. We basically follow the model architecture of Wang et al. (2018). For each token, a quality vector is formed as:

$$q_j = \text{Concat}(\overleftarrow{z_j}, \overrightarrow{z_j}, e^t_{j-1}, e^t_{j+1}, f^{mm}_j), \quad (1)$$

where $\overleftarrow{z_j}, \overrightarrow{z_j}$ are state vectors produced by the bi-directional Transformer, and e^t_{j-1}, e^t_{j+1} are embedding vectors. The "mismatching feature" f^{mm}_j is formed by extracting the score corresponding

to y_j, the highest score in the distribution, their difference, and an indicator of whether y_j has the highest score. After this, the quality vectors are viewed as another sequence and encoded by the Bi-LSTM/Transformer Quality Estimator to predict the QE score. The loss function for training is mean squared error which is typical for regression tasks.

2.2 Pre-trained Translation Models

Bilingual Expert We start with a short description for the model of Wang et al. (2018). The model can be seen as a token-level reconstruction-styled translation model: each target word y_j is predicted given a source sentence and all other target words $\{\ldots, y_{j-1}, y_{j+1}, \ldots\}$. This setting is different to the traditional MT scenario where only previous target words can be seen. The model uses the encoder–decoder architecture. An encoder is applied over the source tokens to obtain the contextual representations of the source sentence. A bidirectional pair of decoders (one forward and one backward) are adopted to encode the target translation sentence, while conditioning on the source sentence via attention mechanism. Formally, for source tokens $\{x_1, \ldots, x_{m_s}\}$ and translation tokens $\{y_1, \ldots, y_{m_t}\}$, the forward and backward target representations $\{\overrightarrow{z_1}, \ldots, \overrightarrow{z_{m_t}}\}$ and

a) Bilingual Expert

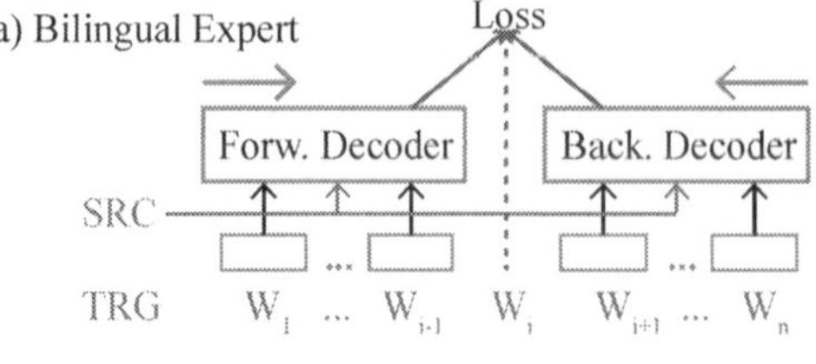

b) Elmo Style

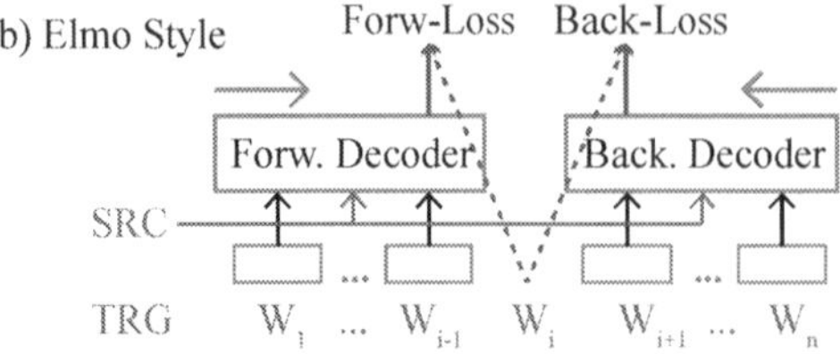

c) BERT Style

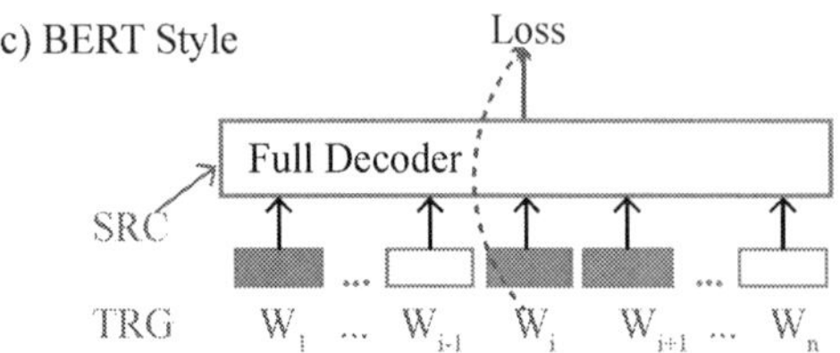

Figure 2: Illustration of reconstruction loss for the token "W_i" in different pre-training strategies. a) In Bilingual Expert, one reconstruction loss is computed for each token, conditioned on the entire target context provided by the Forward and Backward decoders. b) With Elmo-Style, it is equivalent to training bidirectional translation models. Two reconstruction losses are computed for each token, each only depending on one side of the context. c) With BERT-Style, certain inputs are masked out (colored in grey) and a masked-LM is learned. One reconstruction loss is computed for each masked token.

$\{\overleftarrow{z_1}, \ldots, \overleftarrow{z_{m_t}}\}$ are computed as:

$$c_1, \ldots, c_{m_s} = \text{Encoder}(x_1, \ldots, x_{m_s}),$$

$$\overrightarrow{z_1}, \ldots, \overrightarrow{z_{m_t}} = \overrightarrow{\text{Decoder}}(y_1, \ldots, y_{m_t}, c_1, \ldots, c_{m_s}),$$

$$\overleftarrow{z_1}, \ldots, \overleftarrow{z_{m_t}} = \overleftarrow{\text{Decoder}}(y_1, \ldots, y_{m_t}, c_1, \ldots, c_{m_s}).$$

Both encoder and decoders use Transformer (Vaswani et al., 2017) as their backbone for its better performances in machine translation tasks.

After obtaining these representations, the model is trained with the token reconstruction cross-entropy loss for each target token with contextual information from both sides:

$$\log p(y_j \mid y_{i \neq j}, x) = \text{softmax}(\text{ff}([\overrightarrow{z_j}_{-1}; \overleftarrow{z_j}_{+1}])). \quad (2)$$

Here "ff" denotes a feed-forward layer. Note that we cannot use representations that capture y_j,

therefore, we use the forward representation of the previous token $\overrightarrow{z_j}_{-1}$ and the backward representation of the next token $\overleftarrow{z_j}_{+1}$.

SOURCE In the Bilingual Expert model, each target token is predicted given all target tokens on both sides. However, this training scheme makes too much information visible to the model, such that the model could predict the target word even without seeing the source sentence.

For example, we can easily infer that the missing word in "He loves playing _____ and his favorite basketball player is Michael Jordan" is "basketball". In another words, too much visible information on the target side provides an inductive bias that pushes the model towards learning a bi-directional language model instead of a translation-like model, by omitting the information on the source sentence.

We want to force our model to exploit the relationship between the source tokens and target tokens. Thus, we no longer make the words on both sides visible to our model at the same time. Instead, we separate the two directions, so that the model must predict each target word depending only on the source sentence and target words on one side. More specifically, we compute two losses, ℓ_1 and ℓ_2. The cross-entropy loss ℓ_1 is derived by predicting the target word y_j based on the source sentence $\{x_0, \ldots, x_{m_s}\}$ and left-side target words $\{y_0, \ldots, y_{j-1}\}$. Another cross-entropy loss ℓ_2 is derived by predicting y_j based on the source sentence and right-side target words $\{y_{j+1}, \ldots, y_{m_t}\}$. This training scheme corresponds to the strategy used in ELMo (Peters et al., 2018), but the difference is that here we condition on additional source information, hence the name SOURce-Conditional Elmo-style (SOURCE) model.

Another method to force the model to attend more to source is using BERT (Devlin et al., 2018), which masks several words and try to predict those words at once. Inspired by the work of Cross-lingual BERT (Lample and Conneau, 2019), we choose to use the structure as shown in Figure 2. It can reduce the information seen by the decoder and force it to condition more on the source sentence. Due to limitations on time and computing resources, we did not manage to produce successful results using BERT. This would be an interesting and promising direction to explore in future work.

Dataset	Parallel	QE		
		train	dev	test
En-De-SMT	32.8M	26299	1000	1926
En-De-NMT		13442	1000	1023
En-Ru	8.0M	15089	1000	1023

Table 1: Statistics of the parallel data and QE data.

From empirical results of SOURCE, we find that although the prediction accuracy on MT parallel data decreases, the final performance on QE increases significantly. This shows that decreasing the visible information makes token-prediction more difficult, and forces the model to learn more useful structures from the data, which in turn becomes features of higher quality for the QE task.

2.3 Model Ensemble

We perform model ensembling by stacking, which means we use the prediction results of different models on the development set as new features, and train a simple regression model to predict the actual development set labels. Finally, the regression model is applied on the predictions of different models on test set. We use ridge regression here as the regression model. We also use grid search and cross-validation to select the regularization weight for ridge regression.

We train both the pre-trained MT module and the QE scorer module with different hyper-parameters to produce different models for ensembling. For the pre-trained MT module, toggled hyper-parameters include number of layers, number of self-attention heads, learning rate, label-smoothing rate, warm-up steps, and dropout rates. For the QE scorer module, toggled hyper-parameters include number of layers, hidden size, percentage of augmented data, encoder type (LSTM or Transformer), and dropout rate.

3 Experiments

3.1 Settings

Our system is evaluated on the WMT18/19 QE sentence-level task. The main metric is the Pearson's r correlation score between predicted scores and ground-truth HTER scores. There are other metrics including Mean Absolute Error (MAE) and Root Mean Squared Error (RMSE) for scoring and the Spearman's ρ rank correlation for ranking. We evaluate our models on datasets in the WMT 18/19 shared task with different translation systems: WMT-18 En-De-SMT, WMT-18/19 En-De-NMT, WMT-19 En-Ru-NMT. For experiments on WMT-19 data, we report results based on official evaluation results.

Data For the parallel data used in pre-training of the MT module, we collect large-scale parallel corpora for En-De and En-Ru from the WMT-18 translation task. Officially pre-processed data[1] are utilized. To make it compatible with QE data, we re-escaped certain punctuation tokens. To reduce the corpus size, we further apply a more strict filtering step by discarding sentence pairs with too many overlapping words in their source and target sentences (> 0.9 for En-De, > 0.5 for En-Ru). Finally, we obtain 32.1M EN-De and 7.8M En-Ru sentence pairs and mix it with the training set of the QE data (using post-edited sentences as target). Our mixing strategy is to mix one copy of QE data for every 1M of parallel data. The statistics of the mixed parallel data and QE data are summarized in Table 1.

Following Wang et al. (2018), we also prepare artificial data via round-trip translation (Junczys-Dowmunt and Grundkiewicz, 2016, 2017). Since the QE data are obtained with two kinds of translation systems: SMT and NMT, we also prepare two kinds of artificial data. For simplicity, we take the back-translated corpus by the Edinburgh's translation system,[2] which contains 3.6M back-translated sentences for En-De and 1.9M for En-Ru. We further train a SMT system with Moses and decode the English sentence back to German. For NMT, we simply take a pre-trained NMT system (also Edinburgh's system[3]) for decoding.

Implementation We implement our system from scratch in Python with TensorFlow (Abadi et al., 2015) and OpenNMT (Klein et al., 2017). Because of limited resources, we manually search for good hyper-parameters by heuristics evaluated on the development set. The training of the MT module takes around 4 to 5 days and the training of the QE module takes a couple of hours with one GPU.

---

[1] http://data.statmt.org/wmt18/ translation-task/preprocessed/. According to the official script, the data is processed with tokenization, cleaning and truecase with standard Moses scripts.

[2] http://data.statmt.org/rsennrich/ wmt16_backtranslations/.

[3] http://data.statmt.org/wmt17_systems/.

System	test 2018 En-De-SMT			test 2018 En-De-NMT			
	Pearson r ↑	MAE↓	RMSE↓	Pearson r ↑	MAE↓	RMSE↓	Spearman ρ ↑
Alibaba (ensemble)	**0.7397**	0.0937	0.1362	0.5012	0.1131	0.1742	0.6049
JXNU (ensemble)	0.7000	0.0962	0.1382	0.5129	0.1114	0.1749	0.6052
SOURCE (ours, ensemble)	—	—	—	**0.5474**	0.1123	0.1623	**0.6155**
SOURCE (ours)	**0.6970**	0.1009	0.1409	**0.4956**	0.1197	0.1797	—
Bilingual Expert (our impl.)	0.6645	0.1089	0.1488	0.4447	0.1240	0.1791	—
melaniad	0.4877	0.1316	0.1675	0.4198	0.1359	0.1770	—
cscarton	0.4872	0.1321	0.1714	0.3808	0.1297	0.1785	—

Table 2: Evaluation results on the test sets of WMT-18 En-De-SMT and WMT-18 NMT. The two leading teams only provide ensemble results on 2018 test data. We re-implement Alibaba's single model (Bilingual Expert) and achieved similar results on 2017 data as reported in their paper. We test that Bilingual Expert on 2018 data to make a fair comparison for single model. With limited computational resource, we only run the ensemble for En-De-NMT, because in WMT2019 they only requires NMT submission.

System	En-De-NMT		En-Ru-NMT	
	Pearson r ↑	Spearman ρ ↑	Pearson r ↑	Spearman ρ ↑
UNBABEL	0.5718	0.6221	0.5923	0.5388
SOURCE (ours)	0.5474	0.5947	0.4575	0.4039
NJU	0.5433	0.5694	–	–
ETRI	0.5260	0.5745	0.5327	0.5222

Table 3: Evaluation results on the WMT-19 QE sentence-level shared task. Here we only show the top four teams.

3.2 Results

WMT-18 En-De-SMT Results are shown on the left side of Table 2. We can see that our SOURCE model significantly outperforms the state-of-the-art single model from the previous year (Bilingual Expert) and is comparable to the ensemble model from JXNU.

WMT-18 En-De-NMT We evaluate our model through CodaLab, which is recommended by the host. Results are shown on the right side of Table 2. The results are similar to the SMT ones, our single SOURCE model can obtain results comparable to the best ensemble systems. It is worth mentioning that our ensemble model significantly outperforms the best system from the previous year on both scoring (Pearson r) and ranking (Spearman ρ) subtasks.

WMT-19 En-De-NMT and En-Ru-NMT The official result from WMT-19 is shown in Table 3. Our system achieves the second place on En-De and the third place on En-Ru. It is worth mentioning that due to the limitation of computational resource, we train far fewer models for En-Ru than En-De, so it is reasonable that our system performs much better on the En-De dataset.

4 Conclusion and Discussion

Empirical results indicate that decreasing the visible information makes token-prediction more difficult, and forces the model to learn more useful structures from the data, which in turn becomes features of higher quality for the QE task. The experimental results on WMT-18 shows the effectiveness of our SOURCE model as well as our stacking ensemble strategy. According to the official evaluation results on WMT-19 dataset, our ensemble SOURCE modela chieves the second place on En-De dataset and the third place on En-Ru dataset.

We will explore the BERT-style structure to better condition on source sentences in the future.

References

Martín Abadi, Ashish Agarwal, Paul Barham, Eugene Brevdo, Zhifeng Chen, Craig Citro, Greg S. Corrado, Andy Davis, Jeffrey Dean, Matthieu Devin, Sanjay Ghemawat, Ian Goodfellow, Andrew Harp, Geoffrey Irving, Michael Isard, Yangqing Jia, Rafal Jozefowicz, Lukasz Kaiser, Manjunath Kudlur, Josh Levenberg, Dandelion Mané, Rajat Monga, Sherry

Moore, Derek Murray, Chris Olah, Mike Schuster, Jonathon Shlens, Benoit Steiner, Ilya Sutskever, Kunal Talwar, Paul Tucker, Vincent Vanhoucke, Vijay Vasudevan, Fernanda Viégas, Oriol Vinyals, Pete Warden, Martin Wattenberg, Martin Wicke, Yuan Yu, and Xiaoqiang Zheng. 2015. TensorFlow: Large-scale machine learning on heterogeneous systems. Software available from tensorflow.org.

Dzmitry Bahdanau, Kyunghyun Cho, and Yoshua Bengio. 2014. Neural machine translation by jointly learning to align and translate. *arXiv preprint arXiv:1409.0473*.

Rajen Chatterjee, Matteo Negri, Raphael Rubino, and Marco Turchi. 2018. Findings of the WMT 2018 shared task on automatic post-editing. In *Proceedings of the Third Conference on Machine Translation: Shared Task Papers*, pages 710–725.

Jacob Devlin, Ming-Wei Chang, Kenton Lee, and Kristina Toutanova. 2018. Bert: Pre-training of deep bidirectional transformers for language understanding. *arXiv preprint arXiv:1810.04805*.

Kai Fan, Bo Li, Fengming Zhou, and Jiayi Wang. 2018. "bilingual expert" can find translation errors. *CoRR*, abs/1807.09433.

Marcin Junczys-Dowmunt and Roman Grundkiewicz. 2016. Log-linear combinations of monolingual and bilingual neural machine translation models for automatic post-editing. In *Proceedings of the First Conference on Machine Translation*, pages 751–758, Berlin, Germany.

Marcin Junczys-Dowmunt and Roman Grundkiewicz. 2017. An exploration of neural sequence-to-sequence architectures for automatic post-editing. In *Proceedings of the Eighth International Joint Conference on Natural Language Processing (Volume 1: Long Papers)*, pages 120–129, Taipei, Taiwan.

Hyun Kim and Jong-Hyeok Lee. 2016. A recurrent neural networks approach for estimating the quality of machine translation output. In *Proceedings of the 2016 Conference of the North American Chapter of the Association for Computational Linguistics: Human Language Technologies*, pages 494–498, San Diego, California.

G. Klein, Y. Kim, Y. Deng, J. Senellart, and A. M. Rush. 2017. OpenNMT: Open-Source Toolkit for Neural Machine Translation. *ArXiv e-prints*.

Guillaume Lample and Alexis Conneau. 2019. Cross-lingual language model pretraining. *arXiv preprint arXiv:1901.07291*.

Matthew E. Peters, Mark Neumann, Mohit Iyyer, Matt Gardner, Christopher Clark, Kenton Lee, and Luke Zettlemoyer. 2018. Deep contextualized word representations. In *Proc. of NAACL*.

Matthew Snover, Bonnie Dorr, Richard Schwartz, Linnea Micciulla, and John Makhoul. 2006. A study of translation edit rate with targeted human annotation. In *Proceedings of association for machine translation in the Americas*, volume 200.

Ilya Sutskever, Oriol Vinyals, and Quoc V Le. 2014. Sequence to sequence learning with neural networks. In *Advances in neural information processing systems*, pages 3104–3112.

Ashish Vaswani, Noam Shazeer, Niki Parmar, Jakob Uszkoreit, Llion Jones, Aidan N Gomez, Łukasz Kaiser, and Illia Polosukhin. 2017. Attention is all you need. In *Advances in Neural Information Processing Systems*, pages 5998–6008.

Jiayi Wang, Kai Fan, Bo Li, Fengming Zhou, Boxing Chen, Yangbin Shi, and Luo Si. 2018. Alibaba submission for WMT18 quality estimation task. In *Proceedings of the Third Conference on Machine Translation: Shared Task Papers*, pages 809–815, Belgium, Brussels.

Transformer-based Automatic Post-Editing Model
with Joint Encoder and Multi-source Attention of Decoder

WonKee Lee*, Jaehun Shin*, Jong-hyeok Lee
Department of Computer Science and Engineering,
Pohang University of Science and Technology (POSTECH), Republic of Korea
{wklee, jaehun.shin, jhlee}@postech.ac.kr

Abstract

This paper describes POSTECH's submission to the WMT 2019 shared task on Automatic Post-Editing (APE). In this paper, we propose a new multi-source APE model by extending Transformer. The main contributions of our study are that we 1) reconstruct the encoder to generate a joint representation of translation (*mt*) and its *src* context, in addition to the conventional *src* encoding and 2) suggest two types of multi-source attention layers to compute attention between two outputs of the encoder and the decoder state in the decoder. Furthermore, we train our model by applying various teacher-forcing ratios to alleviate exposure bias. Finally, we adopt the ensemble technique across variations of our model. Experiments on the WMT19 English-German APE data set show improvements in terms of both TER and BLEU scores over the baseline. Our primary submission achieves -0.73 in TER and +1.49 in BLEU compared to the baseline, and ranks second among all submitted systems.

1 Introduction

Automatic Post-Editing (APE) is the task of automatically correcting errors in a given the machine translation (MT) output to generate a better translation (Chatterjee et al., 2018). Because APE can be regarded as a sequence-to-sequence problem, MT techniques have been previously applied to this task. Subsequently, it is only natural that neural APE has been proposed following the appearance of neural machine translation (NMT).

Among the initial approaches to neural APE, a log-linear combination model (Junczys-Dowmunt and Grundkiewicz, 2016) that combines bilingual and monolingual translations yielded the best results. Since then, In order to leverage information from both MT outputs (*mt*) and its corresponding source sentences (*src*), a multi-encoder model (Libovický et al., 2016) based on multi-source translation (Zoph and Knight, 2016) has become the prevalent approach (Bojar et al., 2017). Recently, with the advent of Transformer (Vaswani et al., 2017), most of the participants in the WMT18 APE shared task proposed Transformer-based multi-encoder APE models (Chatterjee et al., 2018).

Previous multi-encoder APE models employ separate encoders for each input (*src*, *mt*), and combine their outputs in various ways: by 1) sequentially applying attention between the hidden state of the decoder and the two outputs (Junczys-Dowmunt and Grundkiewicz, 2018; Shin and Lee, 2018) or 2) simply concatenating them (Pal et al., 2018; Tebbifakhr et al., 2018). However, these approaches seem to overlook one of the key differences between general multi-source translation and APE. Because the errors *mt* may contain are dependent on the MT system, the encoding process for *mt* should reflect its relationship with the source sentence. Furthermore, we believe that it would be helpful to incorporate information from the source sentence, which should ideally be error-free, in addition to the jointly encoded *mt* in generating post-edited sentence.

From these points of view, we propose a multi-source APE model by extending Transformer to contain a joint multi-source encoder and a decoder that involves a multi-source attention layer to combine the outputs of the encoder. Apart from that, we apply various teacher-forcing ratios at training time to alleviate exposure bias. Finally, we ensemble model variants for our submission. The remainder of the paper is organized as follows: Section 2 describes our model architecture.

---

* Both authors equally contributed to this work

Proceedings of the Fourth Conference on Machine Translation (WMT), Volume 3: Shared Task Papers (Day 2) pages 112–117
Florence, Italy, August 1-2, 2019. ©2019 Association for Computational Linguistics

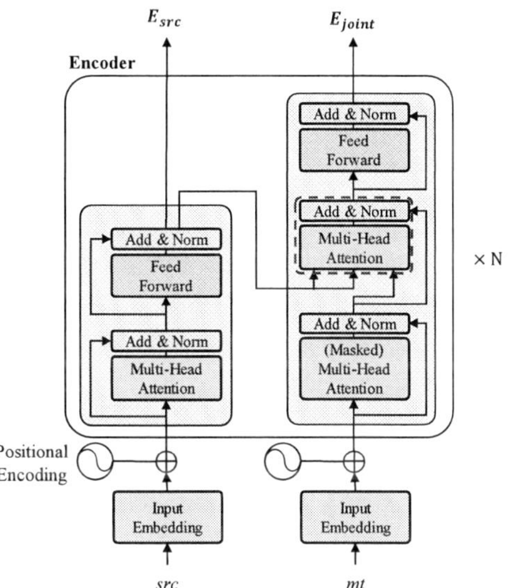

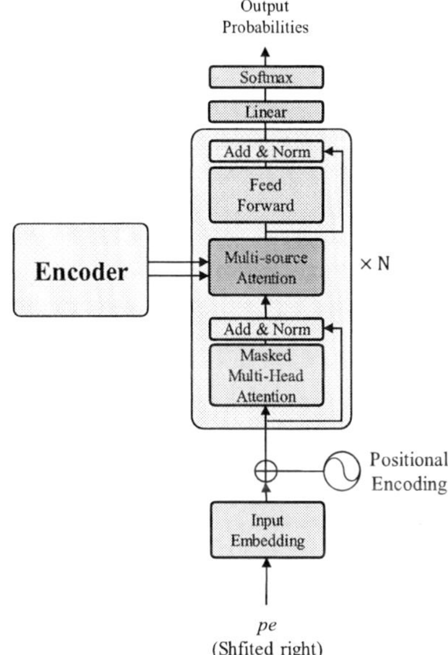

Figure 1: **The architecture of the proposed encoder** – the dashed square indicates the joint hidden representation of two sources

Figure 2: The architecture of the decoder

Section 3 summarizes the experimental results, and Section 4 gives the conclusion.

2 Model Description

We adopt Transformer to the APE problem, which takes multiple inputs (*src*, *mt*) to generate a post-edited sentence (*pe*). In the following subsections, we describe our modified encoder and decoder.

2.1 Encoder

The proposed encoder structure for multi-source inputs, as shown in Figure 1, is an extension of what is introduced in Vaswani et al. (2017) developed considering single-source input. Similar to recent APE studies, our encoder receives two sources: *src* $x = (x_1, ..., x_{T_x})$ and *mt* $y = (y_1, ..., y_{T_y})$, where T_x and T_y denote their sequence lengths respectively, but produce the joint representation $E_{joint} = (e_1^j, ..., e_{T_y}^j)$, in addition to encoded *src* $E_{src} = (e_1^s, ..., e_{T_x}^s)$.

Joint representation. Unlike previous studies, which independently encode two input sources using separate encoding modules, we incorporate *src* context information into each hidden state of *mt* through the single encoding module, resulting in a joint representation of two sources. As shown with the dashed square in Figure 1, jointly represented hidden states are obtained from the residu-

al connection and multi-head attention that takes $H_{src} \in \mathbb{R}^{T_x \times d}$ as keys and values and $H_{mt} \in \mathbb{R}^{T_y \times d}$ as queries. Therefore, the joint representation of each level of the stack ($i = 1, ..., N$) can be expressed with *MultiHead(Q, K, V)* and *LayerNorm* described in Vaswani et al. (2017) as follows:

$$H_{joint}^i = \text{LayerNorm}(H_{mt}^i + C_{src}^i)$$

where

$$C_{src}^i = \text{MultiHead}(H_{mt}^i, H_{src}^i, H_{src}^i) \qquad (1)$$

Stack-level attention. When applying attention across source and target, the original Transformer only considers source hidden states retrieved from the final stack, whereas our encoder feeds into each attention layer the *src* embeddings from the same level, as can be seen in (1).

Masking option. The self-attention layer that is the first attention layer of the *mt* encoding module optionally includes a future mask, which mimics the general decoding process of MT systems that depends only on previously generated words. We conduct experiments (§3.2) for two cases: with and without this option.

2.2 Decoder

Our decoder is an extension of Transformer decoder, in which the second multi-head attention layer that originally only refers to single-source

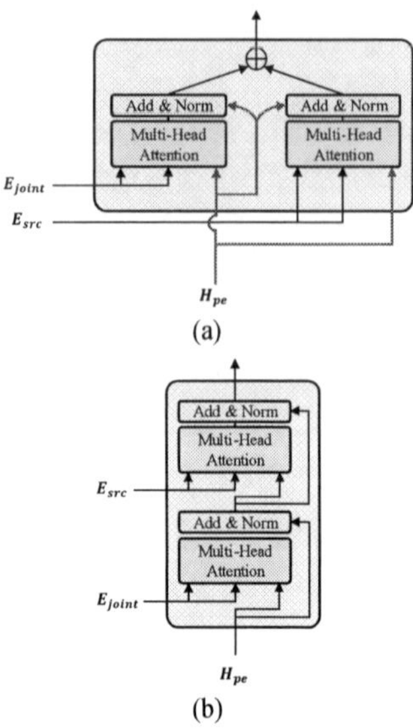

(a)

(b)

Figure 3: Illustrations of the multi-source attention layer. (a) and (b) refer to the linear and sequential combinations, respectively.

encoder states is replaced with a multi-source attention layer. Figure 2 shows our decoder architecture including the multi-source attention layer that attends to both outputs of the encoder. Furthermore, we construct two types of the multi-source attention layer by utilizing different strategies in combining attention over two encoder output states.

Multi-source parallel attention. Figure 3a illustrates the structure of parallel attention. The decoder's hidden state simultaneously attends to each output of the multi-source encoder, followed by residual connection, and the results are linearly combined by summing them at the end:

$$H_{parallel} = H_1 + H_2$$

where

$$H_1 = \text{LayerNorm}\big(H_{pe} + C_{joint}\big)$$
$$H_2 = \text{LayerNorm}\big(H_{pe} + C_{src}\big)$$
$$C_{Joint} = \text{MultiHead}\big(H_{pe}, E_{joint}, E_{joint}\big)$$
$$C_{src} = \text{MultiHead}\big(H_{pe}, E_{src}, E_{src}\big).$$

Note that $H_{pe} \in \mathbb{R}^{T_z \times d}$ denotes the hidden states for decoder input pe $z = (z_1, \dots, z_{T_z})$.

Multi-source sequential attention. As shown in Figure 3b, two outputs of the encoder are sequentially combined with the decoder's hidden state: E_{joint} and the decoder's hidden state are first assigned to multi-head attention and residual con-

Dataset	Triplets	TER
official training set	13,442	14.89
official development set	1,000	15.08
eSCAPE-NMT	7,258,533	60.54
eSCAPE-NMT-filtered	4,303,876	39.65

Table 1: **Dataset statistics** – number of sentence triplets (src, mt, pe) and TER score.

nection layers, then the same operation is performed between the result and E_{src}.

$$H_{seq} = \text{LayerNorm}(H' + C_{src})$$

where

$$H' = \text{LayerNorm}\big(H_{pe} + C_{joint}\big)$$
$$C_{src} = \text{MultiHead}(H', E_{src}, E_{src})$$
$$C_{joint} = \text{MultiHead}\big(H_{pe}, E_{joint}, E_{joint}\big).$$

This approach is structurally equivalent to Junczys-Dowmunt and Grundkiewicz (2018), except that the encoder states being passed on are different.

3　Experiments

3.1　Dataset

We used the WMT19 official English-German APE dataset (Chatterjee et al., 2018) which consists of a training and development set. In addition, we adopted the eSCAPE NMT dataset (Negri et al., 2018) as additional training data. We extracted sentence triplets from the eSCAPE-NMT dataset according to the following criteria, to which the official training dataset mostly adheres. Selected triplets have no more than 70 words in each sentence, a TER less than or equal to 75, and a reciprocal length ratio within the monolingual pair (*mt*, *pe*) less than 1.4. Table 1 summarizes the statistic of the datasets.

3.2　Training Details

Settings. We modified the OpenNMT-py (Klein et al., 2017) implementation of Transformer to build our models. Most hyperparameters such as the dimensionality of hidden states, optimizer settings, dropout ratio, etc. were copied from the "base model" described in Vaswani et al. (2017). We adjusted the warm-up learning steps and batch size per triplets to 18k and ~25k, respectively. For data preprocessing, we employed subword encoding (Kudo, 2018) with 32k shared vocabulary.

114

Teacher-forcing Ratios	Architecture							
	Parallel w/ masking		Parallel w/o masking		Sequential w/ masking		Sequential w/o masking	
	TER	BLEU	TER	BLEU	TER	BLEU	TER	BLEU
w/o tuning	15.06	77.18	15.03	77.29	14.89	77.38	15.10	77.19
1.00	15.02	77.25	14.95	**77.41**	14.83	**77.54**	14.75	**77.68**
0.95	15.07	77.24	14.94	77.24	14.83	77.41	**14.53**	77.36
0.90	**14.75**	**77.54**	14.94	77.26	14.79	77.40	14.99	77.26
0.85	14.86	77.37	14.95	77.30	**14.73**	77.50	14.76	77.56
0.80	14.98	77.06	**14.93**	77.15	14.83	77.44	15.34	76.79

Table 2: **Results of training variants** – the columns correspond to their architectures and the rows correspond to their teacher-forcing ratios. The bold values indicate the best result in the metrics for each architecture. "w/o tuning" refer to generic model.

Two-step training. We separated the training process into two steps: the first phase for training a generic model, and the second phase to fine-tune the model. For the first phase, we trained the model with a union dataset that is the concatenation of eSCAPE-NMT-filtered, and the upsampled official training set by copying 20 times. After reaching the convergence point in the first phase, we fine-tuned the model by running the second phase using only the official training set.

Model variations. In our experiment, we constructed four types of models in terms of the existence of the encoder future mask and the type of the multi-source attention layer in the decoder as follows:

- **Parallel w/ masking** where the model involves the multi-source parallel attention layer with the encoder mask.

- **Parallel w/o masking** in which the encoder mask is excluded from Parallel w/ masking.

- **Sequential w/ masking** where the model involves the multi-source sequential attention layer with the encoder mask.

- **Sequential w/o masking** in which the encoder mask is excluded from Seq. w/ masking.

Teacher-forcing ratio. During training, because the decoder takes as input the target shifted to the right, the ground-truth words are passed to the decoder. However, at inference time, the decoder consumes only previously produced output words, causing exposure bias. To overcome this problem, we have empirically adjusted the teacher-forcing ratio in the second phase of training, so that teacher-forcing is applied stochastically in such a way that given a ratio α, the greedy decoding output of the previous step is fed into the next input with a probability of $1 - \alpha$.

Ensemble. To leverage all variants in different architectures and teacher-forcing ratios, we combined them using an ensemble approach according to the following three criteria:

- Ens_set_1: top-N candidates among all variants in terms of TER.

- Ens_set_2: top-N candidates for variants in each architecture, in terms of TER.

- Ens_set_3: two candidates for variants in each architecture, achieving the best TER and BLEU scores, respectively.

3.3 Results

We trained a generic model for each of the four model variations mentioned in §3.2. Then, we fine-tuned those models using various teacher-forcing ratios. For evaluation, we used TER (Snover et al., 2006) and BLEU (Papineni et al., 2002) scores on the WMT official development dataset. Table 2 shows the scores of the generic and fine-tuned models according to their architectures and teacher-forcing ratios. The result shows that adjusting teacher-forcing ratio helps improve the post-editing performance of the models.

Table 3 gives the results of the ensemble models. The ensemble models had slightly worse TER scores ($+0.02 \sim +0.13$) than the best TER score in the fine-tuned variants, but better BLEU scores ($+0.09 \sim +0.27$) than the best BLEU score. We

Models	TER	BLEU	Submission Name
Ens_set_1-top4	14.66	77.79	–
Ens_set_1-top6	14.62	77.79	–
Ens_set_1-top8	14.62	77.81	–
Ens_set_2-top1	14.58	77.86	Contrastive (top1Ens4)
Ens_set_2-top2	**14.55**	**77.95**	Primary (top2Ens8)
Ens_set_3	14.61	77.86	Contrastive (var2Ens8)

Table 3: **Results of ensemble models** – "Submission Name" indicates the names (types) for the submission. The bold values indicate the best result in each metric.

Systems	TER	BLEU
UNBABEL_Primary	**16.06**	75.96
POSTECH_Primary (top2Ens8)	16.11	**76.22**
POSTECH_Contrastive (var2Ens8)	16.13	76.21
USSAR-DFKI_Contrastive	16.15	75.75
POSTECH_Contrastive (top1Ens4)	16.17	76.15
Tebbifakhr et al. (2018)	16.46	75.53
Junczys-Dowmunt and Grundkiewicz (2018)	16.50	75.44
Shin and Lee (2018)	16.70	75.14
Baseline	16.84	74.73

Table 4: **Submission results** – the top-5 systems among official results of the WMT19 APE shared task. We also include the previous round results for comparison. The bold values indicate the best result in each metric.

selected the three best ensemble models for submission, expecting to reap the benefits from leveraging different architectures in the decoding process. The names and types for submission are noted in Table 3.

Submission results. The results of primary and contrastive submission on the official test set are reported in Table 4. Our primary submission achieves improvements of -0.73 in TER and +1.49 in BLEU compared to the baseline, and shows better results than the state-of-the-art of the last round with -0.35 in TER and +0.69 in BLEU. While our primary system ranks second out of 18 systems submitted this year, it shows the highest BLEU score.

4   Conclusion

In this paper, we present POSTECH's submissions to the WMT19 APE shared task. We propose a new Transformer-based APE model comprising a joint multi-source encoder and a decoder with two types of multi-source attention layers. The proposed encoder generates a joint representation for MT output with optional masking, in addition to the encoded source sentence. The proposed decoder employs two types of multi-source attention layers according to the post-editing strategy. We refine the eSCAPE-NMT dataset and apply two-step training with various teacher-forcing ratios. Finally, our ensemble models showed improvements in terms of both TER and BLEU, and outperform not only the baseline but also the best model from the previous round of the task.

References

Ondřej Bojar, Rajen Chatterjee, Christian Federmann, Yvette Graham, Barry Haddow, Shujian Huang, Matthias Huck, Philipp Koehn, Qun Liu, and Varvara Logacheva. 2017. Findings of the 2017 conference on machine translation (wmt17). In *Proceedings of the Second Conference on Machine Translation*, page 169-214.

Rajen Chatterjee, Matteo Negri, Raphael Rubino, and Marco Turchi. 2018. Findings of the WMT 2018 Shared Task on Automatic Post-Editing. In *Proceedings of the Third Conference on Machine Translation: Shared Task Papers*, page 710-725.

Marcin Junczys-Dowmunt, and Roman Grundkiewicz. 2016. Log-linear Combinations of Monolingual and Bilingual Neural Machine Translation Models for Automatic Post-Editing. In *Proceedings of the*

First Conference on Machine Translation: Volume 2, Shared Task Papers, page 751-758.

Marcin Junczys-Dowmunt, and Roman Grundkiewicz. 2018. MS-UEdin Submission to the WMT2018 APE Shared Task: Dual-Source Transformer for Automatic Post-Editing. In *Proceedings of the Third Conference on Machine Translation: Shared Task Papers*, page 822-826.

Guillaume Klein, Yoon Kim, Yuntian Deng, Jean Senellart, and Alexander Rush. 2017. OpenNMT: Open-Source Toolkit for Neural Machine Translation. *Proceedings of ACL 2017, System Demonstrations*, 67-72.

Taku Kudo. 2018. Subword Regularization: Improving Neural Network Translation Models with Multiple Subword Candidates. In *Proceedings of the 56th Annual Meeting of the Association for Computational Linguistics (Volume 1: Long Papers)*, page 66-75.

Jindřich Libovický, Jindřich Helcl, Marek Tlustý, Ondřej Bojar, and Pavel Pecina. 2016. CUNI System for WMT16 Automatic Post-Editing and Multimodal Translation Tasks. In *Proceedings of the First Conference on Machine Translation: Volume 2, Shared Task Papers*, page 646-654.

Matteo Negri, Marco Turchi, Rajen Chatterjee, and Nicola Bertoldi. 2018. ESCAPE: a Large-scale Synthetic Corpus for Automatic Post-Editing. In *Proceedings of the Eleventh International Conference on Language Resources and Evaluation (LREC-2018)*.

Santanu Pal, Nico Herbig, Antonio Krüger, and Josef van Genabith. 2018. A Transformer-Based Multi-Source Automatic Post-Editing System. In *Proceedings of the Third Conference on Machine Translation: Shared Task Papers*, page 827-835.

Kishore Papineni, Salim Roukos, Todd Ward, and Wei-Jing Zhu. 2002. BLEU: a method for automatic evaluation of machine translation. In *Proceedings of the 40th annual meeting on association for computational linguistics*, page 311-318.

Jaehun Shin, and Jong-hyeok Lee. 2018. Multi-encoder Transformer Network for Automatic Post-Editing. In *Proceedings of the Third Conference on Machine Translation: Shared Task Papers*, page 840-845.

Matthew Snover, Bonnie Dorr, Richard Schwartz, Linnea Micciulla, and John Makhoul. 2006. A study of translation edit rate with targeted human annotation. In *Proceedings of association for machine translation in the Americas*.

Amirhossein Tebbifakhr, Ruchit Agrawal, Matteo Negri, and Marco Turchi. 2018. Multi-source transformer with combined losses for automatic post editing. In *Proceedings of the Third Conference on Machine Translation: Shared Task Papers*, page 846-852.

Ashish Vaswani, Noam Shazeer, Niki Parmar, Jakob Uszkoreit, Llion Jones, Aidan N Gomez, Łukasz Kaiser, and Illia Polosukhin. 2017. Attention is all you need. In *Advances in Neural Information Processing Systems*, page 5998-6008.

Barret Zoph, and Kevin Knight. 2016. Multi-Source Neural Translation. In *Proceedings of NAACL-HLT*, page 30-34.

Unbabel's Submission to the WMT2019 APE Shared Task: BERT-based Encoder-Decoder for Automatic Post-Editing

António V. Lopes
Unbabel

M. Amin Farajian
Unbabel

Gonçalo M. Correia
Instituto de Telecomunicações

Jonay Trenous
Unbabel

André F. T. Martins
Unbabel

{antonio.lopes, amin, sony,andre.martins}@unbabel.com
goncalo.correia@lx.it.pt

Abstract

This paper describes Unbabel's submission to the WMT2019 APE Shared Task for the English-German language pair. Following the recent rise of large, powerful, pretrained models, we adapt the BERT pretrained model to perform Automatic Post-Editing in an encoder-decoder framework. Analogously to dual-encoder architectures we develop a BERT-based encoder-decoder (BED) model in which a single pretrained BERT encoder receives both the source `src` and machine translation `mt` strings. Furthermore, we explore a conservativeness factor to constrain the APE system to perform fewer edits. As the official results show, when trained on a weighted combination of in-domain and artificial training data, our BED system with the conservativeness penalty improves significantly the translations of a strong Neural Machine Translation (NMT) system by -0.78 and $+1.23$ in terms of TER and BLEU, respectively. Finally, our submission achieves a new state-of-the-art, ex-aequo, in English-German APE of NMT.

1 Introduction

Automatic Post Editing (APE) aims to improve the quality of an existing Machine Translation (MT) system by learning from human edited samples. It first started by the automatic article selection for English noun phrases (Knight and Chander, 1994) and continued by correcting the errors of more complex statistical MT systems (Bojar et al., 2015, 2016; Chatterjee et al., 2018a). In 2018, the organizers of the WMT shared task introduced, for the first time, the automatic post-editing of neural MT systems (Chatterjee et al., 2018b).

Despite its successful application to SMT systems, it has been more challenging to automatically post edit the strong NMT systems (Junczys-Dowmunt and Grundkiewicz, 2018). This mostly is due to the fact that high quality NMT systems make fewer mistakes, limiting the improvements obtained by state-of-the-art APE systems such as self-attentive transformer-based models (Tebbifakhr et al., 2018; Junczys-Dowmunt and Grundkiewicz, 2018). In spite of these findings and considering the dominance of the NMT approach in both the academic and industrial applications, the WMT shared task organizers decided to move completely to the NMT paradigm this year and ignore the SMT technology. They also provide the previous year in-domain training set (i.e. $13k$ of <src,mt,pe> triplets) further increasing the difficulty of the task.

Training state-of-the-art APE systems capable of improving high quality NMT outputs requires large amounts of training data, which is not always available, in particular for this WMT shared task. Augmenting the training set with artificially synthesized data is one of the popular and effective approaches for coping with this challenge. It was first used to improve the quality of NMT systems (Sennrich et al., 2016) and then it was applied to the APE task (Junczys-Dowmunt and Grundkiewicz, 2016). This approach, however, showed limited success on automatically post editing the high quality translations of APE systems.

Transfer learning is another solution to deal with data sparsity in such tasks. It is based on the assumption that the knowledge extracted from other well-resourced tasks can be transferred to the new tasks/domains. Recently, large models pre-trained on multiple tasks with vast amounts of data, for instance BERT and MT-DNN (Devlin et al., 2018a; Liu et al., 2019), have obtained state-of-the-art results when fine-tuned over a small set of training samples. Following Correia and Martins (2019), in this paper we use BERT (Devlin et al., 2018a) within the encoder-decoder framework (§2.1) and formulate the task of Automatic

Proceedings of the Fourth Conference on Machine Translation (WMT), Volume 3: Shared Task Papers (Day 2) pages 118–123
Florence, Italy, August 1-2, 2019. ©2019 Association for Computational Linguistics

Post Editing as generating `pe` which is (possibly) the modified version of `mt` given the original source sentence `src`. As discussed in §2.1, instead of using multi-encoder architecture, in this work we concatenate the `src` and `mt` with the BERT special token (i.e. `[SEP]` and feed them to our single encoder.

We also introduce the *conservativeness penalty*, a simple yet effective mechanism that controls the freedom of our APE in modifying the given MT output. As we show in §2.2, in the cases where the automatic translations are of high quality, this factor forces the APE system to do less modifications, hence avoids the well-known problem of over-correction.

Finally, we augmented our original in-domain training data with a synthetic corpus which contains around $3M$ `<src,mt,pe>` triplets (§3.1). As discussed in §4, our system is able to improve significantly the MT outputs by -0.78 TER (Snover et al., 2016) and $+1.23$ BLEU (Papineni et al., 2002), achieving an ex-aequo first-place in the English-German track.

2 Approach

In this section we describe the main features of our APE system: the *BERT-based encoder-decoder* (BED) and the *conservativeness penalty*.

2.1 BERT-based encoder-decoder

Following (Correia and Martins, 2019) we adapt the BERT model to the APE task by integrating the model in an encoder-decoder architecture. To this aim we use a single BERT encoder to obtain a joint representation of the `src` and `mt` sentence and a BERT-based decoder where the multi-head context attention block is initialized with the weights of the self-attention block. Both the encoder and the decoder are initialized with the pre-trained weights of the multilingual BERT[1] (Devlin et al., 2018b). Figure 1 depicts our BED model.

Instead of using multiple encoders to separately encode `src` and `mt`, we use BERT pre-training scheme, where the two strings after being concatenated by the `[SEP]` special symbol are fed to the single encoder. We treat these sentences as `sentenceA` and `sentenceB` in (Devlin et al., 2018b) and assign different segment embeddings to each of them. This emulates a similar setting

[1]https://github.com/google-research/bert

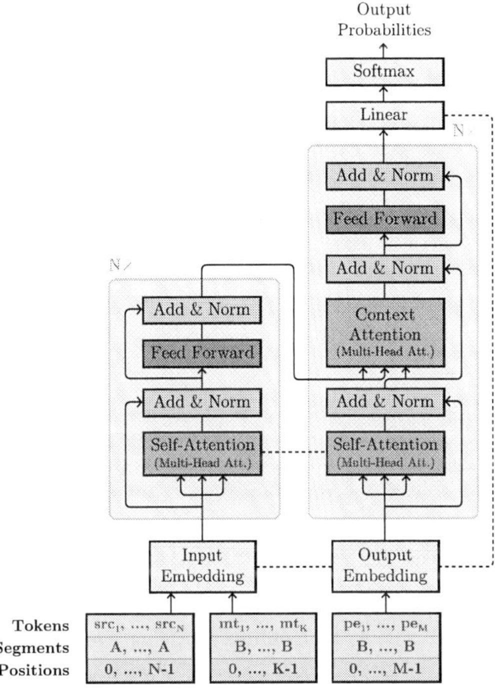

Figure 1: BERT encoder decoder, taken from Correia and Martins (2019).

to (Junczys-Dowmunt and Grundkiewicz, 2018) where a dual-source encoder with shared parameters is used to encode both input strings.

On the target side, following (Correia and Martins, 2019) we use a single decoder where the context attention block is initialized with the self attention weights, and all the weights of the self-attention are shared with the respective self-attention weights in the encoder.

2.2 Conservativeness penalty

With domain specific NMT systems making relatively few translation errors, APE systems face new challenges. This means more careful decisions have to be made by the APE system, making the least possible edits to the raw `mt`. To this aim, we introduce our "conservativeness" penalty developed on the *post editing penalty* proposed by (Junczys-Dowmunt and Grundkiewicz, 2016). It is a simple yet effective method to penalize/reward hypotheses in the beam, at inference time, that diverge far from the original input.

More formally, let V be the source and target vocabulary. We define $V_c = \{V_{src} \cup V_{mt}\}$ as the conservative tokens of an APE triplet, where $V_{src}, V_{mt} \subset V$ are the `src` and `mt` tokens, respectively. For the sake of argument we define V_c for decoding a single APE triplet, which can be generalized to batch decoding with V_c defined for each batch element. Given the $|V|$ sized vector of candidates h_t at each decoding step t, we modify the score/probability of each candidate v as:

$$h_t(v) = \begin{cases} h_t(v) - c & \text{if } v \in V \setminus V_c \\ h_t(v) & \text{otherwise} \end{cases} \quad (1)$$

where c is the conservativeness penalty, penalizing (or rewarding for negative values) all tokens of V not present in V_c. Note that, this penalty can be applied to either the raw non-normalized outputs of the model (logit) or the final probabilities (log probabilities).

As the log probabilities and logit scores have different bounds of $(-\infty, 0)$ and $(-\infty, +\infty)$, respectively, c is set accordingly. Hence, for positive values of conservativeness the aim is to avoid picking tokens not in the `src` and `mt`, thus, limiting the number of corrections. On the other hand, negative values enable over correction.

Moreover, in order to apply the penalty in the log probabilities, there are some considerations to take into account as we don't renormalize after the transformation. For positive values, the factor lowers the probability of all non conservative tokens, either increasing the confidence of an already picked conservative token, or favouring these tokens that are close to the best candidate – thus being closer to scores rather than probabilities. In contrast, negative penalties might require carefully selected values and truncating at the upper boundary – we did not experiment with negative values in this work, however the Quality Estimation shared task winning system used an APE-QE system with negative conservativeness (Kepler et al., 2019).

In contrast with Junczys-Dowmunt and Grundkiewicz, our model takes into account both `src` and `mt`, allowing to copy either of them directly. This is beneficial to handle proper nouns as they should be preserved in the post edition without any modification. Moreover, instead of setting the penalty as a fixed value of -1, we define it as a hyperparameter which enables a more dynamic control of our model's post-editions to the `mt` input.

3 Experiments

3.1 Data

This year for the English-German language pair the participants were provided an in-domain training set and the eSCAPE corpus, an artificially synthesized generic training corpus for APE (Negri et al., 2018). In addition to these corpora, they were allowed to use any additional data to train their systems. Considering this, and the fact that the in-domain training set belongs to the IT domain, we decided to use our own synthetic training corpus. Thus, we trained our models on a combination of the in-domain data released by the APE task organizers and this synthetic dataset.

In-domain training set: we use the $13k$ triplets of `<src,mt,pe>` in the IT domain without any preprocessing as they are already preprocessed by the shared task organizers. Despite the previous year where the `mt` side was generated either by a phrase-based or a neural MT system, this year all the source sentences were translated only by a neural MT system unknown to the participants.

Synthetic training set: instead of the eSCAPE corpus provided by the organizers we created our own synthetic corpus using the parallel data provided by the Quality Estimation shared task[2]. We found this corpus closer to the IT domain which is the target domain of the APE task. To create this corpus we performed the following steps:

1. Split the corpus into 5 folds f_i.

2. Use OpenNMT (Klein et al., 2017) to train 5 LSTM based translation models, one model $\mathcal{M}_i$ for every subset created by removing fold f_i from the training data.

3. Translate each fold f_i using the translation Model $\mathcal{M}_i$.

4. Join the translations to get an unbiased machine translated version of the full corpus.

5. Remove empty lines.

The final corpus has $3.3M$ triplets. We then oversampled the in-domain training data 20 times (Junczys-Dowmunt and Grundkiewicz, 2018) and used them together with our synthetic data to train our models.

---

[2]Dataset can be found under Additional Resouces at `http://www.statmt.org/wmt19/qe-task.html`

System	Beam	↓w/o c	↓best c	↓worst c
MT Baseline	-	15.08	-	-
BED	4	15.65	-	-
	6	15.61	-	-
+ logprobs	4	-	**14.84** $(c = 1.5)$	15.06 $(c = 2.3)$
	6	-	**14.87** $(c = 1.5)$	15.01 $(c = 2.5)$
+ logits	4	-	15.03 $(c = 1.7)$	15.25 $(c = 0.9)$
	6	-	15.05 $(c = 1.7)$	15.23 $(c = 0.9)$

Table 1: TER scores of the baseline NMT system and our BERT encoder-decoder `ape` model. The columns "w/o c", "best c", and "worst c" presents the scores of our system without the conservativeness penalty, with the best and the worst conservativeness penalty settings on our dev corpus, respectively. "logprobs" and "logits" refer, respectively, to the state where we apply the conservativeness factor (see §2.2)

3.2 BED training

We follow Correia and Martins for training our BERT-based Encoder-Decoder APE models. In particular, we set the learning rate to $5e^{-5}$ and use *bertadam* optimizer to perform $200k$ steps from which $20k$ are warmup steps. We set the effective batch size to 2048 tokens. Furthermore, we also use a shared matrix for the input and output token embedddings and the projection layer (Press and Wolf, 2017). Finally, we share the self-attention weights between the encoder and the decoder and initialize the multi-head attention of the decoder with the self-attention weights of the encoder.

Similarly to Junczys-Dowmunt (2018), we apply a data weighting strategy during training. However, we use a different weighting approach, where each sample s_i is assigned a weight, w_{s_i}, defined as $1 - TER(s_i)$. This results in assigning higher weights to the samples with less MT errors and vice versa, which might sound counter intuitive since in the APE task the goal is to learn more from the samples with larger number of errors. However, in this task, where the translations are provided by strong NMT systems with very small number of errors, our APE system needs to be conservative and learn to perform limited number of modifications to the `mt`.

3.3 BED decoding

In the decoding step we perform the standard beam decoding with our conservativeness factor. We fine tuned the this factor on the dev set provided by the organizers. Furthermore, in our experiments we set restrict the search to $c \in [0, +5]$ and use beam sizes of 4 and 6. In our preliminary experiments larger beam sizes didn't help to improve the performance further. Finally, we used

the evaluation script available on the website to access the performance of our model.

4 Results and discussion

In our preliminary experiments we noticed that using the pure BED model does not improve the quality of the translations provided by strong NMT systems. As Table 1 shows, it actually degrades the performance by -0.57 TER scores. Although the scores in Correia and Martins are actually closer to the baseline, we find that using the BED model only, without controlling the conservativeness to the original MT can lead to baseline level scores (on dev). Hence, we applied different conservativeness penalties during the beam decoding and as the results in Table 1 show, different values for this hyperparameter significantly changes the performance of our model. For the sake of compactness, here we present only the best (i.e. `best c`) and worst (i.e. `worst c`) scores by our model, to compare the effect of this factor.

Furthermore, intuitively, logits stands as the best candidate to apply the penalty, not only it was done in a similar fashion previously (Junczys-Dowmunt and Grundkiewicz, 2018), but also, after the normalization of the weights, the conservative tokens should have large peaks while having a stable behaviour. However, we achieved our best scores with penalties over the log probabilities, suggesting pruning hypothesis directly after normalizing the logits leads to more conservative outputs. Nonetheless, we leave as future work further investigations on the impact of pruning before and after normalizing the logits, as well as exploring renormalization of the log probabilities. Finally, we hypothesize that not only our BED model but also other APE models could benefit from the conservativeness penalty. We, however, leave it to be explored in future work.

Regarding the performance of our model on the official test set, as the results of Table 2 show, we outperform last year's winning systems by almost -0.4 TER and $+0.5$ BLEU, which for strong performing NMT systems is significant. In addition, our submission ranks first in the official results [3], *ex aequo* with 3 other systems. Table 3 depicts the official results of the shared task, considering only the best submission of each team.

	↓TER	↑BLEU
Baseline	16.84	74.73
(Tebbifakhr et al., 2018)	16.46	75.53
Primary	**16.08**	**75.96**
Contrastive	16.21	75.70

Table 2: Submission at the WMT APE shared task.

Although in this paper we did not present an ablation analysis (due to time constraints), we hypothesize that three BED training and decoding techniques used in this work were influential on the final result obtained for this task: i) the synthetic training corpus contains more IT domain samples than the generic eSCAPE corpus, making it a suitable dataset to train APE systems for this domain; ii) the data weighting mechanism enforces the system to be more conservative and learn fewer edits which is crucial for strong specialized NMT engines, and, finally, iii) the conservativeness factor is crucial to avoid the well-known problem of over-correction posed generally by APE systems over the high quality NMT outputs, guaranteeing faithfulness to the original MT.

5   Conclusion

We presented Unbabel's submissions to the APE shared task at WMT 2019 for the English-German language pair. Our model uses the BERT pre-trained language model within the encoder-decoder framework and applies a conservative factor to control the faithfulness of APE system to the original input stream.

The result of the official evaluation show that our system is able to effectively detect and correct the few errors made by the strong NMT system, improving the score by -0.8 and $+1.2$ in terms of TER and BLEU, respectively.

---

[3]Available at http://www.statmt.org/wmt19/ ape-task.html under *Results*.

System	↓Ter	↑BLEU
Ours (Unbabel)	**16.06**⋆	75.96
POSTECH	16.11⋆	**76.22**
USSAR DFKI	16.15⋆	75.75
FBK	16.37⋆	75.71
UdS MTL	16.77	75.03
IC USFD	16.78	74.88
Baseline	16.84	74.73
ADAP DCU	17.07	74.30

Table 3: APE Results as provided by the shared task organizers. We only present the best score of each team. ⋆ indicates not statistically significantly different, *ex aequo*.

Finally, using APE to improve strong in-domain Neural Machine Translation systems is increasingly more challenging, and ideally the editing system will tend to perform less and less modifications of the raw mt. In line with Junczys-Dowmunt and Grundkiewicz's suggestion, studying how to apply APE to engines in generic data (domain agnostic) can be a more challenging task, as it would require more robustness and generalization of the APE system.

Acknowledgments

The authors would like to thank the anonymous reviewers for the feedback. Moreover, we would like to thank António Góis, Fábio Kepler, and Miguel Vera for the fruitful discussions and help. We would also like to thank the support provided by the EU in the context of the PT2020 project (contracts 027767 and 038510), by the European Research Council (ERC StG DeepSPIN 758969), and by the Fundação para a Ciência e Tecnologia through contract UID/EEA/50008/2019.

References

Ondřej Bojar, Rajen Chatterjee, Christian Federmann, Yvette Graham, Barry Haddow, Matthias Huck, Antonio Jimeno Yepes, Philipp Koehn, Varvara Logacheva, Christof Monz, Matteo Negri, Aurelie Neveol, Mariana Neves, Martin Popel, Matt Post, Raphael Rubino, Carolina Scarton, Lucia Specia, Marco Turchi, Karin Verspoor, and Marcos Zampieri. 2016. Findings of the 2016 conference on machine translation. In *Proceedings of the First Conference on Machine Translation*, pages 131–198, Berlin, Germany. Association for Computational Linguistics.

Ondřej Bojar, Rajen Chatterjee, Christian Federmann,

Barry Haddow, Matthias Huck, Chris Hokamp, Philipp Koehn, Varvara Logacheva, Christof Monz, Matteo Negri, Matt Post, Carolina Scarton, Lucia Specia, and Marco Turchi. 2015. Findings of the 2015 workshop on statistical machine translation. In *Proceedings of the Tenth Workshop on Statistical Machine Translation*, pages 1–46, Lisbon, Portugal. Association for Computational Linguistics.

Rajen Chatterjee, Matteo Negri, Raphael Rubino, and Marco Turchi. 2018a. Findings of the WMT 2018 shared task on automatic post-editing. In *Proceedings of the Third Conference on Machine Translation: Shared Task Papers*, pages 710–725, Belgium, Brussels. Association for Computational Linguistics.

Rajen Chatterjee, Matteo Negri, Raphael Rubino, and Marco Turchi. 2018b. Findings of the WMT 2018 shared task on automatic post-editing. In *Proceedings of the Third Conference on Machine Translation: Shared Task Papers*, pages 710–725, Belgium, Brussels. Association for Computational Linguistics.

Gonçalo Correia and André Martins. 2019. A simple and effective approach to automatic post-editing with transfer learning. In *Proceedings of the 57th annual meeting on association for computational linguistics*. Association for Computational Linguistics.

Jacob Devlin, Ming-Wei Chang, Kenton Lee, and Kristina Toutanova. 2018a. Bert: Pre-training of deep bidirectional transformers for language understanding. *arXiv preprint arXiv:1810.04805*.

Jacob Devlin, Ming-Wei Chang, Kenton Lee, and Kristina Toutanova. 2018b. Bert: Pre-training of deep bidirectional transformers for language understanding. *arXiv preprint arXiv:1810.04805*.

Marcin Junczys-Dowmunt. 2018. Microsoft's submission to the wmt2018 news translation task: How i learned to stop worrying and love the data. In *Proceedings of the Third Conference on Machine Translation: Shared Task Papers*, pages 425–430.

Marcin Junczys-Dowmunt and Roman Grundkiewicz. 2016. Log-linear combinations of monolingual and bilingual neural machine translation models for automatic post-editing. In *Proceedings of the First Conference on Machine Translation*, pages 751–758, Berlin, Germany. Association for Computational Linguistics.

Marcin Junczys-Dowmunt and Roman Grundkiewicz. 2018. MS-UEdin submission to the WMT2018 APE shared task: Dual-source transformer for automatic post-editing. In *Proceedings of the Third Conference on Machine Translation: Shared Task Papers, WMT 2018, Belgium, Brussels, October 31 - November 1, 2018*, pages 822–826.

Fabio Kepler, Jonay Trénous, Marcos Treviso, Miguel Vera, António Góis, M. Amin Farajian, António V. Lopes, and André F. T. Martins. 2019. Unbabels participation in the wmt19 translation quality estimation shared task. In *Proceedings of the Fourth Conference on Machine Translation*, Florence, Italy. Association for Computational Linguistics.

Guillaume Klein, Yoon Kim, Yuntian Deng, Jean Senellart, and Alexander M. Rush. 2017. OpenNMT: Open-source toolkit for neural machine translation. In *Proc. ACL*.

Kevin Knight and Ishwar Chander. 1994. Automated postediting of documents. In *Proceedings of the Twelfth AAAI National Conference on Artificial Intelligence*, AAAI'94, pages 779–784. AAAI Press.

Xiaodong Liu, Pengcheng He, Weizhu Chen, and Jianfeng Gao. 2019. Multi-task deep neural networks for natural language understanding. *arXiv preprint arXiv:1901.11504*.

Matteo Negri, Marco Turchi, Rajen Chatterjee, and Nicola Bertoldi. 2018. escape: a large-scale synthetic corpus for automatic post-editing. In *LREC 2018, Eleventh International Conference on Language Resources and Evaluation*, pages 24–30. European Language Resources Association (ELRA).

Kishore Papineni, Salim Roukos, Todd Ward, and Wei-Jing Zhu. 2002. Bleu: a method for automatic evaluation of machine translation. In *Proceedings of the 40th annual meeting on association for computational linguistics*, pages 311–318. Association for Computational Linguistics.

Ofir Press and Lior Wolf. 2017. Using the output embedding to improve language models. In *Proceedings of the 15th Conference of the European Chapter of the Association for Computational Linguistics: Volume 2, Short Papers*, pages 157–163, Valencia, Spain. Association for Computational Linguistics.

Rico Sennrich, Barry Haddow, and Alexandra Birch. 2016. Improving neural machine translation models with monolingual data. In *Proceedings of the 54th Annual Meeting of the Association for Computational Linguistics (Volume 1: Long Papers)*, pages 86–96, Berlin, Germany. Association for Computational Linguistics.

Matthew Snover, Bonnie Dorr, Richard Schwartz, Linnea Micciulla, and John Makhoul. 2016. A study of translation edit rate with targeted human annotation. In *Proceedings of association for machine translation in the Americas*, pages Vol. 200, No. 6.

Amirhossein Tebbifakhr, Ruchit Agrawal, Matteo Negri, and Marco Turchi. 2018. Multi-source transformer with combined losses for automatic post editing. In *Proceedings of the Third Conference on Machine Translation: Shared Task Papers*, pages 846–852, Belgium, Brussels. Association for Computational Linguistics.

USAAR-DFKI – The Transference Architecture for English–German Automatic Post-Editing

Santanu Pal[1,2], Hongfei Xu[1,2], Nico Herbig[2], Antonio Krüger[2], Josef van Genabith[1,2]

[1]Department of Language Science and Technology,
Saarland University, Germany
[2]German Research Center for Artificial Intelligence (DFKI),
Saarland Informatics Campus, Germany
{santanu.pal, josef.vangenabith}@uni-saarland.de
{hongfei.xu, nico.herbig, krueger, josef.van_genabith}@dfki.de

Abstract

In this paper we present an English–German Automatic Post-Editing (APE) system called *transference*, submitted to the APE Task organized at WMT 2019. Our *transference* model is based on a multi-encoder transformer architecture. Unlike previous approaches, it (i) uses a transformer encoder block for src, (ii) followed by a transformer decoder block, but without masking, for self-attention on mt, which effectively acts as second encoder combining $src \rightarrow mt$, and (iii) feeds this representation into a final decoder block generating pe. This model improves over the raw black-box neural machine translation system by 0.9 and 1.0 absolute BLEU points on the WMT 2019 APE development and test set. Our submission ranked 3rd, however compared to the two top systems, performance differences are not statistically significant.

1 Introduction & Related Work

Automatic post-editing (APE) is a method that aims to automatically correct errors made by machine translation (MT) systems before performing actual human post-editing (PE) (Knight and Chander, 1994), thereby reducing the translators' workload and increasing productivity (Pal et al., 2016a; Parra Escartín and Arcedillo, 2015b,a; Pal et al., 2016a). Recent advances in APE research are directed towards neural APE based on neural MT where APE systems can be viewed as a 2nd-stage MT system, translating predictable error patterns in MT output to their corresponding corrections. APE training data minimally involves MT output (mt) and the human post-edited (pe) version of mt, but additionally using the source (src) has been shown to provide further benefits (Bojar et al., 2015, 2016, 2017). Based on the training process, APE systems can be categorized as either single-source ($mt \rightarrow pe$) or multi-

source ($\{src, mt\} \rightarrow pe$) approaches. This integration of source-language information in APE is intuitively useful in conveying context information to improve APE performance. Neural APE was first proposed by Pal et al. (2016b) and Junczys-Dowmunt and Grundkiewicz (2016). A multi-source neural APE system can be configured either by using a single encoder that encodes the concatenation of src and mt (Niehues et al., 2016) or by using two separate encoders for src and mt and passing the concatenation of both encoders' final states to the decoder (Libovický et al., 2016). A small number of multi-source neural APE approaches were proposed in the WMT 2017 APE shared task. The two-encoder architecture (Junczys-Dowmunt and Grundkiewicz, 2017; Chatterjee et al., 2017; Varis and Bojar, 2017) of multi-source models utilizes both the source text (src) and the MT output (mt) to predict the post-edited output (pe) in a single end-to-end neural architecture.

In the WMT 2018 APE shared task, further multi-source APE architectures based on the transformer model (Vaswani et al., 2017) have been presented. The winning team for the NMT task in WMT 2018 Tebbifakhr et al. (2018) employ sequence-level loss functions in order to avoid exposure bias during training and to be consistent with the automatic evaluation metrics. (Pal et al., 2018) proposed an APE model that uses two separate self-attention-based encoders to encode mt and src, followed by a self-attended joint encoder that attends over a combination of the two encoded sequences and is used by the decoder for generating the post-edited sentence pe. Shin and Lee (2018) propose that each encoder has its own self-attention and feed-forward layer to process each input separately. On the decoder side, they add two additional multi-head attention layers, one for $src \rightarrow mt$ and another for $src \rightarrow pe$. There-

Proceedings of the Fourth Conference on Machine Translation (WMT), Volume 3: Shared Task Papers (Day 2) pages 124–131
Florence, Italy, August 1-2, 2019. ©2019 Association for Computational Linguistics

after another multi-head attention between the output of those attention layers helps the decoder to capture common words in mt which should remain in pe. The WMT 2018 winner for the PBSMT task (Junczys-Dowmunt and Grundkiewicz, 2018) also presented transformer-based multi-source APE called a dual-source transformer architecture. They use two encoders and stack an additional cross-attention component for $src \rightarrow pe$ above the previous cross-attention for $mt \rightarrow pe$. Comparing Shin and Lee (2018)'s approach with the winner system, there are only two differences in the architecture: (i) the cross-attention order of $src \rightarrow mt$ and $src \rightarrow pe$ in the decoder, and (ii) the winner system additionally shares parameters between two encoders.

In this work, we present a multi-source neural APE architecture called *transference*[1]. Our model contains (i) a source encoder (enc_{src}) which encodes src information, (ii) a second encoder ($enc_{src \rightarrow mt}$) which can also be viewed as a standard transformer decoding block, however, without masking, and (iii) a decoder (dec_{pe}) which captures the final representation from $enc_{src \rightarrow mt}$ via cross-attention. We thus recombine the different blocks of the transformer architecture and repurpose them for the APE task in a simple yet effective way. The intuition behind our architecture is to generate better representations via both self- and cross-attention and to further facilitate the learning capacity of the feed-forward layer in the decoder block.

The rest of the paper is organized as follows. In 2, we describe the *transference* architecture; 3 describes our experimental setup; 4 reports the results of our approach against the baseline; and finally, 5 concludes the paper with directions for future work.

2   Transference Model for APE

We propose a multi-source transformer model called *transference* (Figure 1), which takes advantage of both the encodings of src and mt and attends over a combination of both sequences while generating the post-edited sentence. The second encoder, $enc_{src \rightarrow mt}$, is identical to the transformer's decoder block but uses no masking in the self-attention layer, thus having one self-attention

<hr>

[1]Our implementation is available at `https://github.com/santanupal1980/Transference.git`

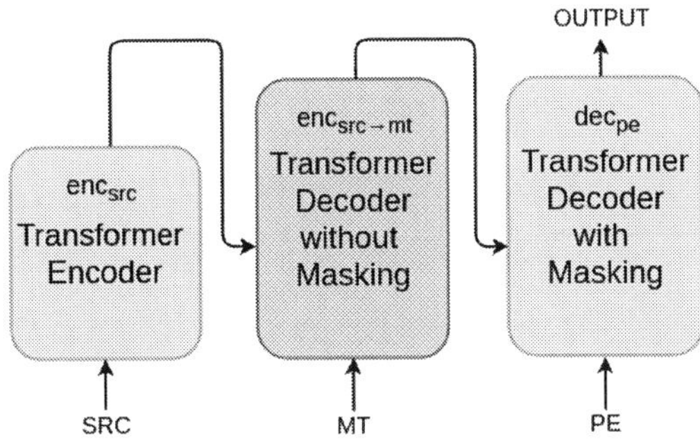

Figure 1: The *transference* model architecture for APE ($\{\mathbf{src}, \mathbf{mt}\}_{\mathbf{tr}} \rightarrow \mathbf{pe}$).

layer and an additional cross-attention layer for $src \rightarrow mt$. Here, the enc_{src} encoder and the dec_{pe} decoder are equivalent to the original transformer for neural MT (Vaswani et al., 2017). Put differently, our multi-source APE implementation extends Vaswani et al. (2017) by introducing an additional encoding block by which src and mt communicate with the decoder.

3   Experiments

We compare our approach against the *raw MT* output provided by the 1st-stage MT system. We evaluate the systems using BLEU (Papineni et al., 2002) and TER (Snover et al., 2006).

3.1   Data

For our experiments, we use the English–German WMT 2019 (Chatterjee et al., 2018) neural APE data. All released APE datasets consist of English–German triplets containing source English text (src) from the IT domain, the corresponding German translations (mt) from a 1st-stage NMT system, and the corresponding human-post-edited version (pe). Table 1 presents the statistics of the released data. As this released APE dataset is small in size (see Table 1), the synthetic eScape APE corpus (Negri et al., 2018), consisting of more than 7M triples, is available as an additional resource. All datasets, except for the eScape corpus, do not require any preprocessing in terms of encoding, tokenization or alignment.

For cleaning the noisy eScape dataset containing many unrelated language words (e.g. Chinese), we perform the following two steps: (i) we use the cleaning process described in Pal et al. (2015), and (ii) we execute the Moses (Koehn et al., 2007) corpus cleaning scripts with minimum and maximum number of tokens set to 1 and 100, respectively.

125

Corpus	Sentences	
	Overall	Cleaning
Train	13,442	-
Dev	1,000	-
Test	1,023	-
eScape	7.2M	6.5M

Table 1: Statistics of the WMT 2019 English-German APE Shared Task Dataset.

(iii) After cleaning, we perform punctuation normalization, and then use the Moses tokenizer to tokenize the eScape corpus with 'no-escape' option. Finally, we apply true-casing.

3.2 Experiment Setup

We split the released data (13.4K) into two sets; we use the first 12K for training and the remaining 1.4K as validation data. The development set (Dev) released by WMT2019[2] is used as test data for our experiment. We build two models *transference4M* and *transferenceALL* using slightly different training procedures.

For *transference4M*, we first train on a training set called eScape4M combined with the first 12k of the provided NMT training data. This eScape4M data is prepared using in-domain (for our case the 12K training data) bilingual cross-entropy difference for data selection as described in Axelrod et al. (2011). The difference in cross-entropy is computed based on two language models (LM): a domain-specific LM is estimated from the in-domain (12K) PE corpus (lm_i) and the out-domain LM (lm_o) is estimated from the eScape corpus. We rank the eScape corpus by assigning a score to each of the individual sentences which is the sum of the three cross-entropy (H) differences. For a jth sentence pair src_j–mt_j–pe_j, the score is calculated based on Equation 1.

$$\begin{aligned}
score = & |H_{src}(src_j, lm_i) - H_{src}(src_j, lm_o)| \\
& + |H_{mt}(mt_j, lm_i) - H_{mt}(mt_j, lm_o)| \\
& + |H_{pe}(pe_j, lm_i) - H_{pe}(pe_j, lm_o)| \quad (1)
\end{aligned}$$

For *transferenceALL*, we initially train on the complete eScape dataset (eScapeAll) combined with the first 12k of the training data. The eScapeAll data is sorted based on their in-domain similarities as described in Equation 1.

Both models are then fine-tuned towards the real data, by training again solely on the first 12k segments of the provided data. For both models, we perform checkpoint averaging using the 8 best checkpoints. We report the results on the development set provided by WMT2019, which we use as a test set.

To handle out-of-vocabulary words and to reduce the vocabulary size, instead of considering words, we consider subword units (Sennrich et al., 2016) by using byte-pair encoding (BPE). In the preprocessing step, instead of learning an explicit mapping between BPEs in the src, mt and pe, we define BPE tokens by jointly processing all triplets. Thus, src, mt and pe derive a single BPE vocabulary. Since mt and pe belong to the same language (DE) and src is a close language (EN), they naturally share a good fraction of BPE tokens, which reduces the vocabulary size.

3.3 Hyper-parameter Setup

We follow a similar hyper-parameter setup for all reported systems. All encoders (for $\{src, mt\}_{tr} \rightarrow pe$), and the decoder, are composed of a stack of $N_{src} = N_{mt} = N_{pe} = 6$ identical layers followed by layer normalization. We set all dropout values in the network to 0.1. During training, we employ label smoothing with value ϵ_{ls} = 0.1. The learning rate is varied throughout the training process, and increasing for the first training steps $warmup_{steps}$ = 8000 and afterwards decreasing as described in (Vaswani et al., 2017). All remaining hyper-parameters are set analogously to those of the transformer's *base* model.

At training time, the batch size is set to 25K tokens, with a maximum sentence length of 256 subwords, and a vocabulary size of 28K. After each epoch, the training data is shuffled. During decoding, we perform beam search with a beam size of 4. We use shared embeddings between mt and pe in all our experiments.

4 Results

The results of our two models, *transference4M* and *transferenceALL*, in comparison to the baseline *raw MT* are presented in Table 2 and 3. Table 2 reports results on the WMT2019 development set (Dev), Table 3 on the WMT2019 test set (Test).

---

[2]It is to be noted that, the released development set and test set are same as in WMT2018.

Exp No.	Models	Dev	
		BLEU ↑	TER ↓
Baseline			
1	*raw MT*	76.76	15.08
No fine-tuning			
2	*transference4M* (CONTRASTIVE)	77.11 (+0.35)	14.94 (-0.14)
3	*transferenceALL*	77.25 (+0.49)	14.87 (-0.21)
Fine tune with 12K			
4	*transference4M*	77.22 (+0.46)	14.89 (-0.19)
5	*transferenceALL*	77.39 (+0.63)	14.71 (-0.37)
Average 8 checkpoints on fine tuned models			
6	*transference4M*	77.27 (+0.51)	14.88 (-0.20)
7	*transferenceALL* (PRIMARY)	**77.67 (+0.91)**	**14.52 (-0.56)**

Table 2: Evaluation results on the WMT APE 2019 development set for the EN-DE NMT task.

Exp No.	Models	Test	
		BLEU ↑	TER ↓
Baseline			
1	*raw MT*	74.73	16.84
Submission			
2	*transference4M* (CONTRASTIVE)	73.97 (-0.76)	17.31 (+0.47)
3	*transferenceALL* (PRIMARY)	**75.75 (+1.02)**	**16.15 (-0.69)**

Table 3: Evaluation results on the WMT APE 2019 test set for the EN-DE NMT task.

4.1 Baselines

The *raw MT* output in Table 2 and Table 3 is a strong black-box NMT system (i.e., 1st-stage MT) on Dev and Test respectively. We report its performance observed with respect to the ground truth (pe), i.e., the post-edited version of mt. The original MT system scores 76.76 BLEU points and 15.08 TER on Dev as well as 74.73 BLEU points and 16.84 TER on Test.

4.2 Transference Transformer for APE

Table 2 shows the results of our *transference* architecture on the Dev set, where our two experimental setups *transference4M* (Exp 2) and *transferenceALL* (Exp 3) improve the performance over the baseline system. Compared to *transference4M* (Exp 2), our *transferenceALL* (Exp 3) performs better in terms of both BLEU and TER on the Dev set. Moreover, fine-tuning our transference models (Exp 4 and 5 in Table 2) yields further performance gains. Additionally averaging the 8 best checkpoints of our fine-tuned version models (Exp 6 and 7) provides further improvements. All models except *transference4M* (CONTRASTIVE, our *contrastive* submission in WMT2019 APE task)

yield statistically significant results ($p < 0.001$) over the *raw MT* baseline. *transferenceALL* (PRIMARY, our *primary* submission in WMT2019 APE task) (Exp 7) also provides statistically significant improvement over *transference4M* (Exp 6). For these and all following significance tests we employ the method by Clark et al. (2011)[3]. Table 2 shows that our APE architecture *transferenceALL* (PRIMARY) (Exp 7) significantly improves over the already very good NMT system by about +0.91 BLEU and -0.56 TER.

Table 3 presents the results of our submissions on the Test set in the WMT 2019 EN-DE APE task. We submitted *transference4M* (CONTRASTIVE) system – a weak model having performance close to the baseline, (i) to check whether in-domain data provides any gain in performance on the Test set or not, (ii) to create another baseline trained on in-domain data, by which we could analyze our PRIMARY transference model's capability of transfer learning. So far, we could not find an explanation why our CONTRASTIVE system behaves completely different on the Test set compared to the Dev

---

[3] https://github.com/jhclark/multeval

set. However, our primary submission *transferenceALL* (PRIMARY) shows similar performance on the WMT2019 Test set as on the Dev set. Overall our *transferenceALL* (PRIMARY) submission achieves statistically significant +1.02 absolute BLEU point and -0.69 absolute in TER improvements in performance over the baseline on the Test set.

4.3 Discussion

It is important to note that raw MT provides a strong baseline. Our proposed *transference* model (*transferenceALL*) shows statistically significant improvements in terms of BLEU and TER compared to this baseline even before fine-tuning, and further improvements after fine-tuning. Finally, after averaging the 8 best checkpoints, our *transferenceALL* model also shows consistent improvements in comparison to the baseline and other experimental setups.

Table 4 shows the performance of our *transferenceALL* model compared to the winner system of WMT 2018 ($wmt18_{Best}$) for the NMT task (Tebbifakhr et al., 2018) on Dev and Test data. The primary submission of $wmt18_{Best}$ scores 14.78 in TER and 77.74 in BLEU on the Dev set and 16.46 in TER and 75.53 in BLEU on the Test set. In comparison to $wmt18_{Best}$, our *transferenceALL* model achieves better scores in TER on both the Dev and Test set, however, in terms of BLEU the score acquired by our *transferenceALL* model is slightly worse for the Dev set, while some improvements were achieved on the Test data. In comparison to the $wmt2019_{Best}$ system, which achieved 16.06 in TER and 75.95 in BLEU according to the official released results[4], we do not used BERT (Devlin et al., 2018) in our system. Even though $wmt2019_{Best}$ integrated BERT, there is no statistical significant performance difference to our primary submission. Moreover, our system does not perform ensembling of multiple models, as the 2nd best system in WMT 2019, which achieves 16.11 in TER and 76.22 in BLEU.

We believe the reasons for the effectiveness of our approach to be as follows. (1) Our $enc_{src \to mt}$ contains two attention mechanisms: one is self-attention and another is cross-attention. The self-attention layer is not masked here; therefore, the cross-attention layer in $enc_{src \to mt}$ is informed by both previous and future time-steps from the self-

attended representation of mt (enc_{mt}) and additionally from enc_{src}. As a result, each state representation of $enc_{src \to mt}$ is learned from the context of src and mt. This might produce better representations for dec_{pe} which can access the combined context. In contrast, in $wmt18_{Best}$, the dec_{pe} accesses the concatenated encoded representations from src and mt encoder jointly. (2) Since pe is a post-edited version of mt, sharing the same language, mt and pe are quite similar compared to src. Therefore, attending over a fine-tuned representation from mt along with src, which is what we have done in this work, might be a reason for the better results compared to those achieved by attending over concatenated encoded information from src and mt directly.

5 Conclusions and Future Work

In this paper, we presented our submissions to the APE shared task at WMT 2019. We extend the transformer-based architecture to a multi-encoder transformer-based model that extends the standard transformer blocks in a simple and effective way for the APE task. Our model makes use of two separate encoders to encode src and mt; the second encoder additionally attends over a combination of both sequences to prepare the representation for the decoder to generate the post-edited translation. The proposed model outperforms the best-performing system of WMT 2018 on the Test data. Our primary submission ranked 3rd, however compared to other two top systems, the performance differences are not statistically significant.

Taking a departure from traditional transformer-based encoders, which perform self-attention only, our second encoder also performs cross-attention to produce representations for the decoder based on both src and mt. Our proposed multi-encoder transformer-based architecture is also generic and can be used for any multi-modal (or multi-source) task, e.g., multi-modal translation, multi-modal summarization.

Acknowledgments

This research was funded in part by the German research foundation (DFG) under grant number GE 2819/2-1 (project MMPE) and the German Federal Ministry of Education and Research (BMBF) under funding code 01IW17001 (project Deeplee). The responsibility for this publication

---

[4] http://www.statmt.org/wmt19/ape-task.html

Models	Dev		Test	
	BLEU $\uparrow$	TER $\downarrow$	BLEU $\uparrow$	TER $\downarrow$
$wmt2018_{Best}$	77.74	14.78	75.53	16.46
transferenceALL	77.67 (-0.07)	**14.52 (-0.26)**	**75.75 (+0.22)**	**16.15 (-0.31)**

Table 4: Comparison with $wmt2018_{Best}$ on the WMT APE 2018 Dev/Test set for the EN-DE NMT task.

lies with the authors. We also want to thank the reviewers for their valuable input, and the organizers of the shared task. We also thank the NVIDIA Corporation for providing a GPU through the NVIDIA GPU Grant.

References

Amittai Axelrod, Xiaodong He, and Jianfeng Gao. 2011. Domain Adaptation via Pseudo In-domain Data Selection. In *Proceedings of the Conference on Empirical Methods in Natural Language Processing*, EMNLP '11, pages 355–362.

Ondřej Bojar, Rajen Chatterjee, Christian Federmann, Yvette Graham, Barry Haddow, Shujian Huang, Matthias Huck, Philipp Koehn, Qun Liu, Varvara Logacheva, Christof Monz, Matteo Negri, Matt Post, Raphael Rubino, Lucia Specia, and Marco Turchi. 2017. Findings of the 2017 Conference on Machine Translation (WMT17). In *Proceedings of the Second Conference on Machine Translation, Volume 2: Shared Task Papers*, pages 169–214, Copenhagen, Denmark. Association for Computational Linguistics.

Ondřej Bojar, Rajen Chatterjee, Christian Federmann, Yvette Graham, Barry Haddow, Matthias Huck, Antonio Jimeno Yepes, Philipp Koehn, Varvara Logacheva, Christof Monz, Matteo Negri, Aurelie Neveol, Mariana Neves, Martin Popel, Matt Post, Raphael Rubino, Carolina Scarton, Lucia Specia, Marco Turchi, Karin Verspoor, and Marcos Zampieri. 2016. Findings of the 2016 Conference on Machine Translation. In *Proceedings of the First Conference on Machine Translation*, pages 131–198, Berlin, Germany. Association for Computational Linguistics.

Ondřej Bojar, Rajen Chatterjee, Christian Federmann, Barry Haddow, Matthias Huck, Chris Hokamp, Philipp Koehn, Varvara Logacheva, Christof Monz, Matteo Negri, Matt Post, Carolina Scarton, Lucia Specia, and Marco Turchi. 2015. Findings of the 2015 Workshop on Statistical Machine Translation. In *Proceedings of the Tenth Workshop on Statistical Machine Translation*, pages 1–46, Lisbon, Portugal. Association for Computational Linguistics.

Rajen Chatterjee, M. Amin Farajian, Matteo Negri, Marco Turchi, Ankit Srivastava, and Santanu Pal. 2017. Multi-Source Neural Automatic Post-Editing: FBK's participation in the WMT 2017 APE shared task. In *Proceedings of the Second Conference on Machine Translation, Volume 2: Shared Task Papers*, pages 630–638, Copenhagen, Denmark. Association for Computational Linguistics.

Rajen Chatterjee, Matteo Negri, Raphael Rubino, and Marco Turchi. 2018. Findings of the WMT 2018 Shared Task on Automatic Post-Editing. In *Proceedings of the Third Conference on Machine Translation, Volume 2: Shared Task Papers*, Brussels, Belgium. Association for Computational Linguistics.

Jonathan H. Clark, Chris Dyer, Alon Lavie, and Noah A. Smith. 2011. Better Hypothesis Testing for Statistical Machine Translation: Controlling for Optimizer Instability. In *Proceedings of the 49th Annual Meeting of the Association for Computational Linguistics: Human Language Technologies: Short Papers - Volume 2*, HLT '11, pages 176–181, Stroudsburg, PA, USA. Association for Computational Linguistics.

Jacob Devlin, Ming-Wei Chang, Kenton Lee, and Kristina Toutanova. 2018. Bert: Pre-training of deep bidirectional transformers for language understanding. *arXiv preprint arXiv:1810.04805*.

Marcin Junczys-Dowmunt and Roman Grundkiewicz. 2016. Log-linear Combinations of Monolingual and Bilingual Neural Machine Translation Models for Automatic Post-Editing. In *Proceedings of the First Conference on Machine Translation*, pages 751–758, Berlin, Germany.

Marcin Junczys-Dowmunt and Roman Grundkiewicz. 2017. The AMU-UEdin Submission to the WMT 2017 Shared Task on Automatic Post-Editing. In *Proceedings of the Second Conference on Machine Translation, Volume 2: Shared Task Papers*, pages 639–646, Copenhagen, Denmark. Association for Computational Linguistics.

Marcin Junczys-Dowmunt and Roman Grundkiewicz. 2018. MS-UEdin Submission to the WMT2018 APE Shared Task: Dual-Source Transformer for Automatic Post-Editing. In *Proceedings of the Third Conference on Machine Translation, Volume 2: Shared Task Papers*, pages 835–839, Belgium, Brussels. Association for Computational Linguistics.

Kevin Knight and Ishwar Chander. 1994. Automated Postediting of Documents. In *Proceedings of the Twelfth National Conference on Artificial Intelligence (Vol. 1)*, AAAI '94, pages 779–784, Seattle, Washington, USA.

Philipp Koehn, Hieu Hoang, Alexandra Birch, Chris Callison-Burch, Marcello Federico, Nicola Bertoldi, Brooke Cowan, Wade Shen, Christine Moran, Richard Zens, Chris Dyer, Ondřej Bojar, Alexandra Constantin, and Evan Herbst. 2007. Moses: Open Source Toolkit for Statistical Machine Translation. In *Proceedings of the 45th Annual Meeting of the ACL on Interactive Poster and Demonstration Sessions*, pages 177–180, Prague, Czech Republic.

Jindřich Libovický, Jindřich Helcl, Marek Tlustý, Ondřej Bojar, and Pavel Pecina. 2016. CUNI System for WMT16 Automatic Post-Editing and Multimodal Translation Tasks. In *Proceedings of the First Conference on Machine Translation*, pages 646–654, Berlin, Germany. Association for Computational Linguistics.

Matteo Negri, Marco Turchi, Rajen Chatterjee, and Nicola Bertoldi. 2018. ESCAPE: a Large-scale Synthetic Corpus for Automatic Post-Editing. In *Proceedings of the Eleventh International Conference on Language Resources and Evaluation (LREC 2018)*, Miyazaki, Japan. European Language Resources Association (ELRA).

Jan Niehues, Eunah Cho, Thanh-Le Ha, and Alex Waibel. 2016. Pre-Translation for Neural Machine Translation. In *Proceedings of COLING 2016, the 26th International Conference on Computational Linguistics: Technical Papers*, pages 1828–1836, Osaka, Japan. The COLING 2016 Organizing Committee.

Santanu Pal, Nico Herbig, Antonio Krger, and Josef van Genabith. 2018. A Transformer-Based Multi-Source Automatic Post-Editing System. In *Proceedings of the Third Conference on Machine Translation, Volume 2: Shared Task Papers*, pages 840–848, Belgium, Brussels. Association for Computational Linguistics.

Santanu Pal, Sudip Naskar, and Josef van Genabith. 2015. UdS-sant: English–German hybrid machine translation system. In *Proceedings of the Tenth Workshop on Statistical Machine Translation*, pages 152–157, Lisbon, Portugal. Association for Computational Linguistics.

Santanu Pal, Sudip Kumar Naskar, and Josef van Genabith. 2016a. Multi-Engine and Multi-Alignment Based Automatic Post-Editing and Its Impact on Translation Productivity. In *Proceedings of COLING 2016, the 26th International Conference on Computational Linguistics: Technical Papers*, pages 2559–2570, Osaka, Japan.

Santanu Pal, Sudip Kumar Naskar, Mihaela Vela, and Josef van Genabith. 2016b. A Neural Network Based Approach to Automatic Post-Editing. In *Proceedings of the 54th Annual Meeting of the Association for Computational Linguistics (Volume 2: Short Papers)*, pages 281–286, Berlin, Germany. Association for Computational Linguistics.

Kishore Papineni, Salim Roukos, Todd Ward, and Wei-Jing Zhu. 2002. BLEU: A Method for Automatic Evaluation of Machine Translation. In *Proceedings of the 40th Annual Meeting on Association for Computational Linguistics*, ACL '02, pages 311–318, Philadelphia, Pennsylvania.

Carla Parra Escartín and Manuel Arcedillo. 2015a. Living on the Edge: Productivity Gain Thresholds in Machine Translation Evaluation Metrics. In *Proceedings of the Fourth Workshop on Post-editing Technology and Practice*, pages 46–56, Miami, Florida (USA). Association for Machine Translation in the Americas (AMTA).

Carla Parra Escartín and Manuel Arcedillo. 2015b. Machine Translation Evaluation Made Fuzzier: A Study on Post-Editing Productivity and Evaluation Metrics in Commercial Settings. In *Proceedings of the MT Summit XV*, Miami (Florida). International Association for Machine Translation (IAMT).

Rico Sennrich, Barry Haddow, and Alexandra Birch. 2016. Neural Machine Translation of Rare Words with Subword Units. In *Proceedings of the 54th Annual Meeting of the Association for Computational Linguistics, ACL 2016, August 7-12, 2016, Berlin, Germany, Volume 1: Long Papers*.

Jaehun Shin and Jong-Hyeok Lee. 2018. Multi-encoder Transformer Network for Automatic Post-Editing. In *Proceedings of the Third Conference on Machine Translation, Volume 2: Shared Task Papers*, pages 853–858, Belgium, Brussels. Association for Computational Linguistics.

Matthew Snover, Bonnie Dorr, Richard Schwartz, Linnea Micciulla, and John Makhoul. 2006. A study of Translation Edit Rate with Targeted Human Annotation. In *Proceedings of Association for Machine Translation in the Americas*, pages 223–231, Cambridge, Massachusetts, USA.

Amirhossein Tebbifakhr, Ruchit Agrawal, Rajen Chatterjee, Matteo Negri, and Marco Turchi. 2018. Multi-Source Transformer with Combined Losses for Automatic Post Editing. In *Proceedings of the Third Conference on Machine Translation, Volume 2: Shared Task Papers*, pages 859–865, Belgium, Brussels. Association for Computational Linguistics.

Dusan Varis and Ondřej Bojar. 2017. CUNI System for WMT17 Automatic Post-Editing Task. In *Proceedings of the Second Conference on Machine Translation, Volume 2: Shared Task Papers*, pages 661–666, Copenhagen, Denmark. Association for Computational Linguistics.

Ashish Vaswani, Noam Shazeer, Niki Parmar, Jakob Uszkoreit, Llion Jones, Aidan N Gomez, Łukasz Kaiser, and Illia Polosukhin. 2017. Attention Is All You Need. In I. Guyon, U. V. Luxburg, S. Bengio,

H. Wallach, R. Fergus, S. Vishwanathan, and R. Garnett, editors, *Advances in Neural Information Processing Systems 30*, pages 5998–6008. Curran Associates, Inc.

APE through neural and statistical MT with augmented data:
ADAPT/DCU submission to the WMT 2019 APE Shared task

Dimitar Shterionov   **Joachim Wagner**   **Félix do Carmo**

ADAPT Centre, School of Computing, Dublin City University, Dublin, Ireland

{firstname}.{lastname}@adaptcentre.ie

Abstract

Automatic post-editing (APE) can be reduced to a machine translation (MT) task, where the source is the output of a specific MT system and the target is its post-edited variant. However, this approach does not consider context information that can be found in the original source of the MT system. Thus a better approach is to employ multi-source MT, where two input sequences are considered – the original source and the MT output.

Extra context information can be introduced in the form of extra tokens that identify certain global properties of a group of segments, added as a prefix or a suffix to each segment. Successfully applied in domain adaptation of MT as well as on APE, this technique deserves further attention. In this work we investigate multi-source neural APE (or NPE) systems with training data which has been augmented with two types of extra context tokens. We experiment with authentic and synthetic data provided by WMT 2019 and submit our results to the APE shared task. We also experiment with using statistical machine translation (SMT) methods for APE. While our systems score bellow the baseline, we consider this work a step towards understanding the added value of extra context in the case of APE.

1   Introduction

Automatic post-editing (APE) aims at improving text that was previously translated by Machine Translation (MT). An APE system is typically trained on triplets composed of: a segment in the source language, a translation hypothesis of that segment by an MT system, and the edited version of that hypothesis, created by a human translator.

Currently, neural machine translation (NMT) systems are the state-of-the-art in MT, achieving quality beyond that of phrase-based statistical MT (SMT) (Bentivogli et al., 2016; Shterionov et al.,

2018). NMT output is more fluent but may contain issues related to accuracy. However, automatic post-editing of NMT output has proved to be a challenging task (Chatterjee et al., 2018).

In terms of post-editing technology, neural methods as well represent the current state-of-the-art (do Carmo et al., 2019). And while neural post-editing (NPE) has shown substantial improvements when applied on PBSMT output, it has not been as effective in improving output from NMT systems. One of the reasons is that NMT and NPE typically use similar approaches, which can make the latter redundant, as it can be assimilated by the former, e.g., in some cases, by increasing the number of layers of the network. One alternative is to explore features of the data not available while training MT systems. In this paper, we explore the effect of adding tokens that identify partitions in the training data which may be relevant to guide the behaviour of the NPE system. Examples of such tokens are related to basic source and/or target sentence length or to more sophisticated analyses of the text. In this work, we explore two features: *sentence length* and *topic*.

2   Related Work

Adding a token to the input of a sequence model to shape its behaviour is not a new idea. Mikolov and Zweig (2012) aim at improving neural language models and avoid the data fragmentation in multiple datasets by using Latent Dirichlet Allocation (Blei et al., 2003) to construct context vectors and represent topics. Sennrich et al. (2016a) call the added token a 'side constraint', which informs the system about target side features, such as honorific forms of treatment, tense, number, gender, or other grammatical or discourse features, which may not exist or be different in the source side. The authors use an automatic annotator of politeness in the tar-

Proceedings of the Fourth Conference on Machine Translation (WMT), Volume 3: Shared Task Papers (Day 2) pages 132–138
Florence, Italy, August 1-2, 2019. ©2019 Association for Computational Linguistics

get sentences in the training set, which places a token at the end of each sentence to control the politeness level of the output of an NMT model. Yamagishi et al. (2016) also use target side annotations during training to control active versus passive voice in the output. Vanmassenhove et al. (2018) used prefixed tokens identifying the gender of the author to aid the MT system in correctly presenting gender features in discourse.

Special input tokens have also been used to aid training of single models on multilingual translation tasks: Johnson et al. (2017) prefix each source sentence in an NMT system with a token to indicate the target language, training a multilingual model on a scenario with multiple source and target languages. This approach is at the background of the research on zero-shot translation. In the context of low-resource languages, Mattoni et al. (2017) add two tokens, one to specify the source language and another to specify the target language. In their case, the source-language token is used for language specific tokenisation. Similarly, Zhou et al. (2018) found that adding tokens that encode the source and target language family, e. g. `source-family:Germanic` and `target-family:Slavic` for English-Czech translation, may improve the accuracy of the NMT outputs for low-resource languages.

Added tokens in APE were used in a scenario where SMT and NMT outputs were trained jointly in a single model (Pylypenko and Rubino, 2018). An artificial token was added to the data to indicate the system the segments had been produced from. However, this strategy was not very successful, especially when editing NMT output.

Our current work further explores the strategy of adding such tokens about data partitions in NPE. Partitions are derived according to topic models or sentence lengths. Topic models are trained separately on the provided data and aim to identify the topic of each segment of the data.

3 Data and Labels

While the shared task is open to using additional data sources, we only use the data sets linked on the shared task website, aiming at better result reproducibility: i. e. (a) the authentic English-German WMT 2018 APE shared task data (Turchi et al., 2018), (b) the synthetic English-German data of the WMT 2016 AmuNMT system (Junczys-Dowmunt and Grundkiewicz, 2016),

(c) the NMT part of the synthetic English-German data of the eSCAPE corpus (Negri et al., 2018), (d) the authentic English-Russian data new in the WMT 2019 APE shared task provided by Microsoft[1] and (e) the synthetic English-Russian data of the eSCAPE corpus.

3.1 Training Data

For the EN-DE experiments, we used the 500k and 4M triplets defined in (Junczys-Dowmunt and Grundkiewicz, 2016). For EN-RU, we used the 8M triplets from the eSCAPE project. Table 1 and Table 2 show statistics about the data used to train our systems.

Size	EN-DE	EN-RU
small	268 840	301 780
medium	795 208	N/A
large	4 660 020	8 037 141

Table 1: Number of SRC-NMT-PE triplets distributed over three data sets used in our experiments.

3.2 Induction of Topic Clusters

We induce ten topic clusters for each language pair using Scikit-Learn's implementation of Latent Dirichlet Allocation (LDA) (Blei et al., 2003). We use the English side of the data. The data is the concatenation of the authentic and a sample of the synthetic data. For English-German, we sample 50k segments each of AmuNMT (500k) and eSCAPE data (7M). For English-Russian, we sample 100k of eSCAPE data. The data was cleaned of stop words and words that occur less than five times or in more than 90% of segments.

3.3 Topic Classification

We split the data for training the LDA models, into ten files according to the induced topics and then label each sentence of *all* data according to the most similar topic file. We measure similarity with cosine similarity on character n-gram tf-idf vector representations ($n = 5, 6, 7$). Before n-gram extraction, segments are lowercased and e-mail addresses, URL numbers and characters repeated more than three times are normalised. For tf-idf values, we use plus one smoothing and we avoid zero and negative idf values by adding two to the number of documents. To represent topic clusters, we use the average of its segment vectors.

---

[1] `http://www.statmt.org/wmt19/ape-task.html` accessed during the task and last 2019-04-30

Size	EN-DE			EN-RU		
	SRC	NMT	PE	SRC	NMT	PE
small	10 771	15 477	18 088	9 125	14 783	15 761
medium	48 227	48 257	48 869	N/A		
large	50 327	50 538	50 790	53 030	50 646	52 970

Table 2: Vocabulary sizes (after applying BPE on the train data set).

3.4 Length Partitions

Another way of partitioning the data is by sentence length. We use the length of the source side of each segment, i. e. the English side to create a partitioning of the data according to the number of tokens. We choose the partition boundaries as thresholds on the number of tokens keeping each partition similar in size within the sample data. Size is measured as $\sum_i s_i^e$ where s_i is the number of tokens in the ith segment and $e = 0.5$. This is a compromise between counting segments ($e = 0$) and counting tokens ($e = 1$).

3.5 Pre-processing for APE Training

We use the available authentic and synthetic data as is. The authentic data, the synthetic AmuNMT data and the synthetic EN-RU eSCAPE data used for training are already tokenised, thus no further tokenisation is conducted. We do not apply lower- nor true-casing, aiming to learn how to correct errors related to the casing. We learn a byte-pair encoding (Sennrich et al., 2016b) of 50 000 operations from our training data which we then apply to split each data set into subword units. After that, the corresponding partition tokens are attached to each segment. In particular, the partition labels are attached to both source and MT segments, i.e., the two sources in our multi-source NPE systems.

4 Experiments

4.1 Objectives

Our experiments aim at two objectives: (i) to investigate the effect of extra information in the form of prefix tokens for NPE; and (ii) to assess whether monolingual SMT[2], can be effective for post-editing of NMT output. The latter is driven by the idea of added benefits from interleaving different MT technologies.

We conduct three types of NPE experiments – (a) baseline experiments, using no extra tokens to build a set of baseline systems; (b) length tokens – prefixed with tokens stating the data partition based on the length and (c) topic tokens – data is prefixed with tokens stating the data partition based on the LDA clustering. For the SMT experiments no additional tokens were attached to the text. We assumed that such augmentation of the source side would increase the difference with respect to word alignment and thus it would have a negative impact on the quality of the system.

4.2 Models

NPE We trained 15 NPE systems: *small*, *medium* and *large* for EN-DE and *small* and *large* for EN-RU, on the data discussed in Section 3.1, for the three different prefix token settings – no token, topic token, length token. For all of them, we employed Marian-NMT[3] to train multi-source sequence-to-sequence models (multi-s2s) with LSTM units.[4] The two sources are the actual source-side data (EN) from the training corpus and its translation (DE or RU). We used cross-entropy as validation metric and the max-length was 150 tokens. The training stops after 5 epochs with no improvement, i.e., early stopping.

SMT We trained 5 SMT models (*small*, *medium* and *large* for EN-DE and *small* and *large* for EN-RU) using Moses (Koehn et al., 2007) release 4.0, Giza++ (Och and Ney, 2003) for word alignment and a 5-gram KenLM language model (Heafield, 2011). Models are tuned with Mert (Och, 2003). We ought to stress that these models are monolingual, i.e., trained only on the original MT output as source and its post-edited variant as target.

---

[2]In this work, we use the term *monolingual* to define an MT system where the source and the target are in the same language, e.g. the source is a translated sentence in German and the target is its post-edited variant.

[3]https://marian-nmt.github.io/
[4]Options: –mini-batch-fit, –workspace 9000, –layer-normalization, –dropout-rnn 0.2 –dropout-src 0.1 –dropout-trg 0.1, –early-stopping 5, –max-length 150 –max-length-crop, –valid-freq 2000 –save-freq 2000 –disp-freq 1000

4.3 Evaluation and selection for WMT submission

We evaluated our models using BLEU (Papineni et al., 2002) and TER (Snover et al., 2006). For the former, we used the *multi-bleu* implementation provided alongside Moses; and for the latter we used the script provided by the WMT organisation.

We computed BLEU and TER using the human PE side of the data as reference, and the NPE output as hypothesis, e.g. TER(*npe,pe*). We also computed BLEU and TER scores for the original data, i.e. in this case the reference again is the human PE but the hypothesis is the NMT part of the training data: TER(*nmt,pe*). We present our results on the development set in Tables 3 and 4 for EN-DE and EN-RU, respectively. We denote the scores for the original (baseline) MT output with *MT*. Scores are scaled between 0 and 100.

	Model	Prefix	BLEU ↑	TER ↓
MT	Baseline	N/A	76.94	15.08
NPE	small	N/A	63.28	24.09
	medium	N/A	70.57	18.81
	large	N/A	70.29	19.89
	small	topic	60.41	28.59
	medium	topic	73.08	17.81
	large	**topic**	**75.82**	**15.89**
	small	length	62.56	26.91
	medium	length	73.74	17.26
	large	**length**	**75.85**	**15.91**
SMT	small	N/A	76.82	15.33
	medium	**N/A**	**77.04**	**15.17**
	large	N/A	76.82	15.26

Table 3: BLEU and TER scores for the EN-DE NPE and SMT models (dev set). Rows in **bold** indicate submitted system results.

For submission to the shared task, we selected the best models, according to TER, available at the submission deadline. For EN-DE, these are: the NPE-large-topic (primary), the NPE-large-length and the SMT-medium; for EN-RU these are the NPE-large-length (primary) and the SMT-small. In the result tables these are marked in **bold**.

5 Results and Analysis

5.1 Development Observations

Table 3 and Table 4 show the evaluation scores (BLEU and TER) on the development set results. In our experiments, the ranking of the systems'

	Model	Prefix	BLEU ↑	TER ↓
MT	Baseline	N/A	80.22	13.13
NPE	small	N/A	50.76	34.45
	large	N/A	59.01	28.01
	small	topic	48.30	41.19
	large	topic	75.39	16.18
	small	length	44.68	44.57
	large	**length**	**73.67**	**19.74**
SMT	**small**	**N/A**	**79.40**	**13.68**

Table 4: BLEU and TER scores for the EN-RU NPE and SMT models (dev set). Rows in **bold** indicate submitted system results.

performance scores is always the same, no matter if we use TER or BLEU.

We can see that all NPE systems in our experiments, whether or not they are augmented with informative tokens, are unable to perform as well as the original NMT translations. So, our NPE systems are not fulfilling their main function. Still, it is worth analysing the evolution of scores from system to system.

As expected, in general, the larger the systems, the better the results. This is most visible in the EN-DE experiments, for which we trained systems in a three-size scale. Systems with small amounts of training data deteriorate the scores very much, which makes them not viable. For augmented systems, in both languages, the addition of more data has a very visible effect, with the largest systems having the best results. The same is not true for the systems with no tokens, in which medium-sized systems achieve better scores than large ones. For the SMT systems, size of the training data was the only factor we tested, but the scores are very close for all systems, with medium-sized systems achieving slightly better results.

The addition of the tokens also has a positive effect in the scores, especially for systems trained with medium-sized and large-sized datasets. For EN-DE, in the systems trained with a small volume of data, the highest scores are for systems with no tokens. But for medium-sized trained systems, the addition of the token *length* achieves the best results. For large systems, the scores are much closer to each other, but augmented systems beat the system with no tokens. In EN-RU, the advantages of adding the tokens is also more visible for the larger datasets, with *topic* as the token that enables the highest scores.

Surprisingly, the APE systems using SMT are the best performing ones, beating all neural ones. In fact, their scores are very close to the original ones, and very consistent, seeming not to be sensitive to the increase in the volumes of training data.

5.2 Final Systems

As noted in Section 4.3 we submitted three systems for EN-DE: the NPE-large-*topic* (as primary), the NPE-large-*length* and the SMT-medium. Only the SMT system scores above the original MT system, and only in terms of BLEU. For EN-RU, we submitted two systems: NPE-large-*length* (as primary) and the SMT-small. None of the system improved on the original MT data, but the SMT system was close. The baseline scores compared to our systems' scores are presented in Table 5 and Table 6.

	System	Model	Prefix	BLEU ↑	TER ↓
MT	Baseline	N/A	N/A	74.73	16.84
NPE	Primary	large	topic	74.29	17.29
	Contrastive I	large	length	74.01	17.41
SMT	Contrastive II	medium	N/A	74.30	17.07

Table 5: BLEU and TER scores for submitted and baseline systems for the EN-DE language pair.

	System	Model	Prefix	BLEU ↑	TER ↓
MT	Baseline	N/A	N/A	76.20	16.16
NPE	Primary	large	length	72.90	18.31
SMT	Contrastive	small	N/A	75.27	16.59

Table 6: BLEU and TER scores for submitted and baseline systems for the EN-RU language pair.

We believe one of the main factors for these results is the initially high quality of the baseline MT systems. The inherent nature of APE systems dictates that they generate a whole new sentence when the inputs are passed through the model. However, in cases when no or barely any changes are required, it will be desirable not generate a new sentence, i.e. the post-edit, but to retain the original one, as any transformation process would be likely to impede the quality. In future work, we will look into combining NPE models with Quality Estimation (QE), to filter NMT output by expected quality and thus control over-correction: the NPE system will then only present alternatives for sentences that require improvements.

6 Conclusions

Although our NPE systems do not fulfill their main aim (improving the output of an NMT system), this paper highlights the potential of two strategies for APE which explore the thin improvement margins allowed by NMT output.

The augmentation strategy is a simple process that requires no system development, but presents its own challenges. The tokens that are used must be informative, so as to guide the NPE system to features in the datasets with a very close relation to the editing patterns the system is supposed to learn. Future work should check the topic model and if necessary switch to a more suitable model. Other types of tokens should also be tested. Furthermore, data augmentation in APE implies pre-analysis of the datasets, since the same tokens are not applicable to different datasets nor use-cases.

The strategy of applying a different MT paradigm, SMT for APE of NMT output, yielded interesting results, albeit still not being able to improve the original NMT output. The margin of development of SMT systems may be limited, but this is also worth experimenting, in view of the challenges APE currently faces with NMT output.

Furthermore, we outlined a hypothesis about the reasons why the post-edited texts score below the baseline system. In particular, we believe this result has to do with the high quality of the baseline MT systems: this implies that some segments should not be post-edited, but our APE system attempted to edit every sentence. We plan to incorporate QE and data selection to mitigate this over-correction issue, offering an APE suggestion only when editing is necessary.

7 Acknowledgements

This research is supported by Science Foundation Ireland through the ADAPT Centre for Digital Content Technology, which is funded under the SFI Research Centres Programme (Grant 13/RC/2106) and is co-funded under the European Regional Development Fund. Félix do Carmo collaborates in this project in the ambit of a European Unions Horizon 2020 research and innovation programme, under the EDGE COFUND Marie Skłodowska-Curie Grant Agreement no. 713567. This publication has emanated from research supported in part by a research grant from Science Foundation Ireland (SFI) under Grant Number 13/RC/2077.

References

Luisa Bentivogli, Arianna Bisazza, Mauro Cettolo, and Marcello Federico. 2016. Neural versus Phrase-Based Machine Translation Quality: a Case Study. In *Proceedings of the 2016 Conference on Empirical Methods in Natural Language Processing*, pages 257–267, Austin, Texas. Association for Computational Linguistics.

David M. Blei, Andrew Y. Ng, and Michael I. Jordan. 2003. Latent Dirichlet allocation. *Journal of Machine Learning Research*, 3:993–1022.

Félix do Carmo, Dimitar Shterionov, Joachim Wagner, Murhaf Hossari, Eric Paquin, and Joss Moorkens. 2019. A review of the state-of-the-art in automatic post-editing. *Under review for publication: Machine Translation.*

Rajen Chatterjee, Matteo Negri, Raphael Rubino, and Marco Turchi. 2018. Findings of the WMT 2018 shared task on automatic post-editing. In *Proceedings of the Third Conference on Machine Translation: Shared Task Papers*, pages 710–725, Belgium, Brussels. Association for Computational Linguistics.

Kenneth Heafield. 2011. KenLM: faster and smaller language model queries. In *Proceedings of the EMNLP 2011 Sixth Workshop on Statistical Machine Translation*, pages 187–197, Edinburgh, Scotland, United Kingdom.

Melvin Johnson, Mike Schuster, Quoc V. Le, Maxim Krikun, Yonghui Wu, Zhifeng Chen, Nikhil Thorat, Fernanda Viégas, Martin Wattenberg, Greg Corrado, Macduff Hughes, and Jeffrey Dean. 2017. Google's multilingual neural machine translation system: Enabling zero-shot translation. *Transactions of the Association for Computational Linguistics*, 5:339–351.

Marcin Junczys-Dowmunt and Roman Grundkiewicz. 2016. Log-linear combinations of monolingual and bilingual neural machine translation models for automatic post-editing. In *Proceedings of the First Conference on Machine Translation*, pages 751–758, Berlin, Germany. Association for Computational Linguistics.

Philipp Koehn, Hieu Hoang, Alexandra Birch, Chris Callison-Burch, Marcello Federico, Nicola Bertoldi, Brooke Cowan, Wade Shen, Christine Moran, Richard Zens, Chris Dyer, Ondrej Bojar, Alexandra Constantin, and Evan Herbst. 2007. Moses: Open source toolkit for statistical machine translation. In *Proceedings of the 45th Annual Meeting of the Association for Computational Linguistics Companion Volume Proceedings of the Demo and Poster Sessions*, pages 177–180, Prague, Czech Republic. Association for Computational Linguistics.

Giulia Mattoni, Pat Nagle, Carlos Collantes, and Dimitar Shterionov. 2017. Zero-shot translation for low-resource indian languages. In *Proceedings of MT Summit XVI – Vol.2 Commercial MT Users and Translators Track*, pages 1–10, Nagoya, Aichi, Japan. Asia-Pacific Association for Machine Translation.

Tomas Mikolov and Geoffrey Zweig. 2012. Context dependent recurrent neural network language model. In *Spoken Language Technologies*. IEEE.

Matteo Negri, Marco Turchi, Rajen Chatterjee, and Nicola Bertoldi. 2018. ESCAPE: a large-scale synthetic corpus for automatic post-editing. In *Proceedings of the 11th Language Resources and Evaluation Conference*, Miyazaki, Japan. European Language Resource Association.

Franz Josef Och. 2003. Minimum error rate training in statistical machine translation. In *Proceedings of the 41st Annual Meeting of the Association for Computational Linguistics*, pages 160–167, Sapporo, Japan. Association for Computational Linguistics.

Franz Josef Och and Hermann Ney. 2003. A systematic comparison of various statistical alignment models. *Computational Linguistics*, 29(1):19–51.

Kishore Papineni, Salim Roukos, Todd Ward, and Wei-Jing Zhu. 2002. BLEU: A Method for Automatic Evaluation of Machine Translation. In *Proceedings of the 40th Annual Meeting on Association for Computational Linguistics*, pages 311–318, Philadelphia, Pennsylvania, USA.

Daria Pylypenko and Raphael Rubino. 2018. DFKI-MLT system description for the WMT18 automatic post-editing task. In *Proceedings of the Third Conference on Machine Translation: Shared Task Papers*, pages 836–839, Belgium, Brussels. Association for Computational Linguistics.

Rico Sennrich, Barry Haddow, and Alexandra Birch. 2016a. Controlling politeness in neural machine translation via side constraints. In *Proceedings of the 2016 Conference of the North American Chapter of the Association for Computational Linguistics: Human Language Technologies*, pages 35–40, San Diego, California. Association for Computational Linguistics.

Rico Sennrich, Barry Haddow, and Alexandra Birch. 2016b. Neural machine translation of rare words with subword units. In *Proceedings of the 54th Annual Meeting of the Association for Computational Linguistics (Volume 1: Long Papers)*, pages 1715–1725, Berlin, Germany. Association for Computational Linguistics.

Dimitar Shterionov, Riccardo Superbo, Pat Nagle, Laura Casanellas, Tony O'Dowd, and Andy Way. 2018. Human versus automatic quality evaluation of NMT and PBSMT. *Machine Translation*, 32(3):217–235.

Matthew Snover, Bonnie Dorr, Richard Schwartz, Linnea Micciulla, and John Makhoul. 2006. A study of translation edit rate with targeted human annotation.

In *AMTA 2006. Proceedings of the 7th Conference of the. Association for Machine Translation of the Americas. Visions for the Future of Machine Translation*, pages 223–231, Cambridge, Massachusetts, USA.

Marco Turchi, Matteo Negri, and Rajen Chatterjee. 2018. WMT18 APE shared task: En-DE NMT train and dev data. LINDAT/CLARIN digital library at the Institute of Formal and Applied Linguistics (ÚFAL), Faculty of Mathematics and Physics, Charles University.

Eva Vanmassenhove, Christian Hardmeier, and Andy Way. 2018. Getting gender right in neural machine translation. In *Proceedings of the 2018 Conference on Empirical Methods in Natural Language Processing*, pages 3003–3008, Brussels, Belgium. Association for Computational Linguistics.

Hayahide Yamagishi, Shin Kanouchi, Takayuki Sato, and Mamoru Komachi. 2016. Controlling the voice of a sentence in Japanese-to-English neural machine translation. In *Proceedings of the 3rd Workshop on Asian Translation (WAT2016)*, pages 203–210, Osaka, Japan. The COLING 2016 Organizing Committee.

Zhong Zhou, Matthias Sperber, and Alexander Waibel. 2018. Massively parallel cross-lingual learning in low-resource target language translation. In *Proceedings of the Third Conference on Machine Translation: Research Papers*, pages 232–243, Belgium, Brussels. Association for Computational Linguistics.

Effort-Aware Neural Automatic Post-Editing

Amirhossein Tebbifakhr[1,2]**, Matteo Negri**[1]**, Marco Turchi**[1]
[1] Fondazione Bruno Kessler, Via Sommarive 18, Povo, Trento - Italy
[2] University of Trento, Italy
{atebbifakhr,negri,turchi}@fbk.eu

Abstract

For this round of the WMT 2019 APE shared task, our submission focuses on addressing the "over-correction" problem in APE. Over-correction occurs when the APE system tends to rephrase an already correct MT output, and the resulting sentence is penalized by a reference-based evaluation against human post-edits. Our intuition is that this problem can be prevented by informing the system about the predicted quality of the MT output or, in other terms, the expected amount of needed corrections. For this purpose, following the common approach in multilingual NMT, we prepend a special token to the beginning of both the source text and the MT output indicating the required amount of post-editing. Following the best submissions to the WMT 2018 APE shared task, our backbone architecture is based on multi-source Transformer to encode both the MT output and the corresponding source text. We participated both in the English-German and English-Russian subtasks. In the first subtask, our best submission improved the original MT output quality up to +0.98 BLEU and -0.47 TER. In the second subtask, where the higher quality of the MT output increases the risk of over-correction, none of our submitted runs was able to improve the MT output.

1 Introduction

Automatic Post-Editing (APE) is the task of correcting the possible errors in the output of a Machine Translation (MT) system. It is usually considered as a supervised sequence-to-sequence task, which aims to map the output of MT system to a better translation i.e. post-edited output, by leveraging a three-way parallel corpus containing (*source text*, *mt output*, *post-edited output*). Considering the MT output as a source sentence and the post-edited output as a target sentence, this problem can be cast as a monolingual translation task and be addressed with different MT solutions (Simard et al., 2007; Pal et al., 2016). However, it has been proven that better performance can be obtained by not only using the raw output of the MT system but also by leveraging the source text (Chatterjee et al., 2017). In the last round of the APE shared task (Chatterjee et al., 2018a), the top-ranked systems (Tebbifakhr et al., 2018; Junczys-Dowmunt and Grundkiewicz, 2018) were based on Transformer (Vaswani et al., 2017), the state-of-the-art architecture in neural MT (NMT), with two encoders to encode both source text and MT output. Although using these systems to post-edit the output of Phrase-Based Statistical Machine Translation (PBSMT) system resulted in a large boost in performance, smaller improvements were observed over neural MT outputs. Indeed, the good performance of the NMT systems leaves less room for improvement and poses the risk of over-correcting the MT output. Over-correction occurs when the APE system rephrases an already correct MT output. Although the post edited out put can still be a correct translation, it is penalized in terms of reference-based evaluation metrics, since it differs from the reference post-edited output.

With the steady improvement of NMT technology on the one side, and the adoption of reference-based evaluation metrics that penalizes correct but unnecessary corrections on the other side, tackling this problem has become a priority. In order to respond to this priority, for this round of the shared task our submission focuses on addressing the over-correction problem. Over-correction has been already addressed before by integrating Quality Estimation (QE) and APE system in three different ways (Chatterjee et al., 2018b), namely: *i)* as an *activator*, to decide whether to apply post-editing or not, using a threshold on the estimated

Proceedings of the Fourth Conference on Machine Translation (WMT), Volume 3: Shared Task Papers (Day 2) pages 139–144
Florence, Italy, August 1-2, 2019. ©2019 Association for Computational Linguistics

quality of the MT output, *ii)* as a *guidance*, to post-edit only the parts of a text that have poor estimated quality, *iii)* as a *selector*, to select the best output by comparing the estimated quality of the MT output and the automatically post-edited output. Our approach is a mixture of the first two. While in all previous scenarios the decision is made externally to the APE system, we allow the APE system to implicitly make the decision and in a softer manner. Instead of choosing between "*do*" and "*do not*" post-edit, we let the system decide which post-editing strategy to apply, choosing between three strategies: no post-editing (i.e. leaving the sentence untouched), light post-editing (i.e. a conservative modification) and heavy post-editing (i.e. an aggressive modification). To this aim, similar to the idea of multilingual NMT (Johnson et al., 2017), a special token is added to the beginning of both the source text and the MT output indicating the required amount of post-editing. Similar to last year's submission (Tebbifakhr et al., 2018), we use Transformer architecture with two encoders for encoding the source text and the MT output, while we share the parameters of the two encoders and tie the embeddings and decoder's softmax layer weights (Junczys-Dowmunt and Grundkiewicz, 2018).

We participated in both the APE sub-tasks proposed this year, which respectively consist in post-editing the output of English-German and English-Russian NMT systems. Our experiments show that, on the development sets for both language directions, prepending the special token can improve the performance of the APE system up to 0.5 BLEU points. However, predicting the correct token at test time, when the quality of the MT output is unknown, is still challenging and can harm the systems' performance. In the English-German subtask, our top system improves the MT output up to -0.47 TER and +0.98 BLEU points. In the English-Russian subtask, due to the high quality of the MT segments, none of our submitted systems was able to improve the MT output, emphasizing the need for further research towards more reliable solutions to the over-correction problem.

2 System Architecture

The backbone architecture of our system is based on the state-of-the-art architecture in NMT i.e. Transformer (Vaswani et al., 2017). Like most NMT models, it follows the encoder-decoder framework, where an encoder encodes the input sentence into a continuous space, and a decoder decodes this encoded representation into the output sentence. However, we use two encoders in order to process both the source text and the MT output. By attending to the concatenation of the representation of the source and MT sentences, the decoder generates the post-edited output. Following Junczys-Dowmunt and Grundkiewicz (2018), we share all the parameters between the encoders, and we use shared embedding weights across all encoders and the decoder and tie them to decoder's softmax layer weights.

In order to tackle the over-correction problem and to induce a post-editing strategy that resembles the work of a human post-editor, we add a special token to the beginning of both the source text and the MT output indicating the amount of required post-editing. In this paper, we use three different tokens, namely "*no post-edit*" (no edits are required), "*light post-edit*" (minimal edits are required), and "*heavy post-edit*" (a large number of edits are required). However, the number of tokens can be increased/decreased to provide more fine/coarse-grained information to the APE system, but this is beyond the scope of this paper. Before training, we first compute the TER (Snover et al., 2006) score between the MT output and the post-edited output, then we add the *no post-edit* token to samples with zero TER score, *light post-edit* to samples with non-zero TER score smaller than 40, and finally *heavy post-edit* to samples with TER score larger than 40. According to (Turchi et al., 2013, 2014), 40 TER is the level of quality above which a human translator tends to rewrite the post-edited sentence from scratch.

At testing time, since the post-edited output is not available, we need to predict the proper token for the input sample. For predicting the proper token, we test two approaches. The first one, namely BERT, is based on a text classifier obtained by fine-tuning BERT (Devlin et al., 2018) on the in-domain data, which classifies the MT output into the three defined classes. The second one, namely SIM, is an information retrieval approach, that, given a query containing the source and the MT sentence to be post-edited, retrieves the most similar triplet (source, MT sentence and post-edit) from the training data using an inverted index. Then, similarly to (Farajian et al., 2017), the retrieved triplets are ranked based on the average of the sentence-level BLEU scores (Chen and Cherry, 2014) between *a)* the source segment in the query and the retrieved source sentence and *b)* the MT segment in the query and the retrieved MT sentence. For the most similar triplet, the TER between the MT sentence and the post-edit is computed and the token created. For highly repetitive and homogeneous corpora, the similarity between the top retrieved triplet and the query is quite high, but this is not always the case. So, to limit the risk of assigning a token obtained from the top triplet, but with a low similarity, a threshold (τ) is set. If the average sentence-level BLEU of the top retrieved triplet is above τ, the relative token is associated to the query, otherwise the most frequent token in the training data is used. Once the token is obtained, it is added to the source and the sentence to be post-edited during inference.

3   Experimental Settings

3.1   Data

The official training data of the APE shared task contains a small amount of in-domain data, in which the post-edited outputs are real human post-edits. To overcome the lack of data and to train neural APE models, the organizers also provided a large amount of synthetic data. For the En-Ru subtask, they provided the eSCAPE dataset (Negri et al., 2018), which is produced from a parallel corpus by considering the target sentences as artificial human post-edits and machine-translated source sentences as MT output. For the En-De subtask, in addition to the eSCAPE dataset, another synthetic dataset was made available, which is created using round-trip translation from a German monolingual corpus (Junczys-Dowmunt and Grundkiewicz, 2016). We clean the English to German/Russian eSCAPE dataset by removing *i)* samples with a length ratio between source text and post-edited output which is too different than the average and *ii)* samples where the source text language is not English or post-edited output language is not German/Russian. In order to reduce the vocabulary size, we apply Byte Pair Encoding (BPE) (Sennrich et al., 2016). We learn the BPE merging rules on the union of the source text, MT output and post-edit output to obtain a shared vocabulary.

3.2   Hyperparameters

In our APE system, we use 32K merging rules for applying BPE. We employ OpenNMT-tf toolkit (Klein et al., 2017) to implement our system. We use 512 dimensions for the word embedding and 6 layers for both the encoders and the decoder, each containing 512 units and a feed-forward network with 1,024 dimensions. We set the attention and residual dropout probabilities, as well as the label-smoothing parameter to 0.1. For training the system, we use Adam optimizer (Kingma and Ba, 2014) with effective batch size of 8,192 tokens and the warm-up strategy introduced by (Vaswani et al., 2017) with warm-up steps equal to 8,000. We also employ beam search with beam width of 4.

3.3   Evaluation Metrics

We use two different evaluation metrics to assess the quality of our APE systems: *i)* TER (Snover et al., 2006), the official metric for the task, computed based on the edit distance between the given hypothesis and the reference and *ii)* BLEU (Papineni et al., 2002), as the geometric average of $n-$gram precisions in the given hypothesis multiplied by the brevity penalty.

4   Results

For both subtasks, we train our APE systems with and without prepending the token. We start the training of the APE systems on the union of the synthetic data and 20-times over-sampled in-domain data. Then, we fine-tune the best performing checkpoint on the development set only on the in-domain data. The best performance on the development sets for En-De and En-Ru is reported in Tables 1 and 2 respectively.

As shown in Table 1, both APE systems, with the oracle token and without the token (lines 2 and 3), improve the quality of the MT output for En-De subtask. This improvement is larger when the token indicating the required amount of post-editing is provided to the system. This observation confirms the need for guiding the APE system to adopt different post-editing strategies according to the MT quality. For the En-Ru subtask, as shown in line 2 and 3 of Table 2, although none of the two systems can improve over the MT output, the system with the token has better performance compared to the one without. However, during testing, the oracle token is not available and

Systems	TER ($\downarrow$)	BLEU ($\uparrow$)
MT Output	15.08	76.76
Without Token	14.65	77.55
Token (ORACLE)	14.38	77.85
Token (BERT)	15.54	76.56
Token (SIM)	15.31	77.06
Robust (BERT)	15.04	77.24
Robust (SIM)	15.07	77.24

Table 1: Performance of the APE systems, on the English-German development set.

Systems	TER ($\downarrow$)	BLEU ($\uparrow$)
MT Output	13.12	79.97
Without Token	14.92	78.17
Token (ORACLE)	14.77	78.51
Token (BERT)	15.72	77.28
Token (SIM)	15.07	77.97
Robust (BERT)	15.85	77.19
Robust (SIM)	15.04	78.09

Table 2: Performance of the APE systems, on the English-Russian development set.

we need to predict the proper token for each input sample. We run our post-editing system using the predicted tokens obtained by the approach based on the BERT text classifier (BERT) and the information retrieval method (SIM). [1] As reported in the lower part of both tables, performance drops when the predicted tokens are prepended to the source text and the MT output instead of the oracle tokens. On the one side, this shows that the errors made by our predicting approaches hurt the work of the APE. On the other side, this drop in performance confirms that the APE system is able to leverage the token when generating the post-edited output. In order to make the APE robust to the wrong token, we run the fine-tuning step on in-domain data using noisy tokens instead of oracle ones. To add noise to the tokens, we replace 30 percent of the tokens in the in-domain train data with a different token, randomly sampled from the two wrong labels. As shown in the

---

[1] The most frequent label in the En-Ru in-domain dataset is *"no post-edit"*, while for En-De is *"light post-edit"*. The τ values are 0.75 for En-Ru and 0.5 for En-De.

Systems	TER ($\downarrow$)	BLEU ($\uparrow$)
MT Output	16.84	74.73
Primary	16.37	75.71
Contrastive	16.61	75.28

Table 3: Performance of the APE systems, on the English-German test set.

Systems	TER ($\downarrow$)	BLEU ($\uparrow$)
MT Output	16.16	76.20
Primary	19.34	72.42
Contrastive	19.48	72.91

Table 4: Performance of the APE systems, on the English-Russian test set.

last two lines of each table, adding noise to the tokens during training improves the results. In En-De, both approaches (BERT and SIM) have similar performance, while in En-Ru, the approach based on retrieving similar samples outperforms the approach using the text classifier. This is due to the fact that in En-Ru the majority token is "no post-edit" and the information retrieval approach tends to choose the majority token when the similarity is above the threshold resulting in more conservative post-editing. We submitted our best performing system without prepending the token as our *Primary* submission, and the best robust system with predicted tokens using the retrieval approach as our *Contrastive* submission. The results on English-German and English-Russian test sets are reported in Tables 3 and 4 respectively. These results confirm our findings on the dev data showing that *i)* the APE system is not able to improve the quality of the baseline for En-Ru, while it has limited gains for En-De and *ii)* the addition of the token seems to be more useful for En-Ru than for En-De, resulting in a small gain in BLEU compared to the system without prepending the token.

5   Conclusions

For this round of the APE shared task, we focused on the over-correction problem. In order to address this problem, we augmented the input of the APE system with a token to guide the system to be conservative when the MT output has high quality and aggressive with low-quality MT segments. Our experiments showed that it can result in better performance when the added token is accurate. In fact, when the token has to be predicted during testing, it results in lower APE performance. In order to make the APE system robust to this noise, we fine-tune the APE system on in-domain data by altering a portion of the tokens in the data. This can help the system to be more robust against the noisy token at test time, but it still shows lower performance than the system without the token. We learned that it is necessary for the system to be aware of the quality of the MT output before applying the post-editing. However, predicting the quality of the MT output is still an open problem which has to be addressed.

References

Rajen Chatterjee, M. Amin Farajian, Matteo Negri, Marco Turchi, Ankit Srivastava, and Santanu Pal. 2017. Multi-source neural automatic post-editing: FBK's participation in the WMT 2017 APE shared task. In *Proceedings of the Second Conference on Machine Translation*, pages 630–638, Copenhagen, Denmark. Association for Computational Linguistics.

Rajen Chatterjee, Matteo Negri, Raphael Rubino, and Marco Turchi. 2018a. Findings of the WMT 2018 shared task on automatic post-editing. In *Proceedings of the Third Conference on Machine Translation: Shared Task Papers*, pages 710–725, Belgium, Brussels. Association for Computational Linguistics.

Rajen Chatterjee, Matteo Negri, Marco Turchi, Frédéric Blain, and Lucia Specia. 2018b. Combining quality estimation and automatic post-editing to enhance machine translation output. In *Proceedings of the 13th Conference of the Association for Machine Translation in the Americas (Volume 1: Research Papers)*, pages 26–38, Boston, MA. Association for Machine Translation in the Americas.

Boxing Chen and Colin Cherry. 2014. A systematic comparison of smoothing techniques for sentence-level bleu. In *Proceedings of the Ninth Workshop on Statistical Machine Translation*, pages 362–367.

Jacob Devlin, Ming-Wei Chang, Kenton Lee, and Kristina Toutanova. 2018. BERT: pre-training of deep bidirectional transformers for language understanding. *CoRR*, abs/1810.04805.

M Amin Farajian, Marco Turchi, Matteo Negri, and Marcello Federico. 2017. Multi-domain neural machine translation through unsupervised adaptation. In *Proceedings of the Second Conference on Machine Translation*, pages 127–137.

Melvin Johnson, Mike Schuster, Quoc V. Le, Maxim Krikun, Yonghui Wu, Zhifeng Chen, Nikhil Thorat, Fernanda Viégas, Martin Wattenberg, Greg Corrado, Macduff Hughes, and Jeffrey Dean. 2017. Google's multilingual neural machine translation system: Enabling zero-shot translation. *Transactions of the Association for Computational Linguistics*, 5:339–351.

Marcin Junczys-Dowmunt and Roman Grundkiewicz. 2016. Log-linear Combinations of Monolingual and Bilingual Neural Machine Translation Models for Automatic Post-Editing. In *Proceedings of the First Conference on Machine Translation: Volume 2, Shared Task Papers*, pages 751–758. Association for Computational Linguistics.

Marcin Junczys-Dowmunt and Roman Grundkiewicz. 2018. MS-UEdin submission to the WMT2018 APE shared task: Dual-source transformer for automatic post-editing. In *Proceedings of the Third Conference on Machine Translation: Shared Task Papers*, pages 822–826, Belgium, Brussels. Association for Computational Linguistics.

D. P. Kingma and J. Ba. 2014. Adam: A Method for Stochastic Optimization. *ArXiv e-prints*.

Guillaume Klein, Yoon Kim, Yuntian Deng, Jean Senellart, and Alexander Rush. 2017. OpenNMT: Open-Source Toolkit for Neural Machine Translation. In *Proceedings of ACL 2017, System Demonstrations*, pages 67–72, Vancouver, Canada.

M. Negri, M. Turchi, R. Chatterjee, and N. Bertoldi. 2018. eSCAPE: a Large-scale Synthetic Corpus for Automatic Post-Editing. *ArXiv e-prints*.

Santanu Pal, Sudip Kumar Naskar, Mihaela Vela, and Josef van Genabith. 2016. A neural network based approach to automatic post-editing. In *Proceedings of the 54th Annual Meeting of the Association for Computational Linguistics (Volume 2: Short Papers)*, volume 2, pages 281–286.

Kishore Papineni, Salim Roukos, Todd Ward, and Wei-Jing Zhu. 2002. BLEU: A Method for Automatic Evaluation of Machine Translation. In *Proceedings of the 40th Annual Meeting on Association for Computational Linguistics*, ACL '02, pages 311–318, Philadelphia, Pennsylvania. Association for Computational Linguistics.

Rico Sennrich, Barry Haddow, and Alexandra Birch. 2016. Neural Machine Translation of Rare Words with Subword Units. In *Proceedings of the 54th Annual Meeting of the Association for Computational Linguistics (Volume 1: Long Papers)*, pages 1715–1725, Berlin, Germany. Association for Computational Linguistics.

Michel Simard, Nicola Ueffing, Pierre Isabelle, and Roland Kuhn. 2007. Rule-based translation with statistical phrase-based post-editing. In *Proceedings of the Second Workshop on Statistical Machine Translation*, pages 203–206. Association for Computational Linguistics.

Matthew Snover, Bonnie Dorr, Richard Schwartz, Linnea Micciulla, and John Makhoul. 2006. A Study of Translation Edit Rate with Targeted Human Annotation. In *Proceedings of Association for Machine Translation in the Americas*, pages 223–231, Cambridge, Massachusetts, USA.

Amirhossein Tebbifakhr, Ruchit Agrawal, Matteo Negri, and Marco Turchi. 2018. Multi-source transformer with combined losses for automatic post editing. In *Proceedings of the Third Conference on Machine Translation: Shared Task Papers*, pages 846–852, Belgium, Brussels. Association for Computational Linguistics.

Marco Turchi, Matteo Negri, and Marcello Federico. 2013. Coping with the subjectivity of human judgements in MT quality estimation. In *Proceedings of the Eighth Workshop on Statistical Machine Translation*, pages 240–251, Sofia, Bulgaria. Association for Computational Linguistics.

Marco Turchi, Matteo Negri, and Marcello Federico. 2014. Data-driven annotation of binary MT quality estimation corpora based on human post-editions. *Machine Translation*, 28(3):281–308.

Ashish Vaswani, Noam Shazeer, Niki Parmar, Jakob Uszkoreit, Llion Jones, Aidan N Gomez, Łukasz Kaiser, and Illia Polosukhin. 2017. Attention is All you Need. In I Guyon, U V Luxburg, S Bengio, H Wallach, R Fergus, S Vishwanathan, and R Garnett, editors, *Advances in Neural Information Processing Systems 30*, pages 5998–6008. Curran Associates, Inc.

UdS Submission for the WMT 19 Automatic Post-Editing Task

Hongfei Xu
Saarland University
DFKI
hfxunlp@foxmail.com

Qiuhui Liu
China Mobile Online Services
liuqiuhui@cmos.chinamobile.com

Josef van Genabith
Saarland University
DFKI
josef.van_genabith@dfki.de

Abstract

In this paper, we describe our submission to the English-German APE shared task at WMT 2019. We utilize and adapt an NMT architecture originally developed for exploiting context information to APE, implement this in our own transformer model and explore joint training of the APE task with a de-noising encoder.

1 Introduction

The Automatic Post-Editing (APE) task is to automatically correct errors in machine translation outputs. This paper describes our submission to the English-German APE shared task at WMT 2019. Based on recent research on the APE task (Junczys-Dowmunt and Grundkiewicz, 2018) and an architecture for the utilization of document-level context information in neural machine translation (Zhang et al., 2018b), we re-implement a multi-source transformer model for the task. Inspired by Cheng et al. (2018), we try to train a more robust model by introducing a multi-task learning approach which jointly trains APE with a de-noising encoder.

We made use of the artificial eScape data set (Negri et al., 2018) provided for the task, since the multi-source transformer model contains a large number of parameters and training with large amounts of supplementary synthetic data can help regularize its parameters and make the model more general. We then tested the BLEU scores between machine translation results and corresponding gold standard post-editing results on the original development set, the training set and the synthetic data as shown in Table 1.

dev	train	eScape
77.15	77.42	37.68

Table 1: BLEU Scores of Data Sets

Table 1 shows that there is a significant gap between the synthetic eScape data set (Negri et al., 2018) and the real-life data sets (the development set and the original training set from post-editors), potentially because Negri et al. (2018) generated the data set in a different way compared to Junczys-Dowmunt and Grundkiewicz (2016) and very few post-editing actions are normally required due to the good translation quality of neural machine translation (Bahdanau et al., 2014; Gehring et al., 2017; Vaswani et al., 2017) which significantly reduces errors in machine translation results and makes the post-editing results quite similar to raw machine translation outputs.

2 Our Approach

We simplify and employ a multi-source transformer model (Zhang et al., 2018b) for the APE task, and try to train a more robust model through multi-task learning.

2.1 Our Model

The transformer-based model proposed by Zhang et al. (2018b) for utilizing document-level context information in neural machine translation has two source inputs which can also be a source sentence along with the corresponding machine translation output and therefore caters for the requirements of APE. Since both source sentence and machine translation outputs are important for the APE task (Pal et al., 2016; Vu and Haffari, 2018), we remove the context gate used to restrict the information flow from the first input to the final output in their architecture, and obtain the model we used for our submission shown in Figure 1.

The model first encodes the given source sentence with stacked self-attention layers, then "post-edits" the corresponding machine translation result through repetitively encoding the machine translation result (with a self-attention

Proceedings of the Fourth Conference on Machine Translation (WMT), Volume 3: Shared Task Papers (Day 2) pages 145–150
Florence, Italy, August 1-2, 2019. ©2019 Association for Computational Linguistics

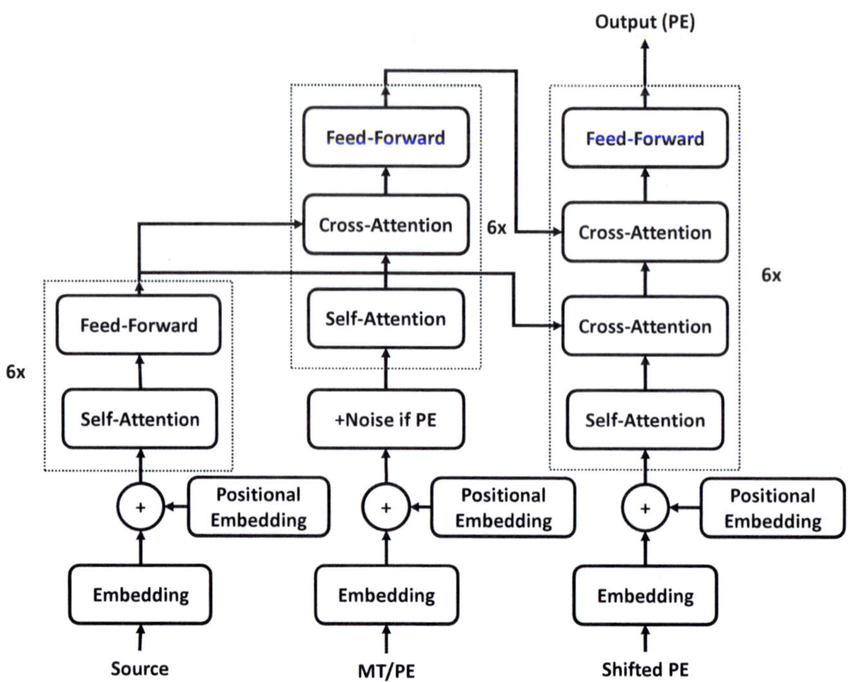

Figure 1: Our Transformer-Based Multi-Source Model for the APE Task

layer), attending to the source sentence (with a cross-attention layer) and processing the collected information (with a feed-forward neural network). Finally, the decoder attends to representations of the source sentence and the machine translation result and generates the post-editing result.

Compared to the multi-source transformer model used by Junczys-Dowmunt and Grundkiewicz (2018), this architecture has one more cross-attention module in the encoder for machine translation outputs to attend to the source input which makes the parameter sharing of layers between two encoders impossible, but we think this cross-attention module can help the de-noising task. The embedding of source, machine translation outputs and post-editing results is still shared as Junczys-Dowmunt and Grundkiewicz (2018) advised.

2.2 Joint Training with De-noising Encoder

Table 1 shows a considerable difference between the synthetic data set (Negri et al., 2018) and the real data set. To enable the model to handle more kinds of errors, we simulate new "machine translation outputs" through adding noise to the corresponding post-editing results. Following Cheng et al. (2018), we add noise directly to the look-up embedding of post-editing results instead of ma-

nipulating post-editing sequences.

Since the transformer (Vaswani et al., 2017) does not apply any weight regularization, we assume that the model can easily learn to reduce noise by enlarging weights, and propose to add adaptive noise to the embedding:

$$emb_{out} = emb + strength * \overline{abs(emb)} * N \quad (1)$$

where emb is the embedding matrix, $strength$ is a number between $[0.0, +\infty)$ to control the strength of noise, N is the noise matrix of the same shape as emb. We explore both standard Gaussian distribution and uniform distribution of $[-1.0, -1.0]$ as N. In this way the noise will automatically grow with the growing embedding weights.

Given that the transformer translation model (Vaswani et al., 2017) incorporates word order information through adding positional embedding to word embedding, we add noise to the combined embedding. In this case, the noise can both affect the word embedding (replacing words with their synonyms) and positional embedding (swapping word orders).

During training, we use the same model, and achieve joint training by randomly varying inputs: the inputs for the APE task are {source, mt, pe}, while those for the de-noising encoder task are {source, pe+noise, pe} where "source", "mt" and "pe" stand for the source sentence, the corresponding output from the machine translation system and the correct post-editing result. The final loss for joint training is:

$$loss = \lambda * loss_{\text{ape}} + (1 - \lambda) * loss_{\text{de-noising}} \quad (2)$$

i.e. the loss between the APE task and the de-noising encoder task are balanced by λ in this way.

3 Experiments

We implemented our approaches based on the Neutron implementation (Xu and Liu, 2019) for transformer-based neural machine translation.

3.1 Data and Settings

We only participated in the English to German task, and we used both the training set provided by WMT and the synthetic eSCAPE corpus (Negri et al., 2018). We first re-tokenized[1] and true-cased both data sets with tools provided by Moses (Koehn et al., 2007), then cleaned the data sets with scripts ported from the Neutron implementation, and the original training set was up-sampled 20 times as in (Junczys-Dowmunt and Grundkiewicz, 2018). We applied joint Byte-Pair Encoding (Sennrich et al., 2016) with $40k$ merge operations and 50 as the vocabulary threshold for the BPE. We only kept sentences with a max of 256 sub-word tokens for training, and obtained a training set of about $6.5M$ triples with a shared vocabulary of 42476. We did not apply any domain adaptation approach for our submission considering that (Junczys-Dowmunt and Grundkiewicz, 2018) shows few improvements, but advanced domain adaption (Wang et al., 2017) or fine-tuning (Luong and Manning, 2015) methods may still bring some improvements. The training set was shuffled for each training epoch.

Like Junczys-Dowmunt and Grundkiewicz (2018), all embedding matrices were bound with the weight of the classifier. But for tokens which in fact do never appear in post-editing outputs in the shared vocabulary, we additionally remove their weights in the label smoothing loss and set corresponding biases in the decoder classifier to -10^{32}.

Unlike Zhang et al. (2018b), the source encoder, the machine translation encoder and the decoder had 6 layers. The hidden dimension of the

position-wise feed-forward neural network was 2048, the embedding dimension and the multi-head attention dimension were 512. We used a dropout probability of 0.1, and employed label smoothing (Szegedy et al., 2016) value of 0.1. We used the Adam optimizer (Kingma and Ba, 2015) with 0.9, 0.98 and 10^{-9} as β_1, β_2 and ϵ. The learning rate schedule from Vaswani et al. (2017) with $8,000$ as the number of warm-up steps[2] was applied. We trained our models for only 8 epochs with at least $25k$ post-editing tokens in a batch, since we observed over-fitting afterwards. For the other hyper parameters, we used the same as the transformer base model (Vaswani et al., 2017).

During training, we kept the last 20 checkpoints saved with an interval of $1,500$ training steps (Vaswani et al., 2017; Zhang et al., 2018a), and obtained 4 models for each run through averaging every 5 adjacent checkpoints.

For joint training, we simply used 0.2 as the strength of noise ($strength$), and 0.5 as λ for joint training. Other values may provide better performance, but we did not have sufficient time to try this for our submission.

During decoding, we used a beam size of 4 without any length penalty.

3.2 Results

We first evaluated case-sensitive BLEU scores[3] on the development set, and results of all our approaches and baselines are shown in Table 2.

"MT as PE" is the do-nothing baseline which takes the machine translation outputs directly as post-editing results. "Processed MT" is the machine translation outputs through preprocessing (re-tokenizing and truecasing) and post-processing (de-truecasing and re-tokenizing without "-a" argument[4]) but without APE. "Base", "Gaussian" and "Uniform" stand for our model trained only for the APE task, jointly trained with Gaussian noise and uniform noise, respectively. We reported the minimum and the maximum BLEU scores of the 4 averaged models for

---

[1] using arguments: -a -no-escape

[2] https://github.com/tensorflow/tensor2tensor/blob/master/tensor2tensor/models/transformer.py#L1623.

[3] https://github.com/moses-smt/mosesdecoder/blob/master/scripts/generic/multi-bleu.perl.

[4] "-a" indicates tokenizing in the aggressive mode, which normally helps reduce vocabulary size. The official data sets were tokenized without this argument, so we have to recover our post-editing outputs.

each experiment. "Ensemble x5" is the ensemble of 5 models from joint training, 4 of which were averaged models with highest BLEU scores on the development set, another one was the model saved for each training epoch with lowest validation perplexity.

Models	BLEU
MT as PE	76.76
Processed MT	76.61
Base	$76.91 \sim 77.13$
Gaussian	$76.94 \sim 77.08$
Uniform	$77.01 \sim 77.10$
Ensemble x5	**77.22**

Table 2: BLEU Scores on the Development Set

Table 2 shows that the performance got slightly hurt (comparing "Processed MT" with "MT as PE") with pre-processing and post-processing procedures which are normally applied in training seq2seq models for reducing vocabulary size. The multi-source transformer (Base) model achieved the highest single model BLEU score without joint training with the de-noising encoder task. We think this is perhaps because there is a gap between the generated machine translation outputs with noise and the real world machine translation outputs, which biased the training.

Even with the ensembled model, our APE approach does not significantly improve machine translation outputs measured in BLEU (+0.46). We think human post-editing results may contain valuable information to guide neural machine translation models in some way like Reinforcement-Learning, but unfortunately, due to the high quality of the original neural machine translation output, only a small part of the real training data in the APE task are actually corrections from post editors, and most data are generated from the neural machine translation system, which makes it like adversarial training of neural machine translation (Yang et al., 2018) or multipass decoding (Geng et al., 2018).

All our submissions were made by jointly trained models because the performance gap between the best and the worst model of jointly trained models is smaller, which means that jointly trained models may have smaller variance.

Results on the test set from the APE shared task organizers are shown in Table 3. Even the ensemble of 5 models did not result in significant differences especially in BLEU scores.

Models	TER	BLEU
MT as PE	16.84	74.73
Gaussian	16.79	75.03
Uniform	16.80	75.03
Ensemble x5	16.77	75.03

Table 3: Results on the Test Set

4 Related Work

Pal et al. (2016) applied a multi-source sequence-to-sequence neural model for APE, and Vu and Haffari (2018) jointly trained machine translation with the post editing sequence prediction task (Berard et al., 2017). Though all previous approaches get significant improvements over Statistical Machine Translation outputs, benefits with APE on top of Neural Machine Translation outputs are not very significant (Chatterjee et al., 2018).

On the other hand, advanced neural machine translation approaches may also improve the APE task, such as: combining advances of the recurrent decoder (Chen et al., 2018), the Evolved Transformer architecture (So et al., 2019), Layer Aggregation (Dou et al., 2018) and Dynamic Convolution structures (Wu et al., 2019).

5 Conclusion

In this paper, we described details of our approaches for our submission to the WMT 19 APE task. We borrowed a multi-source transformer model from the context-dependent machine translation task and applied joint training with a denoising encoder task for our submission.

Acknowledgments

Hongfei Xu is supported by a doctoral grant from China Scholarship Council ([2018]3101, 201807040056). This work is supported by the German Federal Ministry of Education and Research (BMBF) under the funding code 01IW17001 (Deeplee). We thank the anonymous reviewers for their instructive comments.

References

Dzmitry Bahdanau, Kyunghyun Cho, and Yoshua Bengio. 2014. Neural machine translation by jointly learning to align and translate. *arXiv preprint arXiv:1409.0473.*

Alexandre Berard, Laurent Besacier, and Olivier Pietquin. 2017. LIG-CRIStAL submission for the wmt 2017 automatic post-editing task. In *Proceedings of the Second Conference on Machine Translation, Volume 2: Shared Task Papers*, pages 623–629, Copenhagen, Denmark. Association for Computational Linguistics.

Rajen Chatterjee, Matteo Negri, Raphael Rubino, and Marco Turchi. 2018. Findings of the WMT 2018 shared task on automatic post-editing. In *Proceedings of the Third Conference on Machine Translation, Volume 2: Shared Task Papers*, pages 723–738, Belgium, Brussels. Association for Computational Linguistics.

Mia Xu Chen, Orhan Firat, Ankur Bapna, Melvin Johnson, Wolfgang Macherey, George Foster, Llion Jones, Mike Schuster, Noam Shazeer, Niki Parmar, Ashish Vaswani, Jakob Uszkoreit, Lukasz Kaiser, Zhifeng Chen, Yonghui Wu, and Macduff Hughes. 2018. The best of both worlds: Combining recent advances in neural machine translation. In *Proceedings of the 56th Annual Meeting of the Association for Computational Linguistics (Volume 1: Long Papers)*, pages 76–86, Melbourne, Australia. Association for Computational Linguistics.

Yong Cheng, Zhaopeng Tu, Fandong Meng, Junjie Zhai, and Yang Liu. 2018. Towards robust neural machine translation. In *Proceedings of the 56th Annual Meeting of the Association for Computational Linguistics (Volume 1: Long Papers)*, pages 1756–1766, Melbourne, Australia. Association for Computational Linguistics.

Zi-Yi Dou, Zhaopeng Tu, Xing Wang, Shuming Shi, and Tong Zhang. 2018. Exploiting deep representations for neural machine translation. In *Proceedings of the 2018 Conference on Empirical Methods in Natural Language Processing*, pages 4253–4262. Association for Computational Linguistics.

Jonas Gehring, Michael Auli, David Grangier, Denis Yarats, and Yann N. Dauphin. 2017. Convolutional sequence to sequence learning. In *Proceedings of the 34th International Conference on Machine Learning*, volume 70 of *Proceedings of Machine Learning Research*, pages 1243–1252, International Convention Centre, Sydney, Australia. PMLR.

Xinwei Geng, Xiaocheng Feng, Bing Qin, and Ting Liu. 2018. Adaptive multi-pass decoder for neural machine translation. In *Proceedings of the 2018 Conference on Empirical Methods in Natural Language Processing*, pages 523–532, Brussels, Belgium. Association for Computational Linguistics.

Marcin Junczys-Dowmunt and Roman Grundkiewicz. 2016. Log-linear combinations of monolingual and bilingual neural machine translation models for automatic post-editing. In *Proceedings of the First Conference on Machine Translation*, pages 751–758, Berlin, Germany. Association for Computational Linguistics.

Marcin Junczys-Dowmunt and Roman Grundkiewicz. 2018. MS-UEdin submission to the wmt2018 ape shared task: Dual-source transformer for automatic post-editing. In *Proceedings of the Third Conference on Machine Translation, Volume 2: Shared Task Papers*, pages 835–839, Belgium, Brussels. Association for Computational Linguistics.

Diederik P. Kingma and Jimmy Ba. 2015. Adam: A method for stochastic optimization. In *3rd International Conference on Learning Representations, ICLR 2015, San Diego, CA, USA, May 7-9, 2015, Conference Track Proceedings*.

Philipp Koehn, Hieu Hoang, Alexandra Birch, Chris Callison-Burch, Marcello Federico, Nicola Bertoldi, Brooke Cowan, Wade Shen, Christine Moran, Richard Zens, Chris Dyer, Ondrej Bojar, Alexandra Constantin, and Evan Herbst. 2007. Moses: Open source toolkit for statistical machine translation. In *Proceedings of the 45th Annual Meeting of the Association for Computational Linguistics Companion Volume Proceedings of the Demo and Poster Sessions*, pages 177–180, Prague, Czech Republic. Association for Computational Linguistics.

Minh-Thang Luong and Christopher D. Manning. 2015. Stanford neural machine translation systems for spoken language domain. In *International Workshop on Spoken Language Translation*, Da Nang, Vietnam.

Matteo Negri, Marco Turchi, Rajen Chatterjee, and Nicola Bertoldi. 2018. ESCAPE: a Large-scale Synthetic Corpus for Automatic Post-Editing. In *Proceedings of the Eleventh International Conference on Language Resources and Evaluation (LREC 2018)*, Miyazaki, Japan. European Language Resources Association (ELRA).

Santanu Pal, Sudip Kumar Naskar, Mihaela Vela, and Josef van Genabith. 2016. A neural network based approach to automatic post-editing. In *Proceedings of the 54th Annual Meeting of the Association for Computational Linguistics (Volume 2: Short Papers)*, pages 281–286, Berlin, Germany. Association for Computational Linguistics.

Rico Sennrich, Barry Haddow, and Alexandra Birch. 2016. Neural machine translation of rare words with subword units. In *Proceedings of the 54th Annual Meeting of the Association for Computational Linguistics (Volume 1: Long Papers)*, pages 1715–1725. Association for Computational Linguistics.

David R. So, Chen Liang, and Quoc V. Le. 2019. The evolved transformer. *CoRR*, abs/1901.11117.

C. Szegedy, V. Vanhoucke, S. Ioffe, J. Shlens, and Z. Wojna. 2016. Rethinking the inception architecture for computer vision. In *2016 IEEE Conference on Computer Vision and Pattern Recognition (CVPR)*, pages 2818–2826.

Ashish Vaswani, Noam Shazeer, Niki Parmar, Jakob Uszkoreit, Llion Jones, Aidan N Gomez, Ł ukasz Kaiser, and Illia Polosukhin. 2017. Attention is all you need. In I. Guyon, U. V. Luxburg, S. Bengio, H. Wallach, R. Fergus, S. Vishwanathan, and R. Garnett, editors, *Advances in Neural Information Processing Systems 30*, pages 5998–6008. Curran Associates, Inc.

Thuy-Trang Vu and Gholamreza Haffari. 2018. Automatic post-editing of machine translation: A neural programmer-interpreter approach. In *Proceedings of the 2018 Conference on Empirical Methods in Natural Language Processing*, pages 3048–3053, Brussels, Belgium. Association for Computational Linguistics.

Rui Wang, Andrew Finch, Masao Utiyama, and Eiichiro Sumita. 2017. Sentence embedding for neural machine translation domain adaptation. In *Proceedings of the 55th Annual Meeting of the Association for Computational Linguistics (Volume 2: Short Papers)*, pages 560–566, Vancouver, Canada. Association for Computational Linguistics.

Felix Wu, Angela Fan, Alexei Baevski, Yann Dauphin, and Michael Auli. 2019. Pay less attention with lightweight and dynamic convolutions. In *International Conference on Learning Representations*.

Hongfei Xu and Qiuhui Liu. 2019. Neutron: An Implementation of the Transformer Translation Model and its Variants. *arXiv preprint arXiv:1903.07402*.

Zhen Yang, Wei Chen, Feng Wang, and Bo Xu. 2018. Improving neural machine translation with conditional sequence generative adversarial nets. In *Proceedings of the 2018 Conference of the North American Chapter of the Association for Computational Linguistics: Human Language Technologies, Volume 1 (Long Papers)*, pages 1346–1355, New Orleans, Louisiana. Association for Computational Linguistics.

Biao Zhang, Deyi Xiong, and jinsong su jinsong. 2018a. Accelerating neural transformer via an average attention network. In *Proceedings of the 56th Annual Meeting of the Association for Computational Linguistics (Volume 1: Long Papers)*, pages 1789–1798. Association for Computational Linguistics.

Jiacheng Zhang, Huanbo Luan, Maosong Sun, Feifei Zhai, Jingfang Xu, Min Zhang, and Yang Liu. 2018b. Improving the transformer translation model with document-level context. In *Proceedings of the 2018 Conference on Empirical Methods in Natural Language Processing*, pages 533–542, Brussels, Belgium. Association for Computational Linguistics.

Terminology-Aware Segmentation and Domain Feature for the WMT19 Biomedical Translation Task

Casimiro Pio Carrino, Bardia Rafieian, Marta R. Costa-jussà, José A. R. Fonollosa
{casimiro.pio.carrino, bardia.rafieian}@upc.edu,
{marta.ruiz, jose.fonollosa}@upc.edu,
TALP Research Center
Universitat Politècnica de Catalunya, Barcelona

Abstract

In this work, we give a description of the TALP-UPC systems submitted for the WMT19 Biomedical Translation Task. Our proposed strategy is NMT model-independent and relies only on one ingredient, a biomedical terminology list. We first extracted such a terminology list by labelling biomedical words in our training dataset using the BabelNet API. Then, we designed a data preparation strategy to insert the terms information at a token level. Finally, we trained the Transformer model (Vaswani et al., 2017) with this terms-informed data. Our best-submitted system ranked 2nd and 3rd for Spanish-English and English-Spanish translation directions, respectively.

1 Introduction

Domain adaptation in Neural Machine Translation (NMT) remains one of the main challenges (Koehn and Knowles, 2017). Domain-specific translations are especially relevant for industrial applications where there is a need for achieving both fluency and terminology in translations. Current state-of-the-art NMT systems achieve high performances when trained with large-scale parallel corpora. However, most of the time, large-scale parallel corpora are not available for specific domains. Consequently, NMT models perform poorly for domain-specific translation when trained in low-resource scenario (Chu and Wang, 2018). Several works have been proposed to overcome the lack of domain parallel data by levering on both monolingual domain data (Domhan and Hieber, 2017; Currey et al., 2017) and parallel out-of-domain data (Wang et al., 2017; van der Wees et al., 2017) to improve the performance of domain-specific systems. Furthermore, some attempts have been made to directly insert external knowledge into NMT models through termi-

nology (Chatterjee et al., 2017) and domain information (Kobus et al., 2016). In this work, we designed a data preparation strategy for domain-specific translation systems to enrich data with terminology information without affecting the model architecture. The approach consists on two main steps: 1) Retrieve a biomedical terms list from on our training data 2) use terms to add a domain feature on the source side and define a terminology-aware segmentation. The data preparation is a model-independent process which generates terms-informed token representations that can be used to train any NMT model. For the Biomedical WMT19 task, we decided to train one of the state-of-the-art neural models, the transformer (Vaswani et al., 2017). In our knowledge, this is the first attempt to design a domain-specific text segmentation based on a given terminology list. The rest of the paper is organized as follows. In Sec. 2, we described how terminology is extracted from BabelNet; in Sec. 3 and 4, we defined the terminology-aware segmentation and the domain feature approach, respectively; in Sec. 5, we described the experiments performed, the performance evaluation and the results of the WMT19 competition. Finally, Sec. 6 describes the conclusion and future works.

2 BabelNet

In our work, in order to collect biomedical terms, the domain category of each word was detected with the help of BabelNet (Navigli and Ponzetto, 2012). Specifically, we extracted a list of biomedical terms from our training data using the BabelNet API. To capture biomedical-related domains, we refer to the "biomedical" definition in the BabelNet as stated, "The science of dealing with the maintenance of health and the prevention and treatment of disease". Moreover,

Proceedings of the Fourth Conference on Machine Translation (WMT), Volume 3: Shared Task Papers (Day 2) pages 151–155
Florence, Italy, August 1-2, 2019. ©2019 Association for Computational Linguistics

a biomedical word has BabelNet relations with bio-science, technology, medical practice, medical speciality, neurology and orthopaedics. Consequently, we identified related BabelNet domains to the "biomedical" domain which are: Health and Medicine, Chemistry and Mineralogy, Biology and Engineering and Technology. Based on these domains, we then used the BabelNet API to find the domain of each word in the training dataset by searching through the BabelNet multilingual dictionary. Since a word can have multiple Babel synsets and domains, we collected a domain according to the key concept of a word. For our experiments, we created a list of 10,000 biomedical terms for both English and Spanish.

3 Terminology-aware segmentation

We propose the so-called "bpe-terms segmentation" consisting of both subwords and terms tokens. The idea is to overcome the open-vocabulary problem with subwords and at the same time have the ability to add domain features for terms at the word level. The procedure is rather simple. After learning the bpe codes (Sennrich et al., 2015), they are applied to segment the sentences by explicitly excluding terms belonging to a given domain terminology list. The resulting sentence is a mixture of both subwords and term tokens. In Table 1, we show the differences between standard bpe-segmentation and our bpe-terms segmentation. Unlike general domain words, biomedical terms are not divided into subwords producing a shorter sequence of tokens. It is also important to notice that all the terms that are not present in the terminology list, like "hypertension" and "clot" in the examples, might be split into subwords. These examples show how the effectiveness of bpe-term segmentation depends entirely on the size and quality of the terminology list.

4 Domain features

Following the domain control approach (Kobus et al., 2016), we enrich the data with a word-level binary feature by means of the biomedical terminology. Every word belonging to the terminology list has been labelled as biomedical, while all others as a general domain. The resulting binary feature is then embedded into a dense vector and combined with the word vector. The most common combination strategy consists in concatenating the feature embedding with the word embedding. However, we introduced an additional Multi-Layer perception with one hidden layer after the concatenation. This operation maps the resulting embedding into a new vector that might be more useful for the translation task. More precisely, given the word embedding $\mathbf{x_w} \in R^n$ and the feature embedding $\mathbf{x_f} \in R^m$, the resulting vector $\hat{\mathbf{x}} \in R^d$ is computed as:

$$\hat{\mathbf{x}} = g([\mathbf{x_w}, \mathbf{x_f}]\mathbf{W} + \mathbf{b})$$

where $\mathbf{W} \in R^{n+m,d}$ is the weight matrix, $\mathbf{b} \in R^d$ is the bias term and g is a nonlinear functions for the hidden layer that is applied element-wise. In our experiments, due to the binary nature of the domain feature, we set $m = 3$ as its embedding dimension. The word embedding dimension is set to $n = 512$ instead.

5 Experiments

This section describes the experiments we performed. We first start with the data collection and preprocessing processes. Then, we describe trained systems and their evaluations. Finally, we present the results of the competition in terms of BLEU score. (Papineni et al., 2002).

5.1 Data collection

We gathered data from the resources provided in the official WMT19 web page and from the OPUS collection. For our submissions, all the available biomedical parallel sentences for en/es are chosen both in plain text and Dublin Core format. Then, data have been parsed and merged to create the training and validation sets. Finally, we cleaned the datasets by removing empty sentences and duplicates. In particular, we selected Scielo (Soares et al., 2018), (Neves et al., 2016), UFAL, Pubmed, Medline, IBECS (Villegas et al., 2018) and EMEA (Tiedemann, 2012) sources for the training set and Khresmoi (Dušek et al., 2017) for the validation set.

5.2 Data preprocessing

Data are preprocessed following the standard pipeline by normalizing punctuation, tokenization and true-casing. We also removed sentences longer than 80 tokens and shorter than 2 tokens. For the previous steps, we used the scripts found in the Moses distribution (Koehn et al., 2007). Eventually, we trained shared byte-pairs encoding (BPE) (Sennrich et al., 2015) on both source and

Segmentation	Sentence
Bpe	"the intr@@ ig@@ u@@ ing pro@@ ble@@ m of **cal@@ ci@@ fic@@ ation** and **os@@ s@@ ific@@ ation** ; ne@@ ed to un@@ der@@ st@@ and it for the comp@@ re@@ h@@ ens@@ ion of **b@@ one phys@@ io@@ path@@ ology** ." "inhibition of **T@@ AF@@ I** activity also resulted in a tw@@ of@@ old increase in clot lysis whereas inhibition of both factor XI and **T@@ AF@@ I** activity had no additional effect . " "a 5@@ 7-@@ year-old male with **hepatos@@ plen@@ omegaly** , **p@@ ancy@@ topenia** and hypertension ."
Bpe-terms	"the intr@@ ig@@ u@@ ing pro@@ ble@@ m of **calcification** and **ossification** ; ne@@ ed to un@@ der@@ st@@ and it for the comp@@ re@@ h@@ ens@@ ion of **bone physiopathology** ." inhibition of **TAFI** activity also resulted in a tw@@ of@@ old increase in clot lysis whereas inhibition of both factor XI and **TAFI** activity had no additional effect . "a 5@@ 7-@@ year-old male with **hepatosplenomegaly** , **pancytopenia** and hypertension ."

Table 1: Different segmentation for some sample sentences extracted from the training data. Biomedical terms are in bold type to highlight the effect of the segmentation on them.

	Training set	**Validation set**
es/en	2812577	500

Table 2: The total number of parallel sentences in the training and validation sets after the preprocessing step.

target data with a number of maximum BPE symbols of 50k. The statistics of the final datasets in terms of the total number of lines are shown in Table 2.

5.3 Training with data enriched with terms information

Our strategy involves a data preparation designed to enrich the sentences with terminology information at the token level before the actual training takes place. There are two important components, the bpe-terms segmentation and the domain feature approach as explained in Sec. 3 and Sec. 4. Both of them are based on the terminology

list that was created using the BabelNet API as described in Sec 2. The bpe-terms segmentation is applied to both the source and target side. Instead, the domain feature approach is applied only on the source side. After that, the resulting terms-informed data are used to train the NMT Transformer model. (Vaswani et al., 2017). Thereafter, three different experiments have been performed:

1. The first experiment combined both the terminology-aware segmentation and the domain feature.

2. The second, instead, make just use of the bpe-terms segmentation.

3. The third experiment combined both the terminology-aware segmentation and the domain feature. Additionally, both the vocabularies among source and target and the embedding weights between encoder and decoder are shared during the training.

<table>
<tr><td rowspan="2">System</td><td>en2es</td><td>es2en</td></tr>
<tr><td>WMT18</td><td>WMT18</td></tr>
<tr><td>baseline</td><td>40.84</td><td>43.70</td></tr>
<tr><td>bpe-terms src-tgt + domain feature</td><td>44.26</td><td>43.49</td></tr>
<tr><td>bpe-terms src-tgt + shared vocab & embs</td><td>44.04</td><td>43.84</td></tr>
<tr><td>bpe-terms src-tgt</td><td>44.09</td><td>44.84</td></tr>
</table>

Table 3: The BLEU scores calculated on the WMT18 test set for the three systems compared with the baseline.

<table>
<tr><td rowspan="2">System</td><td colspan="2">en2es</td><td colspan="2">es2en</td></tr>
<tr><td>WMT19 (All)</td><td>WMT19 (OK)</td><td>WMT18 (All)</td><td>WMT19 (OK)</td></tr>
<tr><td>bpe-terms src-tgt</td><td>43.40</td><td>46.09</td><td>37.92</td><td>43.55</td></tr>
<tr><td>bpe-terms src-tgt + domain feature</td><td>43.01</td><td>45.68</td><td>37,21</td><td>42.70</td></tr>
<tr><td>bpe-terms src-tgt + shared vocab & embs</td><td>43.92</td><td>46.83</td><td>39.41</td><td>45.09</td></tr>
</table>

Table 4: The BLEU scores calculated on the WMT19 test set for the three systems.

Furthermore, we trained a baseline model with standard BPE segmentation to make a comparison with the three proposed experiments. All the models have maximum vocabulary size of 50k tokens. However, the final vocabulary size is affected by both the bpe-terms segmentation and the shared vocabularies between source and target side. It turns out that only the baseline and the third experiment had a vocabulary size of 50k tokens. For the training, we used the Transformer (Vaswani et al., 2017) implementation with its default parameters found in the OpenNMT toolkit (Klein et al.).

5.4 Evaluation and results

We evaluated all the models calculating the BLEU score on the WMT18 test set with the 'multi-bleu-detok.sh' script in the Moses distribution (Koehn et al., 2007). For the WMT19 competition, we first calculated the averages of the training checkpoints that achieved the highest BLEU scores on the validation set. Then, we submitted these averages as our best models. The results for both WMT18 and WMT19 test sets are shown in table 3 and 4. In Table 5, we also calculated how many biomedical terms are found in the validation and WMT18/WMT19 test sets to have an idea of the coverage of the terminology list on the out-of-training data. On the WMT18 test set, our proposed models performed better than the baseline, indicating that the Transformer model (Vaswani et al., 2017) took advantages from the bpe-terms segmentation. On the contrary, the domain feature approach overall hurts the test set performances. The best performing system evaluated on the WMT19 test set is the one with bpe-terms seg-

mentation plus shared vocabulary and embedding layers for both source/target and encoder/decoder layers, respectively, showing consistency across both es/en direction. As a result, we placed 2nd for es2en and 3rd for en2es in the WMT19 competition.

<table>
<tr><td></td><td>Validation set</td><td>WMT18</td><td>WMT19</td></tr>
<tr><td>es</td><td>713</td><td>355</td><td>399</td></tr>
<tr><td>en</td><td>831</td><td>363</td><td>502</td></tr>
</table>

Table 5: The number of biomedical terms from the terminology list found in the validation set and the WMT18 and WMT19 test sets.

6 Conclusions and future works

In this article, we described the TALP-UPC systems submitted to the WMT19 Biomedical Translation Task. Our experiments show an NMT model-independent approach that benefits from terminology to improve translations in the biomedical domain. The future efforts will be devoted to extending our bpe-terms segmentation by taking into account multi-word terms extracted from available biomedical glossaries and collecting a terminology list independent from training data.

Acknowledgments

This work is partially supported by Lucy Software / United Language Group (ULG) and the Catalan Agency for Management of University and Research Grants (AGAUR) through an Industrial PhD Grant. This work is also supported in part by the Spanish Ministerio de

Economía y Competitividad, the European Regional Development Fund and the Agencia Estatal de Investigación, through the postdoctoral senior grant Ramón y Cajal, contract TEC2015-69266-P (MINECO/FEDER, EU) and contract PCIN-2017-079 (AEI/MINECO).

References

Rajen Chatterjee, Matteo Negri, Marco Turchi, Marcello Federico, Lucia Specia, and Frédéric Blain. 2017. Guiding neural machine translation decoding with external knowledge. In *WMT*.

Chenhui Chu and Rui Wang. 2018. A survey of domain adaptation for neural machine translation. *CoRR*, abs/1806.00258.

Anna Currey, Antonio Valerio Miceli Barone, and Kenneth Heafield. 2017. Copied monolingual data improves low-resource neural machine translation. In *WMT*.

Tobias Domhan and Felix Hieber. 2017. Using target-side monolingual data for neural machine translation through multi-task learning. In *Proceedings of the 2017 Conference on Empirical Methods in Natural Language Processing*, pages 1500–1505, Copenhagen, Denmark. Association for Computational Linguistics.

Ondřej Dušek, Jan Hajič, Jaroslava Hlaváčová, Jindřich Libovický, Pavel Pecina, Aleš Tamchyna, and Zdeňka Urešová. 2017. Khresmoi summary translation test data 2.0. LINDAT/CLARIN digital library at the Institute of Formal and Applied Linguistics (ÚFAL), Faculty of Mathematics and Physics, Charles University.

G. Klein, Y. Kim, Y. Deng, J. Senellart, and A. M. Rush. OpenNMT: Open-Source Toolkit for Neural Machine Translation. *ArXiv e-prints*.

Catherine Kobus, Josep Maria Crego, and Jean Senellart. 2016. Domain control for neural machine translation. *CoRR*, abs/1612.06140.

Philipp Koehn, Hieu Hoang, Alexandra Birch, Chris Callison-Burch, Marcello Federico, Nicola Bertoldi, Brooke Cowan, Wade Shen, Christine Moran, Richard Zens, Chris Dyer, Ondřej Bojar, Alexandra Constantin, and Evan Herbst. 2007. Moses: Open source toolkit for statistical machine translation. In *Proceedings of the 45th Annual Meeting of the ACL on Interactive Poster and Demonstration Sessions*, ACL '07, pages 177–180, Stroudsburg, PA, USA. Association for Computational Linguistics.

Philipp Koehn and Rebecca Knowles. 2017. Six challenges for neural machine translation. In *Proceedings of the First Workshop on Neural Machine Translation*, pages 28–39, Vancouver. Association for Computational Linguistics.

Roberto Navigli and Simone Paolo Ponzetto. 2012. Babelnet: The automatic construction, evaluation and application of a wide-coverage multilingual semantic network. *Artificial Intelligence*, 193:217 – 250.

Mariana Neves, Antonio Jimeno Yepes, and Aurélie Névéol. 2016. The scielo corpus: a parallel corpus of scientific publications for biomedicine. In *Proceedings of the Tenth International Conference on Language Resources and Evaluation (LREC 2016)*, Paris, France. European Language Resources Association (ELRA).

Kishore Papineni, Salim Roukos, Todd Ward, and Wei-Jing Zhu. 2002. Bleu: A method for automatic evaluation of machine translation. In *Proceedings of the 40th Annual Meeting on Association for Computational Linguistics*, ACL '02, pages 311–318, Stroudsburg, PA, USA. Association for Computational Linguistics.

Rico Sennrich, Barry Haddow, and Alexandra Birch. 2015. Neural machine translation of rare words with subword units. *CoRR*, abs/1508.07909.

Felipe Soares, Viviane Moreira, and Karin Becker. 2018. A large parallel corpus of full-text scientific articles. In *Proceedings of the Eleventh International Conference on Language Resources and Evaluation (LREC-2018)*. European Language Resource Association.

Jörg Tiedemann. 2012. Parallel data, tools and interfaces in opus. In *Proceedings of the Eight International Conference on Language Resources and Evaluation (LREC'12)*, Istanbul, Turkey. European Language Resources Association (ELRA).

Ashish Vaswani, Noam Shazeer, Niki Parmar, Jakob Uszkoreit, Llion Jones, Aidan N Gomez, Ł ukasz Kaiser, and Illia Polosukhin. 2017. Attention is all you need. In I. Guyon, U. V. Luxburg, S. Bengio, H. Wallach, R. Fergus, S. Vishwanathan, and R. Garnett, editors, *Advances in Neural Information Processing Systems 30*, pages 5998–6008. Curran Associates, Inc.

Marta Villegas, Ander Intxaurrondo, Aitor Gonzalez-Agirre, Montserrat Marimon, and Martin Krallinger. 2018. The mespen resource for english-spanish medical machine translation and terminologies: Census of parallel corpora, glossaries and term translations. *Language Resources and Evaluation*.

Rui Wang, Andrew Finch, Masao Utiyama, and Eiichiro Sumita. 2017. Sentence embedding for neural machine translation domain adaptation. In *Proceedings of the 55th Annual Meeting of the Association for Computational Linguistics (Volume 2: Short Papers)*, pages 560–566, Vancouver, Canada. Association for Computational Linguistics.

Marlies van der Wees, Arianna Bisazza, and Christof Monz. 2017. Dynamic data selection for neural machine translation. *CoRR*, abs/1708.00712.

Exploring Transfer Learning and Domain Data Selection for the Bio-medical translation

Noor-e-Hira[1], Sadaf Abdul Rauf[1,2], Kiran kiani[1], Ammara Zafar[1] and Raheel Nawaz[3]
[1] Fatima Jinnah Women University, Pakistan
[2] LIMSI-CNRS, France
[3] Manchester Metropolitan University, UK
sadaf.abdulrauf@limsi.fr
{noorehira94,kianithe1,ammarazafar11}@gmail.com

Abstract

Transfer Learning and Selective data training are two of the many approaches being extensively investigated to improve the quality of Neural Machine Translation systems. This paper presents a series of experiments by applying transfer learning and selective data training for participation in the Bio-medical shared task of WMT19. We have used Information Retrieval to selectively choose related sentences from out-of-domain data and used them as additional training data using transfer learning. We also report the effect of tokenization on translation model performance.

1 Introduction

This paper describes the first system submission by Fatima Jinnah Women University under the NRPU project (NRPU-FJ) for the Bio-medical task. We have built our systems using the paradigm of Neural Machine Translation. We worked on translation between French and English (in both directions) and incorporated domain adaption by using selective data training utilizing information retrieval to retrieve domain related sentences from out-of-domain corpus.

Neural Machine Translation (NMT) (Kalchbrenner and Blunsom, 2013; Sutskever et al., 2014; Cho et al., 2014), is the current state-of-the-art in Machine Translation. Since its arrival, active research is being done to investigate the field and exploit its benefits to produce quality translations. These efforts have resulted in state of the art translation architectures (Vaswani et al., 2017; Gehring et al., 2017). Despite the winning results of NMT over it's counter part Statistical Machine Translation (SMT) for large training corpora; the quality of NMT systems for low resource languages and smaller corpora is still a challenge (Koehn and Knowles, 2017).

To overcome this challenge various studies explore numerous techniques to improve NMT quality especially in low resource settings. Domain adaptation (Freitag and Al-Onaizan, 2016), transfer learning (Zoph et al., 2016; Khan et al., 2018), fine tuning (Dakwale and Monz, 2017; Huck et al., 2018) and data selective training (van der Wees et al., 2017); are few terms being interchangeably used for such techniques as reported in the literature.

As is common in machine learning approaches, the quality of the system being built depends on the data used to train the system. This was true for SMT systems and still holds significance for NMT based systems (Sajjad et al., 2017; Chu et al., 2017). The domain of the training data is crucial to get quality translations. MT performance quickly degrades when the testing domain is different from the training domain. The reason for this degradation is that the learning models closely approximate the empirical distributions of the training data (Lambert et al., 2011). An MT system trained on parallel data from the news domain may not give appropriate translations when used to translate articles from the medical domain.

The availability of language resources has increased over the last decade, previously this was mainly true only for monolingual corpora, whereas parallel corpora were a limited resource for most domains. Most of the parallel data available to the research community was limited to texts produced by international organizations, parliamentary debates or legal texts (proceedings of the Canadian or European Parliament (Koehn, 2006), or of the United Nations,[1] MultiUN.[2] These only covered specific languages and domains which posed a challenge for the porta-

---

[1] https://cms.unov.org/UNCorpus/
[2] http://www.euromatrixplus.net/multi-un

Proceedings of the Fourth Conference on Machine Translation (WMT), Volume 3: Shared Task Papers (Day 2) pages 156–163
Florence, Italy, August 1-2, 2019. ©2019 Association for Computational Linguistics

bility of MT systems across different application domains and also its adaptability with respect to language within the same application domain.

Translation quality of medical texts also suffers due to fewer resources available to train a quality NMT system. Though, medical domain is a growing domain with respect to availability of parallel corpora like scielo (Neves et al., 2016), EMEA (Tiedemann, 2012), Medline (Yepes et al., 2017) and others in making are being made available to the research community.

In this paper we present an approach which aims at increasing the training corpus by mining similar in domain (Bio Med) sentences from out of domain data. We have developed NMT system for English-French language pair, for translation in both directions. Data selective training over cascaded transfer learning, approach has been used to train the model for English to French translation direction; whereas for French to English translation, data selective training approach was used over the whole corpus.

The systems were built with tokenized and untokenized data to study the affect of tokenization in NMT. Tokenization is an important prepossessing step to build MT system. It benefits the MT system by splitting the words into sub-word units, removing punctuations and any other unnecessary tags from the corpus; thus decreasing the vocabulary and helping to translate the unknown words. Tokenization, where, improves the MT system quality it also raises a challenge of developing good quality tokenizers for each language. Studies are performed to investigate tokenization for SMT systems (Zalmout and Habash, 2017; Chung and Gildea, 2009), the question arises how important tokenization is for NMT? Could tokenization be ignored in NMT? (Domingo et al., 2018) investigate tokenization in NMT, to explore the impact of tokenization scheme selected for building NMT, but do not report that, if tokenization is not done, how much will it affect the quality of the NMT system. We present an answer to this question along with other explorations.

The rest of the paper structured as follows; Section 2 provides a brief overview of the related work and background. Section 3 discusses the experimental setup. Results for the different systems are presented in section 3.3. The paper concludes with a brief conclusion.

2 Related Work

This section reports a brief review of the existing literature for machine translation in bio-medical domain. The literature for neural machine translation with the focus of bio-medical domain data is not in abundance. Few studies which we found are discussed followed by a brief overview of transfer learning, domain adaptation and data selective training methods

The system by (Huck et al., 2017) ranked highest in human evaluation in WMT17. They used linguistically informed cascaded word segmentation at the target language side using suffix and compound splitting and BPE. The system was built using attention based gated recurrent units (GRUs).

The techniques used to improve machine translation quality also include selection of best translation among various candidate translations from different translation models. (Grozea, 2018) focuses the mentioned dimension for bio-medical domain NMT system for English Romanian language pair. Percentages were computed for source words which have correspondence in the translation, to select the quality translation. The resultant BLEU scores did not improve more than 0.5.

Khan et al. (2018) trained three NMT systems with different corpus grouping. One experiment included only in-domain corpus, whereas two experiments were performed to train in-domain corpus by initializing the training parameters from general domain system. Learning rate was adjusted to 0.25 and dropout to 0.2, for all the training experiments. The study reveals that training in-domain corpus by transfer learning from general domain corpus increase the MT system quality. The study reports a gain of 4.02 BLEU points over the baseline through transfer learning.

2.1 Transfer Learning

Transfer learning is a process of training a model by utilizing the learned parameters of an already trained model. Learned knowledge of one model is transferred to initiate the training process of a new model for some related models. (Zoph et al., 2016) has defined the process in terms of parent and child model training. The model which is first trained then used to initialize the parameters of a new training process is considered as parent model and the new model which has utilized the knowledge of parent model for its training is considered as child model.

Jointly training both source-target and target-source models minimizes reconstruction errors of monolingual sentences as proposed in the dual learning framework by (He et al., 2016) where two translation models teach each other through a reinforcement learning process. (Wang et al., 2018) also proposed dual transfer learning by sampling several most likely source sentences (target-to-source) to avoid enumerating all source sentences, thus transferring the knowledge from the dual model to boost the training of the primal source-to-target translation.

2.2 Domain adaptation using selective data training

Adaptation using existing parallel texts has shown to be beneficial for translation quality by distributing the probability mass associated with the existing translation phrases. Our method also mostly distributes the probability mass of existing translation phrases and has shown improved results in the paradigm of SMT systems(Abdul-Rauf et al., 2016, 2017). In this study we show the effectiveness of the method in NMT systems. Information retrieval has been previously used in the context of translation model adaptation by (Hildebrand et al., 2005), who use IR to find sentences similar to the test set from the parallel training data. They use the source side of the test data to find related sentences from the parallel corpora. (Lu et al., 2008) use a similar technique of using IR to select and weight portions of existing training data to improve translation performance.

3 Experiments

We have studied two approaches being used to improve NMT in low resource settings. A detailed description of our experiments is provided in this section.

3.1 Corpus

We used in-domain and general domain corpora to train our systems. News-Commentary (Tiedemann, 2012) was used as general domain corpus to perform Information Retrieval for selective data selection. The books corpus was used as the main out-domain corpus. For in-domain corpus we used Medline abstracts training corpus, subset of scielo corpus (Neves et al., 2016), EMEA corpus (Tiedemann, 2012), Medline titles training corpus

Corpus	English	French
In-domain:		
EMEA	12.3M	14.5M
Scielo	0.09M	0.1M
UFAL	1.4M	1.5M
Medline Abstracts	1.4M	1.7M
Medline Titles	6.0M	6.7M
Out-domain:		
Books	2.71M	2.76M
News Commentary (nc)	4.9M	5.9M
NC English IR, top-1 (ncSDE)	1.2M	1.5M
NC French IR, top-2 (ncSDF)	2.1M	2.5M
Development set	1.1M	1.2M
Test set	9.2K	10.9K

Table 1: Train, Development and Test set details in terms of number of words (tokenized).

provided by WMT17 (Yepes et al., 2017), UFAL Medical corpus and Khresmoi corpus. Medline titles corpus was used as test set. Table 1 summarizes the details of our training, development and test corpora.

3.2 Data Selection Procedure

We adopted the technique reported in (Abdul-Rauf and Schwenk, 2011) for our data selection procedure. In-domain Medline titles corpus were used as queries to retrieve related sentences from News Commentary corpus. We had a total of 627,576 queries for data selection. Top n ($1 < n < 10$) relevant sentences were ranked against each query. We used just the unique samples to train the systems.

The data selection process was done on both French and English. For the English News Commentary corpus, English side of Medline titles were used as queries and correspondingly for French News Commentary Corpus as Index using French part of Medline titles as queries. Two separate data selection pipelines were executed to investigate the effect of language used for data selection, inspired by the previous results on choice of translation direction reported in (Abdul-Rauf et al., 2016).

ID	Train Set	Detail	Test	
	English to French		**Un-tokenized**	**tokenized**
	Adding in-domain data to *In-domain* baseline:			
M1	em+sc+medAbs+uf	Baseline-in-domain	12.68	15.65
M2	em+sc+medAbs+uf+ncSDF	M1 $\Rightarrow$ M2	14.57	19.56
M3	em+sc+medAbs+uf+ncSDE	M1 $\Rightarrow$ M3	14.71	19.76
M4	em+sc+medAbs+uf+NewsComentary	M1 $\Rightarrow$ M4	14.54	17.75
	Adding in-domain data to *Out-domain* baseline:			
M5	books	Baseline-outdomain	-	4.53
M6	books+em+sc+medAbs+uf	M5 $\Rightarrow$ M6	-	14.48
M7	books+em+sc+medAbs+uf+ncSDF	M6 $\Rightarrow$ M7	-	16.12
M8	books+em+sc+medAbs+uf-ncSDF+ncSDE+medTitle	M5 $\Rightarrow$ M8	-	21.97
	French to English		**Un-tokenized**	**tokenized**
FE	em+sc+medAbs+uf+ncSDF+ncSDE+medTitle		-	15.94

Table 2: BLEU scores for English to French Models and English to French. $\Rightarrow$ shows the direction of transfer learning while building the models. The best model from IR was chosen which was top2 for French IR and top1 for English IR.

3.3 Training Parameters

We used OpenNMT-py (Klein et al., 2017) to train the models. For English to French translation direction we adopted transfer learning approach along with selective data training. A series of experiments were performed to train a two layer RNN (Recurrent Neural Network) encoder decoder model, having 500 LSTM (Long Short Term Memory) units in each layer. Training was optimized via Adam optimizer and 0.001 learning rate fixed for all the experiments. Whereas for initial experiments we kept the batch size to 64 samples, and afterwards we increased the batch size to 128 samples. Validation was applied after every 10000 steps.

For training NMT system for French to English direction, we followed simple training process. The training model architecture and training parameters were same as for English to French experiments, except that the batch size was set to 128 through out the training process.

4 Results

This section describes the procedure and results of all experiments done by using tokenized and un-tokenized corpora in the training pipeline. Table 2 and Figure 1 show our results in values as well as graphically for English to French. The section is further sub-divided in two sub-sections, Adding in-domain data to *In-domain* baseline (section 4.1)

and Adding in-domain data to *Out-domain* baseline (section 4.2), in which we discuss the results the results on tokenized data following the general MT convention. Effect of tokenization is discussed in the corresponding section 4.3. Experiments were performed with the aim to answer the following research questions:

- How important is the decision for selection of parent model for transfer learning.

- What is the effect of transfer learning when selective data training is initialized from an already trained in-domain model.

- Does selective data training has any benefit over simple training with out-domain corpus.

- How the source or target side data selection affects the translation performance.

- How the performance of a system is affected, if the corpus is not tokenized before starting the training pipeline.

4.1 Adding in-domain data to *In-domain* baseline

Table 1 summarizes the corpora used in our experiments. We have used the general domain News Commentary NC corpus having 4.9M English and 5.9M French tokens to do IR to select medical domain related sentences. We retrieved $top - 10$

sentences from both English and French NC corpus (section 3.2) and built NMT systems to choose the best system. The results of these experiments are graphically depicted in Figure 1. As is evident, selected data training always outperforms the baseline as well as the system built by adding the whole NC corpus to the baseline (row 4 Table 2). We then selected the best systems from both IR pipelines, which were $top-1$ (ncSDE) for English IR yielding 1.2M and 1.5M English and French tokens respectively. For the IR in French direction the best system was $top-2$ (ncSDF) having 2.1M and 2.5M English and French tokens respectively.

Table 2, summarizes the results of all the experiments. We have used short representations to name the corpora used for training. We represented $EMEA$ as em, $Scielo$ as sc, $Medline$ abstracts as $medAbs$, $UFAL$ as uf, selected data of News Commentary using French queries as $ncSDF$, selected data of News Commentary using English queries as $ncSDE$. Right arrow is used to show the application of transfer learning.

For our experiments on transfer learning and selective data training, we first trained a baseline system (M1), by concatenating in-domain EMEA corpus, $Medline$ abstracts corpus, $Scielo$ corpus and $UFAL$ corpus. We didn't add Medline titles corpus in our baseline training pipeline, to get a clear picture of the results of data selective training over transfer learning (as Medline titles were used as a key to select the data from general domain). The BLEU scores of the baseline system, calculated over test set from Medline titles corpus were 15.65.

In the second experiment we applied transfer learning to initialize the selective data training over sentences found by IR from News Commentary French corpus ($ncSDF$) from baseline model. For this experiment data selection was done using the French queries which is the target language in our case. Transfer learning over selective data training improved the system (M2) performance by 4 BLEU points from the baseline. Which is a significant improvement.

The third experiment was done by applying transfer learning to initialize the selective data training from baseline model, but this time data selection was performed using English queries ($ncSDE$). The resulting model (M3) performed better than the baseline with gain of 4.11 BLEU points. Comparing the resulting BLEU scores of

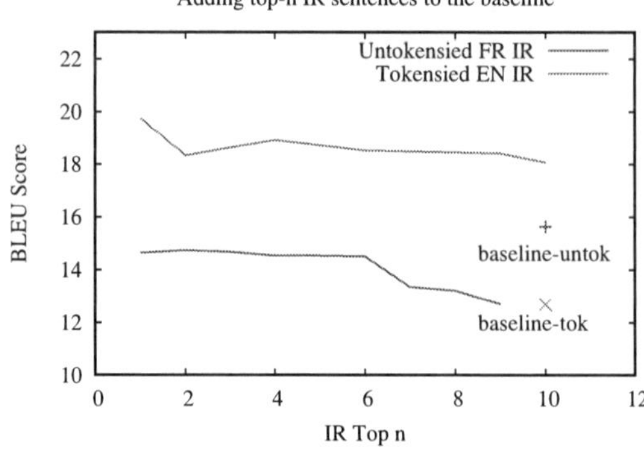

Figure 1: Effect of adding our IR selected data to baseline. In this figure we also show the difference between the the use of tokenized vs untokenized data

both the selective data training experiments, no obvious difference is observed by the change in language to select data.

To explore if selective data training gives any benefit over simple training using whole NC corpus; we built M5. In this experiment we continue to train the baseline system with full News Commentary corpus, which was used for finding domain related sentences for selective data training in above mentioned experiments (M2 and M3). Note that NC corpus is more than double the size of $ncSDE$ and $ncSDF$ (see table 1). The resulting model (M5) only achieved an improvement of 2.1 BLEU points. This clearly demonstrates the efficiency and performance of IR based data selection method.

4.2 Adding in-domain data to *Out-domain* baseline

Table 2 shows the detailed results of our experiments on building NMT systems for English to French translation focusing on the above stated research questions. We first trained the out-domain baseline system (M5) on 2.7M French words of *books* corpus and getting a baseline score of 4.53 BLEU. We applied transfer learning to initialize the training of 17.2M French words of in-domain $em + sc + medAbs + uf$ corpus to train a new model (M6).

We see that starting from an out-domain baseline *books* corpus, the addition of in-domain data drastically improves system performance, giving a total gain of around 10 BLEU points (Table 2 row 6). We did not observe this scale of improvement in previous experiments (section 4.1) when in-domain IR selected data was added to in-domain medical corpora.

Then, we evaluate the performance of cascaded transfer learning over selective data training. We applied transfer learning over the model which was first trained by transferring the parameters of baseline-out-domain to train over major in-domain corpus (M6). However, here we see a similar trend when we apply selective data training using $ncSDF$ (M6 $\Rightarrow$ M7) and resulting improvement is of 1.64 BLEU points. Here, domain data selection exhibited the same trend as we observed in previous section.

In the last experiment we concatenated all the in-domain corpus and trained a model (M8) initiating from out-domain *books* corpus. Interestingly, this is the best result achieved, giving a total improvement of 17.44 BLEU points from the out-domain *books* corpus baseline (4.53 $\Rightarrow$ 21.97). The improvement of 1.64 BLEU points (M6 $\Rightarrow$ M7) achieved with a rather stronger baseline as in the previous section, strengthens our claim of efficiency of our IR based data selection method using selective data training.

4.3 Effect of Tokenization on translation quality

To study the effect of tokenization on performance of NMT systems, we built four models (from M1 to M4) with both tokenized and untokenized corpora. For the experiments done with tokenized corpora we used $MossesTokenizer$ (Koehn et al., 2007), which is reported to yield best results as compared to other tokenizers (Domingo et al., 2018).

Table 2 lists the results of our findings. All the models built using tokenized corpora significantly out-performed their corresponding counterparts built using untokenized corpora.

M1 dropped in performance, by 2.97 BLEU points when trained with untokenized corpora, than its corresponding system trained with tokenized corpora (12.68 $\Leftrightarrow$ 15.65). Same trend is observed in M2 which showed a decline of 4.99 BLEU points by using untokenized corpora during training, in comparison to its training using tokenized corpora (14.57 $\Leftrightarrow$ 19.56). The decline in performance of M3, when trained with untokenized corpora is highest. Its performance decreased by 5.05 BLEU points as compared to training using tokenized corpora. M4 maintained

the trend of decrease in performance when trained with untokenized corpora. It lost 3.21 BLEU points with respect to its corresponding system trained using tokenized corpora. The trend of decline in performance for untokenized corpora can also be observed from Figure 1.

On average the decline in performance of the systems is around 4 BLEU points, which reveals the importance of tokenization of corpora in NMT. This concludes that tokenization of corpora is an important pre-processing step when building NMT systems.

It must be noted here that the selective data training maintained its trend to perform better than the baseline as well as the system built by adding $ncSDE$, $ncSDF$ and the whole NC corpus to the baseline for the systems built using untokenized corpora. Our IR based data selection method still holds it's efficiency claim here (see $M2$ and $M3$ vs $M4$). This adds to the efficacy of the data selective training approach we adapted to build our systems for domain adaptation.

4.4 French to English

To train the system for French to English direction, we followed simple training pipeline with selective data training using both source and target language as selection queries. We concatenated all the in-domain corpus and trained the system with selective data training from News Commentary. This model (FE) gave 15.94 BLEU score on the test set. The reported BLEU scores from WMT official results are 0.1972 and 0.2105 for all and OK sentences respectively.

5 Conclusion

In this paper, we have described our submission to the Bio Medical task based on the sequence-to-sequence NMT architecture for the WMT2019 shared task. In the Bio-medical task we worked on translation between French and English (in both directions). We used transfer learning approach to train our systems along with selective data training using information retrieval techniques.

We performed a series of experiments to investigate a few important research questions. Data selective training, though done with selected corpus smaller in size, yields better results than using the whole out-domain corpus in training for domain adaptation. Our study also adds to the previous results, that tokenization is an important preprocessing step for NMT and it helps significantly improve the system performance.

Over all our system achieved an improvement of 17.44 BLEU points from the out-domain *books* corpus baseline (4.53 $\Rightarrow$ 21.97) by adding all in-domain data. The improvement of 4.11 and 1.64 BLEU points in selective data training from in-domain to in-domain and out-domain to in-domain respectively show the efficiency of our IR based data selection method using selective data training methods.

Acknowledgments

This study is funded by the projects: National Research Program for Universities (NRPU) by Higher Education Commission of Pakistan (5469/Punjab/NRPU/R&D/HEC/2016) and the project Alector (ANR-16-CE28-0005) by Agence National de la Recherche, France.

References

Sadaf Abdul-Rauf and Holger Schwenk. 2011. Parallel sentence generation from comparable corpora for improved SMT. *Machine Translation*, pages 1–35.

Sadaf Abdul-Rauf, Holger Schwenk, Patrik Lambert, and Mohammad Nawaz. 2016. Empirical use of information retrieval to build synthetic data for smt domain adaptation. *IEEE/ACM Transactions on Audio, Speech and Language Processing (TASLP)*, 24(4):745–754.

Sadaf Abdul-Rauf, Holger Schwenk, and Mohammad Nawaz. 2017. Parallel fragments: Measuring their impact on translation performance. *Computer Speech & Language*, 43:56–69.

Kyunghyun Cho, Bart Van Merriënboer, Dzmitry Bahdanau, and Yoshua Bengio. 2014. On the properties of neural machine translation: Encoder-decoder approaches. *arXiv preprint arXiv:1409.1259*.

Chenhui Chu, Raj Dabre, and Sadao Kurohashi. 2017. An empirical comparison of simple domain adaptation methods for neural machine translation. *arXiv preprint arXiv:1701.03214*.

Tagyoung Chung and Daniel Gildea. 2009. Unsupervised tokenization for machine translation. In *Proceedings of the 2009 Conference on Empirical Methods in Natural Language Processing: Volume 2-Volume 2*, pages 718–726. Association for Computational Linguistics.

Praveen Dakwale and Christof Monz. 2017. Fine-tuning for neural machine translation with limited degradation across in-and out-of-domain data. *Proceedings of the XVI Machine Translation Summit*, page 117.

Miguel Domingo, Mercedes Garcia-Martinez, Alexandre Helle, and Francisco Casacuberta. 2018. How much does tokenization affect in neural machine translation? *arXiv preprint arXiv:1812.08621*.

Markus Freitag and Yaser Al-Onaizan. 2016. Fast domain adaptation for neural machine translation. *arXiv preprint arXiv:1612.06897*.

Jonas Gehring, Michael Auli, David Grangier, Denis Yarats, and Yann N Dauphin. 2017. Convolutional sequence to sequence learning. In *Proceedings of the 34th International Conference on Machine Learning-Volume 70*, pages 1243–1252. JMLR. org.

Cristian Grozea. 2018. Ensemble of translators with automatic selection of the best translation–the submission of fokus to the wmt 18 biomedical translation task–. In *Proceedings of the Third Conference on Machine Translation: Shared Task Papers*, pages 644–647.

Di He, Yingce Xia, Tao Qin, Liwei Wang, Nenghai Yu, Tieyan Liu, and Wei-Ying Ma. 2016. Dual learning for machine translation. In *Advances in Neural Information Processing Systems*, pages 820–828.

Almut Silja Hildebrand, Matthias Eck, Stephan Vogel, and Alex Waibel. 2005. Adaptation of the translation model for statistical machine translation based on information retrieval. In *Proceedings of the Meeting of the European Association for Machine Translation (EAMT)*, Budapest, Hungary.

Matthias Huck, Fabienne Braune, and Alexander Fraser. 2017. Lmu munichs neural machine translation systems for news articles and health information texts. In *Proceedings of the Second Conference on Machine Translation*, pages 315–322.

Matthias Huck, Dario Stojanovski, Viktor Hangya, and Alexander Fraser. 2018. Lmu munichs neural machine translation systems at wmt 2018. In *Proceedings of the Third Conference on Machine Translation: Shared Task Papers*, pages 648–654.

Nal Kalchbrenner and Phil Blunsom. 2013. Recurrent continuous translation models. In *Proceedings of the 2013 Conference on Empirical Methods in Natural Language Processing*, pages 1700–1709.

Abdul Khan, Subhadarshi Panda, Jia Xu, and Lampros Flokas. 2018. Hunter nmt system for wmt18 biomedical translation task: Transfer learning in neural machine translation. In *Proceedings of the Third Conference on Machine Translation: Shared Task Papers*, pages 655–661.

Guillaume Klein, Yoon Kim, Yuntian Deng, Jean Senellart, and Alexander M Rush. 2017. Opennmt: Open-source toolkit for neural machine translation. *arXiv preprint arXiv:1701.02810*.

Philipp Koehn. 2006. Europarl: A parallel corpus for statistical machine translation.

Philipp Koehn, Hieu Hoang, Alexandra Birch, Chris Callison-Burch, Marcello Federico, Nicola Bertoldi, Brooke Cowan, Wade Shen, Christine Moran, Richard Zens, et al. 2007. Moses: Open source toolkit for statistical machine translation. In *Proceedings of the 45th annual meeting of the association for computational linguistics companion volume proceedings of the demo and poster sessions*, pages 177–180.

Philipp Koehn and Rebecca Knowles. 2017. Six challenges for neural machine translation. *arXiv preprint arXiv:1706.03872*.

Patrik Lambert, Holger Schwenk, Christophe Servan, and Sadaf Abdul-Rauf. 2011. Investigations on translation model adaptation using monolingual data. In *Proceedings of the Sixth Workshop on Statistical Machine Translation*, pages 284–293, Edinburgh, Scotland. Association for Computational Linguistics.

Yajuan Lu, Jin Huang, and Qun Liu. 2008. Improving statistical machine translation performance by training data selection and optimization. In *Proceedings of the 2007 Joint Conference on Empirical Methods in Natural Language Processing and Computational Natural Language Learning (EMNLP-CoNLL)*.

Mariana Neves, Antonio Jimeno Yepes, and Aurlie Nvol. 2016. The scielo corpus: a parallel corpus of scientific publications for biomedicine. In *Proceedings of the Tenth International Conference on Language Resources and Evaluation (LREC 2016)*, Paris, France. European Language Resources Association (ELRA).

Hassan Sajjad, Nadir Durrani, Fahim Dalvi, Yonatan Belinkov, and Stephan Vogel. 2017. Neural machine translation training in a multi-domain scenario. *arXiv preprint arXiv:1708.08712*.

Ilya Sutskever, Oriol Vinyals, and Quoc V Le. 2014. Sequence to sequence learning with neural networks. In *Advances in neural information processing systems*, pages 3104–3112.

Jrg Tiedemann. 2012. Parallel data, tools and interfaces in opus. In *Proceedings of the Eight International Conference on Language Resources and Evaluation (LREC'12)*, Istanbul, Turkey. European Language Resources Association (ELRA).

Ashish Vaswani, Noam Shazeer, Niki Parmar, Jakob Uszkoreit, Llion Jones, Aidan N Gomez, Łukasz Kaiser, and Illia Polosukhin. 2017. Attention is all you need. In *Advances in neural information processing systems*, pages 5998–6008.

Yijun Wang, Yingce Xia, Li Zhao, Jiang Bian, Tao Qin, Guiquan Liu, and T Liu. 2018. Dual transfer learning for neural machine translation with marginal distribution regularization. In *Proceedings of the Thirty-Second AAAI Conference on Artificial Intelligence*.

Marlies van der Wees, Arianna Bisazza, and Christof Monz. 2017. Dynamic data selection for neural machine translation. *arXiv preprint arXiv:1708.00712*.

Antonio Jimeno Yepes, Aurélie Névéol, Mariana Neves, Karin Verspoor, Ondrej Bojar, Arthur Boyer, Cristian Grozea, Barry Haddow, Madeleine Kittner, Yvonne Lichtblau, et al. 2017. Findings of the wmt 2017 biomedical translation shared task. In *Proceedings of the Second Conference on Machine Translation*, pages 234–247.

Nasser Zalmout and Nizar Habash. 2017. Optimizing tokenization choice for machine translation across multiple target languages. *The Prague Bulletin of Mathematical Linguistics*, 108(1):257–269.

Barret Zoph, Deniz Yuret, Jonathan May, and Kevin Knight. 2016. Transfer learning for low-resource neural machine translation. *arXiv preprint arXiv:1604.02201*.

Huawei's NMT Systems for the WMT 2019 Biomedical Translation Task

Wei Peng*, Jianfeng Liu
Artificial Intelligence Application Research Center
Huawei Technologies
Shenzhen, PRC
`peng.wei1@huawei.com`
`liujianfeng@huawei.com`

Liangyou Li*, Qun Liu
Noah's Ark Lab
Huawei Technologies
Hong Kong, PRC
`liliangyou@huawei.com`
`qun.liu@huawei.com`

Abstract

This paper describes Huawei's neural machine translation systems for the WMT 2019 biomedical translation shared task. We trained and fine-tuned our systems on a combination of out-of-domain and in-domain parallel corpora for six translation directions covering English–Chinese, English–French and English–German language pairs. Our submitted systems achieve the best BLEU scores on English–French and English–German language pairs according to the official evaluation results. In the English–Chinese translation task, our systems are in the second place. The enhanced performance is attributed to more in-domain training and more sophisticated models developed. Development of translation models and transfer learning (or domain adaptation) methods has significantly contributed to the progress of the task.

1 Introduction

In recent years, neural machine translation (NMT) has achieved substantial progress and outperforms statistical machine translation (SMT), especially when large volumes of parallel corpora are available. However, compared to out-of-domain (OOD) data, in-domain data is typically in a small volume and hard to obtain. Therefore, a lot of research focuses on how to make use of OOD data to improvement in-domain NMT systems. Among them, a well-accepted method for domain adaptation is to fine-tune a pre-trained baseline model using in-domain data (Koehn and Knowles, 2017; Luong and Manning, 2015; Freitag and Al-Onaizan, 2016).

In this paper, we present Huawei's practices on adapting our NMT systems from general-domain to in-domain. In addition to fine-tuning our OOD systems on in-domain data, we also resort to a broader spectrum of domain adaptation settings (Chu and Wang, 2018), including training models from scratch on a mixture of shuffled OOD and in-domain data and ensemble various models at the decoding stage. Final systems are submitted to the biomedical shared task of WMT 2019 on six translation directions for English–Chinese, English–French and English–German language pairs.

This paper is organized as below: Section 2 illustrates the system architecture followed by details of parallel corpora for training in Section 3. Section 4 presents our experimental settings. Results are presented and discussed in Section 5. In Section 6, we conclude the paper and unveil future work.

2 System Architecture

Our systems are implemented in TensorFlow 1.8 platform with the Transformer architecture (Vaswani et al., 2017) which consists of an encoder stack and a decoder stack with multi-head attention mechanisms. Each encoder layer consists of two sub-layers: a multi-head self-attention layer and a feed-forward layer with `relu` as the activation function. Compared to the encoder, each decoder layer includes an additional sub-layer to attend to outputs of the encoder. The hyperparameters used in our systems are defined in Table 1 which follow the transformer-big settings in Vaswani et al. (2017).

Hyperparameters	Values
Encoder Layers	6
Decoder Layers	6
Embedding Units	1,024
Attention Heads	16
Feed-forward Hidden Units	4,096

Table 1: Hyperparameters of our systems.

Co-first author

Proceedings of the Fourth Conference on Machine Translation (WMT), Volume 3: Shared Task Papers (Day 2) pages 164–168
Florence, Italy, August 1-2, 2019. ©2019 Association for Computational Linguistics

3 Parallel Corpora

In this section, we present the parallel corpora used to train and evaluate translation models. The statistics of the data used is shown in Table 2. The OOD parallel corpora are collected from a number of sources. In addition to WMT parallel corpora for the news translation task, we also gather data from OPUS.[1] For English–Chinese tasks, we also include in-house data. The data generated by back-translating WMT monolingual corpus is named as "BT" data. Data from other sources such as the UM-Corpus (Tian et al., 2014) and Wikipedia are also included.

The in-domain data is from WMT biomedical translation shared task website.[2] More specifically, the in-domain data are gathered from the following sources (shown in Table 2):

- The EMEA corpus (Tiedemann, 2012). The EMEA corpus encompasses biomedical documents from the European Medicines Agency (EMEA). This corpus is a major component of in-domain training data.

- The UFAL medical corpus collection.[3] The extracted EN–FR parallel corpus contains data predominantly from PatTR Medical data whilst EMEA (OpenSubtitles and crawled) contributing to approximately one-third of the EN–DE data. PathTR is a parallel EN–DE and EN–FR corpus extracted from the MAREC patent collection and it has been used for this task since 2014, containing aligned sentence segments from patent titles, abstracts, and claims.[4]

- A small portion of in-domain data are from Medline and Pubmed.[5] This source of data is provided by the WMT Biomedical task organizers.

4 Experiments

The data depicted in Table 2 are mixed, pre-processed and split into training and development sets. The development data is created by random

Corpus	EN–ZH	EN–FR	EN–DE
OOD Parallel	48.94M	66.33M	22.28M
BT	6.12M	-	24.19M
UM-Corpus	875K	-	-
Wikipedia	-	818K	2.46M
UFAL	-	2.81M	3.04M
EMEA	-	1.09M	1.11M
Medline [6]	-	55K	29K
Pubmed	-	613K	-
Total	55.93M	71.72M	53.11M

Table 2: Corpora statistics in the numbers of sentence pairs after cleaning.

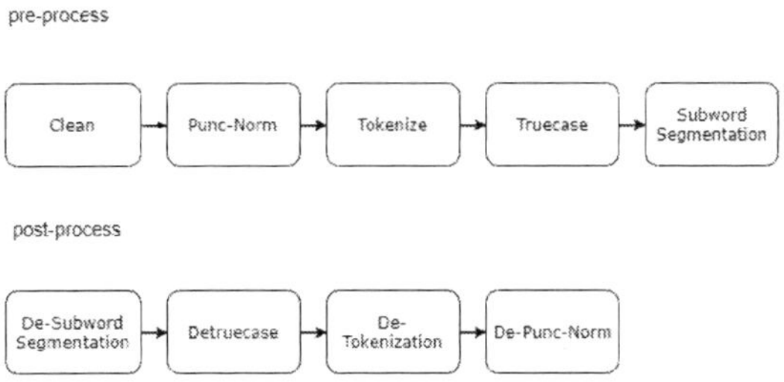

pre-process

Clean → Punc-Norm → Tokenize → Truecase → Subword Segmentation

post-process

De-Subword Segmentation → Detruecase → De-Tokenization → De-Punc-Norm

Figure 1: Data Processing Pipeline

selection 1% from the mixed data sets. We also pre-processed the WMT 2018 test data and treated it as test data to benchmark the models trained under various settings.

4.1 Pre-processing and Post-processing

We noticed that the data processing procedure is an important factor in enhancing the quality of training data and thus the performance of trained models. Our pre-processing pipeline is composed of a number of steps (depicted in Figure 1). The data is undergone data cleaning, puncture normalization (Punc-Norm), tokenization, truecasing and subword segmentation:

- Data cleaning addresses the issues of noisy training data. For example, we remove sentence pairs which are potentially misaligned according to scores from fast-align. We also remove sentence pairs if the ratio of language-specific characters is lower than a threshold. As we found parallel corpora of a language pair may contain sentences pairs which are in a third language, we apply language detection[7] and filtering as well.

---

[1] http://opus.nlpl.eu/
[2] http://www.statmt.org/wmt19/biomedical-translation-task.html
[3] https://ufal.mff.cuni.cz/ufal_medical_corpus
[4] https://www.cl.uni-heidelberg.de/statnlpgroup/pattr/
[5] https://github.com/biomedical-translation-corpora/corpora

[7] https://github.com/aboSamoor/polyglot

- After cleaning data, a few common steps used for machine translation are applied by using scripts from Moses (Koehn et al., 2007). Punc-Norm deals with variations of punctuation in different languages (i.e., French, German) by normalizing them into a standard form. Tokenization is a language-dependent process of splitting a sentence into a sequence of tokens. Truecasing models are trained for each language and applied appropriate case forms on words.

- In order to alleviate the out-of-vocabulary problem, subword segmentation (Sennrich et al., 2016) is used as well. Instead of training an individual segmentation model for each language independently, we directly use subsets of the multilingual vocabularies[8] from the BERT (Devlin et al., 2018) project.[9] It is generated by the WordPiece (Schuster and Nakajima, 2012) model trained on Wikipedia dump. A greedy algorithm is then applied to segment a word in our corpus into a sequence of subwords according to the vocabulary if applicable. For example, "Bitstream" is segmented into "Bit" and "##stream".

After decoding, the outputs are post-processed by combining subwords, de-truecasing and de-tokenization. Punctuation is also converted back to their original form in a specific language when translating to Chinese, French and German.

4.2 Training and Decoding Details

The models are trained in two different ways: (1) Mixed: the model is simply trained on a mixture of data without differentiating OOD and in-domain data. The data is shuffled randomly and there is no oversampling technique applied; (2) Fine-tuned: the baseline model is first pre-trained on the OOD parallel corpus and then fine-tuned on the in-domain data.

All systems are trained for 400K steps, except that, in the Fine-tuned setting, we further fine-tune base systems for 300K unless early stopped. The training was performed on GPU clusters with 4 or 8 Tesla V100. Follow Transformer, we use Adam as a optimizer and a dynamic learning rate with a

linear warmup and root-squared decay. The batch size is set to be 3K source or target words on each GPU card.

We average top 10 checkpoints (Vaswani et al., 2017) evaluated against the development set as the final model for decoding. The beam size is set to 4 and a length penalty weight factor with a value 1 is used (Wu et al., 2016).

We further optionally apply ensemble decoding to combine best models trained in the two settings mentioned above. Ensemble decoding (or prediction) is an approach combining multiple predictors to reduce the errors. It has been widely used in improving NMT performance.

5 Experimental Results

We experimented with more than twenty models in total trained on different combinations of various data and under different settings. `sacrebleu.py` (Post, 2018) and `multi-bleu.perl` from Moses[10] are used to evaluate translations on the development and test data. Table 3 shows BLEU scores on WMT 2018 test set under different settings. We found that models from fine-tuning on in-domain data outperform models trained on the mixed data set when reasonable volumes of in-domain data are available (e.g., on EN–FR and EN–DE). By contrast, the mixed method performs the best on EN–ZH where we do not have genuine in-domain data for fine-tuning. Another interesting finding is that the ensemble decoding consistently takes the middle place when we simply combine the best two models under the three settings. We presume this is caused by domain issues as at least one of the two models used was not well trained on in-domain data.

The results in terms of official BLEU scores of our submissions for WMT 2019 are presented in Table 4 and Table 5. Our final systems achieve the best BLEU scores on English–French and English–German language pairs according to the official evaluation results. In the English–Chinese translation task, our systems are in the second place. We can also find from the tables that training with the mixed data, fine-tuning on in-domain data have contributed to a number of winning models on different language pairs. While the mixed method works better than the Fine-tuned method on English–Chinese and English–

---

[8]Vocabulary size for EN–ZH: 42K (ZH), 46K (EN); Vocabulary size for EN–DE: 58K (DE), 58K (EN); Vocabulary size for EN–FR: 59K (FR), 58K (EN).

[9]https://github.com/google-research/bert

[10]https://github.com/moses-smt/mosesdecoder

BLEU Scores on WMT 18 Data

Models	EN2ZH	ZH2EN	EN2DE	DE2EN	EN2FR	FR2EN
Baseline	33.49	19.46	24.4	27.98	30.57	35.40
Fine-tuned	31.65	21.46	**26.56**	**32.8**	**34.38**	**40.56**
Mixed	**34.36**	**24.37**	24.54	29.18	31.88	36.46
Ensemble (top 2)	34.27	23.41	25.28	32.36	34.30	38.77

Table 3: BLEU scores of the trained models measured against a subset of the test data for WMT 18 biomedical task (bold fonts show the best scores).

German, the fine-tuned method outperforms on French–English (EN2FR Run1) due to a reasonable volume of high-quality in-domain data included. It is noted that the submission (EN2FR Run3) based on the ensemble decoding method has resulted in much lower performance.

According to our experiments and experiences, we reached the same conclusion as that from the WMT biomedical task organizers (Neves et al., 2018): the enhanced performance is attributed to more in-domain training and more sophisticated models developed (i.e., Transformers). The development of translation models and transfer learning (or domain adaptation) methods have significantly contributed to the progress of the task.

6 Conclusions

In this paper, we present Huawei's neural machine translation systems for the WMT 2019 biomedical translation shared task. More than twenty models have been trained and tested under different training settings on three language pairs (six translation directions), i.e., English–Chinese, English–French and English–German. A number of pre-processing and post-processing techniques have been employed to enhance the quality of the data. Our final systems rank the best BLEU scores on English–French and English–German language pairs and the second on English–Chinese according to the official evaluation results in terms of BLEU scores.

Acknowledgments

We would like to express our gratitude to colleagues from HUAWEI Noah's Ark Lab and HUAWEI AARC for their continuous support. We also appreciate the organizers of WMT 19 Biomedical Translation Task for their prompt replies to our inquiries.

References

Chenhui Chu and Rui Wang. 2018. A survey of domain adaptation for neural machine translation. In *Proceedings of the 27th International Conference on Computational Linguistics*, pages 1304–1319, Santa Fe, New Mexico, USA. Association for Computational Linguistics.

Jacob Devlin, Ming-Wei Chang, Kenton Lee, and Kristina Toutanova. 2018. Bert: Pre-training of deep bidirectional transformers for language understanding. arXiv:1810.04805.

Markus Freitag and Yaser Al-Onaizan. 2016. Fast domain adaptation for neural machine translation.

Philipp Koehn, Hieu Hoang, Alexandra Birch, Chris Callison-Burch, Marcello Federico, Nicola Bertoldi, Brooke Cowan, Wade Shen, Christine Moran, Richard Zens, Chris Dyer, Ondrej Bojar, Alexandra Constantin, and Evan Herbst. 2007. Moses: Open source toolkit for statistical machine translation. In *Proceedings of the 45th Annual Meeting of the Association for Computational Linguistics Companion Volume Proceedings of the Demo and Poster Sessions*, pages 177–180, Prague, Czech Republic. Association for Computational Linguistics.

Philipp Koehn and Rebecca Knowles. 2017. Six challenges for neural machine translation. In *Proceedings of the First Workshop on Neural Machine Translation*, pages 28–39, Vancouver, Canada. Association for Computational Linguistics.

Minh-Thang Luong and Christopher D. Manning. 2015. Stanford neural machine translation systems for spoken language domain. In *International Workshop on Spoken Language Translation*, Da Nang, Vietnam.

Mariana L. Neves, Antonio Jimeno-Yepes, Aurélie Névéol, Cristian Grozea, Amy Siu, Madeleine Kittner, and Karin M. Verspoor. 2018. Findings of the wmt 2018 biomedical translation shared task: Evaluation on medline test sets. In *Proceedings of the Third Conference on Machine Translation: Shared Task Papers*, pages 324–339, Belgium, Brussels. Association for Computational Linguistics.

WMT 19 Submission	EN2ZH	ZH2EN	EN2DE	DE2EN	EN2FR	FR2EN
Best Official	**42.34**	**34.13**	**27.89**	**28.82**	**39.95**	**35.56**
ARC Run 1	35.47	30.07	**27.89**	28.71	**39.95**	35.51
ARC Run 2	35.47	30.05	27.86	28.79	36.67	35.51
ARC Run 3	35.47	30.05	27.85	**28.82**	36.19	**35.56**
ARC Best Model	Mixed	Mixed	Mixed	Mixed	Fine-tuned	Fine-tuned

Table 4: Official BLEU scores of ARC submission for WMT 19 biomedical task test sets with all sentences (bold fonts show the best official scores).

WMT 19 Submission	EN2ZH	ZH2EN	EN2DE	DE2EN	EN2FR	FR2EN
Best Official	**43.92**	**35.61**	**35.39**	**38.84**	**42.41**	**38.24**
ARC Run 1	37.09	32.15	**35.39**	38.66	**42.41**	38.18
ARC Run 2	37.09	32.16	35.28	38.80	38.89	38.18
ARC Run 3	37.09	32.16	35.26	**38.84**	38.29	**38.24**
ARC Best Model	Mixed	Mixed	Mixed	Mixed	Fine-tuned	Fine-tuned

Table 5: Official BLEU scores of our submissions for WMT 19 biomedical task with OK-aligned test sets (bold fonts show the best official scores).

Matt Post. 2018. A call for clarity in reporting BLEU scores. In *Proceedings of the Third Conference on Machine Translation: Research Papers*, pages 186–191, Belgium, Brussels. Association for Computational Linguistics.

Mike Schuster and Kaisuke Nakajima. 2012. Japanese and korean voice search. In *International Conference on Acoustics, Speech and Signal Processing*, pages 5149–5152.

Rico Sennrich, Barry Haddow, and Alexandra Birch. 2016. Neural machine translation of rare words with subword units. In *Proceedings of the 54th Annual Meeting of the Association for Computational Linguistics (Volume 1: Long Papers)*, pages 1715–1725, Berlin, Germany. Association for Computational Linguistics.

Liang Tian, Derek F. Wong, Lidia S. Chao, Paulo Quaresma, Francisco Oliveira, Yi Lu, Shuo Li, Yiming Wang, and Longyue Wang. 2014. Um-corpus: A large english-chinese parallel corpus for statistical machine translation. In *Proceedings of the Ninth International Conference on Language Resources and Evaluation (LREC'14)*, pages 1837–1842, Reykjavik, Iceland. European Language Resources Association (ELRA).

Jörg Tiedemann. 2012. Parallel data, tools and interfaces in opus. In *Proceedings of the Eight International Conference on Language Resources and Evaluation (LREC'12)*, pages 2214–2218, Istanbul, Turkey. European Language Resources Association (ELRA).

Ashish Vaswani, Noam Shazeer, Niki Parmar, Jakob Uszkoreit, Llion Jones, Aidan N Gomez, Łukasz Kaiser, and Illia Polosukhin. 2017. Attention is all you need. In I. Guyon, U. V. Luxburg, S. Bengio, H. Wallach, R. Fergus, S. Vishwanathan, and R. Garnett, editors, *Advances in Neural Information Processing Systems 30*, pages 5998–6008. Curran Associates, Inc.

Yonghui Wu, Mike Schuster, Zhifeng Chen, Quoc V. Le, Mohammad Norouzi, Wolfgang Macherey, Maxim Krikun, Yuan Cao, Qin Gao, Klaus Macherey, Jeff Klingner, Apurva Shah, Melvin Johnson, Xiaobing Liu, Łukasz Kaiser, Stephan Gouws, Yoshikiyo Kato, Taku Kudo, Hideto Kazawa, Keith Stevens, George Kurian, Nishant Patil, Wei Wang, Cliff Young, Jason Smith, Jason Riesa, Alex Rudnick, Oriol Vinyals, Greg Corrado, Macduff Hughes, and Jeffrey Dean. 2016. Google's neural machine translation system: Bridging the gap between human and machine translation. *CoRR*, abs/1609.08144.

UCAM Biomedical translation at WMT19: Transfer learning multi-domain ensembles

Danielle Saunders[†] and **Felix Stahlberg**[†] and **Bill Byrne**[‡†]

[†]Department of Engineering, University of Cambridge, UK

[‡]SDL Research, Cambridge, UK

Abstract

The 2019 WMT Biomedical translation task involved translating Medline abstracts. We approached this using transfer learning to obtain a series of strong neural models on distinct domains, and combining them into multi-domain ensembles. We further experiment with an adaptive language-model ensemble weighting scheme. Our submission achieved the best submitted results on both directions of English-Spanish.

1 Introduction

Neural Machine Translation (NMT) in the biomedical domain presents challenges in addition to general domain translation. Firstly, available corpora are relatively small, exacerbating the effect of noisy or poorly aligned training data. Secondly, individual sentences within a biomedical document may use specialist vocabulary from small domains like health or statistics, or may contain generic language. Training to convergence on a single biomedical dataset may therefore not correspond to good performance on arbitrary biomedical test data.

Transfer learning is an approach in which a model is trained using knowledge from an existing model (Khan et al., 2018). Transfer learning typically involves initial training on a large, general domain corpus, followed by fine-tuning on the domain of interest. We apply transfer learning iteratively on datasets from different domains, obtaining strong models that cover two domains for both directions of the English-German language pair, and three domains for both directions of English-Spanish.

The domain of individual documents in the 2019 Medline test dataset is unknown, and may vary sentence-to-sentence. Evenly-weighted ensembles of models from different domains can give good results in this case (Freitag and Al-Onaizan, 2016). However, we suggest a better approach would take into account the likely domain, or domains, of each test sentence. We therefore investigate applying Bayesian Interpolation for language-model based multi-domain ensemble weighting.

1.1 Iterative transfer learning

Transfer learning has been used to adapt models both across domains, e.g. news to biomedical domain adaptation, and within one domain, e.g. WMT14 biomedical data to WMT18 biomedical data (Khan et al., 2018). For en2de and de2en we have only one distinct in-domain dataset, and so we use standard transfer learning from a general domain news model.

For es2en and en2es, we use the domain-labelled Scielo dataset to provide two distinct domains, health and biological sciences ('bio'), in addition to the complete biomedical dataset (Neves et al., 2016). We therefore experiment with iterative transfer learning, in which a model trained with transfer learning is then trained further on the original domain.

NMT transfer learning for domain adaptation involves using the performance of a model on some general domain A to improve performance on some other domain B: $A \rightarrow B$. However, if the two domains are sufficiently related, we suggest that task B could equally be used for transfer learning A: $B \rightarrow A$. The stronger general model A could then be used to achieve even better performance on other tasks: $B \rightarrow A \rightarrow B$, $B \rightarrow A \rightarrow C$, and so on.

1.2 Adaptive decoding

Previous work on transfer learning typically aims to find a single model that performs well on a known domain of interest (Khan et al., 2018).

Proceedings of the Fourth Conference on Machine Translation (WMT), Volume 3: Shared Task Papers (Day 2) pages 169–174
Florence, Italy, August 1-2, 2019. ©2019 Association for Computational Linguistics

The biomedical translation task offers a scenario in which the test domain is unknown, since individual Medline documents can have very different styles and topics. Our approach is to decode such test data with an ensemble of distinct domains.

For intuitive ensemble weights, we use sequence-to-sequence Bayesian Interpolation (BI) as described in Saunders et al. (2019), which also contains a more in-depth derivation and discusses possible hyperparameter configurations. We consider models $p_k(\mathbf{y}|\mathbf{x})$ trained on K domains, used for $T = K$ domain decoding tasks. We assume throughout that $p(t) = \frac{1}{T}$, i.e. that tasks are equally likely absent any other information. Weights $\lambda_{k,t}$ define a task-conditional ensemble. At step i, where $h_i = \mathbf{y}_{1:i-1}$ is decoding history:

$$p(y_i|h_i, \mathbf{x}) = \sum_{k=1}^{K} p_k(y_i|h_i, \mathbf{x}) \sum_{t=1}^{T} p(t|h_i, \mathbf{x})\lambda_{k,t} \tag{1}$$

This is an adaptively weighted ensemble where, for each source sentence $\mathbf{x}$ and output hypothesis $\mathbf{y}$, we re-estimate $p(t|h_i, \mathbf{x})$ at each step:

$$p(t|h_i, \mathbf{x}) = \frac{p(h_i|t, \mathbf{x})p(t|\mathbf{x})}{\sum_{t'=1}^{T} p(h_i|t', \mathbf{x})p(t'|\mathbf{x})} \tag{2}$$

$p(h_i|t, \mathbf{x})$ is found from the last score of each model:

$$p(h_i|t, \mathbf{x}) = p(y_{i-1}|h_{i-1}, t, \mathbf{x}) \tag{3}$$
$$= \sum_{k} p_k(y_{i-1}|h_{i-1}, t, \mathbf{x})\lambda_{k,t}$$

We use G_t, an n-gram language model trained on source training sentences from task t, to estimate initial task posterior $p(t|\mathbf{x})$:

$$\frac{p(\mathbf{x}|t)p(t)}{\sum_{t'=1}^{T} p(\mathbf{x}|t')p(t')} = \frac{G_t(\mathbf{x})^\alpha}{\sum_{t'=1}^{T} G_{t'}(\mathbf{x})^\alpha} \tag{4}$$

Here α is a smoothing parameter. If $\overline{G}_{k,t} = \sum_{\mathbf{x} \in \text{Test}_t} G_k(\mathbf{x})$, we take:

$$\lambda_{k,t} = \frac{\overline{G}_{k,t}^\alpha}{\sum_{k'} \overline{G}_{k',t}^\alpha} \tag{5}$$

Figure 1 demonstrates this adaptive decoding when weighting a biomedical and a general (news) domain model to produce a biomedical sentence. The model weights are even until biomedical-specific vocabulary is produced, at which point the in-domain model dominates.

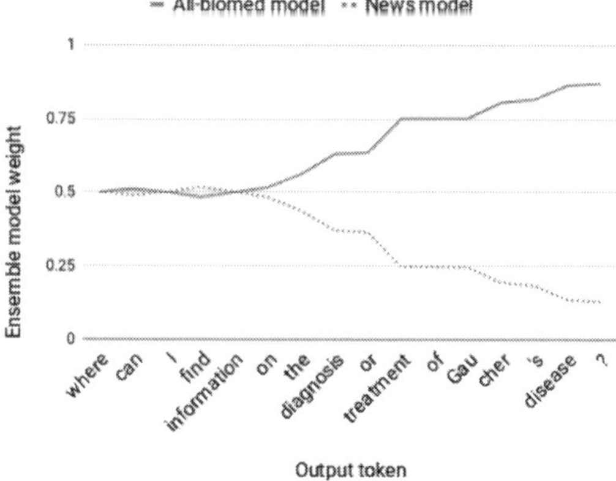

Figure 1: Adaptively adjusting model weights during decoding with Bayesian Interpolation

1.3 Related work

Transfer learning has been applied to NMT in many forms. Luong and Manning (2015) use transfer learning to adapt a general model to in-domain data. Zoph et al. (2016) use multilingual transfer learning to improve NMT for low-resource languages. Chu et al. (2017) introduce mixed fine-tuning, which carries out transfer learning to a new domain combined with some original domain data. Kobus et al. (2017) train a single model on multiple domains using domain tags. Khan et al. (2018) sequentially adapt across multiple biomedical domains to obtain one single-domain model.

At inference time, Freitag and Al-Onaizan (2016) use uniform ensembles of general and fine-tuned models. Our Bayesian Interpolation experiments extend previous work by Allauzen and Riley (2011) on Bayesian Interpolation for language model combination.

2 Experimental setup

2.1 Data

We report on two language pairs: Spanish-English (es-en) and English-German (en-de). Table 1 lists the data used to train our biomedical domain evaluation systems. For en2de and de2en

---

[1] https://ufal.mff.cuni.cz/ufal_medical_corpus
[2] Dušek et al. (2017)
[3] Neves et al. (2016)
[4] https://github.com/biomedical-translation-corpora/medline (Yepes et al., 2017)
[5] http://www.himl.eu/test-sets

	Domain	Training datasets	Sentence pairs	Dev datasets	Sentence pairs
es-en	All-biomed	UFAL Medical[1] Scielo[3] Medline titles[4] Medline training abstracts Total (pre) / post-filtering	639K 713K 288K 83K (1723K) / **1291K**	Khresmoi[2]	1.5K
	Health	Scielo health only Total post-filtering	587K **558K**	Scielo 2016 health	5K
	Bio	Scielo bio only Total post-filtering	126K **122K**	Scielo 2016 bio	4K
en-de	All-biomed	UFAL Medical Medline training abstracts Total (pre) / post-filtering	2958K 33K (2991K) / **2156K**	Khresmoi Cochrane[5]	1.5K 467

Table 1: Biomedical training and validation data used in the evaluation task. For both language pairs identical data was used in both directions.

we additionally reuse strong general domain models trained on the WMT19 news data, including filtered Paracrawl. Details of data preparation and filtering for these models are discussed in Stahlberg et al. (2019).

For each language pair we use the same training data in both directions, and use a 32K-merge source-target BPE vocabulary (Sennrich et al., 2016) trained on the 'base' domain training data (news for en-de, Scielo health for es-en)

For the biomedical data, we preprocess the data using Moses tokenization, punctuation normalization and truecasing. We then use a series of simple heuristics to filter the parallel datasets:

- Detected language filtering using the Python `langdetect` package[6]. In addition to mis-labelled sentences, this step removes many sentences which are very short or have a high proportion of punctuation or HTML tags.

- Remove sentences containing more than 120 tokens or fewer than 3.

- Remove duplicate sentence pairs

- Remove sentences where the ratio of source to target tokens is less than 1:3.5 or more than 3.5:1

- Remove pairs where more than 30% of either sentence is the same token.

2.2 Model hyperparameters and training

We use the Tensor2Tensor implementation of the Transformer model with the `transformer_big` setup for all NMT models (Vaswani et al., 2018). By default this model size limits batch size of

2K due to memory constraints. We delay gradient updates by a factor of 8, letting us effectively use a 16K batch size (Saunders et al., 2018). We train each domain model until it fails to improve on the domain validation set in 3 consecutive checkpoints, and perform checkpoint averaging over the final 10 checkpoints to obtain the final model (Junczys-Dowmunt et al., 2016).

At inference time we decode with beam size 4 using SGNMT (Stahlberg et al., 2017). For BI we use 2-gram KENLM models (Heafield, 2011) trained on the source training data for each domain. For validation results we report cased BLEU scores with SacreBLEU (Post, 2018)[7]; test results use case-insensitive BLEU.

2.3 Results

Our first experiments involve iterative transfer learning in es2en and en2es to obtain models on three separate domains for the remaining evaluation. We use health, a relatively clean and small dataset, as the initial domain to train from scratch. Once converged, we use this to initialise training on the larger, noiser all-biomed corpus. When the all-biomed model has converged, we use it to initialise training on the health data and bio data for stronger models on those domains. Figure 2 shows the training progression for the health and all-biomed models, as well as the standard transfer learning case where we train on all-biomed from scratch.

Table 2 gives single model validation scores for es2en and en2es models with standard and iterative transfer learning. We find that the all-biomed domain gains 1-2 BLEU points from transfer learning. Moreover, the health domain gains on

---

[6]`https://pypi.org/project/langdetect/`

[7]SacreBLEU signature: `BLEU+case.mixed +numrefs.1+smooth.exp+tok.13a+version.1.3.2`

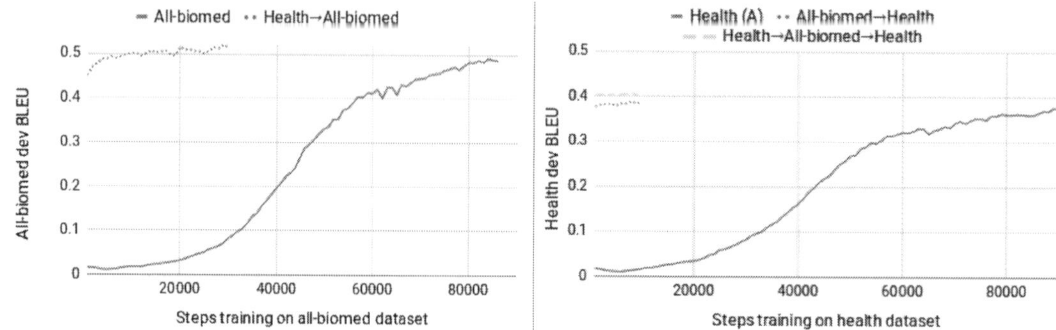

Figure 2: Transfer learning for es2en domains. Left: standard transfer learning improves performance from a smaller (health) to a larger (all-biomed) domain. Right: returning to the original domain after transfer learning provides further gains on health.

Transfer learning schedule	es2en			en2es		
	Khresmoi	Health	Bio	Khresmoi	Health	Bio
Health	45.1	35.7	34.0	41.2	34.7	36.1
All-biomed	49.8	35.4	35.7	43.4	33.9	37.5
All-biomed → Health	48.9	36.4	35.9	43.0	35.2	38.0
All-biomed → Bio	48.0	34.6	37.2	43.2	34.1	40.5
Health → All-biomed	**52.1**	36.7	37.0	44.2	35.0	39.0
Health → All-biomed → Health	51.1	**37.0**	37.2	44.0	**36.3**	39.5
Health → All-biomed → Bio	50.6	36.0	**38.0**	**45.2**	35.3	**41.3**

Table 2: Validation BLEU for English-Spanish models with transfer learning. We use the final three models in our submission.

all domains from iterative transfer learning relative to training from scratch and relative to standard transfer learning(All-biomed → Health), despite being trained twice to convergence on health.

We submitted three runs to the WMT19 biomedical task for each language pair: the best single all-biomed model, a uniform ensemble of models on two en-de and three es-en domains, and an ensemble with Bayesian Interpolation. Tables 3 and 4 give validation and test scores.

We find that a uniform multi-domain ensemble performs well, giving 0.5-1.2 BLEU improvement on the test set over strong single models. We see small gains from using BI with ensembles on most validation sets, but only on en2es test.

Following test result release, we noted that, in general, we could predict BI ($\alpha = 0.5$) performance by comparing the uniform ensemble with the oracle model performing best on each validation domain. For en2es uniform ensembling underperforms the health and bio oracle models on their validation sets, and the uniform ensemble slightly underperforms BI on the test data. For en2de, by contrast, uniform ensembling is consistently better than oracles on the dev sets, and outperforms BI on the test data. For de2en and es2en,

uniform ensembling performs similarly to the oracles, and performs similarly to BI.

From this, we hypothesise that BI ($\alpha = 0.5$) has a tendency to converge to a single model. This is effective when single models perform well (en2es) but ineffective if the uniform ensemble is predictably better than any single model (en2de). Consequently in Table 5 we experiment with BI ($\alpha = 0.1$). In this case BI matches or out-performs the uniform ensemble. Notably, for en2es, where BI ($\alpha = 0.5$) performed well, taking $\alpha = 0.1$ does not harm performance.

3 Conclusions

Our WMT19 Biomedical submission covers the English-German and English-Spanish language pairs, achieving the best submitted results on both directions of English-Spanish. We use transfer learning iteratively to train single models which perform well on related but distinct domains, and show further gains from multi-domain ensembles. We explore Bayesian Interpolation for multi-domain ensemble weighting, and find that a strongly smoothed case gives small gains over uniform ensembles.

	es2en				en2es			
	Khresmoi	**Health**	**Bio**	**Test**	**Khresmoi**	**Health**	**Bio**	**Test**
Health → All-biomed	52.1	36.7	37.0	42.4	44.2	35.0	39.0	44.9
Health → All-biomed → Health	51.1	37.0	37.2	-	44.0	36.3	39.5	-
Health → All-biomed → Bio	50.6	36.0	38.0	-	45.2	35.3	41.3	-
Uniform ensemble	**52.2**	36.9	37.9	**43.0**	**45.1**	35.6	40.2	45.4
BI ensemble (α=0.5)	52.1	**37.0**	**38.1**	42.9	44.5	**35.7**	**41.2**	**45.6**

Table 3: Validation and test BLEU for models used in English-Spanish language pair submissions.

	de2en			en2de		
	Khresmoi	**Cochrane**	**Test**	**Khresmoi**	**Cochrane**	**Test**
News	43.8	46.8	-	30.4	40.7	-
News → All-biomed	44.5	47.6	27.4	31.1	39.5	26.5
Uniform ensemble	45.3	48.4	**28.6**	**32.6**	42.9	**27.2**
BI ensemble (α=0.5)	**45.4**	**48.8**	28.5	32.4	**43.1**	26.4

Table 4: Validation and test BLEU for models used in English-German language pair submissions.

	es2en	en2es	de2en	en2de
Uniform	**43.2**	45.3	28.3	25.9
BI (α=0.5)	43.0	**45.5**	28.2	25.2
BI (α=0.1)	**43.2**	**45.5**	**28.5**	**26.0**

Table 5: Comparing uniform ensembles and BI with varying smoothing factor on the WMT19 test data. Small deviations from official test scores on submitted runs are due to tokenization differences. $\alpha = 0.5$ was chosen for submission based on results on available development data.

Acknowledgments

This work was supported by EPSRC grant EP/L027623/1 and has been performed using resources provided by the Cambridge Tier-2 system operated by the University of Cambridge Research Computing Service[8] funded by EPSRC Tier-2 capital grant EP/P020259/1.

References

Cyril Allauzen and Michael Riley. 2011. Bayesian Language Model Interpolation for Mobile Speech Input. In *Proceedings of the Twelfth Annual Conference of the International Speech Communication Association*.

Chenhui Chu, Raj Dabre, and Sadao Kurohashi. 2017. An empirical comparison of domain adaptation methods for neural machine translation. In *Proceedings of the 55th Annual Meeting of the Association for Computational Linguistics (Volume 2: Short Papers)*, pages 385–391.

Ondřej Dušek, Jan Hajič, Jaroslava Hlaváčová, Jindřich Libovický, Pavel Pecina, Aleš Tamchyna, and Zdeňka Urešová. 2017. Khresmoi summary translation test data 2.0. LINDAT/CLARIN digital library at the Institute of Formal and Applied Linguistics (ÚFAL), Faculty of Mathematics and Physics, Charles University.

Markus Freitag and Yaser Al-Onaizan. 2016. Fast domain adaptation for Neural Machine Translation. *CoRR*, abs/1612.06897.

Kenneth Heafield. 2011. KenLM: Faster and smaller language model queries. In *Proceedings of the Sixth Workshop on Statistical Machine Translation*, pages 187–197.

Marcin Junczys-Dowmunt, Tomasz Dwojak, and Rico Sennrich. 2016. The AMU-UEDIN submission to the WMT16 news translation task: Attention-based NMT models as feature functions in phrase-based SMT. In *Proceedings of the First Conference on Machine Translation*, pages 319–325, Berlin, Germany. Association for Computational Linguistics.

Abdul Khan, Subhadarshi Panda, Jia Xu, and Lampros Flokas. 2018. Hunter nmt system for wmt18 biomedical translation task: Transfer learning in neural machine translation. In *Proceedings of the Third Conference on Machine Translation: Shared Task Papers*, pages 655–661.

Catherine Kobus, Josep Crego, and Jean Senellart. 2017. Domain control for neural machine translation. In *Proceedings of the International Conference Recent Advances in Natural Language Processing, RANLP 2017*, pages 372–378.

Minh-Thang Luong and Christopher D Manning. 2015. Stanford Neural Machine Translation systems for spoken language domains. In *Proceedings of the International Workshop on Spoken Language Translation*, pages 76–79.

Mariana L Neves, Antonio Jimeno-Yepes, and Aurélie Névéol. 2016. The ScieLO Corpus: a Parallel Corpus of Scientific Publications for Biomedicine. In *LREC*.

Matt Post. 2018. A call for clarity in reporting BLEU scores. *CoRR*, abs/1804.08771.

---

[8]http://www.hpc.cam.ac.uk

Danielle Saunders, Felix Stahlberg, Adrià de Gispert, and Bill Byrne. 2018. Multi-representation ensembles and delayed sgd updates improve syntax-based nmt. In *Proceedings of the 56th Annual Meeting of the Association for Computational Linguistics (Volume 2: Short Papers)*, pages 319–325.

Danielle Saunders, Felix Stahlberg, Adrià de Gispert, and Bill Byrne. 2019. Domain adaptive inference for neural machine translation. In *Proceedings of the 57th Annual Meeting of the Association for Computational Linguistics*.

Rico Sennrich, Barry Haddow, and Alexandra Birch. 2016. Neural Machine Translation of Rare Words with Subword Units. In *Proceedings of the 54th Annual Meeting of the Association for Computational Linguistics*, volume 1, pages 1715–1725.

Felix Stahlberg, Eva Hasler, Danielle Saunders, and Bill Byrne. 2017. SGNMT–A Flexible NMT Decoding Platform for Quick Prototyping of New Models and Search Strategies. In *Proceedings of the 2017 Conference on Empirical Methods in Natural Language Processing: System Demonstrations*, pages 25–30.

Felix Stahlberg, Danielle Saunders, Adrià de Gispert, and Bill Byrne. 2019. CUED@WMT19:EWC&LMs. In *Proceedings of the Fourth Conference on Machine Translation: Shared Task Papers*. Association for Computational Linguistics.

Ashish Vaswani, Samy Bengio, Eugene Brevdo, Francois Chollet, Aidan N. Gomez, Stephan Gouws, Llion Jones, Łukasz Kaiser, Nal Kalchbrenner, Niki Parmar, Ryan Sepassi, Noam Shazeer, and Jakob Uszkoreit. 2018. Tensor2Tensor for Neural Machine Translation. *CoRR*, abs/1803.07416.

Antonio Jimeno Yepes, Aurélie Névéol, Mariana Neves, Karin Verspoor, Ondrej Bojar, Arthur Boyer, Cristian Grozea, Barry Haddow, Madeleine Kittner, Yvonne Lichtblau, et al. 2017. Findings of the wmt 2017 biomedical translation shared task. In *Proceedings of the Second Conference on Machine Translation*, pages 234–247.

Barret Zoph, Deniz Yuret, Jonathan May, and Kevin Knight. 2016. Transfer Learning for Low-Resource Neural Machine Translation. In *Proceedings of the 2016 Conference on Empirical Methods in Natural Language Processing*, pages 1568–1575.

BSC Participation in the WMT Translation of Biomedical Abstracts

Felipe Soares
Barcelona Supercomputing Center (BSC)
`felipe.soares@bsc.es`

Martin Krallinger
Centro Nacional de Investigaciones
Oncológicas (CNIO)
Barcelona Supercomputing Center (BSC)
`martin.krallinger@bsc.es`

Abstract

This paper describes the machine translation systems developed by the Barcelona Supercomputing (BSC) team for the biomedical translation shared task of WMT19. Our system is based on Neural Machine Translation unsing the OpenNMT-py toolkit and Transformer architecture. We participated in four translation directions for the English/Spanish and English/Portuguese language pairs. To create our training data, we concatenated several parallel corpora, both from in-domain and out-of-domain sources, as well as terminological resources from UMLS.

1 Introduction

In this paper, we present the system developed at the Barcelona Supercomputing Center (BSC) for the Biomedical Translation shared task in the Fourth Conference on Machine Translation (WMT19), which consists in translating scientific texts from the biological and health domain.

Our participation in this task considered the English/Portuguese and English/Spanish language pairs, with translations in both directions. For that matter, we developed a machine translation (MT) system based on neural machine translation (NMT), using OpenNMT-py (Klein et al., 2017).

2 Related Works

Previous participation in biomedical translation tasks include the works of Costa-Jussà et al. (2016) which employed Moses Statistic Machine Translation (SMT) to perform automatic translation integrated with a neural character-based recurrent neural network for model re-ranking and bilingual word embeddings for out of vocabulary (OOV) resolution. Given the 1000-best list of SMT translations, the RNN performs a rescoring and selects the translation with the highest score.

The OOV resolution module infers the word in the target language based on the bilingual word embedding trained on large monolingual corpora. Their reported results show that both approaches can improve BLEU scores, with the best results given by the combination of OOV resolution and RNN re-ranking. Similarly, Ive et al. (2016) also used the n-best output from Moses as input to a re-ranking model, which is based on a neural network that can handle vocabularies of arbitrary size.

More recently, Tubay and Costa-jussÃ (2018) employed multi-source language translation using romance languages to translate from Spanish, French, and Portuguese to English. They used data from SciELO and Medline abstracts to train a Transformer model with individual languages to English and also with all languages concatenated to English.

In the last WMT biomedical translation challenge (2018) (Neves et al., 2018), the submission that achieved the best BLEU scores for the ES/EN and PT/EN, in both directions, were the ones submited by the UFRGS team (Soares and Becker, 2018), followed by the TALP-UPC (Tubay and Costa-jussÃ, 2018) in the ES/EN direction and the UHH-DS in the EN/PT directions.

3 Resources

In this section, we describe the language resources used to train both models, which are from two main types: corpora and terminological resources.

3.1 Corpora

We used both in-domain and general domain corpora to train our systems. For general domain data, we used the books corpus (Tiedemann, 2012), which is available for several languages, included the ones we explored in our systems, and the JRC-Acquis (Tiedemann, 2012). As for in-domain data, we included several different corpora:

Proceedings of the Fourth Conference on Machine Translation (WMT), Volume 3: Shared Task Papers (Day 2) pages 175–178
Florence, Italy, August 1-2, 2019. ©2019 Association for Computational Linguistics

- The corpus of full-text scientific articles from Scielo (Soares et al., 2018a), which includes articles from several scientific domains in the desired language pairs, but predominantly from biomedical and health areas.

- A subset of the UFAL medical corpus[1], containing the Medical Web Crawl data for the English/Spanish language pair.

- The EMEA corpus (Tiedemann, 2012), consisting of documents from the European Medicines Agency.

- A corpus of theses and dissertations abstracts (BDTD) (Soares et al., 2018b) from CAPES, a Brazilian governmental agency responsible for overseeing post-graduate courses. This corpus contains data only for the English/Portuguese language pair.

- A corpus from Virtual Health Library[2] (BVS), containing also parallel sentences for the language pairs explored in our systems.

Table 1 depicts the original number of parallel segments according to each corpora source. In Section 4.1, we detail the pre-processing steps performed on the data to comply with the task evaluation.

Corpus	Sentences	
	EN/ES	EN/PT
Books	93,471	-
UFAL	286,779	-
Full-text Scielo	425,631	2.86M
JRC-Acquis	805,757	1.64M
EMEA	-	1.08M
CAPES-BDTD	-	950,252
BVS	737,818	631,946
Total	2.37M	7.19M

Table 1: Original size of individual corpora used in our experiments

3.2 Terminological Resources

Regarding terminological resources, we extracted parallel terminologies from the Unified Medical Language System[3] (UMLS). For that matter, we

used the MetamorphoSys application provided by U.S. National Library of Medicine (NLM) to subset the language resources for our desired language pairs. Our approach is similar to what was proposed by Perez-de Viñaspre and Labaka (2016).

Once the resource was available, we imported the MRCONSO RRF file to an SQL database to split the data in a parallel format in the two language pairs. Table 2 shows the number of parallel concepts for each pair.

Language Pair	Concepts
EN/ES	14,399
EN/PT	26,194

Table 2: Number of concepts from UMLS for each language pair

4 Experimental Settings

In this section, we detail the pre-processing steps employed as well as the architecture of the Transformer.

4.1 Pre-processing

As detailed in the description of the biomedical translation task, the evaluation is based on texts extracted from Medline. Since one of our corpora, the one comprised of full-text articles from Scielo, may contain a considerable overlap with Medline data, we decided to employ a filtering step in order to avoid including such data.

The first step in our filter was to download metadata from Pubmed articles in Spanish and Portuguese. For that matter, we used the Ebot utility[4] provided by NLM using the queries *POR[la]* and *ESP[la]*, retrieving all results available. Once downloaded, we imported them to an SQL database which already contained the corpora metadata. To perform the filtering, we used the *pii* field from Pubmed to match the Scielo unique identifiers or the title of the papers, which would match documents not from Scielo.

Once the documents were matched, we removed them from our database and partitioned the data in training and validation sets. Table 3 contains the final number of sentences for each language pair and partition.

[1]https://ufal.mff.cuni.cz/ufal_
medical_corpus
[2]http://bvsalud.org/
[3]https://www.nlm.nih.gov/research/
umls/
[4]https://www.ncbi.nlm.nih.gov/Class/
PowerTools/eutils/ebot/ebot.cgi

Language	Train	Dev
EN/ES	2.35M	22,670
EN/PT	7.17M	24,206

Table 3: Final corpora size for each language pair

4.2 NMT System

As for the NMT system, we employed the OpenNMT-py toolkit (Klein et al., 2017) to train three MT systems, one for (Spanish,Portuguese)→English, another one for (English,Spanish)→Portuguese and a third one for (English,Portuguese)→Spanish. Tokenization was performed using the SentecePiece[5] unsupervised tokenizer with a vocabulary size of 32,000. The tokenization was done for each MT system (e.g. concatenated English, Spanish and Portuguese to generate one of the models).

The parameters of our network are as follows. Encoder and Decoder: Transformer; Word vector size: 1024; Layers for encoder and decoder: 6; Attention heads: 16; RNN size: 1024; Hidden transformer feed-forward: 4096; Batch size: 4096.

To train our system, we used the an IBM cluster with 2 Power-9 CPUs and with four NVIDIA Tesla V100 GPUs. The models with the best perplexity value were chosen as final models. During translation, OOV words were replace by their original word in the source language, all other OpenNMT-py options for translation were kept as default.

5 Results

We now detail the results achieved by our Transformer systems on the official test data used in the shared task. Table 4 shows the BLEU scores (Papineni et al., 2002) for our systems and for the submissions made by other teams. For the ES/EN language pair, we figured in 5 out of 11, while for EN/ES in 4 out of 8.

However, one should also take in account the confidence interval of the average of the results. By performing a t-test on the ES/EN results, we found out that the mean of the BLEU scores is 0.4366 (p-value < 0.01 with confidence interval (95%) between 0.4145 and 0.4857. This means that only the submissions from UCAM can be said to be better than the average. Similarly, the

[5]https://github.com/google/
sentencepiece

team from UHH-DS is has statistically lower performance than the average. Meanwhile, all other teams, including ours, are statistically tied around the mean, meaning that there is no sufficient information to difference the performance from one system to another.

Similarly, for the EN/ES language pair, we performed the same statistical test and achieved p-value < 0.01. The reported mean is 0.4675, with confidence interval (95%) between 0.4489 and 0.4861. Thus, Only submissions 2 and 3 from UCAM can be said to be better than average, while the submission from MT-UOC-UPF performed worse than the average. All other teams, including ours, are statistically tied around the mean, without evidence that there is any significant difference among the systems.

Unfortunately, no other team participated on the PT/EN and EN/PT language pairs.

6 Conclusions

We presented the BSC machine translation system for the biomedical translation shared task in WMT19. For our submission, we trained three Transformers NMT systems with multilingual implementation for the English/Spanish and English/Portuguese language pairs.

For model building, we included several corpora from biomedical and health domain, and from out-of-domain data that we considered to have similar textual structure, such as JRC-Acquis and books. Prior training, we also pre-processed our corpora to ensure, or at least minimize the risk, of including Medline data in our training set, which could produce biased models, since the evaluation was carried out on texts extracted from Medline.

Regarding future work, we are planning on optimizing our systems by studying the use of synthetic data from back-translation of monolingual to increase NMT performance (Sennrich et al., 2016) by providing additional training data.

Acknowledgements

This work was supported by the Encargo de Gestion SEAD-BSC of the Spanish National Plan for the Advancement of Language technologies, the ICTUSnet INTERREG Sudoe programme, the European Union Horizon2020 eTransafe (grant agreemed 777365) project, and the Amazon AWS Cloud Credits for Research.

Teams	Runs	ES/EN	EN/ES	PT/EN	EN/PT
BSC	1	0.4356	0.4701	0.3990	0.4811
MT-UOC-UPF	1	0.4159	0.4219	-	-
Talp_upc	1	0.4509	0.4568	-	-
Talp_upc	2	0.4355	0.4609	-	-
Talp_upc	3	0.4270	0.4683	-	-
UCAM	1	0.4770	0.4834	-	-
UCAM	2	**0.4833**	0.4891	-	-
UCAM	3	0.4811	**0.4896**	-	-
UHH-DS	1	0.3969	-	-	-
UHH-DS	2	0.3999	-	-	-
UHH-DS	3	0.3997	-	-	-

Table 4: Official BLEU scores for the English/Spanish and English/Portuguese language pairs in both translation directions for the well aligned sentences of the test set. Bold numbers indicate the best result for each direction.

References

Marta R Costa-Jussà, Cristina España-Bonet, Pranava Madhyastha, Carlos Escolano, and José AR Fonollosa. 2016. The talp–upc spanish–english wmt biomedical task: Bilingual embeddings and char-based neural language model rescoring in a phrase-based system. In *Proceedings of the First Conference on Machine Translation: Volume 2, Shared Task Papers*, volume 2, pages 463–468.

Julia Ive, Aurélien Max, and François Yvon. 2016. Limsi's contribution to the wmt'16 biomedical translation task. In *First Conference on Machine Translation*, volume 2, pages 469–476.

G. Klein, Y. Kim, Y. Deng, J. Senellart, and A. M. Rush. 2017. OpenNMT: Open-Source Toolkit for Neural Machine Translation. *ArXiv e-prints*.

Mariana Neves, Antonio Jimeno Yepes, Aurélie Névéol, Cristian Grozea, Amy Siu, Madeleine Kittner, and Karin Verspoor. 2018. Findings of the wmt 2018 biomedical translation shared task: Evaluation on medline test sets. In *Proceedings of the Third Conference on Machine Translation, Volume 2: Shared Task Papers*, pages 328–343, Belgium, Brussels. Association for Computational Linguistics.

Kishore Papineni, Salim Roukos, Todd Ward, and Wei-Jing Zhu. 2002. Bleu: a method for automatic evaluation of machine translation. In *Proceedings of the 40th annual meeting on association for computational linguistics*, pages 311–318. Association for Computational Linguistics.

Rico Sennrich, Barry Haddow, and Alexandra Birch. 2016. Improving neural machine translation models with monolingual data. In *Proceedings of the 54th Annual Meeting of the Association for Computational Linguistics (Volume 1: Long Papers)*, volume 1, pages 86–96.

Felipe Soares and Karin Becker. 2018. Ufrgs participation on the wmt biomedical translation shared task. In *Proceedings of the Third Conference on Machine Translation, Volume 2: Shared Task Papers*, pages 673–677, Belgium, Brussels. Association for Computational Linguistics.

Felipe Soares, Viviane Moreira, and Karin Becker. 2018a. A Large Parallel Corpus of Full-Text Scientific Articles. In *Proceedings of the Eleventh International Conference on Language Resources and Evaluation (LREC 2018)*, Miyazaki, Japan. European Language Resources Association (ELRA).

Felipe Soares, Gabrielli Yamashita, and Michel Anzanello. 2018b. A parallel corpus of theses and dissertations abstracts. In *The 13th International Conference on the Computational Processing of Portuguese (PROPOR 2018)*, Canela, Brazil. Springer International Publishing.

Jörg Tiedemann. 2012. Parallel data, tools and interfaces in opus. In *Proceedings of the Eight International Conference on Language Resources and Evaluation (LREC'12)*, Istanbul, Turkey. European Language Resources Association (ELRA).

Brian Tubay and Marta R. Costa-jussÃ. 2018. Neural machine translation with the transformer and multi-source romance languages for the biomedical wmt 2018 task. In *Proceedings of the Third Conference on Machine Translation, Volume 2: Shared Task Papers*, pages 678–681, Belgium, Brussels. Association for Computational Linguistics.

Olatz Perez-de Viñaspre and Gorka Labaka. 2016. Ixa biomedical translation system at wmt16 biomedical translation task. In *Proceedings of the First Conference on Machine Translation*, pages 477–482, Berlin, Germany. Association for Computational Linguistics.

The MLLP-UPV Spanish-Portuguese and Portuguese-Spanish Machine Translation Systems for WMT19 Similar Language Translation Task

Pau Baquero-Arnal, Javier Iranzo-Sánchez, Jorge Civera, Alfons Juan

Machine Learning and Language Processing (MLLP) research group
Valencian Research Institute for Artificial Intelligence (VRAIN)
Universitat Politècnica de València
Camí de Vera s/n, 46022, València, Spain
`{pabaar,jairsan,jcivera,ajuan}@vrain.upv.es`

Abstract

This paper describes the participation of the MLLP research group of the Universitat Politècnica de València in the WMT 2019 Similar Language Translation Shared Task. We have submitted systems for the Portuguese $\leftrightarrow$ Spanish language pair, in both directions. They are based on the Transformer architecture as well as on a novel architecture called 2D alternating RNN. Both systems have been domain adapted through fine-tuning that has been shown to be very effective.

1 Introduction

In this paper we describe the supervised Statistical Machine Translation (MT) systems developed by the MLLP research group of the Universitat Politècnica de València for the Related Languages Translation Shared Task of the *ACL 2019 Fourth Conference on Machine Translation* (WMT19). For this task, we participated in both directions of the Portuguese $\leftrightarrow$ Spanish language pair using Neural Machine Translation (NMT) models. This paper introduces a novel approach to translation modeling that is currently being developed. We report results for this approach and compare them with models based on the well-performing Transformer (Vaswani et al., 2017) NMT architecture. A domain adapted version of this latter system achieves the best results out of all submitted systems on both directions of the shared task.

The paper is organized as follows. Section 2 describes the architecture and settings of the novel 2D RNN model. Section 3 describes our baseline systems and the results obtained. Section 4 reports the results obtained by means of the fine-tuning technique. Section 5 reports comparative results with respect to the systems submitted by the other competition participants. Section 6 outlines our conclusions for this shared task.

2 2D Alternating RNN

In this section, we will describe the general architecture of the 2D alternating RNN model. The 2D alternating RNN is a novel translation architecture in development by the MLLP group. This architecture approaches the machine translation problem with a two-dimensional view, much in the same manner as Kalchbrenner et al. (2015); Bahar et al. (2018) and Elbayad et al. (2018). This view is based on the premise that translation is fundamentally a two-dimensional problem, where each word of the target sentence can be explained in some way by all the words in the source sentence. Two-dimensional translation models define the distribution $p(e_i | f_0^J, e_0^{i-1})$ by jointly encoding the source sentence (f_0^J) and the target history (e_0^{i-1}), whereas the usual translation models encode them separately, in separate components usually called "encoder" and "decoder".

The proposed architecture is depicted in Figure 1. It defines a two-dimensional translation model by leveraging already known recurrent cells, such as LSTMs or GRU, without any further modification.

As many other translation models, we have a context vector which is projected to vocabulary size and a softmax (σ) is applied to obtain the probability distribution of the next word at timestep i:

$$p(e_i = x | f_0^J, e_0^{i-1}) = \sigma(W c_i)_x \qquad (1)$$

To explain how this context vector is drawn from a two-dimensional processing style, we need to define a grid with two dimensions: one for the source, and one for the target. From this point, we will define a layer-like structure called block, where each block of the model has such a grid as the input, and another one as the output.

Proceedings of the Fourth Conference on Machine Translation (WMT), Volume 3: Shared Task Papers (Day 2) pages 179–184
Florence, Italy, August 1-2, 2019. ©2019 Association for Computational Linguistics

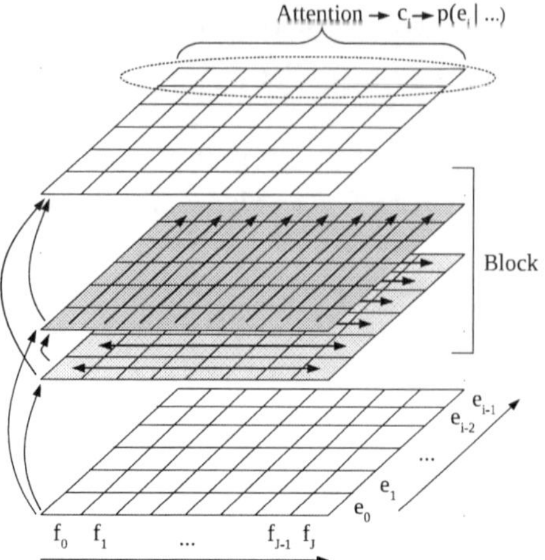

Figure 1: The 2D alternating RNN architecture. White grids on the top and bottom represent the input/output of a block. Arrows in grey grids represent the RNNs, while the arrows on the left depict how the layers are interconnected. Arrows on the bottom and bottom right indicate the source and target dimensions.

The first grid that serves as input to this two-dimensional architecture has each cell s_{ij}^0 containing the concatenation of the source embedding in position j and the target embedding in position $i - 1$:

$$s_{ij}^0 = \begin{bmatrix} f_j \\ e_{i-1} \end{bmatrix} \qquad (2)$$

Each block of the model has two recurrent cells: one along the source dimension and another one along the target dimension. They process each row or column independently of one another. The horizontal cell is bidirectional and receives the grid s^l as its input:

$$h_{ij}^l = \begin{bmatrix} \mathrm{RNN}_{h1}(h_{i,j-1}^l, s_{ij}^{l-1}) \\ \mathrm{RNN}_{h2}(h_{i,j+1}^l, s_{ij}^{l-1}) \end{bmatrix} \qquad (3)$$

The vertical cell receives the concatenation of h^l and s^l:

$$k_{ij}^l = \mathrm{RNN}_k(k_{i-1,j}^l, [s_{ij}^{l-1}; h_{ij}^l]) \qquad (4)$$

The output of the block is the concatenation of the output of both cells:

$$s_{ij}^l = \begin{bmatrix} h_{ij}^l \\ k_{ij}^l \end{bmatrix} \qquad (5)$$

From the output of the last block, s^L, we generate a context vector as follows:

$$c_i = \mathrm{Attention}([s_{i0}^L, \ldots, s_{iJ}^L]) \qquad (6)$$

The Attention function extracts a single vector from a set of vectors leveraging an attention mechanism. That is, it scores the vectors according to a learned linear scoring function, which is followed by a softmax to extract scores; and with those scores it performs a weighted sum to obtain a context vector.

3 Baseline systems

This section describes training corpora as well as the baseline model architectures and configurations adopted to train our NMT systems. As said in Section 1, two different model architectures were trained: the Transformer architecture (Vaswani et al., 2017) and our proposed 2D alternating RNN architecture. BLEU (Papineni et al., 2002) scores were computed with the `multi-bleu` utility from Moses (Koehn et al., 2007).

3.1 Corpus description and data preparation

The training data is made up of the JCR, Europarl, news-commentary and wikititles corpora. Table 1 shows the number of sentences, number of words and vocabulary size of each corpus. The provided development data was split equally in two disjoint sets, and one was used as development set and the other as test set.

Corpus	Sent.(K)	Words(M)		Vocab.(K)	
		Es	Pt	Es	Pt
JCR	1650	42	40	264	264
Europarl	1812	53	52	177	156
news	48	1	1	49	47
wikititles	621	1	1	292	295
dev	1.5	0	0	6	6
test	1.5	0	0	6	6
Total	4131	98	96	623	604

Table 1: Statistics of the data sets used to train the Spanish ↔ Portuguese MT systems.

The data was processed using the standard Moses pipeline (Koehn et al., 2007), specifically, punctuation normalization, tokenization and truecasing. Then, we applied 32K BPE (Sennrich et al., 2016b) operations, learned jointly over the source and target languages. We included in the

180

vocabulary only those tokens occurring at least 10 times in the training data.

3.2 Transformer baseline models

For the Transformer (Vaswani et al., 2017) models, we used the "Base" configuration (512 model size, 2048 feed-forward size), trained on one GPU. The batch size was 4000 tokens, and we carried out gradient accumulation by temporarily storing gradients and updating the weights every 4 batches. This setup allowed us to train models using an effective batch size of 16000 tokens. We used dropout (Srivastava et al., 2014) with 0.1 probability of dropping, and label smoothing (Szegedy et al., 2016) where we distribute 0.1 of the probability among the target vocabulary. We stored a checkpoint every 10000 updates, and for inference we used the average of the last 8 checkpoints.

We used the Adam optimizer (Kingma and Ba, 2015) with $\beta_1 = 0.9$, $\beta_2 = 0.98$. The learning rate was updated following an inverse square-root schedule, with an initial learning rate of $5 \cdot 10^{-4}$ and 4000 warm-up updates.

The models were built using the fairseq toolkit (Ott et al., 2019).

3.3 2D alternating RNN baseline model

For the 2D alternating RNN models, we used GRU as the recurrent cell, 256 for the embedding size and 128 as the number of units of each layer of the block. The model consisted of a single block. The batch size was 20 sentences, with a maximum length of 75 subword units.

We used the Adam optimizer with $\beta_1 = 0.9$, $\beta_2 = 0.98$. The learning rate was initialized at 10^{-3} and kept constant, but halved after 3 checkpoints without improving the development perplexity. A checkpoint was saved every 5000 updates. The model was built using our own toolkit. Due to time constraints, the 2D alternating model was only trained for the Portuguese → Spanish direction.

3.4 Results

Table 2 shows the evaluation results for the Portuguese→Spanish systems, and Table 3 shows the evaluation results for our Spanish→Portuguese Transformer system. For the Portuguese → Spanish direction, the Transformer model obtains 57.4 BLEU in the test set, and 51.9 in the hidden test set of the competition.

System	BLEU	
	test	test-hidden
Transformer	57.4	51.9
2D altern. RNN	55.1	49.7

Table 2: Baseline BLEU scores on the Portuguese → Spanish task.

System	BLEU	
	test	test-hidden
Transformer	51.2	45.5

Table 3: Baseline BLEU scores on the Spanish → Portuguese task.

The 2D alternating model achieves 55.1 and 49.7 BLEU, respectively. These results show how, even though it is in early stages of development, the 2D alternating RNN model is able to obtain competitive results for this task that are not very far from those obtained by the state-of-the-art Transformer architectures. It is worth noting that this has been achieved with a model that has significantly fewer parameters (14.9M) than its Transformer counterpart (60.2M).

4 Fine-tuning

NMT models perform best when trained with data from the domain of the test data. However, most available parallel corpora belong to institutional documents or internet-crawled content domains, so it is common to find situations where there is a domain mismatch between train and test data. In such cases, small amounts of in-domain data can be used to improve system performance by carrying out an additional training step, often referred to as the fine-tuning step, using the in-domain data after the main training finishes. This technique has been used to adapt models trained with general domain corpora to specific domains with only small amounts of in-domain data (Luong and Manning, 2015; Sennrich et al., 2016a).

In order to empirically test if this is one of such cases, we have trained two language models, one using only the presumably out-of-domain data (the train corpora from Table 1), and one using only the in-domain development data. The models were 4-gram language models trained using the SRI Language Modelling Toolkit (Stolcke et al., 2011). We then computed the perplexity of the test set using these two language models. The model that was trained with the out-of-domain data obtains a per-

System	BLEU	
	test	test-hidden
Transformer	57.4	51.9
+ fine-tuned	72.4	66.6
2D altern. RNN	55.1	49.7
+ fine-tuned	64.0	-

Table 4: Comparative BLEU scores of the Transformer and 2D alternating RNN models on the Portuguese → Spanish task.

System	BLEU	
	test	test-hidden
Transformer	51.3	45.5
+ fine-tuned	70.7	64.7

Table 5: Comparative BLEU scores of the Transformer model on the Spanish → Portuguese task.

plexity of 298.0, whereas the model that used the in-domain data obtains a perplexity of 81.9. This result shows that there is in a fact a domain mismatch between the train and test data, which supports the idea of carrying out fine-tuning.

We applied this to both translation directions, using the first part of the development data as in-domain training data, and the second part as a new dev set. One checkpoint was stored after every fine-tuning epoch, and we monitored model performance on the new dev set in order to stop fine-tuning once the BLEU results started decreasing. For the Transformer models, we used the same learning rate as when training stopped, while for the 2D alternating models we used 10^{-3}.

Tables 4 and 5 compare the BLEU scores achieved by the fine-tuned systems with that of the baseline non fine-tuned ones on the Portuguese→Spanish and Spanish→Portuguese tasks, respectively.

Table 4 shows that for this particular task, fine-tuning is a key step for achieving very substantial performance gains: in the Portuguese→Spanish task, we obtained a 15.0 BLEU improvement in the test set and a 14.7 BLEU improvement in the hidden test set for the Transformer model. The 2D alternating RNN obtained a 8.9 BLEU improvement thanks to fine-tuning. This also applies to the Spanish→Portuguese task, shown in Table 5: we obtained a 19.4 BLEU improvement in the test set, and a 19.2 BLEU improvement in the hidden test set after applying fine-tuning.

In order to understand the impact and behaviour

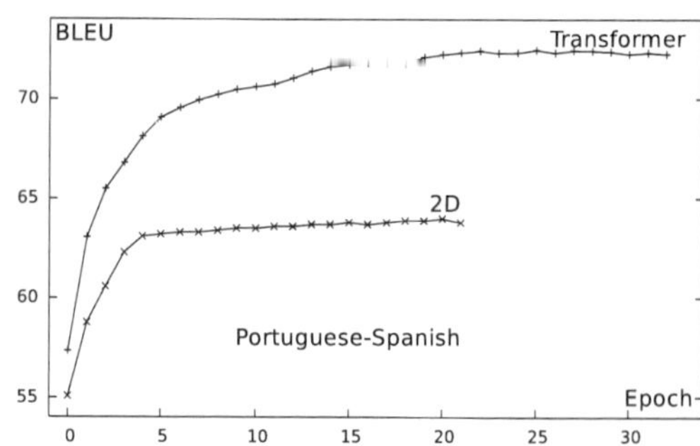

Figure 2: BLEU scores as a function of the number of fine-tuning epochs on the Transformer and 2D alternating RNN models for the Portuguese→Spanish task.

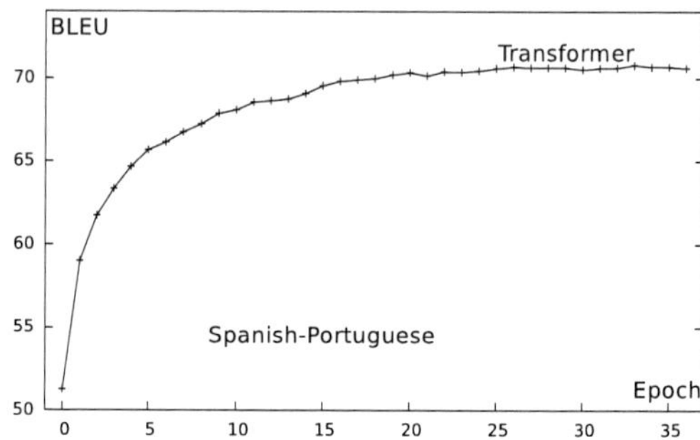

Figure 3: BLEU scores as a function of the number of fine-tuning epochs on the Transformer model for the Spanish→Portuguese task.

of the fine-tuning process, we have analyzed the model's performance as a function of the number of fine-tuning epochs. Figure 2 shows the impact of the fine-tuning step for the Transformer and 2D alternating RNN models on the Portuguese → Spanish task, while Figure 3 shows the results of the fine-tuning step applied to the Transformer model on the Spanish → Portuguese task. In both language pairs, the first epochs are the most beneficial for system performance, and additional fine-tuning epochs bring diminishing returns until the BLEU curve flattens.

5 Comparative results

We now move on to the results for the primary submissions of all participants in the Shared Task. We chose to send our fine-tuned Transfomer systems as primary submissions to both tasks after reviewing the results on the provided test set (Section 4). The submission was made with the checkpoint that achieved the best performance on the fine-tuning dev data. Table 6 shows the results

Team	BLEU	TER
MLLP	**66.6**	**19.7**
NICT	59.9	25.3
U. Helsinki	58.4	25.3
Kyoto U.	56.9	26.9
BSC	54.8	29.8
UBC-NLP	52.3	32.9

Table 6: Primary submission results of the Portuguese → Spanish shared task in the hidden test set.

Team	BLEU	TER
MLLP	**64.7**	**20.8**
UPC-TALP	62.1	23.0
NICT	53.3	29.1
U. Helsinki	52.0	29.4
UBC-NLP	46.1	36.0
BSC	44.0	37.5

Table 7: Primary submission results of the Spanish → Portuguese shared task in the hidden test set.

of the Portuguese→Spanish task, while Table 7 shows the results of the Spanish→Portuguese task; both in BLEU and TER (Snover et al., 2006).

In both tasks, our system outperformed all other participants by a significant margin. In the Portuguese→Spanish task, our submission outperforms the next best system by 6.7 BLEU and 5.6 TER. In a similar manner, our submission to the Spanish → Portuguese task improves the results of the second-best submission by 2.6 BLEU and 2.2 TER points. We attribute our success to the domain adaptation carried out by means of the fine-tuning technique. We have been able to apply this technique by using part of the competition's development data as in-domain training data.

6 Conclusions

We have taken on the similar language task with the same approaches that we found useful for other kinds of translation tasks. NMT models, specifically the Transformer architecture, fare well in this task without making any specific adaptation to the similar-language setting. In fact, we achieved the best results among the participants using a general domain-adaptation approach.

For this particular task, the use of in-domain data to carry out fine-tuning has allowed us to obtain remarkable results that significantly outperform the next best systems in both Portuguese→Spanish and Spanish→Portuguese.

We believe these results are explained by the domain difference between training and test data, and are unrelated to the similarity between Spanish and Portuguese.

We have introduced the 2D alternating RNN model, a novel NMT architecture, that has been tested in the Portuguese→Spanish task. With small embedding and hidden unit sizes and a shallow architecture, we achieved similar performance to the Transformer model, although the difference between them increases after applying fine-tuning.

In terms of future work, we plan to fully develop the 2D alternating RNN model in order to support larger embedding and hidden unit sizes as well as deeper architectures using more regularization. All these improvements should allow us to increase the already good results achieved by this model.

Acknowledgments

The research leading to these results has received funding from the European Union's Horizon 2020 research and innovation programme under grant agreement no. 761758 (X5gon); the Government of Spain's research project Multisub, ref. RTI2018-094879-B-I00 (MCIU/AEI/FEDER, EU) and the Generalitat Valenciana's predoctoral research scholarship ACIF/2017/055.

References

Parnia Bahar, Christopher Brix, and Hermann Ney. 2018. Towards two-dimensional sequence to sequence model in neural machine translation. In *Proceedings of the 2018 Conference on Empirical Methods in Natural Language Processing*, pages 3009–3015, Brussels, Belgium. Association for Computational Linguistics.

Maha Elbayad, Laurent Besacier, and Jakob Verbeek. 2018. Pervasive attention: 2D convolutional neural networks for sequence-to-sequence prediction. In *Proceedings of the 22nd Conference on Computational Natural Language Learning*, pages 97–107, Brussels, Belgium. Association for Computational Linguistics.

Nal Kalchbrenner, Ivo Danihelka, and Alex Graves. 2015. Grid long short-term memory. *arXiv preprint*.

Diederik P. Kingma and Jimmy Ba. 2015. Adam: A Method for Stochastic Optimization. In *Proceedings of the 3rd International Conference for Learning Representations*, San Diego, California, USA.

Philipp Koehn, Hieu Hoang, Alexandra Birch, Chris Callison-Burch, Marcello Federico, Nicola Bertoldi, Brooke Cowan, Wade Shen, Christine Moran, Richard Zens, Chris Dyer, Ondrej Bojar, Alexandra Constantin, and Evan Herbst. 2007. Moses: Open source toolkit for statistical machine translation. In *ACL 2007, Proceedings of the 45th Annual Meeting of the Association for Computational Linguistics, June 23-30, 2007, Prague, Czech Republic.*

Minh-Thang Luong and Christopher D. Manning. 2015. Stanford neural machine translation systems for spoken language domain. In *International Workshop on Spoken Language Translation.*

Myle Ott, Sergey Edunov, Alexei Baevski, Angela Fan, Sam Gross, Nathan Ng, David Grangier, and Michael Auli. 2019. fairseq: A fast, extensible toolkit for sequence modeling. *arXiv preprint arXiv:1904.01038.*

Kishore Papineni, Salim Roukos, Todd Ward, and Wei-Jing Zhu. 2002. Bleu: a method for automatic evaluation of machine translation. In *Proceedings of the 40th Annual Meeting of the Association for Computational Linguistics, July 6-12, 2002, Philadelphia, PA, USA.*, pages 311–318.

Rico Sennrich, Barry Haddow, and Alexandra Birch. 2016a. Improving neural machine translation models with monolingual data. In *Proceedings of the 54th Annual Meeting of the Association for Computational Linguistics, ACL 2016, August 7-12, 2016, Berlin, Germany, Volume 1: Long Papers.*

Rico Sennrich, Barry Haddow, and Alexandra Birch. 2016b. Neural machine translation of rare words with subword units. In *Proceedings of the 54th Annual Meeting of the Association for Computational Linguistics, ACL 2016, August 7-12, 2016, Berlin, Germany, Volume 1: Long Papers.*

Matthew Snover, Bonnie Dorr, Richard Schwartz, Linnea Micciulla, and John Makhoul. 2006. A study of translation edit rate with targeted human annotation. In *Proceedings of association for machine translation in the Americas*, volume 200.

Nitish Srivastava, Geoffrey E. Hinton, Alex Krizhevsky, Ilya Sutskever, and Ruslan Salakhutdinov. 2014. Dropout: a simple way to prevent neural networks from overfitting. *Journal of Machine Learning Research*, 15(1):1929–1958.

Andreas Stolcke, Jing Zheng, Wen Wang, and Victor Abrash. 2011. SRILM at Sixteen: Update and Outlook. In *Proceedings of the 2011 IEEE Workshop on Automatic Speech Recognition and Understanding (ASRU)*, Waikoloa, Hawaii, USA.

Christian Szegedy, Vincent Vanhoucke, Sergey Ioffe, Jonathon Shlens, and Zbigniew Wojna. 2016. Rethinking the inception architecture for computer vision. In *2016 IEEE Conference on Computer Vision and Pattern Recognition, CVPR 2016, Las Vegas, NV, USA, June 27-30, 2016*, pages 2818–2826.

Ashish Vaswani, Noam Shazeer, Niki Parmar, Jakob Uszkoreit, Llion Jones, Aidan N. Gomez, Lukasz Kaiser, and Illia Polosukhin. 2017. Attention is all you need. In *Advances in Neural Information Processing Systems 30: Annual Conference on Neural Information Processing Systems 2017, 4-9 December 2017, Long Beach, CA, USA*, pages 6000–6010.

The TALP-UPC System for the WMT Similar Language Task: Statistical vs Neural Machine Translation

Magdalena Biesialska   **Lluis Guardia**   **Marta R. Costa-jussà**
TALP Research Center, Universitat Politècnica de Catalunya, 08034 Barcelona
`magdalena.biesialska@upc.edu lluis.guardia@alu-etsetb.upc.edu`
`marta.ruiz@upc.edu`

Abstract

Although the problem of similar language translation has been an area of research interest for many years, yet it is still far from being solved. In this paper, we study the performance of two popular approaches: statistical and neural. We conclude that both methods yield similar results; however, the performance varies depending on the language pair. While the statistical approach outperforms the neural one by a difference of 6 BLEU points for the Spanish-Portuguese language pair, the proposed neural model surpasses the statistical one by a difference of 2 BLEU points for Czech-Polish. In the former case, the language similarity (based on perplexity) is much higher than in the latter case. Additionally, we report negative results for the system combination with back-translation.

Our TALP-UPC system submission won 1st place for Czech→Polish and 2nd place for Spanish→Portuguese in the official evaluation of the 1st WMT Similar Language Translation task.

1 Introduction

Much research work has been done on language translation in the past decades. Given recent success of various machine translation (MT) systems, it is not surprising that some could consider similar language translation an already solved task. However, there are still remaining challenges that need to be addressed, such as limited resources or out-of-domain. Apart from these well-known, standard problems, we have discovered other under-researched phenomena within the task of similar language translation. Specifically, there exist languages from the same linguistic family that have a high degree of difference in alphabets, as it is the case for Czech-Polish, which may pose a challenge for MT systems.

Neural MT has achieved the best results in many tasks, outperforming former statistical MT (SMT) methods (Sennrich et al., 2016a). However, there are tasks where previous statistical MT approaches are still competitive, such as unsupervised machine translation (Artetxe et al., 2018; Lample et al., 2018). Motivated by the close proximity between the languages at hand and limited resources, in this article we aimed to determine whether the neural or the statistical approach is a better one to solve the given problem.

We report our results in the 1st Similar Language Translation WMT task (Barrault et al., 2019). In the official evaluation, our Czech→Polish and Spanish→Portuguese translation systems were ranked 1st and 2nd respectively. The main contributions of our work are the neural and statistical MT systems trained for similar languages, as well as the strategies for adding monolingual corpora in neural MT. Additionally, we report negative results on the system combination by using back-translation and Minimum Bayes Risk (Kumar and Byrne, 2004) techniques.

2 Background

In this section, we provide a brief overview of statistical (phrase-based) and neural-based MT approaches as well as strategies for exploiting monolingual data.

2.1 Phrase-based Approach

Phrase-based (PB) statistical MT (Koehn et al., 2003) translates by concatenating at a phrase level the most probable target given the source text. In this context, a phrase is a sequence of words, regardless if it is a phrase or not from the linguistic point of view. Phrases are extracted from word alignments between both languages in a large parallel corpus, based on the probabilistic study, which identifies each phrase with several features,

Proceedings of the Fourth Conference on Machine Translation (WMT), Volume 3: Shared Task Papers (Day 2) pages 185–191
Florence, Italy, August 1-2, 2019. ©2019 Association for Computational Linguistics

such as conditional probabilities. The collection of scored phrases constitutes the translation model.

In addition to this model, there are also other models to help achieve a better translation, such as the reordering model, which helps in a better ordering of the phrases; or the language model, trained from a monolingual corpus in the target language helping to obtain a better fluency in the translation. The weights of each of these models are optimized by tuning over a validation set. Based on these optimized combinations, the decoder uses beam search to find the most probable output given an input. Figure 1 shows a diagram of the phrase-based MT approach.

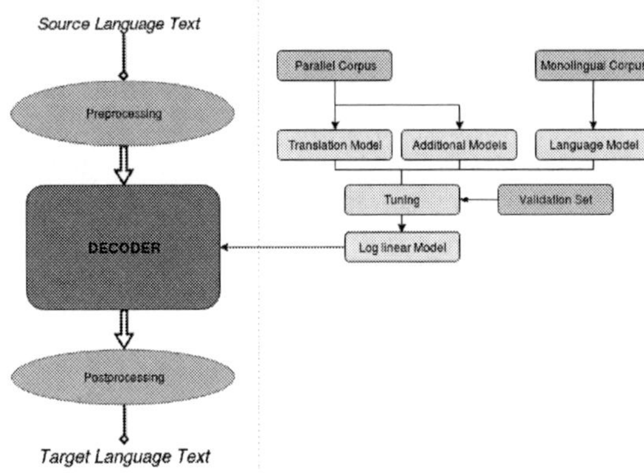

Figure 1: Basic schema of a phrase-based MT system

2.2 Neural Approach

Neural networks (NNs) have been successful in many Natural Language Processing (NLP) tasks in recent years. NMT systems, which use end-to-end NN models to encode a source sequence in one language and decode a target sequence in the second language, early on demonstrated performance on a par with or even outperformed traditional phrase-based SMT systems (Kalchbrenner and Blunsom, 2013; Cho et al., 2014; Sutskever et al., 2014; Bahdanau et al., 2015; Sennrich et al., 2016a; Zhou et al., 2016; Wu et al., 2016).

Previous state-of-the-art NMT models used predominantly bi-directional recurrent neural networks (RNN) equipped with Long-Short Term Memory (LSTM; Hochreiter and Schmidhuber 1997) units or Gated Recurrent Units (GRU; Cho et al. 2014) both in the encoder and the decoder combined with the attention mechanism (Bahdanau et al., 2015; Luong et al., 2015). There were also approaches, although less common, to leverage convolutional neural networks (CNN) for

sequence modeling (Kalchbrenner et al., 2016; Gehring et al., 2017).

In this work, we focus on the most current state-of-the-art NMT architecture, the Transformer (Vaswani et al., 2017), which shows significant performance improvements over traditional sequence-to-sequence models. Interestingly, while the Transformer employs many concepts that were used earlier in encoder-decoder RNN and CNN based models, such as: residual connections (He et al., 2016b), position embeddings (Gehring et al., 2017), attention; the Transformer architecture relies solely on the self-attention mechanism without resorting to either recurrence or convolution.

The variant of the self-attention mechanism implemented by the Transformer, multi-head attention, allows to model dependencies between all tokens in a sequence irrespective of their actual position. More specifically, the representation of a given word is produced by means of computing a weighted average of attention scores of all words in a sentence.

Adding Monolingual Data Although our proposed statistical MT model incorporates monolingual corpora, the supervised neural MT approach is not capable to make use of such data. However, recent studies have reported notable improvements in the translation quality when monolingual corpora were added to the training corpora, either through back-translation (Sennrich et al., 2016b) or copied corpus (Currey et al., 2017). Encouraged by those results and given the similarity of languages at hand, we propose to exploit monolingual data by leveraging back-translation as well as by simply copying target-side monolingual corpus and use it together with the original parallel data.

3 System Combination with Back-translation

In this paper, we propose to combine the results of both phrase-based and NMT systems at the sentence level. However, differently from the previous work of Marie and Fujita (2018), we aimed for a conceptually simple combination strategy.

In principle, for every sentence generated by the two alternative systems we used the BLEU score (Papineni et al., 2002) to select a sentence with the highest translation quality. Each of the translations was back-translated (i.e. translated from the target language to the source language). Instead of using only one system to perform back-translation, we used both PB and neural MT systems and weighted them equally. See Figure 2 for a graphical representation of this strategy.

This approach was motivated by the recent success of different uses of back-translation in neural MT studies (Sennrich et al., 2016b; Lample et al., 2018). The final test set was composed of sentences produced by the system that obtained the highest score based on the quality of the combined back-translation.

4   Experimental Framework

In this section we describe the data sets, data preprocessing as well as training and evaluation details for the PB and neural MT systems and the system combination.

4.1   Data and Preprocessing

Both submitted systems are constrained, hence they don't use any additional parallel or monolingual corpora except for the datasets provided by the organizers. For both Czech-Polish and Spanish-Portuguese, we used all available parallel training data, which in the case of Czech-Polish consisted of about 2.2 million sentences and about 4.5 million sentences in the case of Spanish-Portuguese. Also, we used all the target-side monolingual data, which was 1.2 million sentences for Polish and 10.9 million sentences for Portuguese.

Preprocessing   Our NMT model was trained on a combination of the original Czech-Polish parallel corpus together with pseudo-parallel corpus obtained from translating Polish monolingual data to Czech with Moses. Additionally, the development corpus was split into two sets: first containing 2k sentences and second containing 1k sentences, where the former was added to the training data and the latter was used for validation purposes.

Our Phrase-Based model was trained on a combination of the original Spanish-Portuguese parallel corpus together with 2k sentences from the dev corpus. Specifically, the development corpus was split into two sets: first containing 2k sentences and second containing 1k sentences, where the former was added to the training data and the latter was used for validation purposes.

Then we followed the standard preprocessing scheme, where training, dev and test data are nor-malized, tokenized and truecased using *Moses*[1] scripts. Additionally, training data was also cleaned with `clean-corpus-n.perl` script from *Moses*. Finally, to allow open-vocabulary, we learned and applied byte-pair encoding (BPE)[2] for the concatenation of the source and target languages with 16k operations. The postprocessing was done in reverse order and included detruecasing and detokenization.

4.2   Parameter Details

Phrase-based   For the Phrase-based systems we used Moses (Koehn et al., 2007), which is a statistical machine translation system. In order to build our model, we used generally the default parameters which include: grow-diagonal-final-and word alignment, lexical msd-bidirectional-fe reordering model trained, lexical weights, binarized and compacted phrase table with 4 score components and 4 threads used for conversion, 5-gram, binarized, loading-on-demand language model with Kneser-Ney smoothing and trie data structure without pruning; and MERT (Minimum Error Rate Training) optimisation with 100 n-best list generated and 16 threads.

Neural-based   Our neural network model is based on the Transformer architecture (as described in section 2.2) implemented by Facebook in the *fairseq* toolkit[3]. The following hyperparameter configuration was used: 6 attention layers in the encoder and the decoder, with 4 attention heads per layer, embedding dimension of 512, maximum number of tokens per batch set to 4000, Adam optimizer with $\beta_1 = 0.90$, $\beta_2 = 0.98$, varied learning rate with the inverse square root of the step number (warmup steps equal 4000), dropout regularization and label smoothing set to 0.1, weight decay and gradient clipping threshold set to 0.

System Combination   The key parameter in the system combination with back-translation, explained in section 3, is the score. Hence, we used the BLEU score (Papineni et al., 2002) at the sentence level, implemented as *sentence-bleu* in *Moses*. Furthermore, we assigned equal weights to both phrase and neural-based translations and back-translations.

---

[1] https://github.com/moses-smt/mosesdecoder
[2] https://github.com/rsennrich/subword-nmt
[3] https://github.com/pytorch/fairseq

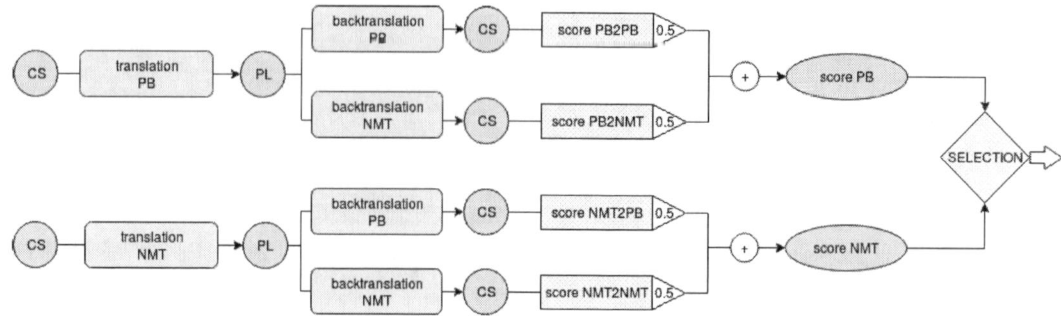

Figure 2: Scheme of the system combination approach

As contrastive approaches for system combination, we used two additional strategies: Minimum Bayes Risk (Kumar and Byrne, 2004) and the length ratio. In the former case, we used the implementation available in *Moses*. In the latter approach, the ratio was computed as the number of words in the translation divided by the number of words in the source input. Sentence translations that gave a length ratio closer to 1 were selected. In the case of ties, we kept the sentence from the system that scored the best according to Table 3.

5 Results

The results provided in Table 1 show BLEU scores for the direct phrase-based and neural-based MT systems. Also, we report on experiments with incorporating monolingual data in two ways: either using a monolingual corpus both on the source and target sides (*monolingual*) or using the back-translation system to produce a translation of a monolingual corpus (*pseudo corpus*). Interestingly, we observe that the *monolingual* approach harms the performance of the system even in the case of similar languages. With regard to the Spanish-Portuguese language pair, due to the large size of the monolingual corpora as well as the time constraint, we were unable to finish training of our NMT model with the pseudo corpus.

Table 1: Phrase-based (PB) and Neural-based (NMT) results.

	CS-PL	ES-PT
PB	9.87	64.96
NMT	11.69	58.40
NMT + monolingual	10.91	52.37
NMT + pseudo corpus	12.76	–

As presented in Table 3, our proposed system combinations, employing either MBR or the back-translation approach, did not achieve any signif-

Table 2: Back-translation system results.

1st system	2nd system	**PL-CS**	**PT-ES**
PB	PB	44.34	84.62
	NMT	24.51	66.15
NMT	PB	32.47	63.37
	NMT	27.31	60.01

Table 3: System Combination results.

	CS-PL	**ES-PT**
MBR	12.75	62.17
Back-translation	10.71	64.97

icant improvements. The MBR strategy was applied to all systems from Table 1, which means that for the Czech-Polish pair we used 4 systems and for Spanish-Portuguese we used 3 systems. Back-translation results were evaluated with respect to the systems in Table 2 and the system combination with back-translation was created using the best two systems from Table 1.

In order to analyze the reason behind the weak performance of the system combination with back-translation, we evaluated the correlation between the quality of each translated sentence (generated using PB and NMT systems) and the quality of back-translations (both for PB and NMT systems) on the validation set. For any combination, Czech-Polish or Spanish-Portuguese, correlation varies between 0.2 and 0.4, which explains the poor performance of back-translation as a quality estimation metric.

6 Discussion

Although Czech and Polish belong to the same family of languages (Slavic) and share the same subgroup (Western Slavic), the BLEU score obtained by our winning system is relatively low comparing to other pairs of similar languages (e.g. Spanish and Portuguese). It may seem surprising considering some common characteristics shared by both languages, such as 7 noun cases, 2 number cases, 3 noun gender cases as well as 3 tenses among others.

Low performance on this task could be explained by the language distance. Considering the metric proposed by Gamallo et al. (2017), which is based on perplexity as a distance measure between languages, the distance between Czech and Polish is 27 while for Spanish-Portuguese is 7. The very same metric used to evaluate the distance of Czech and Polish from other Slavic languages (i.e. Slovak and Russian) shows that Polish is the most distant language within this group (see Table 4). In general, distances between Latin languages are smaller than between Slavic ones.

Table 4: Distances between Slavic and Latin languages. Examples across families.

Slavic		Latin		Mix	
pair	dist.	pair	dist.	pair	dist.
CS-PL	27	ES-PT	7	ES-CS	37
CS-SL	8	ES-FR	15	ES-PL	44
CS-RU	21	ES-RO	20	PT-CS	31
PL-SL	24	PT-FR	15	PT-PL	38
PL-RU	34	PT-RO	22		

While Czech and Polish languages are highly inflected, which poses a challenge, we hypothesize that one of the reasons for the low BLEU score lies also in the difference of the alphabets. Even though both alphabets are based on the Latin script, they include letters with diacritics – *ą, ć, ę, ł, ń, ó, ś, ź, ż* in Polish, and *á, č, ď, é, ě, ch, í, ň, ó, ř, š, ť, ú, ů, ý, ž* in Czech. The total number of unique letters in Polish is 32, while in the Czech language there are 42 letters. Moreover, some letters are used only in the case of foreign words, such as *q, x* (in Czech and Polish), *w* (in Czech), and *v* (in Polish).

7 Future Work

In the future we plan to extend our research in the following directions. First, we would like to explore how removing diacritics on the source-side would impact the performance of our system for the Czech-Polish language pair. Furthermore, we would like to study the performance of our system combination while applying various quality estimation approaches. We would be interested in experimenting with the reward score introduced by He et al. (2016a), which is a linear combination of language model score and the reconstruction probability of the back-translated sentence, as well as

with other quality measures implemented in the *OpenKiwi* (Kepler et al., 2019) toolkit[4].

Acknowledgments

The authors want to thank Pablo Gamallo, José Ramom Pichel Campos and Iñaki Alegria for sharing their valuable insights on their language distance studies.

This work is supported in part by the Spanish Ministerio de Economía y Competitividad, the European Regional Development Fund and the Agencia Estatal de Investigación, through the postdoctoral senior grant Ramón y Cajal, the contract TEC2015-69266-P (MINECO/FEDER,EU) and the contract PCIN-2017-079 (AEI/MINECO).

References

Mikel Artetxe, Gorka Labaka, and Eneko Agirre. 2018. Unsupervised statistical machine translation. In *Proceedings of the 2018 Conference on Empirical Methods in Natural Language Processing*, Brussels, Belgium. Association for Computational Linguistics.

Dzmitry Bahdanau, Kyunghyun Cho, and Yoshua Bengio. 2015. Neural machine translation by jointly learning to align and translate. In *3rd International Conference on Learning Representations, ICLR 2015, San Diego, CA, USA, May 7-9, 2015, Conference Track Proceedings*.

Loïc Barrault, Ondřej Bojar, Marta R. Costa-jussà, Christian Federmann, Mark Fishel, Yvette Graham, Barry Haddow, Matthias Huck, Philipp Koehn, Shervin Malmasi, Christof Monz, Mathias Müller, Santanu Pal, Matt Post, and Marcos Zampieri. 2019 Findings of the 2019 conference on machine translation (wmt19). In *Proceedings of the Fourth Conference on Machine Translation, Volume 2: Shared Task Papers*, Florence, Italy. Association for Computational Linguistics.

Kyunghyun Cho, Bart van Merrienboer, Çaglar Gülçehre, Dzmitry Bahdanau, Fethi Bougares, Holger Schwenk, and Yoshua Bengio. 2014. Learning phrase representations using RNN encoder-decoder for statistical machine translation. In *Proceedings of the 2014 Conference on Empirical Methods in Natural Language Processing, EMNLP 2014, October 25-29, 2014, Doha, Qatar*, pages 1724–1734.

Anna Currey, Antonio Valerio Miceli Barone, and Kenneth Heafield. 2017. Copied monolingual data improves low-resource neural machine translation. In *Proceedings of the Second Conference on Machine Translation*, pages 148–156, Copenhagen, Denmark. Association for Computational Linguistics.

---

[4]https://github.com/Unbabel/OpenKiwi

Pablo Gamallo, José Ramom Pichel, and Iñaki Alegria. 2017. From language identification to language distance. *Physica A: Statistical Mechanics and its Applications*, 484:152 – 162.

Jonas Gehring, Michael Auli, David Grangier, Denis Yarats, and Yann N. Dauphin. 2017. Convolutional sequence to sequence learning. In *Proceedings of the 34th International Conference on Machine Learning - Volume 70*, ICML'17, pages 1243–1252.

Di He, Yingce Xia, Tao Qin, Liwei Wang, Nenghai Yu, Tie-Yan Liu, and Wei-Ying Ma. 2016a. Dual learning for machine translation. In *Advances in Neural Information Processing Systems*, pages 820–828.

Kaiming He, Xiangyu Zhang, Shaoqing Ren, and Jian Sun. 2016b. Deep residual learning for image recognition. In *Proceedings of the IEEE conference on computer vision and pattern recognition*, pages 770–778.

Sepp Hochreiter and Jürgen Schmidhuber. 1997. Long short-term memory. *Neural Comput.*, 9(8):1735–1780.

Nal Kalchbrenner and Phil Blunsom. 2013. Recurrent continuous translation models. In *Proceedings of the 2013 Conference on Empirical Methods in Natural Language Processing*, pages 1700–1709. Association for Computational Linguistics.

Nal Kalchbrenner, Lasse Espeholt, Karen Simonyan, Aäron van den Oord, Alex Graves, and Koray Kavukcuoglu. 2016. Neural machine translation in linear time. *CoRR*, abs/1610.10099.

Fábio Kepler, Jonay Trénous, Marcos Treviso, Miguel Vera, and André FT Martins. 2019. Openkiwi: An open source framework for quality estimation. *arXiv preprint arXiv:1902.08646*.

Philipp Koehn, Hieu Hoang, Alexandra Birch, Chris Callison-Burch, Marcello Federico, Nicola Bertoldi, Brooke Cowan, Wade Shen, Christine Moran, Richard Zens, et al. 2007. Moses: Open source toolkit for statistical machine translation. In *Proceedings of the 45th annual meeting of the association for computational linguistics companion volume proceedings of the demo and poster sessions*, pages 177–180.

Philipp Koehn, Franz J. Och, and Daniel Marcu. 2003. Statistical phrase-based translation. In *Proceedings of the 2003 Human Language Technology Conference of the North American Chapter of the Association for Computational Linguistics*, pages 127–133.

Shankar Kumar and William Byrne. 2004. Minimum Bayes-risk decoding for statistical machine translation. In *HLT-NAACL 2004: Main Proceedings*, pages 169–176, Boston, Massachusetts, USA. Association for Computational Linguistics.

Guillaume Lample, Myle Ott, Alexis Conneau, Ludovic Denoyer, and Marc'Aurelio Ranzato. 2018. Phrase-based & neural unsupervised machine translation. In *Proceedings of the 2018 Conference on Empirical Methods in Natural Language Processing*, pages 5039–5049, Brussels, Belgium. Association for Computational Linguistics.

Thang Luong, Hieu Pham, and Christopher D. Manning. 2015. Effective approaches to attention-based neural machine translation. In *Proceedings of the 2015 Conference on Empirical Methods in Natural Language Processing*, pages 1412–1421, Lisbon, Portugal. Association for Computational Linguistics.

Benjamin Marie and Atsushi Fujita. 2018. A smorgasbord of features to combine phrase-based and neural machine translation. In *Proceedings of the 13th Conference of the Association for Machine Translation in the Americas (Volume 1: Research Papers)*, pages 111–124, Boston, MA. Association for Machine Translation in the Americas.

Kishore Papineni, Salim Roukos, Todd Ward, and Wei-Jing Zhu. 2002. Bleu: a method for automatic evaluation of machine translation. In *Proceedings of the 40th annual meeting on association for computational linguistics*, pages 311–318. Association for Computational Linguistics.

Rico Sennrich, Barry Haddow, and Alexandra Birch. 2016a. Edinburgh neural machine translation systems for WMT 16. In *Proceedings of the First Conference on Machine Translation*, pages 371–376, Berlin, Germany. Association for Computational Linguistics.

Rico Sennrich, Barry Haddow, and Alexandra Birch. 2016b. Improving neural machine translation models with monolingual data. In *Proceedings of the 54th Annual Meeting of the Association for Computational Linguistics (Volume 1: Long Papers)*, pages 86–96, Berlin, Germany. Association for Computational Linguistics.

Ilya Sutskever, Oriol Vinyals, and Quoc V Le. 2014. Sequence to sequence learning with neural networks. In Z. Ghahramani, M. Welling, C. Cortes, N. D. Lawrence, and K. Q. Weinberger, editors, *Advances in Neural Information Processing Systems 27*, pages 3104–3112. Curran Associates, Inc.

Ashish Vaswani, Noam Shazeer, Niki Parmar, Jakob Uszkoreit, Llion Jones, Aidan N Gomez, Łukasz Kaiser, and Illia Polosukhin. 2017. Attention is all you need. In *Advances in Neural Information Processing Systems*, pages 5998–6008.

Yonghui Wu, Mike Schuster, Zhifeng Chen, Quoc V. Le, Mohammad Norouzi, Wolfgang Macherey, Maxim Krikun, Yuan Cao, Qin Gao, Klaus Macherey, Jeff Klingner, Apurva Shah, Melvin Johnson, Xiaobing Liu, Lukasz Kaiser, Stephan Gouws, Yoshikiyo Kato, Taku Kudo, Hideto

Kazawa, Keith Stevens, George Kurian, Nishant Patil, Wei Wang, Cliff Young, Jason Smith, Jason Riesa, Alex Rudnick, Oriol Vinyals, Greg Corrado, Macduff Hughes, and Jeffrey Dean. 2016. Google's neural machine translation system: Bridging the gap between human and machine translation. *CoRR*, abs/1609.08144.

Jie Zhou, Ying Cao, Xuguang Wang, Peng Li, and Wei Xu. 2016. Deep recurrent models with fast-forward connections for neural machine translation. *TACL*, 4:371–383.

Machine Translation from an Intercomprehension Perspective

Yu Chen   **Tania Avgustinova**
Department of Language Science and Technology
Saarland University, Saarbrücken, Germany
{yuchen, tania}@coli.uni-sb.de

Abstract

Within the first shared task on machine translation between similar languages, we present our first attempts on Czech to Polish machine translation from an intercomprehension perspective. We propose methods based on the mutual intelligibility of the two languages, taking advantage of their orthographic and phonological similarity, in the hope to improve over our baselines. The translation results are evaluated using BLEU. On this metric, none of our proposals could outperform the baselines on the final test set. The current setups are rather preliminary, and there are several potential improvements we can try in the future.

1 Introduction

A special type of semi-communication can be experienced by speakers of similar languages, where all participant use their own native languages and still successfully understand each other. On the other hand, in countries with more than one official languages, even if these languages are mutually intelligible. While it is a common practice to use English as a pivot language for building machine translation systems for under-resourced language pairs. If English turns out to be typologically quite distant from both the source and the target languages, this circumstance easily results in accumulation of errors. Hence, the interesting research question is how to put the similarity between languages into use for translation purposes in order to alleviate the problem caused by the lack of data or limited bilingual resources.

Slavic languages are well-known for their close relatedness, which may be traced to common ancestral forms both in the oral tradition and in written text communication. Sharing many common features, including an inventory of cognate sound-meaning pairings, they are to various degrees mutually intelligible, being at the same time so differ-

ent that translating between them is never an easy task. For example, all Slavic languages have rich morphology, but inflections systematically differ from one language to another, which makes it impossible to have a uniform solution for translating between them or to a third language.

We chose to work on the language pair Czech-Polish from the West Slavic subgroup. In an intercomprehension scenario, when participants in a multilingual communication speak their native languages, Czechs and Poles are able to understand each other to a considerable extent, mainly due to objectively recognisable and subjectively perceived linguistic similarities. As Czech-English and Polish-English translation pairs are challenging enough, this naturally motivates the search for direct translation solutions instead of a pivot setup.

We first briefly introduce the phenomenon of intercomprehension between Slavic languages and our idea how to take advantage of it for machine translation purposes. The next section spreads out our plans on Czech-Polish translation by exploring the similarities and differences between the two languages. Then, we explain how we organized the experiments that lead to our submissions to the shared task. We conclude with a discussion of the translation results and an outlook.

2 Slavic Intercomprehension

Intercomprehension is a special form of multilingual communication involving receptive skills when reconstructing the meaning in inter-lingual contexts under concrete communicative situation It is common practice for millions of speakers, especially those of related languages. In order to interpret the message encoded in a foreign but related language, they rely on linguistic and non-linguistic elements existing for similar situations

Proceedings of the Fourth Conference on Machine Translation (WMT), Volume 3: Shared Task Papers (Day 2) pages 192–196
Florence, Italy, August 1-2, 2019. ©2019 Association for Computational Linguistics

in their own linguistic repertoire.

Languages from the same family exhibit systematic degrees of mutual intelligibility which may be in many cases asymmetric. Czech and Polish belong to the West Slavic subgroup and related both genetically and typologically. It could be shown, for example, that the Poles understood written Czech better than the Czechs understood written Polish, while the Czechs understood spoken Polish better than the Poles understood spoken Czech (Golubović, 2016). How can this be useful for machine translation? In order to tackle the Czech-to-Polish machine translation problem from an intercomprehension point of view, we currently focus on orthographic and phonological similarities between the two languages that could provide us with relevant correspondences in order to establish inter-lingual transparency and reveal cognate units and structures.

3 Approach

3.1 Orthographic correspondences

Both orthographic systems are based on the Latin alphabet with diacritics, but the diacritical signs in the two languages are rather different. Czech has a larger set of letters with diacritics, while Polish uses digraphs more often. There are two basic diacritical signs in Czech: the acute accent (´) used to mark a long vowel and the háček (ˇ) in the consonants which becomes the acute accent for d' and t'. The diacritics used in the Polish alphabet are the kreska (graphically similar to the acute accent) in the letters ć, ń, ó, ś, ź; the kreska ukośna (stroke) in the letter ł. ; the kropka (overdot) in the letter ż; and the ogonek ("little tail") in the letters ą, ę. The Czech letters á, č, d', é, ě, ch, í, ň, ř, š, t', ú, ů, ý, ž as well as q, v, and x do not exist in Polish, and the Polish letters ą, ć, ę, ł, ń, ś, w, ż and ź are not part of the Czech alphabet.

In a reading intercomprehension scenario, it is natural for people to simply ignore unknown elements around graphemes that they are familiar with. That is, when facing unknown alphabet with "foreign" diacritical signs, the reader is most likely to drop them and treat the respective letters as the corresponding plain Latin ones. Experiments showed that efficiency of intercomprehension is significantly improved if the text is manually transformed to mimic the spelling in the reader's language (Jágrová, 2016). However, such rewriting requires a huge effort from a bilingual linguist and cannot be easily applied to large amount of data. An alternative to the manual rewriting is to utilize the correspondence rules using Minimum Description Length (MDL) principle (Grünwald, 2007). Most of the around 3000 rules generated from a parallel cognate list of around 1000 words are not deterministic. We use only the rules converting Czech letters that do not exist in Polish, as listed in Table 1, to avoid over-transformation.

CZ	PL
Áá	Aa
Čč	Cz cz
Ďď	Dź dź
Ěě	Je je
Éé	Ee
Íí	Ii
Ňň	Nn
Řř	Rz rz
Šš	Sz sz
Ťť	Ćć
Ůů	Óó
Vv	Ww
Xx	Ks ks
Ýý	Yy
Žž	Źź

Table 1: Orthographic correspondence list

3.2 Phoneme correspondences

Czech and Polish are both primarily phonemic with regard to their writing system, which is reflected in the alphabets. That is, graphemes consistently correspond to phonemes of the language, but the relation between spelling and pronunciation is more complex than a one-to-one correspondence. In addition, Polish uses more digraphs, such as ch, cz, dz, dź, dż, rz, and sz. In both languages, some graphemes have been merged due to historical reasons and at the same time some changes in phonology have not been reflected in spelling.

It is well-known, that people often try to pronounce the foreign texts in a way closer to their own language. Moreover, hearing the correct pronunciation sometimes helps them to infer the meaning more easily, in particular, loanwords / internationalisms and the pan-Slavic vocabulary.

To be able to make use of phonological information within a machine translation system, we

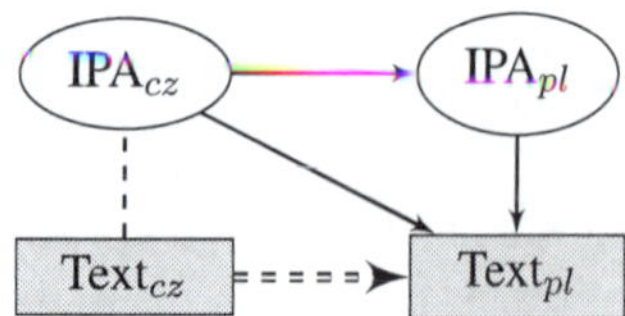

Figure 1: Phoneme-infused translation setup

propose a multi-source multi-target structure as shown in Figure 1, which considers the IPA transcription of the text as a text in a "new" closely related language. More specifically, for the translation from Czech to Polish, the source languages of the multilingual system include ordinary Czech and IPA-transcribed Czech. So, three different translation paths are competing with each other to produce the final translations.

4 Experiments

4.1 Data and baselines

We used the provided parallel corpora Europarl, Wiki Titles, JRC-Acquis and the monolingual corpus News Crawl 2018 for Polish. We extract randomly two disjoint subsets from the development set of the shared task: one with 2000 sentences and another one with 1000 sentences. During the development phase, all systems are optimized for the BLEU score on the first set and the second set is used as a blind test set. The results reported in the next section refer to BLEU scores (Papineni et al., 2002) on the official test set unless specified otherwise.

For the purpose of more thorough comparisons, we build three baseline systems in different paradigms, one phrase based statistical machine translation system (PBSMT) with the Moses toolkit (Koehn et al., 2007) and two neural machine translation (NMT) system with the marian toolkit (Junczys-Dowmunt et al., 2018). All baselines apply the same pre- and post-processing steps. Preprocessing consists of tokenization, truecasing and removing sentences with more than 100 tokens. Postprocessing consists of detruecasing and detokenization. All these steps use scripts included in the Moses toolkit.

The PBSMT baseline uses both the target side of the parallel corpora and the monolingual corpus provided for the language model. 5-gram language models are first built individually from each corpus and then interpolated with KenLM (Heafield et al., 2013) given the development. We

run *fast_align* (Dyer et al., 2013) on the parallel corpora to obtain word alignments in both directions. Then, phrase pairs with less than 6 tokens are extracted to construct a translation model based on the alignments. Weights for the features in the translation model are determined with the Minimal Error Rate Training (MERT) (Och, 2003).

A byte pair encoding (BPE) (Sennrich et al., 2015) is applied to the training data to reduce the vocabulary to 36,000 units for the NMT systems. The first NMT system utilized only the parallel data. It is a single sequence-to-sequence model with single-layer RNNs in both the encoder and the decoder. The embedding size is 512 and the RNN state size is 1024.

The architecture of our second NMT baseline follows the architecture described in (Vaswani et al., 2017). We first train a shallow model from Polish to Czech with only the parallel corpora in order to translate the complete monolingual Polish corpus into Czech for a synthesized parallel corpus, which is concatenated with the original data to produce new training data (Sennrich et al., 2016). We then train four left-to-right (L2R) deep Transformer-based models and four right-to-left (R2L) models. The ensemble decoder combines the four L2R models to generate an n-best list, which is rescored using the R2L models to produce the final translation.

System	BLEU
PBSMT	11.58
Deep RNN	9.56
Transformer-based	
+ Ensemble	
+ Rerenking	13.46

Table 2: Czech-Polish baselines on development test

Table 2 lists the BLEU scores of the baselines. To our surprise, the simple "old-fashioned" PBSMT system surpassed the RNN-based NMT system and was close to the Transformer-based ensemble. In fact, the translations produced by the Transformer-based NMT are not significantly better than those from the PBSMT.

4.2 Translation results

The outcome of various experiments based on the produced baseline systems is presented here by first looking into the PBSMT and then into the

Transformer-based NMT.

Note that we actually made a mistake inserting the source segments into each translation segment for the final submission. Therefore, the results reported here are all produced after the submission by re-evaluating the clean sgm files. All the scores are cased BLEU scores calculated with the nist evaluation script *mteval-v14.perl*.

4.2.1 Modifying PBSMT

Our PBSMT experiments start with applying a joint BPE model to the training sets, both parallel and monolingual, similarly to the approach introduced by (Kunchukuttan and Bhattacharyya, 2016).

Given the lexical similarity between Czech and Polish, a joint BPE model identifies a small cognate vocabulary of subwords from which words in both languages can be composed. This step eventually identifies the orthographic correspondences as described in Section 3.1. BPE operations ex-

Corpus	%
Acquis	119.23
Europarl	118.09
WikiTitles	238.96
News 2018	145.81

Table 3: Sentence expansion due to BPE operatios Sentence length ratio (%)

pand the sentences (ratio shown in Table 3), therefore we increase the order of the language model from 5 to 7 and the maximal phrase length in the translation model from 5 to 6. We also apply character replacements following the list shown in Table 1. Table 4 lists the results of the 3 combina-

	BLEU$_{dev}$	**BLEU**$_{test}$
PBSMT baseline	11.58	9.62
+ BPE	12.21	7.90
+ replacement	11.53	5.31*
+ BPE + replacement	11.89	6.71*

Table 4: Translation results of PBSMT systems
* marks the system trained on partial development set

tions of these two operations. The translation does not seem to benefit from the character replacement. The BPE operation does not improve the system over the test set either, despite that a minor change was recorded on the development test set.

	BLEU$_{dev}$	**BLEU**$_{test}$
Transformer baseline	13.46	11.54
+replacement	13.33	11.25*
Phoneme-based		4.90
+reranking		5.88

Table 5: Translation results of NMT systems
* marks the system trained on partial development set

4.2.2 Modifying NMT

Table 5 shows the results from the second group of experiments. We have applied the same character replacement to our Transformer-based NMT system, but the impact is again minimal.

As for the phoneme-based system, we first convert all the data into IPA transcriptions using the finite state transducer (FST) model from (Deri and Knight, 2016) with the Carmel toolkit (Graehl, 2019) according to the languages. Consequently, we have 4 versions of the same messages: Czech texts, Czech IPA transcriptions, Polish texts and Polish IPA transcriptions. Considering proximity between the texts and the transcriptions, we use two separate BPE's: one for the texts and another one for the transcriptions. To construct the multiway NMT system illustrated in Figure 1, we gather 3 pairs of parallel texts together: (IPA$_{cs}$, Text$_{pl}$), (IPA$_{cs}$, IPA$_{pl}$) and (IPA$_{pl}$, Text$_{pl}$). We add tokens to each source sentences to mark the source and target sentence language (Ha et al., 2016). Then, such a concatenated parallel corpus is used to train a Transformer-based NMT system. The test set is sent through this multiway system to create an n-best list, which is scored with the original Transformer-based baseline.

Due to deadline constraints, we do not have enough time for thorough experiments on this setup. Such a design seems to degrade the system significantly, but it is also clear that such an architecture is producing very different predictions for the translation.

5 Discussions

This contribution describes our submission to the shared task on similar language translation. It is our first attempt to make use of orthographic and phonological correspondences between two closely related languages, Czech and Polish, inspired by their mutual intelligibility.

The current setups are rather preliminary. Currently, none of our methods improves the baselines on the final test set. There are several potential improvements we can try in the future.

A fixed short replacement list we used is just a small portion of the orthographic correspondence rules. We are considering to integrate the orthographic correspondences with a BPE model as our next step.

Regarding the phoneme based system, the next thing to investigate is the choice of grapheme-to-phoneme (g2p) tools. It is not yet clear which g2p tool and which phoneme transcription set suit our purpose the best. Grouping similar phonemes is one of the potential direction to explore.

References

Aliya Deri and Kevin Knight. 2016. Grapheme-to-phoneme models for (almost) any language. In *Proceedings of the 54th Annual Meeting of the Association for Computational Linguistics (Volume 1: Long Papers)*, volume 1, pages 399–408.

Chris Dyer, Victor Chahuneau, and Noah A. Smith. 2013. A simple, fast, and effective reparameterization of IBM model 2. In *Proceedings of the 2013 Conference of the North American Chapter of the Association for Computational Linguistics: Human Language Technologies*, pages 644–648, Atlanta, Georgia. Association for Computational Linguistics.

Jelena Golubović. 2016. *Mutual intelligibility in the Slavic language area*. Ph.D. thesis, University of Groningen.

Jonathan Graehl. 2019. Carmel finite-state toolkit.

Peter D Grünwald. 2007. *The minimum description length principle*. The MIT Press.

Thanh-Le Ha, Jan Niehues, and Alexander H. Waibel. 2016. Toward multilingual neural machine translation with universal encoder and decoder. *CoRR*, abs/1611.04798.

Kenneth Heafield, Ivan Pouzyrevsky, Jonathan H. Clark, and Philipp Koehn. 2013. Scalable modified Kneser-Ney language model estimation. In *Proceedings of the 51st Annual Meeting of the Association for Computational Linguistics*, pages 690–696, Sofia, Bulgaria.

Klára Jágrová. 2016. Adaptation towards a reader's language: The potential for increasing the intelligibility of polish texts for czech readers. In *12th European Conference on Formal Description of Slavic Languages*.

Melvin Johnson, Mike Schuster, Quoc V Le, Maxim Krikun, Yonghui Wu, Zhifeng Chen, Nikhil Thorat, Fernanda Viégas, Martin Wattenberg, Greg Corrado, et al. 2017. Google's multilingual neural machine translation system: Enabling zero-shot translation. *Transactions of the Association for Computational Linguistics*, 5:339–351.

Marcin Junczys-Dowmunt, Roman Grundkiewicz, Tomasz Dwojak, Hieu Hoang, Kenneth Heafield, Tom Neckermann, Frank Seide, Ulrich Germann, Alham Fikri Aji, Nikolay Bogoychev, André F. T. Martins, and Alexandra Birch. 2018. Marian: Fast neural machine translation in C++. In *Proceedings of ACL 2018, System Demonstrations*, pages 116–121, Melbourne, Australia. Association for Computational Linguistics.

Philipp Koehn, Hieu Hoang, Alexandra Birch, Chris Callison-Burch, Marcello Federico, Nicola Bertoldi, Brooke Cowan, Wade Shen, Christine Moran, Richard Zens, Chris Dyer, Ondřej Bojar, Alexandra Constantin, and Evan Herbst. 2007. Moses: Open source toolkit for statistical machine translation. In *Proceedings of the 45th Annual Meeting of the ACL on Interactive Poster and Demonstration Sessions*, ACL '07, pages 177–180, Stroudsburg, PA, USA. Association for Computational Linguistics.

Anoop Kunchukuttan and Pushpak Bhattacharyya. 2016. Learning variable length units for smt between related languages via byte pair encoding. *arXiv preprint arXiv:1610.06510*.

Franz Josef Och. 2003. Minimum error rate training in statistical machine translation. In *Proceedings of the 41st Annual Meeting on Association for Computational Linguistics - Volume 1*, ACL '03, pages 160–167, Stroudsburg, PA, USA. Association for Computational Linguistics.

Kishore Papineni, Salim Roukos, Todd Ward, and Wei-Jing Zhu. 2002. Bleu: a method for automatic evaluation of machine translation. In *Proceedings of 40th Annual Meeting of the Association for Computational Linguistics*, pages 311–318, Philadelphia, Pennsylvania, USA. Association for Computational Linguistics.

Rico Sennrich, Barry Haddow, and Alexandra Birch. 2015. Neural machine translation of rare words with subword units. *CoRR*, abs/1508.07909.

Rico Sennrich, Barry Haddow, and Alexandra Birch. 2016. Improving neural machine translation models with monolingual data. In *Proceedings of the 54th Annual Meeting of the Association for Computational Linguistics (Volume 1: Long Papers)*, pages 86–96, Berlin, Germany. Association for Computational Linguistics.

Ashish Vaswani, Noam Shazeer, Niki Parmar, Jakob Uszkoreit, Llion Jones, Aidan N Gomez, Ł ukasz Kaiser, and Illia Polosukhin. 2017. Attention is all you need. In I. Guyon, U. V. Luxburg, S. Bengio, H. Wallach, R. Fergus, S. Vishwanathan, and R. Garnett, editors, *Advances in Neural Information Processing Systems 30*, pages 5998–6008. Curran Associates, Inc.

Utilizing Monolingual Data in NMT for Similar Languages: Submission to Similar Language Translation Task

Jyotsana Khatri, Pushpak Bhattacharyya
Department of Computer Science and Engineering,
Indian Institute of Technology Bombay
`{jyotsanak,pb}@cse.iitb.ac.in`

Abstract

This paper describes our submission to Shared Task on Similar Language Translation in Fourth Conference on Machine Translation (WMT 2019). We submitted three systems for Hindi $\rightarrow$ Nepali direction in which we have examined the performance of a Recursive Neural Network (RNN) based Neural Machine Translation (NMT) system, a semi-supervised NMT system where monolingual data of both languages is utilized using the architecture by (Artetxe et al., 2017) and a system trained with extra synthetic sentences generated using copy of source and target sentences without using any additional monolingual data.

1 Introduction

In this paper, we present the submission for Similar Language Translation Task in WMT 2019. The task focuses on improving machine translation results for three language pairs Czech-Polish (Slavic languages), Hindi-Nepali (Indo-Aryan languages) and Spanish-Portuguese (Romance languages). The main focus of the task is to utilize monolingual data in addition to parallel data because the provided parallel data is very small in amount. The detail of task is provided in (Barrault et al., 2019). We participated for Hindi-Nepali language pair and submitted three systems based on NMT for Hindi $\rightarrow$ Nepali direction. We have utilized monolingual data of both languages and also trained an NMT system with copy data from both sides with no additional monolingual data.

The rest of the paper is organized as follows: We start with introduction to NMT, followed by a list of some of the existing methods for how to utilize monolingual data in NMT. A brief introduction to unsupervised and semi-supervised NMT is provided. We also describe in brief about two existing popular methods of training cross-lingual word embeddings in an unsupervised way. In Section 4.3 we describe our three submitted systems for the task.

2 Neural Machine Translation

Many architectures have been proposed for neural machine translation. Most famous one is RNN based encoder-decoder proposed in (Cho et al.), where encoder and decoder are both recursive neural networks, encoder can be bi-directional. After this attention based sequence to sequence models where attention is utilized to improve performance in NMT are proposed in (Bahdanau et al., 2014), (Luong et al., 2015). Attention basically instructs the system about which words to focus more, while generating a particular target word. Transformer based encoder-decoder architecture for NMT is proposed in (Vaswani et al., 2017), which is completely based on self-attention and positional encoding. This does not follow recurrent architecture. Positional encoding provides the system with information of order of words.

NMT needs lots of parallel data to train a system. This task basically focuses on how to improve performance for languages which are similar but resource scarce. There are many language pairs for which parallel data does not exist or exist in a very small amount. In past, to improve the performance of NMT systems various techniques like Back-Translation (Sennrich et al., 2016a), utilizing other similar language pairs through pivoting (Cheng et al., 2017) or transfer learning (Zoph et al., 2016), complete unsupervised architectures (Artetxe et al., 2017) (Lample et al., 2018) and many others have been proposed.

2.1 Utilizing monolingual data in NMT

There has been good amount of work done on how we can utilize monolingual data to improve performance of an NMT system. Back-Translation

Proceedings of the Fourth Conference on Machine Translation (WMT), Volume 3: Shared Task Papers (Day 2) pages 197–201
Florence, Italy, August 1-2, 2019. ©2019 Association for Computational Linguistics

was introduced by (Sennrich et al., 2016b), to utilize monolingual data of target language. This requires a translation system in opposite direction. In (Sennrich et al., 2016b), a method where empty sentences are provided in the input for target side monolingual data is also evaluated, back-translation performs better than this. In iterative Back-Translation, systems in both directions improve each other (Hoang et al., 2018), it is done in an incremental fashion. To generate back-translated data, current system in opposite direction is utilized. In (Currey et al., 2017) , target side monolingual data is copied to generate source synthetic translations and the system is trained by combining this synthetic data with parallel data. In (Zhang and Zong, 2016), source side monolingual data is utilized to iteratively generate synthetic sentences from the same model. In (Domhan and Hieber, 2017), there is a separate layer for target side language model in training, decoder utilize both source dependent and source independent representations to generate a particular target word. In (Burlot and Yvon, 2018), it is claimed that quality of back-translated sentences is important.

Recently many systems have been proposed for Unsupervised NMT, where only monolingual data is utilized. The Unsupervised NMT approach proposed in (Artetxe et al., 2017) follows an architecture where encoder is shared and decoder is separate for each language. Encoder tries to map sentences from both languages in the same space, which is supported by cross-lingual word embeddings. They fix cross-lingual word embeddings in the encoder while training, which helps in generating cross-lingual sentence representations in the same space.

The system with one shared encoder and two separate decoders with no parallel data is trained by iterating between Denoising and Back-Translation. Denoising tries to generate the correct sentence from noisy sentences, in that way the decoder is learning how to generate sentences in that particular language. These noisy sentences are created by shuffling words within a window. If the system is only trained with denoising then it may turn out to be a denoising auto-encoder. So they have also introduced back-translation in the training process to introduce translation task. Training is done by alternating between denoising and back-translation for mini-batches if parallel data

is not available. In a semi-supervised setting if some amount of parallel data is available, training alternates between denoising, back-translation and parallel sentences. In (Lample et al., 2018), encoder and decoder both are shared between the languages. Training is done by alternating between denoising and back-translation. Initialization is performed using a system trained on word-word translated sentences which is performed using cross-lingual word embeddings trained using MUSE(Conneau et al., 2017). They also utilize a discriminator which tries to identify the language from the encoder representations, this leads to adversarial training.

2.2 Cross-lingual word embeddings

Cross-lingual word embeddings tries to map two word embedding spaces of different languages in the same space. The basic assumption for generating the cross-lingual word embeddings in most papers is that both the embedding spaces must be isometric. Cross-lingual word embeddings is generated by learning a linear transformation which minimizes the distances between words given in a dictionary. There are many methods proposed for training cross-lingual word embeddings in an unsupervised way. While training cross-lingual word embeddings in an unsupervised manner there is no dictionary available, only the monolingual embeddings are available. In (Artetxe et al., 2018), cross lingual word embeddings are generated following a series of steps which involves: normalization of the embeddings so they can be used together to utilize for a distance metric, unsupervised initialization using normalized embeddings, self-learning framework using adversarial training where it iterates between creating the dictionary and finding the optimal mapping, and some weighting refinement over this. Through these steps a transformation of these spaces to a common space is learnt. In (Conneau et al., 2017) an adversarial training process is followed where discriminator tries to correctly identify the language using its representation and the mapping matrix W tries to confuse the discriminator.

3 System Overview

This section describes the specification of the systems submitted in detail. We have submitted systems for Hindi-Nepali language pair in Hindi $\rightarrow$ Nepali direction. Hindi and Nepali both are Indo-Aryan languages and are very similar to each other. They share a significant portion of the vocabulary and similar word orders. The three submitted systems are:

- A pure RNN based NMT system

- Semi-supervised RNN based NMT system

- Utilization of copied data in RNN based NMT

First system is pure RNN based NMT system. To train this we have utilized only parallel corpora.
Second system is trained using a semi-supervised NMT system where monolingual data from both languages is utilized. We have utilized architecture proposed in (Artetxe et al., 2017) where encoder is shared and decoders are separate for each language and model is trained by alternating between denoising and back-translation. This architecture can also be utilized for completely unsupervised setting.
Third system is also a pure RNN based NMT system where additional parallel data (synthetic data) is created by copying source side sentences to target side and target side sentences to source side, but we do this only for the available parallel sentences, no additional monolingual data is utilized. In this way the amount of available data becomes three times of the original data. All the data is combined together, shuffled and then provided to the NMT system, there is no identification provided to distinguish between parallel data and copy data.
To train all three systems we have utilized the implementation of (Artetxe et al., 2017).

4 Experimental Details

4.1 Dataset

We have utilized monolingual corpora of both languages in our primary system. The dataset details are given in Table 1. Hindi-Nepali parallel data is provided in the task, which contains 65505 sentences. Hindi monolingual corpora is IITB Hindi monolingual corpora (Kunchukuttan et al., 2018). Nepali monolingual sentences are created using the monolingual data of Wikipedia and Common-Crawl provided for Parallel corpus filtering task [1]

---

by separating each sentence using | and keeping sentences of length 500 and less.

Dataset	Number of sentences
Hindi-Nepali Parallel Data	65,505
IITB Hindi Monolingual Corpora	45,075,242
Nepali Monolingual corpora	6,688,559

Table 1: Dataset details

4.2 Preprocessing

Sentences are preprocessed using tokenization and Byte Pair Encoding (BPE). Sentences are tokenized for both hindi and nepali using IndicNLP[2] library. This tokenized data is preprocessed using BPE. Number of merge operations for BPE is set to 20000 for both languages and learnt separately for each language. The results may improve if we learn BPE jointly because both languages are similar. Byte pair Encoding is learnt using the implementation by (Sennrich et al., 2016b).
Monolingual embeddings are trained using Fast-Text[3] (Bojanowski et al., 2017) using bpe applied monolingual data for both languages. The dimension of embeddings is set to 100. Cross-lingual embeddings are created using VecMap (Artetxe et al., 2018).

4.3 System detail

Table 2 reports BLEU score for the test and dev data for all three systems. We have not utilized dev data while training. We have used encoder and decoder with 2 layers, 600 hidden units each, GRU cells, batch size of 50 and maximum sentence length of 50. Adam optimizer is used with learning rate 0.0002. We have trained all three systems with fixed 300000 iterations. The number of sentences in test and dev data is 1567 and 3000 respectively. The BLEU score for test data is provided by task organizers and for dev data BLEU score is calculated using multi-bleu.pl from moses toolkit (Koehn et al., 2007).

---

[1] http://www.statmt.org/wmt19/ parallel-corpus-filtering.html

System	Test	Dev
Basic	3.5	4.6
With Monolingual Data	2.8	3.27
With copy data	2.7	4.38

Table 2: Experimental results (BLEU scores)

4.4 Results

As it is clear from the results in Table 2 that the system with only parallel data is performing better than when we are utilizing monolingual data. To answer why this is happening, a study of size and quality of monolingual data, the study of ratio of monolingual and parallel data provided to the system is required. The intuition behind using copied data with parallel data is, that both the languages are similar and this may provide more data to the system. But the results show the system is getting confused as we are providing all the data together without any distinguishing mark between parallel and copied sentences. For the same sentence both original translation and its copy is given in the output which may be causing confusion.

5 Summary

In this paper we have explained about systems submitted for Similar Language Translation task in WMT 2019. We have reported results for a semi-supervised technique which utilizes denoising and back-translation. We have utilized lots of monolingual data together with available parallel data for training a neural machine translation system which share encoder and have separate decoders for each language, in a semi-supervised setting. A study of size and quality of monolingual data is required to analyze the performance which is left as future work. We have also explained results for utilizing copied data with parallel data and compared both the above mentioned techniques with a pure RNN based NMT system.

References

Mikel Artetxe, Gorka Labaka, and Eneko Agirre. 2018. A robust self-learning method for fully unsupervised cross-lingual mappings of word embeddings. In *Proceedings of the 56th Annual Meeting of the Association for Computational Linguistics (Volume 1: Long Papers)*, pages 789–798.

Mikel Artetxe, Gorka Labaka, Eneko Agirre, and Kyunghyun Cho. 2017. Unsupervised neural machine translation. *arXiv preprint arXiv:1710.11041*.

Dzmitry Bahdanau, Kyunghyun Cho, and Yoshua Bengio. 2014. Neural machine translation by jointly learning to align and translate. *arXiv preprint arXiv:1409.0473*.

Loïc Barrault, Ondřej Bojar, Marta R. Costa-jussà, Christian Federmann, Mark Fishel, Yvette Graham, Barry Haddow, Matthias Huck, Philipp Koehn, Shervin Malmasi, Christof Monz, Mathias Müller, Santanu Pal, Matt Post, and Marcos Zampieri. 2019. Findings of the 2019 conference on machine translation (wmt19). In *Proceedings of the Fourth Conference on Machine Translation, Volume 2: Shared Task Papers*, Florence, Italy. Association for Computational Linguistics.

Piotr Bojanowski, Edouard Grave, Armand Joulin, and Tomas Mikolov. 2017. Enriching word vectors with subword information. *Transactions of the Association for Computational Linguistics*, 5:135–146.

Franck Burlot and François Yvon. 2018. Using monolingual data in neural machine translation: a systematic study. In *Proceedings of the Third Conference on Machine Translation: Research Papers*, pages 144–155.

Yong Cheng, Qian Yang, Yang Liu, Maosong Sun, and Wei Xu. 2017. Joint training for pivot-based neural machine translation. In *IJCAI*, pages 3974–3980.

Kyunghyun Cho, Bart van Merriënboer Caglar Gulcehre, Dzmitry Bahdanau, Fethi Bougares Holger Schwenk, and Yoshua Bengio. Learning phrase representations using rnn encoder–decoder for statistical machine translation.

Alexis Conneau, Guillaume Lample, Marc'Aurelio Ranzato, Ludovic Denoyer, and Hervé Jégou. 2017. Word translation without parallel data. *arXiv preprint arXiv:1710.04087*.

Anna Currey, Antonio Valerio Miceli Barone, and Kenneth Heafield. 2017. Copied monolingual data improves low-resource neural machine translation. In *Proceedings of the Second Conference on Machine Translation*, pages 148–156.

Tobias Domhan and Felix Hieber. 2017. Using target-side monolingual data for neural machine translation through multi-task learning. In *Proceedings of the 2017 Conference on Empirical Methods in Natural Language Processing*, pages 1500–1505.

Vu Cong Duy Hoang, Philipp Koehn, Gholamreza Haffari, and Trevor Cohn. 2018. Iterative back-translation for neural machine translation. In *Proceedings of the 2nd Workshop on Neural Machine Translation and Generation*, pages 18–24.

---

[2] https://github.com/anoopkunchukuttan/indic_nlp_library
[3] https://fasttext.cc/

Philipp Koehn, Hieu Hoang, Alexandra Birch, Chris Callison-Burch, Marcello Federico, Nicola Bertoldi, Brooke Cowan, Wade Shen, Christine Moran, Richard Zens, et al. 2007. Moses: Open source toolkit for statistical machine translation. In *Proceedings of the 45th annual meeting of the association for computational linguistics companion volume proceedings of the demo and poster sessions*, pages 177–180.

Anoop Kunchukuttan, Pratik Mehta, and Pushpak Bhattacharyya. 2018. The iit bombay english-hindi parallel corpus. In *Proceedings of the Eleventh International Conference on Language Resources and Evaluation (LREC-2018)*.

Guillaume Lample, Myle Ott, Alexis Conneau, Ludovic Denoyer, et al. 2018. Phrase-based & neural unsupervised machine translation. In *Proceedings of the 2018 Conference on Empirical Methods in Natural Language Processing*, pages 5039–5049.

Thang Luong, Hieu Pham, and Christopher D Manning. 2015. Effective approaches to attention-based neural machine translation. In *Proceedings of the 2015 Conference on Empirical Methods in Natural Language Processing*, pages 1412–1421.

Rico Sennrich, Barry Haddow, and Alexandra Birch. 2016a. Improving neural machine translation models with monolingual data. In *Proceedings of the 54th Annual Meeting of the Association for Computational Linguistics (Volume 1: Long Papers)*, volume 1, pages 86–96.

Rico Sennrich, Barry Haddow, and Alexandra Birch. 2016b. Neural machine translation of rare words with subword units. In *Proceedings of the 54th Annual Meeting of the Association for Computational Linguistics (Volume 1: Long Papers)*, volume 1, pages 1715–1725.

Ashish Vaswani, Noam Shazeer, Niki Parmar, Jakob Uszkoreit, Llion Jones, Aidan N Gomez, Łukasz Kaiser, and Illia Polosukhin. 2017. Attention is all you need. In *Advances in neural information processing systems*, pages 5998–6008.

Jiajun Zhang and Chengqing Zong. 2016. Exploiting source-side monolingual data in neural machine translation. In *Proceedings of the 2016 Conference on Empirical Methods in Natural Language Processing*, pages 1535–1545.

Barret Zoph, Deniz Yuret, Jonathan May, and Kevin Knight. 2016. Transfer learning for low-resource neural machine translation. In *Proceedings of the 2016 Conference on Empirical Methods in Natural Language Processing*, pages 1568–1575.

Neural Machine Translation: Hindi ⇔ Nepali

Sahinur Rahman Laskar, Partha Pakray and **Sivaji Bandyopadhyay**
Department of Computer Science and Engineering
National Institute of Technology Silchar
Assam, India
{sahinurlaskar.nits, parthapakray, sivaji.cse.ju}@gmail.com

Abstract

With the extensive use of Machine Translation (MT) technology, there is progressively interest in directly translating between pairs of similar languages. Because the main challenge is to overcome the limitation of available parallel data to produce a precise MT output. Current work relies on the Neural Machine Translation (NMT) with attention mechanism for the similar language translation of WMT19 shared task in the context of Hindi-Nepali pair. The NMT systems trained the Hindi-Nepali parallel corpus and tested, analyzed in Hindi ⇔ Nepali translation. The official result declared at WMT19 shared task, which shows that our NMT system obtained Bilingual Evaluation Understudy (BLEU) score 24.6 for primary configuration in Nepali to Hindi translation. Also, we have achieved BLEU score 53.7 (Hindi to Nepali) and 49.1 (Nepali to Hindi) in contrastive system type.

1 Introduction

MT acts as an interface, which handles language perplexity issues using automatic translation in between pair of diverse languages in Natural Language Processing (NLP). Although, corpus-based based MT system overcome limitations of rule-based MT system such as dependency on linguistic expertise, the complexity of various tasks of NLP and language diversity for Interlingua-based MT system (Dave et al., 2001). But it needs sufficient parallel corpus to get optimize MT output. The NMT falls under the category of corpus-based MT system, which provides better accuracy than Statistical Machine Translation (SMT), corpus-based MT system. The NMT system used to overcome the demerits of SMT, such as the issue of accuracy and requirement of large datasets. Recurrent Neural Network (RNN) encoder-decoder NMT system, which assists encoding of a variable-length source sentence into a

fixed-length vector and same is decoded to generate the target sentence (Cho et al., 2014). The simple RNN adopted Long Short Term Memory (LSTM), which is a gated RNN used to improve the translation quality of longer sentences. The importance of LSTM component is to learn long term features for encoding and decoding. Besides, LSTM, other aspects that improve the performance of the NMT system like the requirement of test-time decoding using beam search, input feeding using attention mechanism (Luong et al., 2015). The reason behind the massive unfolding of the NMT system over SMT is the ability of context analysis and fluent translation (Mahata et al., 2018; Pathak and Pakray, 2018; Pathak et al., 2018).

Motivated by the merits of the NMT over other MT systems and the importance of direct translation in between pairs of similar languages, current work has investigated similar language pair namely, Hindi-Nepali, for translation from Hindi to Nepali and vice-versa using the NMT system. Due to lack of background work of similar language pair translation, the specific translation work for Hindi ⇔ Nepali is still in its infancy. To examine the efficiency of our NMT systems, the predicted translations exposed to automatic evaluation using the BLEU score (Papineni et al., 2002).

The rest of the paper is structured as follows: Section 2, details of the system description is presented. Section 3, result and analysis are discussed and lastly, Section 4, concludes the paper with future scope.

2 System Description

The key steps of system architecture are data preprocessing, system training and system testing and same have been described in the subsequent subsections. We have used OpenNMT (Klein et al.,

Proceedings of the Fourth Conference on Machine Translation (WMT), Volume 3: Shared Task Papers (Day 2) pages 202–207
Florence, Italy, August 1-2, 2019. ©2019 Association for Computational Linguistics

2017) and Marian NMT (Junczys-Dowmunt et al., 2018) toolkit to train and test the NMT system. The OpenNMT, an open source toolkit for NMT, which prioritizes efficiency, modularity and support significant research extensibility. Likewise, Marian, a research-friendly tookit based on dynamic computation graphs written in purely C++, which achieved high training and translation speed for NMT.

2.1 Data Preprocessing

During the preprocessing step, source and target sentences of raw data are tokenized using Amun toolkit and makes a vocabulary size of dimension 66000, 50000 for Nepali-Hindi parallel sentence pairs, which indexes the words present in the training process. All unique words are listed out in dictionary files. The details of the data set are discussed next.

Data The NMT system has been trained using parallel source-target sentence pairs for Hindi and Nepali, where Hindi and Nepali are the source and target language and vice-versa. The training corpus has been compiled manually by back-translation using Google translator[1] from the Wikipedia source of Hindi language,[2] Nepali language,[3] and source of Bible[4] and as well as dataset provided by the WMT19 organizer (Barrault et al., 2019). The test data provided by the organizer for Hindi to Nepali translation consists of 1,567 number of instances and for Nepali to Hindi translation consists of 2,000 number of instances, have been used to check the translational effect of the trained system. Also, validate using a subset of training corpus containing 500 instances. The details of the corpus statistics are shown in Table 1. The NMT system has been trained and tested in three different configurations such as Run-1, Run-2, and Run-3 using primary and contrastive system type, which are summarized in Table 2 and 3.

2.2 System Training

After preprocessing the data, the source and target sentences were trained using our NMT systems for translation prediction in case of both Hindi to Nepali and Nepali to Hindi. Our NMT systems adopted OpenNMT and Marian NMT to train parallel training corpora using sequence-to-

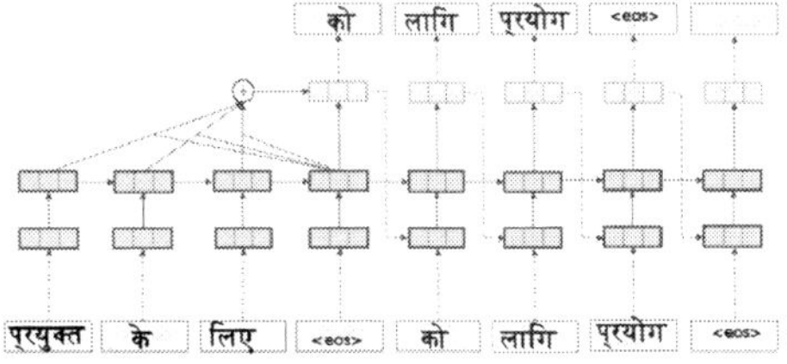

Figure 1: NMT System Architecture.

sequence RNN having attention mechanism. In NMT system architecture, encoder and decoder are the main components of the system. The encoder consists of a two-layer network of LSTM units, having 500 nodes in each layer, which transforms the variable length input sentence of the source language into a fixed size summary vector. After that, a two-layer LSTM decoder having 500 hidden units, process the summary vector (output of encoder) to generate target sentence as output. Multiple Graphics Processing Units (GPU) were used to increase the performance of training. The minimum batch size is set to 2000 for memory requirements, a drop out of 0.1 and enable layer normalization, which guarantees that memory will not grow during training that result in a stable training run.

NMT System with Attention Mechanism The main disadvantage of the basic encoder-decoder model is that it transforms the source sentence into a fixed length vector. Therefore, there is a loss of information in case of a long sentence. The encoder is unable to encode all valuable information into the summary vector. Hence, an attention mechanism is introduced to handle such an issue. The encoder design is the main difference between basic encoder-decoder model and attention model. In the attention model, a context vector is taken as input by the decoder, unlike a summary vector in the basic encoder-decoder model. The context vector is computed using convex coefficients, are called attention weights, which measure how much important is the source word in the generation of the current target word.

Figure 1 presents the NMT system architecture, where attention mechanism and input feeding are used to translate Hindi source sentence "प्रयुक्त के लिए" into the Nepali target sentence "को लागि प्रयोग" (Luong et al., 2015). Here, $<$ $eos >$ marks the end of a sentence.

---

[1] https://translate.google.com/
[2] https://en.wikipedia.org/wiki/Hindi
[3] https://en.wikipedia.org/wiki/Nepali_language
[4] https://www.bible.com

Nature of corpus	Name of Corpus/Source	Number of instances
Training	WMT19 Organizer	65,505
	Bible + Wikipedia	1,81,368
	(using Back-translation)	
	Total	2,46,873
Test	Hindi to Nepali	1,567
	Nepali to Hindi	2,000
Validation	WMT19 Organizer	500

Table 1: Corpus Statistics.

Configuration	Tools	Training Data (No. of instances)
Primary (NMT-1): Run-1	Marian NMT	65,505 (WMT19 Organizer)
Contrastive (NMT-2): Run-2	OpenNMT	1,33,526 (65,505: WMT19 Organizer + Bible + Wikipedia)
Contrastive (NMT-3): Run-3	Marian NMT	2,46,873 (65,505: WMT19 Organizer + Bible + Wikipedia)

Table 2: Different configuration, tools and training data used for Hindi-Nepali Translation.

Configuration	Tools	Training Data (No. of instances)
Primary (NMT-1): Run-1	Marian NMT	65,505 (WMT19 Organizer)
Contrastive (NMT-2): Run-2	Marian NMT	1,33,526 (65,505: WMT19 Organizer + Bible + Wikipedia)
Contrastive (NMT-3): Run-3	OpenNMT	2,46,873 (65,505: WMT19 Organizer + Bible + Wikipedia)

Table 3: Different configuration, tools and training data used for Nepali-Hindi Translation.

2.3 System Testing

During system testing phase, the trained system is carried out on test sentences as mentioned in Section 2.1 provided by the WMT19 organizer for predicting translations.

3 Result and Analysis

The official results of the competition are reported by WMT19 organizer (Barrault et al., 2019) and the same are presented in Table 4, 5, 6 and 7 respectively.

A total of six, five teams participated in Hindi to Nepali and Nepali to Hindi translation using primary and contrastive system type. In the primary system type of Hindi to Nepali translation, our NMT system attained a lower BLEU score and a higher BLEU score in Nepali to Hindi translation than other participated teams. However, in both directions of Hindi-Nepali translation under contrastive configuration our system (Marian) obtained excellent BLEU score 53.7 (Hindi to Nepali), 49.1 (Nepali to Hindi). Moreover, it has been observed that our system's BLEU score of Marian outperforms OpenNMT in both directions of Hindi-Nepali translation under contrastive as well as primary configuration.

Analysis To analyze the best and worst performance of our NMT system, considered the sample sentences from test data provided by the organizer and predicted target sentences on the same test data by our NMT system and Google translator. In the case of a short, medium, long sentences of best performance are given in Table 8, our NMT system provides a perfect prediction like Google translation for the given test sentences. In Table 9, the worst case prediction sentences are presented. In Segment Id = 136, our NMT system's prediction is wrong. The predicted target sentence is in a different language in Segment Id = 25 and also, in case of a long sentence as given in Segment Id = 153, the prediction is not precise. However, Google translation yields accurate prediction in the same sentences.

Segment Id=306: Source Language=Nepali, Target Language=Hindi	
Source Test Sentence	तपाईं यो खाता मेट्न निश्चित हुनुहुन्छ ?
Generated Target Sentence	क्या आप निश्चित हैं कि आप इस खाते को विलोपित करना चाहते हैं?
Google Translation	क्या आप वाकई इस खाते को हटाना चाहते हैं ?

Segment Id=1: Source Language=Nepali, Target Language=Hindi	
Source Test Sentence	तपाईंले उपलब्ध गराउनु भएको इमेल ठेगाना वैध छैन ।
Generated Target Sentence	आपने जो ईमेल पता दिया है वह वैध नहीं है.
Google Translation	आपके द्वारा प्रदान किया गया ईमेल पता मान्य नहीं है ।

Segment Id=43: Source Language=Nepali, Target Language=Hindi	
Source Test Sentence	तपाईंले समर्थन गर्ने लगइन विधि प्रयोग गरी रहनुभएको र तपाईंको पासवर्ड सही रुपले लेख्नु भएको निश्चित गर्न जाँच गर्नुहोस् । याद गर्नुहोस्, धेरै पासवर्डहरू सम्वेदनशील हुन्छन्; तपाईंको क्याप्स लक चालु भैरहेको हुनसक्छ ।
Generated Target Sentence	जांच करें कि आपके कूटशब्द की वर्तनी शुद्ध है और फिर आप एक समर्थित लॉगिन विधि का प्रयोग कर रहे हैं. याद रखें कि बहुत से कूटशब्द कुछ बड़े-छोटे अक्षरों के प्रति संवेदनशील होते हैं; आपका कैप्सलाक ऑन हो सकता है.
Google Translation	यह पुष्टि करने के लिए जांचें कि आप लॉगिन विधि का उपयोग कर रहे हैं और अपना पासवर्ड सही तरीके से लिख रहे हैं । याद रखें, कई पासवर्ड पर्यायवाची हैं; आपका कैप्स लॉक चालू हो सकता है ।

Table 8: Best Performance examples in Nepali to Hindi translation.

Segment Id=136: Source Language=Nepali, Target Language=Hindi	
Source Test Sentence	मेनु सिर्जना गर्न असफल (सम्भवत% 1 छुटेको वा बिग्रिएको हुनुपर्छ)
Generated Target Sentence	पियर से प्रमाण पत्र लेने में असमर्थ
Google Translation	मेनू बनाने में विफलता (शायद% 1 को हटाया जाना चाहिए या क्षतिग्रस्त होना चाहिए)

Segment Id=25: Source Language=Nepali, Target Language=Hindi	
Source Test Sentence	डा. जिव फाइल "% 1" म्याक्रो फाइल भएकाले यसले आकृति समावेश गर्दैन ।
Generated Target Sentence	Die Audiodatei für dieses Ereignis existiert nicht.
Google Translation	डॉ। लाइव फ़ाइल "% 1" एक मैक्रो फ़ाइल है क्योंकि इसमें आकृति शामिल नहीं है ।

Segment Id=153: Source Language=Nepali, Target Language=Hindi	
Source Test Sentence	या त फोल्डरहरूलाई छुट्टछुट्टै चयन गरेर, र/वा सबै स्थानीय फोल्डरहरू, सबै टाढाको फोल्डरहरू, वा दुवै चयन गरेर तपाईंले स्रोतको रूपमा कम्तीमा पनि एउटा फोल्डरलाई निर्दिष्ट गर्नु पर्दछ ।
Generated Target Sentence	आप कम से कम एक फ़ोल्डर को एक स्रोत के रूप में जरूर निर्दिष्ट करें. या तो फ़ोल्डर को निजी रूप से चुनते हुये, और / या सारे स्थानीय फोल्ड को चुनते हुये, सारे दूरस्थ फ़ोल्डर , या दोनों.
Google Translation	आपको या तो फ़ोल्डर को अलग-अलग, और / या सभी स्थानीय फ़ोल्डर, सभी दूर फ़ोल्डर, या दोनों का चयन करके स्रोत के रूप में कम से कम एक फ़ोल्डर निर्दिष्ट करना होगा।

Table 9: Worst Performance examples in Nepali to Hindi translation.

Moreover, the BLEU scores of the test set translated by the Google translator with the test set provided by the organizer show close to each other for both target language Hindi and Nepali, as shown in Table 10.

Target Language	BLEU Score
Hindi	0.405171
Nepali	0.332679

Table 10: BLEU scores of Hindi and Nepali target language for test data and test set translation by Google translator.

Team	BLEU Score	Type	System
Panlingua-KMI	11.5	Primary	PBSMT
CMUMEA N	11.1	Primary	AUGTRAN
TeamZeroGang	8.2	Primary	-
NITS-CNLP	**3.7**	**Primary**	**NMT-1 (Marian)**

Table 4: BLEU scores result of participated teams at WMT19 shared task in Hindi to Nepali translation.

Team	BLEU Score	Type	System
NITS-CNLP	**24.6**	**Primary**	**NMT-1 (Marian)**
CMUMEA N	12.1	Primary	AUGTRAN
Panlingua-KMI	9.8	Primary	PBSMT
TeamZeroGang	9.1	Primary	-
CFILT_IITB	2.7	Primary	WITH MONOLINGUAL

Table 5: BLEU scores result of participated teams at WMT19 shared task in Nepali to Hindi translation.

Team	BLEU Score	Type	System
NITS-CNLP	**53.7**	**Contrastive**	**NMT-3 (Marian)**
TeamZeroGang	8.2	Contrastive	-
NITS-CNLP	**3.6**	**Contrastive**	**NMT-2 (OpenNMT)**
CFILT_IITB N	3.5	Contrastive	Basic

Table 6: BLEU scores result of participated teams at WMT19 shared task in Hindi to Nepali translation.

Team	BLEU Score	Type	System
NITS-CNLP	**49.1**	**Contrastive**	**NMT-3 (Marian)**
TeamZeroGang	9.1	Contrastive	-
Panlingua-KMI	4.2	Contrastive	NMT
Panlingua-KMI	3.6	Contrastive	NMT-Transformer
NITS-CNLP	**1.4**	**Contrastive**	**NMT-2 (OpenNMT)**

Table 7: BLEU scores result of participated teams at WMT19 shared task in Nepali to Hindi translation.

4 Conclusion and Future Scope

In this work, our NMT systems adopted attention mechanism to predict translation of similar language pair namely, Hindi to Nepali and vice-versa. In the current competition, in primary configuration, our NMT system obtained BLEU score 24.6 in Nepali to Hindi translation and BLEU score 3.7 in Hindi to Nepali translation. On the other hand, in contrastive configuration, our NMT system acquired BLEU score 53.7 (Hindi to Nepali), 49.1 (Nepali to Hindi). However, close analysis of generated target sentences on given test sentences remarks that our NMT systems need to improve in case of wrong translation, translation in a different language. Moreover, BLEU scores presented in Table 10, pointed out that is case of both target language Hindi and Nepali, the scores are in relatively stable in both directions of Hindi-Nepali translation like our systems (both Marian and OpenNMT) in contrastive configuration (as mentioned in Table 6 and 7) but unlike in primary configuration (Marian) (as mentioned in Table 4 and 5). Hence, more experiments and comparative analysis will be needed in future work to reason about Marian outperforms OpenNMT in both directions i.e. Hindi to Nepali and Nepali to Hindi translation. In the future work, more number of instances in Hindi-Nepali pair, different Indian similar language pair like Bengali-Assamese, Telugu-Kannada, Hindi-Punjabi, shall be considered for machine translation, which may be possible to overcome the limitation of available parallel data to produce precise MT output.

Acknowledgement

Authors would like to thank WMT19 Shared task organizers for organizing this competition and also, thank Centre for Natural Language Processing (CNLP) and Department of Computer Science and Engineering at National Institute of Technology, Silchar for providing the requisite support and infrastructure to execute this work.

References

Loïc Barrault, Ondřej Bojar, Marta R. Costa-jussà, Christian Federmann, Mark Fishel, Yvette Graham, Barry Haddow, Matthias Huck, Philipp Koehn, Shervin Malmasi, Christof Monz, Mathias Müller, Santanu Pal, Matt Post, and Marcos Zampieri. 2019. Findings of the 2019 conference on machine translation (wmt19). In *Proceedings of the Fourth Conference on Machine Translation, Volume 2: Shared Task Papers*, Florence, Italy. Association for Computational Linguistics.

Kyunghyun Cho, Bart van Merrienboer, Caglar Gulcehre, Dzmitry Bahdanau, Fethi Bougares, Holger Schwenk, and Yoshua Bengio. 2014. Learning phrase representations using rnn encoder–decoder for statistical machine translation. In *Proceedings of the 2014 Conference on Empirical Methods in Natural Language Processing (EMNLP)*, pages 1724–1734, Doha, Qatar. Association for Computational Linguistics.

Shachi Dave, Jignashu Parikh, and Pushpak Bhattacharyya. 2001. Interlingua-based english–hindi machine translation and language divergence. *Machine Translation*, 16(4):251–304.

Marcin Junczys-Dowmunt, Roman Grundkiewicz, Tomasz Dwojak, Hieu Hoang, Kenneth Heafield, Tom Neckermann, Frank Seide, Ulrich Germann, Alham Fikri Aji, Nikolay Bogoychev, André F. T. Martins, and Alexandra Birch. 2018. Marian: Fast neural machine translation in C++. In *Proceedings of ACL 2018, System Demonstrations*, pages 116–121, Melbourne, Australia. Association for Computational Linguistics.

Guillaume Klein, Yoon Kim, Yuntian Deng, Jean Senellart, and Alexander Rush. 2017. Opennmt: Open-source toolkit for neural machine translation. In *Proceedings of ACL 2017, System Demonstrations*, pages 67–72, Vancouver, Canada. Association for Computational Linguistics.

Thang Luong, Hieu Pham, and Christopher D. Manning. 2015. Effective approaches to attention-based neural machine translation. In *Proceedings of the 2015 Conference on Empirical Methods in Natural Language Processing*, pages 1412–1421, Lisbon, Portugal. Association for Computational Linguistics.

Sainik Kumar Mahata, Dipankar Das, and Sivaji Bandyopadhyay. 2018. Mtil2017: Machine translation using recurrent neural network on statistical machine translation. *Journal of Intelligent Systems*, pages 1–7.

Kishore Papineni, Salim Roukos, Todd Ward, and Wei-Jing Zhu. 2002. Bleu: A method for automatic evaluation of machine translation. In *Proceedings of the 40th Annual Meeting on Association for Computational Linguistics*, ACL '02, pages 311–318, Stroudsburg, PA, USA. Association for Computational Linguistics.

Amarnath Pathak and Partha Pakray. 2018. Neural machine translation for indian languages. *Journal of Intelligent Systems*, pages 1–13.

Amarnath Pathak, Partha Pakray, and Jereemi Bentham. 2018. English–mizo machine translation using neural and statistical approaches. *Neural Computing and Applications*, 30:1–17.

NICT's Machine Translation Systems
for the WMT19 Similar Language Translation Task

Benjamin Marie   Raj Dabre   Atsushi Fujita

National Institute of Information and Communications Technology

3-5 Hikaridai, Seika-cho, Soraku-gun, Kyoto, 619-0289, Japan

{bmarie, raj.dabre, atsushi.fujita}@nict.go.jp

Abstract

This paper presents the NICT's participation in the WMT19 shared Similar Language Translation Task. We participated in the Spanish–Portuguese task. For both translation directions, we prepared state-of-the-art statistical (SMT) and neural (NMT) machine translation systems. Our NMT systems with the Transformer architecture were trained on the provided parallel data enlarged with a large quantity of back-translated monolingual data. Our primary submission to the task is the result of a simple combination of our SMT and NMT systems. According to BLEU, our systems were ranked second and third respectively for the Portuguese-to-Spanish and Spanish-to-Portuguese translation directions. For contrastive experiments, we also submitted outputs generated with an unsupervised SMT system.

1 Introduction

This paper describes the machine translation (MT) systems built for the participation of the National Institute of Information and Communications Technology (NICT) in the WMT19 shared Similar Language Translation Task. We participated in Spanish–Portuguese (es-pt) in both translation directions. We chose this language pairs to explore the potential of unsupervised MT for very close languages with large monolingual data, and to compare it with supervised MT systems trained on large bilingual data.

We participated under the team name "NICT." All our systems were *constrained*, i.e., we used only the parallel and monolingual data provided by the organizers to train and tune the MT systems. For both translation directions, we trained supervised neural MT (NMT) and statistical MT (SMT) systems, and combined them through n-best list reranking using different informative features as proposed by Marie and Fujita (2018a). This simple combination method, in conjunction with the exploitation of large back-translated monolingual data (Sennrich et al., 2016a), performed among the best MT systems in this task.

The remainder of this paper is organized as follows. Section 2 introduces the data preprocessing. Section 3 describes the details of our NMT and SMT systems, and also our unsupervised SMT systems. Then, the combination of NMT and SMT is described in Section 4. Empirical results produced with our systems are presented in Section 5, and Section 6 concludes this paper.

2 Data Preprocessing

2.1 Data

As parallel data to train our systems, we used all the provided data. As monolingual data, we used the provided "News Crawl" corpora that are sufficiently large and in-domain to train our unsupervised systems and be used for generating useful pseudo-parallel data through back-translation. To tune/validate our systems, we used the provided development data.

2.2 Tokenization, Truecasing, and Cleaning

We used the tokenizer and truecaser of `Moses` (Koehn et al., 2007). The truecaser was trained on one million tokenized lines extracted randomly from the monolingual data. Truecasing was then performed on all the tokenized data. For cleaning, we only applied the `Moses` script `clean-corpus-n.perl` to remove lines in the parallel data containing more than 80 tokens and replaced characters forbidden by `Moses`. Note that we did not perform any punctuation normalization. Table 1 presents the statistics of the parallel and monolingual data, respectively, after preprocessing.

208

Proceedings of the Fourth Conference on Machine Translation (WMT), Volume 3: Shared Task Papers (Day 2) pages 208–212
Florence, Italy, August 1-2, 2019. ©2019 Association for Computational Linguistics

Corpus	#sent. pairs		#sent. tokens	
	es	pt	es	pt
Parallel	3.41M	3.41M	87.38M	84.69M
Development	3,000	3,000	69,704	68,284
Monolingual	40.88M	7.61M	1.22B	171.15M

Table 1: Statistics of our preprocessed data.

3 MT Systems

3.1 NMT

For our NMT systems, we adopt the Transformer architecture (Vaswani et al., 2017). We chose `Marian` (Junczys-Dowmunt et al., 2018)[1] to train our NMT systems since it supports state-of-the-art features and is one of the fastest NMT frameworks publicly available. In order to limit the size of the vocabulary of the NMT models, we segmented tokens in the parallel data into sub-word units via byte pair encoding (BPE) (Sennrich et al., 2016b) using 30k operations. BPE segmentations were jointly learned on the training parallel data for the source and target languages. All our NMT systems were consistently trained on 4 GPUs,[2] with the parameters for `Marian` listed in Table 2. To improve translation quality, we added 5M synthetic sentence pairs, obtained through back-translating (Sennrich et al., 2016a) the first 5M sentences from the monolingual corpora, to the original parallel data for training. We performed NMT decoding with an ensemble of a total of four models according to the best BLEU (Papineni et al., 2002) scores on the development data produced by four independent training runs using the same training parameters.

3.2 SMT

We trained SMT systems using `Moses`.[3] Word alignments and phrase tables were obtained from the tokenized parallel data using `mgiza`. Source-to-target and target-to-source word alignments were symmetrized with the `grow-diag-final-and` heuristic. We also trained `MSLR` (monotone, swap, discontinuous-left, discontinuous-right) lexicalized reordering model. We trained one 4-gram language models on the entire monolingual data concatenated to the target side of the parallel data using `LMPLZ`

```
--type transformer
--max-length 80
--mini-batch-fit --valid-freq
5000 --save-freq 5000
--workspace 8000 --disp-freq
500 --beam-size 12 --normalize
1 --valid-mini-batch 16
--overwrite --early-stopping
5 --cost-type ce-mean-words
--valid-metrics ce-mean-words
translation --keep-best
--enc-depth 6 --dec-depth
6 --transformer-dropout
0.1 --learn-rate 0.0003
--dropout-src 0.1
--dropout-trg 0.1 --lr-warmup
16000 --lr-decay-inv-sqrt
16000 --lr-report
--label-smoothing 0.1
--devices 0 1 2 3 --dim-vocabs
30000 30000 --optimizer-params
0.9 0.98 1e-09 --clip-norm 5
--sync-sgd --tied-embeddings
--exponential-smoothing
```

Table 2: Parameters of Marian used for training our NMT systems.

(Heafield et al., 2013). Our systems used the default distortion limit of 6. We tuned the SMT model weights with `KB-MIRA` (Cherry and Foster, 2012) and selected the weights giving the best BLEU score on the development data after 15 iterations.

3.3 Unsupervised SMT

We also built an SMT system, without any supervision, i.e., using only but all the provided monolingual data for training. We chose unsupervised SMT (USMT) over unsupervised NMT (UNMT) since previous work (Artetxe et al., 2018b) has shown that USMT slightly outperforms UNMT and that we expect USMT to work well for this language pair that involves only very few word reorderings.

We built USMT systems using a framework similar to the one proposed in Marie and Fujita (2018b). The first step of USMT is the induction of a phrase table from the monolingual corpora. We first collected phrases of up to six tokens from the monolingual News Crawl corpora

---

[1] `https://marian-nmt.github.io/`, version 1.6.0

[2] NVIDIA® Tesla® P100 16Gb.

[3] `https://github.com/moses-smt/mosesdecoder/`

using `word2phrase`.[4] As phrases, we also considered all the token types in the corpora. Then, we selected the 300k most frequent phrases in the monolingual corpora to be used for inducing a phrase table. All possible phrase pairs are scored, as in Marie and Fujita (2018b), using bilingual word embeddings, and the 300 target phrases with the highest scores were kept in the phrase table for each source phrase. In total, the induced phrase table contains 90M (300k×300) phrase pairs. For this induction, bilingual word embeddings of 512 dimensions were obtained using word embeddings trained with `fastText`[5] and aligned in the same space using unsupervised `Vecmap` (Artetxe et al., 2018a). For each one of these phrase pairs a total of four scores, to be used as features in the phrase table were computed to mimic phrase-based SMT: forward and backward phrase and lexical translation probabilities. Finally, the phrase table was plugged into a `Moses` system that was tuned on the development data using `KB-MIRA`. We performed four refinement steps to improve the system using at each step 3M synthetic parallel sentences generated, from sentences randomly sampled from the monolingual data, by the forward and backward translation systems, instead of using only either forward (Marie and Fujita, 2018b) or backward translations (Artetxe et al., 2018b). We report on the performance of the systems obtained after the fourth refinement step.

4 Combination of NMT and SMT

Our primary submission for WMT19 is the result of a simple combination of NMT and SMT. Indeed, as demonstrated by Marie and Fujita (2018a), and despite the simplicity of the method used, combining NMT and SMT makes MT more robust and can significantly improve translation quality, even when SMT greatly underperforms NMT. Moreover, due to the very few word reorderings to perform and the morphological similarity between Spanish and Portuguese, we can expect SMT to perform closely to NMT while remaining different and complementary. Following Marie and Fujita (2018a), our combination of NMT and SMT works as follows.

4.1 Generation of n-best Lists

We first produced the six 100-best lists of translation hypotheses generated by four NMT left-to-right models individually, by their ensemble, and by one right-to-left model. Unlike `Moses`, `Marian` must use a beam of size k to produce a k-best list during decoding. However, using a larger beam size during decoding for NMT may worsen translation quality (Koehn and Knowles, 2017). Consequently, we also produced with `Marian` the 12-best lists and merged them with `Marian`'s 100-best lists to obtain lists containing up to 112 hypotheses,[6] or up to 672 hypotheses after merging all the lists produced by NMT. In this way, we make sure that we still have hypotheses of good quality in the lists despite using a larger beam size. We also generated 100-best translation hypotheses with SMT.[7] Finally, we merged the lists produced by `Marian` and `Moses`.

4.2 Reranking Framework and Features

We rescored all the hypotheses in the resulting lists with a reranking framework using SMT and NMT features to better model the fluency and the adequacy of each hypothesis. This method can find a better hypothesis in these merged n-best lists than the one-best hypothesis originated by either `Moses` or `Marian`. We chose `KB-MIRA` as a rescoring framework and used a subset of the features proposed in Marie and Fujita (2018a). As listed in Table 3, it includes the scores given by the four left-to-right NMT models used to perform ensemble decoding (see Section 3.1). We also used as features the scores given by the right-to-left NMT model that we trained for each translation direction with the same parameters as left-to-right NMT models. The right-to-left NMT model achieving the best BLEU score on the development data, was selected, giving us another feature for each translation direction. All the following features we used are described in details by Marie and Fujita (2018a). We computed sentence-level translation probabilities using the lexical translation probabilities learned by `mgiza` during the training of our SMT systems. The language model trained for SMT was also used to score the transla-

---

[6]Note that we did not remove duplicated hypotheses that may appear, for instance, in both 12-best and 100-best lists.

[7]We used the option `distinct` in `Moses` to avoid duplicated hypotheses, i.e., with the same content but obtained from different word alignments, and consequently to increase diversity in the generated n-best lists.

---

[4]`https://code.google.com/archive/p/word2vec/`

[5]`https://github.com/facebookresearch/fastText`

Feature	Description
L2R (4)	Scores given by each of the 4 left-to-right `Marian` models
R2L (1)	Scores given by 1 right-to-left `Marian` models
LEX (4)	Sentence-level translation probabilities, for both translation directions
LM (1)	Scores given by the language model used by our SMT system
LEN (2)	Difference between the length of the source sentence and the length of the translation hypothesis, and its absolute value

Table 3: Set of features used by our reranking systems. The column "Feature" refers to the same feature name used in Marie and Fujita (2018a). The numbers in parentheses indicate the number of scores in each feature set.

System	es→pt		pt→es	
	dev	test	dev	test
SMT	55.6	-	60.4	-
NMT	53.8	-	61.3	-
Reranked SMT+NMT	57.2	53.3	61.9	59.9
USMT	51.4	47.9	57.9	54.9

Table 4: Results (BLEU). Since the translation reference of the test data was not released at the time of writing this paper, we could not compute BLEU scores on the test data for the configurations that we did not submit to the tasks and put "-" instead.

tion hypotheses. To account for hypotheses length, we added the difference, and its absolute value, between the number of tokens in the translation hypothesis and the source sentence.

The reranker was trained on n-best lists produced by decoding the same development data that we used to validate NMT system's training and to tune SMT's model weights.

5 Results

The results for both translation directions are presented in Table 4. As expected, we obtained very high BLEU scores that point out that the proximity between the two languages has a key role in the success of MT. Also, due to the many characteristics shared by both languages, especially regarding word orderings and morphology, we can observe that SMT performed as good as NMT. Combining SMT and NMT through reranking derived our best results with, for instance, a substantial improvement of 1.6 BLEU points for es→pt on the development data.

USMT also achieved very high BLEU scores: only 5.4 BLEU points below our primary model for es→pt on the test data. The USMT performance points out that training MT systems with large bilingual data may be unnecessary for very close languages, such as Spanish and Portuguese.

6 Conclusion

We participated in the Spanish–Portuguese translation task and compared a strong supervised MT system with USMT. While our supervised MT system significantly outperformed USMT, we showed that USMT for close languages has the potential to be a reasonable alternative since it can deliver a good translation quality without requiring manual creation of large parallel data for training.

Acknowledgments

We would like to thank the reviewers for their useful comments and suggestions. This work was conducted under the program "Research and Development of Enhanced Multilingual and Multipurpose Speech Translation Systems" of the Ministry of Internal Affairs and Communications (MIC), Japan.

References

Mikel Artetxe, Gorka Labaka, and Eneko Agirre. 2018a. A robust self-learning method for fully unsupervised cross-lingual mappings of word embeddings. In *Proceedings of the 56th Annual Meeting of the Association for Computational Linguistics (Volume 1: Long Papers)*, pages 789–798, Melbourne, Australia. Association for Computational Linguistics.

Mikel Artetxe, Gorka Labaka, and Eneko Agirre. 2018b. Unsupervised statistical machine translation. In *Proceedings of the 2018 Conference on Empirical Methods in Natural Language Processing*, pages 3632–3642, Brussels, Belgium. Association for Computational Linguistics.

Colin Cherry and George Foster. 2012. Batch tuning strategies for statistical machine translation. In *Proceedings of the 2012 Conference of the North American Chapter of the Association for Computational Linguistics: Human Language Technologies*, pages 427–436, Montréal, Canada. Association for Computational Linguistics.

Kenneth Heafield, Ivan Pouzyrevsky, Jonathan H. Clark, and Philipp Koehn. 2013. Scalable modified Kneser-Ney language model estimation. In *Proceedings of the 51st Annual Meeting of the Association for Computational Linguistics (Volume 2: Short Papers)*, pages 690–696, Sofia, Bulgaria. Association for Computational Linguistics.

Marcin Junczys-Dowmunt, Roman Grundkiewicz, Tomasz Dwojak, Hieu Hoang, Kenneth Heafield, Tom Neckermann, Frank Seide, Ulrich Germann, Alham Fikri Aji, Nikolay Bogoychev, André F. T. Martins, and Alexandra Birch. 2018. Marian: Fast neural machine translation in C++. In *Proceedings of ACL 2018, System Demonstrations*, pages 116–121. Association for Computational Linguistics.

Philipp Koehn, Hieu Hoang, Alexandra Birch, Chris Callison-Burch, Marcello Federico, Nicola Bertoldi, Brooke Cowan, Wade Shen, Christine Moran, Richard Zens, Chris Dyer, Ondrej Bojar, Alexandra Constantin, and Evan Herbst. 2007. Moses: Open source toolkit for statistical machine translation. In *Proceedings of the 45th Annual Meeting of the Association for Computational Linguistics Companion Volume Proceedings of the Demo and Poster Sessions*, pages 177–180. Association for Computational Linguistics.

Philipp Koehn and Rebecca Knowles. 2017. Six challenges for neural machine translation. In *Proceedings of the First Workshop on Neural Machine Translation*, pages 28–39, Vancouver. Association for Computational Linguistics.

Benjamin Marie and Atsushi Fujita. 2018a. A smorgasbord of features to combine phrase-based and neural machine translation. In *Proceedings of the 13th Conference of the Association for Machine Translation in the Americas (Volume 1: Research Papers)*, pages 111–124. Association for Machine Translation in the Americas.

Benjamin Marie and Atsushi Fujita. 2018b. Unsupervised neural machine translation initialized by unsupervised statistical machine translation. *CoRR*, abs/1810.12703.

Kishore Papineni, Salim Roukos, Todd Ward, and Wei-Jing Zhu. 2002. Bleu: a method for automatic evaluation of machine translation. In *Proceedings of 40th Annual Meeting of the Association for Computational Linguistics*, pages 311–318, Philadelphia, Pennsylvania, USA. Association for Computational Linguistics.

Rico Sennrich, Barry Haddow, and Alexandra Birch. 2016a. Improving neural machine translation models with monolingual data. In *Proceedings of the 54th Annual Meeting of the Association for Computational Linguistics (Volume 1: Long Papers)*, pages 86–96. Association for Computational Linguistics.

Rico Sennrich, Barry Haddow, and Alexandra Birch. 2016b. Neural machine translation of rare words with subword units. In *Proceedings of the 54th Annual Meeting of the Association for Computational Linguistics (Volume 1: Long Papers)*, pages 1715–1725, Berlin, Germany. Association for Computational Linguistics.

Ashish Vaswani, Noam Shazeer, Niki Parmar, Jakob Uszkoreit, Llion Jones, Aidan N. Gomez, Łukasz Kaiser, and Illia Polosukhin. 2017. Attention is all you need. In *Proceedings of the 30th Neural Information Processing Systems Conference*, pages 5998–6008.

Panlingua-KMI MT System for Similar Language Translation Task at WMT 2019

Atul Kr. Ojha[l], Ritesh Kumar[+], Akanksha Bansal[l], Priya Rani[+]
[l]Panlingua Language Processing LLP, New Delhi, [+]Dr. Bhimrao Ambedkar University, Agra
`(shashwatup9k,akanksha.bansal15,pranijnu)@gmail.com, ritesh78_llh@jnu.ac.in`

Abstract

The present paper enumerates the development of Panlingua-KMI Machine Translation (MT) systems for Hindi ↔ Nepali language pair, designed as part of the Similar Language Translation Task at the WMT 2019 Shared Task. The Panlingua-KMI team conducted a series of experiments to explore both the phrase-based statistical (PBSMT) and neural methods (NMT). Among the 11 MT systems prepared under this task, 6 PBSMT systems were prepared for Nepali-Hindi, 1 PBSMT for Hindi-Nepali and 2 NMT systems were developed for Nepali↔ Hindi. The results show that PBSMT could be an effective method for developing MT systems for closely-related languages. Our Hindi-Nepali PBSMT system was ranked 2nd among the 13 systems submitted for the pair and our Nepali-Hindi PBSMT system was ranked 4th among the 12 systems submitted for the task.

1 Introduction

Automated translation between languages from the same family is a challenging task. While similarity among language pairs may seem to be an advantageous situation in terms of the possibility of developing better performing machine translation systems even with low quantity of resources (like low volume of parallel data), the challenge is to figure out how exactly the advantage can be leveraged and what could be the best method to do it.

The area of Statistical Machine Translation (SMT) has witnessed a continuous rise for the last two decades. The availability of open source toolkits, like Moses (Koehn et al., 2007), have also provided it an impetus. However, neural models have garnered much attention in recent times as they provide robust solutions to machine translation tasks. Their popularity is heightened further with the availability of Neural Machine Translation (NMT) open source toolkits such as OpenNMT (Klein et al., 2017), which provides an almost out-of-the-box solution for developing the first NMT systems as well as experimenting with different kinds of architectures and hyper-parameters (which is crucial for developing a good NMT system). Keeping in view the recent results obtained in MT developments, we experimented with both PBSMT as well as NMT models and evaluated how different models perform in comparison to each other. In general, NMT systems are extremely data-hungry and require huge amounts of parallel data to give a good system. The team was motivated to know if NMT could perform better than PBSMT systems even with low volume of data and without making use of monolingual data when the language pairs were closely-related.

Thus, the broad objectives behind conducting these experiments were,

a) to compare the performance of SMT and NMT in case of closely-related, relatively low-resourced language pairs, and

b) to find how SMT can be made to perform better for closely-related language pairs.

2 System Overview

This section provides an overview of the systems developed for the WMT 2019 Shared Task. In these experiments, the Panlingua-KMI team explored both phrase-based statistical (Koehn et al., 2003) method and neural method for Nepali-Hindi and Hindi-Nepali language pairs. For this purpose, 11 MT systems were developed including 6 Phrase-based Statistical Machine Translation (PBSMT) for Nepali-Hindi, 1 PBSMT for Hindi-Nepali, 2 NMT for Nepali-Hindi and 2 NMT for

Proceedings of the Fourth Conference on Machine Translation (WMT), Volume 3: Shared Task Papers (Day 2) pages 213–218
Florence, Italy, August 1-2, 2019. ©2019 Association for Computational Linguistics

Hindi-Nepali. The system details are provided in the following subsections.

2.1 Phrase-based SMT Systems

These systems were built on the Moses open source toolkit using the KenLM language model (Heafield, 2011) and GIZA++ aligner. 'Grow-diag-final-and heuristic' parameters were used to extract phrases from the corresponding parallel corpora. In addition to this, KenLM was used to build 5-gram language models. The pre-processing was done to handle noise in data (for example, hyperlink, non-UTF characters etc), the details of which are provided below in section 3.1.

2.2 Neural Machine Translation System

OpeNMT (pytorch port of this toolkit) was used to build 2 NMT systems. The first system was built with 2 layers using LSTM model while the second system was built with 6 layers using the Transformer model. 500 hidden units were used.

2.3 Assessment

Assessment of these systems was done on the standard automatic evaluation metrics: BLEU (Papineni et al., 2002) and Translation Error Rate (TER) (Snover et al., 2006). TER was evaluated only for systems whose BLEU score was above 5. In addition to these, the errors of the developed systems were also analysed.

3 Experiments

This section briefly describes the experiment settings for developing the systems.

3.1 Corpus Size

The parallel dataset for these experiments was provided by the *WMT Similar Translation Shared Task* [1] organisers and the Nepali monolingual dataset was taken from *WMT 2019 Shared Task: Parallel Corpus Filtering for Low-Resource Conditions* [2] (Barrault et al., 2019). The monolingual dataset for Hindi was procured from *Workshop on Asian Translation Shared Task 2018* (Nakazawa et al., 2018). The parallel data was sub-divided into training, tuning and monolingual sets, as detailed in Table 1.

Nepali-Hindi and Hindi-Nepali MT systems were

[1]http://www.statmt.org/wmt19/similar.html
[2]http://www.statmt.org/wmt19/parallel-corpus-filtering.html

Language Pair	Training	Tuning	Monolingual
Nepali↔ Hindi	65505	3000	-
Nepali	-	-	92296
Hindi	-	-	104967

Table 1: Statistics of Parallel and Monolingual Sentences of the Nepali and Hindi Languages

tested on 2,000 and 1567 test sentences respectively.

3.2 Pre-processing

The following pre-processing steps were performed as part of the experiments:

a) Both corpora were tokenized and cleaned (sentences of length over 40 / 80 words were removed).

b) True-casing of Latin characters in the corpora was performed. Even though neither of the language pairs use Latin-based scripts, this was needed as the corpora for training as well as testing contained some Latin characters as well.

All these processes were performed using Moses scripts. However, the tokenization was done by the RGNLP team tokenizer (Ojha et al., 2018). This tokenizer was used since Moses does not provide tokenizer for Indic languages. Also the RGNLP tokenizer ensured that the canonical Unicode representation of the characters are retained.

3.3 Development of MT Systems

The pre-processed dataset was used to develop three MT models per language pair – two different phrase-based statistical machine translation system using different language models and one neural MT system using the encoder-decoder framework. Both of these are discussed in the following subsections.

3.3.1 Training and Development of PBMST Systems

As mentioned above, we used the Moses open source toolkit for the development of the PBSMT system. The translation model (TM) and language models (LM) were trained independently and combined in a log-linear scheme where both the models were assigned a different weight using the Minimum Error Rate (MERT) Training tuning algorithm (Och and Ney, 2003). In addition, 3,000 parallel sentences were used for Nepali-Hindi and Hindi-Nepali language pairs to tune the systems.

The details of the experiments are as follows:

I) Nepali-Hindi PBSMT - 6 different experiments (3 each for dataset with sentences of length up to 40 words and 80 words) were conducted for Nepali-Hindi PBSMT system. The difference among the experiments were only with respect to pre-processing alterations. It was used to gauge the effect of different pre-processing steps on the performance of MT system for closely-related languages. The following pre-processing alternations were used -

    a experiments without lowercasing

    b experiments without removing utterances with non-UTF characters

    c experiments with complete pre-processing including lowercasing and getting rid of utterances with non-UTF characters.

II) Hindi-Nepali PBSMT - Based on our experience with Nepali-Hindi system, we developed only one system for Hindi-Nepali pair, using the dataset with complete pre-processing including lowercasing and getting rid of utterances with non-UTF characters.

3.3.2 Training and Developments of NMT Systems

The OpenNMT toolkit was used to develop the NMT systems. The training was done on two layers of LSTM network with 500 hidden units at both, the encoder and decoder models for 1,00,000 epochs. The variability of the parameters was limited with the use of default hyper-parameters configuration. Any unknown words in the translation were replaced with the word in the source language bearing the highest attention weight. All the NMT experiments were carried out only with a dataset that contained sentences with length of up to 40 words.

The hyper-parameters and details of the architecture used for the experiments are as below.

    a **LSTM Model -** This system was built using 2-layer LSTM model (Hochreiter and Schmidhuber, 1997). Our settings followed the Open-NMT training guidelines that indicate that the default training setup is reasonable for training of any language pairs. The model is trained on 1,00,000 epochs, using Adam with a default learning rate of 0.002 and mini-batches of 40 with 500 hidden units. Vocabulary size of 32308 and 32895 for Nepali-Hindi and Hindi-Nepali language pairs respectively was extracted. A static NMT-setup was maintained with the use of same hyper-parameters setting across two language pairs.

    b **Transformer Model -** Another NMT system was developed using the Transformer model (implemented in pytorch port of OpenNMT) with 6 layers. The Nepali-Hindi system was trained for 20,000 epochs and Hindi-Nepali for 10,000 epochs. All other hyper-parameters were kept at default values in the OpenNMT implementation.

3.4 Post-processing

In the end, the translations of the test data using PBSMT systems were post-processed using methods including de-tokenization, de-truecasing for English tokens to improve the accuracy rate of the translated outputs.

4 Evaluation and Error Analysis

This section discusses the results of automatic evaluation, human evaluation, and comparative analysis of the PBSMT and NMT systems.

4.1 Automatic Evaluation Results

Both the PBSMT and NMT systems were evaluated using the reference set provided by the shared task organizers. The standard MT evaluation metrics, BLEU (Papineni et al., 2002) score and TER (Snover et al., 2006), were used for the automatic evaluation. These results were prepared on the Primary and Contrastive system submission which are depicted in the graph provided below as *_P and *_C, where P stands for Primary and C stands for Contrastive, respectively. The results of only the highest scoring system across both language pairs are presented in this paper. It gives a quantitative picture of particular differences across different teams, especially with reference to evaluation scores (Figure 1 and 2).

The Panlingua-KMI PBSMT system produced fourth and second best results for Nepali-Hindi and Hindi-Nepali language pair respectively, across 6 teams and 12-13 systems. Also for PBSMT systems, the Hindi-Nepali language pair

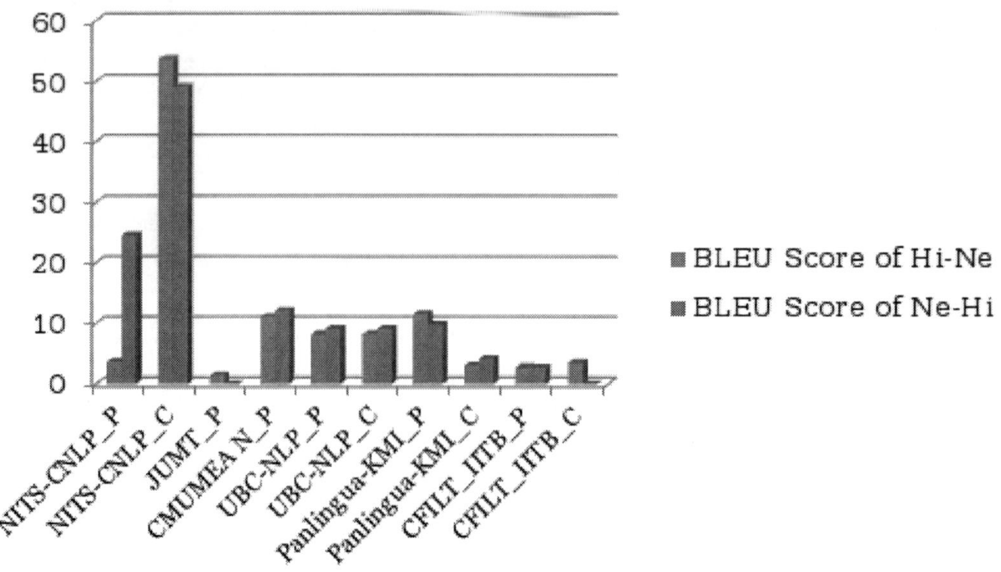

Figure 1: Accuracy of Nepali-Hindi and Hindi-Nepali MT System at BLEU Metric

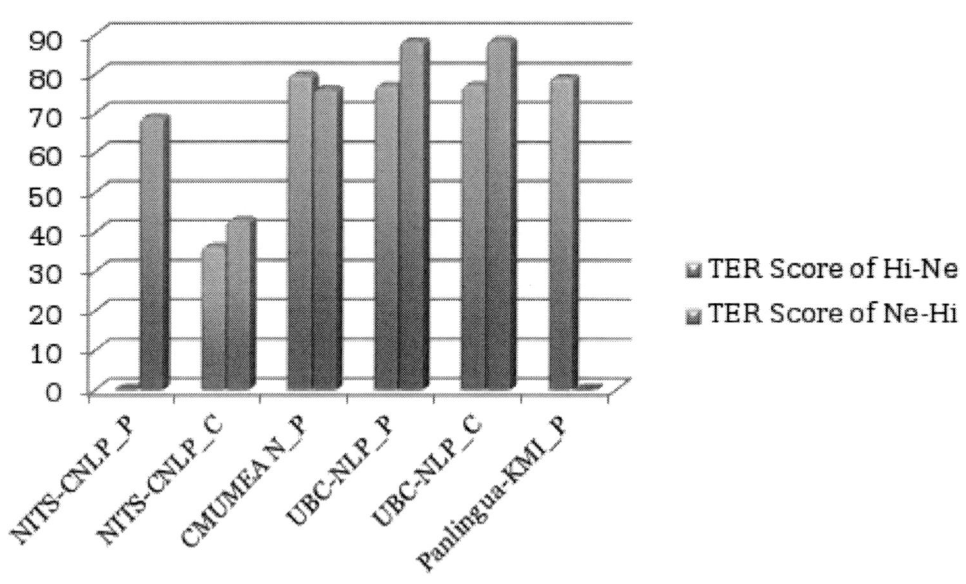

Figure 2: Accuracy of Nepali-Hindi and Hindi-Nepali MT System at TER Metric

showed better results in terms of both the metrics (11.5 in BLEU, 79.1 in TER) while the Nepali-Hindi language pair scored 9.8 in BLEU, 91.3 in TER.

4.2 Comparative Analysis of the PBSMT and NMT Systems

Across both the language pairs, PBSMT performed better than NMT as its accuracy rate was higher in BLEU and lower in TER metrics as shown in Figures 1 and 2. On further manual inspection of the outputs produced by Nepali-Hindi and Hindi-Nepali PBSMT, NMT-LSTM and

NMT-Transformer systems, we found that the outputs produced by the PBSMT seemed better than those produced by the NMT systems (shown in Figures 3 and 4).

Source Sentence	यो पर्याप्त प्राविधिक त्रुटि हो जसमा सञ्जाल सञ्चारका लागि आवश्यक यन्त्र (सकेट) सिर्जना हुन सकेन ।
PBSMT Output	इस पर्याप्त तकनीकी त्रुटि है जहाँ नेटवर्क संवाद के लिए आवश्यक उपकरण (सॉकेट) बनाने नहीं हो सका .
NMT Output	वाकई में हार त्रुटि है .
NMT-Transformer Output	यह पर्याप्त तकनीकी नहीं हो सकती . नेटवर्क संवाद के लिए आपको धन्यवाद .
Source Sentence	% 1 सिमलिङ्क सिर्जना गर्न सकेन। कृपया अनुमति जाँच गर्नुहोस् ।
PBSMT Output	% 1 के लिए सिमलिंक बनाने नहीं कर सका . कृपया अनुमतियाँ जाँचें .
NMT Output	% 1 के लिए सिमलिंक बनाने में . कृपया अनुमतियाँ जाँचें .
NMT-Transformer Output	% 1 के लिए सिमलिंक बनाने में असफल . कृपया अनुमतियाँ जाँचें .
Source Sentence	FITS न्यून/ अधिक मानहरू गणना गर्न असक्षम भयो ।
PBSMT Output	एफआईटीएस कम / बड़ा - मान गणना नहीं कर में अक्षम .
NMT Output	एफआईटीएस विक्रेताओं : मूल्य गणना करने में अक्षम .
NMT-Transformer Output	वी - केलेन्डर
Source Sentence	पाठ आदेशले हालसम्म काम गरेको छैन । '% 1' आदेशलाई उपेक्षा गरिएको छ ।
PBSMT Output	पाठ कमांड अभी कार्य नहीं कर रहा है . ' % 1 ' आदेशलाई नज़र अंदाज़ किया गया है .
NMT Output	
NMT-Transformer Output	कमांड अभी भी जुड़े हैं . लिलो कहता है . Comment
Source Sentence	असक्रिय भएको अवधि पछि वालेट बन्द गर्नुहोस् जब वालेट बन्द हुन्छ यसलाई फेरि पहुँच गर्न पासवर्डको आवश्यकता पर्दछ ।
PBSMT Output	असक्रिय के साथ अवधि के बाद वैलेट बंद करें जब वैलेट बंद होता है इसे फिर से पर पहुँच नहीं पासवर्ड की आवश्यकता आवश्यक है .
NMT Output	@ action : button
NMT-Transformer Output	विंडो को विस्फोट से उड़ाएं जब उन्हें बंद किया जाए Name

Figure 3: Comparative Analysis of Nepali-Hindi PB-SMT, NMT and NMT-Transformer MT's Output

Source Sentence	युनिक्स सॉकेट (वर्तमान होस्ट तथा वर्तमान उपयोक्ता के लिए विशिष्ट)
PBSMT Output	युनिक्स सकेट (वर्तमान होस्ट र हालको प्रयोगकर्ताका लागि विशिष्ट)
NMT Output	युनिक्स सकेट वस्तुहरु जित्दछ र हालको प्रयोगकर्ता बढाउनुहोस्
NMT-Transformer Output	युनिक्स सकेट र होस्ट र हालको प्रयोगकर्ता वोरोध गर्यो
Source Sentence	सर्वर से कोटा जानकारी प्राप्त करने के दौरान त्रुटि हुई% 1
PBSMT Output	सर्भरबाट कोटा जानकारी प्राप्ती गर्दा त्रुटि हुई% 1
NMT Output	सर्भरले जडान जानकारी प्राप्त गर्दा त्रुटि : % 1
NMT-Transformer Output	कोटा जानकारी प्राप्त गर्दा त्रुटि थियो : % 1
Source Sentence	जब कोई अनुप्रयोग बटुआ खोलने की कोशिश करता है तो बताएँ (P)
PBSMT Output	जब कुनै अनुप्रयोग वालेट खोल्न प्रयास गर्दछ भने प्रोम्ट गर्नुहोस् (P)
NMT Output	अनुप्रयोग कुञ्जी खोल्न प्रयास गर्दछ Name
NMT-Transformer Output	अनुप्रयोग सुरुआतमा वालेट खोल्न प्रयास गर्दछ
Source Sentence	POP सर्वर %s से जोड़ने में विफल: निवेदित सत्यापन यांत्रिकी के लिए कोई समर्थन नहीं.
PBSMT Output	पप सर्भरमा %s बाट थम्दा विफल: अनुरोध गरिएको प्रमाणीकरण संयन्त्रको लागि कुनै समर्थन नहीं.
NMT Output	पप सर्भर जानकारीMissing थपिने सुविधाइरूका लागि समर्थन सन्दर्भ QXml
NMT-Transformer Output	पप पप सर्भरबाट समर्थन गर्दैन
Source Sentence	सोलारिस समर्थन कुछ भागों को सन ओएस 5 के विलियम लेफ़ेब्रे के "टॉप" यूटिलिटी से (अनुमति से) लिया गया है.
PBSMT Output	सोलारिस समर्थन केही भागों लाई १८७८ OS ५ का विलियम लेफ़ेब्रे का "टॉप" यूटिलिटी बाट (अनुमति से) गरिएको छ है.
NMT Output	
NMT-Transformer Output	सोलारिस समर्थन र लेख ठेगानाहरु

Figure 4: Comparative Analysis of Hindi-Nepali PB-SMT, NMT and NMT-Transformer MT's Output

NMT's result was affected primarily due to over-generation, NER issues, OOV (Out-of-Vocabulary), and word-order, hence, unable to provide output of 27 source sentences for Nepali-Hindi and 12 source sentences for Hindi-Nepali. The PBSMT's results were also influenced by the above-mentioned factors, but despite that, output of each source sentence was produced.

5 Conclusion

The entire series of experiments revealed several aspects of developing NMT system for closely-related languages. It may seem that NMT performs better than SMT on fluency level (3 and 4) but the relation between source and target language is erroneous, thereby, resulting in poor BLEU score and higher TER. Also, alterations at pre-processing stage do not render any improvement in SMT systems, thus, strengthening the importance of lower casing and excluding non-UTF characters from the data sets. It was also observed that datasets with maximum length of sentences upto 40 words performed better than those with upto 80 words.

The larger picture, based on these experiments, reveal that similarities between two languages did not yield any advantage, as expected at the initial stage. Thus it could be concluded that similar features shared between two languages do not have any significant effect on the performance of the MT systems, at least, as long as the standard methodologies are employed for developing the systems. In order to make use of the similarity in between the language pairs, some more sophisticated methods need to be explored and is a matter of further research.

Acknowledgments

We are grateful to the organizers of WMT Similar Translation Shared Task 2019 for providing us the Nepali-Hindi Parallel Corpus and evaluation scores. We would also like to acknowledge the WMT 2019 Corpus Filtering Shared Task and WAT 2018 for releasing Nepali and Hindi monolingual corpus respectively.

References

Loïc Barrault, Ondřej Bojar, Marta R. Costa-jussà, Christian Federmann, Mark Fishel, Yvette Graham, Barry Haddow, Matthias Huck, Philipp Koehn, Shervin Malmasi, Christof Monz, Mathias Müller,

Santanu Pal, Matt Post, and Marcos Zampieri. 2019. Findings of the 2019 conference on machine translation (wmt19). In *Proceedings of the Fourth Conference on Machine Translation, Volume 2: Shared Task Papers*, Florence, Italy. Association for Computational Linguistics.

Kenneth Heafield. 2011. Kenlm: Faster and smaller language model queries. In *Proceedings of the sixth workshop on statistical machine translation*, pages 187–197. Association for Computational Linguistics.

Sepp Hochreiter and Jürgen Schmidhuber. 1997. Long short-term memory. *Neural computation*, 9(8):1735–1780.

Guillaume Klein, Yoon Kim, Yuntian Deng, Jean Senellart, and Alexander M Rush. 2017. Opennmt: Open-source toolkit for neural machine translation. *arXiv preprint arXiv:1701.02810*.

Philipp Koehn, Hieu Hoang, Alexandra Birch, Chris Callison-Burch, Marcello Federico, Nicola Bertoldi, Brooke Cowan, Wade Shen, Christine Moran, Richard Zens, et al. 2007. Moses: Open source toolkit for statistical machine translation. In *Proceedings of the 45th annual meeting of the association for computational linguistics companion volume proceedings of the demo and poster sessions*, pages 177–180.

Philipp Koehn, Franz Josef Och, and Daniel Marcu. 2003. Statistical phrase-based translation. In *Proceedings of the 2003 Conference of the North American Chapter of the Association for Computational Linguistics on Human Language Technology-Volume 1*, pages 48–54. Association for Computational Linguistics.

Toshiaki Nakazawa, Shohei Higashiyama, Chenchen Ding, Raj Dabre, Anoop Kunchukuttan, W. P. Pa, Isao Goto, Hideya Mino, K. Sudoh, and Sadao Kurohashi. 2018. Overview of the 5th workshop on asian translation. In *Proceedings of the 5th Workshop on Asian Translation (WAT2018)*.

Franz Josef Och and Hermann Ney. 2003. A systematic comparison of various statistical alignment models. *Computational linguistics*, 29(1):19–51.

Atul Kr Ojha, Koel Dutta Chowdhury, Chao-Hong Liu, and Karan Saxena. 2018. The rgnlp machine translation systems for wat 2018. In *Proceedings of the 5th Workshop on Asian Translation (WAT2018)*.

Kishore Papineni, Salim Roukos, Todd Ward, and Wei-Jing Zhu. 2002. Bleu: a method for automatic evaluation of machine translation. In *Proceedings of the 40th annual meeting on association for computational linguistics*, pages 311–318. Association for Computational Linguistics.

Matthew Snover, Bonnie Dorr, Richard Schwartz, Linnea Micciulla, and John Makhoul. 2006. A study of translation edit rate with targeted human annotation. In *Proceedings of association for machine translation in the Americas*, volume 200.

UDS–DFKI Submission to the WMT2019 Similar Language Translation Shared Task

Santanu Pal[1,3], Marcos Zampieri[2], Josef van Genabith[1,3]
[1]Department of Language Science and Technology, Saarland University, Germany
[2]Research Institute for Information and Language Processing, University of Wolverhampton, UK
[3]German Research Center for Artificial Intelligence (DFKI),
Saarland Informatics Campus, Germany
`santanu.pal@uni-saarland.de`

Abstract

In this paper we present the UDS-DFKI system submitted to the Similar Language Translation shared task at WMT 2019. The first edition of this shared task featured data from three pairs of similar languages: Czech and Polish, Hindi and Nepali, and Portuguese and Spanish. Participants could choose to participate in any of these three tracks and submit system outputs in any translation direction. We report the results obtained by our system in translating from Czech to Polish and comment on the impact of out-of-domain test data in the performance of our system. UDS-DFKI achieved competitive performance ranking second among ten teams in Czech to Polish translation.

1 Introduction

The shared tasks organized annually at WMT provide important benchmarks used in the MT community. Most of these shared tasks include English data, which contributes to make English the most resource-rich language in MT and NLP. In the most popular WMT shared task for example, the News task, MT systems have been trained to translate texts from and to English (Bojar et al., 2016, 2017).

This year, we have observed a shift on the dominant role that English on the WMT shared tasks. The News task featured for the first time two language pairs which did not include English: German-Czech and French-German. In addition to that, the Similar Language Translation was organized for the first time at WMT 2019 with the purpose of evaluating the performance of MT systems on three pairs of similar languages from three different language families: Ibero-Romance, Indo-Aryan, and Slavic.

The Similar Language Translation (Barrault et al., 2019) task provided participants with train-

ing, development, and testing data from the following language pairs: Spanish - Portuguese (Romance languages), Czech - Polish (Slavic languages), and Hindi - Nepali (Indo-Aryan languages). Participant could submit system outputs to any of the three language pairs in any direction. The shared task attracted a good number of participants and the performance of all entries was evaluated using popular MT automatic evaluation metrics, namely BLEU (Papineni et al., 2002) and TER (Snover et al., 2006).

In this paper we describe the UDS-DFKI system to the WMT 2019 Similar Language Translation task. The system achieved competitive performance and ranked second among ten entries in Czech to Polish translation in terms of BLEU score.

2 Related Work

With the widespread use of MT technology and the commercial and academic success of NMT, there has been more interest in training systems to translate between languages other than English (Costa-jussà, 2017). One reason for this is the growing need of direct translation between pairs of similar languages, and to a lesser extent language varieties, without the use of English as a pivot language. The main challenge is to overcome the limitation of available parallel data taking advantage of the similarity between languages. Studies have been published on translating between similar languages (e.g. Catalan - Spanish (Costa-jussà, 2017)) and language varieties such as European and Brazilian Portuguese (Fancellu et al., 2014; Costa-jussà et al., 2018). The study by Lakew et al. (2018) tackles both training MT systems to translate between European–Brazilian Portuguese and European–Canadian French, and two pairs of similar languages Croatian–Serbian

Proceedings of the Fourth Conference on Machine Translation (WMT), Volume 3: Shared Task Papers (Day 2) pages 219–223
Florence, Italy, August 1-2, 2019. ©2019 Association for Computational Linguistics

and Indonesian–Malay.

Processing similar languages and language varieties has attracted attention not only in the MT community but in NLP in general. This is evidenced by a number of research papers published in the last few years and the recent iterations of the VarDial evaluation campaign which featured multiple shared tasks on topics such as dialect detection, morphosyntactic tagging, cross-lingual parsing, cross-lingual morphological analysis (Zampieri et al., 2018, 2019).

3 Data

We used the Czech–Polish dataset provided by the WMT 2019 Similar Language Translation task organizers for our experiments. The released parallel dataset consists of out-of-domain (or general-domain) data only and it differs substantially from the released development set which is part of a TED corpus. The parallel data includes Europarl v9, Wiki-titles v1, and JRC-Acquis. We combine all the released data and prepare a large out-domain dataset.

3.1 Pre-processing

The out-domain data is noisy for our purposes, so we apply methods for cleaning. We performed the following two steps: (i) we use the cleaning process described in Pal et al. (2015), and (ii) we execute the Moses (Koehn et al., 2007) corpus cleaning scripts with minimum and maximum number of tokens set to 1 and 100, respectively. After cleaning, we perform punctuation normalization, and then we use the Moses tokenizer to tokenize the out-domain corpus with 'no-escape' option. Finally, we apply true-casing.

The cleaned version of the released data, i.e., the General corpus containing 1,394,319 sentences, is sorted based on the score in Equation 1. Thereafter, We split the entire data (1,394,319) into two sets; we use the first 1,000 for validation and the remaining as training data. The released development set (Dev) is used as test data for our experiment. It should be noted noted that, we exclude 1,000 sentences from the General corpus which are scored as top (i.e., more in-domain like) during the data selection process.

We prepare two parallel training sets from the aforementioned training data: (i) *transference500K*(presented next), collected 500,000 parallel data through data selection method (Axelrod et al., 2011), which are very similar to the in-domain data (for our case the development set), and (ii) *transferenceALL*, utilizing all the released out-domain data sorted by Equation 1.

The *transference500K*training set is prepared using in-domain (development set) bilingual cross-entropy difference for data selection as was described in Axelrod et al. (2011). The difference in cross-entropy is computed based on two language models (LM): a domain-specific LM is estimated from the in-domain (containing 2050 sentences) corpus (lm_i) and the out-domain LM (lm_o) is estimated from the eScape corpus. We rank the eScape corpus by assigning a score to each of the individual sentences which is the sum of the three cross-entropy (H) differences. For a jth sentence pair src_j–trg_j, the score is calculated based on Equation 1.

$$score = |H_{src}(src_j, lm_i) - H_{src}(src_j, lm_o)| \\ + |H_{trg}(trg_j, lm_i) - H_{trg}(trg_j, lm_o)| \quad (1)$$

4 System Architecture - The Transference Model

Our *transference* model extends the original transformer model to multi-encoder based transformer architecture. The *transformer* architecture (Vaswani et al., 2017) is built solely upon such attention mechanisms completely replacing recurrence and convolutions. The transformer uses positional encoding to encode the input and output sequences, and computes both self- and cross-attention through so-called multi-head attentions, which are facilitated by parallelization. We use multi-head attention to jointly attend to information at different positions from different representation subspaces.

The first encoder (enc_1) of our model encodes word form information of the source (f_w), and a second sub-encoder (enc_2) to encode sub-word (byte-pair-encoding) information of the source (f_s). Additionally, a second encoder ($enc_{src \rightarrow mt}$) which takes the encoded representation from the enc_1, combines this with the self-attention-based encoding of f_s (enc_2), and prepares a representation for the decoder (dec_e) via cross-attention. Our second encoder ($enc_{1 \rightarrow 2}$) can be viewed as a transformer based NMT's decoding block, however, without masking. The intuition behind our architecture is to generate better representations via both self- and cross-attention and to further facilitate the learning capacity of the feed-forward layer in the decoder block. In our transference model, one self-attended encoder for f_w, $\mathbf{f_w} = (w_1, w_2, \ldots, w_k)$, returns a sequence of continuous representations, enc_2, and a second self-attended sub-encoder for f_s, $\mathbf{f_s} = (s_1, s_2, \ldots, s_l)$, returns another sequence of continuous representations, enc_2. Self-attention at this point provides the advantage of aggregating information from all of the words, including f_w and f_s, and successively generates a new representation per word informed by the entire f_w and f_s context. The internal enc_2 representation performs cross-attention over enc_1 and prepares a final representation ($enc_{1 \to 2}$) for the decoder (dec_e). The decoder generates the e output in sequence, $\mathbf{e} = (e_1, e_2, \ldots, e_n)$, one word at a time from left to right by attending to previously generated words as well as the final representations ($enc_{1 \to 2}$) generated by the encoder.

We use the scale-dot attention mechanism (like Vaswani et al. (2017)) for both self- and cross-attention, as defined in Equation 2, where Q, K and V are query, key and value, respectively, and d_k is the dimension of K.

$$attention(Q, K, V) = softmax(\frac{QK^T}{\sqrt{d_k}})V \quad (2)$$

The multi-head attention mechanism in the transformer network maps the Q, K, and V matrices by using different linear projections. Then h parallel heads are employed to focus on different parts in V. The ith multi-head attention is denoted by $head_i$ in Equation 3. $head_i$ is linearly learned by three projection parameter matrices: $W_i^Q, W_i^K \in R^{d_{model} \times d_k}$, $W_i^V \in R^{d_{model} \times d_v}$; where $d_k = d_v = d_{model}/h$, and d_{model} is the number of hidden units of our network.

$$head_i = attention(QW_i^Q, KW_i^K, VW_i^V) \quad (3)$$

Finally, all the vectors produced by parallel heads are linearly projected using concatenation and form a single vector, called a multi-head attention (M_{att}) (cf. Equation 4). Here the dimension of the learned weight matrix W^O is $R^{d_{model} \times d_{model}}$.

$$M_{att}(Q, K, V) = Concat_{i:1}^{n}(head_i)W^O \quad (4)$$

5 Experiments

We explore our *transference* model –a two-encoder based transformer architecture, in CS-PL similar language translation task.

5.1 Experiment Setup

For *transferenceALL*, we initially train on the complete out-of-domain dataset (General). The General data is sorted based on their in-domain similarities as described in Equation 1.

transferenceALL models are then fine-tuned towards the 500K (in-domain-like) data. Finally, we perform checkpoint averaging using the 8 best checkpoints. We report the results on the provided development set, which we use as a test set before the submission. Additionally we also report the official test set result.

To handle out-of-vocabulary words and to reduce the vocabulary size, instead of considering words, we consider subword units (Sennrich et al., 2016) by using byte-pair encoding (BPE). In the preprocessing step, instead of learning an explicit mapping between BPEs in the Czech (CS) and Polish (PL), we define BPE tokens by jointly processing all parallel data. Thus, CS and PL derive a single BPE vocabulary. Since CS and PL belong to the similar language, they naturally share a good fraction of BPE tokens, which reduces the vocabulary size.

We pass word level information on the first encoder and the BPE information to the second one. On the decoder side of the transference model we pass only BPE text.

We evaluate our approach with development data which is used as test case before submission. We use BLEU (Papineni et al., 2002) and TER (Snover et al., 2006).

5.2 Hyper-parameter Setup

We follow a similar hyper-parameter setup for all reported systems. All encoders, and the decoder, are composed of a stack of $N_{fw} = N_{fs} = N_{es} = 6$ identical layers followed by layer normalization. Each layer again consists of two sub-layers and a residual connection (He et al., 2016) around each of the two sub-layers. We apply dropout (Srivastava et al., 2014) to the output of each sub-layer, before it is added to the sub-layer input and normalized. Furthermore, dropout is applied to the sums of the word embeddings and the corresponding positional encodings in both encoders as well as the decoder stacks.

We set all dropout values in the network to 0.1. During training, we employ label smoothing with value $\epsilon_{ls} = 0.1$. The output dimension produced by all sub-layers and embedding layers is $d_{model} = 512$. Each encoder and decoder layer contains a fully connected feed-forward network (FFN) having dimensionality of $d_{model} = 512$ for the input and output and dimensionality of $d_{ff} = 2048$ for the inner layers. For the scaled dot-product attention, the input consists of queries and keys of dimension d_k, and values of dimension d_v. As multi-head attention parameters, we employ $h = 8$ for parallel attention layers, or heads. For each of these we use a dimensionality of $d_k = d_v = d_{model}/h = 64$. For optimization, we use the Adam optimizer (Kingma and Ba, 2015) with $\beta_1 = 0.9$, $\beta_2 = 0.98$ and $\epsilon = 10^{-9}$.

The learning rate is varied throughout the training process, and increasing for the first training steps $warmup_{steps} = 8000$ and afterwards decreasing as described in (Vaswani et al., 2017). All remaining hyper-parameters are set analogously to those of the transformer's *base* model. At training time, the batch size is set to 25K tokens, with a maximum sentence length of 256 subwords, and a vocabulary size of 28K. After each epoch, the training data is shuffled. After finishing training, we save the 5 best checkpoints which are written at each epoch. Finally, we use a single model obtained by averaging the last 5 checkpoints. During decoding, we perform beam search with a beam size of 4. We use shared embeddings between CS and PL in all our experiments.

6   Results

We present the results obtained by our system in Table 1.

tested on	model	BLEU	TER
Dev set	Generic	12.2	75.8
Dev set	Fine-tuned*	**25.1**	**58.9**
Test set	Generic	7.1	89.3
Test set	Fine-Tuned*	**7.6**	**87.0**

Table 1: Results for CS–PL Translation; * averaging 8 best checkpoints.

Our fine-tuned system on development set provides significant performance improvement over the generic model. We found +12.9 absolute BLEU points improvement over the generic model. Similar improvement is also observed in terms of TER (-16.9 absolute). It is to be noted that our generic model is trained solely on the clean version of training data.

Before submission, we performed punctuation normalization, unicode normalization, and detokenization for the run.

In Table 2 we present the ranking of the competition provided by the shared task organizers. Ten entries were submitted by five teams and are ordered by BLEU score. TER is reported for all submissions which achieved BLEU score greater than 5.0. The type column specifies the type of system, whether it is a Primary (P) or Constrastive (C) entry.

Team	Type	BLEU	TER
UPC-TALP	P	7.9	85.9
UDS-DFKI	P	**7.6**	**87.0**
Uhelsinki	P	7.1	87.4
Uhelsinki	C	7.0	87.3
Incomslav	C	5.9	88.4
Uhelsinki	C	5.9	88.4
Incomslav	P	3.2	-
Incomslav	C	3.1	-
UBC-NLP	C	2.3	-
UBC-NLP	P	2.2	-

Table 2: Rank table for Czech to Polish Translation

Our system was ranked second in the competition only 0.3 BLEU points behind the winning team UPC-TALP. The relative low BLEU and high TER scores obtained by all teams are due to out-of-domain data provided in the competition which made the task equally challenging to all participants.

7   Conclusion

This paper presented the UDS-DFKI system submitted to the Similar Language Translation shared task at WMT 2019. We presented the results obtained by our system in translating from Czech to Polish. Our system achieved competitive performance ranking second among ten teams in the competition in terms of BLEU score. The fact that out-of-domain data was provided by the organizers resulted in a challenging but interesting scenario for all participants.

In future work, we would like to investigate how effective is the proposed hypothesis (i.e., word-BPE level information) in similar language translation. Furthermore, we would like to explore the similarity between these two languages (and the other two language pairs in the competition) in more detail by training models that can best capture morphological differences between them. During such competitions, this is not always possible due to time constraints.

Acknowledgments

This research was funded in part by the German research foundation (DFG) under grant number GE 2819/2-1 (project MMPE) and the German Federal Ministry of Education and Research (BMBF) under funding code 01IW17001 (project Deeplee). The responsibility for this publication lies with the authors. We would like to thank the anonymous WMT reviewers for their valuable input, and the organizers of the shared task.

References

Amittai Axelrod, Xiaodong He, and Jianfeng Gao. 2011. Domain Adaptation via Pseudo In-domain Data Selection. In *Proceedings of EMNLP*.

Loïc Barrault, Ondřej Bojar, Marta R. Costa-jussà, Christian Federmann, Mark Fishel, Yvette Graham, Barry Haddow, Matthias Huck, Philipp Koehn, Shervin Malmasi, Christof Monz, Mathias Müller, Santanu Pal, Matt Post, and Marcos Zampieri. 2019. Findings of the 2019 Conference on Machine Translation (WMT19). In *Proceedings of WMT*.

Ondřej Bojar, Rajen Chatterjee, Christian Federmann, Yvette Graham, Barry Haddow, Shujian Huang, Matthias Huck, Philipp Koehn, Qun Liu, Varvara Logacheva, et al. 2017. Findings of the 2017 Conference on Machine Translation (WMT17). In *Proceedings of WMT*.

Ondrej Bojar, Rajen Chatterjee, Christian Federmann, Yvette Graham, Barry Haddow, Matthias Huck, Antonio Jimeno Yepes, Philipp Koehn, Varvara Logacheva, Christof Monz, et al. 2016. Findings of the 2016 Conference on Machine Translation. In *Proceedings of WMT*.

Marta R. Costa-jussà. 2017. Why Catalan-Spanish Neural Machine Translation? Analysis, Comparison and Combination with Standard Rule and Phrase-based Technologies. In *Proceedings of VarDial*.

Marta R. Costa-jussà, Marcos Zampieri, and Santanu Pal. 2018. A Neural Approach to Language Variety Translation. In *Proceedings of VarDial*.

Federico Fancellu, Andy Way, and Morgan OBrien. 2014. Standard Language Variety Conversion for Content Localisation via SMT. In *Proceedings of EAMT*.

Kaiming He, Xiangyu Zhang, Shaoqing Ren, and Jian Sun. 2016. Deep Residual Learning for Image Recognition. *Proceedings of CVPR*.

Diederik P Kingma and Jimmy Lei Ba. 2015. Adam: A Method for Stochastic Optimization. *Proceedings of ICLR*.

Philipp Koehn, Hieu Hoang, Alexandra Birch, Chris Callison-Burch, Marcello Federico, Nicola Bertoldi, Brooke Cowan, Wade Shen, Christine Moran, Richard Zens, Chris Dyer, Ondřej Bojar, Alexandra Constantin, and Evan Herbst. 2007. Moses: Open Source Toolkit for Statistical Machine Translation. In *Proceedings of ACL*.

Surafel M Lakew, Aliia Erofeeva, and Marcello Federico. 2018. Neural Machine Translation into Language Varieties. *arXiv preprint arXiv:1811.01064*.

Santanu Pal, Sudip Naskar, and Josef van Genabith. 2015. UdS-sant: English–German hybrid machine translation system. In *Proceedings of WMT*.

Kishore Papineni, Salim Roukos, Todd Ward, and Wei-Jing Zhu. 2002. Bleu: A method for automatic evaluation of machine translation. In *Proceedings of ACL*.

Rico Sennrich, Barry Haddow, and Alexandra Birch. 2016. Neural Machine Translation of Rare Words with Subword Units. In *Proceedings of ACL*.

Matthew Snover, Bonnie Dorr, Richard Schwartz, Linnea Micciulla, and John Makhoul. 2006. A Study of Translation Edit Rate with Targeted Human Annotation. In *Proceedings of AMTA*.

Nitish Srivastava, Geoffrey Hinton, Alex Krizhevsky, Ilya Sutskever, and Ruslan Salakhutdinov. 2014. Dropout: A Simple Way to Prevent Neural Networks from Overfitting. *J. Mach. Learn. Res.*, 15(1):1929–1958.

Ashish Vaswani, Noam Shazeer, Niki Parmar, Jakob Uszkoreit, Llion Jones, Aidan N Gomez, Łukasz Kaiser, and Illia Polosukhin. 2017. Attention Is All You Need. In *Proceedings of NIPS*.

Marcos Zampieri, Shervin Malmasi, Preslav Nakov, Ahmed Ali, Suwon Shon, James Glass, Yves Scherrer, Tanja Samardžić, Nikola Ljubešić, Jörg Tiedemann, Chris van der Lee, Stefan Grondelaers, Nelleke Oostdijk, Dirk Speelman, Antal van den Bosch, Ritesh Kumar, Bornini Lahiri, and Mayank Jain. 2018. Language Identification and Morphosyntactic Tagging: The Second VarDial Evaluation Campaign. In *Proceedings of VarDial*.

Marcos Zampieri, Shervin Malmasi, Yves Scherrer, Tanja Samardžić, Francis Tyers, Miikka Silfverberg, Natalia Klyueva, Tung-Le Pan, Chu-Ren Huang, Radu Tudor Ionescu, Andrei Butnaru, and Tommi Jauhiainen. 2019. A Report on the Third VarDial Evaluation Campaign. In *Proceedings of VarDial*.

Neural Machine Translation of Low-Resource and Similar Languages with Backtranslation

Michael Przystupa
University of British Columbia
<first>.<last>@gmail.com

Muhammad Abdul-Mageed
University of British Columbia
muhammad.mageed@ubc.ca

Abstract

We present our contribution to the WMT19 Similar Language Translation shared task. We investigate the utility of neural machine translation on three low-resource, similar language pairs: Spanish – Portuguese, Czech – Polish, and Hindi – Nepali. Since state-of-the-art neural machine translation systems still require large amounts of bitext, which we do not have for the pairs we consider, we focus primarily on incorporating monolingual data into our models with backtranslation. In our analysis, we found Transformer models to work best on Spanish – Portuguese and Czech – Polish translation, whereas LSTMs with global attention worked best on Hindi – Nepali translation.

1   Introduction

We present our contribution to the WMT 2019 Similar Language Translation shared task, which focused on translation between similar language pairs in low-resource settings (Barrault et al., 2019). Similar languages have advantages that can be exploited when building machine translation systems. In particular, languages that come from the same language family (or that come from related language families) may have in common a multitude of information such as lexical or syntactic structures. This commonality has been exploited in a number of previous works for similar language translation (Haji et al., 2003; Goyal and Lehal, 2009, 2011; Pourdamghani and Knight, 2017).

In this work, we are primarily concerned with neural machine translation (NMT). NMT is a language agnostic framework where language similarities could possibly be exploited to build scalable, state-of-the-art (SOTA) machine translation systems. For example, NMT systems have been used on a number of WMT translation tasks where they enabled highly successful modeling (Bahdanau et al., 2014; Luong et al., 2015; Koehn, 2017; Vaswani et al., 2017; Edunov et al., 2018). A weakness with NMT is its dependence on large bitext corpora. For this reason, researchers have considered ways to mitigate this specific issue.

A prominent approach meant to alleviate need for large parallel data is *backtranslation*. This technique generates synthetic bitext by translating monolingual sentences of the target language into the source language with a pre-existing target-to-source translation system. These noisy source translations are then incorporated to train a new source-to-target MT system (Sennrich et al., 2015a). This approach is instrumental in unsupervised machine translation where authors have shown that, up to a certain amount of bitext, better translation systems can be trained with these unsupervised approaches than supervised methods (Artetxe et al., 2017; Lample et al., 2017, 2018). Backtranslation research has also extended to scenarios of training supervised systems with just synthetic data (Edunov et al., 2018; Marie and Fujita, 2018). Given the success of this approach, it offers a promising avenue to leverage monolingual data for improving translation between similar languages.

Motivated by the success of backtranslation, we focus on leveraging monolingual data to improve NMT systems for similar language pairs. Hence, for our submissions to the shared task, we focus on investigating the effectiveness of synthetic bitext produced with *backtranslation*.

The rest of the paper is organized as follows: We discuss our methods in Section 2, including our NMT models and our decisions for backtranslation. Section 3 is where we describe our analysis of the shared task data. In Section 4, we present our experimental findings, discussing the effectiveness of backtranslation in terms of BLEU

224

Proceedings of the Fourth Conference on Machine Translation (WMT), Volume 3: Shared Task Papers (Day 2) pages 224–235
Florence, Italy, August 1-2, 2019. ©2019 Association for Computational Linguistics

score performance. We conclude in Section 5.

2 Methodology

Here, we outline our approach to improve translation quality for similar languages. This includes description of the two NMT models we considered in our analysis, and our procedure for backtranslating data.

2.1 Model Architectures

Sequence to sequence (seq2seq) models (Vinyals et al., 2015) have emerged as the most prominent architecture in the NMT literature. In seq2seq models, source sentences X are *encoded* as a series of latent representations capturing words in context information. A *decoder* utilizes these hidden states, such as for initialization, to help inform the decoding process for target sentences Y. For our work, we consider both a recurrent neural network (RNN) with *attention* and *Transformer* seq2seq models for our experiments. We briefly introduce each of these next.

Recurrent Neural Network Architecture

There are a number of variations of RNN architectures previously considered for NMT. The one we chose is the default model available in the OpenNMT-py toolkit (Klein et al., 2017). It is an implementation of one of several variations studied by Luong et al. (2015) which focused on understanding attention in depth. It follows the typical seq2eq architecture but includes an attention mechanism which combines the encoder hidden states as a context vector which is added as an additional input to the decoder. We include additional details of this particular model in the supplementary material, and otherwise only mention that both the encoder and decoder are Long Short Term Memory cells (Hochreiter and Schmidhuber, 1997). For the rest of the paper we shall refer to this model as LSTM+Attn when discussing it.

Transformer

The Transformer is a model that uses intra-attention (*self-attention*) instead of sequential hidden states. For translation, it has been shown to train faster compared to RNN-based seq2seq architectures (Vaswani et al., 2017). For brevity, we exclude discussing this model in detail, and instead refer readers to the original paper Vaswani et al. (2017), or alternatively the tutorial by Rush

(2018) which provides a step-by-step guide on the implementation.

2.2 Backtranslation Decisions

Applying backtranslation in practise generally requires a number of decisions such as the amount of synthetic text to add and decoding scheme choice. Both of these considerations have previously been studied by Edunov et al. (2018) which can be applied as general backtranslation guidelines. We largely based our choices off of their findings, but with one discrepancy. In their work, the emphasis was on the number of available training sentence pairs when making backtranslation choices as the key factor.

However, Edunov et al. (2018) do not discuss other aspects of bitext such as sentence length variation, number of words, or even initial bitext quality. This makes it difficult to apply their findings to other bitext corpora based solely on number of sentences. Our assumption when applying findings from Edunov et al. (2018) is that the translation system's BLEU score is more reflective of the expected synthetic sentence quality than the number of sentences used. Our final results suggest this assumption is fairly reasonable. Our Hindi – Nepali translation models, despite having the smallest bitext corpus, performed better on the test sets compared to our Polish – Czech systems following this choice.

Before backtranslating any data, we trained both the Transformer and LSTM+Attn NMT systems with only the provided bitext corpora and calculated the BLEU score on the validation set. Based on our *bitext only* model performances, we then chose the appropriate backtranslation scheme for each language pair. For the Spanish – Portuguese systems we sampled the synthetic source sentences because Edunov et al. (2018) found that for resource rich language pairs this could provide better training signal. For our work, this corresponded to randomly picking each word x_i from the probability distribution for the current position $x_i \sim p(x_i | \mathbf{y}, x_{<i})$. For both Czech – Polish and Hindi – Nepali synthetic sentences, the synthetic source sentences were deterministically produced with greedy decoding, as their validation BLEU scores were much lower. This again was in line with translation behavior of backtranslation found by Edunov et al. (2018).

We used these decoding schemes to backtranslate the available monolingual data with the best corresponding *bitext only* NMT system (either the Transformer or LSTM+Attn model) for each language direction. The two exceptions were Spanish and Hindi, for each of which we had significantly more monolingual data. For Spanish, we only used ~3.3M sentences at most, and for Hindi we only used ~2.4M sentences.

For our experiments, the best performing bitext only systems produced 2 sets of backtranslated text. The first set (which we will refer to as *Synth 1*) included only parts of all the considered monolingual data for a subset of the translation directions. The second set (henceforth referred to as *Synth 2*) consisted of backtranslating all Czech, Polish, Hindi, and Nepali monolingual data and larger portions of the Portuguese and Spanish data. As part of the *Synth 2* data set, we increased the frequency bitext was trained on compared to synthetic bitext. This meant that for every synthetic sentence our models trained on, the model was trained on several sentences of the bitext. This decision was due to the performances we found on our *Synth 1* datasets where several language pairs did not perform as well. In most cases, with the exception of few of our Spanish – Portuguese models, systems trained with these *synthetic* datasets outperformed our bitext only models.

At this point, we had produced 24 models trained on synthetic and real bitext. [1] From these 24 models, we again chose the best performing ones to perform a 3rd round of backtranslation. This 3rd set of backtranslated data (which we refer to as *Synth 3*) followed the same decoding schemes for each language pair as previously discussed. The amount of backtranslation was mostly the same except for the synthetic Portuguese to Spanish data where we backtranslated the largest amount of the available Spanish monolingual data. Exact counts are available in Tables 2,3,4. In the work we report here, we only followed this procedure once. In the future, our goal will be to follow the iterative backtranslation approach proposed by Hoang et al. (2018).

3   Dataset Analysis

In this section, we present an analysis of the shared task data. For additional information, such as our pre-processing of the data, refer to the supplementary material.

To get an understanding of the provided data, we collect statistics including the word and sentence counts, sentence length variation, and token overlap. Table 1 contains information on the approximate sentence and word counts after cleaning the data. Based on the size of the datasets, we hypothesize that our most successful NMT system would be for Spanish – Portuguese (~3.5M sentences), followed by, Czech – Polish (~1.7M sentences), and Hindi – Nepali being the most difficult (~68K sentences).

In addition to this, the sentence length variations in the box-plots of Figure 1 highlight how for Spanish – Portuguese, and Czech – Polish the sentences are generally longer in the bitext compared to Hindi – Nepali. In our experimental results, we reason that part of the success for the LSTM+Attn models on Hindi – Nepali is due to the short sentence lengths. A cited advantage of the Transformer (Vaswani et al., 2017) is its ability to encode longer dependencies, but also see Tang et al. (2018), which on the Hindi – Nepali corpus would not be as much of a requirement due to the shorter bitext.

We also wanted to understand from which perspective each of the language pairs might be considered similar, so we analyzed the overlap between tokens in each language pairs bitext. We tokenized on our cleaned data with the *Tok-Tok Tokenizer* available through the NLTK toolkit.[2] We then calculated the percentage of shared tokens compared to the total tokens at increasingly higher thresholds by token frequency.

Figure 2 shows our findings for the percentage of shared tokens at different thresholds of token frequency. These plots would suggest that although Spanish – Portuguese and Czech – Polish have larger over all token overlap, the most frequent tokens are where much of the language discrepancy is. Czech and Polish in particular, seem to have significantly fewer shared tokens which could suggest a smaller lexical overlap. This could partially be because of differences in alphabets between Czech and Polish. By contrast, Hindi and Nepali seem to share much more in common as we see an increase of overlap for more frequent tokens, but we note this could be an artefact of the small size of the Hindi and Nepali data. We now present our experimental findings.

---

[1]24 = 2 (Transformer vs. RNN) x 2 (*Synth 1* vs. *Synth 2*) x 6 (translation pairs).

[2]https://www.nltk.org/

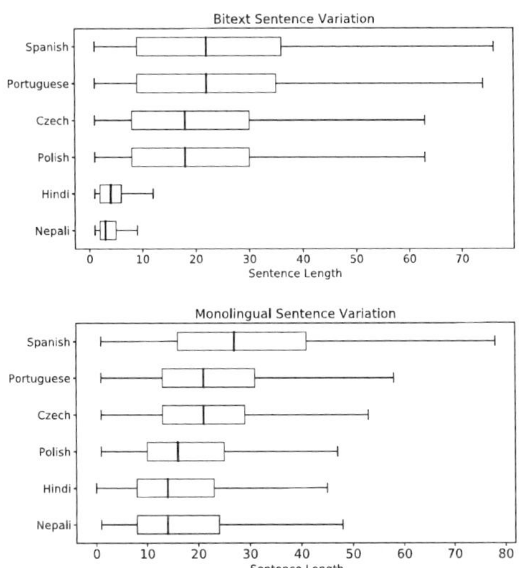

Figure 1: Boxplots showing the variation in sentence lengths between language pairs.

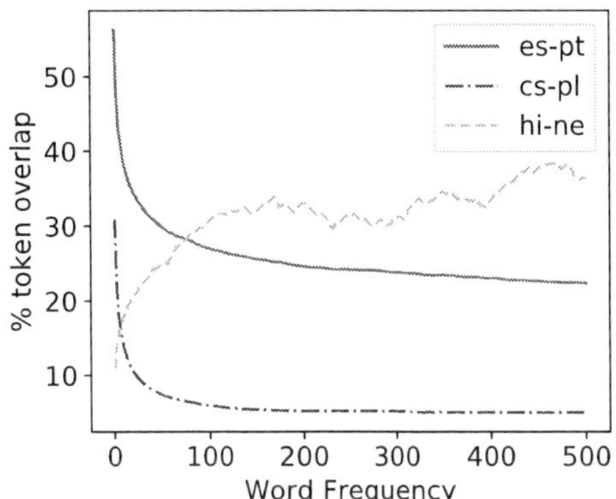

Figure 2: Lexical overlap between language pairs at different thresholds for word frequency.

	Bitext		**Monolingual**	
Lg.	Sentences	Words	Sentences	Words
Es	~3.5M	~90M	~46M	~1.3B
Pt		~87M	~10M	~241M
Cs	~1.7M	~36M	~920K	~20.8M
Pl		~37M	~1.1M	~22M
Hi	~68K	~360K	~44M	~890K
Ne		~337K	~551K	~11M

Table 1: Approximate sentence and word counts for bitext and monolingual data after cleaning the data.

4 Experiments

For all of our experiments, we use OpenNMT-py (Klein et al., 2017) to handle training and build our models. For our LSTM+Attn model, we used the default parameters provided in the OpenNMT-py toolkit. For the Transformer, we used the recommended settings provided by the OpenNMT-py toolkit, with the exception of using 2 layers in the Transformer encoder and decoder instead of 6. We changed the number of Transformer layers because we found in our preliminary results on the bitext only systems that this worked well for each language direction. We did not investigate model architecture and hyperparameter tuning further, and hence we note additional work in this context could lead to better performance (Chen et al., 2018). The exact parameters are listed in the supplemental material. For our final evalua-

tion, we also perform ensemble decoding by using different checkpoints in the optimization process and further details can be found in the supplement material.

We represented the vocabulary for each language with a joint byte-pair encoding (BPE) model (Sennrich et al., 2015b) trained on all available bitext and monolingual data shared between the languages motivated by the work of Lample et al. (2018). Our BPE models were trained with the SentencePiece API and consisted of 20,000 merge operations.[3] The reader may notice that, based on our discussion in Section3, Czech and Polish may not have necessarily benefited from a joint vocabulary. This indeed may be the case, especially as our final results for Czech – Polish translation were the lowest-performing among all our final systems.

We present our findings for each respective language pair on the validation data provided by task organizers. [4] We measure performance on the validation data with the BLEU score based on the BPE representations of sentences using the script that comes with the OpenNMT-py toolkit. Note that for our test data, BLEU score is measured on the detokenized input sequences (i.e., word tokens rather than BPE).

4.1 Spanish ↔ Portuguese Results

Table 2 shows validation results with various amounts of backtranslated text, as well as infor-

---

[3]https://github.com/google/sentencepiece

[4]We provide the formal task evaluation on the TEST data in Section 4.4.

Language	Model	Bitext Only	Synth 1	Synth 2	Synth 3
Es - Pt	Transformer	50.26	47.69	52.63	**52.83**
	LSTM+Attn	48.81	46.08	41.91	
Pt - Es	Transformer	51.72	54.01	53.91	**55.64**
	LSTM+Attn	49.9	50	50.5	

	Synth 1		Synth 2		Synth 3	
	Bitext	*Synthetic*	*Bitext*	*Synthetic*	*Bitext*	*Synthetic*
Es - Pt	3,517,035	2,486,960	3,517,035	3,399,936	7,034,070	3,600,928
Pt - Es	3,517,035	1,597,856	3,517,035	1,940,736	7,034,070	4,033,824

Table 2: Validation BLEU scores from varying quality and amount of backtranslated text for both directions for Spanish – Portuguese translation.

Language	Model	Bitext Only	Synth 1	Synth 2	Synth 3
Cs - Pl	Transformer	13.5	13.59	16.04	**16.32**
	LSTM+Attn	9.91	9.36	11.24	
Pl - Cs	Transformer	13.34	13.84	15.1	**15.57**
	LSTM+Attn	10.01	9.65	10.9	

	Synth 1		Synth 2		Synth 3	
	Bitext	*Synthetic*	*Bitext*	*Synthetic*	*Bitext*	*Synthetic*
Cs - Pl	1,713,570	874,240	3,427,140	1,194,737	3,427,140	1,194,737
Pl - Cs	1,713,570	921,097	3,427,140	921,097	3,427,140	921,097

Table 3: Validation BLEU scores from varying quality and amount of backtranslated text for Czech – Polish translation.

Langauge	Model	Bitext Only	Synth 1	Synth 2	Synth 3
Hi - Ne	Transformer	6.38	6.39	7.74	8.96
	LSTM+Attn	10.71	10.93	9.89	**11.72**
Ne - Hi	Transformer	5.58	13.31	12.21	13.83
	LSTM+Attn	9.48	**14.7**	11.5	14.07

	Synth 1		Synth 2		Synth 3	
	Bitext	*Synthetic*	*Bitext*	*Synthetic*	*Bitext*	*Synthetic*
Hi - Ne	304,955	278,720	304,955	452,304	487,928	452,304
Ne - Hi	609,910	647,360	609,910	2,622,219	2,439,640	2,622,219

Table 4: Validation BLEU scores from varying quality and amount of backtranslated text for both directions of Hindi – Nepali translation.

mation on the size of the training data used for each model. Note that we did not evaluate the *Synth 3* dataset on the LSTM+Attn model which was due to our previous findings and compute resource limitations.

We found that too much of the sampled backtranslated text did not necessarily improve translation quality. Between the *Synth 1* and *Synth 2* synthetic sets, we can see a small drop of performance particularly for Spanish to Portuguese translation where we had much more available monolingual data to backtranslate. In our best performing model, part of this improvement is likely due to us doubling the number of times the bitext was looked at with respect to the synthetic sentences. This is in alignment with previous research findings on the importance of bitext over synthetic sentence pairs (Sennrich et al., 2015a; Edunov et al., 2018).

4.2 Czech ↔ Polish Translation

Table 3 shows our Czech – Polish validation BLEU scores and, like our Spanish – Portuguese systems, excludes results of the LSTM+Attn model on *Synth 3* dataset. Similar to our Spanish – Portuguese models, we found that the most useful change is doubling the amount of times the bitext is trained on. One difference with our Czech – Polish data was that we had upsampled bitext sooner having tried it on the *Synth 2* dataset instead of waiting till *Synth 3*. This discrepancy allowed us to isolate improvements on the *Synth 3* dataset to the quality of synthetic sentences instead of having result confounded with upsampling like with Spanish – Portuguese. As we see in our results from *Synth 2* to *Synth 3*, where the only difference is synthetic sentence quality, we again achieve an improvement in BLEU score.

4.3 Hindi ↔ Nepali Translation

Table 4 show's our results for Hindi – Nepali translation. As our initial models on this particular pair were performing relatively poorly, we decided to train even more frequently on the bitext compared to the amounts considered on the previous language pairs. This decision was in part motivated by the results of Edunov et al. (2018) where upsampling bitext with deterministically backtranslating data in low resource language pairs seemed most effective.

Initially we believed that maintaining a close to 1-to-1 ratio of synthetic to real bitext would always be necessary to achieve better results. For the *Synth 1* dataset, we upsampled the training corpus by 5x's for Hindi to Nepali translation and 10x's for Nepali to Hindi translation. This lead to large improvements for both models when translating from Nepali to Hindi, although it did not provide quite as noticeable improvements for translating Hindi to Nepali. The most likely explanation is the noticeable difference in the amount of synthetic sentences. At least for Nepali to Hindi this choice to maintain the 1-to-1 ratio seemed to work best for Nepali to Hindi as we achieved our best performance on *Synth 1* for this translation direction.

Although generally maintaining close to a *1-to-1 ratio* seems to be important, we note one discrepancy for Hindi to Nepali results. Between the *Synth 1* to *Synth 2* Hindi to Nepali dataset we kept the upsampled bitext fixed while increasing the

	Model	Dataset	Ensemble	Val BLEU	Test BLEU
Es - Pt	Transformer	Synth 3	True	46.41	46.1
Pt - Es	Transformer	Synth 3	True	52.4	52.3
Cs - Pl	Transformer	Synth 3	False	7.88	2.3
Pl - Cs	Transformer	Synth 3	True	8.18	6.9
Hi - Ne	LSTM + Attn	Synth 3	True	10.19	8.2
Ne - Hi	LSTM + Attn	Synth 1	True	10.66	9.1

Table 5: Final BLEU scores on the detokenized translations for the best performing models across all our experiments.

amount of synthetic sentences to closer to a *2 to 3 ratio* of real to synthetic bitext. In the Transformer case, this increase in data seemed beneficial as the BLEU score for the Transformer improved, but seemed to negatively impact the LSTM+Attn model. This raises a potential question on whether considerations of backtranslation could be model dependent. We leave investigating this question as future work.

We further found that there is a limitation to the benefit of upsampling the amount of bitext despite having even more synthetic bitext. For the *Synth 3* datasets, we again returned to maintaining a 1-to-1 ratio of real to synthetic bitext. This lead to upsampling the data 10x's for translating Hindi to Nepali, and 20x's for Nepali to Hindi. This upsampling, along with higher quality synthetic data did seem to benefit both the Transformer ad LSTM+attn model for Hindi to Nepali translation which achieved our best performances. In contrast, as the amount of synthetic data increased for Nepali to Hindi translation, we observed this to negatively impact performance compared to those on the *Synth 1* datasets. Even though the synthetic sentences were produced with a better translation systems, the *Synth 3* dataset performance was still worse.

4.4 Shared Task Evaluation

Official, shared task results for our primary submissions are presented in Table 5 along with a number of important choices we made as to which models to submit. There are a number of interesting behaviors we see in terms of performance from our validation to test sets. In the Spanish – Portuguese translation systems, we can see that the relative BLEU scores between the two directions are fairly stable. This is likely in part due to the sampling process used for backtranslation we used in comparison for the other language pairs which

used greedily decoded sentences. As for the other language pairs, although we originally hypothesized that Czech – Polish would produce better systems than Hindi – Nepali our results seem to suggest the opposite and that we might have overfit the Czech – Polish validation set compared to Hindi – Nepali translation.

5   Conclusion

Our findings are congruent with previous work showing the efficacy of backtranslation as a strategy for improving NMT systems. However, we couch this conclusion with caution. The reason is that tuning the correct amount of included synthetic data is still much dependent on the size of data at hand (which can be limited). Further work is needed before we can reach a more definitive recommendation as to how to perform backtranslation in different contexts, with varying degrees of resource availability.

Acknowledgments

Thank you to Pawel Przystupa and Arun Rajendran for helping evaluate sentence translation quality in Polish and Hindi respectively. Thank you to the organizers, particularly Dr. Marta Costa-Jussa, who helped us through the shared task. We acknowledge the support of the Natural Sciences and Engineering Research Council of Canada (NSERC) and Compute Canada (www.computecanada.ca).

References

Nepali parallel corpus. `https://web.archive.org/web/20160802134929/http://www.cle.org.pk/software/ling_resources/UrduNepaliEnglishParallelCorpus.htm`.

News commentary parallel corpus v11 (2016). `http://www.casmacat.eu/corpus/news-commentary.html`.

Mikel Artetxe, Gorka Labaka, Eneko Agirre, and Kyunghyun Cho. 2017. Unsupervised neural machine translation. *CoRR*, abs/1710.11041.

Dzmitry Bahdanau, Kyunghyun Cho, and Yoshua Bengio. 2014. Neural machine translation by jointly learning to align and translate. *arXiv e-prints*, abs/1409.0473.

Loïc Barrault, Ondřej Bojar, Marta R. Costa-jussà, Christian Federmann, Mark Fishel, Yvette Graham, Barry Haddow, Matthias Huck, Philipp Koehn, Shervin Malmasi, Christof Monz, Mathias Müller, Santanu Pal, Matt Post, and Marcos Zampieri. 2019. Findings of the 2019 conference on machine translation (wmt19). In *Proceedings of the Fourth Conference on Machine Translation, Volume 2: Shared Task Papers*, Florence, Italy. Association for Computational Linguistics.

Sabin Bhatta. 2017. Nepali news classifier. `https://github.com/sndsabin/Nepali-News-Classifier`.

Ondřej Bojar, Vojtěch Diatka, Pavel Rychlý, Pavel Straňák, Vít Suchomel, Aleš Tamchyna, and Daniel Zeman. 2014. HindMonoCorp 0.5. LINDAT/CLARIN digital library at the Institute of Formal and Applied Linguistics (ÚFAL), Faculty of Mathematics and Physics, Charles University.

Ondřej Bojar, Christian Federmann, Mark Fishel, Yvette Graham, Barry Haddow, Philipp Koehn, and Christof Monz. 2018. Findings of the 2018 conference on machine translation (WMT18). In *Proceedings of the Third Conference on Machine Translation: Shared Task Papers*, pages 272–303, Belgium, Brussels. Association for Computational Linguistics.

Mia Xu Chen, Orhan Firat, Ankur Bapna, Melvin Johnson, Wolfgang Macherey, George Foster, Llion Jones, Niki Parmar, Mike Schuster, Zhifeng Chen, Yonghui Wu, and Macduff Hughes. 2018. The best of both worlds: Combining recent advances in neural machine translation. *CoRR*, abs/1804.09849.

Christos-C. 2017. Bible corpus tools. `https://github.com/christos-c/bible-corpus-tools`.

Sergey Edunov, Myle Ott, Michael Auli, and David Grangier. 2018. Understanding back-translation at scale. *CoRR*, abs/1808.09381.

Vishal Goyal and Gurpreet Lehal. 2009. Hindi-punjabi machine transliteration system (for machine translation system).

Vishal Goyal and Gurpreet Singh Lehal. 2011. Hindi to punjabi machine translation system. In *Information Systems for Indian Languages*, pages 236–241, Berlin, Heidelberg. Springer Berlin Heidelberg.

Jan Haji, Petr Homola, and Vladislav Kubo. 2003. A simple multilingual machine translation system. In *In In: Proceedings of the MT Summit IX*.

Vu Cong Duy Hoang, Philipp Koehn, Gholamreza Haffari, and Trevor Cohn. 2018. Iterative back-translation for neural machine translation. In *Proceedings of the 2nd Workshop on Neural Machine Translation and Generation*, pages 18–24, Melbourne, Australia. Association for Computational Linguistics.

Sepp Hochreiter and Jürgen Schmidhuber. 1997. Long short-term memory. *Neural Comput.*, 9(8):1735–1780.

Guillaume Klein, Yoon Kim, Yuntian Deng, Jean Senellart, and Alexander M. Rush. 2017. OpenNMT: Open-source toolkit for neural machine translation. In *Proc. ACL*.

Philipp Koehn. 2005. Europarl: A Parallel Corpus for Statistical Machine Translation. In *Conference Proceedings: the tenth Machine Translation Summit*, pages 79–86, Phuket, Thailand. AAMT, AAMT.

Philipp Koehn. 2017. Neural machine translation. *CoRR*, abs/1709.07809.

Philipp Koehn. 2018. Global voices parallel corpus. `http://casmacat.eu/corpus/global-voices.html`.

Anjinkya Kulkarni. 2016. Ted parallel corpus. `https://github.com/ajinkyakulkarni14/TED-Multilingual-Parallel-Corpus`.

Guillaume Lample, Ludovic Denoyer, and Marc'Aurelio Ranzato. 2017. Unsupervised machine translation using monolingual corpora only. *CoRR*, abs/1711.00043.

Guillaume Lample, Myle Ott, Alexis Conneau, Ludovic Denoyer, and Marc'Aurelio Ranzato. 2018. Phrase-based & neural unsupervised machine translation. *CoRR*, abs/1804.07755.

Minh-Thang Luong, Hieu Pham, and Christopher D. Manning. 2015. Effective approaches to attention-based neural machine translation. *CoRR*, abs/1508.04025.

Benjamin Marie and Atsushi Fujita. 2018. Unsupervised neural machine translation initialized by unsupervised statistical machine translation. *CoRR*, abs/1810.12703.

Nima Pourdamghani and Kevin Knight. 2017. Deciphering related languages. In *Proceedings of the 2017 Conference on Empirical Methods in Natural Language Processing*, pages 2513–2518, Copenhagen, Denmark. Association for Computational Linguistics.

Rudolf Rosa. 2018. Plaintext wikipedia dump 2018. LINDAT/CLARIN digital library at the Institute of Formal and Applied Linguistics (ÚFAL), Faculty of Mathematics and Physics, Charles University.

Alexander Rush. 2018. The annotated transformer. http://nlp.seas.harvard.edu/2018/04/03/attention.html.

Rico Sennrich, Barry Haddow, and Alexandra Birch. 2015a. Improving neural machine translation models with monolingual data. *CoRR*, abs/1511.06709.

Rico Sennrich, Barry Haddow, and Alexandra Birch. 2015b. Neural machine translation of rare words with subword units. *CoRR*, abs/1508.07909.

Ralf Steinberger, Bruno Pouliquen, Anna Widiger, Camelia Ignat, Tomaž Erjavec, Dan Tufiş, and Dániel Varga. 2006. The JRC-Acquis: A multilingual aligned parallel corpus with 20+ languages. In *Proceedings of the Fifth International Conference on Language Resources and Evaluation (LREC'06)*, Genoa, Italy. European Language Resources Association (ELRA).

Gongbo Tang, Mathias Müller, Annette Rios, and Rico Sennrich. 2018. Why self-attention? a targeted evaluation of neural machine translation architectures. *arXiv preprint arXiv:1808.08946*.

Jrg Tiedemann. 2012. Parallel data, tools and interfaces in opus. In *Proceedings of the Eight International Conference on Language Resources and Evaluation (LREC'12)*, Istanbul, Turkey. European Language Resources Association (ELRA).

Ashish Vaswani, Noam Shazeer, Niki Parmar, Jakob Uszkoreit, Llion Jones, Aidan N. Gomez, Lukasz Kaiser, and Illia Polosukhin. 2017. Attention is all you need. *CoRR*, abs/1706.03762.

Oriol Vinyals, Łukasz Kaiser, Terry Koo, Slav Petrov, Ilya Sutskever, and Geoffrey Hinton. 2015. Grammar as a foreign language. In *Advances in neural information processing systems*, pages 2773–2781.

Bitext Word Counts

	Cs	PL	Es	PT	Hi	Ne
Europarl v9	1,4340,556	14,408,072	52,655,739	51,631,991		
Wiki Titles v1	552,136	554,080	1,577,829	1,546,923		
JRC-Acquis	21,465,448	22047909	34513834	32,601,655		
News Commentary v14			1406962	1358467		
Other					306,178	284,419
Dev	59,316	53,710	69,377	67,898	56,465	53,374
Total	36,417,456	37,063,771	90,223,741	87,206,934	362,643	337,793

Table 6: Sentence counts for each dataset after cleaning procedure.

Supplementary Material

A Data Sources

Submissions to the shared task were asked to only use the data provided data from the organizers. This included bitext from a number of different sources of varying utility to training translation systems. For the Spanish – Portuguese and Czech – Polish bitext corpora included the latest JRC-Acquis (Steinberger et al., 2006), Europarl (Koehn, 2005), News Commentary (new) data sets, as well as the Wiki Titles corpus (Bojar et al., 2018). The Hindi – Nepali corpus consists of the KDE, Ubuntu, and Gnome data sets available through Tiedemann (2012).[5] There was also a bilingual dictionary included for Hindi - Nepali language pair but we did not include it in our analysis because they were largely word to word translations. By the same argument, we likely should not have included the Wiki titles data set either as this corpus was also largely word to word translations. An interesting observation from our results is that our Czech – Polish systems ended up doing much worse then our Hindi – Nepali systems suggesting perhaps fewer, longer sentences are indeed more valuable then shorter, near word to word translations.

Additionally, the organizers provided monolingual datasets for Spanish, Portuguese, Czech and Polish. They all largely came from the same sources including the Europarl, JRC-Acquis, New Crawl, and News Commentary datasets. For Hindi and Nepali, we were allowed to use any monolingual data we found. For Hindi monolingual data, we only used the corpora collected by Bojar et al. (2014) which consisted of several million sentences collected from the internet. For Nepali, we largely used corpora provided in the WMT19 Parallel Corpus Filtering shared task which included a filtered Wikipedia dump of Nepali sentences, Global Voices Corpus (Koehn, 2018), the Nepali tagged corpus (nep), and a bible corpus (Christos-C, 2017). Externally, we found 3 additional Nepali corpora including one called the Nepali News corpus (Bhatta, 2017), the Ted Multilingual corpus (Kulkarni, 2016),and an additional Wikipedia dump corpus (Rosa, 2018).

A.1 Data Set Cleaning Information

To clean the datasets, we removed white spaces and re-tabulated the sentence pairs because of formatting errors. Additionally, we removed any pairs which were less than 4 characters long excluding leading and trailing white spaces. Table 6,8 contain the number of word counts per data set considered in this work. Table 7, 9 contain the sentence counts per dataset after the cleaning process.

---

[5]The actual Hi – Ne sources were never disclosed but were confirmed by organizers

232

Bitext Sentence Counts

	CS – PL	ES – PT	HI – NE
Europarl v9	615,115	1,791,082	
Wiki Titles v1	244,028	614,600	
JRC-Acquis	859,382	1,067,198	
News Commentary v14		46,850	
Other			65,506
Dev	3,051	3,001	3,001
Total	1,721,576	3,522,731	68,507

Table 7: Sentence counts for each dataset after cleaning procedure.

Monolingual Datasets Word Counts

	Cs	PL	Es	PT	Hi	Ne
Europarl v9	15,129,685	8,117,153	57,499,268	56,486,759		
New commentary v14	5,699,897		11,879,901	1,611,655		
News Crawl 2007 - 2018		14,348,031	1,311,839,007	183,746,078		
Hindi Monolingual					890,209,442	
Ted Multilingual						32,078
Filtered Wikipedia Dump						2,939,682
Wikipedia Dump						3,477,956
Global Voice						86,703
Nepali Tagged Corpus						51,276
Nepali NewsCorpus						4,616,548
Bible Corpus						769,344
Total	20,829,582	22,465,184	1,381,218,176	241,844,492	890,209,442	11,973,587

Table 8: Sentence counts for each dataset after cleaning procedure.

Monolingual Datasets Sentence Counts

	Cs	Pl	Es	Pt	Hi	Ne
Europarl v9	661,426	380,336	2,004,495	2,004,629		
New commentary v14	259,666		412,791	58,002		
News Crawl 2007 - 2018		814,397	43,807,883	8,299,115		
Hindi Monolingual					44,186,496	
Ted Multilingual Corpora						4,345
Filtered Wikipedia Dump						92,296
Wikipedia Dump						118,519
Global Voice						2,892
Nepali Tagged Corpus						4,287
Nepali NewsCorpus						298,151
Bible Corpus						30,547
Total	921,092	1,194,733	44,486,496	10,361,746	47,108,715	551,037

Table 9: Sentence counts for each dataset after cleaning procedure.

B   Model Information

B.1   Details on RNN with Attention Model

As mentioned in the paper, our RNN architecture is a one of several studied in the work of Luong et al. (2015). The particular model we use can be described with the following equations.

$$z_i = \text{Encoder}(x_i, z_{i-1}) \, , \; \forall i \in T \tag{1}$$

$$\text{score}(z_i, s_j) = z_i W^g s_j \ , \ \forall i \in T \tag{2}$$

$$\alpha_i = \text{softmax}(\text{score}(z_i, s_j)) \ , \ \forall i \in T \tag{3}$$

$$c = \sum_{i=1}^{T} \alpha_i * z_i \tag{4}$$

$$\tilde{s}_{j-1} = W^s[c; s_{j-1}] \tag{5}$$

$$s_j = \text{Decoder}(\tilde{s}_{j-1}, y_j, s_{j-1}) \tag{6}$$

$$p(y_j | y_{<j}, \mathbf{x}) = \text{Generator}(\tilde{s}_j) \tag{7}$$

The *encoder* and *decoder* are Long Short Term Memory (LSTM) RNNs (Hochreiter and Schmidhuber, 1997), where the encoder produces latent representations z_i for each word embedding x_i in the source sentence of length T. Equation 2 refers to *general* attention proposed by Luong et al. (2015), where W^g is learned and Equations 3 and 4 show the application of this global attention mechanism. The *decoder* LSTM then produces hidden states s_j using as input the word embedding y_j, context vector $\tilde{s}_{j-1}$, and previous hidden state s_{j-1}. The context hidden states $\tilde{s}_j$ are how the log-probability of target words are determined and are calculated on the concatenation of context c and previous hidden state s_{j-1} with learned parameters W^s.

B.2   Ensemble Decoding

As a way to further improve translation system quality, previous research has shown that an ensemble of models can improve translation performance (Koehn, 2017). For our work this meant using a window around the best performing single models that we found on the evaluation set. By window we mean we translated the test and evaluation sets with the single best model along with the n checkpoint models before, and n checkpoint models after the single best model.

For our final evaluations this involved either $n = 1$ or $n = 2$ windows around the best performing models. We did not find much difference between the two choices of n as both generally gave only minute improvements to performance. Our checkpoints were saved after every 10,000 mini-batch updates. As an example, generally we found the Transformer worked well with around 50,000 or 60,000 updates. Supposing we found 50,000 steps the best along with picking $n = 1$, we then included the checkpoint at 40,000 updates and 60,000 updates to translate the final model.

B.3   Hyperparameter Information

Table 10 contains the specific parameters for the models used in our analysis. One parameter left out of the tables was the number of updates which in OpenNMT-py is counted per batch update. For the RNN model we found 150,000 steps generally sufficient for our best performances on the Hindi – Nepali data, and at most 60,000 or 50,000 steps with the Transformer sufficient for Spanish – Portuguese and Czech – Polish even with the backtranslated data.

B.4   Tuning results

In Table 11 shows the full results of tuning our models. As a reminder, the BLEU scores were calculated on the byte-pair encoding representations of the sentences instead of the detokenized translations. This is in part why the scores, particularly in some cases, are much higher than the final validation scores reported in the paper.

LSTM Model	
Embed Dim	*500*
RNN Type	LSTM
Num Layers	2
Hidden Dim	500
Input Feeding	True
Attention	Global
Attenion Type	General
Dropout	0.3
Optimization	
Batch Size	32
Batch type	Sentences
Optimizer	SGD
Init Learning Rate	1.0
Learning Rate Schedule	
# Steps before Decay	50,000
Decay Frequency	10,000 steps
Decay Schedule	$lr_{curr} * 0.5$

Transformer	
Embed Dim	*512*
RNN Type	Transformer
Num Layers	2
Hidden Dim	512
Num Heads	8
Attenion Type	Multi-Head
Fully Connected Hidden Size	2048
Dropout	0.1
Position Encoding	Sinusoidal
Optimization	
Batch Size	4096
Batch type	Tokens
Optimizer	Adam
β_2	0.998
Init Learning Rate	2.0
Label Smoothing	0.1
Gradient Accum. Count	2
Learning Rate Schedule	
# Steps before Decay	8000
Decay Schedule	Noam

Table 10: The parameters used for the RNN Model and the Transformer model. Parameters are largely from the OpenNMT-py toolkit suggested parameters.

	Model	Decoding Type	Bitext Only	Bitext + Synth 1	Bitext + Synth 2	Bitext + Synth 3
Es - Pt	Transformer	Sampling	50.26	47.69	52.63	**52.83**
Pt - Es			51.72	54.01	53.91	**55.64**
Cs - Pl		Greedy	13.5	13.59	16.04	**16.32**
Pl - Cs			13.34	13.84	15.1	**15.57**
Hi - Ne			6.38	6.39	7.74	**8.96**
Ne - Hi			5.58	13.31	12.21	**13.83**
Es - PT	LSTM+Attn	Sampling	**48.81**	46.08	41.91	
Pt - Es			49.9	50	**50.5**	
Cs - Pl		Greedy	9.91	9.36	**11.24**	
Pl - Cs			10.01	9.65	**10.9**	
Hi - Ne			10.71	10.93	9.89	**11.72**
Ne - Hi			9.48	**14.7**	11.5	14.07

BLEU Score

Table 11: BLEU scores on the validation set. These scores were calculated on the BPE tokens.

The University of Helsinki submissions to the WMT19 similar language translation task

Yves Scherrer, Rául Vázquez, Sami Virpioja

University of Helsinki
{name.surname}@helsinki.fi

Abstract

This paper describes the University of Helsinki Language Technology group's participation in the WMT 2019 similar language translation task. We trained neural machine translation models for the language pairs Czech ↔ Polish and Spanish ↔ Portuguese. Our experiments focused on different subword segmentation methods, and in particular on the comparison of a cognate-aware segmentation method, Cognate Morfessor, with character segmentation and unsupervised segmentation methods for which the data from different languages were simply concatenated. We did not observe major benefits from cognate-aware segmentation methods, but further research may be needed to explore larger parts of the parameter space. Character-level models proved to be competitive for translation between Spanish and Portuguese, but they are slower in training and decoding.

1 Introduction

Machine translation between closely related languages is, in principle, less challenging than translation between distantly related ones. Sharing large parts of their grammars and vocabularies reduces the amount of effort needed for a machine translation system to be able to generalize (Pourdamghani and Knight, 2017). Nevertheless, and especially since the languages offered in this shared task are to some extent morphologically complex, we assume that proper subword segmentation will be beneficial for neural machine translation (NMT) performance. In particular, we aim at consistent segmentation across both related languages. While generic subword segmentation methods such as BPE (Sennrich et al., 2016), Morfessor (Creutz and Lagus, 2007; Grönroos et al., 2014), or SentencePiece (Kudo and Richardson, 2018) yield improved consistency by concatenat-

ing data from the two languages and training a single segmentation model, the Cognate Morfessor method (Grönroos et al., 2018) explicitly relies on cognate word pairs to enforce consistent segmentation.

The University of Helsinki participated in the similar language translation task for the language pairs Czech ↔ Polish and Spanish ↔ Portuguese, obtaining the following rankings:
– third (out of six) on Portuguese → Spanish,
– fourth (out of five) on Spanish → Portuguese,
– third (out of five) on Czech → Polish,
– first (out of two) on Polish → Czech.

Section 2 describes the different subword segmentation techniques we considered in our work. Section 3 details the training data and our preprocessing pipeline, whereas Section 4 presents the models we evaluated and the models we submitted, together with the results.

2 Subword segmentation

Our experiments focused on four subword segmentation methods, which are summarized shortly in this section.

2.1 Character segmentation

For similar languages, a commonly used segmentation scheme is character-level segmentation, where every character, including the space character, is considered independently. The idea of character-level machine translation for similar languages dates back to SMT times (e.g. Tiedemann, 2009). More recently, character-level NMT has shown promising results for distant languages (Costa-jussà and Fonollosa, 2016; Lee et al., 2017) as well as for similar ones (Costa-jussà et al., 2017).

The advantage of character-level models is that they do not require any other type of preprocessing such as tokenization or truecasing, and that

Proceedings of the Fourth Conference on Machine Translation (WMT), Volume 3: Shared Task Papers (Day 2) pages 236–244
Florence, Italy, August 1-2, 2019. ©2019 Association for Computational Linguistics

the segmentation algorithm is free of hyperparameters. However, character-level NMT models tend to be slow due to the greater length of the sequences.

2.2 Morfessor

Morfessor (Creutz and Lagus, 2002, 2007) is a method for unsupervised morphological segmentation. In contrast to the byte-pair encoding (BPE) algorithm widely adopted in neural machine translation (Sennrich et al., 2016), Morfessor defines a proper statistical model and applies maximum a posteriori estimation for the model parameters. The granularity of the segmentation (and thus size of the subword lexicon) is tunable by inserting a hyperparameter for varying the balance between prior and data likelihood (Kohonen et al., 2010). The prior can be considered as a encoding cost for the subword lexicon, and the likelihood as encoding cost for the corpus given the lexicon. In the first Morfessor variant, Morfessor Baseline (Creutz and Lagus, 2002; Virpioja et al., 2013), the statistical model is a unigram language model, i.e., the subword units are assumed to occur independently in words. Under this assumption, the probability of a sequence of tokens is simplified to be the product of the subword occurrence probabilities, which enables an efficient training algorithm.

The Morfessor Baseline method has been widely tested in automatic speech recognition (ASR) for various languages (Kurimo et al., 2006; Creutz et al., 2007). Smit et al. (2017) report that it performs slightly better in Finnish ASR compared to BPE. Morfessor Baseline and BPE segmentations have not been compared so far with respect to the performance in NMT. However, the Morfessor FlatCat variant (Grönroos et al., 2014) have been tested in English-to-Finnish NMT (Grönroos et al., 2017) and Turkish-to-English NMT (Ataman et al., 2017). While the former does not provide comparison to other segmentation methods, Ataman et al. (2017) report significant improvements over BPE segmentation for Turkish.

2.3 Cognate Morfessor

Cognate Morfessor (Grönroos et al., 2018) is a variant of Morfessor designed to optimize subword segmentation for two related languages so that segmentations are consistent especially for cognates, i.e., word pairs that are similar orthographically, semantically, and distributionally. Cognate Morfessor extends the cost function of Morfessor Baseline (consisting of a lexicon and corpus coding costs) by three lexicon and corpus costs: one for each language, and one for edit operations that transform the cognate forms between the languages. Having more components in the cost function means that they can also be weighted separately; the method has one hyper-parameter for the monolingual corpus costs and one for the edit operations.

The goal of Grönroos et al. (2018) was to improve the translation accuracy from a language with less parallel data (e.g. Estonian) using a related language with more data (e.g. Finnish) in the same NMT system. However, Cognate Morfessor is also a sensible segmentation approach for translating between two related languages. For cognates for which the task is similar to transliteration, the method can learn longer subword chunks that can be transliterated in one step, reducing the average number of tokens per word and improving efficiency compared to character-based models.

Moreover, it can improve the consistency of the segmentation compared to the common approach of concatenating the bilingual corpora and optimizing a joint subword lexicon for them. For example, consider that some common inflection produces a slightly different suffix for the two languages. A joint lexicon is likely to have both suffixes as subword units. Then the suffix for language A may interfere with the segmentation of stems of language B that happen to contain the same string, and vice versa. Cognate Morfessor can avoid such problems by keeping the suffixes in separate lexicons.

2.4 SentencePiece unigram model

As discussed in Section 2.2, Morfessor Baseline defines a unigram language model and determines the size of its lexicon by using a prior probability for the lexicon parameters. A more straightforward approach, first proposed by Varjokallio et al. (2013) for application in ASR, is to fix the lexicon size beforehand and try to find the set of units such that they maximize likelihood of the data for a unigram model. Another heuristic search algorithm for this problem has been proposed by Kudo (2018). In addition, he proposes a subword regularization method for NMT: The unigram language model can be used to generate multiple candidate segmentations to emulate noise and segmentation errors in the data, and thus improve the

Dataset	ES $\leftrightarrow$ PT	CS $\leftrightarrow$ PL
Europarl	1798 k	619 k
JRC-Acquis	1650 k	1311 k
Wikititles	621 k	249 k
News-Commentary	47 k	—
Total	4116 k	2178 k

Table 1: Filtered parallel dataset statistics (sentence pairs).

Direction	Back-trans.	Parallel	Total
PT $\rightarrow$ ES	3405 k	4116 k	7520 k
ES $\rightarrow$ PT	2283 k	4116 k	6399 k
PL $\rightarrow$ CS	765 k	2178 k	2943 k
CS $\rightarrow$ PL	4273 k	2178 k	6451 k

Table 2: Back-translation and training data statistics (sentence pairs).

robustness of the translation. The unigram method by Kudo (2018) is implemented in the Sentence-Piece software (Kudo and Richardson, 2018).

2.5 Byte pair encoding

In Sennrich et al. (2016) the authors adapt the byte pair encoding (BPE) data compression algorithm (Gage, 1994) to the task of word segmentation. They use the idea of the original algorithm, iteratively replacing the most frequent pair of bytes in a sequence with a single and unused byte, on word segmentation by merging characters instead of bytes. This allows for the representation of an open vocabulary through a fixed-size vocabulary of variable-length character sequences.

3 Data

The organizers of the similar languages task provided a fixed set of parallel datasets for training. We filtered these datasets minimalistically, removing empty lines, lines with more than 500 tokens, and lines with source-target length ratio higher than 9.[1] Table 1 reports the sizes of these datasets after filtering.

We trained four character-level NMT systems (see Section 4.1) with these parallel data in order to create back-translations.[2] We created

back-translations from all provided monolingual datasets, starting from the beginning of each dataset. Table 2 lists the amount of back-translated sentence pairs per translation direction and summarizes the amount of training data for the final systems.

For the models based on Morfessor and Cognate Morfessor, all data was normalized, tokenized and truecased with the Moses tools[3], while the models based on SentencePiece were only truecased in the same way. For the character-level models, a second filtering step was applied to remove sentence pairs with less than 20 or more than 1000 characters.

The development and test sets were processed analogously, and the system outputs were detokenized and detruecased with the Moses tools.

4 Experiments and results

All our NMT models are trained with the same translation toolkit – OpenNMT-py (Klein et al., 2017) –, use the same model architecture – the Transformer (Vaswani et al., 2017) –, and the same hyperparameters[4]. Training data are shuffled beforehand.

We set a threshold in terms of epochs for each translation direction, after which we stop model training.[5] This allows us to compare models fairly, as they have all seen the same amount of training data, which is not guaranteed when relying on training time or number of batches.

Results on the development set are shown in Table 3 and discussed in detail below. We report two word-level metrics, BLEU (Papineni et al., 2002) and TER (Snover et al., 2006), as well as two character-level metrics, CharacTer (Wang et al., 2016) and chrF (Popović, 2016). BLEU and chrF are computed with SacreBLEU (Post, 2018).[6] In order to quantify the impact of pre- and post-processing, we compute BLEU scores with the unprocessed reference as well as with an additional reference that has been normalized,

---

order not to impose any prior decision on preprocessing and segmentation.

[3] https://github.com/moses-smt/mosesdecoder/

[4] http://opennmt.net/OpenNMT-py/FAQ.html

[5] Note however that not all character-level models could be trained sufficiently long due to timing constraints.

[6] Signatures: *BLEU+case.mixed+numrefs.1+smooth.exp+tok.13a+version.1.2.12*; *chrF2+case.mixed+numchars.6+numrefs.1+space.False+tok.13a+version.1.2.12*

---

[1] We used the `clean-corpus-n.perl` script of the Moses SMT distribution. See https://github.com/moses-smt/mosesdecoder/

[2] We chose character-level systems for back-translation in

tokenized, truecased and de-truecased and detokenized. Surprisingly, the results with the two references may vary by up to 2 points.

Despite the large amounts of available training data, we chose hyperparameters resulting in rather small vocabulary sizes for all subword splitting schemes, ranging between 2800 and 8900 units per language pair. This choice was guided by three reasons: (1) the competitive performance of character-level models, (2) the desire to force the models to split words across languages, and to do so not only for rare words, and (3) the competitive performance of small vocabulary sizes in related problems such as historical text normalization (Tang et al., 2018).

A general finding, shared by the other participants, is that the scores on the Slavic language pair are much lower than on the Romance language pair. We assume that the Spanish–Portuguese development and test sets are built by translating directly from one language to the other, whereas the Czech–Polish development and test sets had been translated from English independently of each other, leading to much freer translations. If this hypothesis is correct, the automatic evaluation scores for Czech–Polish may in fact underestimate the real translation quality.

4.1 Character-level models

For each translation direction, we train a character-level model on the parallel data only and use this model to create back-translations for the opposing direction. Table 3 show BLEU scores on the development set under the *Characters-Initial* line.

Additional character-level models are trained with included back-translations. Due to their good overall performance, these models were selected as contrastive runs for our submissions . They are referred to as *Characters* in Table 3.

The comparison of development scores shows the impact of back-translations: depending on the translation direction, gains of 2 to 6 BLEU points are observed. There is however no clear correlation between the amount (or proportion) of added back-translations and the scores.

4.2 Morfessor Baseline models

Morfessor Baseline segmentations were trained on the concatenation of the source and language parallel training data using the Morfessor 2.0 software (Virpioja et al., 2013). We used the default

parameters[7] except that we applied log-dampening and a minimum frequency threshold of 5. We selected two corpus weight (α) values, 0.03 and 0.05, for our experiments. Models trained on the latter setting were submitted as contrastive runs.

Results are shown in Table 3. All Morfessor models outperform the character-level models on the processed reference, but not necessarily on the raw reference, suggesting that some normalization and tokenization settings might have been harmful. Unfortunately, we became aware of this issue only after submission.

The differences between the two corpus cost settings are marginal – in general, translation quality slightly improves for one direction but decreases for the other one.

4.3 Cognate Morfessor models

The Cognate Morfessor training method requires cognate word pairs as input. We follow the cognate extraction method presented in Grönroos et al. (2018) with some minor modifications:

- Word-align the parallel corpora of the two cognate languages. We use *eflomal* (Östling and Tiedemann, 2016) and symmetrize the alignment with the *grow-diag-final-and* heuristic.

- Remove all word pairs that contain punctuation or occur less than 5 times.

- Filter the list of word pairs based on Levenshtein distance. If either of the words consists of 4 or fewer characters, an exact match is required. Otherwise, a Levenshtein distance up to a third of the mean of the lengths is allowed.

- Further filter the list to remove one-to-many and many-to-one mappings, keeping only the most frequent pairing.

Cognate Morfessor models have to be trained on the full vocabulary, not only the cognate pairs.[8] Therefore, the list of cognate pairs is complemented with unaligned source-only and target-only items. This resulted in a training vocabulary of 140 227 entries for Spanish–Portuguese (63 355 cognate pairs + 35 351 monolingual ES words +

---

[7]https://morfessor.readthedocs.io/en/latest/cmdtools.html#morfessor

[8]See https://github.com/Waino/morfessor-cognates.

Model	Parameters	Train. epochs	Vocab. size	Proc ref BLEU	Raw reference BLEU	TER	cTER	chrF2
ES → PT								
Characters-Initial		5.0	562	52.46	53.90	27.00	19.61	76.72
‡ Characters		1.8	813	54.62	56.20	25.63	18.07	77.96
Morfessor Baseline	$\alpha = 0.03$	2.5	3090	57.43	56.14	26.38	18.36	77.88
‡ Morfessor Baseline	$\alpha = 0.05$	2.5	5187	56.94	55.28	28.76	18.64	77.43
Cognate Morfessor	$\alpha = 0.001$	2.5	2818	57.26	55.89	27.85	18.76	77.58
* Cognate Morfessor	$\alpha = 0.01$	2.5	3884	56.92	55.41	27.60	18.61	77.45
SentencePiece Unigram	$|V| = 5000$	2.5	7668	**59.76**	**57.79**	**25.58**	**17.55**	**78.52**
Byte Pair Encoding	$|V| = 5000$	2.5	6224	58.79	56.92	26.01	17.86	78.25
PT → ES								
Characters-Initial		4.0	562	55.38	56.20	26.35	18.68	78.24
‡ Characters		2.0	834	60.69	**62.10**	**22.61**	15.68	**81.47**
Morfessor Baseline	$\alpha = 0.03$	2.5	3090	62.78	60.77	23.30	15.81	81.32
‡ Morfessor Baseline	$\alpha = 0.05$	2.5	5187	**62.89**	60.87	23.42	**15.63**	81.34
Cognate Morfessor	$\alpha = 0.001$	2.5	2818	60.05	58.11	27.67	15.91	80.95
* Cognate Morfessor	$\alpha = 0.01$	2.5	3884	61.41	59.48	25.67	16.01	81.16
SentencePiece Unigram	$|V| = 5000$	2.5	7664	62.06	60.27	24.68	16.75	80.05
Byte Pair Encoding	$|V| = 5000$	2.5	6225	61.52	59.77	25.22	17.18	79.58
CS → PL								
Characters-Initial		11.1	419	8.51	8.64	79.16	68.33	35.97
‡ Characters		5.5	486	10.45	10.60	76.91	61.89	39.75
Morfessor Baseline	$\alpha = 0.03$	5.5	4181	**12.17**	**11.90**	75.27	61.83	40.72
‡ Morfessor Baseline	$\alpha = 0.05$	5.5	7255	11.93	11.71	76.12	62.29	40.46
Cognate Morfessor	$\alpha = 0.001$	5.5	2884	12.13	11.88	**75.24**	61.65	40.88
* Cognate Morfessor	$\alpha = 0.01$	5.5	4186	11.90	11.66	75.76	**61.00**	**40.96**
SentencePiece Unigram	$|V| = 5000$	5.5	8841	9.98	9.74	77.25	66.37	37.39
Byte Pair Encoding	$|V| = 5000$	5.5	6264	10.01	9.80	77.10	66.32	37.39
PL → CS								
Characters-Initial		11.2	419	11.14	11.34	71.06	71.77	34.39
‡ Characters		3.0	868	14.98	15.33	66.69	64.77	38.35
Morfessor Baseline	$\alpha = 0.03$	3.0	4181	15.68	15.39	66.06	64.55	39.22
‡ Morfessor Baseline	$\alpha = 0.05$	3.0	7255	15.80	15.52	66.45	64.36	39.30
Cognate Morfessor	$\alpha = 0.001$	3.0	2884	**16.02**	**15.73**	**65.82**	**64.12**	39.56
* Cognate Morfessor	$\alpha = 0.01$	3.0	4186	15.75	15.48	66.09	64.71	**39.20**
SentencePiece Unigram	$|V| = 5000$	3.0	8682	13.56	13.28	67.44	69.03	36.93
Byte Pair Encoding	$|V| = 5000$	3.0	5939	14.29	14.08	67.39	68.30	37.49

Table 3: Key figures and results of our experiments on the development set. All scores are percentage values. *Proc ref* refers to a preprocessed and postprocessed version of the reference. Primary submissions are marked with *, contrastive submissions with ‡.

Model	BLEU	TER
ES → PT		
Characters	**52.8**	**28.6**
Morfessor Baseline ($\alpha = 0.05$)	51.0	33.1
Cognate Morfessor ($\alpha = 0.01$)	52.0	29.4
PT → ES		
Characters	**59.1**	25.5
Morfessor Baseline ($\alpha = 0.05$)	58.6	**25.1**
Cognate Morfessor ($\alpha = 0.01$)	58.4	25.3
CS → PL		
Characters	5.9	88.4
Morfessor Baseline ($\alpha = 0.05$)	7.0	**87.3**
Cognate Morfessor ($\alpha = 0.01$)	**7.1**	87.4
PL → CS		
Characters	6.6	80.2
Morfessor Baseline ($\alpha = 0.05$)	**7.2**	79.6
Cognate Morfessor ($\alpha = 0.01$)	7.0	**79.4**

Table 4: Official results of the submitted systems. BLEU scores are based on *mt-eval-v13b*. The Cognate Morfessor systems are primary submissions.

41 521 monolingual PT words) and 183 706 entries for Czech–Polish (34 291 cognate pairs + 71 416 monolingual CS words + 77 999 monolingual PL words). It clearly appears that the number of cognate pairs is proportionally much lower for Czech–Polish than for Spanish–Portuguese, and further experiments will be required to quantify the impact of the cognate extraction heuristics on these results.

Cognate Morfessor has two hyper-parameters: the monolingual corpus cost (α) and the edit operation weight. We keep the recommended value of 10 for the edit operation and experiment with two values of α, 0.01 and 0.001. Moreover, we disable the word-final epsilon symbol, which had been introduced by Grönroos et al. (2018) to account for situations where two aligned words do not have the same number of morphs. An inspection of our data showed that this configuration occurred very rarely in both language families.

The *Cognate Morfessor* lines in Table 3 show the NMT results obtained with these models. Again, the choice of α value does not have a consistent impact on the results. The cognate Morfessor models consistently outperform the character models when evaluated against the processed reference, but not when evaluated against the raw ref-

erence. They obtain very similar results compared to the standard Morfessor approach.

Based on the results obtained on the development data and the ability to specifically simulate the conditions of closely related morphologically rich languages, we selected the Cognate Morfessor models with $\alpha = 0.01$ as our primary systems.

4.4 SentencePiece unigram models

We trained the segmentation models only on the available parallel datasets for each language pair, following the findings of our submission to the WMT18 translation task (Raganato et al., 2018). We specified a vocabulary size of 5,000 tokens for each language and we took advantage from the tokenizer integrated in the SentencePiece implementation (Kudo and Richardson, 2018) by training the models on non-tokenized data. We applied the same truecasing models as before.

Results reported in Table 3 show that the models trained on SentencePiece-encoded data are consistently behind the Morfessor Baseline and Cognate Morfessor ones, except for the Spanish–Portuguese translation direction. This might be caused by the choice of vocabulary size used and the selected epoch in the table. These models had not converged at the reported time, results were chosen such that different models could be comparable. Once converged, they achieved better BLEU scores, but still fall behind the Cognate Morfessor models.

4.5 Byte pair encoding models

We ran further contrastive experiments using the well-known BPE segmentation (Sennrich et al., 2016). Since the BPE models serve here only for comparison purposes, we set them to be as comparable as possible to the other experiments. For this reason, we jointly trained them on the parallel datasets for each language pair and specified them to have 5,000 merge operations. Said segmentation models were trained on previously tokenized and truecased data.

5 Test results

We submitted three systems per language pair. The official results are reproduced in Table 4. The good performance of the character-level models on Spanish–Portuguese and Portuguese–Spanish can be attributed to the absence of pre- and post-processing, as illustrated in Table 3, rather than to the underlying model architecture. The two Morfessor systems can be considered equivalent, as no clear winner emerges. The two official evaluation metrics BLEU and TER do not rank the systems consistently.

Character-level metrics were not provided by the organizers, but follow-up experiments showed that chrF2 yields the same rankings as BLEU, whereas CharacTer deviates from BLEU and TER.

The results of our submissions – and of many competitors in this shared task – lie very closely together. Before drawing any conclusions, it would therefore be useful to perform statistical significance testing. MultEval (Clark et al., 2011) provides significance scores through bootstrap resampling, but requires the output from multiple training runs of the same translation system. Unfortunately, we were not able to complete multiple training runs of our models due to time constraints.

6   Conclusions

The University of Helsinki participation focused on a single aspect of neural machine translation, namely subword segmentation. Subword segmentation that is consistent across the two languages has shown numerous benefits in translation quality, especially with respect to morphologically complex languages and for the translation (or transliteration) of rare words.

One of the investigated subword segmentation algorithms, Cognate Morfessor, was previously used successfully in a multilingual setting (translating from English to two related languages, Finnish and Estonian), and it seemed appealing to us to test this approach on similar language pairs from the Romance and Slavic language families. We contrasted the Cognate Morfessor models with three generic segmentation approaches: character segmentation, Morfessor Baseline, and SentencePiece. Our results did not show conclusive evidence that Cognate Morfessor would outperform the segmentation algorithms that did not use the information on cognates, but we have only explored a small area of the parameter space. In particular, the impact of the vocabulary size – independently of the segmentation method – on translation quality should be investigated further.

One rather surprising finding is the competitiveness of character-based models in the test evaluation for the Romance languages. This suggests that rule-based preprocessing and postprocessing

scripts such as tokenization, punctuation normalization etc. can have a significant impact on the resulting output and penalize systems that rely on these scripts. Note, however, that models with a few thousand vocabulary units are typically much more efficient than pure character-level models in terms of training and decoding.[9]

It is obvious that other aspects than subword segmentation may have a decisive impact on translation quality: parallel corpus filtering methods, the amount and quality of back-translations, as well as fine-tuning towards the target domain are known to be important factors. We have not considered these factors in our submissions, but the shared task setup provides an interesting test bed for further experiments.

Acknowledgments

We would like to thank Stig-Arne Grönroos for the help with Cognate Morfessor.

The authors gratefully acknowledge the support of the Academy of Finland through project 314062 from the ICT 2023 call on Computation, Machine Learning and Artificial Intelligence. The authors also acknowledge CSC – IT Center for Science, Finland, for computational resources.

 This work is part of the FoTran project, funded by the European Research Council (ERC) under the European Union's Horizon 2020 research and innovation programme (grant agreement No 771113).

References

Duygu Ataman, Matteo Negri, Marco Turchi, and Marcello Federico. 2017. Linguistically motivated vocabulary reduction for neural machine translation from Turkish to English. *The Prague Bulletin of Mathematical Linguistics*, 108(1):331–342.

Jonathan H. Clark, Chris Dyer, Alon Lavie, and Noah A. Smith. 2011. Better hypothesis testing for statistical machine translation: Controlling for optimizer instability. In *Proceedings of the 49th Annual Meeting of the Association for Computational Linguistics: Human Language Technologies*, pages 176–181, Portland, Oregon, USA. Association for Computational Linguistics.

---

[9]For instance, the PL $\rightarrow$ CS Cognate Morfessor model took 66 hours of training on a single GPU to complete three full epochs, whereas the character-level model took 116 hours for three epochs. Decoding of both development and test set took about 20 minutes with the former and 45 minutes with the latter.

Marta R. Costa-jussà, Carlos Escolano, and José A. R. Fonollosa. 2017. Byte-based neural machine translation. In *Proceedings of the First Workshop on Subword and Character Level Models in NLP*, pages 154–158, Copenhagen, Denmark. Association for Computational Linguistics.

Marta R. Costa-jussà and José A. R. Fonollosa. 2016. Character-based neural machine translation. In *Proceedings of the 54th Annual Meeting of the Association for Computational Linguistics (Volume 2: Short Papers)*, pages 357–361, Berlin, Germany. Association for Computational Linguistics.

Mathias Creutz, Teemu Hirsimäki, Mikko Kurimo, Antti Puurula, Janne Pylkkönen, Vesa Siivola, Matti Varjokallio, Ebru Arisoy, Murat Saraçlar, and Andreas Stolcke. 2007. Morph-based speech recognition and modeling of out-of-vocabulary words across languages. *ACM Transactions on Speech and Language Processing*, 5(1):3:1–3:29.

Mathias Creutz and Krista Lagus. 2002. Unsupervised discovery of morphemes. In *Proceedings of the ACL 2002 Workshop on Morphological and Phonological Learning*, volume 6 of *MPL '02*, pages 21–30, Stroudsburg, PA, USA. Association for Computational Linguistics.

Mathias Creutz and Krista Lagus. 2007. Unsupervised models for morpheme segmentation and morphology learning. *ACM Transactions on Speech and Language Processing*, 4(1).

Philip Gage. 1994. A new algorithm for data compression. In *C Users J*, pages 23–28.

Stig-Arne Grönroos, Sami Virpioja, and Mikko Kurimo. 2017. Extending hybrid word-character neural machine translation with multi-task learning of morphological analysis. In *Proceedings of the Second Conference on Machine Translation*, pages 296–302, Copenhagen, Denmark. Association for Computational Linguistics.

Stig-Arne Grönroos, Sami Virpioja, and Mikko Kurimo. 2018. Cognate-aware morphological segmentation for multilingual neural translation. In *Proceedings of the Third Conference on Machine Translation: Shared Task Papers*, pages 386–393, Belgium, Brussels. Association for Computational Linguistics.

Stig-Arne Grönroos, Sami Virpioja, Peter Smit, and Mikko Kurimo. 2014. Morfessor FlatCat: An HMM-based method for unsupervised and semi-supervised learning of morphology. In *Proceedings of COLING 2014, the 25th International Conference on Computational Linguistics: Technical Papers*, pages 1177–1185, Dublin, Ireland. Dublin City University and Association for Computational Linguistics.

Guillaume Klein, Yoon Kim, Yuntian Deng, Jean Senellart, and Alexander Rush. 2017. OpenNMT: Open-source toolkit for neural machine translation. In *Proceedings of ACL 2017, System Demonstrations*, pages 67–72, Vancouver, Canada. Association for Computational Linguistics.

Oskar Kohonen, Sami Virpioja, and Krista Lagus. 2010. Semi-supervised learning of concatenative morphology. In *Proceedings of the 11th Meeting of the ACL Special Interest Group on Computational Morphology and Phonology*, pages 78–86, Uppsala, Sweden. Association for Computational Linguistics.

Taku Kudo. 2018. Subword regularization: Improving neural network translation models with multiple subword candidates. In *Proceedings of the 56th Annual Meeting of the Association for Computational Linguistics (Volume 1: Long Papers)*, pages 66–75, Melbourne, Australia. Association for Computational Linguistics.

Taku Kudo and John Richardson. 2018. SentencePiece: A simple and language independent subword tokenizer and detokenizer for neural text processing. In *Proceedings of the 2018 Conference on Empirical Methods in Natural Language Processing: System Demonstrations*, pages 66–71, Brussels, Belgium. Association for Computational Linguistics.

Mikko Kurimo, Antti Puurula, Ebru Arisoy, Vesa Siivola, Teemu Hirsimäki, Janne Pylkkönen, Tanel Alumäe, and Murat Saraclar. 2006. Unlimited vocabulary speech recognition for agglutinative languages. In *Proceedings of the 2006 Human Language Technology Conference of the North American Chapter of the Association of Computational Linguistics (HLT-NAACL)*, HLT-NAACL '06, pages 487–494, Stroudsburg, PA, USA. Association for Computational Linguistics.

Jason Lee, Kyunghyun Cho, and Thomas Hofmann. 2017. Fully character-level neural machine translation without explicit segmentation. *Transactions of the Association for Computational Linguistics*, 5:365–378.

Robert Östling and Jörg Tiedemann. 2016. Efficient word alignment with Markov Chain Monte Carlo. *Prague Bulletin of Mathematical Linguistics*, 106:125–146.

Kishore Papineni, Salim Roukos, Todd Ward, and Wei-Jing Zhu. 2002. Bleu: a method for automatic evaluation of machine translation. In *Proceedings of 40th Annual Meeting of the Association for Computational Linguistics*, pages 311–318, Philadelphia, Pennsylvania, USA. Association for Computational Linguistics.

Maja Popović. 2016. chrF deconstructed: beta parameters and n-gram weights. In *Proceedings of the First Conference on Machine Translation*, pages 499–504, Berlin, Germany. Association for Computational Linguistics.

Matt Post. 2018. A call for clarity in reporting BLEU scores. In *Proceedings of the Third Conference on Machine Translation: Research Papers*, pages 186–191, Belgium, Brussels. Association for Computational Linguistics.

Nima Pourdamghani and Kevin Knight. 2017. Deciphering related languages. In *Proceedings of the 2017 Conference on Empirical Methods in Natural Language Processing*, pages 2513–2518, Copenhagen, Denmark. Association for Computational Linguistics.

Alessandro Raganato, Yves Scherrer, Tommi Nieminen, Arvi Hurskainen, and Jörg Tiedemann. 2018. The University of Helsinki submissions to the WMT18 news task. In *Proceedings of the Third Conference on Machine Translation: Shared Task Papers*, pages 488–495, Belgium, Brussels. Association for Computational Linguistics.

Rico Sennrich, Barry Haddow, and Alexandra Birch. 2016. Neural machine translation of rare words with subword units. In *Proceedings of the 54th Annual Meeting of the Association for Computational Linguistics (Volume 1: Long Papers)*, pages 1715–1725, Berlin, Germany. Association for Computational Linguistics.

Peter Smit, Sami Virpioja, and Mikko Kurimo. 2017. Improved subword modeling for WFST-based speech recognition. In *Proc. Interspeech 2017*, pages 2551–2555.

Matthew Snover, Bonnie Dorr, Richard Schwartz, Linnea Micciulla, and John Makhoul. 2006. A study of translation edit rate with targeted human annotation. In *Proceedings of Association for Machine Translation in the Americas*.

Gongbo Tang, Fabienne Cap, Eva Pettersson, and Joakim Nivre. 2018. An evaluation of neural machine translation models on historical spelling normalization. In *Proceedings of the 27th International Conference on Computational Linguistics*, pages 1320–1331, Santa Fe, New Mexico, USA. Association for Computational Linguistics.

Jörg Tiedemann. 2009. Character-based PSMT for closely related languages. In *Proceedings of EAMT 2009*, page 12–19, Barcelona, Spain.

Matti Varjokallio, Mikko Kurimo, and Sami Virpioja. 2013. Learning a subword vocabulary based on unigram likelihood. In *IEEE Automatic Speech Recognition and Understanding Workshop, (ASRU 2013), Olomouc, Czech Republic, December 8-12, 2013*.

Ashish Vaswani, Noam Shazeer, Niki Parmar, Jakob Uszkoreit, Llion Jones, Aidan N Gomez, Ł ukasz Kaiser, and Illia Polosukhin. 2017. Attention is all you need. In I. Guyon, U. V. Luxburg, S. Bengio, H. Wallach, R. Fergus, S. Vishwanathan, and R. Garnett, editors, *Advances in Neural Information Processing Systems 30*, pages 5998–6008. Curran Associates, Inc.

Sami Virpioja, Peter Smit, Stig-Arne Grönroos, and Mikko Kurimo. 2013. Morfessor 2.0: Python implementation and extensions for Morfessor Baseline. Report 25/2013 in Aalto University publication series SCIENCE + TECHNOLOGY, Department of Signal Processing and Acoustics, Aalto University, Helsinki, Finland.

Weiyue Wang, Jan-Thorsten Peter, Hendrik Rosendahl, and Hermann Ney. 2016. CharacTer: Translation edit rate on character level. In *Proceedings of the First Conference on Machine Translation*, pages 505–510, Berlin, Germany. Association for Computational Linguistics.

Dual Monolingual Cross-Entropy-Delta Filtering of Noisy Parallel Data

Amittai Axelrod   **Anish Kumar**   **Steve Sloto**

DiDi AI Labs

Los Angeles, CA

`amittai@didiglobal.com`

Abstract

We introduce a purely monolingual approach to filtering for parallel data from a noisy corpus in a low-resource scenario. Our work is inspired by Junczys-Dowmunt (2018), but we relax the requirements to allow for cases where no parallel data is available. Our primary contribution is a dual monolingual cross-entropy delta criterion modified from Cynical data selection (Axelrod, 2017), and is competitive (within 1.8 BLEU) with the best bilingual filtering method when used to train SMT systems. Our approach is featherweight, and runs end-to-end on a standard laptop in three hours.

1 Introduction

The 2018 WMT shared task on parallel corpus filtering (Koehn et al., 2018) required participants to select subcorpora of 10M and 100M words from an extremely noisy 1B word German-English parallel corpus from Paracrawl (Buck and Koehn, 2016). These subcorpora were then used to train machine translation systems, and evaluated on held-out test sets. The best submission (Junczys-Dowmunt, 2018) comprised:

1. a filter based on language ID

2. a dual conditional cross-entropy filter to determine whether the halves of a sentence pair were of roughly equal translation probability

3. a cross-entropy difference filter to prioritize in-domain sentence pairs

The 2019 WMT shared task on parallel corpus filtering (Koehn et al., 2019) was set for low-resource conditions, with the goal of translating Wikipedia texts both Sinhala-to-English and Nepali-to-English (Guzmán et al., 2019).

We participated only in the Sinhala-English track, basing our system on that of Junczys-Dowmunt (2018) but extensively modified for the

2019 low-resource scenario. As compared to their work, ours comprised: a minor upgrade of their first element, a relaxation of the second, a modern replacement for the third, and an additional length-based filter. The resulting entirely monolingual pipeline to filter noisy parallel data proved to be competitive with the other multilingual entries when used to train downstream SMT systems.

2 Related Work

We now describe the Junczys-Dowmunt (2018) system that was the inspiration for ours.

2.1 2018 Language ID Filter

The first feature used the `langid` Python module to classify the language of each half of each sentence pair to a language. Any sentence pair where either half was classified as being in an incorrect language was removed, and sentence pairs with correctly-classified halves were kept.

2.2 2018 Dual Conditional Cross-Entropy

The dual conditional cross-entropy filtering method rewards sentence pairs with minimal *symmetric translation disagreement*. That is the difference in average (per-word) conditional cross-entropy of the sentence pair halves:

$$|H_{F \to E}(s_E|s_F) - H_{E \to F}(s_F|s_E)|$$

For a sentence pair (s_E, s_F), the per-word conditional cross-entropy $H_{F \to E}(s_E|s_F)$ of one half of the sentence pair is computed by a translation model $F \to E$, and the corresponding $H_{E \to F}(s_F|s_E)$ of the other half of the sentence pair is computed by a translation model in the opposite direction. The two translation models are trained in inverse directions on the same parallel corpus, so they should be equally expressive.

However, the difference in translation scores does not take into account whether the scores

Proceedings of the Fourth Conference on Machine Translation (WMT), Volume 3: Shared Task Papers (Day 2) pages 245–251
Florence, Italy, August 1-2, 2019. ©2019 Association for Computational Linguistics

are good or not. A perfectly translated sentence pair where the translation models agree perfectly would have the same score as a poorly translated sentence pair where the translation models also agree. This same weakness is found in the cross-entropy difference criterion (Moore and Lewis, 2010) on which the conditional cross-entropy difference is based. To force the better sentence pair to have a lower feature score than the other pair, Junczys-Dowmunt (2018) add a term consisting of the average per-word conditional cross-entropy of the two halves. Worse sentences have higher entropy, so a score of 0 remains ideal. The equation for the dual conditional cross-entropy is thus:

$$h(s_E, s_F) = | \underset{F \to E}{H}(s_E|s_F) - \underset{E \to F}{H}(s_F|s_E) |$$
$$+ \frac{1}{2} \big(\underset{F \to E}{H}(s_E|s_F) + \underset{E \to F}{H}(s_F|s_E) \big) \tag{1}$$

The first term is the translation disagreement, and the second term is the average entropy. The score is exponentiated so that good sentence pairs have a feature score of 1, and bad sentence pairs have a score of 0:

$$f(s_E, s_F) = e^{-h(s_E, s_F)}$$

In describing their approach, Junczys-Dowmunt (2018) criticize the Moore and Lewis (2010) cross-entropy difference method for "missing" an adequacy component. This is misguided, as the Moore-Lewis method was originally designed for language modeling and was only later repurposed for machine translation. In MT, the two halves of a sentence pair might be fluent but not express the same thing, and so the notion of *adequacy* is used to describe how well the halves correspond in meaning. In language modeling, there is no such thing as a sentence pair, and there should not be much doubt that a sentence rather adequately (and tautologically) manages to express exactly that which it *does* express. It would be more proper to state that the omission of adequacy is a weakness of the bilingual extension of Moore-Lewis to machine translation by Axelrod et al. (2011).

2.3 2018 Moore-Lewis Filtering

The third and final feature in the best 2018 system was a monolingual (English) cross-entropy difference (Moore and Lewis, 2010) score:

$$H_{in}(s_E) - H_{out}(s_E) \tag{2}$$

The cross-entropies H were computed using language models trained on 1M sentences of WMT news data as in-domain, and 1M random Paracrawl sentences as out-of-domain data. This is an ideal setup for cross-entropy difference, as Equation 2 fundamentally assumes that the two corpora are as different as possible.

3 Cynical Data Selection

Both the relaxation of the dual conditional cross-entropy filter and our replacement of the cross-entropy difference filter are based on Cynical data selection (Axelrod, 2017), described below. The Moore-Lewis cross-entropy difference approach fundamentally views the training data as being either *in*-domain or *out/general*-domain. This stark distinction is not realistic. Cynical data selection relaxes that assumption, and starts with one corpus of *representative* data (REPR), and one of *available* data (AVAIL). The representative data is exactly that: representative of what we would like to be translating. The *available* data is similarly the data pool from which one can select a subcorpus. No relationship is assumed between the *representative* and *available* corpora, nor between the domains they cover.

The algorithm incrementally grows a corpus of sentences, selecting from AVAIL, in order to better model REPR. First, it estimates the perplexity of a language model trained on the already-selected data and evaluated on the REPR corpus. Next, for each sentence still available, it estimates the change in that perplexity (or entropy, ΔH) that would result from adding it as a new sentence to the LM training data and re-training the LM (Sethy et al., 2006). The sentence with the lowest cross-entropy delta is removed from AVAIL, added to the selected pile, and the process repeats. Identifying the next single sentence to add is $O(n^2)$ and not computationally practical, but it <u>is</u> efficient to find the best word v in the vocabulary V_{REPR} to add once to the selected data. From there, it is now practical to pick the best sentence still in AVAIL that contains that word. The $n + 1^{th}$ iteration, after selecting n sentences, is:

1. Find the single word $v \in V_{repr}$ that would most lower the entropy (evaluated on REPR) of a language model, trained on the n already-selected sentences plus the one-word sentence "v".

2. Find the single sentence $s \in$ AVAIL containing v that would (also) most lower the entropy (evaluated on REPR) of a language model trained on the n sentences plus s.

3. Remove s from AVAIL, update the language model with the count c of all words in s, and add s to the selected sentences.

The cross-entropy delta ΔH is the change in the entropy of a language model, evaluated on a constant test set, after adding a new entry to the language model's training corpus. This is straightforward to compute, as there is a entropic length penalty for increasing the size of the training corpus, and an entropy gain for adding new information to the training set. This was first formulated by Sethy et al. (2006) as "relative entropy", and clarified by Axelrod (2017) as:

$$
\Delta H_{n \to n+1} = H_{n+1} - H_n
$$

$$
\Delta H_{n \to n+1} = \underbrace{\log \frac{W_n + w_{n+1}}{W_n}}_{Penalty}
$$

$$
+ \underbrace{\sum_{v \in V_{\text{REPR}}} \frac{C_{\text{REPR}}(v)}{W_{\text{REPR}}} \log \frac{C_n(v)}{C_n(v) + c_{n+1}(v)}}_{Gain}
$$

$$(3)$$

The penalty term depends on the length w_{n+1} of the $n + 1^{th}$ line, and the size in words W_n of the already-selected data. The gain term depends on the empirical probability of each word v in the REPR corpus, and then the count C_n of the word so far in the n selected lines, and the count c_{n+1} of the word in the $n + 1^{th}$ line.

4 Sinhala-English Data

The 2019 iteration of the shared task focused exclusively on filtering a noisy parallel corpus for low-resource language pairs, and had considerably less data than the 2018 German-English task. Table 1 shows that only 645k lines of parallel Sinhala-English were provided in total– less than the small 1M German-English sentence pair subsets used to train the dual NMT engines for the scoring function of Junczys-Dowmunt (2018).

4.1 Data

The 2019 Si-En parallel data was drawn from conversations and technical manuals, unlike the wiki-based evaluation data. Larger and more relevant,

Corpus	Lines	Tok (Si)	Tok (En)
Open Subtitles	601,164	3.4M	3.6M
Ubuntu	45,617	175k	151k
Total	646,781	3.5M	3.7M

Table 1: Parallel Data for Sinhala-English

yet monolingual, corpora were provided from both Wikipedia and Common Crawl, detailed in Table 2.

Corpus	Lines	Tokens
Sinhala Wikipedia	156k	4.7M
English Wikipedia	67.8M	1.9B
Sinhala Common Crawl	5.2M	110M
English Common Crawl	380M	8.9B
English Subset Wikipedia	150k	5.5M
English Subset Common Crawl	6M	123M

Table 2: Corpus statistics for provided monolingual data in Sinhala and English, and an English subset of comparable size to the Sinhala data.

The provided monolingual English data was several orders of magnitude larger than the Sinhala data, which would have made it difficult to create equally strong (or weak) monolingual models used in this work. We therefore assembled a monolingual English corpus comparable in size and content to the Sinhala one by randomly selecting 150k lines from Wikipedia and 6M lines from Common Crawl. We used SentencePiece (Kudo and Richardson, 2018), with `model_type=word`, to preprocess the Sinhala and English sides separately, producing a fairly word-like vocabulary of 100k subwords for each language. Each SentencePiece model was trained on 1M lines of monolingual data: 150k Wiki + 850k Common Crawl.

5 Our Submission

We used the feature framework from Junczys-Dowmunt (2018) as the basis for ours. For each sentence pair (s_{Si}, s_{En}) in the noisy corpus, we computed a final score $f(s_{Si}, s_{En}) \in [0, 1]$ by multiplying each of the individual feature scores for the sentence pair:

$$
f(s_{Si}, s_{En}) = \prod_i f_i(s_{Si}, s_{En}) \qquad (4)
$$

The feature scores, and therefore the final score, all had the same range of $[0, 1]$. For evaluation, the lines were sorted from highest to lowest over-all score, and then selected in that order until the number of selected English words reached the evaluation threshold. Any feature score being 0 effectively removed that sentence pair from consideration. The selected subsets were then submitted for evaluation by the task organizers. The following are the monolingual features we used to score the noisy parallel data.

5.0 Length Ratio Feature

We added one feature as compared to Junczys-Dowmunt (2018), based on the length ratio of the two halves of the sentence pair, penalizing sentence pairs with sides of disparate lengths. The provided clean, parallel, training data in Table 1 is inconclusive regarding the expected Si-to-En length ratio, as one of the parallel corpora had more English tokens than Sinhala, and the other had the reverse. The ratios were approximately inverses, so we set the desired ratio to be 1 and penalized sentence pair scores according to how divergent the parallel segment's length ratio was from 1. A sentence pair with a length ratio within two orders of magnitude, *i.e.* $e^{-2} < \frac{si}{en} < e^2$, or $|ln(\frac{si}{en})| < 2$, received a feature score of 1, or no penalty. The feature score was set to 0.5 if $2 < |ln(\frac{si}{en})| < 3$. For $3 < |ln(\frac{si}{en})|$ the feature was 0.35. For pairs where both segments contained fewer than six tokens, we applied less strict penalties as ratios are more likely to vary with shorter segment lengths. For such pairs, we assigned a score of 0.5 if the ratio is greater than 4 orders of magnitude, 0.75 if between 3 and 4, and 0.9 if within 2-3 factors. We also observed that large numbers of non-parallel Paracrawl sentence pairs contained mostly numbers on one side. Any sentence pair where at least 15% of either half was only numerals received a score of 0.

5.1 Language ID Feature

As with the 2018 task, a considerable quantity of the provided Paracrawl data was not in the correct language. Following Junczys-Dowmunt (2018), we classified the halves of the sentence pair using the `langid` Python module and assigned 0 to any sentence pair with an incorrectly-labeled half. If the correct languages were selected, then the feature value was the product of the `langid` confidence scores. Inspecting the filter output showed that it was not strong enough. The `langid` classification had many false positives, as well as

source-side (Sinhala) sentences that were mixed with a significant amount of English. The shared task's hard limit on the number of selectable words made it important to minimize the amount of English on the Sinhala side. The languages have non-overlapping writing scripts, so it was easy to detect erroneous characters. We therefore multiplied the lang_id score by the proportion of characters (excluding numerals and punctuation) in each sentence that belong to the correct Unicode block, resulting in an overall language ID feature that slightly extends the original.

5.2 Dual Monolingual Cross-Entropy Deltas

Junczys-Dowmunt (2018) trained MT systems on clean parallel data for the 2018 task, but used only the translation probability of each to score the Paracrawl data and not the translation output itself. The motivation for training the dual NMT systems on the same parallel corpus was to ensure that the models would have similar BLEU scores and translation probabilities for the halves of a truly parallel sentence pair.

We did not have enough good parallel data for Sinhala and English, which ruled out training models on identical information. However, perhaps the translation models themselves were not inherently necessary as long as similar scores could be obtained. Language models require less training data than an MT engine to be reliable, and can also output an average per-word probability for a sentence– and we were provided with good monolingual data. We set out to construct language models with similar *amounts* of information hoping they might have similar perplexities for the halves of a parallel sentence pair, and different perplexities for a non-parallel pair. The result was a relaxation of the dual conditional translation cross-entropy feature that only required monolingual data, and used equal relative informativeness instead of equal translation probability.

5.2.1 Setting Up Language Models

N-gram language models in different languages are not comparable. Differences in morphology can lead to significant differences in word counts, data sparsity, and thus how well a fixed model architecture can represent the language. Instead of multilingual word embeddings using sparse data (Artetxe and Schwenk, 2019), we simply used SentencePiece to force the Sinhala and English corpora to have the same size vocabulary (100k subwords). First, we hoped a standard lexicon size would mitigate the effect of morphology differences affecting sentence length and word sparsity. Secondly, we hoped it would encourage language models trained on similar– but not parallel– English and Sinhala texts to have similar perplexities over each half of a parallel test set.

This would mean the two LMs had similar estimates of how much information is in each half of the parallel data. The two halves of the parallel corpus presumably contain the same amount of actual information, but two LMs would only come up with the same estimate if they themselves contained comparable amounts of information, even if they did not the same information.

To test this, we trained 4-gram language models using KenLM (Heafield, 2011) on the Sinhala monolingual data and the restricted-size English data in Table 2, both unprocessed and after tokenizing with SentencePiece. The models were evaluated on the provided parallel `valid` and `test` sets. Table 3 shows that, indeed, forcing English and Sinhala LMs to have identical vocabulary sizes was enough to obtain nearly identical perplexities on the halves of a parallel corpus, even though the language models were trained on similar but not parallel data.

Corpus	valid	test
Sinhala, untok	1,759.8	1,565.9
English, untok	1,069.2	985.3
Sinhala, tok=SP	**320.5**	**299.2**
English, tok=SP	**302.5**	**292.7**

Table 3: Using SentencePiece to equalize LM perplexities in different languages on the dev sets.

5.2.2 Parallel Scoring with Monolingual LMs

Wse used the "greedy cross-entropy delta" term from Cynical data selection in a novel way: to score each side of the Paracrawl data as a memoryless stream of text. In this setup, we had a language model trained on the monolingual Wikipedia data, which is the REPR corpus, and representative of the kind of data the organizers will evaluate on. We compute the ΔH of adding each sentence s in Paracrawl to the REPR corpus, retraining a LM on REPR+s, and recomputing the perplexity on REPR corpus. After computing all of the ΔH scores for the Paracrawl data, cynical data selection would normally extract the best one, in-

corporate it into the training set, and iterate. Instead, we modified the public implementation[1] of Cynical data selection to not update anything, and the scoring is done in a single pass as done by Sethy et al. (2006).

The difference between a LM perplexity and the ΔH score is that the LM quantifies the likelihood, and the ΔH score quantifies informativeness. The ΔH score estimates, for a fixed REPR corpus: does this next line contain any information at all about REPR that we do not already know? A negative score would indicate a estimated decrease in entropy, so adding this line should improve a model trained on the selected data.

We constructed monolingual Sinhala and English LMs with similar perplexities on a parallel test set that resembled the task evaluation, so we hoped that sentences with equal ΔH scores according to these two models could be parallel. Or, at least, that sentences with disparate ΔH scores would be deemed not-parallel, and filtered out.

One could simply replace the translation system conditional cross-entropies in Equation 1 with the cross-entropies from the two comparable language models just described. However, that would only characterize the fluency, without any sense of the content. It is not clear whether identical perplexities or identical ΔH scores is a better indicator of "these sentences are parallel": being equally likely and being equally informative are each positive indicators. The goal of the shared task was to assemble the parallel corpus that produced the best downstream MT system for Wikipedia test; prioritizing informative sentences seemed more important here than prioritizing likely ones. Our version of Equation 1 thus used Equation 3's ΔH scores, dual monolingual cross-entropy deltas, for each sentence pair (s_{Si}, s_{En}), instead of dual bilingual conditional cross-entropies:

$$|\Delta H_{En}(s_{En}|\text{REPR}_{En}) - \Delta H_{Si}(s_{Si}|\text{REPR}_{Si})|$$
$$+\frac{1}{2}\left(\Delta H_{En}(s_{En}|\text{REPR}_{En}) + \Delta H_{Si}(s_{Si}|\text{REPR}_{Si})\right)$$
$$(5)$$

This was exponentiated to be in the range of $[0, 1]$.

5.3 Dual Monolingual Cynical Data Selection

The final feature from (Junczys-Dowmunt, 2018) was a monolingual Moore-Lewis score, intended to bias the filtering towards in-domain news data.

---

[1] `github.com/amittai/cynical`

However, the Moore-Lewis method for data selection has some notable flaws, as described in Axelrod (2017). The biggest is that it has no sense of *sufficiency*: while it is not helpful to see an identical sentence pair 10,000 times, the Moore-Lewis criterion will assign the same score to all copies. Cynical data selection selects sentences only if they contribute <u>new</u> information to the set of sentences already selected, and has previously been shown to help domain adaptation in SMT (Santamaría and Axelrod, 2017) and NMT (Zhang et al., 2019), and a variation of it was used for the 2018 corpus filtering task (Erdmann and Gwinnup, 2018). As a side effect, Cynical selection eliminates the need for explicit vocabulary coverage features that were used in the previous shared task (Lo et al., 2018; Azpeitia et al., 2018).

For each language, we used Cynical data selection to rank the sentences in the noisy corpus. We set the Paracrawl data to be the *Available* set, and the clean monolingual Wikipedia data to be the *Representative* set. This selects the subset of Paracrawl that best models monolingual Wikipedia. The re-ranked Paracrawl corpus was then scored by converting the Cynical ranking to a percentage and subtracted from 1. Thus the sentence selected as number 15,000 out of 3M would have a score of $1 - \frac{15k}{3M}$, and 1 would be the best score and 0 the worst. The ranking score for a sentence pair was the product of the monolingual rank scores for each half.

tio feature was overly complicated and not aggressive enough; the Si→En NMT systems tended to stutter to produce English sentences of appropriate length. Discarding anything with a length difference > 20% would probably have been better.

The official evaluation results were a pleasant surprise. Table 4 shows the top and bottom scores for each evaluation category, providing context for our submission. We were in the bottom third of the SMT systems, yet within 1.8 BLEU of the best system at 1M, and 1.3 BLEU of the best system at 5M. This is rather competitive for a gratuitously-monolingual approach to a bilingual task!

Our submitted system, like roughly 30% of the submissions, was not suitable for filtering data for a low-resource NMT pipeline. However, the NMT systems trained on 1M words were several BLEU points better than systems trained on 5M words, so training an NMT system on small amounts of data is unpredictable. Better feature engineering would certainly help.

System	1M SMT	1M NMT	5M SMT	5M NMT
Rank 1	4.27	6.39	4.94	4.44
DiDi	2.53	0.19	3.70	0.20
Rank 10	0.92	0.03	2.73	0.10

Table 4: Bleu scores on `test` for systems trained on subsets with 1M and 5M English words of the noisy Paracrawl data.

6 Results and Discussion

Our submission was entirely monolingual, and used parallel data only to sanity-check the language models trained in Section 5.2.1. Furthermore, all of the preprocessing, language modeling, data selection, and feature computation in this work was run on a laptop. As such, we had no expectations for whether our method would be effective compared against bilingual or multilingual methods trained for days on GPU machines.

We tried to predict results using NMT systems after the submission deadline, thanks to the scripts, code, and standard settings provided by the organizers, but all of our system BLEU scores (Papineni et al., 2002) were under 0.20 and worse than a random baseline. While the evaluation campaign cutoff was set to be 1M or 5M English words, the Sinhala sides of our filtered corpus contained only 740k and 3.6M words respectively. Our length ra-

7 Conclusion

We presented a purely monolingual method, based on cynical data selection (Axelrod, 2017), for filtering noisy parallel data. Our approach is a relaxation of the dual conditional cross-entropy method of Junczys-Dowmunt (2018), that does require any parallel data. As secondary contributions, we have used Cynical data selection in a streaming scenario for the first time, and used relative *informativeness* to judge the relationship between the halves of a sentence pair. While our method does not outperform most parallel approaches, it is competitive, and more suitable for scenarios with little or no parallel data. Furthermore, our work is also undemanding of computational resources, as it ran end-to-end on a single laptop in a couple hours, and should integrate well into a feature ensemble for real-world deployment.

References

Mikel Artetxe and Holger Schwenk. 2019. Margin-based Parallel Corpus Mining with Multilingual Sentence Embeddings. *ACL (Association for Computational Linguistics).*

Amittai Axelrod. 2017. Cynical Selection of Language Model Training Data. *arXiv [cs.CL].*

Amittai Axelrod, Xiaodong He, and Jianfeng Gao. 2011. Domain Adaptation Via Pseudo In-Domain Data Selection. *EMNLP (Empirical Methods in Natural Language Processing).*

Andoni Azpeitia, Thierry Etchegoyhen, and Eva Martínez garcia. 2018. STACC, OOV Density and N-gram Saturation: Vicomtech's Participation in the WMT 2018 Shared Task on Parallel Corpus Filtering. *WMT Conference on Statistical Machine Translation.*

Christian Buck and Philipp Koehn. 2016. Findings of the WMT 2016 Bilingual Document Alignment Shared Task. *WMT Conference on Statistical Machine Translation.*

Grant Erdmann and Jeremy Gwinnup. 2018. Coverage and Cynicism: The AFRL Submission to the WMT 2018 Parallel Corpus Filtering Task. *WMT Conference on Statistical Machine Translation.*

Francisco Guzmán, Peng-Jen Chen, Myle Ott, Juan Pino, Guillaume Lample, Philipp Koehn, Vishrav Chaudhary, and Marc'Aurelio Ranzato. 2019. Two New Evaluation Datasets for Low-Resource Machine Translation: Nepali-English and Sinhala-English. *arXiv [cs.CL].*

Kenneth Heafield. 2011. KenLM : Faster and Smaller Language Model Queries. *WMT (Workshop on Statistical Machine Translation).*

Marcin Junczys-Dowmunt. 2018. Dual Conditional Cross-Entropy Filtering of Noisy Parallel Corpora. *WMT Conference on Statistical Machine Translation.*

Philipp Koehn, Francisco Guzmán, Vishrav Chaudhary, and Juan Pino. 2019. Findings of the WMT 2019 Shared Task on Parallel Corpus Filtering for Low-Resource Conditions. *WMT Conference on Statistical Machine Translation.*

Philipp Koehn, Huda Khayrallah, Kenneth Heafield, and Mikel Forcada. 2018. Findings of the WMT 2018 Shared Task on Parallel Corpus Filtering. *WMT Conference on Statistical Machine Translation.*

Taku Kudo and John Richardson. 2018. SentencePiece: A Simple and Language Independent Subword Tokenizer and Detokenizer for Neural Text Processing. *EMNLP (Empirical Methods in Natural Language Processing) System Demonstrations.*

Chi-kiu Lo, Michel Simard, Darlene Stewart, Samuel Larkin, Cyril Goutte, and Patrick Littell. 2018. Accurate Semantic Textual Similarity for Cleaning Noisy Parallel Corpora using Semantic Machine Translation Evaluation Metric: The NRC Supervised Submissions to the Parallel Corpus Filtering task. *WMT Conference on Statistical Machine Translation.*

Robert C Moore and William D Lewis. 2010. Intelligent Selection of Language Model Training Data. *ACL (Association for Computational Linguistics).*

Kishore Papineni, Salim Roukos, Todd Ward, and Weijing Zhu. 2002. BLEU: A Method for Automatic Evaluation of Machine Translation. *ACL (Association for Computational Linguistics).*

Lucía Santamaría and Amittai Axelrod. 2017. Data Selection with Cluster-Based Language Difference Models and Cynical Selection. *IWSLT (International Workshop on Spoken Language Translation).*

Abhinav Sethy, Panayiotis G. Georgiou, and Shrikanth Narayanan. 2006. Text Data Acquisition for Domain-Specific Language Models. *EMNLP (Empirical Methods in Natural Language Processing).*

Xuan Zhang, Pamela Shapiro, Gaurav Kumar, Paul McNamee, Marine Carpuat, and Kevin Duh. 2019. Curriculum Learning for Domain Adaptation in Neural Machine Translation. *NAACL (North American Association for Computational Linguistics).*

NRC Parallel Corpus Filtering System for WMT 2019

Gabriel Bernier-Colborne
NRC-CNRC
National Research Council Canada
2107, chemin de la Polytechnique
Montreal, Quebec H3T 1J4, Canada
Gabriel.Bernier-Colborne@nrc-cnrc.gc.ca

Chi-kiu Lo
NRC-CNRC
National Research Council Canada
1200 Montreal Road
Ottawa, Ontario K1A 0R6, Canada
Chikiu.Lo@nrc-cnrc.gc.ca

Abstract

We describe the National Research Council Canada team's submissions to the parallel corpus filtering task at the Fourth Conference on Machine Translation.

1 Introduction

The WMT19 shared task on parallel corpus filtering was essentially the same as last year's edition (Koehn et al., 2018b), except under low-resource conditions: the language pairs were Nepali-English and Sinhala-English instead of German-English, and the data participants were allowed to use was constrained. The aim of the challenge was to identify high-quality sentence pairs in a noisy corpus crawled from the web using ParaCrawl (Koehn et al., 2018a), in order to train machine translation (MT) systems on the clean data. Specifically, participating systems must produce a score for each sentence pair in the test corpora, this score indicating the quality of that pair. Then samples containing 1M or 5M words would be used to train MT systems. Participants were ranked based on the performance of these MT systems on a test set of Wikipedia translations (Guzmán et al., 2019), as measured by BLEU (Papineni et al., 2002). Participants were provided with a few small sources of parallel data, covering different domains, for each of the two low-resource languages, as well as a third, related language, Hindi (which uses the same script as Nepali). The provided data also included much larger monolingual corpora for each of the four languages (en, hi, ne, si).

Cleanliness or quality of parallel corpora for MT systems is affected by a wide range of factors, e.g., the parallelism of the sentence pairs, the fluency of the sentences in the output language, etc. Previous work (Goutte et al., 2012; Simard, 2014)

showed that different types of errors in the parallel training data degrade MT quality in different ways.

Intuitively, cross-lingual semantic textual similarity is one of the most important properties of high-quality sentence pairs. Lo et al. (2016) scored cross-lingual semantic textual similarity in two ways, either using a semantic MT quality estimation metric, or by first translating one of the sentences using MT, and then comparing the result to the other sentence, using a semantic MT evaluation metric. At last year's edition of the corpus filtering task, Lo et al. (2018)'s supervised submissions were developed in the same philosophy using a new semantic MT evaluation metric, YiSi-1.

This year, the National Research Council (NRC) Canada team submitted 4 systems to the corpus filtering task, which use different strategies to evaluate the parallelism of sentence pairs. Two of these systems exploit the quality estimation metric YiSi-2, the third uses a deep Transformer network (Vaswani et al., 2017), and the fourth is an ensemble combining these approaches.

In this paper, we describe the 4 systems we submitted, which have three main components: pre-filtering rules, sentence pair scoring, and re-ranking to improve vocabulary coverage. The systems vary in the way they score sentence pairs. Official results indicate our best systems were ranked 3rd or 4th out of over 20 submissions in most test settings, the ensemble system providing the most robust results.

2 System architecture

There are a wide range of factors that determine whether a sentence pair is good for training MT systems. Some of the more important properties of a good training corpus include:

Proceedings of the Fourth Conference on Machine Translation (WMT), Volume 3: Shared Task Papers (Day 2) pages 252–260
Florence, Italy, August 1-2, 2019. ©2019 Association for Computational Linguistics

- High parallelism in the sentence pairs, that constitutes translation adequacy.

- High fluency and grammaticality, especially for sentences in the output language, that constitutes translation fluency.

- High vocabulary coverage, especially in the input language, which should help make the translation system more robust.

- High variety of sentence lengths, which should also improve robustness.

The systems developed by the NRC exploit different strategies to identify a set of sentence pairs that has these properties. The four systems shared the same pipeline architecture:

1. Initial filtering to remove specific types of noise

2. Sentence pair scoring

3. Re-ranking to improve vocabulary coverage

The difference between our 4 submissions is in the way sentence pairs were scored. We used YiSi-2 for two of our submissions, a deep Transformer network exploiting transfer learning for the third, and an ensemble that combines scores from YiSi-2 and several deep Transformer networks.

2.1 Initial filtering

The pre-filtering steps of our submissions are mostly the same as those in Lo et al. (2018). We remove: 1) duplicates after masking email, web addresses and numbers, 2) the majority of number mismatches, 3) sentences in the wrong language according to the `pyCLD2` language detector[1] and 4) long sentences (either side has more than 150 tokens).

An additional pre-filtering rule included in this year's submissions is the removal of pairs where over 50% of the Nepali/Sinhalese text is comprised of English, numbers or punctuation.

2.2 Sentence pair scoring

We experimented with different strategies to score sentence pairs. These are described in the following subsections.

2.2.1 YiSi-2: cross-lingual semantic MT evaluation metric

YiSi[2] is a unified semantic MT quality evaluation and estimation metric for languages with different levels of available resources. YiSi-1 measures the similarity between a machine translation and human references by aggregating weighted distributional (lexical) semantic similarities, and optionally incorporating shallow semantic structures.

YiSi-2 is the bilingual, reference-less version, which uses bilingual word embeddings to evaluate cross-lingual lexical semantic similarity between the input and MT output. While YiSi-1 successfully served in the WMT2018 parallel corpus filtering task, YiSi-2 showed comparable accuracy on identifying clean parallel sentences on a hand-annotated subset of test data in our internal experiments (Lo et al., 2018).

Like YiSi-1, YiSi-2 can exploit shallow semantic structures as well. However, there is no semantic role labeler for Nepali/Sinhalese readily available off-the-shelf, thus the version of YiSi-2 used in this work is purely based on cross-lingual lexical semantic similarity. In addition, instead of evaluating through the bag of trigrams to reward the same word order between the two sentences as in YiSi-1, YiSi-2 evaluates through the bag of unigrams to allow reordering between the two sentences in the two languages. Here is a simplified version of YiSi without using shallow semantic structures and bag of n-grams (it is the same as the original version of YiSi (Lo, 2019) with the hyperparameter β set to 0 and n to 1):

$$v(u) = \text{embedding of unit } u$$
$$w(u) = idf(u) = log(1 + \frac{|\mathbb{U}|+1}{|\mathbb{U}_{\exists u}|+1})$$
$$s(e, f) = cos(v(e), v(f))$$

$$s_p(\overrightarrow{e}, \overrightarrow{f}) = \frac{\sum_a \max_b w(e_a) \cdot s(e_a, f_b)}{\sum_a w(e_a)}$$

$$s_r(\overrightarrow{e}, \overrightarrow{f}) = \frac{\sum_b \max_a w(f_b) \cdot s(e_a, f_b)}{\sum_b w(f_b)}$$

$$\text{precision} = s_p(\overrightarrow{e_{\text{sent}}}, \overrightarrow{f_{\text{sent}}})$$
$$\text{recall} = s_r(\overrightarrow{e_{\text{sent}}}, \overrightarrow{f_{\text{sent}}})$$

$$\text{YiSi} = \frac{\text{precision} \cdot \text{recall}}{\alpha \cdot \text{precision} + (1-\alpha) \cdot \text{recall}}$$

$$\text{YiSi-2} = \text{YiSi}(E\text{=NE/SI}, F\text{=EN})$$

---

[1] https://github.com/aboSamoor/pycld2

[2] YiSi is the romanization of the Cantonese word 意思 ('meaning').

model	lang.	training data				dict.	size
		domain	#sent	#word		#pair	#vocab
supervised	ne	IT and religious	563k	8M		—	34k
	en			5M			46k
	si	IT and subtitles	647k	6M			43k
	en			5M			33k
unsupervised	ne	wiki	92k	5M		9k	55k
	en	news	779M	13B			3M
	si	wiki	156k	8M		8k	72k
	en	news	779M	13B			3M

Table 1: Statistics of data used to train the bilingual word embeddings for evaluating cross-lingual lexical semantic similarity in YiSi-2.

where $\mathbb{U}$ is the set of all tested sentences in the same language of the word unit u; α is the ratio of precision and recall in the final YiSi score. In this experiment, we set α to 0.5 for a balanced ratio of precision and recall.

This year, we experimented with two methods to build the bilingual word embeddings for evaluating cross-lingual lexical semantic similarity in YiSi-2. The *supervised* bilingual word embeddings are trained on the parallel data provided using `bivec` (Luong et al., 2015). The *unsupervised* (weakly supervised, to be precise) bilingual word embeddings are built by transforming monolingual `w2v` (Mikolov et al., 2013) embeddings of each language into the same vector space using `vecmap` (Artetxe et al., 2016). Table 1 shows the statistics of the data used to train the two bilingual word embedding models. Common Crawl data was not used to train the bilingual word embeddings.

2.2.2 Deep Transformer Network (XLM)

The other approach we tested to score sentence pairs exploits self-supervised cross-lingual language model pre-training (Lample and Conneau, 2019) of a deep Transformer network, followed by a fine-tuning stage where we teach the network to distinguish real (good) parallel sentences from bad ones. We thereby transfer over knowledge acquired from a token-level (cross-lingual) language modelling task to a sentence-level (cross-lingual) discourse modelling task, i.e. predicting whether two sentences are translations of each other. This approach allows us to exploit both monolingual and parallel text during the unsupervised pre-training phase, therefore allowing us to profit from the greater availability of monolingual data.

Our use of XLM for sentence pair scoring is similar to the Zipporah system (Xu and Koehn, 2017), in that we train a model to discriminate between positive examples of actual translations and procedurally generated negative examples, then use the predicted probability of the positive class to score sentence pairs. The way we generate negative examples, which we will explain below, is also similar, but the model itself is very different.

Lample and Conneau (2019) introduced self-supervised cross-lingual language model pre-training of deep Transformer networks, and released a system called XLM (for cross-lingual language model).[3] The cross-lingual LM pre-training task is similar to the masked language model (MLM) pre-training used in BERT (Devlin et al., 2018), but the model can exploit cross-lingual context, as we will explain below. The architecture of XLM is a Transformer network like BERT, but it incorporates language embeddings in the input representation layer.

We used XLM to train a model using almost all the available data, except for the monolingual English Common Crawl data. This includes both monolingual and parallel data, and includes the Hindi datasets. All the data was preprocessed[4] using XLM's preprocessing tools, which include the Moses tokenizer (which defaults to English for both Nepali and Sinhala) and a script to remove accents and convert to lower case.

We then applied byte pair encoding[5] (BPE; Sen-

---

[3]`https://github.com/facebookresearch/XLM`

[4]The Nepali-English dictionary was first converted to the same format as the rest of the parallel data (two separate, line-aligned files).

[5]We used fastBPE (`https://github.com/glample/fastBPE`).

nrich et al., 2016a,b) to the training and test data, after learning 80K BPE codes on the concatenation of 3 monolingual corpora (of similar sizes) representing the 3 languages present in the test set (selected from sources similar to the benchmark, comprised of Wikipedia translations):

- Sinhala: all of Sinhala Wikipedia and all of Sinhala Common Crawl, for a total of 5.3 million sentences

- Nepali: all of Nepali Wikipedia, all of Nepali Common Crawl, and 1.6M sentences sampled from the monolingual Hindi corpus, for a total of 5.3 million sentences

- English: 5.3 million sentences sampled from English Wikipedia

Once BPE was applied to all the training data, for each language and language pair, we kept 5K sentence pairs for validation, and used the rest for training. Statistics on the data used to train the deep Transformer network are shown in Table 2. In all, this data contains around 1 billion tokens, with a vocabulary[6] size of 95056 (including BPE codes and single characters).

The size differences between the training sets of the 4 languages (between 3.6 and 10 million sentences) and 3 language pairs (between 577K and 642K sentence pairs) were assumed to be unimportant, as XLM samples the languages during training, such that under-represented languages are sampled more frequently.[7]

To teach the Transformer network to distinguish good translations from bad ones, we generated negative examples based on the positive examples in the (clean) parallel training data, in a manner similar to that of Xu and Koehn (2017), but adapted to address one of the types of noise in the (noisy) test data, that is sentence pairs where either side (or both) are not in the right language. Note that corpus filtering systems often use language identification to heuristically filter out this type of noise, but we found it important to provide our system this type of negative example to help it learn to assign them low scores.

For each of the positive examples in the (clean) parallel training data, we generate negative examples that are either inadequate or lack fluency (or both), the idea being that such sentences are not useful for training MT systems. Specifically, we generate 4 negative examples using the following 4 procedures:

1. Swap sentence in source or target with a confounding sentence randomly drawn from the test corpora (from either source or target, regardless of which side is being swapped).

2. Shuffle words in source or target. Make sure the one we shuffle contains at least 2 words.

3. Do both 1 and 2. Do these separately, so we may corrupt the same side twice, or both sides, but in different ways.

4. Either copy source as target, copy target as source or swap source and target. This is meant to learn to detect noise due to the source and/or target being in the wrong language.

Sampling negative examples from the test corpus (in method 1) was meant to teach the model something about the language used in the test data. We feared that this might teach the model that sentences like those in the test corpora are always negative, so we also tested an alternative source of confounding sentences, that is to draw them from the positive examples instead (in any language).

Note that sentence pairs where the target was identical to the source were removed before generating the data for fine-tuning. Not translating certain words does happen in practice (e.g. names, loan words) but if the whole text is a copy of the source, it is not very informative on the task of translating, and in the case of corpus filtering, it may be confounding, as we know some of the noise in the test data is comprised of identical or very similar text segments in the same language. We also removed pairs where both source and target contained a single word.

The model was trained using a fork of XLM which we modified to allow for fine-tuning on pre-labeled sentence pairs (rather than positive examples only, from which negative examples are generated on-the-fly by XLM).

We start by pre-training the model on both monolingual and cross-lingual (masked) language

---

[6]We compute the vocabulary on the data used to learn the BPE codes, after applying BPE to it.

[7]We still recommend minding the size differences between languages, as the sampling function currently implemented in XLM will not behave as intended if the differences are too great.

Lang(s)	Training data sources	Nb training sentences	Nb validation sentences
hi	IITB (mono)	10M (sampled)	5000
si	Wiki, CC	5.2M	2500 each Wiki and CC
ne	Wiki, CC	3.6M	2500 each Wiki and CC
en	Wiki	10M (sampled)	5000
hi–en	IITB (para)	600K (sampled)	5000
si–en	Open Subtitles, GNOME/KDE/Ubuntu	642K	2500 each
ne–en	Bible, Global Voices, Penn Treebank, GNOME/KDE/Ubuntu, ne–en dictionary	577K	500 Treebank and 4500 Bible

Table 2: Data used to train the deep Transformer network. CC means Common Crawl. For more information on the data sources, see the overview paper on the corpus filtering task.

model tasks. The task can be defined as follows: given a sequence of words in which certain words have been masked, predict the masked words based on the observable ones. The sequence of words can be one or more sentences in a single language, or a parallel pair of sentences in two different languages. In the bilingual case, the model can learn to use cross-lingual context in order to predict words, that is to use not only the context in the language the word belongs to, but also the translation of that context (and the word itself) in another language. Note that the input representation layer in XLM includes language embeddings, which are added to the input representation of each token. We thus specify the language of the texts being fed to the (multilingual) encoder.

Then we fine-tune the model on a sentence pair classification (SPC) task, which can be defined as follows: given two sentences, a source and a target, is the target a valid (i.e. adequate and fluent) translation of the source. This is done only on parallel data, and instead of using only real examples of translations, as during pre-training, we train on both positive and negative examples (in a ratio of 1:4).

During fine-tuning, we can choose to keep training the model on the language modeling tasks, to avoid overfitting the new data or forgetting too much about the old. We tested this approach, using only monolingual data for the language model task during fine-tuning – this was done for practical reasons, to avoid having the model update its language model on the negative examples in the parallel training sets used for fine-tuning.[8]

To set the hyperparameters, we used the default values or those used by Lample and Conneau (2019), with a few exceptions. We reduced the

number of layers from 12 to 6 and the embedding size from 1024 to 512. We reduced the maximum batch size for pre-training from 64 to 32 (because of limited GPU memory), with around 4000 tokens per batch, and used a learning rate of 2e-4 for pre-training. For fine-tuning, we used a batch size of 8 and a learning rate of 1e-5.

It is worth noting that this model was supposed to be pre-trained for a week or more, but we discovered an issue with our data and had to restart pre-training the day before the deadline, so we were only able to pre-train it for 16 hours or so. Our preliminary experiments suggest we could have reduced the perplexity of the (monolingual and cross-lingual) LM by two thirds or more if we had pre-trained fully, but we do not know what effect this would have had on the sentence pair scoring task. We also had to foreshorten fine-tuning, as we only had time to do a few epochs. It is also worth noting that we only had time to evaluate MT quality on a 1M-word sample of Sinhala before the deadline, which may have made our model selection suboptimal.

2.3 Re-ranking to improve vocabulary coverage

Our scoring mechanisms process each sentence pair independently, therefore we sometimes observe redundancy in the top-ranking sentences, as well as a somewhat limited coverage of the words of the source language. To mitigate this issue, we applied a form of re-ranking to improve source token coverage. Going down the ranked list of (previously scored) sentence pairs, we applied a penalty to the pair's score if it did not contain at least one "new" source-language word bigram, i.e., a pair of consecutive source-language tokens not observed in previous (higher-scoring) sentence pairs. The penalty was simply a 20% score discount. This had the effect of down-ranking sen-

---

[8] Our fork of XLM was created simply to accommodate fine-tuning on pre-labeled examples, and was not fool-proof in this respect.

Source of confounders	Fine-tuning tasks	Acc (hi–en)	Acc (ne–en)	Acc (si–en)	Acc (avg)
Test set	SPC only	96.3	99.3	94.8	96.8
Test set	SPC+MLM	92.8	98.2	88.3	93.1
Train set	SPC only	95.6	95.7	93.2	94.8
Train set	SPC+MLM	93.7	93.4	91.1	92.8

Table 3: Sentence pair classification accuracy of XLM model on dev sets. *Confounders* are sentences that we draw at random to create inadequate translations.

	ne-en		si-en	
system	1M-word	5M-word	1M-word	5M-word
Zipporah*	3.40	4.22	4.16	4.77
random	1.30	3.01	1.43	3.33
Zipporah	4.14	**4.42**	4.12	**4.96**
YiSi-2-sup	3.86	3.76	4.85	4.71
YiSi-2-unsup	**4.42**	3.91	3.97	4.56
XLM-v2-spc	4.14	4.09	4.52	4.72
XLM-v2-spc-mlm	3.96	3.69	4.37	4.68
XLM-v3-spc-mlm	3.89	3.91	4.12	4.66
ensemble	3.94	3.95	**4.89**	4.85

Table 4: Uncased BLEU scores on the official dev ("dev-test") sets achieved by the SMT systems trained on the 1M- and 5M-word corpora subselected by the scoring systems. For XLM, v2 is the version that selects confounders from the test corpora, whereas v3 selects them from the training data, and spc-mlm means that both SPC and MLM were used for fine-tuning. *These results for the Zipporah baseline were reported by the task organizers, and the SMT architecture was different from our systems. We obtained Zipporah's score lists and trained our own SMT systems using the data selected from those lists, and results are shown in the third row.

tences that were too similar to a previously selected sentence.

2.4 Ensembling

To combine the output of different sentence pair scoring methods, we use the following, rank-based function:

$$s^*(e, f) = 1 - \frac{1}{|S| \times N} \sum_{s \in S} r(s(e, f))$$

where N is the number of sentence pairs, S is the set of scoring functions, and $r(s(e, f))$ returns the rank of the pair of sentences (e, f) according to score s.

3 Experiments and results

3.1 Intrinsic evaluation of XLM

To evaluate the deep Transformer model intrinsically, we can look at its accuracy on the sentence pair classification task used to fine-tune it. Table 3 shows the accuracy on the dev sets for all three language pairs. The table shows the results obtained using 4 different configurations for training, with the confounding sentences being drawn either from the training data or test data, and using either sentence pair classification (SPC) only or both SPC and the (monolingual) masked language model (MLM) for fine-tuning. First, we see that the accuracy scores are high,[9] so the model is good at discriminating real translations from procedurally generated bad ones.

The results also suggest that including the (monolingual) MLM task during fine-tuning is a hindrance, since the model achieves lower accuracy. However, it is important to note that we did no hyperparameter tuning, had to use a smaller model because of time and resource limitations, and did not have time to fully train any of the models tested. More extensive testing would be required to assess the usefulness of multi-task fine-tuning.

If we analyze the scores output by the model on the test data (i.e. the predicted probability of

---

[9]Picking the most frequent class would achieve 80% accuracy, as 80% of the examples are negative.

langs	system	SMT		NMT	
		1M-word	5M-word	1M-word	5M-word
ne–en	YiSi-2-sup	3.55 (10)	4.07 (T-14)	3.06 (12)	1.34 (10)
	YiSi-2-unsup	4.04 (T-4)	4.14 (T-12)	3.74 (8)	0.98 (16)
	XLM-v2-spc	3.92 (7)	**4.51 (4)**	4.03 (7)	**1.40 (9)**
	ensemble	**4.10 (3)**	4.30 (8)	**4.58 (5)**	1.10 (14)
si–en	YiSi-2-sup	3.87 (6)	4.39 (9)	**4.97 (3)**	**1.58 (9)**
	YiSi-2-unsup	3.14 (13)	4.29 (10)	2.41 (12)	0.68 (15)
	XLM-v2-spc	3.80 (T-8)	4.42 (T-7)	1.63 (15)	0.91 (13)
	ensemble	**4.19 (3)**	**4.54 (4)**	4.06 (4)	1.39 (11)

Table 5: BLEU scores (and ranking, out of 21 submissions for ne–en and 23 for si–en) of NRC's submissions on the test sets. The best of our submissions in each test setting is bolded.

the positive class), we see that the model predicts that a vast majority of sentences pairs are not valid translations of each other, their score being below 0.5. We briefly inspected the top-scoring sentences in the test set,[10] and in the case of ne–en, these seem to contain a lot of biblical texts, which suggests a domain bias, as the ne–en fine-tuning data included biblical texts.

3.2 MT quality check

We used the software provided by the task organizers to extract the 1M-word and 5M-word samples from the original test corpora, using the scores of each of our 4 systems in turn. We then trained SMT systems using the extracted data. The SMT systems were trained using Portage (Larkin et al., 2010) with components and parameters similar to the German-English SMT system in Williams et al. (2016). The MT systems were then evaluated on the official dev set ("dev-test"). Table 4 shows their BLEU scores. We have also included the results of a random scoring baseline (with initial filtering and token coverage re-ranking), as well as those of Zipporah.

These results show that all our BLEU scores are above the random baseline, and some of our systems outperform Zipporah when using a 1M-word sample (for both ne–en and si–en), but not when using a larger, 5M-word sample. We also see that our ensembling method produced good results on si–en, but not on ne–en, where individual systems fared better.

It is also interesting to note that in some cases, the 5M-word sample produced poorer MT results than the 1M-word sample. In fact, we see that

the 1M-word samples selected by our best systems produce similar MT quality than the 5M-word samples selected by Zipporah.

Based on these results, we decided to submit the Transformer model that was fine-tuned on v2 of the fine-tuning data (where confounders were drawn from the test corpora), using SPC only, as well as both YiSi models and an ensemble of these three models.

4 Official Results

Table 5 presents the BLEU scores of our 4 systems on the test sets, using either 1M-word or 5M-word samples. Our best systems were ranked 3rd or 4th out of over 20 submissions in most test settings, except when using NMT on a 5M-word sample. It is worth noting that we were not able to conduct any NMT tests during development due to resource limitations, and were thus unable to tune any of our systems for this test setting.

If we compare the results of our 4 systems, the ensemble system performed best in 4 of 8 test settings, whereas XLM and YiSi (supervised) were best in 2 settings each. The ensemble system was most robust with an average score of 3.53 over all 8 test settings.

In the case of NMT, BLEU scores are much lower when using 5M-word rather than 1M-word samples, and this was true for other top systems, which suggests there is less that 5M words worth of parallel data in the test corpora that are useful (i.e. not too noisy) for NMT training. In the case of SMT, BLEU scores are slightly higher when using the larger samples, which suggests SMT is more robust to noise in the training data. Finally, it is worth noting that our best scores and rankings are similar for both language pairs.

---

[10]We used the XLM model's scores directly for this, and did not apply re-ranking.

5 Conclusion

In this paper, we presented the NRC's submissions to the WMT19 parallel corpus filtering task. Official results indicate our best systems were ranked 3rd or 4th out of over 20 submissions in most test settings, except when using NMT on a 5M-word sample, and that the ensemble system provided the most robust results. Further experimentation is required to understand why the sentence pair rankings produced by our systems work well for NMT if we take a small sample of top-ranked pairs, but less well if we take larger samples. A better way of re-ranking the pairs to optimize vocabulary coverage may lead to improved MT performance. Future work could also include using self-training to adapt the Transformer network to the test data, by iteratively selecting the most likely good examples in the test data and updating the language model and/or sentence pair classification model using these examples.

Acknowledgments

We thank the anonymous reviewers for their helpful suggestions on this paper.

References

Mikel Artetxe, Gorka Labaka, and Eneko Agirre. 2016. Learning principled bilingual mappings of word embeddings while preserving monolingual invariance. In *Proceedings of the 2016 Conference on Empirical Methods in Natural Language Processing*, pages 2289–2294.

Jacob Devlin, Ming Wei Chang, Kenton Lee, and Kristina Toutanova. 2018. BERT: pre-training of deep bidirectional transformers for language understanding. *CoRR*, abs/1810.04805.

Cyril Goutte, Marine Carpuat, and George Foster. 2012. The impact of sentence alignment errors on phrase-based machine translation performance. In *Proceedings of the Tenth Conference of the Association for Machine Translation in the Americas*.

Francisco Guzmán, Peng-Jen Chen, Myle Ott, Juan Pino, Guillaume Lample, Philipp Koehn, Vishrav Chaudhary, and Marc'Aurelio Ranzato. 2019. Two new evaluation datasets for low-resource machine translation: Nepali-english and sinhala-english. *CoRR*, abs/1902.01382.

Philipp Koehn, Kenneth Heafield, Mikel L. Forcada, Miquel Esplà-Gomis, Sergio Ortiz-Rojas, Gema Ramírez Sánchez, Víctor M. Sánchez Cartagena, Barry Haddow, Marta Bañón, Marek Střelec, Anna Samiotou, and Amir Kamran. 2018a. ParaCrawl corpus version 1.0. LINDAT/CLARIN digital library at the Institute of Formal and Applied Linguistics (ÚFAL), Faculty of Mathematics and Physics, Charles University.

Philipp Koehn, Huda Khayrallah, Kenneth Heafield, and Mikel Forcada. 2018b. Findings of the wmt 2018 shared task on parallel corpus filtering. In *Proceedings of the Third Conference on Machine Translation, Volume 2: Shared Task Papers*, Brussels, Belgium. Association for Computational Linguistics.

Guillaume Lample and Alexis Conneau. 2019. Cross-lingual language model pretraining. *CoRR*, abs/1901.07291.

Samuel Larkin, Boxing Chen, George Foster, Uli Germann, Eric Joanis, J. Howard Johnson, and Roland Kuhn. 2010. Lessons from NRC's Portage System at WMT 2010. In *5th Workshop on Statistical Machine Translation (WMT 2010)*, pages 127–132.

Chi-kiu Lo. 2019. YiSi - a unified semantic mt quality evaluation and estimation metric for languages with different levels of available resources. In *Proceedings of the Fourth Conference on Machine Translation: Shared Task Papers*, Florence, Italy. Association for Computational Linguistics.

Chi-kiu Lo, Cyril Goutte, and Michel Simard. 2016. CNRC at Semeval-2016 task 1: Experiments in crosslingual semantic textual similarity. In *Proceedings of the 10th International Workshop on Semantic Evaluation (SemEval-2016)*, pages 668–673.

Chi-kiu Lo, Michel Simard, Darlene Stewart, Samuel Larkin, Cyril Goutte, and Patrick Littell. 2018. Accurate semantic textual similarity for cleaning noisy parallel corpora using semantic machine translation evaluation metric: The NRC supervised submissions to the parallel corpus filtering task. In *Proceedings of the Third Conference on Machine Translation. Shared Task Papers*, pages 908–916, Belgium, Brussels. Association for Computational Linguistics.

Minh-Thang Luong, Hieu Pham, and Christopher D. Manning. 2015. Bilingual word representations with monolingual quality in mind. In *NAACL Workshop on Vector Space Modeling for NLP*, Denver, United States.

Tomas Mikolov, Ilya Sutskever, Kai Chen, Greg Corrado, and Jeffrey Dean. 2013. Distributed representations of words and phrases and their compositionality. In *Proceedings of the 26th International Conference on Neural Information Processing Systems*, NIPS'13, pages 3111–3119, USA. Curran Associates Inc.

Kishore Papineni, Salim Roukos, Todd Ward, and Wei-Jing Zhu. 2002. BLEU: a method for automatic evaluation of machine translation. In *40th Annual Meeting of the Association for Computational Linguistics (ACL-02)*, pages 311–318, Philadelphia, Pennsylvania.

Rico Sennrich, Barry Haddow, and Alexandra Birch. 2016a. Edinburgh neural machine translation systems for WMT 16. In *Proceedings of the First Conference on Machine Translation*, pages 371–376, Berlin, Germany. Association for Computational Linguistics.

Rico Sennrich, Barry Haddow, and Alexandra Birch. 2016b. Neural machine translation of rare words with subword units. In *Proceedings of the 54th Annual Meeting of the Association for Computational Linguistics (Volume 1: Long Papers)*, pages 1715–1725, Berlin, Germany. Association for Computational Linguistics.

Michel Simard. 2014. Clean data for training statistical MT: the case of MT contamination. In *Proceedings of the Eleventh Conference of the Association for Machine Translation in the Americas*, pages 69–82, Vancouver, BC, Canada.

Ashish Vaswani, Noam Shazeer, Niki Parmar, Jakob Uszkoreit, Llion Jones, Aidan N Gomez, Łukasz Kaiser, and Illia Polosukhin. 2017. Attention is all you need. In *Advances in Neural Information Processing Systems*, pages 5998–6008.

Philip Williams, Rico Sennrich, Maria Nadejde, Matthias Huck, Barry Haddow, and Ondřej Bojar. 2016. Edinburgh's statistical machine translation systems for wmt16. In *Proceedings of the First Conference on Machine Translation*, pages 399–410, Berlin, Germany. Association for Computational Linguistics.

Hainan Xu and Philipp Koehn. 2017. Zipporah: a fast and scalable data cleaning system for noisy web-crawled parallel corpora. In *Proceedings of the 2017 Conference on Empirical Methods in Natural Language Processing*, pages 2945–2950, Copenhagen, Denmark. Association for Computational Linguistics.

Low-Resource Corpus Filtering using Multilingual Sentence Embeddings

Vishrav Chaudhary[♦] **Yuqing Tang**[♦] **Francisco Guzmán**[♦] **Holger Schwenk**[♦] **Philipp Koehn**[■]

[♦]Facebook AI   [■]Johns Hopkins University

{vishrav,yuqtang,fguzman,schwenk}@fb.com phi@jhu.edu

Abstract

In this paper, we describe our submission to the WMT19 low-resource parallel corpus filtering shared task. Our main approach is based on the LASER toolkit (Language-Agnostic SEntence Representations), which uses an encoder-decoder architecture trained on a parallel corpus to obtain multilingual sentence representations. We then use the representations directly to score and filter the noisy parallel sentences without additionally training a scoring function. We contrast our approach to other promising methods and show that LASER yields strong results. Finally, we produce an ensemble of different scoring methods and obtain additional gains. Our submission achieved the best overall performance for both the Nepali–English and Sinhala–English 1M tasks by a margin of 1.3 and 1.4 BLEU respectively, as compared to the second best systems. Moreover, our experiments show that this technique is promising for low and even no-resource scenarios.

1 Introduction

The availability of high-quality parallel training data is critical for obtaining good translation performance, as neural machine translation (NMT) systems are less robust against noisy parallel data than statistical machine translation (SMT) systems (Khayrallah and Koehn, 2018). Recently, there is an increased interest in the filtering of noisy parallel corpora (such as Paracrawl[1]) to increase the amount of data that can be used to train translation systems (Koehn et al., 2018).

While the state-of-the-art methods that use NMT models have proven effective in mining parallel sentences (Junczys-Dowmunt, 2018) for high-resource languages, their effectiveness has not been tested in low-resource languages. The implications of low availability of training data for parallel-scoring methods is not known yet.

For the task of low-resource filtering (Koehn et al., 2019), we are provided with a very noisy 40.6 million-word (English token count) Nepali–English corpus and a 59.6 million-word Sinhala–English corpus crawled from the web as part of the Paracrawl project. The challenge consists of providing scores for each sentence pair in both noisy parallel sets. The scores will be used to subsample sentence pairs that amount to 1 million and 5 million English words. The quality of the resulting subsets is determined by the quality of a statistical machine translation (Moses, phrase-based (Koehn et al., 2007)) and the neural machine translation system `fairseq` (Ott et al., 2019) trained on this data. The quality of the machine translation system will be measured by BLEU score using SacreBLEU (Post, 2018) on a held-out test set of Wikipedia translations for Sinhala–English and Nepali–English from the `flores` dataset (Guzmán et al., 2019).

In our submission for this shared task, we use of multilingual sentence embeddings obtained from LASER[2] which uses an encoder-decoder architecture to train a multilingual sentence representation model using a relatively small parallel corpus. Our experiments demonstrate that the proposed approach outperforms other existing approaches. Moreover we make use of an ensemble of multiple scoring functions to further boost the filtering performance.

---

[1]http://www.paracrawl.eu/

[2]https://github.com/facebookresearch/LASER

Proceedings of the Fourth Conference on Machine Translation (WMT), Volume 3: Shared Task Papers (Day 2) pages 261–266
Florence, Italy, August 1-2, 2019. ©2019 Association for Computational Linguistics

2 Methodology

The WMT 2018 shared task for parallel corpus filtering (Koehn et al., 2018)[3] introduced several methods to tackle a high-resource German-English data condition.While many of these methods were successful to filter out noisy translations, few have been tried under low-resource conditions. In this paper, we address the problem of low-resource sentence filtering using sentence-level representations and compare them to other popular methods used in high-resource conditions.

The LASER model (Artetxe and Schwenk, 2018a) makes use of multilingual sentence representations to gauge the similarity between the source and the target sentence. It has provided state-of-the-art performance on the BUCC corpus mining task and has also been effective in filtering WMT Paracrawl data (Artetxe and Schwenk, 2018a). However, these tasks only considered high-resource languages, namely French, German, Russian and Chinese. Fortunately, this technique has also been effective on zero-shot cross-lingual natural language inference in the XNLI dataset (Artetxe and Schwenk, 2018b) which makes it promising for the low resource scenario being focused in this shared task. In this paper, we propose to use an adaptation of LASER to low-resource conditions to compute the similarity scores to filter out noisy sentences.

For comparison to LASER, we also establish initial benchmarks using Bicleaner and Zipporah, two popular baselines which have been used in the Paracrawl project; and dual conditional cross-entropy, which has proven to be state-of-the-art for the high-resource corpus filtering task (Koehn et al., 2018). We explore the performance of the techniques under similar pre-processing conditions regarding language identification filtering and lexical overlap. We observe that LASER scores provide a clear advantage for this task. Finally, we perform ensembling of the scores coming from different methods. We observe that when LASER scores are included in the mix, the boost in performance is relatively minor. In the rest of this section we discuss the settings for each of the methods applied.

2.1 LASER Multilingual Representations

The underlying idea is to use the distances between two multilingual representations as a notion of parallelism between the two embedded sentences (Schwenk, 2018). To do this, we first train an encoder that learns to produce a multilingual, fixed-size sentence representation; and then compute a distance between two sentences in the learned embedding space. In addition, we use a *margin* criterion, which uses a k nearest neighbors approach to normalize the similarity scores given that cosine similarity is not globally consistent (Artetxe and Schwenk, 2018a).

Encoder The multilingual encoder consists of a bidirectional LSTM, and our sentence embeddings are obtained by applying max-pooling over its output. We use a single encoder and decoder in our system, which are shared by all languages involved. For this purpose, we trained multilingual sentence embeddings on the provided parallel data only (see Section 3.2 for details).

Margin We follow the definition of *ratio*[4] from (Artetxe and Schwenk, 2018a). Using this, the similarity score between two sentences (x, y) can be computed as

$$\frac{2k \cos(x, y)}{\sum_{y' \in \text{NN}_k(x)} \cos(x, y') + \sum_{x' \in \text{NN}_k(y)} \cos(x', y))}$$

where $\text{NN}_k(x)$ denotes the k nearest neighbors of x in the other language, and analogously for $\text{NN}_k(y)$. Note that this list of nearest neighbors does not include duplicates, so even if a given sentence has multiple occurrences in the corpus, it would have (at most) one entry in the list.

Neighborhood Additionally, we explored two ways of sampling k nearest neighbors. First a *global* method, in which we used the neighborhood comprised of the noisy data along with the clean data. Second a *local* method, in which we only scored the noisy data using the noisy neighborhood, or the clean data using the clean neighborhood.[5]

---

[3]http://statmt.org/wmt18/
parallel-corpus-filtering.html

[4]We explored the *absolute*, *distance* and *ratio* margin criteria, but the latter worked best

[5]this last part was only done for training an ensemble

2.2 Other Similarity Methods

Zipporah (Xu and Koehn, 2017; Khayrallah et al., 2018), which is often used as a baseline comparison, uses language model and word translation scores, with weights optimized to separate clean and synthetic noise data. In our setup, we trained Zipporah models for both language pairs Sinhala–English and Nepali–English. We used the open source release[6] of the Zipporah tool without modifications. All components of the Zipporah model (probabilistic translation dictionaries and language models) were trained on the provided clean data (excluding the dictionaries). Language models were trained using KenLM (Heafield et al., 2013) over the clean parallel data. We are not using the provided monolingual data, as per default setting. We used the development set from the `flores` dataset for weight training.

Bicleaner (Sánchez-Cartagena et al., 2018) uses lexical translation and language model scores, and several shallow features such as: respective length, matching numbers and punctuation. As with Zipporah, we used the open source Bicleaner[7] toolkit unmodified out-of-the-box. Only the provided clean parallel data was used to train this model. Bicleaner uses a rule-based component to identify noisier examples in the parallel data and trains a classifier to learn how to separate them from the rest of the training data. The use of language model features is optional. We only used models without a language model scoring component.[8]

Dual Conditional Cross-Entropy One of the best performing methods on this task was dual conditional cross-entropy filtering (Junczys-Dowmunt, 2018), which uses a combination of forward and backward models to compute a cross-lingual similarity score. In our experiments, for each language pair, we used the provided clean training data to train neural machine translation models in both translation directions: source-to-target and target-to-source. Given such a translation model M, we force-decode sentence pairs (x, y) from the noisy parallel corpus and obtain the cross entropy score

$$H_M(y|x) = \frac{1}{|y|} \sum_{t=1}^{|y|} \log p_M(y_t|y_{[1,t-1]}, x) \quad (1)$$

Forward and backward cross entropy scores, $H_F(y|x)$ and $H_B(x|y)$ respectively, are then averaged with an additional penalty on a large difference between the two scores $|H_F(y|x) - H_B(x|y)|$.

$$\text{score}(x, y) = \frac{H_F(y|x) + H_B(x|y)}{2} \quad (2)$$
$$- |H_F(y|x) - H_B(x|y)|$$

The forward and backward models are five-layer encoder/decoder transformers trained using `fairseq` with parameters identical to the ones used in the baseline `flores` model [9]. The models were trained on the clean parallel data for 100 epochs. For the Nepali-English task, we also explored using Hindi-English data without major differences in results. We used the `flores` development set to pick the model that maximizes BLEU scores.

2.3 Ensemble

To leverage over the strengths and weaknesses of different scoring systems, we explored the use of a binary classifier to build an ensemble. While it's trivial to obtain positives (e.g. the clean training data), mining negatives can be a daunting task. Hence, we use positive-unlabeled (PU) learning (Mordelet and Vert, 2014), which allows us to obtain classifiers without having to curate a dataset of explicit positive and negatives. In this setting our positive labels come from the clean parallel data while the unlabeled data comes from the noisy set.

To achieve this, we apply bagging of 100 weak, biased classifiers (i.e. with a 2:1 bias for unlabeled data vs. positive label data). We use support vector machines (SVM) with a radial basis kernel, and we randomly sub-sample the set of features for training each base classifier, helping keep them diverse and low-capacity.

We ran two iterations of training of this ensemble. In the first iteration we used the original positive and unlabeled data described above. For the second iteration, we used the learned classifier to re-label the training data. We explored several re-labeling approaches (e.g. setting a threshold that maximizes F_1 score). However, we found that setting a class boundary to preserve the original positives-to-unlabeled ratio worked best. We also observed that the performance deteriorated after two iterations.

---

[6]`https://github.com/hainan-xv/zipporah`
[7]`https://github.com/bitextor/bicleaner`
[8]We found that including a LM as a feature resulted in almost all sentence pairs receiving a score of 0.

[9]`https://github.com/facebookresearch/`
`flores#train-a-baseline-transformer-model`

3 Experimental Setup

We experimented with various methods using a setup that closely mirrors the official scoring of the shared task. All methods are trained on the provided clean parallel data (see Table 1). We did not use the given monolingual data. For development purposes, we used the provided `flores` dev set. For evaluation, we trained machine translation systems on the selected subsets (1M, 5M) of the noisy parallel training data using `fairseq` with the default `flores` training parameter configuration. We report SacreBLEU scores on the `flores` devtest set. We selected our main system based on the best scores on the devtest set for the 1M condition.

	si-en	ne-en	hi-en
Sentences	646k	573k	1.5M
English words	3.7M	3.7M	20.7M

Table 1: Available bitexts to train the filtering approaches.

3.1 Preprocessing

We applied a set of filtering techniques similar to the ones used in LASER (Artetxe and Schwenk, 2018a) and assigned a score of -1 to the noisy sentences based on incorrect language on either the source or the target side or having an overlap of at least 60% between the source and the target tokens. We used fastText[10] for language id filtering. Since LASER computes similarity scores for a sentence pair using these filtering techniques, we experimented by adding these to the other models we used for this shared task.

3.2 LASER Encoder Training

For our experiments and the official submission, we trained a multilingual sentence encoder using the permitted resources in Table 1. We trained a single encoder using all the parallel data for Sinhala–English, Nepali–English and Hindi–English. Since Hindi and Nepali share the same script, we concatenated their corpora into a single parallel corpus. To account for the difference in size of the parallel training data, we over-sampled the Sinhala–English and Nepali/Hindi-English bitexts in a ratio of 5:3. This resulted in roughly 3.2M training sentences for each language direction, i.e. Sinhala and combined Nepali-Hindi.

The models were trained using the same setting as the public LASER encoder which involves normalizing texts and tokenization with Moses tools (falling back to the English mode). We first learn a joint 50k BPE vocabulary on the concatenated training data using fastBPE[11]. The encoder sees Sinhala, Nepali, Hindi and English sentences at the input, without having any information about the current language. This input is always translated into English.[12] We experimented with various techniques to add noise to the English input sentences, similar to what is used in unsupervised neural machine translation, e.g. (Artetxe et al., 2018; Lample et al., 2018), but this did not improve the results.

The encoder is a five-layer BLSTM with 512 dimensional layers. The LSTM decoder has one hidden layer of size 2048, trained with the Adam optimizer. For development, we calculate similarity error on the concatenation of the `flores` dev sets for Sinhala–English and Nepali–English. Our models were trained for seven epochs for about 2.5 hours on 8 Nvidia GPUs.

4 Results

From the results in Table 2, we observe several trends: (*i*) the scores for the 5M condition are generally lower than for the 1M condition. This condition appears to be exacerbated by the application of language id and overlap filtering. (*ii*) LASER shows consistently good performance. The *local* neighborhood works better than the *global* one. In that setting, LASER is on average 0.71 BLEU above the best non-LASER system. These gaps are higher for the 1M condition (0.94 BLEU). (*iii*) The best ensemble configuration provides small improvements over the best LASER configuration. For Sinhala–English the best configuration includes every other scoring method (ALL). For Nepali–English the best configuration is an ensemble of LASER scores. (*iv*) Dual cross entropy shows mixed results. For Sinhala–English, it only works once the language id filtering is enabled which is consistent with previous observations (Junczys-Dowmunt, 2018). For Nepali–English, it provides scores well below the rest of the scoring methods. Note that we did not perform an architecture exploration.

---

[10]9https://fasttext.cc/docs/en/language-identification.html

[11]https://github.com/glample/fastBPE

[12]This means that we have to train an English autoencoder. This didn't seem to hurt, since the same encoder also handles the three other languages

Method	ne-en		si-en	
	1M	**5M**	**1M**	**5M**
Zipporah				
base	5.03	2.09	4.86	4.53
+ LID	5.30	1.53	5.53	3.16
+ Overlap	5.35	1.34	5.18	3.14
Dual X-Ent.				
base	2.83	1.88	0.33	4.63[+]
+ LID	2.19	0.82	6.42	3.68
+ Overlap	2.23	0.91	6.65	4.31
Bicleaner				
base	5.91	2.54[+]	6.20	4.25
+ LID	5.88	2.09	6.36	3.95
+ Overlap	6.12[+]	2.14	6.66[+]	3.26
LASER				
local	*7.37**	**3.15**	*7.49**	5.01
global	6.98	*2.98**	7.27	4.76
Ensemble				
ALL	6.17	2.53	**7.64**	**5.12**
LASER *glob. + loc.*	**7.49**	2.76	7.27	*5.08**

Table 2: SacreBLEU scores on the `flores` devtest set. In **bold**, we highlight the best scores for each condition. In *italics**, we highlight the runner up. We also signal the best non-LASER method with [+].

Submission For the official submission, we used the *ALL* ensemble for the Sinhala–English task and the LASER *global + local* ensemble for the Nepali–English task. We also submitted the LASER *local* as a contrastive system. As we can see in Table 3, the results from the main and contrastive submissions are very close. In one case, the contrastive solution (a single LASER) model yields better results than the ensemble. These results placed our 1M submissions 1.3 and 1.4 BLEU points above the runner ups for the Nepali–English and Sinhala–English tasks, respectively. As noted before, our systems perform worse on the 5M condition. We also noted that the numbers in Table 2 differ slightly from the ones reported in (Koehn et al., 2019). We attribute this difference to the effect of training in 4 (ours) gpus vs. 1 (theirs).

Method	ne-en		si-en	
	1M	**5M**	**1M**	**5M**
Main - Ensemble	6.8	2.8	**6.4**	4.0
Constr - LASER *local*	**6.9**	2.5	6.2	3.8
Best (other)	5.5	**3.4**	5.0	**4.4**

Table 3: Official results of the main and secondary submissions on the `flores` test set evaluated with the NMT configuration. For comparison, we include the best scores by another system.

4.1 Discussion

One natural question to explore is how would the LASER method benefit if it had access to additional data. To explore this, we used the LASER open-source toolkit, which provides a trained encoder covering 93 languages, but does not include Nepali. In Table 4, we observe that the pre-trained LASER model outperforms the LASER *local* model by 0.4 BLEU. For Nepali–English the situation reverses: LASER *local* provides much better results. However, the results of the pre-trained LASER are only slightly worse that those of Bicleaner (6.12) which is the best non-LASER method. This suggests that LASER can function well in zero-shot scenarios (i.e. Nepali–English), but it works even better when it has additional supervision for the languages it is being tested on.

Method	ne-en		si-en	
	1M	**5M**	**1M**	**5M**
Pre-trained LASER	6.06	1.49	**7.82**	**5.56**
LASER *local*	**7.37**	**3.15**	7.49	5.01

Table 4: Comparison of results on the `flores` devtest set using the constrained and the pre-trained vesions of LASER.

5 Conclusions and Future Work

In this paper, we describe our submission to the WMT low-resource parallel corpus filtering task. We use of multilingual sentence embeddings from LASER to filter noisy sentences. We observe that LASER can obtain better results than the baselines by a wide margin. Incorporating scores from other techniques and creating an ensemble provides additional gains. Our main submission to the shared task is based on the best of the ensemble configuration and our contrastive submission is based on the best LASER configuration. Our systems perform the best on the 1M condition for the Nepali–English and Sinhala–English tasks. We analyze the performance of a pre-trained version of LASER and observe that it can perform the filtering task well even in zero-resource scenarios, which is very promising.

In the future, we want to evaluate this technique for high-resource scenarios and observe whether the same results transfer to that condition. Moreover we plan to investigate how the size of training data (parallel, monolingual) impact low-resource sentence filtering task.

References

Mikel Artetxe, Gorka Labaka, Eneko Agirre, and Kyunghyun Cho. 2018. Unsupervised neural machine translation. In *International Conference on Learning Representations (ICLR)*.

Mikel Artetxe and Holger Schwenk. 2018a. Margin-based Parallel Corpus Mining with Multilingual Sentence Embeddings. *arXiv preprint arXiv:1811.01136*.

Mikel Artetxe and Holger Schwenk. 2018b. Massively Multilingual Sentence Embeddings for Zero-Shot Cross-Lingual Transfer and Beyond. *arXiv preprint arXiv:1812.10464*.

Francisco Guzmán, Peng-Jen Chen, Myle Ott, Juan Pino, Guillaume Lample, Philipp Koehn, Vishrav Chaudhary, and Marc'Aurelio Ranzato. 2019. Two new evaluation datasets for low-resource machine translation: Nepali-english and sinhala-english. *arXiv preprint arXiv:1902.01382*.

Kenneth Heafield, Ivan Pouzyrevsky, Jonathan H. Clark, and Philipp Koehn. 2013. Scalable modified Kneser-Ney language model estimation. In *Proceedings of the 51st Annual Meeting of the Association for Computational Linguistics*, pages 690–696, Sofia, Bulgaria.

Marcin Junczys-Dowmunt. 2018. Dual conditional cross-entropy filtering of noisy parallel corpora. In *Proceedings of the Third Conference on Machine Translation, Volume 2: Shared Task Papers*, pages 901–908, Belgium, Brussels. Association for Computational Linguistics.

Huda Khayrallah and Philipp Koehn. 2018. On the impact of various types of noise on neural machine translation. In *Proceedings of the 2nd Workshop on Neural Machine Translation and Generation*, pages 74–83, Melbourne, Australia. Association for Computational Linguistics.

Huda Khayrallah, Hainan Xu, and Philipp Koehn. 2018. The JHU parallel corpus filtering systems for WMT 2018. In *Proceedings of the Third Conference on Machine Translation, Volume 2: Shared Task Papers*, pages 909–912, Belgium, Brussels. Association for Computational Linguistics.

Philipp Koehn, Francisco Guzmán, Vishrav Chaudhary, and Juan M. Pino. 2019. Findings of the wmt 2019 shared task on parallel corpus filtering for low-resource conditions. In *Proceedings of the Fourth Conference on Machine Translation, Volume 2: Shared Task Papers*, Florence, Italy. Association for Computational Linguistics.

Philipp Koehn, Hieu Hoang, Alexandra Birch, Chris Callison-Burch, Marcello Federico, Nicola Bertoldi, Brooke Cowan, Wade Shen, Christine Moran, Richard Zens, Ondrej Bojar Chris Dyer, Alexandra Constantin, and Evan Herbst. 2007. Moses: Open source toolkit for statistical machine translation. In *Annual Meeting of the Association for Computational Linguistics (ACL), demo session*.

Philipp Koehn, Huda Khayrallah, Kenneth Heafield, and Mikel L Forcada. 2018. Findings of the WMT 2018 shared task on parallel corpus filtering. In *Proceedings of the Third Conference on Machine Translation, Volume 2: Shared Task Papers*, pages 726–739, Belgium, Brussels. Association for Computational Linguistics.

Guillaume Lample, Myle Ott, Alexis Conneau, Ludovic Denoyer, and Marc'Aurelio Ranzato. 2018. Phrase-based & neural unsupervised machine translation. In *Empirical Methods in Natural Language Processing (EMNLP)*, pages 5039–5049, Belgium, Brussels. Association for Computational Linguistics.

Fantine Mordelet and J-P Vert. 2014. A bagging svm to learn from positive and unlabeled examples. *Pattern Recognition Letters*, 37:201–209.

Myle Ott, Sergey Edunov, Alexei Baevski, Angela Fan, Sam Gross, Nathan Ng, David Grangier, and Michael Auli. 2019. fairseq: A fast, extensible toolkit for sequence modeling. In *Proceedings of NAACL-HLT 2019: Demonstrations*.

Matt Post. 2018. A call for clarity in reporting bleu scores. In *Proceedings of the Third Conference on Machine Translation (WMT), Volume 1: Research Papers*, volume 1804.08771, pages 186–191, Belgium, Brussels. Association for Computational Linguistics.

Víctor M Sánchez-Cartagena, Marta Bañón, Sergio Ortiz Rojas, and Gema Ramírez. 2018. Prompsit's submission to WMT 2018 parallel corpus filtering shared task. In *Proceedings of the Third Conference on Machine Translation: Shared Task Papers*, pages 955–962, Belgium, Brussels. Association for Computational Linguistics.

Holger Schwenk. 2018. Filtering and mining parallel data in a joint multilingual space. In *Proceedings of the 56th Annual Meeting of the Association for Computational Linguistics (Short Papers)*, pages 228–234, Australia, Melbourne. Association for Computational Linguistics.

Hainan Xu and Philipp Koehn. 2017. Zipporah: a fast and scalable data cleaning system for noisy web-crawled parallel corpora. In *Proceedings of the 2017 Conference on Empirical Methods in Natural Language Processing*, pages 2945–2950, Denmark, Cophenhagen. Association for Computational Linguistics.

Quality and Coverage:
The AFRL Submission to the WMT19 Parallel Corpus Filtering For Low-Resource Conditions Task

Grant Erdmann, Jeremy Gwinnup

Air Force Research Laboratory

`grant.erdmann@us.af.mil, jeremy.gwinnup.1@us.af.mil`

Abstract

The WMT19 Parallel Corpus Filtering For Low-Resource Conditions Task aims to test various methods of filtering noisy parallel corpora, to make them useful for training machine translation systems. This year the noisy corpora are from the relatively low-resource language pairs of English-Nepali and English-Sinhala. This papers describes the Air Force Research Laboratory (AFRL) submissions, including preprocessing methods and scoring metrics. Numerical results indicate a benefit over baseline and the relative effects of different options.

1 Introduction

For this task the participants were provided with a corpus of parallel data in English-Nepali (en-ne) and English-Sinhala (en-si). Both parallel and monolingual training datasets were provided in these languages. The task organizers built statistical machine translation (SMT) and neural machine translation (NMT) systems from the scores produced, based on parallel training sets of 1M (one million) and 5M English words.

Subset selection techniques often strive to reduce a set to the most useful. For the shared task one should avoid selecting:

- A line with undue repetition of content of other selected lines. This repetition can extend training times and/or skew the translation system to favor this type of line.

- Long lines, which will be ignored in training the MT systems.

In addition to adapting the corpus to the building of a general-purpose MT system, we must also deal with significant noise. The main types of noise present in the given data are:

- Not natural language

- One or both languages are incorrect

- Lines are not translations of each other

In contrast to our WMT18 submission (Erdmann and Gwinnup, 2018), we include a text quality metric in the subcorpus-building process, rather than combining it afterward.

2 Preprocessing

As a first step, a rough preprocessing filter is applied to the data.

We remove lines where either language text contains more than 80 words, since the test systems use a maximum of 80 words per line. We also remove lines where the language ID probabilities from fastText (Joulin et al., 2016b,a) do not match the expected languages (using the pre-built language ID models of the authors).

This preprocessed text is used to generate the scores that determine a line's usefulness. We note that there are many fewer preprocessing steps than our previous system (Erdmann and Gwinnup, 2018). We can simplify preprocessing because inclusion of a text quality metric during subcorpus-building will avoid other forms of noise in the process.

3 Coverage Metric

Our metric for subcorpus-building uses both a coverage metric and a text quality metric.

We first give our coverage metric (Gwinnup et al., 2016). Let us select a subcorpus S from a larger corpus C to maximize its similarity to a representative corpus T. Let our preferred subselected subcorpus size be τ times the size of T. Let $\mathcal{V}$ be a set of vocabulary elements of interest. Defining $c_v(X)$ to be the count of the occurrence

Proceedings of the Fourth Conference on Machine Translation (WMT), Volume 3: Shared Task Papers (Day 2) pages 267–270
Florence, Italy, August 1-2, 2019. ©2019 Association for Computational Linguistics

of feature $v \in \mathcal{V}$ in a given corpus X, the coverage g is given by

$$g(S, T, \tau) = \frac{\sum_{v \in \mathcal{V}} f(\min(c_v(S), c_v^\tau(T)))}{\sum_{v \in \mathcal{V}} f(c_v^\tau(T)) + p_v(S, T, \tau)} \quad (1)$$

where the oversaturation penalty $p_v(S, T, \tau)$ is

$$\max(0, c_v(S) - c_v^\tau(T)) \left[f(c_v^\tau(T) + 1) - f(c_v^\tau(T)) \right].$$

Here f can be any submodular function, but we choose exclusively $f(x) = \log(1 + x)$. The scaled count $c_v^\tau(T) = \tau c_v(T)$ accounts for the preferred size of the selected subcorpus differing from the size of T.

4　Text Quality Metric

To create a text quality metric, we use the given clean parallel data to create a MT system. We use the MT system to translate both pre-filtered noisy parallel corpora into English.

This allows us to compute the Meteor (Denkowski and Lavie, 2014) score of the given English lines, using the translated English as a reference. The Meteor metric was chosen due to its using deeper linguistic information than BLEU. The text quality metric of a subcorpus is given by its average:

$$h(S) = \frac{\sum_{s \in S} m(s)}{\sum_{s \in S} 1} \quad (2)$$

where $m(s)$ is the text quality metric (e.g., Meteor) score of line s. This corpus metric is defined to be zero for the empty corpus: $h(\emptyset) = 0$.

The overall score of a subcorpus is given by the product of the coverage metric (1) and the quality metric (2):

$$F(S, T, \tau) = g(S, T, \tau)h(S) \quad (3)$$

5　Subcorpus-Building Algorithm

To build a subcorpus, we iterate the following two steps until the selected subcorpus is large enough:

1. Add the line that has the best effect on the overall score F from (3).

2. If removal of any line would improve F, find the line with the largest improvement. Remove it, unless infinite cycling would result.

This is a greedy algorithm, with review after each selection.

6　Application

This section outlines the particulars of the method applied to the given data for this task. Pre-filtering removed a significant percentage of the noisy parallel corpora prior to scoring. The thresholds for language identification were set empirically. For en-ne we used 40% for English and 1% for Nepali. For en-si we used 10% for both English and Sinhala. After filtering for language identification and a maximum of 80 words, 0.9M of the 2.2M lines remained for en-ne and 1.2M of the 3.4M lines remained for en-si.

We trained phrase-based Moses (Koehn et al., 2007) systems with the small amount of "clean" training data provided by the organizers. These training corpora were normalized as necesssary to remove systematic representation oddities, mostly in punctuation. The Moses systems employ a hierarchical reordering model (Galley and Manning, 2008) and 5-gram operation sequence model (Durrani et al., 2011). The 5-gram English language model used by both systems was trained with the constrained monolingual corpus from our WMT15 (Gwinnup et al., 2015) efforts.

These Moses MT systems were used to translate the pre-filtered datasets. The Meteor score of the given English lines was computed, using translated English as a reference.

The pre-filtered parallel corpora were lowercased and tokenized with tools from Moses. We built a 2000-word-vocabulary SentencePiece (Kudo and Richardson, 2018) model on the given monolingual corpora for each language. The pre-filtered parallel corpora were processed with these models prior to subcorpus-building.

Our subcorpus-building procedure was followed, producing a subcorpus that we ranked by the order a line was added to the subcorpus. This can produce too few scored lines for the 1M-word or 5M-word subcorpora, so we order the scores of the remaining lines by their text quality metric (i.e., Meteor) scores alone. We submitted scores generated by two values of τ for each language pair. The smaller value of τ produced a 50k-line subcorpus, and the larger value of τ produced 150k lines. Our expectation was that the smaller subcorpus would be best in the 1M-word case, and the larger subcorpus in the 5M-word case. For these cases the selected corpora were roughly the same size as the training sets.

7 Numerical Results

The official results of the WMT19 Parallel Filtering Task are given by Bojar et al. (2019).

Here we give some general findings by using the given Moses-EMS configuration for the task. Tables 1–2 give numerical results of this test. BLEU scores are uncased and produced during the Moses-EMS run. We see that the parallel filtering methods we expected to be best do in fact improve on the Zipporah (Xu and Koehn, 2017) baseline.

The smaller, 50k-line subcorpus shows increases of by 0.24 BLEU for 1M en-ne and 0.15 BLEU for 1M en-si. The larger, 150k-line subcorpus shows increases of by 0.11 BLEU for 5M en-ne and 0.32 BLEU for 5M en-si. Picking the best results over all our experiments shows greater improvements over baseline: 0.48 BLEU for 1M en-ne, 0.46 BLEU for 1M en-si, 0.11 BLEU for 5M en-ne, and 0.44 BLEU for 5M en-si.

The tables show that the subcorpus-building process normally improves over scoring by the text quality metric score alone (the row labelled "quality", which is equivalent to either building an empty subcorpus or choosing $F = h$ in (3)). These improvements are largest and most consistent in the 1M-word tests. We expect that the larger sets might be struggling to find helpful data in the noisy corpora, essentially converging to the text-quality-metric-only score.

We tested excluding the text quality metric from the selection process (i.e., choosing $F = g$ in (3)), and these tests are given in the table rows labelled "coverage". As in (Erdmann and Gwinnup, 2018), we saw great benefit from including the text quality using an MT system, even in this low-resource setting.

Varying the number of grams considered in the subcorpus-building algorithm's vocabulary yielded small and inconsistent changes over unigram selection. We have no insight into which linguistic or corporeal features make it beneficial to consider 2-grams in English-Nepali but slightly detrimental in English-Sinhala.

8 Conclusions

We have presented the techniques we used in our submissions to the WMT19 Parallel Corpus Filtering For Low-Resource Conditions Task. Numerical results show our method to be a fraction of a BLEU point better than the Zipporah baseline for training the SMT system.

Table 1: Results for English-Nepali. Line counts are in thousands and (English) word counts in millions. The two bolded rows are the official AFRL submissions.

Type	Lines selected	Words selected	1M SMT BLEU	5M SMT BLEU
quality	N/A	N/A	2.91	4.26
coverage	50	1.4	1.79	4.17
1-gram	**50**	**1.0**	**3.64**	**4.14**
2-gram	50	1.1	3.88	4.21
3-gram	50	1.2	3.84	4.17
4-gram	50	1.2	3.78	4.23
1-gram	75	1.4	3.50	4.25
1-gram	100	1.9	3.47	4.12
coverage	150	3.8	1.24	3.84
1-gram	**150**	**3.1**	**3.55**	**4.33**
1-gram	225	4.8	3.53	4.12
Zipporah	N/A	N/A	3.40	4.22

Table 2: Results for English-Sinhala. Line counts are in thousands and (English) word counts in millions. The two bolded rows are the official AFRL submissions.

Type	Lines selected	Words selected	1M SMT BLEU	5M SMT BLEU
quality	N/A	N/A	3.26	5.07
coverage	50	1.4	1.98	5.17
1-gram	**50**	**0.8**	**4.31**	**5.16**
2-gram	50	1.0	4.26	5.15
3-gram	50	1.0	4.22	4.98
4-gram	50	1.1	4.30	5.04
1-gram	75	1.2	4.54	5.21
1-gram	100	1.6	4.49	5.19
coverage	150	4.0	1.40	3.43
1-gram	**150**	**2.6**	**4.62**	**5.09**
1-gram	225	4.3	4.57	4.91
Zipporah	N/A	N/A	4.16	4.77

We expect the optimal choices in our method to vary significantly with language pairs and noisy corpora. This might be in parameters (language ID thresholds, τ, n-gram levels, etc.) or the combination of coverage and metric metrics (product, sum, etc.), the design of the MT system(s) used for the text quality metric (e.g., phrase-based or neural, with their myriad design choices) or the text quality metric itself (Meteor, BEER (Stanojević and Sima'an, 2015), chrF (Popović, 2015), etc.).

Building a machine translation system in each direction would provide us with two text quality metric scores to incorporate into the overall score. We expect this would decrease dependence on the language ID thresholds and produce a somewhat better subcorpus.

Opinions, interpretations, conclusions and recommendations are those of the authors and are not necessarily endorsed by the United States Government. Cleared for public release on 12 Jun 2019. Originator reference number RH-19-119920. Case number 88ABW-2019-2964.

References

Ondřej Bojar, Christian Federmann, Mark Fishel, Yvette Graham, Barry Haddow, Matthias Huck, Philipp Koehn, and Christof Monz. 2019. Findings of the 2019 conference on machine translation (wmt19). In *Proceedings of the Fourth Conference on Machine Translation, Volume 2: Shared Task Papers*, Florence, Italy. Association for Computational Linguistics.

Michael Denkowski and Alon Lavie. 2014. Meteor universal: Language specific translation evaluation for any target language. In *Proceedings of the EACL 2014 Workshop on Statistical Machine Translation*.

Nadir Durrani, Helmut Schmid, and Alexander Fraser. 2011. A joint sequence translation model with integrated reordering. In *Proc. of the 49th Annual Meeting of the Association for Computational Linguistics (ACL '11)*, pages 1045–1054, Portland, Oregon.

Grant Erdmann and Jeremy Gwinnup. 2018. Coverage and cynicism: The AFRL submission to the WMT 2018 parallel corpus filtering task. In *Proceedings of the Third Conference on Machine Translation: Shared Task Papers*, pages 872–876, Belgium, Brussels. Association for Computational Linguistics.

Michel Galley and Christopher D. Manning. 2008. A simple and effective hierarchical phrase reordering model. In *Proceedings of the Conference on Empirical Methods in Natural Language Processing*, EMNLP '08, pages 848–856.

Jeremy Gwinnup, Tim Anderson, Grant Erdmann, Katherine Young, Michaeel Kazi, Elizabeth Salesky, and Brian Thompson. 2016. The AFRL-MITLL WMT16 news-translation task systems. In *Proceedings of the First Conference on Machine Translation*, pages 296–302, Berlin, Germany. Association for Computational Linguistics.

Jeremy Gwinnup, Tim Anderson, Grant Erdmann, Katherine Young, Christina May, Michaeel Kazi, Elizabeth Salesky, and Brian Thompson. 2015. The AFRL-MITLL WMT15 system: There's more than one way to decode it! In *Proceedings of the Tenth Workshop on Statistical Machine Translation*, pages 112–119, Lisbon, Portugal. Association for Computational Linguistics.

Armand Joulin, Edouard Grave, Piotr Bojanowski, Matthijs Douze, Hérve Jégou, and Tomas Mikolov. 2016a. FastText.zip: Compressing text classification models. *arXiv preprint arXiv:1612.03651*.

Armand Joulin, Edouard Grave, Piotr Bojanowski, and Tomas Mikolov. 2016b. Bag of tricks for efficient text classification. *arXiv preprint arXiv:1607.01759*.

Philipp Koehn, Hieu Hoang, Alexandra Birch, Chris Callison-Burch, Marcello Federico, Nicola Bertoldi, Brooke Cowan, Wade Shen, Christine Moran, Richard Zens, Chris Dyer, Ondřej Bojar, Alexandra Constantin, and Evan Herbst. 2007. Moses: Open source toolkit for statistical machine translation. In *Proc. of the 45th Annual Meeting of the ACL on Interactive Poster and Demonstration Sessions*, ACL '07, pages 177–180.

Taku Kudo and John Richardson. 2018. SentencePiece: A simple and language independent subword tokenizer and detokenizer for neural text processing. In *Proceedings of the 2018 Conference on Empirical Methods in Natural Language Processing: System Demonstrations*, pages 66–71, Brussels, Belgium. Association for Computational Linguistics.

Maja Popović. 2015. chrF: character n-gram F-score for automatic MT evaluation. In *Proceedings of the Tenth Workshop on Statistical Machine Translation*, pages 392–395, Lisbon, Portugal. Association for Computational Linguistics.

Miloš Stanojević and Khalil Sima'an. 2015. BEER 1.1: ILLC UvA submission to metrics and tuning task. In *Proceedings of the Tenth Workshop on Statistical Machine Translation*, pages 396–401, Lisbon, Portugal. Association for Computational Linguistics.

Hainan Xu and Philipp Koehn. 2017. Zipporah: a fast and scalable data cleaning system for noisy web-crawled parallel corpora. In *Proceedings of the 2017 Conference on Empirical Methods in Natural Language Processing*, pages 2945–2950, Copenhagen, Denmark. Association for Computational Linguistics.

Webinterpret Submission to the
WMT2019 Shared Task on Parallel Corpus Filtering

Jesús González-Rubio
WebInterpret Inc.
`jesus.gonzalez-rubio@webinterpret.com`

Abstract

This document describes the participation of Webinterpret in the shared task on parallel corpus filtering at the Fourth Conference on Machine Translation (WMT 2019). Here, we describe the main characteristics of our approach and discuss the results obtained on the data sets published for the shared task.

1 Task Description

Parallel corpus filtering task at WMT19 tackles the problem of cleaning noisy parallel corpora. Given a noisy parallel corpus (crawled from the web), participants develop methods to filter it to a smaller size of high quality sentence pairs.

In comparison to the German-English task last year, the organizers now pose the problem under more challenging low-resource conditions including Nepali and Sinhala languages. The organizers provide very noisy 40.6 million-word (English token count) Nepali-English and a 59.6 million-word Sinhala-English corpora. Both raw corpora were crawled from the web as part of the Paracrawl project[1]. Participants are asked to select a subset of sentence pairs that amount to (a) 5 million, and (b) 1 million English words. The quality of the resulting subsets is determined by the quality of a statistical and a neural Machine Translation (MT) systems trained on the selected data. The quality of the translation systems is measured on a held-out test set of Wikipedia translations. Despite the known origin of the test set, the organizers make explicit that the task addresses the challenge of data quality and not domain-relatedness of the data for a particular use case.

For our submission, we propose a variation of coverage augmentation ranking (Haffari et al., 2009; Gascó et al., 2012; González-Rubio, 2014). The main idea underlying our approach is to minimize the amount of unseen events for the model. In MT, these unseen events are words or sequences thereof. These unseen events result in a loss

of model coverage and, ultimately, of translation quality. The main difference of our submission respect to previous approaches is that we do not rely on an in-domain corpus to identify underrepresented events. Instead, we look for the subset of sentences that provide the most coherent coverage among themselves. One of the advantages of this approach is that it does not rely on pretrained models requiring additional data to train. This characteristic fits perfectly with the focus on low-resource languages of this year's task.

The rest of this document is organized as follows. First, we describe the details of our approach. Next, we present the results of our submission. Finally, we close with the conclusions and some ideas for future developments.

2 Sentence Pairs Ranking

Our goal is to rank the sentence pairs in the raw corpora such that the pairs in the top of the ranking are better candidates for training data. As pre-processing, we only apply tokenization via the TokTok tokenizer in the NLTK python package.

First, we filtered out some of the pairs $(\mathbf{x}, \mathbf{y})$ in the raw corpus according to several heuristic rules (Section 2.1). Then, for the remaining pairs, we computed a ranking value $r(\mathbf{x}, \mathbf{y})$ for each of them. This ranking, was the result of the combination of several different ranking functions aiming at capturing the "value" of the sentence pair according to different criteria (Section 2.2 and Section 2.3). Finally, we used the final ranking of each pair to compute its corresponding score as required for the shared task (Section 2.4).

2.1 Initial Rule-based Filtering

We start by describing the set of filtering rules implemented to reduce the amount of candidates to be ranked by the more sophisticated methods Sections 2.2, and 2.3. These rules have been previously proposed and successfully implemented in the literature, for instance (Junczys-Dowmunt, 2018; Rossenbach et al., 2018).

---

[1] `https://paracrawl.eu/`

Proceedings of the Fourth Conference on Machine Translation (WMT), Volume 3: Shared Task Papers (Day 2) pages 271–276
Florence, Italy, August 1-2, 2019. ©2019 Association for Computational Linguistics

Method	Nepali-English (2.2M)		Sinhala-English (3.4M)	
	Sent. pairs	Ratio	Sent. pairs	Ratio
Language Identification	1.65M	74.0%	2.27M	67.7%
Length Ratio	0.86M	38.6%	1.13M	33.8%
Max. Sentence Length	0.24M	10.9%	0.27M	8.1%
Combined	2.11M	94.4%	2.92M	86.8%

Table 1: Amount of sentence pairs (in Millions) filtered out by each filtering method. "Combined" denotes the final amount of sentence pairs filtered out after applying the three methods in sequence.

The filtering rules we implemented for our submission are not language specific, and moreover, they only place very mild assumption on what constitutes a "good" sentence pair. In particular, *maximum sentence length* is a technical restrictions implemented by many MT systems. Given that the translation system is most probably going to ignore them in any case, it makes no sense for us to even rank them. Table 1 displays the amount of sentences pairs filtered out by each method.

Language Identification

We implemented a very straightforward language identification using the Python LangID package. Specifically, we filtered out all those pairs not belonging to the desired pair of languages. For example, each pair $(\mathbf{x}, \mathbf{y})$ in the Nepali-English corpus should satisfy: $\text{LangID}(\mathbf{x}) = $ "ne" and $\text{LangID}(\mathbf{y}) = $ "en", otherwise the sentence pair is filtered out. For Sinhala-English, we require Sinhala as source language: $\text{LangID}(\mathbf{x}) = $ "si".

Length Ratio

As our second heuristic filtering, we chose the ratio between the number of tokens of $\mathbf{x}$ and $\mathbf{y}$. This is a very simple criterion, but efficient to identify mispaired sentences. We limited this ratio to be under 1.7 and smoothed the counts by adding 1 to them. That is, we rejected the sentence pair if:

$$\frac{|\mathbf{x}| + 1}{|\mathbf{y}| + 1} \quad \text{or} \quad \frac{|\mathbf{y}| + 1}{|\mathbf{x}| + 1}$$

where $|\mathbf{x}|$ and $|\mathbf{y}|$ are the number of tokens of $\mathbf{x}$ and $\mathbf{y}$ respectively.

Maximum Sentence Length

Most translation systems have an upper bound for the sentence length. These sentences will be ignored in any case during training so we decided to filter them out directly. If either the source ($\mathbf{x}$) or destination ($\mathbf{y}$) sentence in a pair was over 50 tokens, we filtered out the pair.

2.2 Coverage Ranking

Sparse data problems are ubiquitous in MT (Zipf, 1935). In a learning scenario, this means that some rare events will be missing completely from a training set, even when it is very large. Missing events result in a loss of coverage, a situation where the structure of the model is not rich enough to cover all types of input. An extreme case of this are out-of-vocabulary words for which the MT system will have no information on how to translate them. Therefore, words (or sequences thereof) that do not appear in the training set cannot be adequately translated (Haddow and Koehn, 2012; Sennrich et al., 2016).

According to these considerations, we propose to explicitly measure how well represented are the different words on a potential training corpus $\mathcal{T}$ as a proxy of the actual "value" of such corpus. We define this corpus "value", $V(\mathcal{T})$, as:

$$V(\mathcal{T}) = \sum_{s \in \text{tokens}(\mathcal{T})} \frac{\min(N, c(s, \mathcal{T}))}{N} \quad (1)$$

where function $\text{tokens}(\mathcal{T})$ returns the set of tokens that appear in $\mathcal{T}$, $c(s, \mathcal{T})$ counts how many times a token s appears in $\mathcal{T}$, and N denotes a count above which we consider a token to be adequately represented. After some initial experiments, we used $N = 50$ in our submission.

In order to rank the different sentences in the raw corpora, we implemented a greedy algorithm to create a training corpus $\mathcal{T}$ by iteratively adding sentences to it taken from a given pool. At start, $\mathcal{T} = \varnothing$ and the pool is equal to the sentences that passed the filtering rules in the previous section. The sentence to be added at each step is the one that resulted in a new $\mathcal{T}$ with the highest value as measured by Equation 1. This selected sentence is then removed from the pool and definitely added to $\mathcal{T}$. This process repeats until the pool is empty.

This algorithm has a complexity of $\mathcal{O}(R^2)$ where R is the number of sentences initially in the pool. In Section 3, we describe how we modify this algorithm for the final submission in order to improve its time performance.

In our submission, we considered as tokens n-grams of sizes from one up to four, and computed them for both the source and destination sentences. This resulted in a total of eight ranks per sentence pair. We denote each of them as $r_c(\mathbf{s}, n)$ where $\mathbf{s} \in \{\mathbf{x}, \mathbf{y}\}$, and $1 \leq n \leq 4$.

The main shortcoming of this ranking scheme is that it ignores how the source and destination sentences in a pair relate to each other. Long sentences with multiple tokens will most surely rank high even when the other sentence in the pair carry completely different meaning. In order to counterbalance these undesired effects, we implement a secondary adequacy ranking to measure such correspondence between the sentences on each pair.

2.3 Adequacy Ranking

This ranking function measures how much of the original meaning is expressed in the translation and vice versa. Specifically, we estimate to which extent the words in the original and translated sentences correspond to each other.

We compute this ranking from a simple (but fast) word-to-word translation model (Brown et al., 1993). Given a sentence pair $(\mathbf{x}, \mathbf{y})$, we compute a *source-given-target* score according to the geometric average probability over the words for the IBM model 1 formulation:

$$P_{\mathrm{M1}}(\mathbf{x}, \mathbf{y}) = \sqrt[|\mathbf{x}|]{\frac{\prod_{i=1}^{|\mathbf{x}|} \sum_{j=0}^{|\mathbf{y}|} P(x_i \mid y_j)}{(|\mathbf{y}| + 1)^{|\mathbf{x}|}}} \quad (2)$$

where $P(x_i \mid y_j)$ is the lexical probability of the ith source word in $\mathbf{x}$ given the jth target word in $\mathbf{y}$. For the *target-given-source* direction, source and target sentences swap their roles. We denote these two rankings as $r_a^{\mathrm{M1}}(\mathbf{x}, \mathbf{y})$ and $r_a^{\mathrm{M1}}(\mathbf{y}, \mathbf{x})$.

Additionally, we compute another two rankings based on a *Viterbi* implementation of Equation 2:

$$P_{\mathrm{Mv}}(\mathbf{x}, \mathbf{y}) = \sqrt[|\mathbf{x}|]{\frac{\prod_{i=1}^{|\mathbf{x}|} \max_{j=0}^{|\mathbf{y}|} P(x_i \mid y_j)}{(|\mathbf{y}| + 1)^{|\mathbf{x}|}}} \quad (3)$$

where we replace the summation ($\sum_{j=0}^{|\mathbf{y}|}$) in Equation 2 by a maximization. Again, we calculate both source-given-target and target-given-source directions: $r_a^{\mathrm{Mv}}(\mathbf{x}, \mathbf{y})$ and $r_a^{\mathrm{Mv}}(\mathbf{y}, \mathbf{x})$ respectively.

2.4 Ranking Aggregation

Finally, we combined the different rankings described in previous sections to obtain the final ranking of our submission.

Aggregation of Coverage Rankings

We start combining the eight coverage rankings described in Section 2.2. First, we average the four rankings for $\mathbf{x}$ into a source coverage ranking. Then, we repeat the process for the four destination rankings. Finally, we got the final coverage ranking $r_C(\mathbf{x}, \mathbf{y})$ as the average between the source and destination coverage rankings:

$$r_c(\mathbf{x}, \mathbf{y}) = \frac{\dfrac{\sum_{n=1}^{4} r_c(\mathbf{x}, n)}{4} + \dfrac{\sum_{n=1}^{4} r_c(\mathbf{y}, n)}{4}}{2} \quad (4)$$

where $r_c(\mathbf{x}, n)$ denotes the ranking of sentence $\mathbf{x}$ using n-grams of size n as tokens.

Aggregation of Adequacy Rankings

First, we averaged the two (source-to-destination and destination-to-source) rankings computed with Equation 2. Then, we repeated the process for the two rankings computed with Equation 3. The final adequacy ranking $r_a(\mathbf{x}, \mathbf{y})$ was then obtained as the average of these two rankings:

$$r_a(\mathbf{x}, \mathbf{y}) = \left(\frac{r_a^{\mathrm{M1}}(\mathbf{x}, \mathbf{y}) + r_a^{\mathrm{M1}}(\mathbf{y}, \mathbf{x})}{2} + \frac{r_a^{\mathrm{Mv}}(\mathbf{x}, \mathbf{y}) + r_a^{\mathrm{Mv}}(\mathbf{y}, \mathbf{x})}{2} \right) / 2 \quad (5)$$

Final Submission Scores

Once we had computed for each sentence pair $(\mathbf{x}, \mathbf{y})$ its coverage ($r_c(\mathbf{x}, \mathbf{y})$) and adequacy ($r_a(\mathbf{x}, \mathbf{y})$) rankings, we averaged these two to obtain the final ranking $r(\mathbf{x}, \mathbf{y})$ of the pair:

$$r(\mathbf{x}, \mathbf{y}) = \frac{r_c(\mathbf{x}, \mathbf{y}) + r_a(\mathbf{x}, \mathbf{y})}{2} \quad (6)$$

For the final submission however, the organizers ask to provide a *score* for each pair. Scores do not have to be meaningful, except that higher scores indicate better quality. To do this, we take the simple solution of computing the score $s(\mathbf{x}, \mathbf{y})$ as the number of sentences in the raw corpus $(\mathrm{R})^2$ divided by the final ranking of the sentence pair.

$^2 R = 2235512$ for Nepali-English, and $R = 3357018$ for Sinhala-English.

Additionally, in order to break potential ties, and to provide a smoothing score for filtered out sentences (see Section 2.1), we added to the score the average word probability as described in Equation 2. The final scores in our submission were:

$$s(\mathbf{x}, \mathbf{y}) = \frac{R}{r(\mathbf{x}, \mathbf{y})} + P_{\mathrm{M1}}(\mathbf{x}, \mathbf{y}) \qquad (7)$$

Note that filtered pairs were considered to have an "infinite" ranking which results in $\frac{R}{r(\mathbf{x},\mathbf{y})} - 0$; for unfiltered pairs the value of this fraction is assured to be greater than one.

3 Submission

We submitted three different score files to the shared task. All employ the same score function Equation 7 but use different ranking functions:

- PRIMARY: computed using as ranking function the combination of coverage and adequacy rankings in Equation 6.

- SECONDARYCOV: computed using only the aggregated coverage ranking in Equation 4.

- SECONDARYADE: computed using only the aggregated adequacy ranking in Equation 5.

3.1 Coverage Rankings Computation

As described in Section 2.2, we implemented a greedy algorithm to compute coverage ranking. At each step, the algorithm selects the sentences that provide a largest increase of "value" (Equation 1) to a iteratively increasing training corpus.

The computational cost of this approach is $\mathcal{O}(R^2)$ where R is the number of sentences under consideration. The initial filtering partially alleviates this cost by drastically reducing the amount of sentences to rank. However, it is still a slow process that took about one second per iteration with our Python implementation[3]. To further reduce the computational time of the algorithm, we implemented a batch approach where at each step we selected not a single sentence but a batch of the most "valuable" ones. After some experiments, we chose to select 1000 sentences at each step as a good compromise; running time was reduced by a factor of 1000 while the "value" of the selected training corpus was barely affected.

---

[3] After filtering about 176k pairs remained for Nepali-English, and 442k pairs remained for Sinhala-English.

	Ne–En		Si–En	
	1M	5M	1M	5M
PRIMARY	3.4 3.1	3.3 2.6	3.7 2.1	**4.1** 1.7
SECONDARYCOV	2.9 0.5	4.2 2.4	2.6 0.1	4.0 1.2
SECONDARYADE	**3.5** 3.6	**4.3** 2.4	**3.9** 2.9	**4.1** 1.4

Table 2: Results of our submissions, in BLEU [%]. SMT figures are in blue while NMT is in red. Best results are in bold.

3.2 Adequacy Rankings Computation

The cornerstone of the adequacy ranking described in Section 2.3 is the probabilistic lexicons in Equations 2 and 3. In our submissions, we used the probabilistic lexicons that can be obtained as a sub-product of the training of full statistical MT models. For this end, we used Moses (Koehn et al., 2007) with its default configuration and the parallel data provided by the organizers as training data.

3.3 Evaluation and Results

Participants in the shared task were asked to submit a file with quality scores, one per line, corresponding to the sentence pairs on the Nepali-English and Sinhala-English corpora. The performance of the submissions is evaluated by subsampling 1 million and 5 million word corpora based on these scores, training statistical (Koehn et al., 2007) and neural [4] MT systems with these corpora, and assessing translation quality on blind tests using BLEU (Papineni et al., 2002).

Table 2 shows the scores of our three submissions for each language pair and condition. Of the three, the one based on coverage rankings (SECONDARYCOV) showed a lower performance consistently being outperformed, particularly in the 1 million condition, by both our PRIMARY and SECONDARYADE submissions.

We were surprised by the "poor" performance of coverage ranking. Previous works (Haffari et al., 2009; Gascó et al., 2012) showed quite promised results. However, in contrast to our case, all these assume the availability of a sample of the domain to be translated. We hypothesize that the lack of this in-domain data in conjunction with the eclectic domains of the data to be filtered are the causes of the poor results of this approach. Moreover, the greedy selection implemented may aggravate this issue by taking not-optimal initial decisions from which the algorithm cannot recover.

Another interesting observation is the unintu-

---

[4] https://github.com/facebookresearch/flores

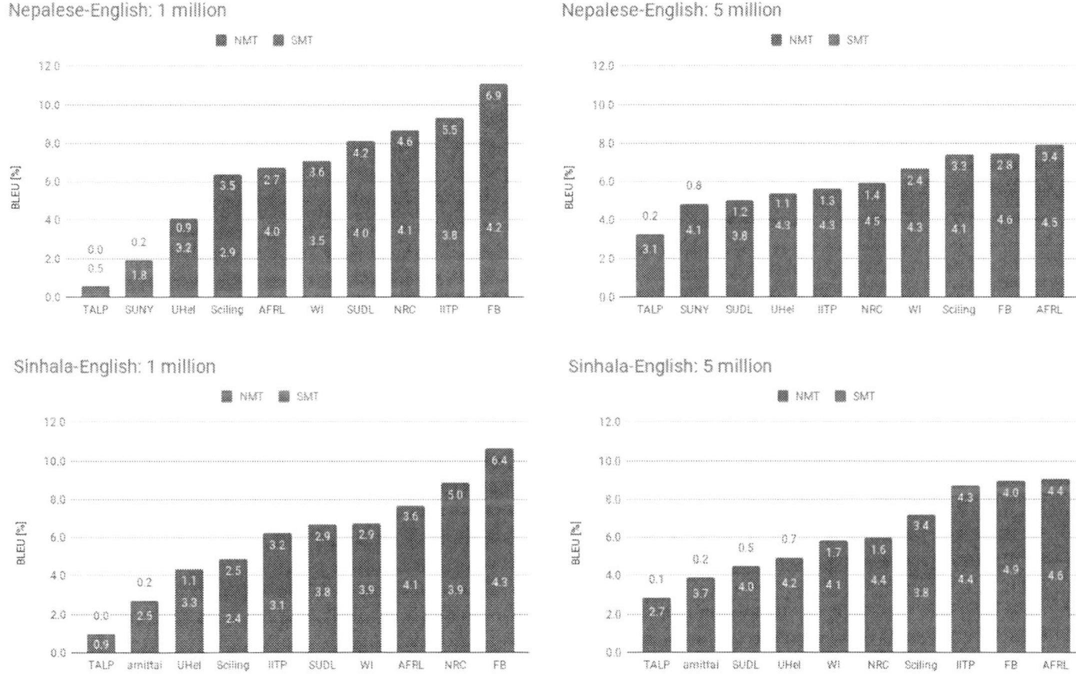

Figure 1: Best results for each team in the competition. We display the participants by increasing sum of BLEU scores for neural and statistical MT models.

itive results for NMT. While SMT results tend to go up as more data is selected, results for NMT tend to show the opposite trend. A fact to consider is that actual BLEU figures are quite low so the actual relevance of these trends are not clear. Additionally, given that this observation is valid other submissions as we will see next, we think this is an issue worthy of further investigation.

After discussing the performance of our submissions, we will compare our best submission on each condition to the rest of participants. Figure 1 summarizes the results of the shared task as reported by the organizers of the task (Bojar et al., 2019). Each sub-figure displays the best submission of each individual participant institution for a particular task and condition. Plots in the upper row show results for Nepalese-English while the bottom row does the same for Sinhala-English. Plots in the left column are for the 1 million condition while results for the 5 million condition are shown in the right column. Stacked bars displayed in the plots denote the BLEU scores for the statistical (blue) and neural (red) systems. We sort them in increasing order according to each system's sum of SMT and NMT scores.

The organizers do not provide confidence intervals for the reported scores so compare results is somehow difficult. Still, as we mention previously, it is surprising the degradation in translation quality for NMT when comparing the 5 million condition to the 1 million condition. Usually, a larger amount of data correlates with an increase in translation quality. In this case, however, scores for SMT barely changed while NMT results went down. This seems to indicate that our methods were not sophisticated enough to find adequate data, or that the really adequate data in the noise corpora amount for less than 5 million words.

Our submission (WI) lays in the upper half among the best submission of the different participants. Regarding Nepalese-English, it scored an aggregated of 7.1 and 6.7 BLEU points for the 1 million and 5 million conditions respectively. This represent respectively about a 64% of the best result submitted for the 1 million condition, and about a 85% of the best result for the 5 million condition. As for the Sinhala–English condition, we scored 6.8 and 5.8 BLEU points which represent a 64% of the best results respectively.

4   Conclusions

We have presented our submission to the WMT19 shared task on parallel corpus filtering. We have mostly explored the application of coverage augmentation ranking techniques with the aim at selecting the subset of sentence pairs that provide the best coherent coverage for the raw sentences.

Results have shown that our proposed coverage approach is not well suited for this particular task. Our secondary submission based on lexical scoring works better in all conditions, and even outperforms our primary submission that combines both coverage and lexical rankings.

One interesting effect seen in the results of the task is the reduced performance on NMT in the presence of more data that can be observed for all participants. Given this, we think that exploring methods able to decide when adding more data will be harmful for performance it is a good research direction to explore.

Acknowledgments

We want to thank the reviewers of the paper for their valuable comments and suggestions. Work funded by WebInterpret Inc.

References

Ondřej Bojar, Christian Federmann, Mark Fishel, Yvette Graham, Barry Haddow, Matthias Huck, Philipp Koehn, Christof Monz, Mathias Müller, and Matt Post. 2019. Findings of the 2019 conference on machine translation (wmt19). In *Proceedings of the Fourth Conference on Machine Translation, Volume 2: Shared Task Papers*.

Peter F. Brown, Vincent J. Della Pietra, Stephen A. Della Pietra, and Robert L. Mercer. 1993. The mathematics of statistical machine translation: parameter estimation. *Computational Linguistics*, 19:263–311.

Guillem Gascó, Martha-Alicia Rocha, Germán Sanchis-Trilles, Jesús Andrés-Ferrer, and Francisco Casacuberta. 2012. Does more data always yield better translations? In *Proceedings of the 13th Conference of the European Chapter of the Association for Computational Linguistics*, pages 152–161.

Jesús González-Rubio. 2014. *On the Effective Deployment of Currrent Machine Translation Technology*. Ph.D. thesis, DSIC, U. Politècnica de València. Supervised by Dr. Daniel Ortiz-Martínez and Prof. Francisco Casacuberta.

Barry Haddow and Philipp Koehn. 2012. Analysing the effect of out-of-domain data on smt systems. In *Proceedings of the Workshop on Statistical Machine Translation*, pages 422–432, Montreal, Canada. Association for Computational Linguistics.

Gholamreza Haffari, Maxim Roy, and Anoop Sarkar. 2009. Active learning for statistical phrase-based machine translation. In *Proceedings of Human Language Technologies: The 2009 Annual Conference of the North American Chapter of the Association for Computational Linguistics*, pages 415–423.

Marcin Junczys-Dowmunt. 2018. Dual conditional cross-entropy filtering of noisy parallel corpora. In *Proceedings of the Third Conference on Machine Translation, Volume 2: Shared Task Papers*, pages 901–908, Belgium, Brussels. Association for Computational Linguistics.

Philipp Koehn, Hieu Hoang, Alexandra Birch, Chris Callison-Burch, Marcello Federico, Nicola Bertoldi, Brooke Cowan, Wade Shen, Christine Moran, Richard Zens, Chris Dyer, Ondrej Bojar, Alexandra Constantin, and Evan Herbst. 2007. Moses: Open Source Toolkit for Statistical Machine Translation. In *Proceedings of ACL 2007, System Demonstrations*.

Kishore Papineni, Salim Roukos, Todd Ward, and Wei-Jing Zhu. 2002. Bleu: a method for automatic evaluation of machine translation. In *Proceedings of the 40th Annual Meeting of the Association for Computational Linguistics*, pages 311–318.

Nick Rossenbach, Jan Rosendahl, Yunsu Kim, Miguel Graa, Aman Gokrani, and Hermann Ney. 2018. The rwth aachen university filtering system for the wmt 2018 parallel corpus filtering task. In *Proceedings of the Third Conference on Machine Translation, Volume 2: Shared Task Papers*, pages 959–967, Belgium, Brussels. Association for Computational Linguistics.

Rico Sennrich, Barry Haddow, and Alexandra Birch. 2016. Neural machine translation of rare words with subword units. In *Proceedings of the 54th Annual Meeting of the Association for Computational Linguistics (Volume 1: Long Papers)*, pages 1715–1725.

George Kingsley Zipf. 1935. *The Psychobiology of Language*. Houghton-Mifflin.

Noisy Parallel Corpus Filtering through Projected Word Embeddings

Murathan Kurfalı[*]
Department of Linguistics
Stockholm University
murathan.kurfali@ling.su.se

Robert Östling[*]
Department of Linguistics
Stockholm University
robert@ling.su.se

Abstract

We present a very simple method for parallel text cleaning of low-resource languages, based on projection of word embeddings trained on large monolingual corpora in high-resource languages. In spite of its simplicity, we approach the strong baseline system in the downstream machine translation evaluation.

1 Introduction

With the advent of web-scale parallel text mining, quality estimation and filtering is becoming an increasingly important step in multilingual NLP. Existing methods focus on languages with relatively large amounts of parallel text available (Schwenk, 2018; Artetxe and Schwenk, 2018), but scaling down to languages with limited amounts of parallel text poses new challenges. We present a method based on projecting word embeddings learned from a monolingual corpus in a high-resource language, to the target low-resource language through whatever parallel text is available.

The goal of participants in the WMT 2019 parallel corpus filtering shared task is to select the 5 million words of parallel sentences producing the highest-quality machine translation system, given a set of automatically crawled sentence candidates of varying quality. It is the continuation of the last year's task (Koehn et al., 2018), except that this year two low-resource languages are used: Nepali and Sinhalese.

2 Related Work

We refer readers to Koehn et al. (2018) for a more thorough review of the methods used in the WMT 2018 parallel corpus filtering shared task, and here review only a few studies of particular relevance to our model.

The Zipporah model of Xu and Koehn (2017) is used as a (strong) baseline in this year's shared task. It aims to find sentences pairs with high adequacy, according to dictionaries generated from an aligned corpora, and fluency modeled by n-gram language models.

Zariņa et al. (2015) use existing parallel corpora to learn word alignments and identify parallel sentences on the assumption that non-parallel sentences have few or none word alignments. In preliminary experiments we also evaluated a variant of this method, but found the resulting machine translation system to produce worse results than the simple approach described below.

Similar to the our model, Bouamor and Sajjad (2018) perform parallel sentence mining through sentence representations obtained by averaging bilingual word embeddings. Based on the cosine similarity, they create a candidate translation list for each sentence on the source side. Then, finding the correct translation is modelled as either a machine translation or binary classification task.

3 Data

In this section, we summarize the target noisy data and the allowed third-party resources where we train our model.

3.1 Target Noisy Corpora

The target noisy parallel corpora provided by the WMT 2019 organizers come from the Paracrawl project[1], and is provided before the standard filtering step to ensure high-recall, low-precision retrieval of parallel sentences.

The noisy corpora have 40.6 million words on the English side (English-Nepali) and 59.6 million words (English-Sinhala). The task is thus to se-

---

[*] Authors contributed equally.

[1] https://paracrawl.eu/

Proceedings of the Fourth Conference on Machine Translation (WMT), Volume 3: Shared Task Papers (Day 2) pages 277–281
Florence, Italy, August 1-2, 2019. ©2019 Association for Computational Linguistics

Language	Word Count	Sentence Count
Sinhala	3,745,282	646,781
Nepali	3,738,058	581,297

Table 1: Word and sentences counts of the "clean" parallel text

lect the approximately 10% highest-quality parallel text.

3.2 Training Data

Participants are allowed to use only the resources provided by the organizers to train systems. The permissible resources include supposedly clean parallel data, consisting of bible translations, Ubuntu localization files as well as movie subtitles. Larger monolingual corpora based on Wikipedia and common crawl data were also provided.[2]

To train our model, we use all the parallel data available for the English-Sinhala and English-Nepali pairs (summarized in Table 1) and the English Wikipedia dump which contains about 2 billion words. We modified the Nepali-English dictionary so that multiple translations were split into separate lines. As manual inspection revealed some problems in this data as well, we ran the same pre-filtering pipeline on it as we used for the noisy evaluation data (see Section 4.1)

4 Method

In this section, we present the components our model used to score the nosiy parallel data.

4.1 Pre-filtering Methods

As many types of poor sentence pairs are easy to detect with simple heuristics, we begin by applying a series of pre-filters. Before pre-filtering, the corpus is normalized through punctuation removal and lowercasing. We pre-filter all parallel data, both the (supposedly) clean and the noisy evaluation sets, using a set of heuristics based heavily on the work of Pinnis (2018):

- **Empty sentence filter:** Remove pairs where either sentence is empty after normalization.

- **Numeral filter:** Remove pairs where either sentence contains 25% or more numerals.

- **Sentence length filter:** Remove pairs where sentence lengths differ by 15 or more words.

- **Foreign writing filter:** Remove pairs where either sentence contains 10% or more words written in the wrong writing system.

- **Long string filter:** Remove pairs containing any token longer than 30 characters.

- **Word length filter:** Remove pairs where either sentence has an average word length of less than 2.

The statistics of each individual filter on the training data and the noisy data are provided in Table 2 and Table 3. In total, the pre-filtering step removed 2,790,557 pairs for the English–Sinhala data and 1,778,339 pairs for English–Nepali. Of all filters, foreign writing and numeral filter seem to be the most useful ones in terms of removing poor data.

Although almost 150 thousand sentence pairs are filtered out in the training data, the rate is considerably less than that of the raw noisy data suggesting that our pre-filters have a low rate of false positives. We further tested our pre-filters on the development data for the MT system evaluation (discarding the result), and found that less than 3% is removed.

4.2 Multilingual word vectors

We first train 300-dimensional FASTTEXT vectors (Bojanowski et al., 2017) with its default parameters using the provided English Wikipedia data.

Our first goal is now to create word vectors for the low-resource languages Sinhala and Nepali, in the same space as the English vectors.

After pre-filtering, we perform word alignment of the provided parallel text using the EFLOMAL tool (Östling and Tiedemann, 2016) with default parameters. Alignment is performed in both directions, and the intersection of both alignments is used. The vector v_i^f for word i in the non-English language f is computed as

$$v_i^f = \sum_j c(i,j) v_j^e$$

that is, the weighted sum of the vectors v_j^e of all aligned English word types j, which have been aligned to the non-English type i with frequency $c(i,j)$. Word types which are aligned less than 20% of the most commonly aligned type are not

---

[2]http://www.statmt.org/wmt19/parallel-corpus-filtering.html

278

	SINHALA		NEPALI	
	Count	**Percentage**	**Count**	**Percentage**
Before filtering	646,781	100	581,297	100
Word length filter	3,149	-0.49	4,133	-0.71
Long string filter	90	-0.01	77	-0.01
Numeral filter	4,803	-0.74	11,981	-2.06
Empty sentence filter	1,859	-0.29	410	-0.07
Sentence length filter	1,140	-0.18	4,501	-0.77
Foreign writing filter	38,965	-6.02	96,161	-16.54
Remaining	596,775	92.27	464,034	79.83

Table 2: Result of pre-filtering the "clean" parallel data.

	SINHALA		NEPALI	
	Count	**Percentage**	**Count**	**Percentage**
Before filtering	3,357,018	100.0	2,235,512	100.0
Word length filter	-7,981	-0.2	-3,015	-0.1
Long string filter	-2,782	-0.1	-4,848	-0.2
Numeral filter	-1,202,438	-35.8	-556,491	-24.9
Empty sentence filter	-7,672	-0.2	-4,378	-0.2
Sentence length filter	-216,486	-6.4	-272,567	-12.2
Foreign writing filter	-1,353,198	-40.3	-937,040	-41.9
Remaining	566,461	16.87	457,173	20.45

Table 3: Result of pre-filtering the noisy data.

counted, to compensate for potentially noisy word alignments. In other words, we let $c(i, j) = 0$ if the actual count is less than $0.2 \max_{j'} c(i, j')$. On average, the vector of each Sinhala word type is projected from 1.66 English word types, and each Nepali word from 1.83 English words types.

4.3 Sentence similarity

Given a sentence pair x and y, our task is to assign a score of translation equivalence. The multilingual word vectors learned in Section 4.2 provide a measure of *word-level* translational equivalence, by using the cosine similarity between the vectors of two words. Since sentence-level equivalence correlates strongly with word-level equivalence, we can approximate the former by looking at pairwise cosine similarity between the words in the sentence pair: $\cos(v_i^e, v_j^f)$. A good translation should tend to have a high value of $\max_j \cos(v_i^e, v_j^f)$ since most English words w_i^e (with vector v_i^e) should have a translationally equivalent word w_j^f (with vector v_j^f) in the other language, and these vectors should be similar.

However, this naive approach suffers from the so-called hubness problem in high-dimensional

	1 Million	5 Million
Sinhala	3.59 (4.65)	0.53 (3.74)
Nepali	4.55 (5.23)	1.21 (1.85)

Table 4: BLEU scores of the NMT system trained on the released development sets. Numbers within parenthesis refer to the baseline scores

spaces (Radovanović et al., 2010), where some words tend to have high similarity to a large number of other words. This can be compensated for by taking the distribution of vector similarities for each word into account (as done in similar contexts by e.g. Conneau et al., 2017; Artetxe and Schwenk, 2018). We use this information in two ways. First, all words which have an average cosine similarity higher than 0.6 to the words in the English sentence are removed since they are unlikely to be informative. We then use as our score the ratio between the highest and the second highest similarity within the sentence, averaged over all remaining words in the sentence.[3]

---

[3]Sentences with vectors for less than half of their words are removed, since we are unable to make a reliable estimate.

	Nepali		Sinhala	
	Sentence Count	Word Count	Sentence Count	Word Count
1 Million	46,529	793,233	55,293	897,198
5 Million	272,605 (248,765)	3,737,250 (3,456,614)	250,767 (279,503)	4,119,591 (3,327,811)

Table 5: Word and sentence counts in the 1 million and 5 million sub-samples according to our model. Numbers in parenthesis refer to the counts of the baseline system (Xu and Koehn, 2017) which is only available only for 5 million sub-sample

5 Results

The quality of the sub-sampled data is assessed according to the BLEU scores of the statistical and neural machine translation systems trained on them.

Here, we present the BLEU scores of the NMT system (Guzmán et al., 2019) which will be used in the official evaluation on the released development set. We evaluate our model via two different sub-samples, one with 1 million and one with 5 million words on the English side. See Table 5 for statistics on the filtered data.

Table 4 presents our results using the NMT system. For Nepali, the performance of our model approaches the strong baseline on both the 1 million and 5 million sub-samples, whereas the NMT system fails completely using the 5 million word Sinhala sub-sample. All BLEU scores are below 6, for our system as well as for the baseline, indicating that there is insufficient data for the NMT system to learn a useful translation model.

6 Conclusion

We have described our submission to the WMT 2019 parallel corpus filtering shared task. Our submission explored the use of multilingual word embeddings for the task of parallel corpus filtering. The embeddings were projected from a high-resource language, to a low-resource language without sufficiently large monolingual corpora, making the approach suitable for a wide range of languages.

Acknowledgments

We would like to thank NVIDIA for their GPU grant.

References

Mikel Artetxe and Holger Schwenk. 2018. Massively multilingual sentence embeddings for zero-shot cross-lingual transfer and beyond. *CoRR*, abs/1812.10464.

Piotr Bojanowski, Edouard Grave, Armand Joulin, and Tomas Mikolov. 2017. Enriching word vectors with subword information. *Transactions of the Association for Computational Linguistics*, 5:135–146.

Houda Bouamor and Hassan Sajjad. 2018. H2@bucc18: Parallel sentence extraction from comparable corpora using multilingual sentence embeddings. In *Proc. Workshop on Building and Using Comparable Corpora*.

Alexis Conneau, Guillaume Lample, Marc'Aurelio Ranzato, Ludovic Denoyer, and Hervé Jégou. 2017. Word translation without parallel data. *arXiv preprint arXiv:1710.04087*.

Francisco Guzmán, Peng-Jen Chen, Myle Ott, Juan Pino, Guillaume Lample, Philipp Koehn, Vishrav Chaudhary, and Marc'Aurelio Ranzato. 2019. Two new evaluation datasets for low-resource machine translation: Nepali-english and sinhala-english. *arXiv preprint arXiv:1902.01382*.

Philipp Koehn, Huda Khayrallah, Kenneth Heafield, and Mikel L Forcada. 2018. Findings of the wmt 2018 shared task on parallel corpus filtering. In *Proceedings of the Third Conference on Machine Translation: Shared Task Papers*, pages 726–739.

Robert Östling and Jörg Tiedemann. 2016. Efficient word alignment with Markov Chain Monte Carlo. *Prague Bulletin of Mathematical Linguistics*, 106:125–146.

Marcis Pinnis. 2018. Tilde's parallel corpus filtering methods for WMT 2018. In *Proceedings of the Third Conference on Machine Translation: Shared Task Papers*, pages 939–945, Belgium, Brussels. Association for Computational Linguistics.

Miloš Radovanović, Alexandros Nanopoulos, and Mirjana Ivanović. 2010. Hubs in space: Popular nearest neighbors in high-dimensional data. *Journal of Machine Learning Research*, 11(Sep):2487–2531.

Holger Schwenk. 2018. Filtering and mining parallel data in a joint multilingual space. In *Proceedings of the 56th Annual Meeting of the Association for Computational Linguistics (Volume 2: Short Papers)*, pages 228–234, Melbourne, Australia. Association for Computational Linguistics.

Hainan Xu and Philipp Koehn. 2017. Zipporah: a fast
and scalable data cleaning system for noisy web-
crawled parallel corpora. In *Proceedings of the 2017
Conference on Empirical Methods in Natural Language Processing*, pages 2945–2950.

Ieva Zariņa, Pēteris Ņikiforovs, and Raivis Skadiņš.
2015. Word alignment based parallel corpora evaluation and cleaning using machine learning techniques. In *Proceedings of the 18th Annual Conference of the European Association for Machine
Translation*.

Filtering of Noisy Parallel Corpora Based on Hypothesis Generation

Zuzanna Parcheta[1]   **Germán Sanchis-Trilles**[1]   **Francisco Casacuberta**[2]
[1]Sciling S.L.,Carrer del Riu 321, Pinedo, 46012, Spain
{zparcheta, gsanchis}@sciling.com
[2]PRHLT Research Center, Camino de Vera s/n, 46022 Valencia, Spain
fcn@prhlt.upv.es

Abstract

The filtering task of noisy parallel corpora in WMT2019 aims to challenge participants to create filtering methods to be useful for training machine translation systems. In this work, we introduce a noisy parallel corpora filtering system based on generating hypotheses by means of a translation model. We train translation models in both language pairs: Nepali–English and Sinhala–English using provided parallel corpora. To create the best possible translation model, we first join all provided parallel corpora (Nepali, Sinhala and Hindi to English) and after that, we applied bilingual cross-entropy selection for both language pairs (Nepali–English and Sinhala–English). Once the translation models are trained, we translate the noisy corpora and generate a hypothesis for each sentence pair. We compute the smoothed BLEU score between the target sentence and generated hypothesis. In addition, we apply several rules to discard very noisy or inadequate sentences which can lower the translation score. These heuristics are based on sentence length, source and target similarity and source language detection. We compare our results with the baseline published on the shared task website, which uses the Zipporah model, over which we achieve significant improvements in one of the conditions in the shared task. The designed filtering system is domain independent and all experiments are conducted using neural machine translation.

1 Introduction

A large amount of parallel corpora can be extracted using web-crawling. This technique of data acquisition is very useful to increase the training set for low-resourced languages. Unfortunately, the extracted data can include noisy sentence pairs, such as unaligned sentences, partially translated pairs, or sentences containing different languages than those intended. For these reasons the creation of systems for filtering of noisy parallel corpora are needed.

In this paper, we introduce a filtering method for noisy parallel corpora based mainly on generating hypotheses for each sentence pair from noisy data and scoring based on hypothesis and target sentence similarity. This technique consists of building the best possible translation engine for each language pair and generating a translation hypothesis for each sentence of the noisy data. Once the hypotheses are generated, we compute the BLEU (Papineni et al., 2002), smoothed by adding one to both numerator and denominator from (Lin and Och, 2004), between each target and hypothesis. To create a translation engine, which will be used for generating hypothesis for each sentence from noisy corpus, we select sentence pairs using bilingual cross-entropy selection (Axelrod et al., 2011) from all parallel corpora provided (Nepali, Sinhala, Hindi to English) jointly. To apply bilingual cross-entropy, we first train language models using the provided monolingual corpora in Nepali, Sinhala and English. In addition, we use some rules to discard useless sentences by filtering according to sentence length, Nepali and Sinhala characters detection, and BLEU scoring between source and target sentences. The last rule is used to discard highly similar sentence pairs.

The paper is structured as follows: Section 2 describes the shared task, the provided data, the subsampling process and the evaluation system. In Section 3 we describe the developed method for filtering noisy data. We describe the experiments conducted and the results. Conclusions and future work are drawn in Section 4.

Proceedings of the Fourth Conference on Machine Translation (WMT), Volume 3: Shared Task Papers (Day 2) pages 282–288
Florence, Italy, August 1-2, 2019. ©2019 Association for Computational Linguistics

2 WMT 2019 shared task on parallel corpus filtering for low-resource conditions

The task "Parallel Corpus Filtering for Low-Resource Conditions"[1] tackles the problem of cleaning noisy parallel corpora for low-resourced language pairs. Given a noisy parallel corpus, participants are required to develop methods to filter it down to a smaller size with a high quality subset. This year there are two language pairs: Nepali–English and Sinhala–English. Participants are asked to provide score files for each sentence in each of the noisy parallel sets. The scores will be used to subsample sentence pairs into two different training set sizes: 1 million and 5 million English words. For this task, very noisy corpora of 40.6 million English words in Nepali–English and 59.6 million English words in Sinhala–English are provided. The data were crawled from the web as part of the Paracrawl project[2]. The quality of the resulting subsets is determined by the quality of a statistical machine translation (SMT) and neural machine translation (NMT) systems trained on this data. The quality of the machine translation system is measured with the sacreBLEU score (Post, 2018) on a held-out test set of Wikipedia translations for Nepali-English (ne–en) and Sinhala-English (si–en). The organisers provide development and test sets for each pair of languages but due to the fact that the task addresses the challenge of data quality and not domain-relatedness of the data for a particular use case, the test sets may be very different from the final official test set in terms of topics.

2.1 Data provided

Organisers provide noisy corpora for the Nepali–English and Sinhala–English language pairs. The main figures of both corpora are shown in Table 1.

In addition, organisers provide links to the permissible third-party sources of bilingual data to be used in the competition. Parallel corpora for the Nepali–English language pair comes from the Bible, Global Voices, Penn Tree Bank, GNOME/KDE/Ubuntu and Nepali Dictionary corpora. For the Sinhala–English language pair, the Open Subtitles and GNOME/KDE/Ubuntu parallel corpora are provided. The main figures of the

---

[1] http://www.statmt.org/wmt19/parallel-corpus-filtering.html

[2] https://paracrawl.eu/

Table 1: Main figures of the noisy corpora for the Nepali–English and Sinhala–English language pairs. k denotes thousands of elements and M denotes millions of elements. $|S|$ stands for number of sentences, $|W|$ for number of running words, and $|V|$ for vocabulary size. Figures computed on tokenised and lowercased corpora.

corpus	language	$|S|$	$|W|$	$|V|$
ne–en	Nepali	2.2M	52.3M	925.3k
	English		56.0M	782.9k
si–en	Sinhala	3.6M	61.2M	822.6k
	English		62.6M	803.0k

parallel corpora are shown in Table 2.

Table 2: Allowed parallel corpora for Nepali–English and Sinhala–English main figures. k denotes thousands of elements and M denotes millions of elements. $|S|$ stands for number of sentences, $|W|$ for number of running words, and $|V|$ for vocabulary size. Figures computed on tokenised and lowercased corpora.

corpus	language	$|S|$	$|W|$	$|V|$
ne–en	Nepali	573k	4.2M	141.3k
	English		4.5M	64.5k
si–en	Sinhala	692k	4.5M	178.5k
	English		5.0M	69.9k

In addition to the parallel data above, monolingual corpora are also provided. The main figures of the monolingual corpora for Nepali, Sinhala and English are shown in Table 3.

Table 3: Main figures of the monolingual data for Nepali, Sinhala and English languages. k denotes thousands of elements and M denotes millions of elements. $|S|$ stands for number of sentences, $|W|$ for number of running words, and $|V|$ for vocabulary size. Figures computed on tokenised and lowercased corpora.

language	$|S|$	$|W|$	$|V|$
Nepali	3.7M	116.1M	1.4M
Sinhala	5.3M	43.2M	766.7k
English	448.2M	760.2M	9.6M

Additional resources provided in the shared task were a Hindi–English (hi–en) parallel corpus and Hindi monolingual data. The main figures of these two corpora are shown in Table 4.

Finally, development and development test sets

Table 4: Main figures of the monolingual (mono.) data for Hindi and bilingual data for Hindi–English (hi–en). k denotes thousands of elements and M denotes millions of elements. $|S|$ stands for number of sentences, $|W|$ for number of running words, and $|V|$ for vocabulary size. Figures computed on tokenised and lowercased corpora.

corpus	lang.	$|S|$	$|W|$	$|V|$
mono.	Hindi	45.1M	838.8k	4.0M
hi–en	Hindi	1.6M	22.4M	333.3k
	English		20.7M	192.5k

are provided in the shared task. Both sets are drawn from Wikipedia articles. These may be very different from the final official test set in terms of topics due to the fact that the task addresses the challenge of data quality and not domain-relatedness of the data. Main figures of development sets are shown in Table 5.

Table 5: Development sets main figures. k denotes thousands of elements. $|S|$ stands for number of sentences, $|W|$ for number of running words, and $|V|$ for vocabulary size. Figures computed on tokenised and lowercased corpora.

corpus	lang.	$|S|$	$|W|$	$|V|$
Validation sets				
ne–en	Nepali	2.6k	10.2k	37.1k
	English		37.1k	10.2k
si–en	Sinhala	2.9k	48.7k	103.3k
	English		53.5k	6.2k
Test sets				
ne–en	Nepali	2.8k	43.2k	10.9k
	English		51.5k	6.4k
si–en	Sinhala	2.8k	46.4k	9.6k
	English		51.0k	6.1k

2.2 Sub-sampling of noisy data

Participants submit files with numerical scores, giving one score per line for the original unfiltered parallel corpus. A tool provided by the organisers takes as input the scores and the noisy parallel corpus. The tool then selects sentences with higher scores to complete the desired 1M and 5M words in target. Systems trained on these data sets are used for evaluation by the organisers.

2.3 Translation evaluation

As specified in the shared task, the evaluation of a selected subset of sentences is done using SMT and NMT. The SMT system is implemented using Moses (Koehn et al., 2007) and the NMT system is built using the FAIRseq (Ott et al., 2019) toolkit. Organisers provided scripts which allow for implementing the same translation system which will be used in the final evaluation. However, we only conducted experiments using NMT. The FAIRseq system tokenises source and target sentences and applies BPE (Sennrich et al., 2016). The tokenisation of Nepali, Sinhala and Hindi sentences is done using the Indic NLP Library[3]. The system (Guzmán et al., 2019) uses a Transformer architecture with 5 encoder and 5 decoder layers, where the number of attention heads, embedding dimension and inner-layer dimension are 2, 512 and 2048, respectively. The model is regularised with dropout, label smoothing and weight decay. The model is optimised with Adam (Kingma and Ba, 2014) using $\beta_1 = 0.9$, $\beta_2 = 0.98$, and $\epsilon = 1e - 8$. The learning rate is fixed to $lr = 1e3$, as described in (Ott et al., 2019). The NMT system from the shared task is trained for 100 epochs and models are saved every 10 epochs. The best model is chosen according to validation set loss function value. The script which allowed us to reproduce the network used in the shared task can be found at https://github.com/facebookresearch/flores. All experiments were performed using NVidia Titan Xp GPUs.

3 System description

In this section, the entire process of sentence scoring is detailed.

Our process for scoring noisy corpora is as follows:

1. We apply bilingual cross-entropy selection (described in 3.1.1) to select the best set of sentences from Nepali, Sinhala and Hindi to English jointly for each language pair: Nepali–English and Sinhala–English.

2. We train an NMT engine using the above selected data for each language pair.

3. Once the NMT engine is trained, we generate a hypothesis for each sentence in the noisy corpus.

---

[3] https://anoopkunchukuttan.github.io/indic_nlp_library/

4. We then compute smoothed BLEU for each target sentence in the noisy corpus, along with its corresponding hypothesis. These computed BLEU scores will be used for the selection of the required subsets of 1M and 5M words of English tokens for the final evaluation.

5. Additionally, we apply a few rules (described in 3.3) to discard some sentences which are considered useless, by replacing their smoothed BLEU score to zero, effectively avoiding that the selection algorithm includes such sentences into the selected subsets.

3.1 Translation engine

The main core of the scoring process is hypothesis generation using a well-trained translation model. To create the translation model we used the NMT system from the shared task and we selected sentences from all provided bilingual corpora in all three language pairs jointly: Nepali, Sinhala and Hindi to English. To select the subset of sentences to train the translation model we used the bilingual cross-entropy selection method (Moore and Lewis, 2010) described in the next subsection.

3.1.1 Bilingual Cross-Entropy selection

We ranked sentences from all bilingual corpora by their perplexity score according to a language model trained on the monolingual corpora in Nepali, Sinhala and English. The perplexity ppl of a string s with empirical ngram distribution p given a language model q is:

$$ppl(s) = 2^{-\sum_{x \in s} p(x) log\, q(x)} = 2^{H(p,q)} \qquad (1)$$

where $H(p, q)$ is the cross-entropy between p and q. Selecting the sentences with the lowest perplexity is therefore equivalent to choosing the sentences with the lowest cross-entropy according to the language model trained on monolingual data. To compute bilingual cross-entropy score $\mathcal{X}(s)$ of a sentence s, we sum the cross-entropy difference over each side of the corpus, both source and target:

$$\mathcal{X}(s) = [H_{M-src}(s) - H_{N-src}(s)] + \qquad (2)$$
$$[H_{M-tgt}(s) - H_{N-tgt}(s)]$$

where $H_{M-src}(s)$ and $H_{M-trg}(s)$ are the cross-entropy of a source/target sentence, respectively, according to a language model trained on the

monolingual data provided, and $H_{N-src}(s)$ and $H_{N-trg}(s)$ are the cross-entropy of a source/target sentence, respectively, according to a language model trained on the noisy corpora. Lower scores are presumed to be better.

3.2 Filtering by hypothesis

Here, the purpose is to filter the noisy data according to the potential smoothed BLEU score of the sentence pair and the generated hypothesis. With the purpose of building a translation system for obtaining this probability, we trained an NMT system with different training set sizes selected using the bilingual cross-entropy technique above. The system was trained for 200 epochs, which was enough to achieve convergence. As development set, and for selecting the best model for computing the BLEU score of the hypothesis associated to a sentence pair, we used the same development set as provided in the shared task. We selected the best epoch according to validation set loss function value. In Table 6 we show sacreBLEU scores for models trained with different number of sentences.

Table 6: Validation sacreBLEU scores for bilingual cross-entropy selection results depending on the number of training sentences for Nepali–English and Sinhala–English. M denotes millions of elements. Best system marked in bold.

Nepali–English	
Training size	Validation
1.0M	11.7
1.5M	12.3
2.0M	12.2
2.5M	12.2
3.0M	**14.9**
3.5M	13.5

Sinhala–English	
Training size	Validation
1.0M	8.3
1.5M	8.8
2.0M	9.8
2.5M	9.5
3.0M	**9.9**
3.5M	9.5

In both language pairs, Nepali–English and Sinhala–English, the best model was achieved using 3M sentences. Once the best models were selected, we translated the noisy corpora and we obtained the hypothesis for each sentence, which allowed us to compute the corresponding smoothed BLEU score. This is the final score provided as competition result. However, and before providing the score, we also applied other filtering strategies, as described in the following subsections.

3.3 Rule based Filtering

After obtaining the hypothesis for each sentence from the noisy corpora, we applied a few rules to filter the sentence pairs. These rules are the following:

1. Remove sentence pairs where the source or target sentence contains more than 250 BPE segments.

2. Remove sentences where the lower-cased source sentence is equal to the lower-cased target sentence.

3. Remove sentence pairs which do not contain any Nepali/Sinhala characters in the source sentence.

4. Remove sentences where the smoothed BLEU score between the source and the target sentence is higher than a fixed threshold μ. We explored different values for this threshold $\mu = \{0.20, 0.25, 0.30, 0.35, 1.0\}$. Note that the space between 0.35 and 1.0 was not explored because values of μ only slightly above 0.35 already implied that no sentences were filtered.

The order in which the rules are applied is important, since sentences that are filtered out with zero score assigned by one rule will not be a candidate for selection in subsequent rules. After applying different threshold values we used the provided script to subsample sentence pairs to amount to 1 million and 5 million English words. The results of training the final NMT system by applying different thresholds μ are shown in Tables 7 and 8.

Finally, we selected thresholds $\mu = 0.35$ for the Nepali–English corpus, and $\mu = 1.00$ (no threshold, all BLEU values between source and target sentences accepted) for the Sinhala–English language pair. In Table 9, the number of removed sentences by each rule are shown.

In total, we discarded 1.2M from Nepali noisy corpus and 1.9M sentences from Sinhala noisy

Table 7: SacreBLEU scores for final NMT system trained using sentences selected with different values of threshold μ for Nepali–English.

Nepali–English			
Eng. words	μ	Valid	Test
	0.20	0.1	0.2
	0.25	3.3	4.1
1M	0.30	3.4	4.2
	0.35	**3.4**	**4.3**
	1.00	2.4	3.0
	0.20	0.2	0.2
	0.25	2.6	3.0
5M	0.30	2.8	3.2
	0.35	**3.0**	**3.4**
	1.00	3.0	3.3

Table 8: SacreBLEU scores for final NMT system trained using sentences selected with different values of threshold μ for Sinhala–English.

Sinhala–English			
Eng. words	μ	Valid	Test
	0.20	2.0	2.4
	0.25	2.2	2.2
1M	0.30	2.3	3.1
	0.35	2.3	2.4
	1.00	**2.4**	**2.3**
	0.20	2.6	2.8
	0.25	3.1	3.0
5M	0.30	3.6	3.4
	0.35	3.3	3.4
	1.00	**4.2**	**4.3**

corpus. The rest of sentences from noisy corpus were scored using target-hypothesis smoothed BLEU described previously.

3.4 Baseline comparision

Once we selected the best models, we compared the obtained sacreBLEU scores with the Zipporah model results published on wmt2019 website. The Zipporah model extracts a bag-of-words translation feature, and trains logistic regression models to classify good data and synthetic noisy data in the proposed feature space. The trained model is used to score parallel sentences in the data pool for selection. In Table 10 we show our result compared to the Zipporah model.

Table 9: Statistics of how many sentences of noisy corpus were set their final score as zero after applying different rules. The number in parenthesis indicates the rule described in the enumerated list above. k denotes thousands of elements and M denotes millions of elements.

Nepali–English	
Rule	Removed sentences
(1) BPE >250	89.4k
(2) src=trg	186.8k
(3) No Nepali symbols	722.7k
(4) src-trg BLEU > 0.35	207.2k

Sinhala–English	
Rule	Removed sentences
(1) BPE >250	76.7k
(2) src=trg	78.3k
(3) No Sinhala symbols	1.7M
(4) src-trg BLEU > 1.00	None

Table 10: SacreBLEU scores for NMT system comparison with the Zipporah model.

Nepali–English		
Eng. words	Model	Test
1M	Sciling	4.3
	Zipporah	**5.2**
5M	Sciling	**3.4**
	Zipporah	1.9
Sinhala–English		
Eng. words	Model	Test
1M	Sciling	2.3
	Zipporah	**4.7**
5M	Sciling	**4.3**
	Zipporah	3.7

4 Conclusions and future work

We introduced filtering of noisy parallel corpora based on hypothesis generation and combined this filtering with several filtering rules. We submitted only the best set of scores for each language pair to the shared task. In both language pairs, Nepali–English and Sinhala–English, we achieved results that performed better than the Zipporah baseline with corpora containing 5M English words. Our conclusion is that the designed filtering method is able to reach better performance when confronted with larger amounts of data.

Future work should concentrate on further improving of our filtering method. We would train a logistic model to combine the BLEU score between the generated hypothesis and target with the BLEU score between source and target instead of threshold values. Also, we would apply data selection techniques such as infrequent n-gram selection (Parcheta et al., 2018) or continuous vector-space representation of sentences (Chinea-Rios et al., 2019).

Acknowledgments

Work partially supported by MINECO under grant DI-15-08169 and by Sciling under its R+D programme. The authors would like to thank NVIDIA for their donation of Titan Xp GPU that allowed to conduct this research.

References

Amittai Axelrod, Xiaodong He, and Jianfeng Gao. 2011. Domain adaptation via pseudo in-domain data selection. In *Proc. of EMNLP*, pages 355–362.

Mara Chinea-Rios, Germán Sanchis-Trilles, and Francisco Casacuberta. 2019. Vector sentences representation for data selection in statistical machine translation. *Computer Speech & Language*, 56:1–16.

Francisco Guzmán, Peng-Jen Chen, Myle Ott, Juan Pino, Guillaume Lample, Philipp Koehn, Vishrav Chaudhary, and Marc'Aurelio Ranzato. 2019. Two new evaluation datasets for low-resource machine translation: Nepali-english and sinhala-english *arXiv preprint arXiv:1902.01382*.

Diederik P. Kingma and Jimmy Ba. 2014. Adam: A method for stochastic optimization. *CoRR*, abs/1412.6980.

Philipp Koehn, Hieu Hoang, Alexandra Birch, Chris Callison-Burch, Marcello Federico, Nicola Bertoldi, Brooke Cowan, Wade Shen, Christine Moran, Richard Zens, et al. 2007. Moses: Open source toolkit for statistical machine translation. In *Proc. of ACL*, pages 177–180.

Chin-Yew Lin and Franz Josef Och. 2004. Automatic evaluation of machine translation quality using longest common subsequence and skip-bigram statistics. In *Proc. of ACL*, pages 605–615.

Robert C. Moore and William Lewis. 2010. Intelligent selection of language model training data. In *Proc. of ACL*, pages 220–224.

Myle Ott, Sergey Edunov, Alexei Baevski, Angela Fan, Sam Gross, Nathan Ng, David Grangier, and

Michael Auli. 2019. fairseq: A fast, extensible toolkit for sequence modeling. *arXiv preprint arXiv:1904.01038*.

Kishore Papineni, Salim Roukos, Todd Ward, and Wei-Jing Zhu. 2002. BLEU: a method for automatic evaluation of machine translation. In *Proc. of ACL*, pages 311–318.

Zuzanna Parcheta, Germán Sanchis-Trilles, and Francisco Casacuberta. 2018. Data selection for nmt using infrequent n-gram recovery. pages 219–228.

Matt Post. 2018. A call for clarity in reporting BLEU scores. In *Proc. of WMT*, pages 186–191.

Rico Sennrich, Barry Haddow, and Alexandra Birch. 2016. Neural machine translation of rare words with subword units. In *Proc. of ACL*, volume 1, pages 1715–1725.

Parallel Corpus Filtering based on Fuzzy String Matching

Sukanta Sen, Asif Ekbal, Pushpak Bhattacharyya
Department of Computer Science and Engineering
Indian Institute of Technology Patna
{sukanta.pcs15,asif,pb}@iitp.ac.in

Abstract

In this paper, we describe the IIT Patna's submission to WMT 2019 shared task on parallel corpus filtering. This shared task asks the participants to develop methods for scoring each parallel sentence from a given noisy parallel corpus. Quality of the scoring method is judged based on the quality of SMT and NMT systems trained on smaller set of high-quality parallel sentences sub-sampled from the original noisy corpus. This task has two language pairs. We submit for both the Nepali-English and Sinhala-English language pairs. We define fuzzy string matching score between English and the translated (into English) source based on Levenshtein distance. Based on the scores, we sub-sample two sets (having 1 million and 5 millions English tokens) of parallel sentences from each parallel corpus, and train SMT systems for development purpose only. The organizers publish the official evaluation using both SMT and NMT on the final official test set. Total 10 teams participated in the shared task and according the official evaluation, our scoring method obtains 2nd position in the team ranking for 1-million Nepali-English NMT and 5-million Sinhala-English NMT categories.

1 Introduction

In this paper, we describe our submission to the WMT 2019[1] parallel corpus filtering task (Koehn et al., 2019). The aim of this shared task is to extract two smaller sets of high-quality parallel sentences from a very noisy parallel corpus. This parallel corpus is crawled from the web as part of the Paracrawl project and contains all kinds of noise (wrong language in source and target, sentence pairs that are not translations of each other, bad language, incomplete or bad translations, etc.).

This task provides the participants two sets of such noisy parallel corpora: one is for Nepali-English with English token count of 40.6 million and another is for Sinhala-English with English token count of 59.6 million. The participants are asked to submit score for each sentence in each of these two parallel corpora (Nepali-English and Sinhala-English). Based on the scores, two smaller sets of parallel sentences that amount to 1 million and 5 millions are extracted from each of those two parallel corpora. The quality of the scoring method is judged based on the quality of the neural machine translation (NMT) and statistical machine translation (SMT) systems trained on these smaller corpora. We participated in both language pair: Nepali-English and Sinhala-English.

Building machine translation (MT) systems, specifically NMT (Kalchbrenner and Blunsom, 2013; Cho et al., 2014; Sutskever et al., 2014; Bahdanau et al., 2015) systems, require supervision of huge amount of high-quality parallel training data. Though recently emerged unsupervised NMT (Artetxe et al., 2018; Lample et al., 2018) has shown promising results on related language pairs, it does not work for distant language pairs like Nepali-English and Sinhala-English (Guzmán et al., 2019). Also, a vast majority of languages in the world fall in the category of low-resource languages as they have too little, if any, parallel data. However, getting parallel training data is not easy as it takes time, money and expert translators. Though we can have parallel data compiled from online sources, it is not reliable as it is often very noisy and poor in quality. It has been found that MT systems are sensitive to noise (Khayrallah and Koehn, 2018). This necessitates to filter out noisy sentences from a large pool of parallel parallel sentences.

Parallel corpus filtering task of WMT 2019 focuses on two new low-resource languages pairs:

---

[1] http://www.statmt.org/wmt19/parallel-corpus-filtering.html

Proceedings of the Fourth Conference on Machine Translation (WMT), Volume 3: Shared Task Papers (Day 2) pages 289–293
Florence, Italy, August 1-2, 2019. ©2019 Association for Computational Linguistics

Nepali-English and Sinhala-English for which we have very little amount of publicly available parallel corpora. We use these parallel corpora for building our scoring scheme based on fuzzy string matching. Total 10 teams participated in the shared task. According the official evaluation, our scoring method obtains 2nd position in the team ranking in two categories: 1-million Nepali-English NMT and 5-million Sinhala-English NMT.

2 Our Approach

The raw parallel corpus is very noisy and main contributing to that is the wrong language. We study both the parallel corpora (Nepali-English and Sinhala-English) and find that there are many parallel sentences which have wrong language at source, target, or both sides. We use language identifier to remove these sentences. The block diagrammatic representation of our approach has been shown in figure 1.

In our scoring scheme, 0 is the lowest score of a parallel sentence. We set score 0 in the following scenarios:

- Wrong source or target: we detect the language of a sentence pair using *langid*[2] and if any of the source or target has wrong language id, we set 0 score to that sentence pair. This helps in filtering out many wrong parallel sentences.

- As official evaluation is done using MT systems trained on sub-sampled sentences having maximum 80 tokens, we set score 0 to all the sentence pairs that have a source or target length more than 80 tokens.

For further scoring, we translate the Nepali (or Sinhala) sentences from remaining parallel sentences into English and find the lexical matching between a English sentence E and translated English E'. To score each pair XX-English (XX is Nepali or Sinhala), we consider four fuzzy string matching scores based on Levenshtein distance (Levenshtein, 1966) between target (English) and source (translated into English). These score are implemented in fuzzywuzzy[3], a python-based string matching package, as:

- *Ratio (R_1)*: ratio between E and E' defined as:

$$\frac{|E| + |E'| - L}{|E| + |E'|} \quad (1)$$

where $|E|$ and $|E'|$ are the lengths of E and E', and L is the Levenshtein distance between E and E'.

- *Partial ratio (R_2)*: same as R_1 but based on sub-string matching. It first finds the best matching sub-string between the two input strings E and E'. Then it finds R_1 between the sub-string and shorter string among the two input strings.

- *Token sort ratio (R_3)*: E and E' are sorted and then R_1 is calculated between the sorted E and E'.

- *Token set ratio (R_4)*: It first removes the duplicate tokens in E and E' and then calculates R_1.

We combine these four scores (R_1, R_2, R_3, R_4) in two different ways (taking arithmetic mean or geometric mean):

$$Score_{AM} = \frac{1}{4} \sum_{i=1}^{4} R_i \quad (2)$$

$$Score_{GM} = \left(\prod_{i=1}^{4} R_i \right)^{\frac{1}{4}} \quad (3)$$

3 Datasets

Source	#Sents	#Tokens
Nepali-English		
Bible	61,645	1,507,905
Global Voices	2,892	75,197
Penn Tree Bank	4,199	88,758
GNOME/KDE/Ubuntu	494,994	2,018,631
Total	563,640	
Sinhala-English		
Open Subtitles	601,164	3,594,769
GNOME/KDE/Ubuntu	45,617	150,513
Total	646,781	

Table 1: Training data sources and number of sentences. These corpora are used to train SMT systems used for fuzzy string matching. **#Sents**: Sentence counts; **#Tokens**: English token counts.

---

[2]https://github.com/saffsd/langid.py
[3]https://github.com/seatgeek/fuzzywuzzy

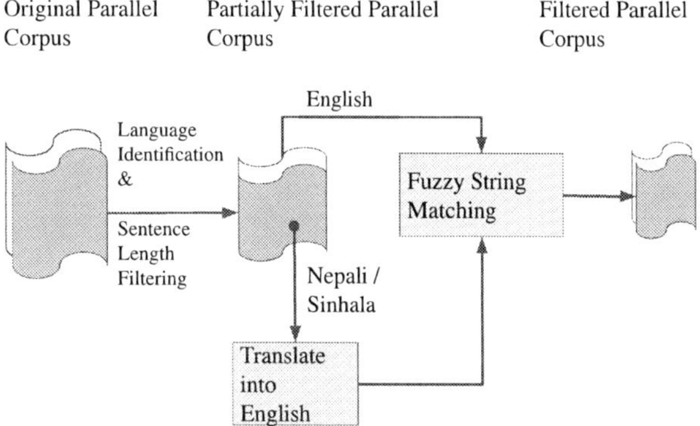

Figure 1: Block diagrammatic representation of our approach. We first apply language identification and set maximum sentence length of up to 80 to get partially filtered corpus from original corpus. Then translate non-English (Nepali / Hindi) sentence into English. Finally, we apply fuzzy string matching between original English and translated English to get filtered corpus.

Set	Nepali-English	Sinhala-English
dev	2,559	2,898
devtest	2,835	2,766

Table 2: Number of sentences in dev and devtest.

This filtering task is focused on two language pairs: Nepali-English with a 40.6 million-word (English token count) and Sinhala-English with a 59.6 million-word for which we develop our method to score each pair of sentences. These parallel corpora are compiled from the web. Apart these two parallel corpora, some other publicly available data are provided for development purpose. Nepali and Sinhala have very little publicly available parallel data. Most of the parallel data for Nepali-English originate from GNOME and Ubuntu handbooks, and rest of the parallel sentences are compiled from Bible corpus (Christodouloupoulos and Steedman, 2015), Global Voices, Penn Tree Bank. For Sinhala-English, we have only two sources of parallel data: OpenSubtitles (Lison et al., 2018), and GNOME and Ubuntu handbooks.

We use only above mentioned, shown in Table 1, parallel data for training phrase-based SMT (Koehn et al., 2003) systems to translate non-English (Nepali and Sinhala) into English for calculating fuzzy string matching scores. Apart from those parallel data, participants are provided with development (*dev*) and development test (*devtest*) sets having parallel sentence counts 2559 and 2835 for Nepali-English, and 2898 and 2766 for

Sinhala-English, respectively. The details of the data are shown in the Table 1 and 2. We tokenize the training, development and test sets in preprocessing stage. For tokenizing Nepali and Sinhala, we use Indic NLP library[4], and for tokenizing English sentences, we use the Moses tokenizer[5].

4 Experiments

For our fuzzy string matching as well as evaluating the quality of the sub-sampled sets, we build XX-English (XX is Nepali or Sinhala) phrase-based SMT (Koehn et al., 2003) system using the Moses tool (Koehn et al., 2007). For training the SMT system we keep the following settings: grow-diag-final-and heuristics for word alignment, msd-bidirectional-fe for reordering model, and 5-gram language model with modified Kneser-Ney smoothing (Kneser and Ney, 1995) using KenLM (Heafield, 2011). The BLEU[6] (Papineni et al., 2002) scores for these SMT systems are 3.7 and 4.6 for Nepali-English and Sinhala-English, respectively.

5 Results

Crude filtering based on language identification and sentence length filtered out almost 77% and 70% parallel sentences from Nepali-English and Sinhala-English corpora, respectively. However,

---

[4]`https://bitbucket.org/anoopk/indic_nlp_library`
[5]`https://github.com/moses-smt/mosesdecoder/blob/RELEASE-3.0/scripts/tokenizer/tokenizer.perl`
[6]We use sacreBLEU (Post, 2018).

Scoring Scheme	1 million				5 million			
	SMT		NMT		SMT		NMT	
	test	*devtest*	*test*	*devtest*	*test*	*devtest*	*test*	*devtest*
Nepali-English								
Arithmetic Mean	3.84	3.64	5.48	5.94	4.34	4.03	1.29	1.25
Geometric Mean	3.89	3.57	5.28	5.57	4.27	4.01	1.32	1.25
Sinhala-English								
Arithmetic Mean	3.07	3.63	3.16	3.70	4.44	5.12	3.87	4.54
Geometric Mean	3.03	3.52	3.01	3.36	4.42	5.17	4.28	5.08

Table 3: Official BLEU scores for 1-million and 5-million sub-sampled sets.

we observe that the language identifier is not efficient in identifying Nepali or Sinhala sentences and misclassifies many sentences. For example, many Nepali sentences are classified as Hindi or Marathi.

Corpus	Before	After
Nepali-English	2,235,512	509,750
Sinhala-English	3,357,018	1,015,504

Table 4: Number of parallel sentences in the raw parallel corpora before and after applying language identification and sentence length based filtering.

Then using the SMT systems as described in Section 4, we translate the Nepali (or Sinhala) sentences from partially filtered parallel corpora into English, and apply fuzzy string matching to score each pair of sentences. We sub-sample sets with 1 million and 5 million English tokens. The size of the sub-sampled sets are shown in the Table 5. To judge the quality of the sub-sampled sets, we train SMT systems following the settings described in 4. We measure the quality of theses sub-samples using BLEU scores shown in Table 6.

Official Evaluation Total 10 teams participated in the shared task. The organizers (Koehn et al., 2019) publish the BLEU scores of the 1-million and 5-million sub-sampled sets on the final official test sets. Official BLEU scores for our systems are shown in the Table 3.

6 Conclusion

In this paper, we report our submission to WMT 2019 shared task on parallel corpus filtering. The aim of this task is to score each parallel sentence from two very noisy parallel corpora: Nepali-English and Sinhala-English. We develop a fuzzy string matching scoring scheme based on Leven-

Scoring Scheme	1 million	5 million
Nepali-English		
Arithmetic Mean	56,868	200,725
Geometric Mean	53,821	185,978
Sinhala-English		
Arithmetic Mean	70,114	264,271
Geometric Mean	67,888	249,275

Table 5: Number of sentences for 1-million and 5-million sub-sampled sets for two scoring schemes.

Scoring Scheme	1 million	5 million
Nepali-English		
Baseline	3.40	4.22
Arithmetic Mean	4.20	3.50
Geometric Mean	4.30	3.80
Sinhala-English		
Baseline	4.16	4.77
Arithmetic Mean	4.20	5.10
Geometric Mean	4.00	5.30

Table 6: BLEU scores on *devtest* for SMT systems trained on two sub-sampled sets. Baseline is the official baseline as reported in shared task page. We use sacreBLEU (Post, 2018).

shtein distance between and English and translated English sentences. Quality of the scoring technique is judged by the quality of SMT and NMT systems. For development purpose, we train only SMT systems to check the quality of the scoring method. Total 10 teams participated in the shared task. The organizers publish the official evaluation using both SMT and NMT on the final official test set. In the team ranking, our scoring method obtains 2nd position in 1-million Nepali-English NMT and 5-million Sinhala-English NMT categories.

References

Mikel Artetxe, Gorka Labaka, Eneko Agirre, and Kyunghyun Cho. 2018. Unsupervised Neural Machine Translation. In *Proceedings of the Sixth International Conference on Learning Representations (ICLR)*.

Dzmitry Bahdanau, Kyunghyun Cho, and Yoshua Bengio. 2015. Neural Machine Translation by Jointly Learning to Align and Translate. In *Proceedings of the 3rd International Conference on Learning Representation (ICLR 2015)*.

Kyunghyun Cho, Bart Van Merriënboer, Dzmitry Bahdanau, and Yoshua Bengio. 2014. On the Properties of Neural Machine Translation: Encoder-decoder Approaches. In *Proceedings of SSST-8, Eighth Workshop on Syntax, Semantics and Structure in Statistical Translation*, pages 103–111.

Christos Christodouloupoulos and Mark Steedman. 2015. A massively parallel corpus: the Bible in 100 languages. *Language resources and evaluation*, 49(2):375–395.

Francisco Guzmán, Peng-Jen Chen, Myle Ott, Juan Pino, Guillaume Lample, Philipp Koehn, Vishrav Chaudhary, and Marc'Aurelio Ranzato. 2019. Two New Evaluation Datasets for Low-Resource Machine Translation: Nepali-English and Sinhala-English. *arXiv preprint arXiv:1902.01382*.

Kenneth Heafield. 2011. KenLM: Faster and Smaller Language Model Queries. In *Proceedings of the Sixth Workshop on Statistical Machine Translation*, pages 187–197. Association for Computational Linguistics.

Nal Kalchbrenner and Phil Blunsom. 2013. Recurrent Continuous Translation Models. In *Proceedings of the 2013 Conference on Empirical Methods in Natural Language Processing (EMNLP 2013)*, pages 1700–1709.

Huda Khayrallah and Philipp Koehn. 2018. On the Impact of Various Types of Noise on Neural Machine Translation. In *Proceedings of the 2nd Workshop on Neural Machine Translation and Generation*, Melbourne, Australia. Association for Computational Linguistics.

Reinhard Kneser and Hermann Ney. 1995. Improved backing-off for m-gram language modeling. In *Acoustics, Speech, and Signal Processing, 1995. ICASSP-95., 1995 International Conference on*, volume 1, pages 181–184. IEEE.

Philipp Koehn, Francisco Guzmán, Vishrav Chaudhary, and Juan M. Pino. 2019. Findings of the WMT 2019 Shared Task on Parallel Corpus Filtering for Low-Resource Conditions. In *Proceedings of the Fourth Conference on Machine Translation, Volume 2: Shared Task Papers*, Florence, Italy. Association for Computational Linguistics.

Philipp Koehn, Hieu Hoang, Alexandra Birch, Chris Callison-Burch, Marcello Federico, Nicola Bertoldi, Brooke Cowan, Wade Shen, Christine Moran, Richard Zens, et al. 2007. Moses: Open Source Toolkit for Statistical Machine Translation. In *Proceedings of the 45th annual meeting of the ACL on interactive poster and demonstration sessions*, pages 177–180. Association for Computational Linguistics.

Philipp Koehn, Franz Josef Och, and Daniel Marcu. 2003. Statistical Phrase-Based Translation. In *Proceedings of the 2003 Conference of the North American Chapter of the Association for Computational Linguistics on Human Language Technology-Volume 1*, pages 48–54. Association for Computational Linguistics.

Guillaume Lample, Alexis Conneau, Ludovic Denoyer, and Marc'Aurelio Ranzato. 2018. Unsupervised Machine Translation using Monolingual Corpora Only. In *Proceedings of the Sixth International Conference on Learning Representations (ICLR)*.

Vladimir I Levenshtein. 1966. Binary codes capable of correcting deletions, insertions, and reversals. In *Soviet physics doklady*, volume 10, pages 707–710.

Pierre Lison, Jörg Tiedemann, and Milen Kouylekov. 2018. Opensubtitles2018: Statistical Rescoring of Sentence Alignments in Large, Noisy Parallel Corpora. In *Proceedings of the Eleventh International Conference on Language Resources and Evaluation (LREC-2018)*.

Kishore Papineni, Salim Roukos, Todd Ward, and Wei-Jing Zhu. 2002. BLEU: a Method for Automatic Evaluation of Machine Translation. In *Proceedings of the 40th annual meeting on association for computational linguistics*, pages 311–318, Philadelphia, Pennsylvania.

Matt Post. 2018. A Call for Clarity in Reporting BLEU Scores. In *Proceedings of the Third Conference on Machine Translation: Research Papers*, pages 186–191, Belgium, Brussels. Association for Computational Linguistics.

Ilya Sutskever, Oriol Vinyals, and Quoc V Le. 2014. Sequence to Sequence Learning with Neural Networks. In *Proceedings of Advances in neural information processing systems (NIPS 2014)*, pages 3104–3112.

The University of Helsinki Submission to the WMT19 Parallel Corpus Filtering Task

Raúl Vázquez, Umut Sulubacak and **Jörg Tiedemann**

University of Helsinki
{name.surname}@helsinki.fi

Abstract

This paper describes the University of Helsinki Language Technology group's participation in the WMT 2019 parallel corpus filtering task. Our scores were produced using a two-step strategy. First, we individually applied a series of filters to remove the *'bad'* quality sentences. Then, we produced scores for each sentence by weighting these features with a classification model. This methodology allowed us to build a simple and reliable system that is easily adaptable to other language pairs.

1 Introduction

Data-driven methodologies define the state of the art in a wide variety of language processing tasks. The availability of well-formed, clean data varies from language to language, and finding such data in sufficient amounts can prove challenging for some of the lower-resourced languages. In particular, the increasingly common neural machine translation systems are highly sensitive to the quality as well as the quantity of training data (Khayrallah and Koehn, 2018), which creates an impediment to achieving good-quality translations in a low-resource scenario.

The web is a massive resource for text data in a wide array of languages. However, it is costly to manually extract high-quality parallel samples from the web, and automatically-crawled datasets such as the ParaCrawl Corpus[1] are typically quite noisy. Designing automatic methods to select high-quality aligned samples from noisy parallel corpora can therefore make crawling the web a more viable option for compiling useful training data.

To emphasize this untapped potential, Koehn et al. (2018) proposed the Shared Task on Parallel Corpus Filtering as part of WMT in 2018. We

participated in this year's task with three sets of quality scores. Each score is a different aggregation of a shared set of features, with each feature representing a local quality estimate focusing on a different aspect. Section 2 contains a brief discussion of this year's shared task. We present our scoring system in Section 3, discussing the filters we used for feature extraction in Section 3.2, and the aggregate scorers in Section 3.3. Finally, we report our contrastive results in Section 4.

2 Task Description

This year, the corpus filtering task organizers decided to pose the problem under more challenging conditions by focusing on low-resource scenarios, as opposed to previous year German–English (Koehn et al., 2018). In particular, two parallel corpora are to be scored for filtering: Nepali–English and Sinhala–English. The task for each participating team is to provide a quality score for each sentence pair in either or both of the corpora. The scores do not have to be meaningful, except that higher scores indicate better quality. The computed scores are then evaluated under four scenarios: training SMT and NMT systems, on samples of 5 million and 1 million words each, where the samples are obtained from the corresponding corpus using the quality scores.

Participants are provided with raw corpora to score, which were crawled using the ParaCrawl pipeline, and consist of 40.6 million (English) words for Nepali–English, and 59.6 million for Sinhala–English. Additionally, some parallel and monolingual corpora were provided for each language pair. We used the parallel datasets to train some of our scoring systems[2]. Some descriptive

---

[1] ParaCrawl can be downloaded from https://paracrawl.eu/

[2] En–Si: OpenSubtitles and GNOME/KDE/Ubuntu; En–Ne: Bible (two translations), Global Voices, Penn Treebank, GNOME/KDE/Ubuntu, and Nepali Dictionary.

Proceedings of the Fourth Conference on Machine Translation (WMT), Volume 3: Shared Task Papers (Day 2) pages 294–300
Florence, Italy, August 1-2, 2019. ©2019 Association for Computational Linguistics

corpus	lang. pair	sent. pairs	EN words
ParaCrawl	EN–NE	2.2M	40.6M
additional	EN–NE	543K	2.9M
ParaCrawl	EN–SI	3.4M	45.5M
additional	EN–SI	647K	3.7M

Table 1: Statistics on the ParaCrawl data and the used parallel data. Only English word counts reported.

statistics of the data we have used can be found in Table 1.

3 Scoring system

We first independently applied a series of filters to the data and computed relevant numerical features with them. We have previously corroborated the filters' effectiveness, since we have used them to clean the noisy datasets provided for this year's news translation task at WMT with satisfactory results. Then, we selected a cut-off value for each filter and trained a classifier over the features to compute a global score for each sentence pair, which we used to rank them.

3.1 Cleaning up the clean training data

Some of our filters require clean data for training. We observed that the provided parallel data still contained quite a lot of noise, and therefore, we applied some additional heuristic filters to clean it further. In particular, we used the following heuristics to remove pairs with characteristics that indicate likely problems in the data:

- Removing all sentence pairs with a length ratio above 3 between the source and the target.

- Removing pairs with very long sentences containing more than 100 words.

- Removing sentences with extremely long words, *i.e.* excluding all sentence pairs with words of 40 or more characters.

- Removing sentence pairs that include HTML or XML tags.

- Removing sentence pairs that include characters outside of the decoding table of Devanagari (for Nepalese) and Sinhala characters besides punctuation and whitespace.

- Removing sentence pairs that include Devanagari or Sinhala characters in English.

The procedure above discarded around 23% of the data for Nepali–English, and we kept around 440k parallel sentences from the original data. For Sinhala–English, we removed about 19% of the data and kept 522k sentence pairs for training.

3.2 Filters

Word alignment. Our first filter applies statistical word alignment models to rank sentence pairs. Word alignment models implement a straightforward way of estimating the likelihood of parallel sentences. In particular, IBM-style alignment models estimate the probability $p(f|a, e)$ of a foreign sentence f given an "emitted" sentence e and an alignment a between them.

We used *eflomal*[3] (Östling and Tiedemann, 2016) for word-level alignment, as it provides significant benefits. First, it is an efficient algorithm based on Gibbs sampling, as opposed to the slower expectation maximization methods commonly used for training. This method is thus able to train and align large quantities of data in a small amount of time. Second, this software allows us to load model priors, a feature we use to initialize the aligner with previously stored model parameters. This is handy for our filtering needs, as we can now train a model on clean parallel data and apply that model to estimate alignment probabilities of noisy data sets.

For obtaining model priors, we use the cleaned training data described above, tokenized with the generic tokenizer from the Moses toolkit (Koehn et al., 2007). We cut all words at 10 characters to improve statistics and training efficiency. With this, we train for both language pairs a Bayesian HMM alignment model with fertilities in both directions, and estimate the model priors from the symmetrized alignment. We then use those priors to run the alignment of the noisy datasets using only a single iteration of the final model to avoid a strong influence of the noisy data on alignment parameters. As it is intractable to estimate a fully normalized conditional probability of a sentence pair under the given higher-level word alignment model, *eflomal* estimates a score based on the maximum unnormalized log-probability of links in the last sampling iteration. In practice, this seems to work well, and we take that value to rank sentence pairs by their alignment quality.

---

[3]Software available from `https://github.com/robertostling/eflomal`

Language model filter. The second filter applies language models for source and target languages. In our approach, we opt for a combination of source and target language models, and focus on the comparison between scores coming from both models. The idea with this filter is to prefer sentence pairs for which the cross-entropy with the clean monolingual language models is low for both languages, and that the absolute difference between the cross-entropy of aligned sentences is low as well. The intuition is that both models should be roughly similarly surprised when observing sentences that are translations of each other. In order to make the values comparable, we trained our language models on parallel data sets.

As both training data sets are rather small, and as we aim for an efficient and cheap filter, we chose a traditional n-gram language model. To further avoid data sparseness and to improve comparability between source and target languages, we also base our language models on BPE-segmented texts (Sennrich et al., 2016) using a BPE model trained on the cleaned parallel data set with 37k merge operations per language. *VariKN*[4] (Siivola et al., 2007b,a) is the perfect toolkit for the purpose of estimating n-gram language models with subword units. It implements Kneser-Ney growing and revised Kneser-Ney pruning methods with the support of n-grams of varying size and the estimation of word likelihoods from text segmented into subword units. In our case, we set the maximum n-gram size to 20, and a pruning threshold of 0.002. Finally, we compute cross-entropies for each sentence in the noisy parallel training data, and store five values as potential features for filtering: the source and target language cross-entropy, $H(S, q_s)$ and $H(T, q_t)$, as well ad the average, max and absolute difference between them, i.e., $avg(H(S, q_s), H(T, q_t))$, $abs(H(S, q_s) - (T, q_t))$ and $max(H(S, q_s), H(T, q_t))$.

Language identifiers. A third filter applies off-the-shelf language identifiers. In particular, we use the Python interface of the Compact Language Detector[5] version 2 (CLD2) from the Google Chrome project, and the widely used `langid.py` package (Lui and Baldwin, 2012), to classify each sentence in the datasets.

We generate 4 features from these classifiers. For each language, we use the reliability score by CLD2 only if the predicted language was correct, and zero otherwise; and we use the detection probability of `langid.py` only if the language was classified correctly, and zero otherwise.

Character scores. Another simple filter computes the proportion of Devanagari, Sinhala and Latin–1 characters in Nepali, Sinhala and English sentences, respectively. For this computation, we ignore all whitespace and punctuation characters using common Unicode character classes.

Terminal punctuation. This heuristic filter generates a penalty score with respect to the co-occurrence of terminal punctuation marks ('.', '…', '?', '!') in a pair of sentences. In order to have a finer granularity than $\{0, 1\}$, we penalize both asymmetry (to catch many-to-one alignments) and large numbers of terminal punctuation (to cover very long sentences, URLs and code). For a given source and target sentence pair, we initialize a score as the absolute difference between source and target terminal punctuation counts. Then, we increment this score by the number of terminal punctuation beyond the first occurrence in both source and target sentences.

The intended effect is for the ideal sentence pair to contain either no terminal punctuation or a single terminal punctuation on either side ($score = 0$). In practice, many sentences are very far from the ideal ($score \gg 100$), and it is counter-intuitive to use a larger positive value to represent a higher penalty. To address both problems, we finally make the following update:

$$score = -log(score + 1)$$

Non-zero numerals. This filter assumes that numerals used to represent quantities and dates will be typically translated in the same format, and penalizes sentence pairs where numerals do not have a one-to-one correspondence or do not occur in the same sequence.

Sinhala uses the same Western Arabic numerals used in the Latin alphabet. Nepali uses Devanagari numerals, following the same decimal system as Western Arabic numerals. This filter takes that into account, and first converts those to digits between $[0, 9]$. After numeric normalization, the filter extracts sequences of numerals from each

---

[4]VariKN is available from `https://vsiivola.github.io/variKN/`

[5]The Python implementation of CLD2 is available at `https://github.com/aboSamoor/pycld2`

pair of sentences, preserving their relative order. Considering that a leading zero can be omitted in some numeric sequences such as in dates and numbered lists, the digit '0' is ignored. Finally, the score is calculated as a similarity measure between the extracted sequences in the range $[0, 1]$ using `SequenceMatcher.ratio()` from Python's `difflib`.

Clean-corpus filter Finally, we use the well-proven *clean-corpus-n* script from Moses to produce a binary feature augmented by a feature that marks sentences including HTML or XML tags.

All in all, we obtain 15 potential features from these filters. However, some of them are to be considered redundant and the information they provide is already encoded in some other variable. For instance, using the reliability score produced by CLD2 together with the prediction probability from `langid.py` would not provide crucial additional information to a model. Table 2 summarizes the filters we used to train our scoring models.

№	Feature	Definition
1	word-align	$\sim p(f\|a, e)$
2	lang-model	$H(S, q_s)$
3		$H(T, q_t)$
4	lang-id	src reliability score
5		tgt reliability score
6	char-score	English chars %
7		Ne/Si chars %
8	term-punct	penalty for asymmetric & excessive term. punct.
9	non-zero	similarity between non-zero digit seq.
10	clean-corpus	1, if kept 0, otherwise

Table 2: List of features extracted from the filters.

3.3 Scorers

We trained a logistic regression classifier and a random forest classifier to score each sentence pair using the features presented in Section 3.2. We trained three independent binary classifiers under the following settings:

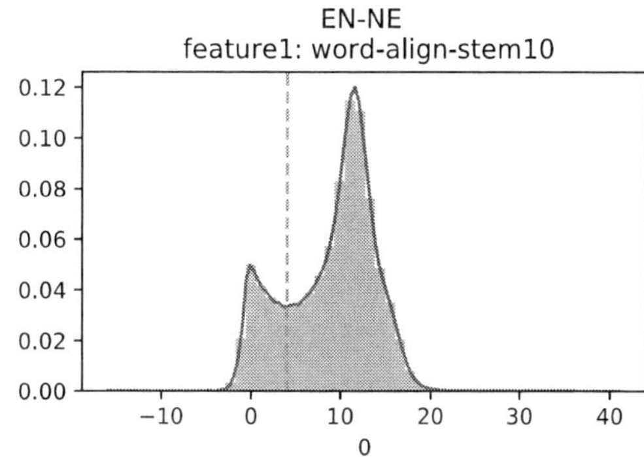

Figure 1: Distribution and cutoff value of feature 1 (word alignment) in the English–Nepali ParaCrawl corpus.

1. Applying all filters to the additional parallel corpora, and using filtered data as positive examples, and filtered-out data as negative examples.

2. Applying all filters to the corresponding ParaCrawl corpus, and using filtered data as positive examples, and a sample of 600k filtered-out examples as negative examples.

3. Applying all filters to both the ParaCrawl and the additional parallel corpora, and using these as positive examples, and a sample of 1M filtered-out examples as negative examples.

	lang. pair	RF AIC	RF BIC	LR AIC	LR BIC
PC	en-ne	17.8	-1.0e+7	-1.3	-2.5e+6
PC+BIC	en-ne	16.8	-1.1e+7	-0.9	-2.9e+6
PC	en-si	15.4	-9.4e+6	-1.5	-2.3e+6
PC+BIC	en-si	15.6	-1.1e+7	-1.4	-2.9e+6

Table 3: AIC and BIC obtained with random forest (RF) and logistic regression (LR) models. Comparison between the first chosen thresholds for ParaCrawl (PC) data and the model that optimizes the information criteria (PC+BIC).

For each filter under the first two scenarios, we adjusted thresholds based on score distributions, attempting to keep a balance between having restrictive thresholds that limited the amount of positive examples, and having lax thresholds

data	langpair	word-align	lang-model (src)	lang-model (tgt)	lang-id (src)	lang-id (tgt)	char-score (%En)	char-score (%Ne/Si)	term-punct	non-zero	clean-corpus
additional clean	ne-en	1	5	0	—	0	0	0	−2	0.5	0
ParaCrawl	ne-en	4	10	9	0	0	0	0	−2	0.5	0
ParaCrawl bestBIC	ne-en	—	—	—	0	0	0	0	−2	0.5	0
additional clean	ne-si	2	6	5	0	0	0	0	−1.5	0.5	0
ParaCrawl	ne-si	3	10	10	0	0	0	0	−1	0.5	0
ParaCrawl bestBIC	ne-si	—	10	10	0	0	0	0	−2	0.5	0

Table 4: Selected threshold value for each feature.

that classified many low-quality examples as positive. In some cases the score distributions were clearly bi-modal, making it easy to determine cut-off values (*e.g.* see Figure 1); while in other cases, we had to opt for a more empirical approach. For this reason, we have a second model that optimizes the Akaike Information Criterion (AIC) (Akaike, 1974) and the Bayes Information Criterion (BIC) (Schwarz et al., 1978) under scenario 2. This model was chosen from among 7 models trained with different reasonable combinations of the features. In Table 3, we compare the information criteria for both models. Finally, under the third scenario we chose to combine the data using the defined cutoff values from the previous two to include a significant amount of examples from both data sets.

Table 4 summarizes the threshold values used for each feature. After applying the filters, we kept 240k sentences ($\approx$ 11% of the total) from the ParaCrawl EN–NE, 230k sentences ($\approx$ 7%) from ParaCrawl EN–SI; 239k ($\approx$ 44%) from the additional clean EN–NE data, and 231k ($\approx$ 36%) from the additional clean EN–SI data. This means that, when combining them for scenario 3, we get 419k sentences ($\approx$ 15%) for EN–NE, and 537k for EN–SI ($\approx$ 14%). In order to avoid overfitting to the negative examples in scenarios 2 and 3, which vastly outnumber the positive ones, we performed stratified sampling of the negative examples where we selected 600K and 1M negative examples, respectively. We then randomly split the data into train (70%) and test (30%) sets.

4 Results

We report the accuracy on the test set achieved by the aforementioned models in Table 5. We do not report the accuracy of the random forest classifiers since they are all $\approx$ 99.99%. This is likely because the algorithm "cuts" through the variables in a similar way to how we chose the threshold values. For the same reason, they are unsuitable for the scoring task at hand. The output produced is a sharp classification that does not help rank the sentences. In contrast, the logarithmic regression model softens the output probabilities, emulating the creation of a composite index when used in combination without the threshold selection procedure.

	lang. pair	accuracy
additional	en-ne	78.21%
ParaCrawl	en-ne	96.09%
ParaCrawl+BIC	en-ne	96.46%
All data	en-ne	86.55%
additional	en-si	78.82%
ParaCrawl	en-si	95.26%
ParaCrawl+BIC	en-si	95.26%
All data	en-si	91.14%

Table 5: Accuracy values on the test data for the trained logistic regression models. Additional refers to the additional parallel clean data provided, ParaCrawl+BIC to the model that optimized the BIC, and All data to scenario 3.

In a final step, we also combined the score given by the regression model with two heuristic features that we deemed to be important for the ranking. One of them is the character score that we introduced earlier, which computes the proportion of language-specific characters in the string ignoring punctuation and whitespace. With this factor, we heavily penalize sentence pairs that contain large portions of foreign text. The second factor is based on the heuristics that translated sentences should exhibit similar lengths in terms of characters. This feature is proven to be efficient for common sentence alignment algorithms, and hence, we add the character length ratio as another factor in the final score. For simplicity, we just multiply the three values without any extra weights to obtain the final ranking score. The system that applies those additional factors is marked with *char-length* in Table 6 with the SMT results on the development test set.

model	NE–EN	SI–EN
baseline	4.22	4.77
logreg	4.91	5.06
+char-length	4.82	5.32
bestBIC	4.63	4.91

Table 6: BLEU scores using SMT on 5 million sampled training examples. The *baseline* refers to the Zipporah model reported by the organizers of the shared task.

We only ran experiments with the provided SMT model. We do not present results from the NMT model, since we encountered complications while running the pre-processing script in the provided development pack for the task. We believe it might be due to character encoding and noise in the data. However, we did not further investigate the source of said problem. The SMT scores are listed in Table 6. We can see that we indeed outperform the baseline model, but the scores are still so low that we deem the resulting models to be essentially useless. The performance for our three attempts are rather similar, with the plain logistic regression model having a slight advantage, and a small improvement provided by the char-length filter for the case of Sinhala–English. For that reason, we selected that model as our final submission, with the plain logreg model as a contrastive run to be evaluated.

By inspecting the provided data we draw the conclusion that the low quality of the final MT models is mainly due to the overall poor quality of the data, rather than solely an issue of the scoring algorithms. The final results of the shared task suggest that it has not been possible to squeeze much more out of the data. As seen in Table 7, submissions for this year demonstrate a narrow range of scores, and our primary submissions rank above average despite their poor performance.

	model	1M	5M	10M
EN–NE	best	4.21	4.62	4.74
	UHel (1)	3.19	3.87	4.31
	average	3.03 ± 1.22	3.60 ± 1.12	3.96 ± 0.89
	UHel (2)	1.29	2.05	3.83
EN–SI	best	4.27	4.76	4.94
	UHel (1)	3.26	3.84	4.12
	average	3.00 ± 1.13	3.43 ± 1.09	3.92 ± 0.87
	UHel (2)	2.28	3.24	3.96

Table 7: An overview of the relative performance (in BLEU scores) of our (1) primary and (2) contrastive SMT models trained on 1, 5, and 10 million samples. The *best* and *average* rows represent the highest score and the mean ± standard deviation among this year's submissions, respectively.

5 Conclusions

In this paper, we presented our rescoring system for the WMT 2019 Shared Task on Parallel Corpus Filtering. Our system is based on contrastive scoring models using features extracted from different kinds of data-driven and heuristic filters. We used these models to assign quality scores to each sentence pair. This methodology allowed us to build a simple and reliable system that is easily adapted to other language pairs. The machine translation quality indeed improves, however, BLEU scores remain particularly low. This raises questions about the general quality of the data. More detailed analyses of the data sets seem to be necessary to draw further conclusions.

Acknowledgments

This work is part of the FoTran project, funded by the European Research Council (ERC) under the European Union's Horizon 2020 research and innovation programme (grant agreement № 771113). as well as the MeMAD project, funded by the European Union's Horizon 2020 Research and Innovation Programme (grant № 780069).

References

Hirotugu Akaike. 1974. A new look at the statistical model identification. In *Selected Papers of Hirotugu Akaike*, pages 215–222. Springer.

Huda Khayrallah and Philipp Koehn. 2018. On the impact of various types of noise on neural machine translation. In *Proceedings of the 2nd Workshop on Neural Machine Translation and Generation*, pages

74–83, Melbourne, Australia. Association for Computational Linguistics.

Philipp Koehn, Hieu Hoang, Alexandra Birch, Chris Callison-Burch, Marcello Federico, Nicola Bertoldi, Brooke Cowan, Wade Shen, Christine Moran, Richard Zens, Chris Dyer, Ondřej Bojar, Alexandra Constantin, and Evan Herbst. 2007. Moses: Open source toolkit for statistical machine translation. In *Proceedings of the 45th Annual Meeting of the ACL on Interactive Poster and Demonstration Sessions*, ACL '07, pages 177–180, Stroudsburg, PA, USA. Association for Computational Linguistics.

Philipp Koehn, Huda Khayrallah, Kenneth Heafield, and Mikel L. Forcada. 2018. Findings of the WMT 2018 shared task on parallel corpus filtering. In *Proceedings of the Third Conference on Machine Translation: Shared Task Papers*, pages 726–739, Belgium, Brussels. Association for Computational Linguistics.

Marco Lui and Timothy Baldwin. 2012. langid.py: An off-the-shelf language identification tool. In *Proceedings of the ACL 2012 System Demonstrations*, pages 25–30, Jeju Island, Korea. Association for Computational Linguistics.

Robert Östling and Jörg Tiedemann. 2016. Efficient word alignment with Markov Chain Monte Carlo. *Prague Bulletin of Mathematical Linguistics*, 106:125–146.

Gideon Schwarz et al. 1978. Estimating the dimension of a model. *The annals of statistics*, 6(2):461–464.

Rico Sennrich, Barry Haddow, and Alexandra Birch. 2016. Neural machine translation of rare words with subword units. In *Proceedings of the 54th Annual Meeting of the Association for Computational Linguistics (Volume 1: Long Papers)*, pages 1715–1725, Berlin, Germany. Association for Computational Linguistics.

Vesa Siivola, Mathias Creutz, and Mikko Kurimo. 2007a. Morfessor and VariKN machine learning tools for speech and language technology. In *8th Annual Conference of the International Speech Communication Association (Interspeech 2007), Antwerp, Belgium, August 27-31, 2007*, pages 1549–1552. ISCA.

Vesa Siivola, Teemu Hirsimäki, and Sami Virpioja. 2007b. On growing and pruning Kneser-Ney smoothed n-gram models. *IEEE Trans. Audio, Speech & Language Processing*, 15(5):1617–1624.

Author Index

Association for Computational Linguistics
209 N. Eighth Street
Stroudsburg, Pennsylvania 18360

ISBN 978-1-5108-9291-0